Lecture Notes in Computer Science 8798

Commenced Publication in 1973
Founding and Former Series Editors:
Gerhard Goos, Juris Hartmanis, and Jan van Leeuwen

More information about this series at http://www.springer.com/series/7409

Valentina Presutti · Eva Blomqvist
Raphaël Troncy · Harald Sack
Ioannis Papadakis · Anna Tordai (Eds.)

The Semantic Web: ESWC 2014 Satellite Events

ESWC 2014 Satellite Events
Anissaras, Crete, Greece, May 25–29, 2014
Revised Selected Papers

Editors
Valentina Presutti
ISTC-CNR
Rome
Italy

Eva Blomqvist
Linköping University
Linköping
Sweden

Raphaël Troncy
EURECOM
Biot
France

Harald Sack
Hasso-Plattner-Institut
Potsdam, Brandenburg
Germany

Ioannis Papadakis
Ionian University
Corfu
Greece

Anna Tordai
Elsevier B.V.
Amsterdem
The Netherlands

ISSN 0302-9743 ISSN 1611-3349 (electronic)
ISBN 978-3-319-11954-0 ISBN 978-3-319-11955-7 (eBook)
DOI 10.1007/978-3-319-11955-7

Library of Congress Control Number: 2014953215

Springer Cham Heidelberg New York Dordrecht London

Printed on acid-free paper

Springer is part of Springer Science+Business Media (www.springer.com)

Preface

The 11th edition of ESWC took place in Crete (Greece), from May 25 to 29, 2014. Its program included three keynotes by: Steffen Staab (Universität Koblenz-Landau), Luciano Floridi (University of Oxford), and Lise Getoor (University of Maryland).

The main scientific program of the conference comprised 50 papers: 41 research and 9 in-use, selected out of 204 submissions, which corresponds to an acceptance rate of 23 % for research papers and of 34.6 % for in-use papers. It was completed by a demonstration and poster session, in which researchers had the chance to present their latest results and advances in the form of live demos. In addition, the conference program included 13 workshops, 8 tutorials, as well as a PhD Symposium, the AI Mashup Challenge, the LinkedUp Challenge, the Semantic Web Evaluation Track (featuring three challenges), the EU Project Networking session, and a panel on "data protection and security on the Web." The PhD Symposium program included 11 contributions, selected out of 15 submissions.

This volume includes the accepted contributions to the demonstration and poster track: 20 poster and 43 demonstration papers, selected out of 113 submissions, which corresponds to an overall acceptance rate of 56 %.

Additionally, this book includes a selection of the best papers from the workshops colocated with the conference, which are distinguished meeting points for discussing ongoing work and the latest ideas in context of the Semantic Web.

From originally 18 workshop submissions the ESWC 2014 workshops Program Committee carefully selected 13 workshops focusing on specific research issues related to the Semantic Web, organized by international renown experts in the respective fields:

- USEWOOD 2014 – Building a Web Observatory for Research on LOD Usage
- WASABI 2014 – Second International Workshop on Semantic Web Enterprise Adoption and Best Practice
- PROFILES 2014 – First International Workshop on Dataset PROFIling and fEderated Search for Linked Data
- SMILE 2014 – International Workshop on Social Media and Linked Data for Emergency Response
- Semantic Sentiment Analysis 2014 – First Workshop on Semantic Sentiment Analysis
- SALAD 2014 – Workshop on Services and Applications over Linked APIs and Data
- EMPIRICAL 2014 – The Empirical Workshop 2014
- Sepublica 2014 – Workshop on Semantics for e-Science in an Intelligent Big Data Context
- HSWI 2014 – Workshop on Human-Semantic Web Interaction
- LIME 2014 – Second International Workshop on Linked Media
- FEOSW 2014 – Second International Workshop on Finance and Economics on the Semantic Web

- WoDOOM 2014 – Third International Workshop on Debugging Ontologies and Ontology Mappings
- KNOW@LOD 2014 – Third International Workshop on Knowledge Discovery and Data Mining Meets Linked Open Data

From the overall 60 papers that were accepted for these workshops, a selection of the best papers has been included in this volume. Each workshop Organizing Committee evaluated the papers accepted in their workshop to propose those to be included in this volume. The authors of the selected papers improved their original submissions, taking into account the comments and feedback obtained during the workshops and the conference. As a result, 12 papers have been selected to be included in this volume.

Finally, we also include two selected papers from the AI Mashup challenges. This year, eight groups registered for the event and five of them qualified to participate in the competition.

As General Chair, Poster and Demo Chairs, Workshop Chair, and AI Mashup Challenge organizer, we would like to thank everybody that has been involved in the organization of ESWC 2014.

Special thanks go to the Poster and Demo Program Committee, to the AI Mashup Challenge reviewers, and to all the workshop organizers and their respective Program Committees that who contributed to making ESWC 2014 workshops a real success.

We would also like to thank the Organizing Committee and especially the local organizers and the Program Chairs for supporting the day-to-day operation and execution of the workshops.

A special thanks also to our Proceedings Chair Anna Tordai, who did a remarkable job in preparing this volume with the kind support of Springer.

Last but not least, thanks to all our sponsors listed in the next pages, for their trust in ESWC.

August 2014

Valentina Presutti
Raphaël Troncy
Eva Blomqvist
Harald Sack
Ioannis Papadakis

Organization

Organizing Committee

General Chair

Valentina Presutti — STLab ISTC-CNR, Italy

Program Chairs

Fabien Gandon — Wimmics, Inria, I3S, CNRS, University of Nice Sophia Antipolis, France

Claudia d'Amato — Department of Computer Science, University of Bari Aldo Moro, Italy

Local Chair

Irini Fundulaki — Institute of Computer Science – FORTH, Greece

Poster and Demo Chairs

Raphaël Troncy — EURECOM, France

Eva Blomqvist — Linköping University, Sweden

Workshop Chair

Harald Sack — Hasso-Plattner-Institute for IT Systems Engineering, University of Potsdam, Germany

Tutorial Chair

Nathalie Aussenac-Gilles — MELODI, IRIT – CNRS, Université de Toulouse, France

PhD Symposium Chairs

Steffen Staab — Institute for Web Science and Technologies – WeST, Universität Koblenz-Landau, Germany

Mathieu d'Aquin — Knowledge Media Institute, The Open University, UK

Semantic Web Evaluation Challenges Coordinator

Milan Stankovic	Université Paris-Sorbonne, STIH and Sépage, France

Semantic Technologies Coordinators

Andrea Giovanni Nuzzolese	University of Bologna/STLab ISTC-CNR, Italy
Anna Lisa Gentile	University of Sheffield, UK
Maribel Acosta Deibe	Karlsruhe Institute of Technology, Germany
Luca Costabello	Inria, France

EU Project Networking Session Chairs

Mari Carmen Suárez-Figueroa	Universidad Politécnica de Madrid, Spain
Alessio Iabichella	STLab ISTC-CNR, Italy
Sergio Consoli	STLab ISTC-CNR, Italy

Publicity Chair

Silvio Peroni	University of Bologna/STLab ISTC-CNR, Italy

Proceedings Chair

Anna Tordai	Elsevier B.V., The Netherlands

Sponsor Chairs

Axel-Cyrille Ngonga Ngomo	University of Leipzig, Germany
Achim Rettinger	Karlsruhe Institute of Technology, Germany

Treasurer

Ioan Toma	STI International, Austria

Local Organization and Conference Administration

Martina Hartl	youvivo GmbH, Germany
Edith Leitner	youvivo GmbH, Germany

Web Site Administrator

Serge Tymaniuk	STI International, Austria

Program Committee

Program Chairs

Fabien Gandon	Wimmics, Inria, I3S, CNRS, University of Nice Sophia Antipolis, France
Claudia d'Amato	Department of Computer Science, University of Bari Aldo Moro, Italy

Track Chairs

Maria Keet	University of KwaZulu-Natal, South Africa
Jérôme Euzenat	Inria and LIG, France
Thomas Lukasiewicz	University of Oxford, UK
Sebastian Rudolph	Technische Universität Dresden, Germany
Laura Hollink	VU University Amsterdam, The Netherlands
Vojtěch Svátek	University of Economics, Prague, Czech Republic
Matthew Rowe	Lancaster University, UK
Maria-Esther Vidal	Universidad Simón Bolívar, Venezuela
Jacopo Urbani	VU University Amsterdam, The Netherlands
Elena Montiel-Ponsoda	Universidad Politécnica de Madrid, Spain
Diana Maynard	University of Sheffield, UK
Nicola Fanizzi	University of Bari Aldo Moro, Italy
Agnieszka Ławrynowicz	Poznan University of Technology, Poland
Payam Barnaghi	CCSR, University of Surrey, UK
Kerry Taylor	CSIRO, Australian National University and University of Melbourne, Australia
Matthias Klusch	German Research Center for Artificial Intelligence, DFKI, Germany
Freddy Lécué	IBM Research, Ireland
Aldo Gangemi	Université Paris 13 – Sorbonne Paris Cité – CNRS, FR/ISTC-CNR, Italy
Krzysztof Janowicz	University of California, Santa Barbara, USA
Renato Iannella	Semantic Identity, Australia
Pompeu Casanovas	Universitat Autònoma de Barcelona, Spain
Massimo Romanelli	Attensity Europe GmbH, Germany
Stefan Rüger	Knowledge Media Institute, The Open University, UK
Evelyne Viegas	Microsoft Research, USA
Milan Stankovic	Université Paris-Sorbonne, STIH and Sépage, France
Erik Cambria	National University of Singapore, Singapore
Diego Reforgiato Recupero	STLab ISTC-CNR, Italy
Iván Cantador	Universidad Autónoma de Madrid, Spain
Tommaso Di Noia	Polytechnic University of Bari, Italy
Angelo Di Iorio	University of Bologna, Italy
Christoph Lange	University of Birmingham, UK

Poster and Demo Session Program Committee

Ghislain Auguste Atemezing
Olivier Aubert
Nathalie Aussenac-Gilles
Tobias Bürger
Elena Cabrio
Vinay Chaudhri
Oscar Corcho
Philippe Cudré-Mauroux
Olivier Curé
Enrico Daga
Emanuele Della Valle
Tommaso Di Noia
Stefan Dietze
John Domingue
Aldo Gangemi
Jose M. Garcia
Anna Lisa Gentile
Jose Manuel Gomez-Perez
Thomas Gottron
Marie Gustafsson Friberger
Claudio Gutierrez
Christophe Guéret
Peter Haase
Karl Hammar
Rinke Hoekstra
Eero Hyvönen
Antoine Isaac
Krzysztof Janowicz
Tomi Kauppinen
Carsten Keßler
Freddy Lecué
Yunjia Li
Erik Mannens
Suvodeep Mazumdar
Raghava Mutharaju
Axel-Cyrille Ngonga Ngomo
Lyndon Nixon
Barry Norton
Andrea Giovanni Nuzzolese
Jeff Z. Pan
Terry Payne
José Luis Redondo-García
Mikko Rinne
Giuseppe Rizzo
Catherine Roussey
Harald Sack
Juan F. Sequeda
Mari Carmen Suárez-Figueroa
He Tan
Vladimir Tarasov
Kerry Taylor
Matthias Thimm
Nicolas Torzec
Victoria Uren
Davy Van Deursen
Marieke Van Erp
Ruben Verborgh
Maria Esther Vidal
Boris Villazón-Terrazas
Ziqi Zhang

Steering Committee

Chair

John Domingue — Knowledge Media Institute, The Open University, UK and STI International, Austria

Members

Grigoris Antoniou — FORTH, Greece
Lora Aroyo — VU University of Amsterdam, The Netherlands

Phillipp Cimiano	Bielefeld University, Germany
Oscar Corcho	Universidad Politécnica de Madrid, Spain
Marko Grobelnik	JSI, Slovenia
Eero Hyvönen	Aalto University, Finland
Axel Polleres	Siemens AG, Austria
Elena Simperl	University of Southampton, UK

Additional Reviewers

Zaenal Akbar
Panos Alexopoulos
Isabelle Augenstein
Hamid Bazoobandi
Michele Catasta
Ronald Denaux
Anna Fensel
Nuria García Santa
Aleix Garrido
Almudena Gonzalez Guimerans
Stijn Heymans
Mouna Kamel
Magnus Knuth
Artem Lutov
Sara Magliacane
Ruslan Mavlyutov
Andriy Nikolov
Vito Claudio Ostuni
Christoph Pinkel
Roman Prokofyev
Jessica Rosati
Marco Luca Sbodio
Ioan Toma
Paolo Tomeo
Cassia Trojahn
Jörg Waitelonis
Honghan Wu
Jiewen Wu

Sponsoring Institutions

LINKEDUP

LDBC
Linked Data Benchmark Council

LINKEDTV

PRELIDA
PRESERVING LINKED DATA

MEDIA
MIXER

fluid
Operations

videolectures.net
exchange ideas & share knowledge

YAHOO! LABS

XLIKE
LiMe

Contents

AI MashUp Challenge

Poster Track

Demo Track

Best Workshop Papers

Ontology Design Patterns: Improving Findability and Composition

Karl Hammar[(✉)]

Jönköping University, P.O. Box 1026, 551 11 Jönköping, Sweden
karl.hammar@jth.hj.se

Abstract. Ontology Design Patterns (ODPs) are intended to guide non-experts in performing ontology engineering tasks successfully. While being the topic of significant research efforts, the uptake of these ideas outside the academic community is limited. This paper summarises issues preventing broader adoption of Ontology Design Patterns among practitioners, with an emphasis on finding and composing such patterns, and presents early results of work aiming to overcome these issues.

Keywords: Ontology Design Pattern · eXtreme Design · Tools

1 Introduction

Ontology Design Patterns (ODPs) were introduced by Gangemi [8] and Blomqvist and Sandkuhl [4] in 2005 (extending upon ideas by the W3C Semantic Web Best Practices and Deployment Working Group[1]), as a means of facilitating practical ontology development. These patterns are intended to help guide ontology engineering work, by packaging best practice into small reusable blocks of ontology functionality, to be adapted and specialised by users in individual ontology development use cases.

This idea has gained some traction within the academic community, as evidenced by the Workshop on Ontology Patterns series of workshops held on conjunction with the International Semantic Web Conference. However, the adoption of ODPs among practitioners is still quite limited. If such patterns are to be accepted as useful artefacts also in practice, it is essential that they [10]:

- model concepts and phenomena that are relevant to practitioners' needs
- are constructed and documented in a manner which makes them accessible and easy to use by said practitioners in real-world use cases
- are accompanied by appropriate methods and tools that support their use by the intended practitioners.

While the first requirement above can be said to be fulfilled by the ODPs published online (the majority of which result from projects and research involving

[1] http://www.w3.org/2001/sw/BestPractices/

V. Presutti et al. (Eds.): ESWC Satellite Events 2014, LNCS 8798, pp. 3–13, 2014.
DOI: 10.1007/978-3-319-11955-7_1

both researchers and practitioners), the latter two requirements have largely been overlooked by the academic community. Many patterns are poorly documented, and at the time of writing, none have been sufficiently vetted to graduate from *submitted* to *published* status in the prime pattern repository online[2]. Toolset support is limited to some of the tasks required when employing patterns, while other tasks are entirely unsupported. Furthermore, the most mature pattern usage support tools are implemented as a plugin for an ontology engineering environment which is no longer actively maintained[3].

In the following paper, these ODP adoption challenges are discussed in more detail, and the author's ongoing work on addressing them is reported. The paper focuses exclusively on Content ODPs as defined in the NeOn Project[4], as this is most common type of Ontology Design Patterns with some 100+ patterns published. The paper is structured as follows: Sect. 2 introduces relevant related published research on ODPs, Sect. 3 focuses on the tasks that need be performed when finding, adapting, and applying patterns, Sect. 4 details the challenges preventing the adoption of ODPs by practitioner ontologists, Sect. 5 proposes solutions to these challenges, Sect. 6 presents the initial results of applying some of those solutions, and Sect. 7 concludes and summarises the paper.

2 Related Work

Ontology Design Patterns were introduced as potential solutions to these types of issues at around the same time independently by Gangemi [8] and Blomqvist and Sandkuhl [4]. The former define such patterns by way of a number of characteristics that they display, including examples such as *"[an ODP] is a template to represent, and possibly solve, a modelling problem"* [8, p. 267] and *"[an ODP] can/should be used to describe a 'best practice' of modelling"* [8, p. 268]. The latter describes ODPs as generic descriptions of recurring constructs in ontologies, which can be used to construct components or modules of an ontology. Both approaches emphasise that patterns, in order to be easily reusable, need to include not only textual descriptions of the modelling issue or best practice, but also some formal ontology language encoding of the proposed solution. The documentation portion of the pattern should be structured and contain those fields or slots that are required for finding and using the pattern.

Since their introduction, ODPs have been the subject of some research and work, see for instance the deliverables of the EU FP6 NeOn Project[5] [5,15] and the work presented at instances of the Workshop on Ontology Patterns[6] at the International Semantic Web Conference. There are to the author's best knowledge no studies indicating ontology engineering performance improvements in terms of time required when using patterns, but results so far indicate that

[2] http://ontologydesignpatterns.org/

[3] XD Tools for NeOn Toolkit, http://neon-toolkit.org/wiki/XDTools.

[4] http://ontologydesignpatterns.org/wiki/Category:ContentOP

[5] http://www.neon-project.org/

[6] http://ontologydesignpatterns.org/wiki/WOP:Main

their usage can help lower the number of modelling errors and inconsistencies in ontologies, and that they are perceived as useful and helpful by non-expert users [3,6].

The use and understanding of ODPs have been heavily influenced by the work taking place in the NeOn Project[7], the results of which include a pattern typology [15], and the eXtreme Design collaborative ontology development methods, based on pattern use [5]. eXtreme Design (XD) is defined as *"a family of methods and associated tools, based on the application, exploitation, and definition of Ontology Design Patterns (ODPs) for solving ontology development issues"* [14, p. 83]. The method is influenced by the eXtreme Programming (XP) [2] agile software development method, and like it, emphasises incremental development, test driven development, refactoring, and a divide-and-conquer approach to problem-solving [13]. Additionally, the NeOn project funded the development of the XD Tools, a set of plugin tools for the NeOn Toolkit IDE intended to support the XD method of pattern use.

Ontology Design Patterns have also been studied within the CO-ODE project [1,7], the results of which include a repository of patterns[8] and an Ontology Pre-Processing Language (OPPL)[9].

3 Using Ontology Design Patterns

The eXtreme Design method provides recommendations on how one should structure an Ontology Engineering project of non-trivial size, from tasks and processes of larger granularity (project initialisation, requirements elicitation, etc.) all the way down to the level of which specific tasks need be performed when employing a pattern to solve a modelling problem. Those specific pattern usage tasks (which are also applicable in other pattern-using development methods) are:

1. Finding patterns relevant to the particular modelling issue
2. Adapting those general patterns to the modelling use case
3. Integrating the resulting specialisation with the existing ontology (i.e., the one being built).

3.1 Finding ODPs

In XD, the task of finding an appropriate design pattern for a particular problem is viewed as a matching problem where a local use case (the problem for which the ontology engineer needs guidance) is matched to a general use case (the intended functionality of the pattern) encoded in the appropriate pattern's documentation. In order to perform such matching, the general use case needs be expressed in a way that enables matching to take place. In practice, pattern

[7] http://www.neon-project.org/
[8] http://odps.sourceforge.net/odp/html/index.html
[9] http://oppl2.sourceforge.net/

intent is encoded using Competency Questions [9], and matching is performed by hand, by the ontology engineer him/herself. XD Tools supports rudimentary keyword-based search across the ontologydesignpatterns.org portal, which can provide the ontology engineer with an initial list of candidate patterns for a given query.

3.2 Specialising ODPs

Having located a pattern appropriate for reuse in a specific scenario, the ontology engineer needs to adapt and specialise said pattern for the scenario in question. The specific steps vary from case to case, but a general approach that works in the majority of cases is as follows:

1. Specialise leaf classes of the subclass tree
2. Specialise leaf properties of the subproperty tree
3. Define domains and ranges of specialised properties to correspond with the specialised classes.

The XD Tools provide a wizard interface that supports each these steps. They also provide a certain degree of validation of the generated specialisations, by presenting the user with a list of generated axioms (expressed in natural language) for the user to reject or accept.

3.3 Integrating ODP Instantiations

Once a pattern has been adapted for use in a particular scenario, the resulting solution module needs to be integrated with the ontology under development. This integration involves aligning classes and properties in the pattern module with existing classes and properties in the ontology, using subsumption or equivalency mappings. This integration process may also include refactoring of the existing ontology, in the case that requirements dictate that the resulting ontology be highly harmonised. There is at the time of writing no known tool support for ODP instantiation integration, and this process is therefore performed entirely by hand.

4 ODP Adoption Challenges

As indicated above, there is a thriving research community studying patterns and developing new candidate ODPs. Unfortunately the adoption of Ontology Design Patterns in the broader Semantic Web community, and in particular among practitioners, is limited. The author has, based on experiences from several studies involving users on different levels (from graduate students to domain experts from industry) [10–12], identified a number of issues that give rise to confusion and irritation among users attempting to employ ODPs, and which are likely to slow uptake of these technologies. Those issues are detailed in the subsequent sections.

4.1 Issues on Finding ODPs

As explained, there are two methods for finding appropriate design patterns for a particular modelling challenge - users can do matching by hand (by consulting a pattern repository and reading pattern documentations one by one), or users can employ the pattern search engine included in XD Tools to suggest candidate patterns. In the former case, as soon as the list of available patterns grows to a non-trivial number (such as in the ontologydesignpatterns.org community portal), users find the task challenging to perform correctly, particularly if patterns are not structured in a way that is consistent with their expectations [10].

In the latter case, signal-to-noise ratio of pattern search engine results is often discouragingly low. In initial experiments (detailed in Sect. 6) the author found that with a result list displaying 25 candidate patterns, the correct pattern was included in less than a third of the cases. In order to guarantee that the correct pattern was included, the search engine had to return more than half of the patterns in the portal, essentially negating the point of using a search engine. Also, the existing pattern search engine included in XD Tools does not allow for filtering the results based on user criteria, which makes it easy for a user to mistakenly import and apply a pattern which is inconsistent with ontology requirements, e.g., on reasoning performance or other constraints.

4.2 Issues on Composing ODPs

The process of integrating a specialised pattern solution module into the target ontology is not supported by any published tools, and consequently relies entirely on the user's ontology engineering skill. Users performing such tasks are often confused by the many choices open to them, and the potential consequences of these choices, not limited to:

- Which mapping axioms should be used between the existing classes and properties and those of the solution module, e.g., equivalency or subsumption?
- Where those pattern instantiation module mapping axioms should be placed: in the target ontology, in the instantiated pattern module, or in a separate mapping module?
- The interoperability effects of customising patterns: for instance, what are the risks in case pattern classes are declared to be subsumed by existing top level classes in the target ontology?
- How selections from the above composition choices affect existing ontology characteristics such as reasoning performance, etc.

4.3 Issues on Pattern and Tooling Quality

Users often express dissatisfaction with the varying degree of documentation quality [10]. While some patterns are documented in an exemplary fashion, many lack descriptions of intents and purpose, consequences of use, or example use cases. Experienced ontology engineers can see through this by studying the accompanying OWL module in order to learn the benefits and drawbacks of a certain pattern, but it is uncommon for non-expert users to do this successfully.

It is not uncommon for patterns to include and build upon other patterns, and these dependencies are not necessarily intuitive or well-explained. On several occasions the author has been questioned by practitioner users as to why, in the ontologydesignpatterns.org repository, the pattern concerning time indexed events makes use of the *Event* class that is defined in the (non time-indexed) *Participation* pattern. The consequence of this dependency structure is of course that any user who models time indexed events using patterns automatically also includes non time-indexed participation representations in their resulting model, which very easily gives rise to modelling mistakes.

In more practical terms, the XD Tools were designed to run as a plugin for the NeOn Toolkit ontology IDE. This IDE unfortunately never gained greater adoption. Additionally, XD Tools and its dependencies require a specific older version of NeOn Toolkit. This means that ontology engineers who want to use newer tools and standards are unable to use XD Tools, but rather have to do their pattern-based ontology engineering without adequate tool support.

5 Improvement Ideas

The author's ongoing research aims to improve upon ODP usage methods and tools, in the process solving some of the issues presented above. To this end, a number of solution suggestions have been developed, and are currently in the process of being tested (some with positive results, see Sect. 6). The following sections present these suggestions and the consequences they would have on both patterns and pattern repositories. Implementation of these suggested improvements within an updated version of the XD Tools targeting the Protégé editor is planned to take place in the coming months.

5.1 Improving ODP Findability

In order to improve recall when searching for suitable ODPs, the author suggests making use of two pieces of knowledge regarding patterns that the current XD Tools pattern search engine does not consider: firstly, that the core intent of the patterns in the index is codified as competency questions, which are structurally similar to such queries that an end-user may pose, and secondly, that patterns are general or abstract solutions to a common problem, and consequently, the specific query that a user inputs needs to be transformed into a more general form in order to match the indexed patterns level of abstraction.

The first piece of knowledge can be exploited by using string distance metrics to determine how similar an input query is to the competency questions associated with a pattern solution. Another approach under study is to employ ontology learning methods to generate graphs from both indexed pattern competency questions and input queries, and then measuring the degree of overlap between concepts referenced in these two graphs.

The second piece of knowledge can be exploited by reusing existing language resources that represent hyponymic relations, such as WordNet. By enriching the indexed patterns with synonyms of disambiguated classes and properties in the pattern, and by enriching the user query using hypernym terms of the query, the degree of overlap between a user query (worded to concern a specific modelling issue) against a pattern competency question (worded to concern a more general phenomenon) can be computed.

5.2 Improving ODP Integration

The challenge of integrating an instantiated pattern module into a target ontology is at its core an ontology alignment challenge. Consequently existing ontology alignment and ontology matching methods are likely to be useful in this context. The behaviour of such systems against very small ontologies such as instantiated pattern modules, is however not well known. The advantage that patterns have over general ontologies in this context is the knowledge that patterns are designed with the very purpose of being adapted and integrated into other ontologies, which is not true in the general ontology alignment use case. Therefore, the pattern creator could a priori consider different ways in which that pattern would best be integrated with an ontology, and construct the pattern in such a way as to make this behaviour known to an alignment system.

The author suggests reusing known good practice from the ontology alignment domain, and combining this with such pattern-specific alignment hints embedded in the individual pattern OWL files. For instance, a pattern class could be tagged with an annotation indicating to a compatible alignment system that this class represents a very high level or foundational concept, and that consequently, it should not be aligned as a subclass; or a pattern class or property could be tagged with annotations indicating labels of suitable sub- or superclasses in the integration step.

Additionally, improved user interfaces would aid non-expert users in applying patterns. Such user interfaces should detail in a graphical or otherwise intuitive manner the consequences of selecting a particular integration strategy, in the case that multiple such strategies are available for consideration.

6 Results

6.1 ODP Search

The author has developed a method of indexing and searching over a set of Ontology Design Patterns based on the ideas presented in Sect. 5. The method combines the existing Lucene-backed Semantic Vectors Search method with a comparison of competency questions based on their relative Levenshtein edit distances, and a comparison of the number of query hypernyms that can be found among the pattern concept synonyms. Each method generates a confidence value between 0 and 1, and these confidence values are added together with equal weight to generate the final confidence value which is used for candidate pattern ordering. While the approach requires further work, early results are promising, as shown in Table 1.

The dataset used in testing was created by reusing the question sets provided by the *Question Answering over Linked Data* (QALD) evaluation campaign. Each question was matched to one or more ODPs suitable for building an ontology supporting the question. This matching was performed by two senior ontology experts independently, and their respective answer sets merged. The two experts reported very similar pattern selections in the cases where only a single pattern candidate existed in the pattern repository compliant with a competency question (e.g., the *Place*[10] or *Information Realization*[11] patterns), but for such competency questions where multiple candidate patterns existed representing different modelling practices (e.g., the *Agent Role*[12] or *Participant Role*[13] patterns), their selections among these candidate patterns diverged. Consequently, the joint testing dataset was constructed via the union of the two experts' pattern selections (representing the possibility of multiple correct modelling choices), rather than their intersection. Recall was defined as the ratio of such expert-provided ODP candidates that the automated system retrieves for a given input question.

Table 1. Recall improvement for ODP search

	XD-SVS	Composite3
R10	6 %	22 %
R15	8 %	31 %
R20	9 %	37 %
R25	14 %	41 %

As shown in the table, the average recall within the first 10, 15, 20 or 25 results is 3–4 times better using the author's composite method (Composite3) than using the existing XD Tools Semantic Vectors Search (XD-SVS). It should be noted that while Composite3 also increases the precision of the results compared to XD-SVS by a similar degree, that resulting precision is still rather poor, at 5–6 %. The potential pattern user will consequently see a lot of spurious results using either of the approaches. This is understood to be a potential usability problem, and an area for further work.

A factor believed to be limiting the success of this method is the fact that resolving ODP concepts and properties to corresponding concepts and properties in natural language resources (in this case WordNet) is an error-prone process.

[10] http://ontologydesignpatterns.org/wiki/Submissions:Place
[11] http://ontologydesignpatterns.org/wiki/Submissions:Information_realization
[12] http://ontologydesignpatterns.org/wiki/Submissions:AgentRole
[13] http://ontologydesignpatterns.org/wiki/Submissions:ParticipantRole

This is largely due to the ambiguity of language and the fact that concepts in ODPs are generally described using only a single label per supported language. If pattern concepts were more thoroughly documented, using for instance more synonymous labels, class sense disambiguation would likely work better, and ODP search consequently work better also. Additionally, WordNet does contain parts of questionable quality (both in terms of coverage and structure), the improvement of which may lead to increased quality of results for dependent methods such as the one presented here.

6.2 ODP Composition

Based on an empirical study of ODP composition as employed in ontology engineering tasks in the IKS Project[14], a number of heuristics for ODP composition have been extracted, and are presently being developed into a Protégé plugin supporting such composition. Most of these heuristics are very simple and make use of basic string matching techniques across labels or concept URIs (e.g., if there is a greatest common substring of more than trivial length, suggest the concept with the longer label as subconcept of the one with the shorter label, etc.). Yet these simple heuristics cover over 60 % of the composition mappings in the source dataset. While end-users would be able to connect such concepts themselves by hand, suggesting them to the user will still save them considerable work, as they do not themselves have to dig through the subsumption hierarchy to locate the classes and properties.

These heuristics are being coupled with a confidence scoring mechanism based on the *scope of control* of an ontology engineering project. This scope defines which namespaces in the project that are allowed to be modified when performing ODP composition. The scope can be set manually by the ontology engineer, but is by default based on the namespaces of open and editable files in the Protégé environment. Redefining the semantics of concepts outside of the scope of control is not recommended. Consequently, composition subsumption axioms in which concepts outside of the scope of control are defined as the subconcepts, are penalised and ranked lower than axioms which do not give rise to such a situation.

From the same study it was observed that all of the mapping axioms used to composite an ODP specialisation module into a resulting ontology were subsumption mappings (i.e., subClassOf or subPropertyOf). Equivalence mappings were not used at all. This may indicate a cognitive understanding of the domain of discourse as being layered, that is to say, that ODP specialisation modules represent a layer of understanding which is more general than the final ontology, but mer specific than the original ODP. For instance, in the ontologies studied, List (an ODP) is specialised as ContentList (an ODP specialisation), which is then composed via subclassing into RadioChannel, Playlist, and NewsStream. If this observation holds also in a larger set of ontologies and ODPs, it may indicate that the border between ODP specialisation and ODP composition is

[14] http://www.iks-project.eu/

not as clear cut as previously thought, and that tooling for specialisation and composition would need be more tightly integrated.

7 Conclusions

This paper has introduced and discussed some concrete challenges regarding the use of Ontology Design Patterns, with an emphasis on tooling-related challenges that prevent non-expert users from performing Ontology Engineering using such patterns. Those challenges primarily concern; (a) the task of finding patterns, (b) decisions to make when integrating pattern based modules with an existing ontology, and, (c) pattern and tooling quality. The author's work aims to overcome these challenges by developing improved methods and accompanying tools for today's Ontology Engineering IDE:s (i.e., Protégé), better supporting each step of ODP application and use.

The author has developed an ODP search method exploiting both the similarity between pattern competency questions and user queries, and the relative abstraction level of general pattern solutions versus concrete user queries, a method shown to increase recall when searching for candidate ODPs significantly. Future work regarding ODP findability includes improving recall and precision further, and to examine which type of criteria users want to be able to filter results based on.

The author has also developed a set of heuristics for ODP composition suggestions, and a confidence scoring method based on the scope of control of an ODP-based ontology engineering project, presently being implemented into a tool for guiding ODP composition. Future work regarding ODP composition includes tackling the more difficult alignments, possibly via enrichment using lexical resources.

References

1. Aranguren, M.E., Antezana, E., Kuiper, M., Stevens, R.: Ontology design patterns for bio-ontologies: a case study on the cell cycle ontology. BMC Bioinf. **9**(Suppl 5), S1 (2008)
2. Beck, K., Andres, C.: Extreme Programming Explained: Embrace Change. Addison-Wesley Professional, Boston (2004)
3. Blomqvist, E., Gangemi, A., Presutti, V.: Experiments on pattern-based ontology design. In: Proceedings of the Fifth International Conference on Knowledge Capture, pp. 41–48. ACM (2009)
4. Blomqvist, E., Sandkuhl, K.: Patterns in ontology engineering: classification of ontology patterns. In: Proceedings of the 7th International Conference on Enterprise Information Systems, pp. 413–416 (2005)
5. Daga, E., Blomqvist, E., Gangemi, A., Montiel, E., Nikitina, N., Presutti, V., Villazon-Terrazas, B.: D2.5.2: pattern based ontology design: methodology and software support. Technical report, NeOn Project (2007)
6. Dzbor, M., Suárez-Figueroa, M.C., Blomqvist, E., Lewen, H., Espinoza, M., Gómez-Pérez, A., Palma, R.: D5.6.2 experimentation and evaluation of the NeOn methodology. Technical report, NeOn Project (2007)

7. Egaña, M., Rector, A.L., Stevens, R., Antezana, E.: Applying ontology design patterns in bio-ontologies. In: Gangemi, A., Euzenat, J. (eds.) EKAW 2008. LNCS (LNAI), vol. 5268, pp. 7–16. Springer, Heidelberg (2008)
8. Gangemi, A.: Ontology design patterns for semantic web content. In: Gil, Y., Motta, E., Benjamins, V.R., Musen, M.A. (eds.) ISWC 2005. LNCS, vol. 3729, pp. 262–276. Springer, Heidelberg (2005)
9. Grüninger, M., Fox, M.S.: The role of competency questions in enterprise engineering. In: Rolstadås, A. (ed.) Benchmarking – Theory and Practice. IFIP AICT, pp. 22–31. Springer, New York (1995)
10. Hammar, K.: Ontology design patterns in use: lessons learnt from an ontology engineering case. In: Proceedings of the 3rd Workshop on Ontology Patterns (2012)
11. Hammar, K.: Towards an Ontology Design Pattern Quality Model. Linköping Studies in Science and Technology, vol. 1606. Linköping University (2013)
12. Hammar, K., Lin, F., Tarasov, V.: Information reuse and interoperability with ontology patterns and linked data. In: Abramowicz, W., Tolksdorf, R., Węcel, K. (eds.) BIS 2010. LNBIP, vol. 57, pp. 168–179. Springer, Heidelberg (2010)
13. Presutti, V., Blomqvist, E., Daga, E., Gangemi, A.: Pattern-based ontology design. In: Suárez-Figueroa, M.C., et al. (eds.) Ontology Engineering in a Networked World, pp. 35–64. Springer, Heidelberg (2012)
14. Presutti, V., Daga, E., Gangemi, A., Blomqvist, E.: eXtreme design with content ontology design patterns. In: Proceedings of the Workshop on Ontology Patterns (WOP 2009), Collocated with ISWC 2009, p. 83 (2009)
15. Presutti, V., Gangemi, A., David, S., Aguado de Cea, G., Suárez-Figueroa, M.C., Montiel-Ponsoda, E., Poveda, M.: D2.5.1: a library of ontology design patterns: reusable solutions for collaborative design of networked ontologies. Technical report, NeOn Project (2007)

Lessons Learned — The Case of CROCUS: Cluster-Based Ontology Data Cleansing

Didier Cherix[2], Ricardo Usbeck[1,2(✉)], Andreas Both[2], and Jens Lehmann[1]

[1] University of Leipzig, Leipzig, Germany
{usbeck,lehmann}@informatik.uni-leipzig.de
[2] R & D, Unister GmbH, Leipzig, Germany
{andreas.both,didier.cherix}@unister.de

Abstract. Over the past years, a vast number of datasets have been published based on Semantic Web standards, which provides an opportunity for creating novel industrial applications. However, industrial requirements on data quality are high while the time to market as well as the required costs for data preparation have to be kept low. Unfortunately, many Linked Data sources are error-prone which prevents their direct use in productive systems. Hence, (semi-)automatic quality assurance processes are needed as manual ontology repair procedures by domain experts are expensive and time consuming. In this article, we present CROCUS – a pipeline for cluster-based ontology data cleansing. Our system provides a semi-automatic approach for instance-level error detection in ontologies which is agnostic of the underlying Linked Data knowledge base and works at very low costs. CROCUS has been evaluated on two datasets. The experiments show that we are able to detect errors with high recall. Furthermore, we provide an exhaustive related work as well as a number of lessons learned.

1 Introduction

The Semantic Web movement including the Linked Open Data (LOD) cloud[1] represents a combustion point for commercial and free-to-use applications. The Linked Open Data cloud hosts over 300 publicly available knowledge bases with an extensive range of topics and DBpedia [1] as central and most important dataset. While providing a short time-to-market of large and structured datasets, Linked Data has yet not reached industrial requirements in terms of provenance, interlinking and especially data quality. In general, LOD knowledge bases comprise only few logical constraints or are not well modelled.

Industrial environments need to provide high quality data in a short amount of time. A solution might be a significant number of domain experts that are checking a given dataset and defining constraints, ensuring the demanded data quality. However, depending on the size of the given dataset the manual evaluation process by domain experts will be time consuming and expensive. Commonly, a dataset is integrated in iteration cycles repeatedly which leads to a

[1] http://lod-cloud.net/

V. Presutti et al. (Eds.): ESWC Satellite Events 2014, LNCS 8798, pp. 14–24, 2014.
DOI: 10.1007/978-3-319-11955-7_2

generally good data quality. However, new or updated instances might be error-prone. Hence, the data quality of the dataset might be contaminated after a re-import.

From this scenario, we derive the requirements for our data quality evaluation process. (1) Our aim is to find singular faults, i.e., unique instance errors, conflicting with large business relevant areas of a knowledge base. (2) The data evaluation process has to be efficient. Due to the size of LOD datasets, reasoning is infeasible due to performance constraints, but graph-based statistics and clustering methods can work efficiently. (3) This process has to be agnostic of the underlying knowledge base, i.e., it should be independent of the evaluated dataset.

Often, mature ontologies, grown over years, edited by a large amount of processes and people, created by a third party provide the basis for industrial applications (e.g., DBpedia). Aiming at short time-to-market, industry needs scalable algorithms to detect errors. Furthermore, the lack of costly domain experts requires non-experts or even layman to validate the data before influencing a productive system. Resulting knowledge bases may still contain errors, however, they offer a fair trade-off in an iterative production cycle.

In this article, we present CROCUS, a cluster-based ontology data cleansing framework. CROCUS can be configured to find several types of errors in a semi-automatic way, which are afterwards validated by non-expert users called quality raters. By applying CROCUS' methodology iteratively, resulting ontology data can be safely used in industrial environments.

On top of our previous work [2] our contributions are as follows: we present (1) an exhaustive related work and classify our approach according to three well-known surveys, (2) a pipeline for semi-automatic instance-level error detection that is (3) capable of evaluating large datasets. Moreover, it is (4) an approach agnostic to the analysed class of the instance as well as the Linked Data knowledge base. (5) we provide an evaluation on a synthetic and a real-world dataset. Finally, (6) we present a number of lessons learned according to error detection in real-world datasets.

2 Related Work

The research field of ontology data cleansing, especially instance data can be regarded threefold: (1) development of statistical metrics to discover anomalies, (2) manual, semi-automatic and full-automatic evaluation of data quality and (3) rule- or logic-based approaches to prevent outliers in application data.

In 2013, Zaveri et al. [10] evaluate the data quality of DBpedia. This manual approach introduces a taxonomy of quality dimensions: (i) accuracy, which concerns wrong triples, data type problems and implicit relations between attributes, (ii) relevance, indicating significance of extracted information, (iii) representational consistency, measuring numerical stability and (iv) interlinking, which looks for links to external resources. Moreover, the authors present a *manual*

Table 1. Table of founded papers for each in [8] defined Dimension on the basis of [9, Tables 8–9]. The blue dimensions are considered in this work.

		Procedure			
	Dimension	Automatic	Semi - Automatic	Manual	Not Specified
Intrisic DQ	Believability			[3]	
	Objectivity			[3]	
	Reputation			[3]	
	Correctness		[4,5]	[3]	
Contextual DQ	Completeness	[6]	[5]	[3]	
	Added Value	[6]		[3]	
	Relevancy			[3]	
	Timeliness			[3]	
	Amount of data			[3]	
Representation	Interpretability			[3]	[7]
	Understandability			[3]	
	Consistency			[3]	[7]
	Conciseness			[3]	[7]
Accessibility	Availability			[3]	[7]
	Response time			[3]	
	Security			[3]	

error detection tool called *TripleCheckMate*[2] and a *semi-automatic* approach supported by the description logic learner (DL-Learner) [11,12], which generates a schema extension for preventing already identified errors. Those methods measured an error rate of 11.93 % in DBpedia which will be a starting point for our evaluation.

A *rule-based* framework is presented by Furber et al. [13] where the authors define 9 rules of data quality. Following, the authors define an error by the number of instances not following a specific rule normalized by the overall number of relevant instances. Afterwards, the framework is able to generate statistics on which rules have been applied to the data. Several *semi-automatic* processes, e.g., [4,5], have been developed to detect errors in instance data of ontologies. Bohm et al. [4] profiled LOD knowledge bases, i.e., *statistical* metadata is generated to discover outliers. Therefore, the authors clustered the ontology to ensure partitions contain only semantically correlated data and are able to detect outliers.

[2] http://github.com/AKSW/TripleCheckMate

Hogan et al. [5] only identified errors in RDF data without evaluating the data properties itself.

In 2013, Kontokostas et al. [14] present an *automatic* methodology to assess data quality via a SPARQL-endpoint[3]. The authors define 14 basic graph patterns (BGP) to detect diverse error types. Each pattern leads to the construction of several cases with meta variables bound to specific instances of resources and literals, e.g., constructing a SPARQL query testing that a person is born before the person dies. This approach is not able to work iteratively to refine its result and is thus not usable in circular development processes.

Bizer et al. [3] present a *manual* framework as well as a browser to filter Linked Data. The framework enables users to define rules which will be used to clean the RDF data. Those rules have to be created manually in a SPARQL-like syntax. In turn, the browser shows the processed data along with an explanation of the filtering.

Network measures like degree and centrality are used by Guer et al. [6] to quantify the quality of data. Furthermore, they present an *automatic* framework to evaluate the influence of each measure on the data quality. The authors proof that the presented measures are only capable of discovering a few quality-lacking triples.

Hogan et al. [7] compare the quality of several Linked Data datasets. Therefore, the authors extracted 14 rules from best practices and publications. Those rules are applied to each dataset and compared against the Page Rank of each data supplier. Thereafter, the Page Rank of a certain data supplier is correlated with the datasets quality. The authors suggest new guidelines to align the Linked Data quality with the users need for certain dataset properties.

A first classification of quality dimensions is presented by Wang et al. [8] with respect to their importance to the user. This study reveals a classification of data quality metrics in four categories, cf. Table 1. Recently, Zaveri et al. [9] present a systematic literature review on different methodologies for data quality assessment. The authors chose 21 articles, extracted 26 quality dimensions and categorized them according to [8]. The results shows which error types exist and whether they are repairable manually, semi-automatic or fully automatic. The presented measures were used to classify CROCUS.

To the best of our knowledge, our tool is the first tool tackling error accuracy (intrinsic data quality), completeness (contextual data quality) and consistency (data modelling) at once in a semi-automatic manner reaching high f1-measure on real-world data.

3 Method

First, we need a standardized extraction of target data to be agnostic of the underlying knowledge base. SPARQL [15] is a W3C standard to query instance data from Linked Data knowledge bases. The `DESCRIBE` query command is a way to retrieve descriptive data of certain instances. However, this query command

[3] http://www.w3.org/TR/rdf-sparql-query/

depends on the knowledge base vendor and its configuration. To circumvent knowledge base dependence, we use *Concise Bounded Descriptions* (CBD) [16]. Given a resource r and a certain description depth d the CBD works as follows: (1) extract all triples with r as subject and (2) resolve all blank nodes retrieved so far, i.e., for each blank node add every triple containing a blank node with the same identifier as a subject to the description. Finally, CBD repeats these steps d times. CBD configured with $d = 1$ retrieves only triples with r as subject although triples with r as object could contain useful information. Therefore, a rule is added to CBD, i.e., (3) extract all triples with r as object, which is called *Symmetric Concise Bounded Description* (SCDB) [16].

Second, CROCUS needs to calculate a numeric representation of an instance to facilitate further clustering steps. Metrics are split into three categories:

(1) The simplest metric counts each property (*count*). For example, this metric can be used if a person is expected to have only one telephone number.

(2) For each instance, the range of the resource at a certain property is counted (*range count*). In general, an undergraduate student should take undergraduate courses. If there is an undergraduate student taking courses with another type (e.g., graduate courses), this metric is able to detect it.

(3) The most general metric transforms each instance into a numeric vector and normalizes it (*numeric*). Since instances created by the SCDB consist of properties with multiple ranges, CROCUS defines the following metrics: (a) numeric properties are taken as is, (b) properties based on strings are converted to a metric by using string length although more sophisticated measures could be used (e.g., n-gram similarities) and (c) object properties are discarded for this metric.

As a third step, we apply the *density-based spatial clustering of applications with noise* (DBSCAN) algorithm [17] since it is an efficient algorithm and the order of instances has no influence on the clustering result. DBSCAN clusters instances based on the size of a cluster and the distance between those instances. Thus, DBSCAN has two parameters: ϵ, the distance between two instances, here calculated by the metrics above and $MinPts$, the minimum number of instances needed to form a cluster. If a cluster has less than $MinPts$ instances, they are regarded as outliers. We report the quality of CROCUS for different values of $MinPts$ in Sect. 4 (Fig. 1).

Finally, identified outliers are extracted and given to human quality judges. Based on the revised set of outliers, the algorithm can be adjusted and constraints can be added to the Linked Data knowledge base to prevent repeating discovered errors.

4 Evaluation

LUBM benchmark. First, we used the LUBM benchmark [18] to create a perfectly modelled dataset. This benchmark allows to generate arbitrary knowledge

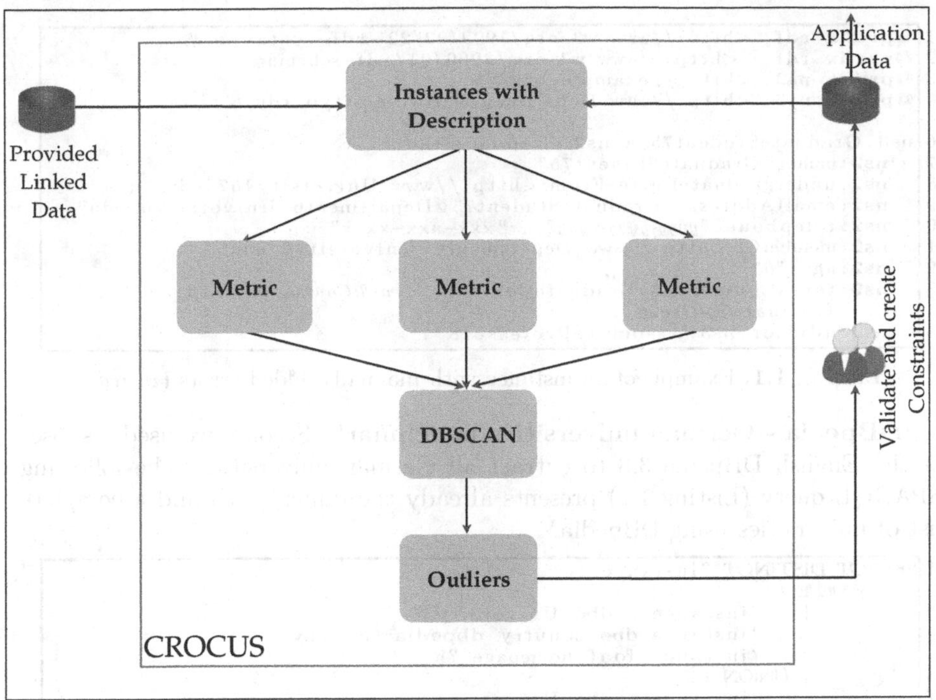

Fig. 1. Architecture of CROCUS.

bases themed as university ontology. Our dataset consists of exactly one university and can be downloaded from our project homepage[4].

The LUBM benchmark generates random but error free data. Thus, we add different errors and error types manually for evaluation purposes:

- *completeness of properties (count)* has been tested with CROCUS by adding a second phone number to 20 of 1874 graduate students in the dataset. The edited instances are denoted as I_{count}.
- *semantic correctness of properties (range count)* has been evaluated by adding for non-graduate students (`Course`) to 20 graduate students ($I_{rangecount}$).
- *numeric correctness of properties (numeric)* was injected by defining that a graduate student has to be younger than a certain age. To test this, 20 graduate students ($I_{numeric}$) age was replaced with a value bigger than the arbitrary maximum age of any other graduate.

For each set of instances holds: $|I_{count}| = |I_{rangecount}| = |I_{numeric}| = 20$ and additionally $|I_{count} \cap I_{rangecount} \cap I_{numeric}| = 3$. The second equation overcomes a biased evaluation and introduces some realistic noise into the dataset. One of those 3 instances is shown in the listing below:

[4] https://github.com/AKSW/CROCUS

```
@prefix rdf: <http://www.w3.org/1999/02/22-rdf-syntax-ns#> .
@prefix rdfs: <http://www.w3.org/2000/01/rdf-schema#> .
@prefix ns2: <http://example.org/#> .
@prefix ns3: <http://www.Department6.University0.edu/> .

ns3:GraduateStudent75 a ns2:GraduateStudent ;
  ns2:name "GraduateStudent75" ;
  ns2:undergraduateDegreeFrom <http://www.University467.edu> ;
  ns2:emailAddress "GraduateStudent75@Department6.University0.edu" ;
  ns2:telephone "yyyy-yyyy-yyyy" , "xxx-xxx-xxxx" ;
  ns2:memberOf <http://www.Department6.University0.edu> ;
  ns2:age "63" ;
  ns2:takesCourse ns3:GraduateCourse21 , ns3:Course39 , ns3:
      GraduateCourse26 ;
  ns2:advisor ns3:AssociateProfessor8 .
```

Listing 1.1. Example of an instance with manually added errors (*in red*).

DBpedia - German universities benchmark. Second, we used a subset of the English DBpedia 3.8 to extract all German universities. The following SPARQL query (Listing 1.2) presents already the difficulty to find a complete list of universities using DBpedia.

```
SELECT DISTINCT ?instance
    WHERE {
         {    ?instance a dbo:University.
              ?instance dbo:country dbpedia:Germany.
              ?instance foaf:homepage ?h.
         } UNION {
              ?instance a dbo:University.
              ?instance dbp::country dbpedia:Germany.
              ?instance foaf:homepage ?h.
         } UNION {
              ?instance a dbo:University.
              ?instance dbp::country "Germany"@en.
              ?instance foaf:homepage ?h.
         }}
```

Listing 1.2. SPARQL query to extract all German universities.

After applying CROCUS to the 208 universities and validating detected instances manually, we found 39 incorrect instances. This list of incorrect instances, i.e., CBD of URIs, as well as the overall dataset can be found on our project homepage. For our evaluation, we used only properties existing in at least 50 % of the instances to reduce the exponential parameter space. Apart from an increased performance of CROCUS we did not find any effective drawbacks on our results.

Results. To evaluate the performance of CROCUS, we used each error type individually on the adjusted LUBM benchmark datasets as well as a combination of all error types on LUBM[5] and the real-world DBpedia subset.

Table 2 shows the f1-measure (F1), precision (P) and recall (R) for each error type. For some values of $MinPts$ it is infeasible to calculate cluster since DBSCAN generates only clusters but is unable to detect outlier. CROCUS is able to detect the outliers with a 1.00 f1-measure as soon as the correct size of $MinPts$ is found.

[5] The datasets can also be found on our project homepage.

Table 2. Results of the LUBM benchmark for all three error types.

	LUBM								
	count			*range count*			*numeric*		
MinPts	F1	P	R	F1	P	R	F1	P	R
2	—	—	—	—	—	—	—	—	—
4	—	—	—	0.49	1.00	0.33	—	—	—
8	—	—	—	0.67	1.00	0.5	—	—	—
10	0.52	1.00	0.35	1.00	1.00	1.00	—	—	—
20	1.00	1.00	1.00	1.00	1.00	1.00	1.00	1.00	1.00
30	1.00	1.00	1.00	1.00	1.00	1.00	1.00	1.00	1.00
50	1.00	1.00	1.00	1.00	1.00	1.00	1.00	1.00	1.00
100	1.00	1.00	1.00	1.00	1.00	1.00	1.00	1.00	1.00

Table 3 presents the results for the combination of all error types for the LUBM benchmark as well as for the German universities DBpedia subset. Combining different error types yielding a more realistic scenario influences the recall which results in a lower f1-measure than on each individual error type. Finding the optimal *MinPts* can efficiently be done by iterating between $[2, \ldots, |I|]$. However, CROCUS achieves a high recall on the real-world data from DBpedia. Reaching a f1-measure of 0.84 for LUBM and 0.91 for DBpedia highlights CROCUS detection abilities.

Table 3. Evaluation of CROCUS against a synthetic and a real-world dataset using all metrics combined.

	LUBM			DBpedia		
MinPts	F1	P	R	F1	P	R
2	0.12	1.00	0.09	0.04	0.25	0.02
4	0.58	1.00	0.41	0.04	0.25	0.02
8	0.84	1.00	0.72	0.04	0.25	0.02
10	0.84	1.00	0.72	0.01	0.25	0.01
20	0.84	1.00	0.72	0.17	0.44	0.10
30	0.84	1.00	0.72	0.91	0.86	0.97
50	0.84	1.00	0.72	0.85	0.80	0.97
100	0.84	1.00	0.72	0.82	0.72	0.97

Table 4. Different error types discovered by quality raters using the German universities DBpedia subset.

Property	Errors
`dbp:staff`, `dbp:established`, `dbp:internationalStudents`	Values are typed as `xsd:string` although they contain numeric types like integer or double.
`dbo:country`, `dbp:country`	`dbp:country` "Germany"@en collides with `dbo:Germany`

In general, CROCUS generated many candidates which were then manually validated by human quality raters, who discovered a variety of errors. Table 4 lists the identified reasons of errors from the German universities DBpedia subset detected as outlier. As mentioned before, some universities do not have a dbo:country property. However, we found a new type of error. Some literals are of type xsd:string although they represent a numeric value. Lists of wrong instances can also be found on our project homepage.

Overall, CROCUS has been shown to be able to detect outliers in synthetic and real-world data and is able to work with different knowledge bases.

5 Lessons Learned

By applying CROCUS on a real-world ontology a set of erroneous candidates is provided to the quality raters. Based on those candidates quality raters and domain experts are able to define constraints to avoid a specific type of failure.

Obviously, there are some failures which are too complex for a single constraint. For instance, an object property with more than one authorized class as range needs another rule for each class, e.g., a property locatedIn with the possible classes Continent, Country, AdminDivision. Any object having this property should only have one instance of Country linked to it. The same holds for an instance of type Continent. However, it is possible to have more than one AdminDivision since each district or state is an AdminDivision.

One possible solution is to create distinct classes for State and District. An even better way is to introduce new subproperties, i.e., locatedInDistrict. Thus, it is possible to define a rule that an object can only have one district. This does not exclude objects with more than one locatedIn associated to an instance of AdminDivision as its range.

6 Conclusion

We presented CROCUS, a novel architecture for cluster-based, iterative ontology data cleansing, agnostic of the underlying knowledge base. With this approach we aim at the iterative integration of data into a productive environment which is a typical task of industrial software life cycles.

The experiments showed the applicability of our approach on a synthetic and, more importantly, a real-world Linked Data set. Finally, CROCUS has already been successfully used on a travel domain-specific productive environment comprising more than 630.000 instances (the dataset cannot be published due to its license).

In the future, we aim at a more extensive evaluation on domain specific knowledge bases. Furthermore, CROCUS will be extended towards a pipeline comprising a change management, an open API and semantic versioning of the underlying data. Additionally, a guided constraint derivation for laymen will be added.

Acknowledgments. This work has been partly supported by the ESF and the Free State of Saxony and by grants from the European Union's 7th Framework Programme provided for the project GeoKnow (GA no. 318159). Sincere thanks to Christiane Lemke

References

1. Lehmann, J., Isele, R., Jakob, M., Jentzsch, A., Kontokostas, D., Mendes, P.N., Hellmann, S., Morsey, M., van Kleef, P., Auer, S., Bizer, C.: DBpedia - a large-scale, multilingual knowledge base extracted from wikipedia. Seman. Web J. (2014)
2. Cherix, D., Usbeck, R., Both, A., Lehmann, J.: Crocus: Cluster-based ontology data cleansing. In: Proceedings of the 2nd International Workshop on Semantic Web Enterprise Adoption and Best Practice (2014)
3. Bizer, C., Cyganiak, R.: Quality-driven information filtering using the wiqa policy framework. Web Semant. Sci. Serv. Agents World Wide Web **7**(1), 1–10 (2009)
4. Böhm, C., Naumann, F., Abedjan, Z., Fenz, D., Grutze, T., Hefenbrock, D., Pohl, M., Sonnabend, D.: Profiling linked open data with ProLOD. In: IEEE 26th International Conference on Data Engineering Workshops ICDEW 2010, pp. 175–178 (2010)
5. Hogan, A., Harth, A., Passant, A., Decker, S., Polleres, A.: Weaving the pedantic web. In: Bizer, C., Heath, T., Berners-Lee, T., Hausenblas, M. (eds.) LDOW. CEUR Workshop Proceedings, vol. 628. CEUR-WS.org (2010)
6. Guéret, C., Groth, P., Stadler, C., Lehmann, J.: Assessing linked data mappings using network measures. In: Simperl, E., Cimiano, P., Polleres, A., Corcho, O., Presutti, V. (eds.) ESWC 2012. LNCS, vol. 7295, pp. 87–102. Springer, Heidelberg (2012)
7. Hogan, A., Umbrich, J., Harth, A., Cyganiak, R., Polleres, A., Decker, S.: An empirical survey of linked data conformance. Web Semant. Sci. Serv. Agents World Wide Web **14**, 14 (2012)
8. Wang, R.Y., Strong, D.M.: Beyond accuracy. what data quality means to data consumers. J. Manage. Inf. Syst. **12**(4), 5–33 (1996)
9. Zaveri, A., Rula, A., Maurino, A., Pietrobon, R., Lehmann, J., Auer, S., Hitzler, P.: Quality assessment methodologies for linked open data. Seman. Web J. (2013) (Submitted)
10. Zaveri, A., Kontokostas, D., Sherif, M.A., Bühmann, L., Morsey, M., Auer, S., Lehmann, J.: User-driven quality evaluation of dbpedia. In: Sabou, M., Blomqvist, E., Noia, T.D., Sack, H., Pellegrini, T. (eds.) I-SEMANTICS, pp. 97–104. ACM (2013)
11. Lehmann, J.: DL-learner: learning concepts in description logics. J. Mach. Learn. Res. **10**, 2639–2642 (2009)
12. Bühmann, L., Lehmann, J.: Pattern based knowledge base enrichment. In: Alani, H., Kagal, L., Fokoue, A., Groth, P., Biemann, C., Parreira, J.X., Aroyo, L., Noy, N., Welty, C., Janowicz, K. (eds.) ISWC 2013, Part I. LNCS, vol. 8218, pp. 33–48. Springer, Heidelberg (2013)
13. Fürber, C., Hepp, M.: Swiqa - a semantic web information quality assessment framework. In: Tuunainen, V.K., Rossi, M., Nandhakumar, J. (eds.) ECIS (2011)
14. Kontokostas, D., Westphal, P., Auer, S., Hellmann, S., Lehmann, J., Cornelissen, R., Zaveri, A.J.: Test-driven evaluation of linked data quality. In: Proceedings of the 23rd International Conference on World Wide Web (2014, to appear)
15. Quilitz, B., Leser, U.: Querying distributed RDF data sources with SPARQL. In: Bechhofer, S., Hauswirth, M., Hoffmann, J., Koubarakis, M. (eds.) ESWC 2008. LNCS, vol. 5021, pp. 524–538. Springer, Heidelberg (2008)
16. Stickler, P.: Cbd-concise bounded description. W3C Member Submission 3 (2005)

17. Ester, M., Kriegel, H.P., Sander, J., Xu, X.: A density-based algorithm for discovering clusters in large spatial databases with noise. In: KDD, vol. 96, pp. 226–231 (1996)
18. Guo, Y., Pan, Z., Heflin, J.: LUBM: A benchmark for OWL knowledge base systems. Web Semant. Sci. Serv. Agents World Wide Web **3**(2–3), 158–182 (2005)

Entity-Based Data Source Contextualization for Searching the Web of Data

Andreas Wagner[1(✉)], Peter Haase[2], Achim Rettinger[1], and Holger Lamm[2]

[1] Karlsruhe Institute of Technology, Karlsruhe, Germany
{a.wagner,rettinger}@kit.edu
[2] Fluid Operations, Walldorf, Germany
peter.haase@fluidops.com

Abstract. To allow search on the Web of data, systems have to combine *data from multiple sources*. However, to effectively fulfill user information needs, systems must be able to "look beyond" exactly matching data sources and offer information from additional/contextual sources (*data source contextualization*). For this, users should be *involved in the source selection process – choosing which sources contribute to their search results*. Previous work, however, solely aims at source contextualization for "Web tables", while relying on schema information and simple relational entities. Addressing these shortcomings, we exploit work from the field of data mining and show how to enable *Web data source contextualization*. Based on a real-world use case, we built a prototype contextualization engine, which we integrated in a system for searching the Web of data. We empirically validated the effectiveness of our approach – achieving performance gains of up to 29 % over the state-of-the-art.

1 Introduction

The amount of RDF on the Web, such as Linked Data, RDFa and Microformats, is large and rapidly increasing. RDF data contains descriptions of entities, with each description being a set of triples: $\{\langle s, p, o\rangle\}$. A triple associates an entity (subject) s with an object o via a predicate p. A set of triples forms a data graph.

Querying of Distributed Data Sources. RDF is oftentimes highly *distributed*, with each data source comprising one or more RDF graphs, cf. Fig. 1.

Example. Catalogs like Eurostat[1] *or Worldbank*[2] *provide finance data, e.g., about the gross domestic product (GDP), which is spread across many sources.*

However, in order to provide the user with her desired information, a system has to *combine such distributed data*. Processing queries in such a manner requires knowledge about what source features which information. This problem is commonly known as *source selection*: a system chooses data sources relevant for a given query (fragment). Previous works selected sources via indexes, e.g., [9,13,18], link-traversal, e.g., [10,13], or by using source meta-data, e.g., [6].

[1] http://ec.europa.eu/eurostat/
[2] http://worldbank.org

V. Presutti et al. (Eds.): ESWC Satellite Events 2014, LNCS 8798, pp. 25–41, 2014.
DOI: 10.1007/978-3-319-11955-7_3

Src. 1. `tec00001` (Eurostat).

```
es:data/tec0001
  rdf:type qb:Observation;
  es-prop:geo es-dic:DE;
  es-prop:unit es-dic:MIO_EUR;
  es-prop:indic_na es-dic:B11;
  sd:time "2010-01-01"^^xs:date;
  sm:obsValue "2496200.0"^^xs:
      double.
```

Src. 2. `gov_q_ggdebt` (Eurostat).

```
es:data/gov_q_ggdebt
  rdf:type qb:Observation;
  es-prop:geo es-dic:DE;
  es-prop:unit es-dic:MIO_EUR;
  es-prop:indic_na es-dic:F2;
  sd:time "2010-01-01"^^xs:date;
  sm:obsValue "1786882.0"^^xs:
      decimal.
```

Src. 3. `NY.GDP.MKTP.CN` (Worldbank).

```
wbi:NY.GDP.MKTP.CN
  rdf:type qb:Observation;
  sd:refArea wbi:classification/country/DE;
  sd:refPeriod "2010-01-01"^^xs:date;
  sm:obsValue "2500090.5"^^xs:double;
  wbprop:indicator wbi:classification/indicator/NY.GDP.MKTP.CN .
```

Fig. 1. Src. 1/3 describes Germany's GDP in 2010. They contextualize each other, as they feature varying observation values and properties for Germany's GDP. Src. 2 provides additional information, as it holds the German debt for 2010. Src. 1–3 each contain one entity: `es:data/tec0001`, `es:data/gov_q_ggdebt`, and `wbi:NY.GDP.MKTP.CN`. Every entity description equals the entire graph contained in its source.

Data Source Contextualization. Existing approaches for source selection aim solely at a mapping of queries/query fragments to sources with *exactly matching* data [6,9,10,13]. In particular, such works do not consider what sources are actually about and how they relate to each other.

Example. Consider a user searching for GDP rates in the EU. A traditional system may discover sources in Eurostat to comprise matching data. However, other sources offer contextual information concerning, e.g., the national debt.

Note, contextual sources are actually not relevant to the user's query, but *relevant to her information need.* Thus, integration of these "additional" sources provides a user with broader results in terms of result dimensions (schema complement) and result entities (entity complement). See our example in Fig. 1.

For enabling systems to identify and integrate sources for contextualization, we argue that *user involvement during source selection* is a key factor. That is, starting with an initial search result (obtained via, e.g., a SPARQL or keyword query), a user should be able to choose and change sources, which are used for result computation. In particular, users should be *recommended contextual sources* at each step of the search process. After modifying the selected sources, the results may be reevaluated and/or the query expanded.

Unfortunately, recent work on data source contextualization focuses on Web tables [2], while using top-level schema such as Freebase. Further, the authors restrict data to a simple relational form. We argue that such a solution is not a good fit for the schemaless, heterogeneous Web of data.

Contributions. This paper continues our work in [20]. More specifically, we provide the following contributions: (1) Previous work on Web table contextualization suffers from inherent drawbacks. Most notably, it is restricted to fixed-structured relational data and requires external schemata to provide additional information. Omitting these shortcomings, we present an entity-based solution for data source contextualization in the Web of data. Our approach is based on well-known data mining strategies and does not require schema information or data adhering to a particular form. (2) We implemented our system, the *data-portal*, based on a real-world use case, thereby showing its practical relevance and feasibility. A prototype version of this portal is publicly available and is currently tested by a pilot customer.[3] (3) We conducted two user studies to empirically validate the effectiveness of the proposed approach: our system outperforms the state-of-the-art with up to 29 %.

Outline. In Sect. 2, we present our use case. We give preliminaries in Sect. 3, outline the approach in Sect. 4, and present its implementation in Sect. 5. We discuss the evaluation in Sect. 6, related work in Sect. 7, and conclude in Sect. 8.

2 Use Case Scenario

In this section, we introduce a real-world use case to *illustrate challenges w.r.t. data source selection during searching the Web of data.* The scenario is provided by a pilot user in the financial industry and available online.[4]

In their daily work, financial researchers heavily rely on a variety of open and closed Web data sources, in order to provide prognoses of future trends. A typical example is the analysis of government debt. During the financial crisis in 2008–2009, most European countries made high debts. To lower doubts about repaying these debts, most countries set up a plan to reduce their public budget deficits. To analyze such plans, a financial researcher requires an overview of public revenue and expenditure in relation to the gross domestic product (GDP). To measure this, she needs information about the deficit target, the revenue/expenditure/deficit, and GDP estimates. This information is publicly available, provided by catalogs like Eurostat and Worldbank. However, it is spread across a huge space of sources. That is, there is no single source satisfying her information needs – instead data from multiple sources has to be identified and combined. To start her search process, a researcher may give "gross domestic product" as keyword query. The result is GDP data from a large number of sources. At this point, data source selection is "hidden" from the researcher, i.e., sources are solely ranked via number and quality of keyword hits. However, knowing *where her information comes from* is critical. In particular, she may want to restrict and/or know the following meta-data:

- General information about the data source, e.g., the name of the author and a short description of the data source contents.

[3] http://data.fluidops.net/

[4] http://data.fluidops.net/resource/Demo_GDP_Germany

- Information about entities contained in the data source, e.g., the single countries of the European Union.
- Description about the dimensions of the observations, e.g., the covered time range or the data unit of the observations.

By means of faceted search, the researcher finally restricts her data source to `tec00001` (Eurostat, Fig. 1) featuring "Gross domestic product at market prices". However, searching the data source space in such a manner requires extensive knowledge. Further, the researcher was not only interested in plain GDP data – she was also looking for *additional information.*

For this, a system should *suggest data sources* that might be of interest, based on sources known to be relevant. These *contextual sources* may feature related, additional information w.r.t. current search results/sources. For instance, data sources containing information about the GDP of further countries or with a different temporal range. *This way, the researcher may discover new sources more easily, as one source of interest links to another – allowing her to explore the space of sources.*

3 Preliminaries

Data Model. Data in this work is represented as RDF:

Definition 1 (RDF Triple, RDF Graph). *Given a set of URIs $\mathcal{U}$, blank nodes $\mathcal{B}$, and a set of literals $\mathcal{L}$, $t = \langle s,p,o \rangle \in \mathcal{U} \cup \mathcal{B} \times \mathcal{U} \times (\mathcal{U} \cup \mathcal{L} \cup \mathcal{B})$ is a* RDF triple. *A* RDF graph *$\mathcal{G} = (\mathcal{V}, \mathcal{E})$ is defined by vertices $\mathcal{V} = \mathcal{U} \cup \mathcal{L} \cup \mathcal{B}$ and a set of triples as edges $\mathcal{E} = \{\langle s,p,o \rangle\}$.*

A data source may contain one or more RDF graphs:

Definition 2 (RDF Data Source). *A data source $D_i \in \mathcal{D}$ is a set of n RDF graphs, i.e., $D_i = \{\mathcal{G}_1^i, \ldots, \mathcal{G}_n^i\}$, with $\mathcal{D}$ as set of all sources.*

Notice, the above definition abstracts from the data access, e.g., via HTTP GET requests. In particular, Definition 2 also covers Linked Data sources, see Fig. 1.

Entity Model. Given a data source D_i, an entity e is a subject that is identified with a URI d_e in $\mathcal{G}_j^i$. Entity e is described via a connected subgraph of $\mathcal{G}_j^i$ containing d_e (called $\mathcal{G}_e$). Subgraphs $\mathcal{G}_e$, however, may be defined in different ways [7]. For our work, we used the *concise bound description*, where all triples with subject d_e are comprised in $\mathcal{G}_e$. Further, if an object is a blank node, all triples with that blank node as subject are also included and so on [7].

Example. We have 3 *subjects in Fig.* 1 *and each of them stands for an entity. Every entity description, $\mathcal{G}_e$, is a one-hop graph. For instance, the description for entity* `es:data/tec0001` *comprises all triples in Src. 1.*

Kernel Functions. We compare different entities by comparing their descriptions, $\mathcal{G}_e$. For this, we make use of kernel functions [19]:

Definition 3 (Kernel function). *Let $\kappa : \mathcal{X} \times \mathcal{X} \mapsto \mathbb{R}$ denote a kernel function such that $\kappa(x_1, x_2) = \langle \varphi(x_1), \varphi(x_2) \rangle$, where $\varphi : \mathcal{X} \mapsto \mathcal{H}$ projects a data space $\mathcal{X}$ to a feature space $\mathcal{H}$ and $\langle \cdot, \cdot \rangle$ refers to the scalar product.*

Note, φ is not restricted, i.e., a kernel is constructed without prior knowledge about φ. We will give suitable kernels for entity descriptions, $\mathcal{G}_e$, in Sect. 4.

Clustering. We use k-means [11] as a simple and scalable algorithm for discovering clusters, C_i, of entities in data sources $\mathcal{D}$. It works as follows [11]:

(1) Choose k initial cluster centers, m_i. (2) Based on a dissimilarity function, dis, an indicator function is given as: $\mathbb{1}(e, C_i)$ is 1 if $dis(e, C_i) < dis(e, C_j), \forall j \neq i$ and 0 otherwise. That is, $\mathbb{1}(e, C_i)$ assigns each entity e to its "closest" cluster C_i. (3) Update cluster centers m_i and reassign, if necessary, entities to new clusters. (4) Stop if convergence threshold is reached, e.g., no (or minimal) reassignments occurred. Otherwise go back to (2). A key problem is defining a dissimilarity function for entities in $\mathcal{D}$. Using kernels we may define such a function – as we will show later, cf. Sect. 4.1.

Problem. We address the problem of finding *contextual data sources* for a given source. Contextual sources should: (a) Add *new entities* that refer to the same real world object as given ones (entity complement). (b) Add entities with same URI identifier, but have *new properties* in their description (schema complement). Note, (a) and (b) are not disjoint, i.e., some entities may be new and add additional properties.

Example. In Fig. 1 *Src. 3 contextualizes Src. 1 in terms of both, entity as well as schema complement. That is, Src. 3 adds entity* `wbi:NY.GDP.MKTP.CN`*, while providing new properties and a different GDP value. In fact, even Src. 2 contextualizes Src. 1, as entities in both sources refer to the real world object "Germany" – one source captures the GDP, while the other describes the debt.*

4 Entity-Based Data Source Contextualisation

Approach. *The intuition behind our approach is simple: if data sources contain similar entities, they are somehow related. In other words, we rely on (clusters of) entities to capture the "latent" semantics of data sources.*

More precisely, we start by extracting entities from given data sources. In a second step, we apply clustering techniques, to mine for entity groups. Notice, for the k-means clustering we employ a kernel function as similarity measure. This way, we abstract from the actual entity representation, i.e., RDF graphs, and use a high-dimensional space (feature space) to increase data comparability/separability [19]. Last, we rely on entity clusters for relating data sources to each other and compute a contextualization score based on these clusters. Note, only the last step is done online – all other steps/computations are offline.

Discussion. We argue our approach to allow for some key advantages: (1) We decouple representation of source content and source similarity, by relying on entities for capturing the overall source semantics. (2) Our solution is highly

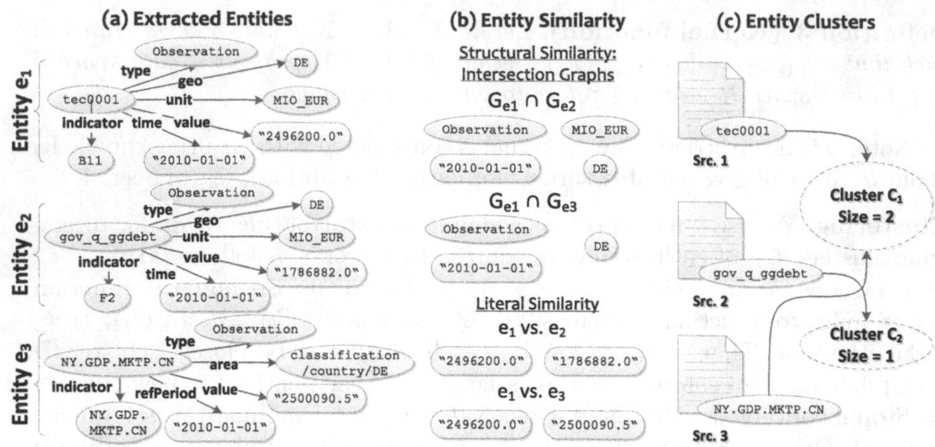

Fig. 2. (a) Extracted entities e_1, e_2 and e_3 from Fig. 1. (b) Structural similarities as intersection graphs $\mathcal{G}_{e1} \cap \mathcal{G}_{e2}$ and $\mathcal{G}_{e1} \cap \mathcal{G}_{e3}$. Literal similarities for entity e_1 vs. e_2 and e_1 vs. e_3. Note, exact matching literals are omitted, as they are covered already by the intersection graphs. Comparison of e_2 vs. e_3 is omitted due to space reasons. (c) Entities grouped in $k = 2$ clusters.

flexible as it allows to "plug-in" application-specific entity definitions/extraction strategies, entity similarity measures, and contextualization heuristics. That is, we solely require an entity to be described as a subgraph, $\mathcal{G}_e$, contained in its data source D. Further, similarity measures may be based on any valid kernel function. Last, various heuristics proposed in [2] could be adapted for our approach. (3) Exploiting clusters of entities allows for a scalable and maintainable approach, as we will outline in the following.

4.1 Related Entities

In order to compare data sources, we first compare their entities with each other. That is, we extract entities, measure similarity between them and finally cluster them (Fig. 2). All of these procedures are offline.

Entity Similarity. We start by extracting entities from each source $D_i \in \mathcal{D}$: First, for scalability reasons, we go over all subjects in RDF graphs in D_i and collect an entity sample, with every entity e having the same probability of being selected. Then, we crawl the concise bound description [7] for each entity e in the sample. For cleaning $\mathcal{G}_e$, we apply standard data cleansing strategies to fix, e.g., missing or wrong data types. Having extracted entities, we define a similarity measure relating pairs of entities. For this, we use two kinds of kernels: (1) kernels for structural similarities κ^s and (2) those for literal similarities κ^l.

With regard to the former, we measure structural "overlaps" between entity descriptions, $\mathcal{G}'_e$ and $\mathcal{G}''_e$, using graph intersections [16]:

Definition 4 (Graph Intersection $\mathcal{G}' \cap \mathcal{G}''$). *Let the intersection between two graphs, denoted as $\bar{\mathcal{G}} = \mathcal{G}' \cap \mathcal{G}''$, be given by $\bar{\mathcal{V}} = \mathcal{V}' \cap \mathcal{V}''$ and $\bar{\mathcal{E}} = \mathcal{E}' \cap \mathcal{E}''$.*

We aim at connected structures in $\mathcal{G}'_e \cap \mathcal{G}''_e$. Thus, we define a path [16]:

Definition 5 (Path). *Let a path in a graph $\mathcal{G}$ be defined as a sequence of vertices and triples $v_1, \langle v_1, p_1, v_2 \rangle, v_2, \ldots, v_n$, with $\langle v_i, p_i, v_{i+1} \rangle \in \mathcal{E}$, having no cycles. The path length is given by the number of contained triples. The set of all paths, up to length l, in $\mathcal{G}$ is denoted as $path_l(\mathcal{G})$.*

The corresponding path kernel is [16]:

Definition 6 (Path Kernel κ^s). *A path kernel is $\kappa^s_{l,\lambda}(\mathcal{G}_1, \mathcal{G}_2) = \sum_{i=1}^{l} \lambda^i \mid \{p \mid p \in paths_i(\mathcal{G}_1 \cap \mathcal{G}_2)\} \mid$, with $\lambda > 0$ as discount factor for path length.*

Note, [16] introduced further kernels, however, we found path kernels to be simple and perform well in our experiments, cf. Sect. 6.

Example. Extracted entities from sources in Fig. 1 are given in Fig. 2-a. In Fig. 2-b, we compare the structure of `tec0001` *(short: e_1) and* `gov_q_ggdebt` *(short: e_2). For this, we compute an intersection: $\mathcal{G}_{e1} \cap \mathcal{G}_{e2}$. This yields a set of 4 paths, each with length 0. The unnormalized kernel value is $\lambda^0 \cdot 4$.*

For literal similarities, one can use different kernels κ^l on, e.g., strings or numbers [19]. For space reasons, we restrict presentation to the string subsequence kernel, κ^l_s [15]. A numerical kernel, κ^l_n, is outlined in our extended report [21].

Definition 7 (String Subsequence Kernel κ^l_s). *Let Σ denote a vocabulary for strings, with each string s as finite sequence of characters in Σ. Let $s[i:j]$ denote a substring $s_i, \ldots, s_j$ of s. Further, let u be a subsequence of s, if indices $i = (i_1, \ldots, i_{|u|})$ exist with $1 \le i_1 \le i_{|u|} \le |s|$ such that $u = s[i]$. The length $l(i)$ of subsequence u is $i_{|u|} - i_1 + 1$. Then, a kernel function κ^l is defined as sum over all common, weighted subsequences for strings s, t: $\kappa^l_\lambda(s,t) = \sum_u \sum_{i:u=s[i]} \sum_{j:u=t[j]} \lambda^l(i)\lambda^l(j)$, with λ as decay factor.*

Example. For instance, strings "MI" and "MIO_EUR" share a common subsequence "MI" with $i = (1, 2)$. Thus, the unnormalized kernel is $\lambda^2 + \lambda^2$.

As literal kernels, κ^l, are only defined for two literals, we sample over every possible literal pair (with the same data type) for two given entities and aggregate the needed kernels for each pair. Finally, we aggregate structure kernel, κ^s and literal kernels, κ^l, resulting in one single kernel [19]:

$$\kappa(e', e'') = \kappa^s(\mathcal{G}_{e'}, \mathcal{G}_{e''}) \bigoplus_{o_1, o_2 \in sample(\mathcal{G}_{e'}, \mathcal{G}_{e''})} \kappa^l(o_1, o_2)$$

We use a weighted summation as aggregation $\oplus$ (we obtained weights experimentally). The dissimilarity between e' and e'' is given as Euclidean distance [22]:

$$dis^2(e', e'') := \|\varphi(e') - \varphi(e'')\|^2 = \kappa(e', e') - 2\kappa(e', e'') + \kappa(e'', e'')$$

Entity Clustering. Using this dissimilarity measure, we may learn clusters of entities. Notice, our algorithm does not separate the input data (graphs $\mathcal{G}_e$), but instead its representation in the feature space. Based on [22], cluster center m_i in the feature space is: $m_i = \frac{1}{|C_i|} \sum \mathbb{1}(\varphi(e), C_i)\varphi(e)$. Distance between a projected entity $\varphi(e)$ and m_i is given by [22]:

$$dis^2(\varphi(e), m_i) = \|\varphi(e) - m_i\|^2 = \kappa(e, e) + f(e, C_i) + g(C_i), \text{ with}$$

$$f(e, C_i) := -\frac{2}{|C_i|} \sum_j \mathbb{1}(\varphi(e_j), C_i)\kappa(e, e_j)$$

$$g(C_i) := \frac{1}{|C_i|^2} \sum_j \sum_l \mathbb{1}(\varphi(e_j), C_i)\mathbb{1}(\varphi(e_l), C_i)\kappa(e_j, e_l)$$

Now, k-means can be applied as introduced in Sect. 3.

Example. In Fig. 2-c, we found two entity clusters. Here, structural similarity was higher for entities e_1 *vs.* e_2 *than for* e_1 *vs.* e_3*. However, numerical similarity between* e_1 *vs.* e_3 *was stronger: "2496200.0" was closer to "2500090.5" as "1786882". As we weighted literal similarity to be more important than structural similarity, this leads to* e_1 *and* e_3 *forming one cluster. In fact, such a clustering is intuitive, as* e_1 *and* e_3 *is about GDP, while* e_2 *is concerned with debt.*

4.2 Related Data Sources

Given a data source D', we score its contextualization w.r.t. another source D'', using entities contained in D' and D''. Note, in contrast to previous work [2], we do not rely on any kind of "external" information, such as top-level schema. Instead, we *solely exploit semantics as captured by entities.*

Contextualisation Score. Similar to [2], we compute two scores, $ec(D'' \mid D')$ and $sc(D'' \mid D')$, for a data source D'', given another source D'. The former is an indicator for the entity complement of D'' w.r.t. D'. That is, *how many new, similar entities* does D'' contribute to given entities in D'. The latter score judges *how many new "dimensions"* are added by D'', to those present in D' (schema complement). Both scores are aggregated to a *contextualization score* for data source D'' given D'.

Let us first define an entity complement score $ec : \mathcal{D} \times \mathcal{D} \mapsto [0, 1]$. We may measure ec simply by counting the overlapping clusters between both sources:

$$ec(D'' \mid D') := \sum_{C_j \in\, cluster(D')} \frac{\mathbb{1}(C_j, D'')|C_j|}{|C_j|}$$

with *cluster* as function mapping data sources to clusters their entities are assigned to. Further, let $\mathbb{1}(C, D)$ by an indicator function, returning 1 if cluster C is associated with data source D via one or more entities.

Considering the schema complement score $sc : \mathcal{D} \times \mathcal{D} \mapsto [0,1]$, we aim to add new dimensions (properties) to those already present. Thus, sc is given as:

$$sc(D'' \mid D') := \sum_{C_j \in \, cluster(D'')} \frac{|props(C_j) \setminus \bigcup_{C_i \in \, cluster(D')} props(C_i)|}{|props(C_j)|}$$

with *props* as function that projects a cluster C to a set of properties, where each property is contained in a description of an entity in C.

Finally, a contextualization score cs is obtained by a monotonic aggregation of ec and sc. In our case, we apply a simple, weighted summation:

$$cs(D'' \mid D') := 1/2 \cdot ec(D'' \mid D') + 1/2 \cdot sc(D'' \mid D')$$

Example. Assuming Src. 1 is given, $cs(D_2 \mid D_1) = cs(D_3 \mid D_1) = 1/2$*, because* $ec(D_3 \mid D_1) = 1$ *and* $sc(D_3 \mid D_1) = 0$ *(the other way around for* $D_2 \mid D_1$*). These scores are meaningful, because* D_2 *adds additional properties (debt), while* D_3 *complements* D_1 *with entities (GDP). See also Fig. 2-c.*

Runtime Behavior and Scalability. Regarding online performance, i.e., computation of contextualization score cs, given the offline learned clusters, we aimed at simple and lightweight heuristics. For ec only an assignment of data sources to clusters (function *cluster*()) and cluster size $|C|$ is needed. Further, measure sc only requires an additional mapping of clusters to "contained" properties (function *props*()). All necessary statistics are easily kept in memory.

With regard to the offline clustering behavior, we expect our approach to perform well, as existing work on kernel k-means clustering showed such approaches to scale to large data sets [1,5,22].

5 Searching the Web of Data via Source Contextualization

Based on our real-world use case (Sect. 2), we show how a source contextualization engine may be *integrated in a real-world query processing system* for the Web of data. Notice, an extended system description is included in our report [21].

Overview. Towards an active *involvement of users in the source selection process*, we implemented a data portal, which offers a *data source space exploration* as well as a *distributed query processing* service.

Using the former, users may explore the space of sources, i.e., search and discover data sources of interest. Here, the contextualization engine fosters discovery of relevant sources during exploration. The query processing service, on the other hand, allows queries to be federated over multiple sources.

Interaction between both services is tight and user-driven. In particular, sources discovered during source exploration may be used for answering queries. On the other hand, sources employed for result computation may be inspected and other relevant sources may be found via contextualization.

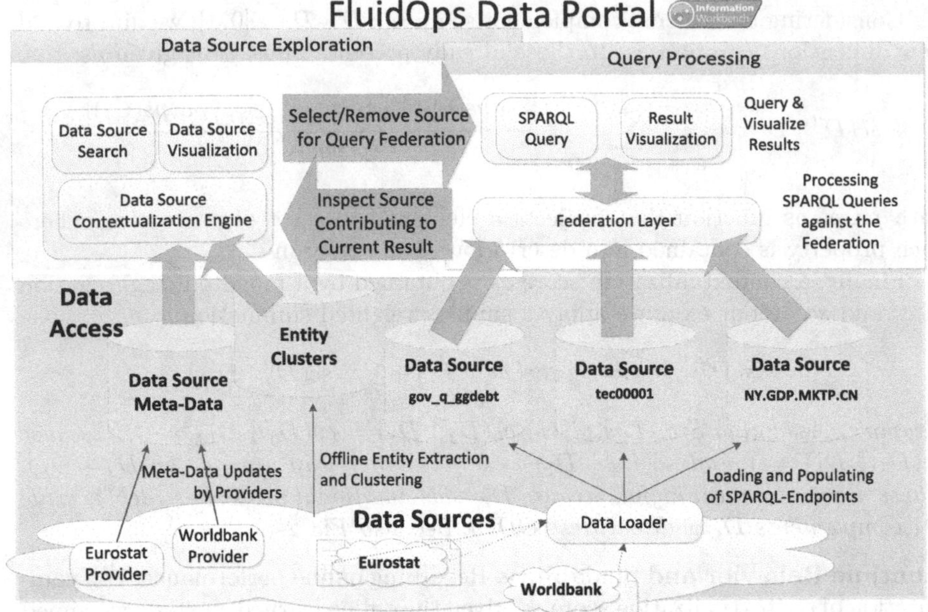

Fig. 3. Our data portal offers two services: source space exploration and query processing. The source contextualization engine is integrated as a key component of the source space exploration. For this, data source meta-data is loaded and entities are extracted/clustered. For query processing, each data source is mapped to a SPARQL endpoint, from which data is accessed via a data-loader.

The data portal is based on the Information Workbench [8] and a running prototype is available.[5] Following our use-case (Sect. 2), we populated the system with statistical data sources from Eurostat and Worldbank. This population involved an extraction of meta-data, which is used to load the sources locally as well as give users insights into the source. Every data source is stored in a triple store – accessible via a SPARQL endpoint. See Fig. 3 for an overview.

Source Exploration and Selection. A typical search process starts with looking for "the right" sources. That is, a user begins with exploration of the data source space. For instance, she may issue a keyword query "gross domestic product", yielding sources with matching words in their meta-data. If this query does not lead to sources suitable for her information need, a faceted search interface or a tag-cloud may be used. For instance, she refines her sources via entity "Germany" in a faceted search, Fig. 4-a. Once the user discovered a source of interest, its structure as well as entity information is shown. For example, a source description for `GDP (current US$)` is given in Fig. 4-b/c. Note, entities used here have been extracted by our approach and are visualized by means of a map. Using these rich source descriptions, a user can get to know the data

[5] http://data.fluidops.net/

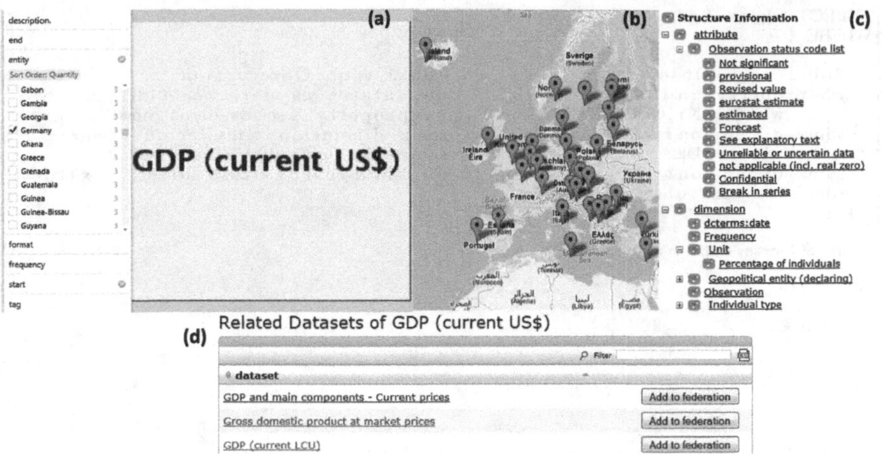

Fig. 4. (a) Faceted search exploration through sources. (b) + (c) Source information for `GDP (current US$)` based on its entities and schema. (d) Contextualization sources for `GDP (current US$)`.

and data sources before issuing queries. Further, for every source a ranked list of contextualization sources is given. For `GDP (current US$)`, e.g., source `GDP at Market Prices` is recommended, Fig. 4-d. This way, the user is guided from one source of interest to another. At any point, she may *select a particular source for querying.* Eventually, she not only knows her relevant sources, but has also gained first insights into data schema and entities.

Processing Queries over Selected Sources. Say, a user has chosen `GDP (current US$)` as well as its contextualization source `GDP at Market Prices` (Fig. 4-d). Due to her previous exploration, she knows that the former provides the German GDP from 2000–2010, while the second source features GDP from years 2011 and 2012. Thus, she may issue a SPARQL query over both sources to visualize the GDP over the years 2000–2012, cf. Fig. 5.

6 Evaluation

We now discuss evaluation results to analyze the *effectiveness* of our approach. We conducted two experiments: (1) Effectiveness w.r.t. a gold standard, thereby measuring the *accuracy of the contextualization score.* (2) Effectiveness w.r.t. data source search result augmentation. In other words, we ask: *How useful are top-ranked contextualization sources in terms of additional information?*

Participants. Experiment (1) and (2) were performed by two different groups, each comprising 14 users. Most participants had an IT background and/or were CS students. Three users came from the finance sector. The users vary in age, 22 to 37 years and gender. All experiments were unsupervised.

```
SELECT ?year ?gdp
WHERE {
  {
   ?obs1 a qb:Observation;
   wb-property:indicator
        wbi-ci:NY.GDP.MKTP.CN;
   sdmx-dimension:refArea
        wbi-cc:DE;
   sdmx-dimension:refPeriod ?year;
   sdmx-measure:obsValue ?gdp.
  }
  UNION
  {
   ?obs2 a qb:Observation;
   qb:dataset es-data:tec00001;
   es-property:geo es-dic:geo#DE;
   sdmx-dimension:timePeriod ?year;
   sdmx-measure:obsValue ?gdp.
   FILTER(?year > "2010-01-01"^^xs:date)
  }
}
```

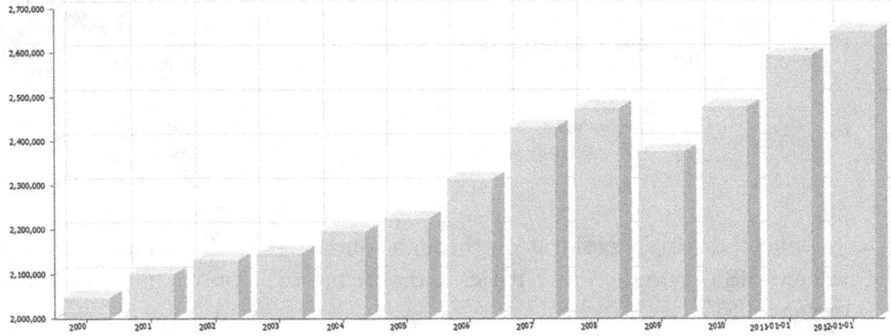

Fig. 5. Query and result visualization for Germany's GDP from 2000–2012. Data sources were selected during source exploration, see Fig. 4.

Data Sources and Clustering. Following our use case in Sect. 2, we employed Linked Data sources from Eurostat[6] and Worldbank[7]. Both provide a large set of data sources comprising statistical information: Eurostat holds $5K$ sources ($8000M$ triples), while Worldbank has $76K$ sources ($167M$ triples). Note, for Eurostat we simply used instances of `void:Dataset` as sources and for Worldbank we considered available dumps as sources. Further, sources varied strongly in their size and # entities. While small sources contained $\leq$10 entities, large sources featured $\geq$1K entities. For extracting/sampling of entities, we restricted attention to instances of `qb:Observation`. We employed the k-means algorithm with $k = 30K$ (chosen based on experiments with different values for k) and initiated the cluster centers via random entities.

Queries. Based on evaluation queries in [2], domain experts constructed 15 queries. A query listing is depicted in Table 1. This query load was designed to be "broad" w.r.t. the following dimensions: (1) We cover a wide range of topics, which may be answered by Eurostat and Worldbank. (2) "Best" results for each query are achieved by using multiple sources from both datasets. (3) # Sources and # entities relevant for a particular query vary.

Systems. We implemented entity-based source contextualization (`EC`) as described in Sect. 4. In particular, we made use of three kernels for capturing

[6] http://eurostat.linked-statistics.org/
[7] http://worldbank.270a.info

Table 1. Queries with their number of relevant entities and sources.

	Keywords	# Entities	# Sources		Keywords	# Entities	# Sources
Q1	Country debt	3,155	1,981	Q9	International trade	2,444	1,085
Q2	Country GDP	4,265	1,969	Q10	National trade	2,971	1,199
Q3	Country population	4,076	3,868	Q11	Price indices	10,490	4,930
Q4	Energy consumption	5,194	651	Q12	Prison population	5,135	629
Q5	Fish species	2,323	157	Q13	Research expenditure	5,287	201
Q6	Fish areas	6,664	316	Q14	School leavers	2,722	637
Q7	Forest area	3,141	707	Q15	Unemployment rate	2,914	266
Q8	Gas emissions	5,470	722	$\sum$		66,251	19,318

entity similarity: a path kernel, a substring kernel, and a numerical kernel [16,19]. As baselines we used two approaches: a schema-based contextualization SC [2] and a keyword-based contextualization KC. SC maps entities in data sources to top-level schemata and finds complementary sources based on schema as well as label similarities of mapped entities. More precisely, the baseline is split in two approaches: SC_{ec} and SC_{sc}. SC_{ec} aims at entity complements, i.e., data sources with similar schema, but different entities. SC_{sc} targets data sources having complementary schema, but holding the same entities. Last, the KC approach treats every data source as a bag-of-words and judges the relevance of a source w.r.t. a query by the number and quality of its matching keywords.

6.1 Effectiveness of Contextualisation Score

Gold Standard. We calculated a simple gold standard that ranks pairs of sources based on their contextualization. That is, for each query in Table 1, we randomly selected one "given" source and 5 "additional" sources – all of which contained the query keywords. Then, 14 users were presented that given source and had to rank how well each of the 5 additional sources contextualizes it (scale on 0–5, where higher is better). To judge the sources' contents, users were given a schema description and a short source extract. We aggregated the user rankings, thereby obtaining a gold standard ranking.

Metric. We applied the footrule distance [12] as rank-distance indicator, which measures the accuracy of the evaluation systems vs. gold standard. Footrule distance is: $\frac{1}{k}\sum_{i=1,\ldots,k}|rank_a(i) - rank(i)|$, with $rank_a(i)$ and $rank(i)$ as approximated and gold standard rank for the "additional" source D_i.

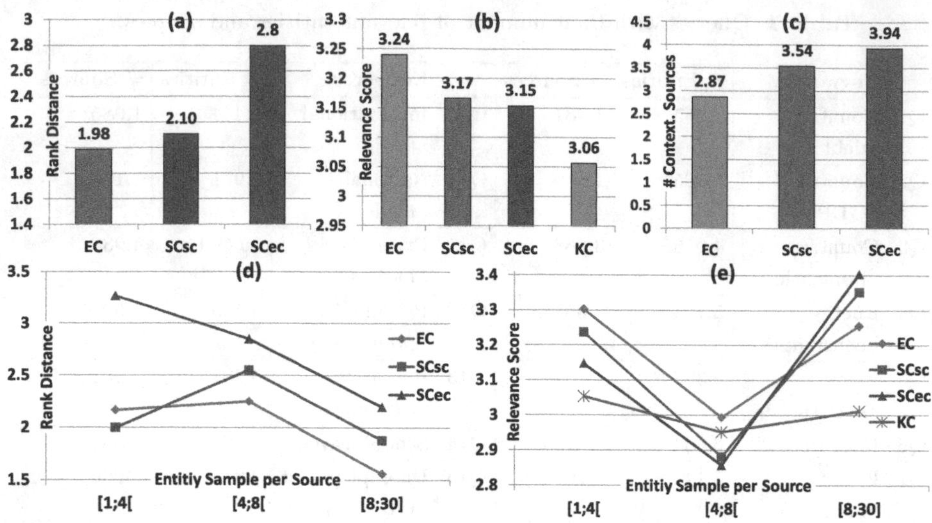

Fig. 6. (a) Exp-1: Rank distance as average over all queries. (b) Exp-2: Relevance score per source, as average over all queries. (c) Exp-2: # Sources for contextualization per source, as average over all queries. (d) Exp-1: Rank distance average over all queries vs. average # sampled entities per source. (e) Exp-2: Relevance score as average over all queries vs. average # sampled entities per source.

Results. Figure 6-a/d give an overview over results of EC and SC. Note, we excluded the KC baseline, because it was too simplistic. That is, reducing sources to bags-of-words, one may only intersect these bags for two given sources. This yielded, however, no meaningful contextualization scores/ranking.

We noticed EC to lead to a good and stable performance over all queries (Fig. 6-a) as well as data source sizes (Fig. 6-d). Overall, EC could outperform $\mathtt{SC}_{sc}$ by 5.7 % and $\mathtt{SC}_{ec}$ by 29 %. Further, as shown in Fig. 6-d, while we observed a decrease in rank distance for all systems in source and entity sample size, EC yielded the best results. We explain these results with our fine-grained source semantics captured by entity clusters. Note, most of our employed contextualization heuristics are very similar to those from SC. However, we observed SC performance to strongly vary with the quality of its schema mappings. Given an accurate classification of entities contained in a particular source, SC was able to effectively relate that source with others. However, if entities were mapped to "wrong" concepts, it greatly affected computed scores. In contrast, our approach relied on clusters learned from instance data, thereby achieving a "more reliable" mapping from sources to their semantics (clusters).

On the other hand, we observed EC to result in equal or, for 2 outlier queries with many "small" sources, worse performance than $\mathtt{SC}_{sc}$ (cf. Fig. 6-d). In particular, given query Q2, $\mathtt{SC}_{sc}$ could achieve a better ranking distance by 20 %. We explain such problematic queries with our simplistic entity sampling. Given small sources, only few entities were included in a sample, which unfortunately pointed to "misleading" clusters. Note, we currently only use a uniform random sample for selecting entities from sources. We expect better results with more refined techniques for discovering important entities for a particular source.

Last, we observed $\texttt{SC}_{ec}$ to lead to much less accurate rankings as $\texttt{SC}_{sc}$ and EC. This is due to exact matching of entity labels: $\texttt{SC}_{ec}$ did not capture common substrings (as EC did), but solely relied on a boolean similarity matching.

6.2 Effectiveness of Augmented Data Source Results

Metric. Following [2], we employ a *reordering of data source search results* as metric: (1) We obtain top 100 data sources via the KC baseline for every query. Here, the order is determined solely by number and quality of keyword hits in the sources' bags-of-words. (2) Via SC and EC we reorder the first 10 results:

For each data source D_i in the top-10 results, we search the top-100 sources for a D_j that contextualizes D_i best. If we find a D_j with contextualization score higher than a threshold, we move D_j after D_i in the top-10 results.

This reordering procedure yields three different top-10 source rankings: one via KC and two (reordered ones) from SC/EC. For every top-10 ranking, users provided a relevance feedback for each source w.r.t. a given query, using a scale 0–5 (higher means "more relevant"). For this, users had a schema description and short source extract for every source. Last, we aggregated these relevancy judgments for each top-10 ranking and query.

Results. User relevance scores are depicted in Fig. 6-b/e. Overall, EC yielded an improved ranking, i.e., it ranked more relevant sources w.r.t. a given query. More precisely, EC outperforms $\texttt{SC}_{sc}$ with 2.5 %, $\texttt{SC}_{ec}$ with 2.8 % and KC with 6.2 %, cf. Fig. 6-b. Furthermore, our EC approach led to stable results over varying source sizes (Fig. 6-e). However, for 2 queries having large sources in their top-100 results, we observed misleading a clustering of sampled entities. Such associated clusters, in turn, led to a bad contextualization, see Fig. 6-e.

Notice that all result reorderings, either by EC or by SC, yielded an improvement (up to 6.2 %) over the plain KC baseline, cf. Fig. 6-b/e. These findings confirm results reported in [2] and clearly show the potential of data source contextualization techniques. In other words, such observations demonstrate the usefulness of contextualization – *participants wanted to have additional/contextualized sources, as provided by EC or SC.*

In Fig. 6-c we show the # sources returned for contextualization of the "original" top-10 sources (obtained via KC). EC returned 19 % less contextualization sources than $\texttt{SC}_{sc}$ and 28 % less than $\texttt{SC}_{ec}$. Unfortunately, as contextualization is a "fuzzy" criteria, we could not determine the total number of relevant sources to be discovered in the top-100. Thus, no recall factor can be computed. However, combined with relevance scores in Fig. 6-b, # sources gives a precision-like indicator. That is, we can compute the average relevance gain per contextualization source: 1.13 EC, 0.89 $\texttt{SC}_{sc}$, and 0.77 $\texttt{SC}_{sc}$, see Fig. 6-b/c. Again, we explain the good "precision" of EC with the fine-grained clustering, providing better and more accurate data source semantics.

Last, it is important to note that, while Exp. 1 (Sect. 6.1*) and Exp. 2 (Sect.* 6.2*) differ greatly in terms of their setting, our observations were still similar: EC outperformed both baselines due to its fine-grained entity clusters.*

7 Related Work

Closest to our approach is work on contextual Web tables [2]. However, [2] focuses on flat entities in tables, i.e., entities adhere to a simple and fixed relational structure. In contrast, we consider entities to be subgraphs contained in data sources. Further, we do not require any kind of "external" information. Most notably, we do not use top-level schemata.

Another line of work is concerned with query processing over distributed RDF data, e.g., [6,9,10,13,18]. During source selection, these approaches frequently exploit indexes, link-traversal, or source meta-data, for mapping queries/query fragments to sources. Our approach is *complementary*, as it enables systems to involve users during source selection. We outlined such an extension of the traditional search process as well as its benefits throughout the paper.

Last, data integration for Web (data) search has received much attention [4]. In fact, some works aim at recommendations for sources to be integrated, e.g., [3, 14,17]. Here, the goal is to give recommendations to identify (integrate) identical entities and schema elements across different data sources.

In contrast, we target a "fuzzy" form of integration, i.e., we do not give exact mappings of entities or schema elements, but merely measure whether or not sources contain entities that might be "somehow" related. In other words, our contextualization score indicates whether sources *might* refer to similar entities and *may* provide contextual information. Furthermore, our approach does not require data sources to adhere to a known schema – instead, we exploit data mining strategies on instance data (entities).

8 Conclusion

We presented a novel approach for Web data source contextualization. For this, we adapted well-known techniques from the field of data mining. More precisely, we provide a framework for source contextualization, to be instantiated in an application-specific manner. By means of a real-world use-case and prototype, we show how source contextualization allows for user involvement during source selection. We empirically validated our approach via two user studies.

References

1. Chitta, R., Jin, R., Havens, T.C., Jain, A.K.: Approximate kernel k-means: solution to large scale kernel clustering. In: SIGKDD (2011)
2. Das Sarma, A., Fang, L., Gupta, N., Halevy, A., Lee, H., Wu, F., Xin, R., Yu, C.: Finding related tables. In: SIGMOD (2012)

3. de Oliveira, H.R., Tavares, A.T., Lóscio, B.F.: Feedback-based data set recommendation for building linked data applications. In: I-SEMANTICS (2012)
4. Doan, A., Halevy, A.Y., Ives, Z.G.: Principles of Data Integration. Morgan Kaufmann, Waltham (2012)
5. Fausser, S., Schwenker, F.: Clustering large datasets with kernel methods. In: ICPR (2012)
6. Görlitz, O., Staab, S.: SPLENDID: SPARQL endpoint federation exploiting VOID descriptions. In: COLD Workshop (2011)
7. Grimnes, G.A., Edwards, P., Preece, A.D.: Instance based clustering of semantic Web resources. In: Bechhofer, S., Hauswirth, M., Hoffmann, J., Koubarakis, M. (eds.) ESWC 2008. LNCS, vol. 5021, pp. 303–317. Springer, Heidelberg (2008)
8. Haase, P., Schmidt, M., Schwarte, A.: The information workbench as a self-service platform for linked data applications. In: COLD Workshop (2011)
9. Harth, A., Hose, K., Karnstedt, M., Polleres, A., Sattler, K., Umbrich, J.: Data summaries for on-demand queries over linked data. In: WWW (2010)
10. Hartig, O., Bizer, C., Freytag, J.-C.: Executing SPARQL queries over the Web of linked data. In: Bernstein, A., Karger, D.R., Heath, T., Feigenbaum, L., Maynard, D., Motta, E., Thirunarayan, K. (eds.) ISWC 2009. LNCS, vol. 5823, pp. 293–309. Springer, Heidelberg (2009)
11. Jain, A.K., Murty, M.N., Flynn, P.J.: Data clustering: a review. ACM Comput. Surv. **31**, 264–323 (1999)
12. Kendall, M., Gibbons, J.D.: Rank Correlation Methods. Edward Arnold, London (1990)
13. Ladwig, G., Tran, T.: Linked data query processing strategies. In: Patel-Schneider, P.F., Pan, Y., Hitzler, P., Mika, P., Zhang, L., Pan, J.Z., Horrocks, I., Glimm, B. (eds.) ISWC 2010, Part I. LNCS, vol. 6496, pp. 453–469. Springer, Heidelberg (2010)
14. Leme, L.A.P.P., Lopes, G.R., Nunes, B.P., Casanova, M.A., Dietze, S.: Identifying candidate datasets for data interlinking. In: Daniel, F., Dolog, P., Li, Q. (eds.) ICWE 2013. LNCS, vol. 7977, pp. 354–366. Springer, Heidelberg (2013)
15. Lodhi, H., Saunders, C., Shawe-Taylor, J., Cristianini, N., Watkins, C.: Text classification using string kernels. J. Mach. Learn. Res. **2**, 419–444 (2002)
16. Lösch, U., Bloehdorn, S., Rettinger, A.: Graph kernels for RDF data. In: Simperl, E., Cimiano, P., Polleres, A., Corcho, O., Presutti, V. (eds.) ESWC 2012. LNCS, vol. 7295, pp. 134–148. Springer, Heidelberg (2012)
17. Nikolov, A., d'Aquin, M.: Identifying relevant sources for data linking using a semantic Web index. In: LDOW Workshop (2011)
18. Nikolov, A., Schwarte, A., Hütter, C.: FedSearch: efficiently combining structured queries and full-text search in a SPARQL federation. In: Alani, H., et al. (eds.) ISWC 2013, Part I. LNCS, vol. 8218, pp. 427–443. Springer, Heidelberg (2013)
19. Shawe-Taylor, J., Cristianini, N.: Kernel Methods for Pattern Analysis. Cambridge University Press, Cambridge (2004)
20. Wagner, A., Haase, P., Rettinger, A., Lamm, H.: Discovering related data sources in data-portals. In: First International Workshop on Semantic Statistics (2013)
21. Wagner, A., Haase, P., Rettinger, A., Lamm, H.: Entity-based data source contextualization for searching the Web of data. Technical report (2013). http://www.aifb.kit.edu/web/Techreport3043
22. Zhang, R., Rudnicky, A.: A large scale clustering scheme for kernel K-Means. In: Pattern Recognition (2002)

Setting the Course of Emergency Vehicle Routing Using Geolinked Open Data for the Municipality of Catania

Sergio Consoli[1(✉)], Aldo Gangemi[1,3], Andrea Giovanni Nuzzolese[1,2], Silvio Peroni[1,2], Diego Reforgiato Recupero[1], and Daria Spampinato[1]

[1] Semantic Technology Laboratory, National Research Council (CNR), Institute of Cognitive Sciences and Technologies, Rome, Italy
{sergio.consoli,diego.reforgiato,daria.spampinato}@istc.cnr.it

[2] Department of Computer Science, University of Bologna, Bologna, Italy
nuzzoles@cs.unibo.it, silvio.peroni@unibo.it

[3] LIPN, University Paris 13, Sorbone Cité, UMR CNRS, Villetaneuse, France
aldo.gangemi@lipn.univ-paris13.fr

Abstract. Linked Open Data (LOD) has gained significant momentum over the past years as a best practice of promoting the sharing and publication of structured data on the semantic Web. Currently LOD is reaching significant adoption also in Public Administrations (PAs), where it is often required to be connected to existing platforms, such as GIS-based data management systems. Bearing on previous experience with the pioneering data.cnr.it, through Semantic Scout, as well as the Agency for Digital Italy recommendations for LOD in Italian PA, we are working on the extraction, publication, and exploitation of data from the Geographic Information System of the Municipality of Catania, referred to as SIT ("Sistema Informativo Territoriale"). The goal is to boost the metropolis towards the route of a modern Smart City by providing prototype integrated solutions supporting transport, public health, urban decor, and social services, to improve urban life. In particular a mobile application focused on real-time road traffic and public transport management is currently under development to support sustainable mobility and, especially, to aid the response to urban emergencies, from small accidents to more serious disasters. This paper describes the results and lessons learnt from the first work campaign, aiming at analyzing, reengineering, linking, and formalizing the Shape-based geo-data from the SIT.

Keywords: Geo-Linked Open Data applications · Linked eGovernment Data extraction and publication · Sustainable mobility · Emergency vehicle routing

---

This work has been supported by the PON R&C project PRISMA, "PiattafoRme cloud Interoperabili per SMArt-government", ref. PON04a2 A Smart Cities, under the National Operational Programme for Research and Competitiveness 2007–2013. Authors are listed in alphabetical order as their contributions are equally distributed.

V. Presutti et al. (Eds.): ESWC Satellite Events 2014, LNCS 8798, pp. 42–53, 2014.
DOI: 10.1007/978-3-319-11955-7_4

1 Preliminary Discussion

In a currently on-going project we are investigating the extraction, enrichment, publication and reuse of Linked Open Data (LOD) [1,2] for the Municipality of Catania (MoC), Italy, by means of the application of latest semantic technologies and software components [3]. The main motivation of the work consists of experimenting social eGovernment systems aimed at optimizing the performance of the Public Administration (PA) of the MoC for the provision of intelligent ICT services to citizens and businesses, supporting the external evaluation of the PA by the detection of the community trust. The work falls within the spirit of the Smart Cities initiatives of the European Commission, which aims at bringing together cities, industry and citizens to improve urban life through more sustainable integrated solutions. Although the methodology has been designed for the case study of the city hall of Catania, the approach is completely generalizable and can be replicated to any PA worldwide. One of the main development objectives of the project consists in conceiving, designing and prototyping applications for the MoC related to certain areas of experimentation, such as online social services and health, traffic management and transport, and urban decor. With the aim of detecting and collecting the required data and processes for these applications, meetings with the Leadership of the Directorate of Information Systems Service of the MoC were carried out.

A particular field of experimentation is specially focused on the management of mobility, i.e. road traffic and public transport. Within this context, the scenario has identified the development of a prototype mobile application implementing a real-time system to inform on the state of roads in urban areas to support sustainable mobility and, in particular, to aid the response to urban emergencies, from small scale accidents to more serious disasters. The system aims at connecting drivers to one another, helping people create local driving communities that work together to improve the quality of everyone's daily driving. That might mean helping them avoid the frustration of sitting in traffic, advising them on unexpected accidents or other traps, or just shaving five minutes off of their regular commute by showing them new routes they never even knew about. But most importantly, the application may have any extremely important role on emergency logistics. Response to an emergency incident requires careful planning and professional execution of plans, when and if an emergency occurs [4]. During these events there is the need to find rapidly the nearest hospitals, or to obtain the best way outs from the emergency zones, or to produce the optimal path connecting two suburbs for redirecting the road traffic, etc. Technically, this system should be able to locate the best path between source and destination not only in a static environment, but particularly in a dynamic one. That is, the user feedback serves at placing in the map some obstacles, or inaccessible zones, coming from accidents or emergency events, and the system responds in real-time producing the optimal path without these forbidden zones. After typing in their destination address, users just drive with the application open on their phone to passively contribute traffic and other road data, but they can also take a more active role by sharing road reports on accidents, advising on unexpected traps, or any other hazards along the way, helping to give other users in the area real-time information about what's to come [5]. For the realization of the app for our case study, it is necessary to process the data and diagrams in the Geographic Information System of the MoC, referred to as SIT: "Sistema Informativo Territoriale" [6]. Therefore it was decided, by mutual agreement with the chief officers and experts of the city hall of Catania, to process the data in order to make them open, interoperable and compatible with the principles of Linked Open Data.

The paper is structured as follows. Background on the state of the art on the use of LOD for PA, often referred to as Linked eGovernment Data [7], is reported in Sect. 2. Techniques and tools used to deal with LOD for the MoC are introduced in Sect. 3, while the extracted ontology is described in Sect. 3.3, along with the means used to consume the accessible data. Section 4 ends the paper with conclusions and the future research where we are directed.

2 Linked eGovernment Data

LOD are currently bootstrapping the Web of Data by converting into RDF and publishing existing datasets available to the general public under open licenses [1,2]. LOD offers the possibility of using data across domains or organisations for purposes like statistics, analysis, maps and publications. These major changes in technology and society are involving also the way of doing politics, administration and the relationship between politicians, public servants and citizens. Transparency, participation and collaboration are the main issues of the integration of citizens in the paradigm of Open Government [8]. Because PAs have large amounts of data which could be made accessible for the purpose of the LOD movement, research on the opening process, data reengineering, linking, formalisation and consumption is of primary interest [9].

The Digital Administration Code incorporates a wide range of best-practices in the usage of Linked eGovernment Data, which can be synthetized as: portals for the supply of the Linked eGovernment Data sets; portals providing raw data sets of LOD for PAs along with technical tools or developer kits for understanding, interpreting, or processing the provided data; existing portals acting as showrooms for best practices for Linked eGovernment Data; mobile apps for smartphones using LOD for PAs [7].

The main thrust on the publication of LOD for PA is coming from big initiatives in the United States (data.gov) [10,11] and the United Kingdom (data.gov.uk) [12], both providing thousands of raw sets of LOD within their portals, but there are also some other experiences and notable initiatives that are in line with the international state of the art. In Germany, one of the first examples for a LOD portal is the one from the state of Baden-Württemberg (opendata.service-bw.de), divided into three main parts: LOD, applications, and tools. In addition to their potentials, Linked eGovernment Data can provide great benefits in the matter of accountability, as shown in the LOD portal example of Kenya (opendata.go.ke).

In addition, LOD have been published in Italy by the city hall of Florence[1], Agency for Digital Italy[2], from the Piedmont region[3], the Chamber of Deputies[4]. Beside these initiatives, another notable for the Italian PA is "data.cnr.it" [13, 14], the open data project of the National Research Council (CNR), designed and maintained by the Semantic Technology Laboratory of ISTC-CNR, and shared with the unit Information Systems Office of CNR.

3 Extraction of Linked eGovernment Data for the MoC

In this section we present the methodology used for the extraction and publication of LOD for the Municipality of Catania. The methods are based on the standards of the W3C[5], on good international practices, on the guidelines issued by the Agency for Digital Italy [15,16] and those by the Italian Index of Public Administration[6], as well as on the in-depth experience of the research participants on this field, in particular related to the development of the "data.cnr.it" [13,14] portal.

3.1 Scenario Analysis

During the phase of selection of the source data, a thorough analysis of the reference domain was made. Thanks to the close interaction with the PA experts of the MoC, the Geographic Information System, SIT [6], was identified as the source dataset for the enrichment and publication of data. The SIT is a data warehouse used for reporting and data analysis, and consisting of databases, hardware, software, and technicians, which manages, develops and integrates information of the province of Catania based on a geographical space [6]. The various territorial levels (hydrography, topography, buildings, infrastructure, technological networks, administrative boundaries and land, ...) form the geo-localised common part of the information flow of the MoC, according to which all the constituent parts are related to each other.

The SIT is designed to contain all the available data of the PA in Catania for the purpose of in-depth knowledge of the local area. Basically tit contains three types of data: *register base*, *registry office*, and *toponymy*, provided in the form of Shape-based files [17] for each data record, i.e. files with extensions: .dbf, .shp, .shx, .sbn, .sbx, .xml. Through the consultation platform on the web it is possible to display the following information: basic cartography; ortho-photos; road graph; buildings with a breakdown by main body of some areas of the city; cadastral sections; data from the 1991 and 2001 census of the population; last Master Plan; gas network on-going works; resident population in selected

1 Available at: http://opendata.comune.fi.it/linked_data.html
2 Available at: http://www.digitpa.gov.it
3 Available at: http://www.dati.piemonte.it/rdf.html
4 Available at: http://dati.camera.it
5 Available at: http://www.w3.org/standards/semanticweb/
6 Available at: http://spcdata.digitpa.gov.it/data.html

areas (municipalities, entire street, polygonal, circular area); total population, distributed into bow street, house number, etc.; breakdown of the population by municipality, blocks, nationality, gender, family components, age, marital status, etc.; extraction and search of resident persons, and their location on the bow streets; competence areas of pharmacies; location and alphanumeric information of: municipality, hospitals, universities, schools, pharmacies, post offices, areas or emergency, public safety, fire departments, public green areas, public community centres, institutions for minors and orphanages. The SIT also includes maps containing geo-referenced information related to: sub-services (electricity-gas-water pipes); data on stoppage areas; occupation stalls; stalls for disadvantaged people; occupation of public land; public transport fleet; management and working state of the fleet; data on lines and stops of public transport; accident traffic data; road signs and markings; maintenance state of roads and sidewalks; management of roadway construction; data of the municipal police; the accounting of the Municipality. Note that the information contained in the SIT are in Italian language, therefore the produced Linked Open Data will be in Italian too (although the whole generation process is completely language-independent).

3.2 Geo-Data Modelling and Reengineering

To reengineer the dataset according to the target conceptual model we used Tabels[7], a software tool developed by the research foundation CTIC, which, using the GeoTools libraries[8], is capable of transforming the information encoded in the shape files into RDF representations. From the shape files supplied for each data record (in particular, the files with extensions .dbf and .shp), Tabels encoded the shape files into RDF triples related to the designed ontology, that it will be described in more detail in Sect. 3.3. On the one hand the characteristics of the table are stored as RDF representation, and, on the other hand, the spatial geometry is modelled on the standard KML representation [18]. At this stage we

Fig. 1. Example of a geo-localised entity of "pharmacies".

[7] Available at: http://idi.fundacionctic.org/tabels/
[8] Available at: http://geotools.org

are mapping to existing vocabularies, in particular NeoGeo[9], suitable for geo-data. The geometric coordinates in KML are expressed according to the Geodetic reference system Gauss-Boaga (or Rome 40). By means of different conversion tools publicly available on-line (e.g. http://www.ultrasoft3d.net/Conversione_Coordinate.aspx), it is possible to produce the coordinates of latitude, longitude and altitude in meters using the Geodetic system WGS84 [19]. In particular, the application of Tabels to each pair of files, .dbf and .shp, of the data tables is able to produce a set of RDF triples stored in a repository with other geometric resources contained in a public server. For example, from the information stored in the database of the SIT representing an entity of "pharmacies" (Fig. 1), Tabels produces the related RDF triples, shown in Fig. 2, and the file with the geometric KML coordinates (Fig. 3).

```
<http://www.essepuntato.it/2013/10/prisma/resource/farmacia/finocchiaro-giuseppa>
a <http://www.essepuntato.it/2013/10/prisma/CATANIA.SDO_Farmacie> ;
    <http://www.essepuntato.it/2013/10/prisma/CODICE-of-CATANIA.SDO_Farmacie>
      "10625" ;
    <http://www.essepuntato.it/2013/10/prisma/MUNI-of-CATANIA.SDO_Farmacie>
      "5" ;
    <http://www.essepuntato.it/2013/10/prisma/Municipali-of-CATANIA.SDO_Farmacie>
      5 ;
    <http://www.essepuntato.it/2013/10/prisma/NOME-of-CATANIA.SDO_Farmacie>
      "FINOCCHIARO GIUSEPPA" ;
    <http://www.essepuntato.it/2013/10/prisma/NUMERO-of-CATANIA.SDO_Farmacie>
      "60" ;
    <http://www.essepuntato.it/2013/10/prisma/OBJECTID-of-CATANIA.SDO_Farmacie>
      1 ;
    <http://www.essepuntato.it/2013/10/prisma/OBJECTID_1-of-CATANIA.SDO_Farmacie>
      1 ;
    <http://www.essepuntato.it/2013/10/prisma/PROPRIETA-of-CATANIA.SDO_Farmacie>
      "FINOCCHIARO GIUSEPPA" ;
    <http://www.essepuntato.it/2013/10/prisma/RECAPITO-of-CATANIA.SDO_Farmacie>
      "VIA SAN GIOVANNI BATTISTA 74" ;
    <http://www.essepuntato.it/2013/10/prisma/Shape-of-CATANIA.SDO_Farmacie>
      "http://www.w3.org/2003/01/geo/wgs84_pos#Point" ;
    <http://www.essepuntato.it/2013/10/prisma/kml-of-CATANIA.SDO_Farmacie>
      <http://www.essepuntato.it/2013/10/prisma/farmacia/kml/Farmacie.1.kml> .
```

Fig. 2. RDF triples produced by Tabels for the example of entity in "pharmacies".

```
<?xml version="1.0" encoding="UTF-8"?>
<kml:kml xmlns:kml="http://earth.google.com/kml/2.1">
    <kml:Document id="featureCollection">
        <kml:Placemark id="Farmacie.1">
            <kml:Point>
                <kml:coordinates>15.0520808419018,37.5490041443454</kml:coordinates>
            </kml:Point>
        </kml:Placemark>
    </kml:Document>
</kml:kml>
```

Fig. 3. KML coordinates produced by Tabels for the example of entity in "pharmacies".

[9] Available at: http://geovocab.org/doc/neogeo.html

Tabels is able to import common file formats, such as XLS or CSV, including shape files. Afterwards it generates automatically a transformation program from the input data files. The generated program is able to transform each row of the input data into a new instance of a RDF class ad-hoc. In addition, each value in the column of the input tables is converted into a new triple where the subject is the instance mentioned, the predicate is a property based on the name of the column header, and the object is the value of the column as a *rdfs:Literal*. It is worth noting that the transformation program automatically generated, is a SPARQL-based script completely customisable by the user. Thus it is possible to change classes, names and associated properties, and then to annotate them appropriately. Once the transformation program is defined, the execution of Tabels generates the corresponding RDF in output, which we make publicly available online through a dedicated SPARQL endpoint. In addition, information regarding each resource object of the ontology data can be obtained through negotiation mechanisms of the content (content negotiation) based on HTTP REST that make them accessible, for example, through a browser or as REST web service. Data consumption is described in more detail in Sect. 3.5.

3.3 Resulting Ontology for the SIT

Starting from the definition of the tables of the SIT, a first version of OWL ontology was developed. This provides classes and properties representing the database entities of the SIT, and is publicly available at the following URI:

http://ontologydesignpatterns.org/ont/prisma/ontology.owl

having the namespace (i.e. the default address of the entities in the ontology):

http://www.ontologydesignpatterns.org/ont/prisma/.

The creation process of this ontology was divided into two main phases and has followed the good practice of formal representation, naming, and semantic assumptions in use in the domain of the Semantic Web and Linked Open Data [15,16]. In the first phase, the entire structure of the tables was converted into a draft OWL ontology, where each table (i.e. each entity type described by the supplied data) is represented by a class and each field of the table by a data property. This translation was carried out in a fully automatic way from the sources provided in XML format (extension .shp.xml) by means of the use of an XSLT transformation. Note that fields with the same name but belonging to different tables have been provided with distinct properties. For example, the fields "Name" of the tables "Nursing Homes" ("Case Riposo") and "Pharmacies" ("Farmacie") have been translated with two different data properties, respectively "Name-of-CATANIA.SDO_NursingHomes" and "Name-of-CATANIA.SDO_Pharmacies".

From this interim draft ontology and from the available data, a first version of the ontology in OWL was produced. At this stage we have followed the suggestions of the W3C Organization Ontology[10], a set of guidelines for generating,

[10] Available at: http://www.w3.org/TR/2014/REC-vocab-org-20140116/

publishing and consuming LOD for organizational structures. In this respect we have named the graph nodes as URIs and pursued the following principles:

- The name of all the classes was taken to the singular (e.g., from "Pharmacies" to "Pharmacy");
- The names of the data properties were aligned when they were clearly showing the same semantics. For example, the properties "Name-of-CATANIA.SDO_NursingHomes" and "Name-of-CATANIA.SDO_Pharmacies" ended in the same property "name", assigned to "NursingHome" and "Pharmacy" as domain or entity class;
- The data properties that seemed to refer to individuals of other classes, probably having foreign key functions on the data base, were transformed into object properties. For example, the property "MUNI-of-CATANIA.SDO_NursingHomes" became "municipality" in order to connect individuals of class "Nursing Home' with individuals of class "Municipality";
- The data properties having values clearly assigned to some resources were transformed into object properties and their values were *reified* as individuals of specially created classes.

All changes made to the intermediate draft ontology for the implementation of the first version of the ontology have been documented in the form of SPARQL CONSTRUCT. This allowed us to create a simple script to convert the data extracted by Tabels in order to make them fully compliant with the final expected ontology, produced as output in RDF format.

3.4 Example of Conversion from the Geo-Data to the Final Ontology

In this section we want to focus on the phase of transformation from shape files to the final RDF ontology by reporting an example. Consider as reference the data record "Traffic Lights" ("Semafori"). The SQL schema of this table includes the fields:

- *ObjectID* - unique number incremented sequentially;
- *Shape* - type Geometry that represents the coordinates defining the geometric characteristics of the entity;
- *Id* - Identification number of type Double;
- *name* - String type name of the entity;
- *Sde_SDE_se* - integer number;
- *Se_ANNO_CAD_DATA* - blob representing the date.

Passing the .shp and .dbf files to Tabels, this generates the transformation program, that is the SPARQL-based script used to import the data (see Fig. 4). As already mentioned, it is possible to edit the script to suit custom requirements. Once any change in the transformation program is completed, it is possible to save and run it, which generates the RDF triples from the table data

```
PREFIX project: <http://www.essepuntato.it/2013/10/prisma/semaforo/>
PREFIX my: <http://www.essepuntato.it/2013/10/prisma/>
PREFIX rdf: <http://www.w3.org/1999/02/22-rdf-syntax-ns#>
PREFIX rdfs: <http://www.w3.org/2000/01/rdf-schema#>
PREFIX dcat: <http://www.w3.org/ns/dcat#>
PREFIX dct: <http://purl.org/dc/terms/>
PREFIX foaf: <http://xmlns.com/foaf/0.1/#>

FOR ?rowId IN rows FILTER get-row(?rowId)
    MATCH [?oBJECTID,?iD,?nOME,?sDESDESE,?geometry,?kml] IN horizontal
    LET ?resource = resource(replace(replace(replace(lower-case(?nOME)," +","-"),"--+","-"),",|\.",""),
                            <http://www.essepuntato.it/2013/10/prisma/resource/semaforo/>)

CONSTRUCT {
    my:TabelsDataCatalog a dcat:Catalog .
    my:TabelsDataCatalog dct:title "Tabels AutoGenerated Catalog" .
    my:TabelsDataCatalog dct:description "Tabels AutoGenerated Catalog" .
    my:TabelsDataCatalog dct:publisher my:TabelsAutoGenerator .
    my:TabelsDataCatalog dcat:dataset my:DataSet
}

CONSTRUCT {
    ?resource a my:CATANIA.SDO_semafori .
    ?resource my:OBJECTID-of-CATANIA.SDO_semafori ?oBJECTID .
    ?resource my:Id-of-CATANIA.SDO_semafori ?iD .
    ?resource my:NOME-of-CATANIA.SDO_semafori ?nOME .
    ?resource my:sde_SDE_se-of-CATANIA.SDO_semafori ?sDESDESE .
    ?resource my:Shape-of-CATANIA.SDO_semafori ?geometry .
    ?resource my:kml-of-CATANIA.SDO_semafori ?kml
}

CONSTRUCT {
    my:CATANIA.SDO_semafori a rdfs:Class
}

CONSTRUCT {
    my:OBJECTID-of-CATANIA.SDO_semafori a rdf:Property .
    my:Id-of-CATANIA.SDO_semafori a rdf:Property .
    my:NOME-of-CATANIA.SDO_semafori a rdf:Property .
    my:sde_SDE_se-of-CATANIA.SDO_semafori a rdf:Property .
    my:Shape-of-CATANIA.SDO_semafori a rdf:Property .
    my:kml-of-CATANIA.SDO_semafori a rdf:Property
}
```

Fig. 4. A view on the transformation program used by Tabels to convert the shape files to RDF for the table "Traffic Lights" ("Semafori").

```
@prefix my: <http://www.essepuntato.it/2013/10/prisma/> .
@prefix : <http://www.essepuntato.it/2013/10/prisma/resource/semaforo/> .

:cso-italia-cso-provincie-vle-ionio a my:CATANIA.SDO_semafori ;
   my:Id-of-CATANIA.SDO_semafori 8 ;
   my:NOME-of-CATANIA.SDO_semafori "C.so Italia-C.so Provincie-V.le Ionio" ;
   my:OBJECTID-of-CATANIA.SDO_semafori 10 ;
   my:Shape-of-CATANIA.SDO_semafori "http://www.w3.org/2003/01/geo/wgs84_pos#Point" ;
   my:kml-of-CATANIA.SDO_semafori
      <http://www.essepuntato.it/2013/10/prisma/semaforo/kml/Semafori.10.kml> ;
   my:sde_SDE_se-of-CATANIA.SDO_semafori 1 .
```

(a)

```
@prefix ont: <http://ontologydesignpatterns.org/ont/prisma/> .
@prefix geo: <http://www.w3.org/2003/01/geo/wgs84_pos#> .

<http://ontologydesignpatterns.org/ont/prisma/semaforo/cso-italia-cso-provincie-vle-ionio>
  a ont:Semaforo ;
  ont:forma geo:Point ;
  ont:identificativoOggetto 10 ;
  ont:nome "C.so Italia-C.so Provincie-V.le Ionio" ;
  ont:sde 1 .
```

(b)

Fig. 5. Top panel (a): RDF/Turtle produced by the transformation program of Tabels for a single entity of the table "Traffic Lights" ("Semafori"). Bottom panel (b): Corresponding final RDF/Turtle ontology obtained through SPARQL CONSTRUCT conversion to fully match the designed ontology.

given as input. Figure 5(a) shows the RDF/Turtle produced by Tabels by using the methodology already described for a single "Traffic Light" entity as example. Figure 5(b) shows the corresponding final ontology of this entity obtained by conversion through SPARQL CONSTRUCT of the related data extracted by Tabels, in order to fully match the designed ontology.

This example further shows the ability and simplicity of the proposed methodology to gather the complex structure of a non-structured database, allowing a rapid analysis, retrieval, and conversion of the data into a structured RDF format, and the publication in the form of Linked Open Data.

3.5 Data Consumption

The produced ontology consists of 854,221 triples and can be publicly queried by selecting the RDF graph called *<prisma>* on the dedicated SPARQL endpoint accessible at http://wit.istc.cnr.it:8894/sparql. Queries can be made by editing the text area available into the interface for the SPARQL query. The SPARQL endpoint is also accessible as a REST web service, whose synopsis is:

- URL ⇒ http://wit.istc.cnr.it:8894/sparql
- Method ⇒ GET
- Parameters ⇒ query (mandatory)
- MIME type supported output ⇒ *text/html*; *text/rdf+n3*; *application/xml*; *application/json*; *application/rdf+xml*.

Data are also accessible through content negotiation. The reference namespace for the ontology is http://www.ontologydesignpatterns.org/ont/prisma/ which is identified by the prefix *prisma-ont*. The namespace associated with the data is, instead http://www.ontologydesignpatterns.org/data/prisma/ which is identified by the prefix *prisma*. These two namespaces allow content negotiation related to the ontology and the associated data. The negotiation can be done either via a web browser (in this case the MIME type of the output is always *text/html*), or by making HTTP REST requests to one of the two namespaces. The synopsis of the REST requests to the web service associated with the namespace identified by the prefix *prisma-ont* is the following:

- URL ⇒ http://www.ontologydesignpatterns.org/ont/prisma/
- Method ⇒ GET
- Parameters ⇒ ID of the ontology object (mandatory the PATH parameter)
- MIME type supported output ⇒ *text/html*; *text/rdf+n3*; *text/turtle*; *text/owl-functional*; *text/owl-manchester*; *application/owl+xml*; *application/rdf+xml*; *application /rdf+json*.

Instead, the synopsis of the REST requests to the web service associated with the namespace identified by the prefix *prisma* is the following:

- URL ⇒ http://www.ontologydesignpatterns.org/data/prisma/
- Method ⇒ GET

- Parameters ⇒ ID of the ontology object (mandatory the PATH parameter)
- MIME type supported output ⇒ *text/html*; *text/rdf+n3*; *text/turtle*; *text/owl-functional*; *text/owl-manchester*; *application/owl+xml*; *application/rdf+xml*; *application /rdf+json*.

4 Conclusion

This paper presents an application of Linked Open Data for PA. The used methodology was implemented by following the standards of the W3C, the good international practices, the guidelines issued by the Agency for Digital Italy and the Italian Index of Public Administration, as well as by the in-depth experience of the research participants in the field. The method was applied to the case study of the PA of the MoC, in particular from their data stored in the Geographic Information System, SIT. By using tools and technologies for the extraction and publication of data, it was possible to produce an ontology of the SIT according to the paradigm of Linked Open Data. The data are publicly accessible to users through queries to a dedicated SPARQL endpoint, or alternatively through calls to dedicate REST web services.

In currently on-going work a mobile application based on this LOD and related to sustainable mobility and emergency vehicle routing is under development and will be released soon. This will support the real-time management of road traffic and public transport, informing citizens on the state of roads in urban areas, in particular during urban emergencies, from small accidents to more serious disasters, and redirecting the road traffic by providing best alternatives routes to find way outs, the nearest hospitals or other locations of interest. The user will be able to contribute traffic and other road data, sharing road reports on accidents, advising on unexpected obstacles or inaccessible zones, or any other hazards along the way, helping to give other users in the area real-time information about what is currently happening. Soon, when the mobile app based on these LOD will be launched, user-centric tests and an experimental evaluation will be object of investigation. Our work is a concrete step supporting the Municipality of Catania to move into the paradigm of Open Government and Linked Data, boosting the metropolis towards the route of a modern Smart City.

References

1. Berners-Lee, T., Chen, Y., Chilton, L., Connolly, D., Dhanaraj, R., Hollenbach, J., Lerer, A., Sheets, D.: Tabulator: exploring and analyzing linked data on the semantic web. In: Proceedings of the 3rd International Semantic Web User Interaction Workshop, SWUI 2006, Athens, USA (2006)
2. Bizer, C., Heath, T., Berners-Lee, T.: Linked Data - the story so far. Int. J. Semant. Web Inf. Syst. **5**(3), 1–22 (2009)
3. Tan, P.N., Steinbach, M., Kumar, V.: Introduction to Data Mining. Addison-Wesley, Boston (2006)

4. Diaz, R., Behr, J., Toba, A., Giles, B., Manwoo, N., Longo, F., Nicoletti, L.: Humanitarian/emergency logistics models: a state of the art overview. vol. 45, pp. 261–268 (2013)
5. Liu, B.: Route finding by using knowledge about the road network. IEEE Trans. Syst. Man Cybern. Part A Syst. Hum. **27**(4), 436–448 (1997)
6. Municipality of Catania: Il Sistema Informativo Territoriale. http://www.sitr.provincia.catania.it:81/il-sit. Accessed Jan 2014
7. Geiger, C.P., von Lucke, J.: Open Government and (Linked) (Open) (Government) (Data). JeDEM - eJournal of eDemocracy and Open Government **4**(2), 265–278 (2012)
8. Geiger, C.P., von Lucke, J.: Open Government Data. In: Parycek, P., Kripp, J.M., Edelmann, N. (eds.) CeDEM11, Proceedings of the International Conference for E-Democracy and Open Government, Edition Donau-Universitat Krems, Austria, pp. 183–194 (2011)
9. Alani, H., Dupplaw, D., Sheridan, J., O'Hara, K., Darlington, J., Shadbolt, N.R., Tullo, C.: Unlocking the potential of public sector information with semantic web technology. In: Aberer, K., et al. (eds.) ASWC 2007 and ISWC 2007. LNCS, vol. 4825, pp. 708–721. Springer, Heidelberg (2007)
10. Ding, L., Difranzo, D., Graves, A., Michaelis, J., Li, X., McGuinness, D., Hendler, J.: Data-gov Wiki: towards linking government data. In: Proceedings of the AAAI 2010 Spring Symposium on Linked Data Meets Artificial Intelligence, Palo Alto, CA, vol. SS-10-07, pp. 38–43. AAAI Press (2010)
11. Ding, L., Lebo, T., Erickson, J.S., DiFranzo, D., Williams, G.T., Li, X., Michaelis, J., Graves, A., Zheng, J.G., Shangguan, Z., Flores, J., McGuinness, D.L., Hendler, J.A.: TWC LOGD: a portal for linked open government data ecosystems. Web Semant. Sci. Serv. Agents World Wide Web **9**(3), 325–333 (2011)
12. Shadbolt, N., O'Hara, K., Berners-Lee, T., Gibbins, N., Glaser, H., Hall, W., Schraefel, M.: Linked Open Government Data: lessons from data.gov.uk. IEEE Intell. Syst. **27**(3), 16–24 (2012)
13. Baldassarre, C., Daga, E., Gangemi, A., Gliozzo, A., Salvati, A., Troiani, G.: Semantic scout: making sense of organizational knowledge. In: Cimiano, P., Pinto, H.S. (eds.) EKAW 2010. LNCS, vol. 6317, pp. 272–286. Springer, Heidelberg (2010)
14. Gangemi, A., Daga, E., Salvati, A., Troiani, G., Baldassarre, C.: Linked Open Data for the Italian PA: the CNR experience. Informatica e Diritto **1**(2), 453–476 (2011)
15. Agency for a Digital Italy: Linee guida per i siti web delle PA. Art. 4 della Direttiva n. 8/2009 del Ministro per la pubblica amministrazione e l'innovazione (2011). http://www.digitpa.gov.it/sites/default/files/linee_guida_siti_web_delle_pa_2011.pdf
16. Agency for a Digital Italy: Linee guida per l'interoperabilità semantica attraverso Linked Open Data. Commissione di coordinamento SPC (2012). http://www.digitpa.gov.it/sites/default/files/allegati_tec/CdC-SPC-GdL6-InteroperabilitaSemOpenData_v2.0_0.pdf
17. Lamb, A., Johnson, L.: Virtual expeditions: Google Earth, GIS, and geovisualization technologies in teaching and learning. Teach. Libr. **37**(3), 81–85 (2010)
18. Dodsworth, E., Nicholson, A.: Academic uses of Google Earth and Google Maps in a library setting. Inf. Technol. Libr. **31**(2), 81–85 (2012)
19. EUROCONTROL: WGS 84 implementation manual. Institute of Geodesy and Navigation (IfEN), University FAF Munich, Germany (1998)

Adapting Sentiment Lexicons Using Contextual Semantics for Sentiment Analysis of Twitter

Hassan Saif[1(✉)], Yulan He[2], Miriam Fernandez[1], and Harith Alani[1]

[1] Knowledge Media Institute, The Open University, Milton Keynes, UK
{h.saif,m.fernandez,h.alani}@open.ac.uk

[2] School of Engineering and Applied Science, Aston University, Birmingham, UK
y.he@cantab.net

Abstract. Sentiment lexicons for sentiment analysis offer a simple, yet effective way to obtain the prior sentiment information of opinionated words in texts. However, words' sentiment orientations and strengths often change throughout various contexts in which the words appear. In this paper, we propose a lexicon adaptation approach that uses the contextual semantics of words to capture their contexts in tweet messages and update their prior sentiment orientations and/or strengths accordingly. We evaluate our approach on one state-of-the-art sentiment lexicon using three different Twitter datasets. Results show that the sentiment lexicons adapted by our approach outperform the original lexicon in accuracy and F-measure in two datasets, but give similar accuracy and slightly lower F-measure in one dataset.

Keywords: Sentiment analysis · Semantics · Lexicon adaptation · Twitter

1 Introduction

Sentiment analysis on Twitter has been attracting much attention recently due to the rapid growth in Twitter's popularity as a platform for people to express their opinions and attitudes towards a great variety of topics. Most existing approaches to Twitter sentiment analysis can be categorised into machine learning [7,11,13] and lexicon-based approaches [2,6,8,15].

Lexicon-based approaches use lexicons of words weighted with their sentiment orientations to determine the overall sentiment in texts. These approaches have shown to be more applicable to Twitter data than machine learning approaches, since they do not require training from labelled data and therefore, they offer a domain-independent sentiment detection [15]. Nonetheless, lexicon-based approaches are limited by the sentiment lexicon used [21]. Firstly, because sentiment lexicons are composed by a generally static set of words that do not cover the wide variety of new terms that constantly emerge in the social web. Secondly, because words in the lexicons have fixed prior sentiment orientations, i.e. each

V. Presutti et al. (Eds.): ESWC Satellite Events 2014, LNCS 8798, pp. 54–63, 2014.
DOI: 10.1007/978-3-319-11955-7_5

term has always the same associated sentiment orientation independently of the context in which the term is used.

To overcome the above limitations, several lexicon bootstrapping and adaptation methods have been previously proposed. However, these methods are either supervised [16], i.e., they require training from human-coded corpora, or based on studying the statistical, syntactical or linguistic relations between words in general textual corpora (e.g., The Web) [17,19] or in static lexical knowledge sources (e.g., WordNet) [5] ignoring, therefore, the specific textual context in which the words appear. In many cases, however, the sentiment of a word is implicitly associated with the semantics of its context [3].

In this paper we propose an unsupervised approach for adapting sentiment lexicons based on the contextual semantics of their words in a tweet corpus. In particular, our approach studies the co-occurrences between words to capture their contexts in tweets and update their prior sentiment orientations and/or sentiment strengths in a given lexicon accordingly.

As a case study we apply our approach on Thelwall-Lexicon [15], which, to our knowledge, is the state-of-the-art sentiment lexicon for social data. We evaluate the adapted lexicons by performing a lexicon-based polarity sentiment detection (positive vs. negative) on three Twitter datasets. Our results show that the adapted lexicons produce a significant improvement in the sentiment detection accuracy and F-measure in two datasets but gives a slightly lower F-measure in one dataset.

In the rest of this paper, related work is discussed in Sect. 2, and our approach is presented in Sect. 3. Experiments and results are presented in Sect. 4. Discussion and future work are covered in Sect. 5. Finally, we conclude our work in Sect. 6.

2 Related Work

Exiting approaches to bootstrapping and adapting sentiment lexicons can be categorised into dictionary and corpus-based approaches. The dictionary-based approach [5,14] starts with a small set of general opinionated words (e.g., good, bad) and lexical knowledge base (e.g., WordNet). After that, the approach expands this set by searching the knowledge base for words that have lexical or linguistic relations to the opinionated words in the initial set (e.g., synonyms, glosses, etc.).

Alternatively, the corpus-based approach measures the sentiment orientation of words automatically based on their association to other strongly opinionated words in a given corpus [14,17,19]. For example, Turney and Littman [17] used *Pointwise Mutual Information* (PMI) to measure the statistical correlation between a given word and a balanced set of 14 positive and negative paradigm words (e.g., good, nice, nasty, poor). Although this work does not require large lexical input knowledge, its identification speed is very limited [21] because it uses web search engines in order to retrieve the relative co-occurrences of words.

Following the aforementioned approaches, several lexicons such as MPQA [20] and SentiWordNet [1] have been induced and successfully used for sentiment analysis on conventional text (e.g., movie review data). However, on Twitter these lexicons are not as compatible due to their limited coverage of Twitter-specific expressions, such as abbreviations and colloquial words (e.g., "`looov`", "`luv`", "`gr8`") that are often found in tweets.

Quite few sentiment lexicons have been recently built to work specifically with social media data, such as Thelwall-Lexicon [16] and Nielsen-Lexicon [8]. These lexicons have proven to work effectively on Twitter data. Nevertheless, such lexicons are similar to other traditional ones, in the sense that they all offer fixed and context-insensitive word-sentiment orientations and strengths. Although a training algorithm has been proposed to update the sentiment of terms in Thelwall-Lexicon [16], it requires to be trained from human-coded corpora, which is labour-intensive to obtain.

Aiming at addressing the above limitations we have designed our lexicon-adaptation approach in away that allows to (i) work in unsupervised fashion, avoiding the need for labelled data, and (ii) exploit the contextual semantics of words. This allows capturing their contextual information in tweets and update their prior sentiment orientation and strength in a given sentiment lexicon accordingly.

3 A Contextual Semantic Approach to Lexicon Adaptation

The main principle behind our approach is that the sentiment of a term is not static, as found in general-purpose sentiment lexicons, but rather depends on the context in which the term is used, i.e., it depends on its contextual semantics.[1] Therefore, our approach functions in two main steps as shown in Fig. 1. First, given a tweet collection and a sentiment lexicon, the approach builds a contextual semantic representation for each unique term in the tweet collection and subsequently uses it to derive the term's contextual sentiment orientation and strength. The SentiCircle representation model is used to this end [10]. Secondly, rule-based algorithm is applied to amend the prior sentiment of terms in the lexicon based on their corresponding contextual sentiment. Both steps are further detailed in the following subsections.

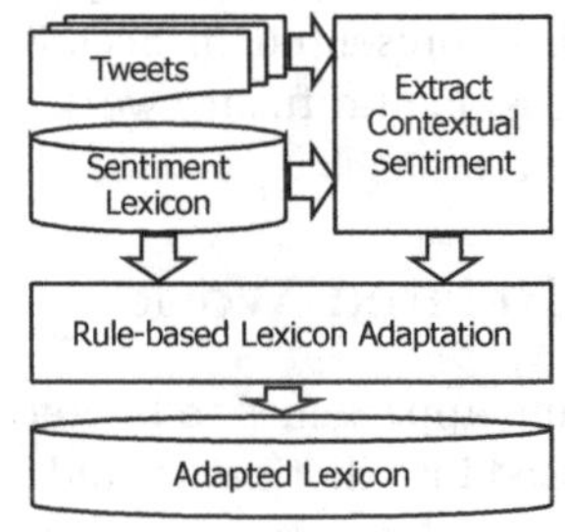

Fig. 1. The systematic workflow of our proposed lexicon adaptation approach.

3.1 Capturing Contextual Semantics and Sentiment

The first step in our pipeline is to capture the words contextual semantics and sentiment in tweets. To this end, we use our previously proposed semantic representation model, SentiCircle [10].

[1] We define context as a textual corpus or a set of tweets.

Following the distributional hypothesis that words that co-occur in similar contexts tend to have similar meaning [18], SentiCircle extracts the contextual semantics of a word from its co-occurrence patterns with other words in a given tweet collection. These patterns are then represented as a geometric circle, which is subsequently used to compute the contextual sentiment of the word by applying simple trigonometric identities on it. In particular, for each unique term m in a tweet collection, we build a two-dimensional geometric circle, where the term m is situated in the centre of the circle, and each point around it represents a context term c_i (i.e., a term that occurs with m in the same context). The position of c_i, as illustrated in Fig. 2, is defined jointly by its Cartesian coordinates x_i, y_i as:

$$x_i = r_i \cos(\theta_i * \pi) \qquad y_i = r_i \sin(\theta_i * \pi)$$

Where θ_i is the polar angle of the context term c_i and its value equals to the prior sentiment of c_i in a sentiment lexicon before adaptation, r_i is the radius of c_i and its value represents the degree of correlation (tdoc) between c_i and m, and can be computed as:

$$r_i = tdoc(m, c_i) = f(c_i, m) \times \log \frac{N}{N_{c_i}}$$

where $f(c_i, m)$ is the number of times c_i occurs with m in tweets, N is the total number of terms, and N_{c_i} is the total number of terms that occur with c_i. Note that all terms' radii in the SentiCircle are normalised. Also, all angles' values are in radian. The trigonometric properties of the SentiCircle allows us to encode the contextual semantics of a term as sentiment orientation and sentiment strength. Y-axis defines the sentiment of the term, i.e., a positive y value denotes a positive sentiment and vice versa. The X-axis defines the sentiment strength of the term. The smaller the x value, the stronger the sentiment.[2] This, in turn, divides the circle into four sentiment quadrants. Terms in the two upper quadrants have a positive sentiment ($\sin\theta > 0$), with upper left quadrant representing stronger positive sentiment since it has larger angle values than those in the top right quadrant. Similarly, terms in the two lower quadrants have negative sentiment values ($\sin\theta < 0$). Moreover, a small region called the "*Neutral Region*" can be defined. This region, as shown in Fig. 2, is located very close to X-axis in the "*Positive*" and the "*Negative*" quadrants only, where terms lie in this region have very weak sentiment (i.e., $|\theta| \approx 0$).

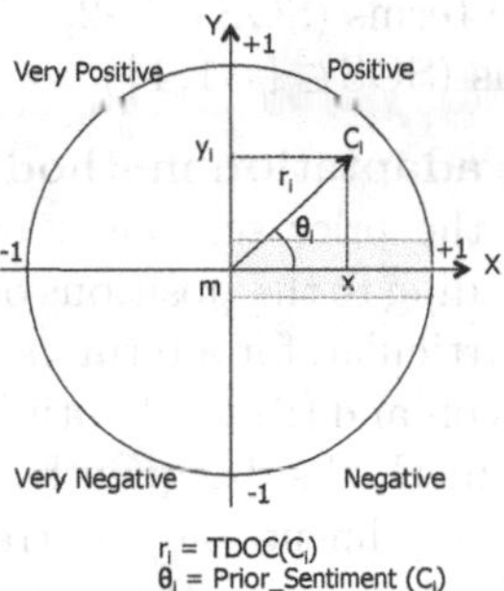

Fig. 2. SentiCircle of a term m. Neutral region is shaded in blue (Color figure online).

Calculating Contextual Sentiment. In summary, the Senti-Circle of a term m is composed by the set of (x, y) Cartesian coordinates of all the context terms

[2] This is because $\cos\theta < 0$ for large angles.

of m. An effective way to compute the overall sentiment of m is by calculating the geometric median of all the points in its SentiCircle. Formally, for a given set of n points $(p_1, p_2, ..., p_n)$ in a Senti-Cirlce Ω, the 2D geometric median g is defined as: $g = \arg\min_{g \in \mathbb{R}^2} \sum_{i=1}^{n} || |p_i - g||_2$. We call the geometric median g the **SentiMedian** as its position in the SentiCircle determines the final contextual-sentiment orientation and strength of m.

Note that the boundaries of the neutral region can be computed by measuring the density distribution of terms in the SentiCircle along the Y-axis. In this paper we use similar boundaries to the ones used in [10] since we use the same evaluation datasets.

3.2 Lexicon Adaptation

The second step in our approach is to update the sentiment lexicon with the terms' contextual sentiment information extracted in the previous step. As mentioned earlier, in this work we use Thelwall-Lexicon [16] as a case study. Therefore, in this section we first describe this lexicon and its properties, and then introduce our proposed adaptation method.

Thelwall-Lexicon consists of 2546 terms coupled with integer values between -5 (very negative) and $+5$ (very positive). Based on the terms' prior sentiment orientations and strengths (SOS), we group them into three subsets of 1919 negative terms (SOS $\in [-2, -5]$), 398 positive terms (SOS $\in [2, 5]$) and 229 neutral terms (SOS $\in \{-1, 1\}$).

The adaptation method uses a set of antecedent-consequent rules that decides how the prior sentiment of the terms in Thelwall-Lexicon should be updated according to the positions of their SentiMedians (i.e., their contextual sentiment). In particular, for a term m, the method checks (i) its prior SOS value in Thelwall-Lexicon and (ii) the SentiCircle quadrant in which the SentiMedian of m resides. The method subsequently chooses the best-matching rule to update the term's prior sentiment and/or strength.

Table 1 shows the complete list of rules in the proposed method. As noted, these rules are divided into *updating rules*, i.e., rules for updating the existing terms in Thelwall-Lexicon, and *expanding rules*, i.e., rules for expanding the lexicon with new terms. The *updating rules* are further divided into rules that deal with terms that have similar prior and contextual sentiment orientations (i.e., both positive or negative), and rules that deal with terms that have different prior and contextual sentiment orientations (i.e., negative prior, positive contextual sentiment and vice versa).

Although they look complicated, the notion behind the proposed rules is rather simple: *Check how strong the contextual sentiment is and how weak the prior sentiment is* $\rightarrow$ *update the sentiment orientation and strength accordingly.* The strength of the contextual sentiment can be determined based on the sentiment quadrant of the SentiMedian of m, i.e., the contextual sentiment is strong if the SentiMedian resides in the "*Very Positive*" or "*Very Negative*"

Table 1. Adaptation rules for Thelwall-Lexicon, where **prior**: prior sentiment value, **StrongQuadrant**: very negative/positive quadrant in the SentiCircle, **Add**: add the term to Thelwall-Lexicon.

Id	Antecedents	Consequent
	Updating rules (similar sentiment orientations)	
1	$(\lvert prior\rvert \leqslant 3) \wedge (SentiMedian \notin StrongQuadrant)$	$\lvert prior\rvert = \lvert prior\rvert + 1$
2	$(\lvert prior\rvert \leqslant 3) \wedge (SentiMedian \in StrongQuadrant)$	$\lvert prior\rvert = \lvert prior\rvert + 2$
3	$(\lvert prior\rvert > 3) \wedge (SentiMedian \notin StrongQuadrant)$	$\lvert prior\rvert = \lvert prior\rvert + 1$
4	$(\lvert prior\rvert > 3) \wedge (SentiMedian \in StrongQuadrant)$	$\lvert prior\rvert = \lvert prior\rvert + 1$
	Updating rules (different sentiment orientations)	
5	$(\lvert prior\rvert \leqslant 3) \wedge (SentiMedian \notin StrongQuadrant)$	$\lvert prior\rvert = 1$
6	$(\lvert prior\rvert \leqslant 3) \wedge (SentiMedian \in StrongQuadrant)$	$prior = -prior$
7	$(\lvert prior\rvert > 3) \wedge (SentiMedian \notin StrongQuadrant)$	$\lvert prior\rvert = \lvert prior\rvert - 1$
8	$(\lvert prior\rvert > 3) \wedge (SentiMedian \in StrongQuadrant)$	$prior = -prior$
9	$(\lvert prior\rvert > 3) \wedge (SentiMedian \in NeutralRegion)$	$\lvert prior\rvert = \lvert prior\rvert - 1$
10	$(\lvert prior\rvert \leqslant 3) \wedge (SentiMedian \in NeutralRegion)$	$\lvert prior\rvert = 1$
	Expanding rules	
11	$SentiMedian \in NeutralRegion$	$(\lvert contextual\rvert = 1) \wedge AddTerm$
12	$SentiMedian \notin StrongQuadrant$	$(\lvert contextual\rvert = 3) \wedge AddTerm$
13	$SentiMedian \in StrongQuadrant$	$(\lvert contextual\rvert = 5) \wedge AddTerm$

quadrants (See Fig. 2). On the other hand, the prior sentiment of m (i.e., $prior_m$) in Thelwall-Lexicon is weak if $|prior_m| \leqslant 3$ and strong otherwise.

For example, the word "`revolution`" in Thelwall-Lexicon has a weak negative sentiment ($prior = -2$) while it has a neutral contextual sentiment since its SentiMedian resides in the neutral region ($SentiMedian \in NeutralRegion$). Therefore, rule number 10 is applied and the term's prior sentiment in Thelwall lexicon will be updated to neutral ($|prior| = 1$). In another example, the words "`Obama`" and "`Independence`" are not covered by the Thelwall-Lexicon, and therefore, they have no prior sentiment. However, their SentiMedians reside in the "*Positive*" quadrant in their SentiCircles, and therefore rule number 12 is applied and both terms will be assigned with a positive sentiment strength of 3 and added to the lexicon consequently.

4 Evaluation Results

We evaluate our approach on Thelwall-Lexicon using three adaptation settings: (i) the *update* setting where we update the prior sentiment of existing terms in the lexicon, (ii) The *expand* setting where we expand Thelwall-Lexicon with new opinionated terms, and (iii) the *update+expand* setting where we try both aforementioned settings together. To this end, we use three Twitter datasets OMD, HCR and STS-Gold. Numbers of positive and negative tweets within these datasets are summarised in Table 2, and detailed in the references added in the

Table 2. Twitter datasets used for the evaluation

Dataset	Tweets	Positive	Negative
Obama-McCain Debate (OMD) [4]	1081	393	688
Health Care Reform (HCR) [12]	1354	397	957
Standford Sentiment Gold Standard (STS-Gold) [9]	2034	632	1402

Table 3. Average percentage of words in the three datasets that had their sentiment orientation or strength updated by our adaptation approach

	OMD	HCR	STS-Gold	Average
Words found in the lexicon	12.43	8.33	8.09	9.61
Hidden words	87.57	91.67	91.91	90.39
Words flipped their sentiment orientation	35.02	35.61	30.83	33.82
Words changed their sentiment strength	61.83	61.95	65.05	62.94
Words remained unchanged	3.15	2.44	4.13	3.24
New opinionated words	23.94	14.30	25.87	21.37

table. To evaluate the adapted lexicons under the above settings, we perform binary polarity classification on the three datasets. To this end, we use the sentiment detection method proposed with Thelwall-Lexicon [15]. According to this method a tweet is considered as positive if its aggregated positive sentiment strength is 1.5 times higher than the aggregated negative one, and negative vice versa.

Applying our adaptation approach to Thelwall-Lexicon results in dramatic changes in it. Table 3 shows the percentage of words in the three datasets that were found in Thelwall-Lexicon with their sentiment changed after adaptation. One can notice that on average 9.61 % of the words in our datasets were found in the lexicon. However, updating the lexicon with the contextual sentiment of words resulted in 33.82 % of these words flipping their sentiment orientation and 62.94 % changing their sentiment strength while keeping their prior sentiment orientation. Only 3.24 % of the words in Thelwall-Lexicon remained untouched. Moreover, 21.37 % of words previously unseen in the lexicon were assigned with contextual sentiment by our approach and added to Thelwall-Lexicon subsequently.

Table 4 shows the average results of binary sentiment classification performed on our datasets using (i) the original Thelwall-Lexicon (*Original*), (ii) Thelwall-Lexicon induced under the *update* setting (*Updated*), and (iii) Thelwall-Lexicon induced under the *update+expand* setting.[3] The table reports the results in accuracy and three sets of precision (P), recall (R), and F-measure (F1), one for positive sentiment detection, one for negative, and one for the average of the two.

[3] Note that in this work we do not report the results obtained under the expand setting since no improvement was observed comparing to the other two settings.

Table 4. Cross comparison results of original and the adapted lexicons

Datasets	Lexicons	Accuracy	Positive Sentiment			Negative Sentiment			Average		
			P	R	F1	P	R	F1	P	R	F1
OMD	Original	66.79	55.99	40.46	46.97	70.64	81.83	75.82	63.31	61.14	61.4
	Updated	**69.29**	58.89	51.4	54.89	74.12	79.51	76.72	66.51	65.45	65.8
	Updated+Expanded	69.2	58.38	53.18	55.66	74.55	78.34	76.4	66.47	65.76	**66.03**
HCR	Original	66.99	43.39	41.31	42.32	76.13	77.64	76.88	59.76	59.47	**59.6**
	Updated	**67.21**	42.9	35.77	39.01	75.07	80.25	77.58	58.99	58.01	58.29
	Updated+Expanded	66.99	42.56	36.02	39.02	75.05	79.83	77.37	58.8	57.93	58.19
STS-Gold	Original	81.32	68.75	73.1	70.86	87.52	85.02	86.25	78.13	79.06	78.56
	Updated	81.71	69.46	73.42	71.38	87.7	85.45	86.56	78.58	79.43	78.97
	Updated+Expanded	**82.3**	70.48	74.05	72.22	88.03	86.02	87.01	79.26	80.04	**79.62**

From these results in Table 4, we notice that the best classification performance in accuracy and F1 is obtained on the STS-Gold dataset regardless the lexicon being used. We also observe that the negative sentiment detection performance is always higher than the positive detection performance for all datasets and lexicons.

As for different lexicons, we notice that on OMD and STS-Gold the adapted lexicons outperform the original lexicon in both accuracy and F-measure. For example, on OMD the adapted lexicon shows an average improvement of 2.46 % and 4.51 % in accuracy and F1 respectively over the original lexicon. On STS-Gold the performance improvement is less significant than that on OMD, but we still observe 1 % improvement in accuracy and F1 comparing to using the original lexicon. As for the HCR dataset, the adapted lexicon gives on average similar accuracy, but 1.36 % lower F-measure. This performance drop can be attributable to the poor detection performance of positive tweets. Specifically, we notice from Table 4 a major loss in the recall on positive tweet detection using both adapted lexicons. One possible reason is the sentiment class distribution in our datasets. In particular, one may notice that HCR is the most imbalanced amongst the three datasets. Moreover, by examining the numbers in Table 3, we can see that HCR presents the lowest number of new opinionated words among the three datasets (i.e., 10.61 % lower than the average) which could be another potential reason for not observing any performance improvement.

5 Discussion and Future Work

We demonstrated the value of using contextual semantics of words for adapting sentiment lexicons from tweets. Specifically, we used Thelwall-Lexicon as a case study and evaluated its adaptation to three datasets of different sizes. Although the potential is palpable, our results were not conclusive, where a performance drop was observed in the HCR dataset using our adapted lexicons. Our initial observations suggest that the quality of our approach might be dependent on the sentiment class distribution in the dataset. Therefore, a deeper investigation in this direction is required.

We used the SentiCircle approach to extract the contextual semantics of words from tweets. In future work we will try other contextual semantic approaches and study how the semantic extraction quality affects the adaptation performance.

Our adaptation rules in this paper are specific to Thelwall-Lexicon. These rules, however, can be generalized to other lexicons, which constitutes another future direction of this work.

All words which have contextual sentiment were used for adaptation. Nevertheless, the results conveyed that the prior sentiments in the lexicon might need to be unchanged for words of specific syntactical or linguistic properties in tweets. Part of our future work is to detect and filter those words that are more likely to have stable sentiment regardless the contexts in which they appear.

6 Conclusions

In this paper we proposed an unsupervised approach for sentiment lexicon adaptation from Twitter data. Our approach extracts the contextual semantics of words and uses them to update the words' prior sentiment orientations and/or strength in a given sentiment lexicon. The evaluation was done on Thelwall-Lexicon using three Twitter datasets. Results showed that lexicons adapted by our approach improved the sentiment classification performance in both accuracy and F1 in two out of three datasets.

Acknowledgment. This work was supported by the EU-FP7 project SENSE4US (grant no. 611242).

References

1. Baccianella, S., Esuli, A., Sebastiani, F.: SentiWordNet 3.0: an enhanced lexical resource for sentiment analysis and opinion mining. In: Seventh Conference on International Language Resources and Evaluation, Valletta, Malta (2010). Accessed May 2010
2. Bollen, J., Mao, H., Zeng, X.: Twitter mood predicts the stock market. Int. J. Comput. Sci. **2**(1), 1–8 (2011)
3. Cambria, E.: An introduction to concept-level sentiment analysis. In: Castro, F., Gelbukh, A., González, M. (eds.) MICAI 2013, Part II. LNCS, vol. 8266, pp. 478–483. Springer, Heidelberg (2013)
4. Diakopoulos, N., Shamma, D.: Characterizing debate performance via aggregated twitter sentiment. In: Proceeding of 28th International Conference on Human Factors in Computing Systems. ACM (2010)
5. Esuli, A., Sebastiani, F.: Determining term subjectivity and term orientation for opinion mining. In: EACL, vol. 6, p. 2006 (2006)
6. Hu, X., Tang, J., Gao, H., Liu, H.: Unsupervised sentiment analysis with emotional signals. In: Proceedings of the 22nd World Wide Web Conference (2013)
7. Kouloumpis, E., Wilson, T., Moore, J.: Twitter sentiment analysis: the good the bad and the OMG! In: Proceedings of the ICWSM, Barcelona, Spain (2011)

8. Nielsen, F.Å.: A new ANEW: evaluation of a word list for sentiment analysis in microblogs (2011). arXiv:http://arxiv.org/abs/1103.2903
9. Saif, H., Fernandez, M., He, Y., Alani, H.: Evaluation datasets for twitter sentiment analysis a survey and a new dataset, the STS-Gold. In: Proceedings of the 1st ESSEM Workshop, Turin, Italy (2013)
10. Saif, H., Fernandez, M., He, Y., Alani, H.: SentiCircles for contextual and conceptual semantic sentiment analysis of Twitter. In: Presutti, V., d'Amato, C., Gandon, F., d'Aquin, M., Staab, S., Tordai, A. (eds.) ESWC 2014. LNCS, vol. 8465, pp. 83–98. Springer, Heidelberg (2014)
11. Saif, H., He, Y., Alani, H.: Semantic sentiment analysis of Twitter. In: Cudré-Mauroux, P., Heflin, J., Sirin, E., Tudorache, T., Euzenat, J., Hauswirth, M., Parreira, J.X., Hendler, J., Schreiber, G., Bernstein, A., Blomqvist, E. (eds.) ISWC 2012, Part I. LNCS, vol. 7649, pp. 508–524. Springer, Heidelberg (2012)
12. Speriosu, M., Sudan, N., Upadhyay, S., Baldridge, J.: Twitter polarity classification with label propagation over lexical links and the follower graph. In: Proceedings of the EMNLP First Workshop on Unsupervised Learning in NLP, Edinburgh, Scotland (2011)
13. Suttles, J., Ide, N.: Distant supervision for emotion classification with discrete binary values. In: Gelbukh, A. (ed.) CICLing 2013, Part II. LNCS, vol. 7817, pp. 121–136. Springer, Heidelberg (2013)
14. Takamura, H., Inui, T., Okumura, M.: Extracting semantic orientations of words using spin model. In: Proceedings of 43rd Annual Meeting on Association for Computational Linguistics (2005)
15. Thelwall, M., Buckley, K., Paltoglou, G.: Sentiment strength detection for the social web. J. Am. Soc. Inform. Sci. Technol. **63**(1), 163–173 (2012)
16. Thelwall, M., Buckley, K., Paltoglou, G., Cai, D., Kappas, A.: Sentiment strength detection in short informal text. J. Am. Soc. Inform. Sci. Technol **61**(12), 2544–2558 (2010)
17. Turney, P., Littman, M.: Measuring praise and criticism: inference of semantic orientation from association. ACM Trans. Inf. Syst. **21**, 315–346 (2003)
18. Turney, P.D., Pantel, P., et al.: From frequency to meaning: vector space models of semantics. J. Artif. Intell. Res. **37**(1), 141–188 (2010)
19. Velikovich, L., Blair-Goldensohn, S., Hannan, K., McDonald, R.: The viability of web-derived polarity lexicons. In: Human Language Technologies, ACL (2010)
20. Wilson, T., Wiebe, J., Hoffmann, P.: Recognizing contextual polarity in phrase-level sentiment analysis. In: Proceedings of Empirical Methods in NLP Conference (EMNLP), Vancouver, Canada (2005)
21. Xu, T., Peng, Q., Cheng, Y.: Identifying the semantic orientation of terms using S-HAL for sentiment analysis. Knowl.-Based Syst. **35**, 279–289 (2012)

RESTful or RESTless – Current State of Today's Top Web APIs

Frederik Bülthoff and Maria Maleshkova(✉)

AIFB, Karlsruhe Institute of Technology (KIT), Karlsruhe, Germany
frederik.buelthoff@student.kit.edu, maria.maleshkova@kit.edu

Abstract. Recent developments in the world of services on the Web show that both the number of available Web APIs as well as the applications built on top is constantly increasing. This trend is commonly attributed to the wide adoption of the REST architectural principles [1]. Still, the development of Web APIs is rather autonomous and it is up to the providers to decide how to implement, expose and describe the Web APIs. The individual implementations are then commonly documented in textual form as part of a webpage, showing a wide variety in terms of content, structure and level of detail. As a result, client application developers are forced to manually process and interpret the documentation. Before we can achieve a higher level of automation and can make any significant improvement to current practices and technologies, we need to reach a deeper understanding of their similarities and differences. Therefore, in this paper we present a thorough analysis of the most popular Web APIs through the examination of their documentation. We provide conclusions about common description forms, output types, usage of API parameters, invocation support, level of reusability, API granularity and authentication details. The collected data builds a solid foundation for identifying deficiencies and can be used as a basis for devising common standards and guidelines for Web API development.

1 Introduction

Recent developments in the world of services on the Web show that both the number of available Web APIs as well as the applications built on top is constantly increasing[1]. Often this proliferation of programmable interfaces that rely solely on the use of URIs, for both resource identification and interaction, and HTTP for message transmission, is attributed to the wide adoption of the REST architectural principles [1]. In particular, Web APIs are characterised by their relative simplicity and their natural suitability for the Web, employing the same technology stack, and these characteristics are exploited by many Web sites like Facebook, Google, Flickr and Twitter who offer easy-to-use, public APIs that provide simple access to some of the resources they hold, thus enabling third-parties to combine and reuse heterogeneous data coming from diverse services in data-oriented service compositions called mashups.

[1] http://blog.programmableweb.com/2013/04/30/9000-apis-mobile-gets-serious/

V. Presutti et al. (Eds.): ESWC Satellite Events 2014, LNCS 8798, pp. 64–74, 2014.
DOI: 10.1007/978-3-319-11955-7_6

Despite their popularity, currently there is no widely accepted understanding of what a Web API is. In fact, while the term 'Web Service' is quite clearly defined [2], Web APIs still lack a broadly accepted definition. Currently the term *Web API* has a general, sometimes even controversial, meaning and is used for depicting HTTP-based component interfaces, frequently being inconsistent about the specific technical and design underpinnings. This situation is undoubtedly driven by the fact that, as opposed to Web service technologies, work around Web APIs has evolved in a rather autonomous way and it is up to the providers to decide how they are going to expose the interface, how they are going to document them and what characteristics these documentations have. As a result, the majority of the Web APIs are described only in human-oriented documentation in textual form, as part of webpages, which is very diverse in terms of structure, content and level of details. Therefore, currently developers have to manually search for suitable documentation, interpret the provided details and implement custom solutions, which are hardly reusable. Such an approach to using Web APIs is very time and effort consuming and will not scale in the context of the growing number of exposed interfaces.

Before any significant impact and improvement can be made to current Web API practices and technologies, we need to reach a deeper understanding of these. This involves, for instance, figuring out how current APIs are developed and exposed, what kind of descriptions are available, how they are represented, how rich these descriptions are, etc. It is only then that we shall be able to clearly identify deficiencies and realise how we can overcome existing limitations, how much of the available know-how on Web services can be applied and in which manner. To this end, we present a thorough analysis over the most popular Web APIs in ProgrammableWeb directory[2].

The remainder of this paper is structured as follows: Sect. 2, describes the methodology used for conducting our Web API study, while Sect. 3 gives the collected data and provides a discussion on identified correlations and trends. Section 4 presents an overview of existing work on analysing Web services and Sect. 5 presents future work and concludes the paper.

2 Survey Setup

The survey was conducted by a single domain expert during December 2013 and January 2014. The dataset, which comprises 45 Web APIs[3] in total, was

[2] http://www.programmableweb.com

[3] Amazon Product Advertising, Amazon S3, BitBucket, Azure (Blob Service), Balanced Payments, Bing Maps REST Services, Bitly, Box, del.icio.us, Disqus, DocuSign Enterprise, Dropbox (Core API), eBay (Shopping API), Etsy, Eventful, Facebook (Graph API), Flickr, Foursquare, Freebase (Search/Reconcile), Geonames, GitHub, Google Custom Search, Google Maps API Web Services, Google Places API, Groupon, Heroku, Instagram, Last.fm, LinkedIn, OpenStreetMap (Editing API), Panoramio, Paypal, Reddit, Salesforce, Tropo, Tumblr, Twilio, Twitpic, Twitter, Wikipedia/Mediawiki, Yahoo! BOSS, Yahoo! BOSS Geo, Yammer, Yelp, Youtube.

primarily composed through the use of the ProgrammableWeb directory. This popular directory provides basic information about Web APIs in general as well as their use in mashups. The latter was used as a metric for the popularity of the Web API. Since we wanted to capture the Web API characteristics that developers are most frequently faced with, we mostly chose the analysed APIs by taking those with the most mashups. This metric is however biased towards older established Web APIs, for which reason we included a third of the entries at random and through other popularity measures[4].

While ProgrammableWeb is considered the largest directory of its kind and, therefore, best suited for this task, the information itself turned out to be in some cases incomplete or out of date, which made some changes to the dataset necessary. These problems included Web APIs that had been discontinued or replaced by others. In addition, similar Web APIs from the same provider, such as the various maps related from Google and Bing, were grouped together as a single entry. As a result, we retained a dataset containing 45 Web APIs.

The survey was conducted by manually analyzing the documentation made available by the Web API providers. The features, which were taken under consideration can be grouped into six categories, which include general Web API information, URI use, HTTP use, input and output data, security and policies as well as common design decisions. The examined criteria were gained from the key architectural principles of REST, the use of the underlying HTTP protocol and from common challenges and design decisions of Web API providers. The results from the survey, as given in Sect. 3 can, therefore, be used as a basis for judging to what extent todays top Web APIs are actually RESTful. The presented categories contain the following features:

1. **General Web API Information** – the APIs size in terms of operations, availability of other protocols and interface descriptions and the type of functionality provided.
2. **URL and Resource Links** – the kind of design schema used in the URL of the Web API and the use of links between API resources.
3. **HTTP Use** – the used HTTP methods and support for alternative HTTP methods, how update operations are implemented, if meaningful HTTP status codes are used in cases of failure and how caching is addressed.
4. **Input and Output Data** – which mechanisms are used for the transmission of input data, what types of input are there and what kind of output formats can be expected.
5. **Security and Policies** – are limitations on the degree of utilization posted and enforced, is authentication necessary and if yes, which authentication scheme is supported.
6. **Common Design Decision** – how are versioning and the selection of the output format realized.

The procedure for gathering the data was straightforward. For each Web API the corresponding ProgrammableWeb webpage and the provider's documentation were opened and examined. The heterogeneous nature of both the

[4] Alexa.com rank and number of tagged questions on StackOverflow.com.

media and the structure of the documentation, as well as various different ways of conveying the same information made any kind of automation of the process unfeasible. Furthermore, some cases of unclear or missing information made it necessary to perform some test interactions with the Web APIs.

3 Survey Results

In this section we describe the results that have been collected as part of the survey on Web APIs. The recorded features have been grouped into six categories, each of which addresses a different aspect of the Web APIs.

General Web API Information. Counting the number of operations supported by the Web API gives us some measure of its size and, therefore, complexity. This metric is easily attained for RPC-style APIs. In the case of resource-oriented or RESTful Web APIs each combination of a resource and a HTTP-verb was counted as an operation. The majority (62 %) of the entries in our dataset had between eleven and one hundred operations, with 38 % in the 11–50 and 24 % in the 51–100 range. The remaining Web APIs were roughly equally divided into a group of smaller (less than 11 operations, 20 %) and larger (more than 100 operations, 18 %) ones. Only two entries (4 %) provided a single operation.

Only a small percentage (20 %) of the Web APIs provided the same service using alternative protocols. For example, Flickr is available through SOAP and through XML-RPC as well, next to their request format self-described as REST. In most cases if an alternative was available, it had been declared as a legacy protocol, not guaranteed to be up to date in functionality and developers were urged to switch to its HTTP-based Web API equivalent. In most cases these were alternative protocols – SOAP or XML-RPC implementations, and had existed before the introduction of their Web API counterparts.

Interface descriptions in a machine-readable format, which in contrast to the textual documentation targeted at humans, can be automatically processed were available for only five Web APIs (11 %) – three using a custom format and one case of JSON Hyper-Schema respectively WSDL. Links to related resources embedded in the response data of Web APIs, which is an alternative to interface descriptions were available in eight cases (18 %). This is necessary for fulfilling the HATEOAS constraint of REST architecture, which requires, that, instead of interacting through a fixed predefined interface the client of a RESTful Web API will transition through application states by following links embedded in the resource representations.

Easier integration of Web APIs into applications can be aided through extensive tooling support. This can either be done directly through Software Development Kits (SDK)s or by providing metadata on the use of the Web API through interface descriptions. We differentiate two types of SDKs – those which are developed and maintained by the provider of the Web API themselves (available in 58 % of the cases) and those provided by third parties (available in 51 % of the cases), but still named and linked to from within official documentation.

In total was at least one SDK available (either official or unofficial) for 76 % of the Web APIs. The most commonly supported platform or programming language was Ruby, closely followed by Python, PHP, Java[5], C#[6], JavaScript and Objective-C[7]. In total, we counted 19 different platforms or programming languages supported by official and 44 by unofficial SDKs.

We can draw two main conclusions based on the gathered data. First, once an HTTP-based Web API is made available, providers tend to abandon and move away from previous interaction protocol implementations, such as SOAP. Second, machine-interpretable interface description formats are rather an exception than a rule. Most providers still prefer to document APIs directly as part of webpages.

URLs and Resource Links. It can be argued that for truly RESTful Web APIs that follow the principle of HATEOAS (Hypermedia as the Engine of Application State) the URL design is opaque because the user of the Web API will never have to construct URLs manually. Nonetheless, the design or structure of the URLs remains a good indicator for the type of the Web API. In addition, we will see that only a small percentage of the Web APIs under consideration aim to follow the HATEOAS principle. We differentiated between three main types of URL design, those that were structured around resources (resouce-oriented) – those that focused on the operations (RPC-style) and those in between (mixed). The latter category contains cases in which some parts, for example search was built in an RPC-style while the rest was structured around resources. The data in Table 1 shows that the majority was resource-oriented, followed by those in RPC-style, with the smallest group being those sorted into the mixed category.

The availability of resource links was previously presented as part of the analysis on interface descriptions. The data in Table 2 incorporates that number in addition to two further use cases: Web APIs with self links include the URL of resources as part of their representation and pagination links provide the user of the Web API with precomposed URLs for paging through datasets. Both help reduce the complexity of using the Web APIs but were only available in 13 % of the analyzed Web APIs.

Table 1. URL design

Description	Number	In %
RESTful	21	47
RPC	15	33
Hybrid	9	13

Table 2. Resource Links

Description	Number	In %
Used at all	11	24
Related resources	8	18
Self	6	13
Pagination	6	13

[5] Java and Android SDKs were both counted as Java.

[6] C# and .NET SKDs were both counted as C#.

[7] Objective-C and iOS SDKs were both counted as Objective-C.

The data indicates that HATEOAS remains one of the most poorly supported constraints of the REST architecture with less than a fifth of the analyzed Web APIs providing links to related resources. A possible explanation is that HATEOAS signifies the largest departure from the previous approaches on Web Services, which heavily relied on predefined interfaces. Notable exceptions include PayPal and Github, which explicitly feature HATEOAS respectively hypermedia links prominently in their documentation.

HTTP Use. As it is to be expected, the two most commonly used HTTP verbs are GET and POST (see Table 3), since both are used by resource-oriented and RPC-style Web APIs. The least popular verb is PATCH. Most Web APIs (58 %) that feature update functionality use PUT or PATCH while 30 % use POST. The remaining 12 % break the idempotency of the GET verb by misusing it for update operations.

In some cases the more uncommonly used HTTP verbs, such as PATCH, are not supported by existing tools and frameworks. Some Web API providers offer, therefore, functionality that allows users to swap out the originally requested HTTP verb with another one, usually POST. Table 4 shows that the most popular way for indicating the original verb is by using a query parameter in the URL of the request. Others simply make no difference between the verb used or allow the requested verb to be set in either a custom header or the URL path. In total, a method override was provided by 42 % of the Web APIs.

Error handling plays a large role in any application. How Web APIs present errors is therefore of particular importance. 71 % of the surveyed Web APIs reused the various predefined status codes of HTTP to indicate an error. In all of those cases the body of the HTTP response did contain further information.

One advantage of using Web APIs and subsequently HTTP is the built-in support for caching, for which only 27 % of the Web APIs explicitly stated their support. Further manual analysis via test invocations showed that an additional six Web APIs did indeed support caching without having documented it.

Table 3. Method support

Description	Number	In %
GET	45	100
POST	34	76
DELETE	21	47
PUT	17	38
HEAD	6	13
PATCH	3	7

Table 4. Method override

Description	Number	In %
Override supported	14	42
Query parameter	6	43
Interchangeable	3	21
Head	3	21
URL path	2	14

Web APIs, which build upon the REST architectural principles, should embrace the HTTP protocol[8]. Adopting the various aspects of HTTP enables the reuse of know-how and best practices gained in making the Web the way it is today. One part of adopting HTTP, means using the status codes defined in the standard, especially those for indicating the various types of errors, which may occur. We found out that the majority of the Web APIs use standard error codes. In contrast, cache support is not widely present, even though it is a feature, which Web API providers can easily support using the built-in mechanisms of HTTP.

Input and Output Data. Using Web APIs means interacting with data. Most requests to Web API will incorporate some input, which can be transmitted in many ways. Table 5 shows that the analyzed Web APIs use four different ways for sending the input, the most popular one being input transmitted as parameters in the query string of the request URL. Another popular transmittal technique encodes the input in the request body, often by using the standard form encoding used by HTML forms on web pages or one of the supported output formats, such as JSON or XML. Many APIs support more than one type input encoding, especially when the output format itself can also be freely chosen.

The input can further be differentiated into several types (see Table 6). All Web APIs under considerations had at least one case in which an input parameter was optional and almost all featured required parameters. In most cases information on which parameters must be provided, which ones are optional and what their associated default values are, is only provided out-of-band in textual documentation. Building valid requests which feature the expected data therefore require careful consideration. Further complexity arises from the fact that most Web APIs incorporate input parameters that (i) state a list or range of valid values (ii) expect data to be encoded using a specific standard (e.g. dates as ISO 8601). (iii) or are of complex nature (e.g. comma separated lists of values).

Table 5. Way of transmitting input

Description	Number	In %
Query	43	96
Body	34	76
Path	25	56
Head	8	18

Table 6. Input datatypes

Description	Number	In %
Optional	45	100
Required	44	98
Alternative/range	43	96
Specified	40	89
Complex	38	84

In contrast to SOAP and XML-RPC, which both use XML as the transport and output format, Web APIs most commonly (89 %) feature support for the

[8] REST is not tied to HTTP, but HTTP it is the base for communication on the world wide web and thus the most popular protocol which REST is applied to.

more compact data representation format JSON[9]. Still, XML remains the second most used data format (58 %). The increasing popularity of JSON is further reflected by the fact that about half of the Web APIs using it, do not provide XML support. Less than a fifth also supported other formats[10]. All of the Web APIs supported either JSON or XML as their primary data representation format. Two Web APIs used their own custom data output format, which in both cases was based on JSON and provided a general structure for all responses.

Our results show that preparing the input in the right format requires additional effort. Each request to a Web API demands careful consideration on which parameters to send, their format and ultimately how to transmit them. In addition, there is no general consensus in Web APIs on how to format even frequently occurring input such as date and time, thus requiring careful manual effort when doing service composition. On the other side of the request are JSON and XML the two main established data interchange formats for output, with JSON rapidly gaining on importance.

Security and Policies. Security and policies or terms of use play an important part in the context of using Web APIs, since they determine the conditions and limits for actually accessing the APIs. Only two of the examined Web APIs did not use any kind of authentication. Roughly a third of the Web APIs require authentication only for operations, which perform data modification, but do not require authentication for reading resources. The most common way of identifying the client application or user is via an API key (also called application id, client id or by similar terms) which is passed along with each request. Other, more secure approaches, are listed in Table 7. The most common approach, used by two thirds of the Web APIs is OAuth in its various protocol versions followed by the basic authentication protocol of HTTP. In those Web APIs that used basic authentication, which sends the provided credentials in plaintext as part of a HTTP header, this authentication method was almost always combined with SSL[11]. In total, SSL was available for 91 % of the Web APIs and its use was mandatory for 41 % of those.

Most Web APIs (89 %) state and implement rate limitations, which restrict the number of invocations in a specific time frame. Consumers of the API have to follow these restrictions in order to prevent their requests or the entire application from being blocked. The limitations are either written down, as part of the documentation, or included with the general terms and conditions. A fifth of the Web APIs use custom HTTP headers to convey information about the remaining quota in every response, thus allowing the client application to dynamically adapt its use pattern.

We can conclude, that the majority of Web APIs use authentication in some form, requiring adopters of these services to both register their application in

[9] JavaScript Object Notation, an open standard for data interchange derived from the JavaScript language.

[10] e.g. including CSV, RDF, YAML, PHP, RSS, Atom, WDDX or form encoded values.

[11] Secure Sockets Layer, a cryptographic protocol which aims to provide communication security over the Internet.

Table 7. Common web API authentication approaches

Authentication mechanisms	Number	In %
OAuth 1.0	20	44
OAuth 2.0	11	24
Custom OAuth	2	4
HTTP basic	8	18
Session	5	11
Custom HMAC	3	7
Other	4	9

Table 8. Common web API versioning techniques

Description	Number	In %
Yes	33	73
No	12	27
URL Path	26	79
Custom header	2	6
Content-negotitiation	2	6
Body	2	6
Subdomain change	1	3

Table 9. Representation format selection

Description	Number	In %
Yes	28	62
No	12	27
Path/File extension	15	54
Query parameter	11	39
Content-negotiation	6	21
Custom header	2	7

advance and tackle the individual authentication scheme used. Our results show that OAuth has the potential to emerge as universally adopted standard for authentication. Almost as common as authentication are limitations on the number of requests per time period that applications can send to Web APIs.

Common Design Decisions. The motivation behind versioning is that Web APIs may change over time and by explicitly distinguishing between versions, new releases will not break compatibility with older API clients. This issue was addressed by 73 % of the examined Web APIs. The most common technique, as shown in Table 8, includes the API version as a prefix in the URL path. Further techniques include a custom HTTP header, standard content negotiation, the specification of versions in the body of the request and switching subdomains. The latter technique was used by Facebook to differentiate their deprecated REST API from their new Graph API.

The way of selecting the output format is another common design decision for Web APIs. Four different techniques (see Table 9) were identified during the survey. In six cases did the Web APIs support more than one way of requesting a specific format. The two most common methods include specifying the format as part of the URL, either as part of the path or as a query parameter. The standard mechanism of HTTP for this purpose, content negotiation (also used for versioning purposes as seen above), was supported by six APIs, followed by the use of a custom HTTP header by two.

Our results show that even though HTTP defines content negotiation using the accept header as the mechanism for representation format selection, is it only supported by a minority of Web APIs. Instead, most Web APIs allow the format to be specified in some way as part of the URL, which allows basic requests to be easily tested in a common web browser. For versioning, including the version identifier as part of the URL is by far the most popular technique.

4 Related Work

The first study on the state of Web APIs was presented by [3] and features a comprehensive overview through the analysis of 222 Web APIs in 2010. While Maleshkova et al. aim to draw conclusions on the state of the entire world of APIs on the Web, we focus on the most popular and common ones, substituting a larger dataset for more and other types of features. Another more recent study from 2012 was provided by Renzel et al. [4], wherein the authors analyze a dataset of twenty Web APIs by a broad range of features, some of which were incorporated in our survey. Similar to our study, the dataset was gained by selecting top ranked entries from the ProgrammableWeb directory, using the number of mashups as the sorting criteria. The rather limited dataset and fast moving developments in the world of services on the web necessitate taking another look at the current state of Web APIs. Other older studies, devoted to investigating Web Services exist. The authors in [5] provide a study on Web services but their data is restricted to only a few characteristics and a single source.

5 Conclusions and Future Work

The results of our survey indicate that Web APIs feature a large amount of heterogeneity in their individual designs, ranging from cases, following the architectural style of REST and its constraints, such as HATEOAS, to those featuring a more RPC-like style. Common service tasks such as composition and invocation, therefore, require more manual effort to smooth over differences in implementations, compared to Web Services that follow a strict standard such as SOAP. Even though REST is only an architectural style, in contrast to a strict standard such as SOAP whose conformity can be validated, a stricter compliance with its guidelines and constraints would already significantly reduce friction in adopting Web APIs for more complex tasks such as the automation of composition and invocation. While some more readily understandable concepts such as using the HTTP verbs have gained widespread adoption, other concepts such as resource linking (HATEOAS) are hardly ever applied. For today's top Web APIs we, therefore, have to conclude that they most commonly remain RESTless.

This area of research has a lot of potential for further work. By building upon the data gained as part of this survey and the previous ones mentioned in the related work section, we could quantify the changes in Web API design over time and possibly gain insight over future developments. Another idea would be to take those parts of the REST principles that we have shown to be poorly applied and work on the problems surrounding their adoption.

References

1. Fielding, R.T.: Architectural styles and the design of network-based software architectures. Ph.D. thesis, University of California (2000)
2. Daigneau, R.: Service design patterns: fundamental design solutions for SOAP/WSDL and RESTful web services. ACM SIGSOFT Softw. Eng. Notes **37**, 40 (2012). (Addison-Wesley (E))
3. Maleshkova, M., Pedrinaci, C., Domingue, J.: Investigating web apis on the world wide web. In: 2010 IEEE 8th European Conference on Web Services (ECOWS), pp. 107–114. IEEE (2010)
4. Renzel, D., Schlebusch, P., Klamma, R.: Today's top "RESTful" services and why they are not RESTful. In: Wang, X.S., Cruz, I., Delis, A., Huang, G. (eds.) WISE 2012. LNCS, vol. 7651, pp. 354–367. Springer, Heidelberg (2012)
5. Li, Y., Liu, Y., Zhang, L., Li, G., Xie, B., Sun, J.: An exploratory study of web services on the internet. In: Proceedings of ICWS, pp. 380–387 (2007)

Ornithology Based on Linking Bird Observations with Weather Data

Mikko Koho[1,2,3](✉), Eero Hyvönen[2,3], and Aleksi Lehikoinen[4]

[1] CSC - IT Center for Science Ltd., Espoo, Finland
mikko.koho@csc.fi
http://www.csc.fi/english

[2] Semantic Computing Research Group (SeCo), Aalto University, Espoo, Finland

[3] Semantic Computing Research Group (SeCo),
University of Helsinki, Helsinki, Finland
eero.hyvonen@aalto.fi
http://www.seco.tkk.fi/

[4] The Finnish Museum of Natural History, University of Helsinki, Helsinki, Finland
aleksi.lehikoinen@helsinki.fi
http://www.luomus.fi/en/

Abstract. This paper presents the first results of a use case of Linked Data for eScience, where 0.5 million rows of bird migration observations over 30 years time span are linked with 0.1 million rows of related weather observations and a bird species ontology. Using the enriched linked data, biology researchers at the Finnish Museum of Natural History will be able to investigate temporal changes in bird biodiversity and how weather conditions affect bird migration. To support data exploration, the data is published in a SPARQL endpoint service using the RDF Data Cube model, on which semantic search and visualization tools are built.

1 Serving Ornithologists with Linked Data

Long-term standardized nature observations provide crucial data for determining population trends in biodiversity management. For example, from monitoring data about bird migration over many years, it is possible to determine trends [13,20] in population size, and annual breeding success [12]. By combining observational data with related datasets, such as weather or pollution data, it is possible to investigate how biodiversity is affected by related phenomena in nature.

This paper presents a use case of adding value to a bird observation dataset by related weather data and a species ontology using the Linked Data [16] approach. We first describe the data, metadata schemas, and ontologies used. After this, publication of the data on a SPARQL endpoint is discussed. Based on the SPARQL endpoint's API, tools and visualizations for researching and exploring the data are being created for the ornithologists, bird watchers and researchers alike, to use—two examples of this are explained in Sect. 3. In conclusion, contributions of our work and related research are discussed.

V. Presutti et al. (Eds.): ESWC Satellite Events 2014, LNCS 8798, pp. 75–85, 2014.
DOI: 10.1007/978-3-319-11955-7_7

2 Data, Metadata, and Ontologies

Data. The bird observation data comes from the Hanko Bird Observatory "Halias" located in Hanko, Finland. The data has been gathered systematically since 1979 and is actively used in scientific research[1].

Nature observation datasets can be divided into two main classes:

1. **Systematic observational datasets.** The methods used in making nature observations are standardized and every species in the research scope is counted. Straightforward to do inference e.g. about spatio-temporal occurence of species.
2. **Open public datasets.** People are free to report nature observations they have made. Methods used in making observations vary and only some portion of observed species may be reported. Any inference done requires knowledge about the way people report observations and results can be misleading.

The Halias dataset is a systematic observational dataset consisting of daily bird counts. All migrating birds are counted daily in a standardized way for four hours starting from sunrise. In addition, local as well as migrating birds outside the standardized observation time are counted for each day. Every observed bird is counted and daily counts are given for each date and species combination.

The weather data comes from a Finnish Meteorological Institute's weather observation station in Russarö, situated less than 6 km away from Halias. The weather observation data consists of measurements of temperature, relative humidity, wind direction (10 min average), wind speed (10 min average), cloud coverage and sea level air pressure, collected every 3 h. Also a total rain amount is given for each day.

Metadata Schema. We have created a data schema for representing the daily bird observations based on the RDF Data Cube Vocabulary[2] of W3C. The schema heavily re-uses—for interoperability reasons—other vocabularies where possible, such as Darwin Core[3], TaxMeOn [21], and data.gov.uk Time Intervals[4].

Observed daily weather variables are aggregated based on needs of this use case. Weather observations that correspond to the standardized observation times of each day are of particular interest. They make it possible to match the weather data and bird migration counts on a shorter time span than the whole day and thus giving better accuracy for finding the connections between them. We calculate average values of the weather variables for the 4-hour standardized observation time. The average values are calculated assuming a linear change in a weather variable's values between the 3-hour observations. The aggregated values of weather variables are then linked directly to the bird observations.

---

[1] See http://www.tringa.fi/web/lintuasemat/hangon-lintuasema/julkaisuluettelo.html for a list of research publications related to observations at Halias.

[2] http://www.w3.org/TR/2014/REC-vocab-data-cube-20140116/

[3] http://rs.tdwg.org/dwc/

[4] http://datahub.io/dataset/data-gov-uk-time-intervals

Wind observations are represented using an ontology of all observed wind speed and direction combinations. The observed winds are then linked with the daily bird observation instances. The schema is documented in detail online[5].

We envision, that by using a standard data model for observations, our forthcoming tools for exploring and visualizing observational data could be applied not only to birds but to other observations, too, and conversely, tools developed by others for the Data Cube model, could be re-used in our case study more easily.

Ontologies. The data is linked with the AVIO Ontology of the Birds of the World [22], based on data from the taxonomic database[6] of the Finnish Museum of Natural History.

For our Halias case study, the original AVIO was refined and extended as follows:

1. Scope of the species ontology was reduced to species observed in Finland. This is due to the need for generating species name abbreviations by certain rules which do not apply globally.
2. Species name abbreviations were added as they are used in the primary data.
3. Species characteristics based on the characteristics system used in Nature Gate service[7] were added.
4. Species conservation statuses were added in both Finnish and EU scope.
5. Rarity classes were added. These are subjective views of rarity of species.

The species characteristics ontology classifies birds in terms of four facet categories: (1) Date and nesting habitat, (2) Coloring and markings, (3) Shape and size, and (4) Behavior. These categories are then divided further into subcategories.

Linked Data Publication. The datasets were combined into a single linked dataset. This linked dataset and the used ontologies compose the whole linked data publication, which consists of 12,315,709 triples.

The data was published as a SPARQL service using the Linked Data Finland (LDF) [9] platform[8]. Based on metadata about the dataset and its graphs, this platform automatically generates APIs and content negotiation services for machines to use, and a homepage for human users with ready to use services, such as Linked Data browsing and editing the data.

The bird observation data is not openly available, but there are ongoing discussions about making the data more openly accessible. Access to the published data is currently restricted to the association that owns the data and collaborating research projects. Nevertheless, the data can be requested for research purposes without any costs.

[5] http://www.essepuntato.it/lode/http://ldf.fi/schema/halias/

[6] http://taxon.luomus.fi/

[7] http://naturegate.fi/

[8] http://www.ldf.fi/

Some structural problems in the original bird observation data were noticed when the transformed linked data was first visualized. There were duplicate species and date combinations with different bird counts, when there should never be more than one of these combinations and the URIs of the observations were created using these combinations. This anomaly was taken into account in the transformation process by creating different URIs for each of the duplicate combinations.

After this, more validation of the data was done in the transformation process and we discovered some other problems of lesser impact, which did not hamper the linked data publication or visualization.

3 Visualizing the Data to Solve Problems

There is a strong connection [1,2,15] between the bird migration magnitude and weather variables of a day in the spring and autumn bird migration periods. Finding these connections from the data however is not a trivial task. Our approach to this problem is to provide data visualization tools based on linked data. Such tools let the ornithologists to explore, find, and visualize relationships between variables in bird and weather observation data. Good visualizations would not only show interesting correlations and patterns in data, but also raise up new questions for further data exploration and research.

Visualizing the data is flexible on top of a SPARQL endpoint with commonly used tools. For example, Sgvizler[9] [19] is a tool that is easy to use for combining SPARQL queries with Google Charts[10] graphics. We next exemplify these possibilities by two visualizations combining bird and weather observations.

Our first visualization originates from the research problem of a collaborating biologist, where he wished to investigate, how local wind conditions affect the migration of different species, or groups of species, during spring and autumn migration. To solve the problem, the visualization of Fig. 1 was created. Here the idea is to use a Circular heat chart[11]. The diagram shows the relationship between wind conditions and observed crane (*Grus grus*) migration in autumn months (September, October, and November). For each observed wind speed and direction combination, the number of migrating cranes during days in which the wind combination is observed, is added up. These sums are then normalized by the number of days with the wind combination to account for the biased occurrence of different wind conditions. Directions in the diagram correspond to wind directions using standard English abbreviations, and distance from the diagram center represents wind speed in meters per second. Migration magnitude increases from gray (no migration) to green. The color scale is normalized so that the deepest green shade corresponds to maximum migration magnitude observed.

During autumn, cranes migrate from breeding areas in Finland to southern wintering areas. As large birds, they are expected to favor tail winds as they

[9] http://dev.data2000.no/sgvizler/

[10] https://developers.google.com/chart/

[11] http://prcweb.co.uk/lab/circularheat/

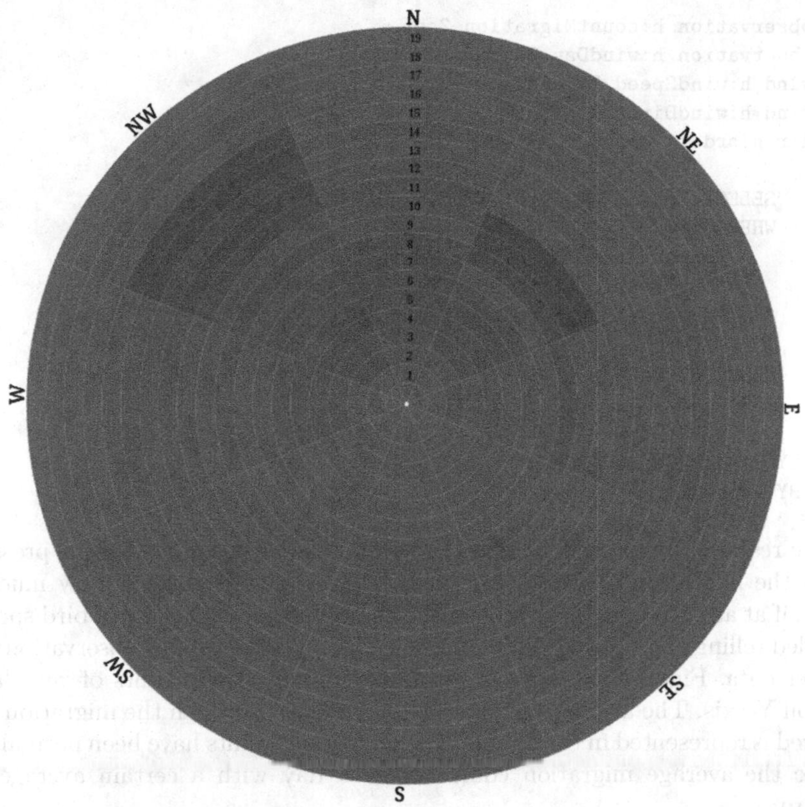

Fig. 1. Diagram of crane migration magnitude on days with different wind conditions in autumn.

migrate southward from Hanko over the Baltic Sea. The example visualization supports this hypothesis.

The visualization is based on a SPARQL query. The graphics were implemented using D3[12] JavaScript library and AngularJS[13] JavaScript framework. The SPARQL query used takes about five seconds to retrieve the results from the LDF platform. Here is the SPARQL query for this visualization:

```
PREFIX rdfs: <http://www.w3.org/2000/01/rdf-schema#>
PREFIX h: <http://ldf.fi/schema/halias/>

SELECT ?order ?speed ((SUM(?cnt)/?days) AS ?normalized)
WHERE {
    ?observation h:observedSpecies ?species .
    ?species rdfs:label"Grus grus".
    ?observation h:season h:autumn .
```

[12] http://d3js.org/

[13] http://angularjs.org/

```
    ?observation h:countMigration ?cnt .
    ?observation h:windDay ?wind .
    ?wind h:windSpeed ?speed .
    ?wind h:windDirection ?dir .
    ?dir h:order ?order .
    {
        SELECT ?wind (COUNT(DISTINCT ?date) AS ?days)
        WHERE {
            ?observation h:refTime ?date .
            ?observation h:windDay ?wind .
            ?observation h:season h:autumn .
        }
        GROUP BY ?wind
    }
}
GROUP BY ?order ?speed ?days
ORDER BY ?speed
```

The research hypothesis behind our second visualization is that air pressure affects the migration of very large birds. However, it is unclear how much it affects, if at all. To solve the problem, the characteristics ontology of bird species is needed telling the sizes of different species, in addition to bird observation and weather data. Figure 2 plots as an example the migration counts of very large birds on Y-axis. The average air pressure of the days in which the migration was observed is represented in the X-axis. The migration counts have been normalized to give the average migration count for each day with a certain average air pressure.

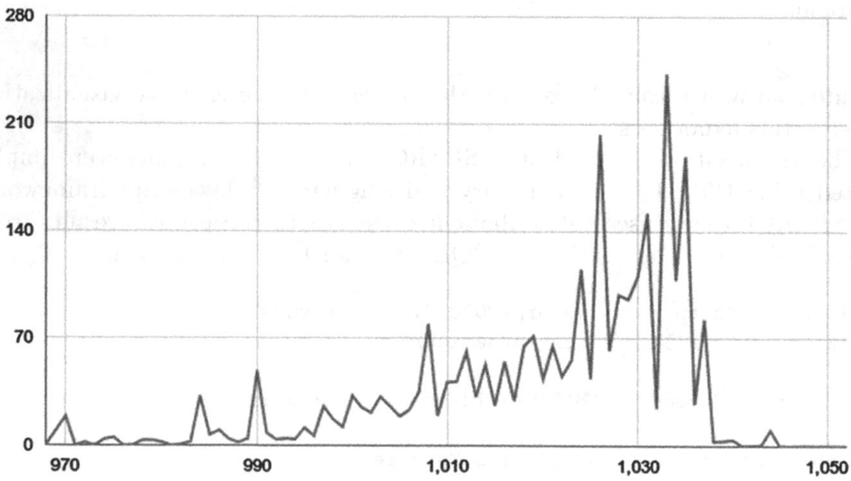

Fig. 2. Average migration count of very large birds in relation to air pressure [hPa].

This visualization was implemented using Sgvizler. It takes about 8 seconds to retrieve the data from the LDF platform using this SPARQL query:

```
PREFIX h: <http://ldf.fi/schema/halias/>
PREFIX bc: <http://ldf.fi/halias/bird-characteristics/>

SELECT  ?pressure ((SUM(?cnt)/?days) AS ?normalized)
WHERE {
    ?observation h:observedSpecies ?species .
    ?species h:hasCharacteristic bc:valtava .
    ?observation h:airPressure ?pressure .
    ?observation h:countMigration ?cnt .
{
SELECT ?pressure (COUNT(DISTINCT ?date) AS ?days)
WHERE {
?observation h:refTime ?date .
?observation h:airPressure ?pressure .
}
GROUP BY ?pressure
}
}
GROUP BY ?pressure ?days
ORDER BY ?pressure
```

Based on the graph, it may be inferred that very large birds migrate mostly during high pressure when there are low chances of rain. As the normal air pressure is around 1013, this seems to be in line with the original hypothesis. Also it was observed that when visualizing the migration magnitude of different bird sizes, smaller birds had higher migration magnitudes at lower air pressures.

Because very low or very high air pressures are rare, a large variance in the values far away from the normal air pressure can be seen in the graph.

4 Discussion

4.1 Contributions

This paper suggests that following advantages may be gained by publishing a statistical dataset using the RDF Data Cube Vocabulary, and by enriching the data by linking it with related datasets:

1. **Better understanding of the primary data.** The weather variables play a key role in the migration magnitude of a single day. Thus by introducing the weather context of the time of observation, a better understanding about the bird observation data can be achieved.
2. **Interoperability.** Efficient use of nature observation data requires standard ways to combine datasets. This can be achieved with by publishing datasets as linked data [16], which makes it also possible to use common tools for data handling and processing [17].

3. **Visualization tools.** It is possible to visualize the data with existing RDF Data Cube visualization tools [14,17] and in the future with new and better tools.
4. **Linking to taxonomic concepts.** By linking to a taxon ontology we are able to express certain taxonomic concepts of the species instead of representing them only by name, which then would need work from an expert to correctly interpret [4,18]. One way to express taxonomic concepts and changes biological conception is to use the TaxMeOn meta-ontology [21].
5. **Data validation.** Structural errors in original data, such as wrong data types or cardinality errors, may cause problems when converting to RDF and thus the conversion may provide information about errors in the original data and help improve data quality.

Performance of SPARQL queries may be an issue in visualizing large linked datasets. The linked dataset used in this research is already large enough to make the data retrieval last several seconds.

4.2 Related Work

There are bird observation analysis systems around, such as eBird[14] used by, e.g., the Audubon Society, that provide visualizations of observations, such as range and point maps and yearly bar charts. The different metrics of observations can be graphed along a timeline and statistics of one species contrasted with others. Furthermore, data mining tools have been applied to observational databases in order to analyze and discover phenomena that take place in nature [7]. Our approach extends these ideas to the Semantic Web, especially to using enriched semantic data based on data linking and ontologies.

The AVIO ontology and species characteristics ontology have been used in our earlier work, the BirdWatch mobile tool for ornithologists [8].

Lots of Linked Data (LD) platforms have emerged on the Web since the publication of the four Linked Data publication principles and the 5-star model[15] [6]. For example, in Life Sciences alone there are LinkedLifeData[16], NeuroCommons[17], Chem2Bio2RDF[18], HCLSIG/LODD[19], BioLOD[20], and Bio2RDF[21]. The Linked Data Finland service used in our case study is based on a "7-star model" with additional services supporting dataset schema documentation, data validation, and data curation [9].

Work in Linked Data visualization [3,11] falls in three categories. One can (1) visualize the structure of data, e.g., ontologies in an ontology editor, (2) present

[14] http://ebird.org/
[15] http://www.w3.org/DesignIssues/LinkedData.html
[16] http://linkedlifedata.com/
[17] http://neurocommons.org/
[18] http://chem2bio2rdf.wikispaces.com/
[19] http://www.w3.org/wiki/HCLSIG/LODD
[20] http://biolod.org/
[21] http://bio2rdf.org/

computed analysis results, e.g., statistics, or (3) use various graphical means for illustrating phenomena, e.g., present data on maps, timelines or using other kind of graphics. Our work is related to the latter two categories, where e.g. business graphics and visualizations been widely and routinely used for data analysis and exploration.

The two visualizations presented in this paper are examples of how Linked Data can be exploited to address research questions in an application domain. Based on the experiments, the SPARQL standard was deemed quite flexible in formulating fairly complex queries, and using visualization frameworks on top of query results was fairly straightforward. Based on our hands-on experiments, data visualization seems to be a promising application dimension of Linked Data. Visualizations, such as our examples, are focused on solving particular problems, but at the same time may well generalize to other use cases by changing the variables involved, such as the species, species group criterion, time frame, or a weather characteristic.

Interest in publishing statistical data as linked data has been growing [5,10] in the past few years and has been studied in many publications. Hausenblas et al. [5] have proposed publishing statistical datasets as linked data using the Statistical Core Vocabulary (SCOVO) and a modelling framework to support this.

Salas et al. [17] present tools OLAP2DataCube and CSV2DataCube for transforming statistical data to RDF Data Cube Vocabulary datasets. Using general purpose link discovery tools for a transformed dataset is shown through an example. Also presented is an extension to OntoWiki for visualizing RDF Data Cube datasets called CubeViz.

Mutlu et al. [14] present a visualization wizard of linked research data that automatically suggests suitable visualizations based on the data and a semantic configuration. Kämpgen and Harth [10] discuss using open-source OLAP systems to visualize statistical Linked Data.

4.3 Future Research

The visualizations have been implemented with this particular use case in mind. We should study if a more general RDF Data Cube visualization approach would suit the needs of this use case. A big challenge with a more general approach comes from the user interface, which should be kept simple and easy to use.

Some existing open source RDF Data Cube visualization services were evaluated when we decided to use the data cube approach, and they were not up to the task at that point. As there seems to have been development in this area, a new evaluation of them would be useful.

This combined data of bird observation counts and weather variables seems interesting for new research in both computer science and biology.

Acknowledgements. This work has been supported by the Ministry of Education and Culture, CSC - IT Center for Science Ltd., National Research Data Initiative

(TTA)(http://www.tdata.fi/en/), and the Linked Data Finland project (http://www.seco.tkk.fi/projects/ldf/) funded by the Finnish Funding Agency for Innovation (Tekes) of 20 partners.

Ornithological society Tringa(http://www.tringa.fi/web/) provided the data used in this research. Hundreds of volunteers at Halias have helped by gathering the data. Miika Alonen from Aalto University's Semantic Computing Research Group (SeCo) gave support in visualizing the data. Jouni Tuominen from SeCo contributed to developing the visualization web service.

References

1. Able, K.P.: The role of weather variables and flight direction in determining the magnitude of nocturnal bird migration. Ecology **54**(5), 1031–1041 (1973). http://www.jstor.org/stable/1935569
2. Alerstam, T.: Optimal bird migration revisited. J. Ornithol. **152**(1), 5–23 (2011). http://dx.doi.org/10.1007/s10336-011-0694-1
3. Dadzie, A.S., Rowe, M.: Approaches to visualising linked data: a survey. Semant. Web **2**(2), 89–124 (2011)
4. Franz, N.M.: Biological taxonomy and ontology development: scope and limitations. Biodivers. Inform. **7**(1), 45–66 (2011)
5. Hausenblas, M., Halb, W., Raimond, Y., Feigenbaum, L., Ayers, D.: SCOVO: using statistics on the web of data. In: Aroyo, L., et al. (eds.) ESWC 2009. LNCS, vol. 5554, pp. 708–722. Springer, Heidelberg (2009)
6. Heath, T., Bizer, C.: Linked Data: Evolving the Web into a Global Data Space, 1st edn. Morgan & Claypool, Palo Alto (2011). http://linkeddatabook.com/editions/1.0/
7. Hochachka, W., Caruana, R., Fink, D., Munson, A., Riedewald, M., Sorokina, D., Kelling, S.: Data-mining discovery of pattern and process in ecological systems. Wildl. Manag. **71**(7), 2427–2437 (2007)
8. Hyvönen, E., Alonen, M., Koho, M., Tuominen, J.: Birdwatch–supporting citizen scientists for better linked data quality for biodiversity management. In: Proceedings of the First International Workshop on Semantics for Biodiversity (S4BioDiv), ESWC 2013. CEUR Workshop Proceedings, vol. 979, May 2013. http://www.ceur-ws.org/Vol-979
9. Hyvönen, E., Alonen, M., Tuominen, J., Mäkelä, E.: Linked data finland: towards a 7-star service platform for linked datasets. In: The First Annual KnowEscape Conference - KnowEscape 2013, November 2013. http://www.seco.tkk.fi/publications/2013/hyvonen-et-al-ldf-2013.pdf
10. Kämpgen, B., Harth, A.: Transforming statistical linked data for use in olap systems. In: Proceedings of the 7th International Conference on Semantic Systems, pp. 33–40. ACM (2011)
11. Katifori, A., Halatsis, C., Lepouras, G., Vassilakis, C., Giannopoulou, E.: Ontology visualization methods–a survey. ACM Comput. Surv. (CSUR) **39**(4), 10 (2007)
12. Kjellén, N.: Annual variation in numbers, age and sex ratios among migrating raptors at falsterbo, sweden from 1986–1995. J. für Ornithologie **139**(2), 157–171 (1998)
13. Lehikoinen, A., et al.: Lintukantojen kehitys hangon lintuaseman aineiston mukaan 1979–2007. Tringa **35**, 313–321 (2008)

14. Mutlu, B., Hoefler, P., Sabol, V., Tschinkel, G., Granitzer, M.: Automated visualization support for linked research data. In: Proceedings of the I-SEMANTICS 2013 Posters & Demonstrations Track, p. 40 (2013)
15. Nisbet, I.C.T., Drury Jr., W.H.: Short-term effects of weather on bird migration: a field study using multivariate statistics. Anim. Behav. **16**(4), 496–530 (1968)
16. Reichman, O., Jones, M.B., Schildhauer, M.P.: Challenges and opportunities of open data in ecology. Science(Washington) **331**(6018), 703–705 (2011)
17. Salas, P.E.R., Auer, S., Breitman, K.K., Casanova, M.A., Martin, M.: Publishing statistical data on the web. Int. J. Semant. Comput. **6**(4), 373–388 (2012)
18. Schulz, S., Stenzhorn, H., Boeker, M.: The ontology of biological taxa. Bioinformatics **24**(13), 313–321 (2008)
19. Skaeveland, M.: Sgvizler: a JavaScript wrapper for easy visualization of sparql result sets. In: Proceedings of the ESWC 2012. Springer-Verlag (2012)
20. Svensson, S.E.: Efficiency of two methods for monitoring bird population levels: breeding bird censuses contra counts of migrating birds. Oikos **30**, 373–386 (1978)
21. Tuominen, J., Laurenne, N., Hyvönen, E.: Biological names and taxonomies on the semantic web – managing the change in scientific conception. In: Antoniou, G., Grobelnik, M., Simperl, E., Parsia, B., Plexousakis, D., De Leenheer, P., Pan, J. (eds.) ESWC 2011, Part II. LNCS, vol. 6644, pp. 255–269. Springer, Heidelberg (2011)
22. Tuominen, J., Laurenne, N., Koho, M., Hyvönen, E.: The birds of the world ontology AVIO. In: Cimiano, P., Fernández, M., Lopez, V., Schlobach, S., Völker, J. (eds.) ESWC 2013. LNCS, vol. 7955, pp. 300–301. Springer, Heidelberg (2013)

Protégé4US: Harvesting Ontology Authoring Data with Protégé

Markel Vigo[(✉)], Caroline Jay, and Robert Stevens

School of Computer Science, University of Manchester, Manchester, UK
{markel.vigo,caroline.jay,robert.stevens}@manchester.ac.uk

Abstract. The inherent complexity of ontologies poses a number of cognitive and perceptual challenges for ontology authors. We investigate how users deal with the complexity of the authoring process by analysing how one of the most widespread ontology development tools (i.e. Protégé) is used. To do so, we build Protégé4US (Protégé for User Studies) by extending Protégé in order to generate log files that contain ontology authoring events. These log files not only contain data about the interaction with the environment, but also about OWL entities and axioms. We illustrate the usefulness of Protégé4US with a case study with 15 participants. The data generated from the study allows us to know more about how Protégé is used (e.g. most frequently used tabs), how well users perform (e.g. task completion times) and identify emergent authoring strategies, including moving down the class hierarchy or saving the current workspace before running the reasoner. We argue that Protégé4US is an valuable instrument to identify ontology authoring patterns.

1 Introduction

Semantic technologies present interaction challenges for both developers of semantic artefacts and their users. This is particularly true for authors of ontologies authored in the Web Ontology Language (OWL), where complex systems of axioms are asserted and then used to draw implications about that ontology. Ontologies are complex artefacts and this complexity comes from different dimensions: the domain, the size of the artefact, the semantics and the interface of the development environment, be the latter a text processor or an IDE for ontology development.

In an initial study with 15 ontology experts we found that, indeed, these complexities cause problems to users along all stages of the authoring process [6]. Exploration, search, building, reasoning, debugging and evaluation pose a number of challenges that users overcome by employing authoring strategies that may be suboptimal. In that study some of the most relevant outcomes in terms of reported problems, and missing or poorly supported features of tools are:

V. Presutti et al. (Eds.): ESWC Satellite Events 2014, LNCS 8798, pp. 86–99, 2014.
DOI: 10.1007/978-3-319-11955-7_8

- Making sense, getting an overview and exploring an ontology is difficult if the ontology is large or the user is not familiar with it.
- The consequences of minor edits can have enormous implications on the underlying ontology. Since current tools are not able to convey these changes the situational awareness of users is dramatically reduced.
- Searching for ontologies and, especially, retrieving components of an external ontology into the active ontology is a missing feature.
- The efficient addition of axioms to large ontologies remains a challenge.
- On-the-fly reasoning capabilities is reported as a desirable feature as users tend to want to frequently run the reasoner to test their latest update or set of modifications.
- Explanations for inconsistencies and inferences tend to be perceived to be overloaded with information, making the debugging of ontologies hard.
- Having predefined 'unit' tests would help in assessing the validity and completeness of ontologies.

Beyond this, little is known about the activity patterns of the ontology authoring process, the details of problems authors encounter and how these difficulties are overcome. The analysis of the literature indicates that tools are normally evaluated against a number of established criteria. What is more, user involvement in the assessment of authoring tools is scarce (see Sect. 2). This may be a consequence of a lack of interest in the human factors of the ontology authoring process as Human-Computer Interaction practices do not pervade all computing disciplines. Additionally, this could also happen because there are not enough instruments to run ontology authoring studies and experiments.

We address this lack of instrumentation by building Protégé4US (Protégé for User Studies), a modification of one of the most widely used ontology authoring environments [1], Protégé. In Sect. 3 we describe how these modifications generate log files containing the interactions of users with the environment and the authoring activities they undertake. Then, in order to corroborate the findings of our preliminary study [6] and find patterns of activity, we run a user study in which 15 participants[1] carry out three authoring tasks with Protégé4US (see Sect. 4). Results in Sect. 5 illustrate the potential of this approach as it facilitates the computation of performance metrics, the number and variety of commands invoked and the patterns in the authoring process. Consequently, the contributions of this paper are twofold:

- We provide an instrument that allows harvesting of ontology authoring events and interaction events.

[1] Four of these participants also took part in the initial interview study [6].

– A study with 15 users carrying out ontology authoring tasks shows the potential of such a tool to expand our knowledge about the ontology authoring process.

2 Related Work

Usability, interoperability, and portability are some of the dimensions identified in a survey about semantic authoring tools of textual content [3]. Only two papers out of the 175 papers that were analysed involved end-users in evaluating the user interface. In both cases enquiry methods were employed *a posteriori* in order to provide evidence about user acceptability of the evaluated tools. Even if the mentioned work focuses on a particular area of the semantic web, it is an indicator of the lack of involvement of users in the development process of ontology authoring tools.

Nevertheless, there are some notable exceptions in the evaluation of ontology authoring tools with users: eight non-expert users carried out a number of basic tasks including ontology loading, entity addition, modification, and removal [4]. After completing their tasks, users were given questionnaires in order to quantify the relevance of tools to accomplish tasks, tool efficiency, user attitude towards tools, and learnability aspects. In another study 28 participants with basic OWL knowledge carried out three tasks with TopBraid Composer and Protégé [2]. Tasks included creating classes and properties, as well as adding subsumption, equivalence, and range axioms. Afterwards, participants were given questionnaires to measure the effectiveness, efficiency, and user experience with the mentioned tools.

A major criticism of existing studies is their sole reliance on questionnaires. In addition to their questionable reliability due to their subjective nature, a key weakness of questionnaires is that preconceived questions get predefined responses and participants are unable to express additional thoughts that would have been interesting for researchers. This is something we addressed in [6] by interviewing ontology authors. While self-reported data can be invaluable in analysing the subjective dimensions of experience, the sole reliance on questionnaires shows an incomplete picture of behaviour analysis. We argue that self-reports should preferably be complemented with objective interaction data. In this sense, the advent of web based authoring environments such as WebProtégé [5] will bring about not only the remote involvement of users, but will also facilitate the analysis of server log data as shown in [7]. While server log analysis allows to increase the involvement of geographically distributed participants, it has several downsides including the lack of contextual information or the difficulty in identifying the tasks and goals of users.

In this paper we present a tool that logs objective interaction and authoring data, Protégé4US; additionally, we conduct a feasibility study of the tool by analysing the data generated by real users carrying out real tasks.

3 Instrumentation of Protégé

We modified Protégé 4.3 by adding event listeners to the interface elements and by logging every class that implemented any user activity. As a consequence, a CSV file that contains the timestamps and information about the events is generated as shown below in an extract from a log file. The first value in each row shows the timestamp in milliseconds, while the second value indicates the type of event. Even though a broad range of events is collected, we can classify these in to three main types: interaction events, authoring events on the current ontology and the commands invoked in the working environment —we assign to each event a value of *1*, *2* or *3* respectively. The third column denotes the Protégé tab that was active when the event occurred as depicted by Fig. 1. The fourth value describes the event and the last column indicates the object of the event: i.e. the specific class that was edited, the reasoner that was invoked or the class that was hovered over.

```
1:  76585,2,Classes,Element edited,Juliette subclass of: Potato and hasCroppingTime
some 'Main cropping'
2:  77786,3,Classes,Save ontology,http://owl.cs.manchester.ac.uk/ontology/start-here.owl
3:  80204,3,Classes,Reasoner invoked,HermiT 1.3.8
4:  80647,1,Classes,Mouse entered, Class hierarchy (inferred)
5:  82910,1,Classes,Element hovered,Early_cropping_potato
6:  83049,1,Classes,Element selected,Early_cropping_potato
7:  83661,1,Classes,Hierarchy expanded,Early_cropping_potato
```

From this we can later reconstruct and analyse the authoring process: line 1 of the log file shows —using a potato ontology we describe later in Sect. 4— how the class of Juliette potatoes is harvested between September and November, as indicated by the value of the hasCroppingTime property, which is 'Main cropping'. After that, line 2 and 3 tell that the ontology was saved and that the HermiT reasoner was invoked right after. Once the reasoner was finished the user entered into the inferred class hierarchy (line 4), and selected the Early_cropping_potato class (line 5–6) in the inferred class hierarchy. Finally line 7 indicates that the hierarchy under this class was expanded.

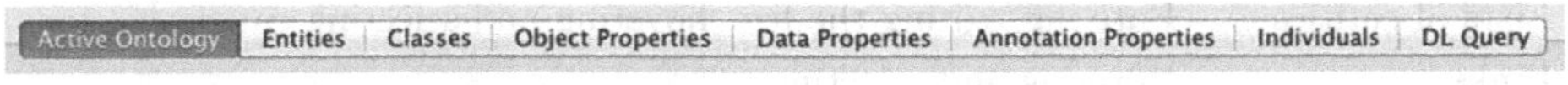

Fig. 1. Default tabs of Protégé 4.3

3.1 Interaction Events

The user interface of Protégé 4.3 is implemented using data structures such as hierarchies and lists that are containers of different types of entities. For instance, the hierarchy data structure can contain classes, properties, data and annotations (see Fig. 2). Similarly, lists expand the description of a particular element (see Fig. 3) and are used to describe classes, properties, data properties, annotations and individuals. Therefore, in Protégé4US the functionalities of hierarchies and lists, and the events triggered by user interaction are analogous regardless of the type of entity they contain. As a result, the interaction events described in Table 1 apply to all hierarchies and lists, irrespective of the type of entity upon which the event is generated.

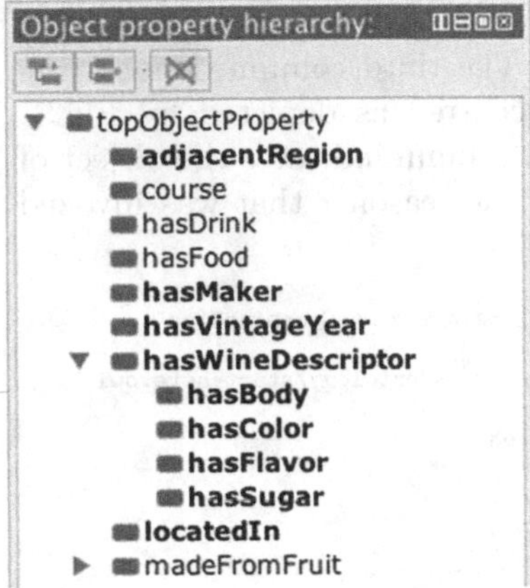

Fig. 2. The hierarchy structure of Protégé 4.3: property hierarchy

Fig. 3. The list structure of Protégé 4.3

Table 1. Interaction events in Protégé4US

Event	Description
Annotations	Hovering and selecting
Lists of entities	Entering/exiting the list, hovering and selecting entities
Links	Hovering and selecting
Hierarchies	Entering/exiting the hierarchy, hovering and selecting entities. Expanding and collapsing entity hierarchies. Hovering tooltips
Individuals	Hovering and selecting
Search result panel	Hovering, selecting and clicking on search results

3.2 Authoring Events

Authoring events are those that modify the state of the ontology. Table 2 does not only describe the CRUD events (create, read, update and delete) that

Table 2. Authoring events in Protégé4US

Event	Description
Add entities	Add child/sibling classes, properties, individuals or annotations
Class conversion	Converting a class into a defined class or a primitive class
Class hierarchy wizard	A hierarchy is added into the current ontology
Characteristics of properties	Check/uncheck the characteristics of properties to make them functional, inverse functional, transitive, symmetric, asymmetric, reflexive or irreflexive
Characteristics of classes	Create a defined class or an inverse of a existing class
Closure	Add a closure
Delete	Delete an entity or a restriction
Duplicate entity	When an entity with the same characteristics as another is created
Entity dragged	Drag & drop an entity in a hierarchy
Entity edited	Create universal, existential and cardinality restrictions to classes. Add domain and ranges to properties
Rename entity	Invoke refactoring to rename an entity

Protégé4US collects, but also gives specific details about the modification of entities in terms of *how*, amongst others, ranges, domains or restrictions are set.

3.3 Environment Commands in Protégé4US

The events shown in Table 3 can be understood as the features added by ontology authoring IDEs on top of the basic functionalities required to build an OWL ontology (see Table 2). These include the events generated by the interaction with buttons that trigger actions, the invocation of the reasoner and explanation handler, and the file saving events.

4 Study

4.1 Participants

Fifteen participants (ten male) in the age range between 22–47 and a median age of 32 took part in our study. They had a background in computer science and worked both in academia or industry. We used snowball sampling to contact

Table 3. Events on the Protégé4US environment

Event	Description
Button clicked	When clicking on the interface buttons to add or remove child/sibling classes, properties, individuals and annotations
Class hierarchy wizard	When the wizard is invoked through *Tools* → *Create class hierarchy...*
Explaining	Invoking the explanation handler to clarify an inference or an inconsistency
History navigation	When the back and forth arrows are clicked, and when the *undo* or *redo* commands are invoked
Reasoning	Events are generated when a reasoner is invoked, when reasoning is finished and when the reasoner is stopped
Search panel	When the user types a query in the search box
Usage panel	When the checkboxes of the usage panel are clicked in order to establish the visualisation criteria: all, disjoints, differents and superclasses
Workspace events	Ontology saved, loaded and set as the active ontology

possible candidates and invited to participate those who reported to be knowledgeable about OWL and Protégé, which is corroborated by the self-reported assessment about these selection criteria in Figs. 4 and 5. Users completed a questionnaire containing 5-point Likert scales in order to answer "Assess your expertise with OWL" and "Assess your expertise with Protégé", where 1 indicated 'Novice' and 5 was for 'Expert'.

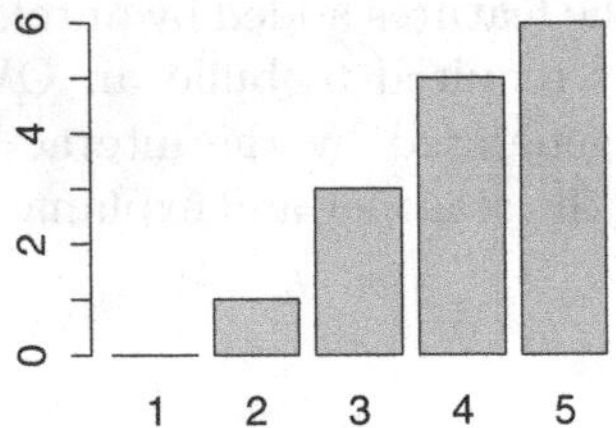

Fig. 4. Reported OWL expertise: 1-novice, 5-expert; X-axis: expertise, Y-axis: frequency

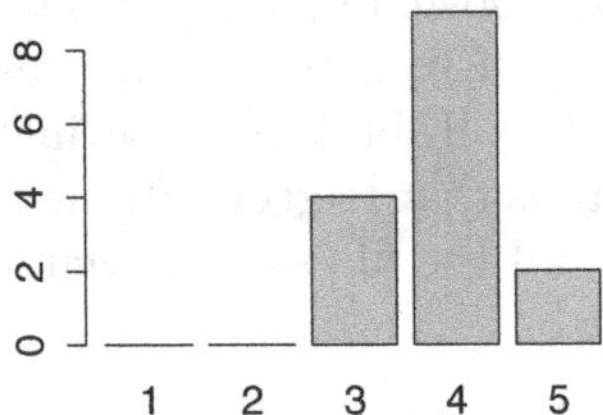

Fig. 5. Reported Protégé expertise: 1-novice, 5-expert; X-axis: expertise, Y-axis: frequency

4.2 Experimental Design

The goal of the tasks was to make an ontology of potatoes that could drive a 'potato finder' application. Participants were told to carry out the following three tasks with an intended incremental difficulty level:

1. Classify the potatoes by cropping times.
2. Import a file containing descriptions of potato yields. Represent the yields of each kind of potato and classify by combinations of yield and cropping time.
3. Add in a representation of culinary role (i.e. preferred way of cooking). Build at least two classes that combine the three axis (culinary role, yield and cropping time).

Participants were also provided with a printed table with the necessary information —cropping time, yield or skin colour— to build the potato ontology. They were also told not to start from scratch, but they should adopt the persona of a 'jobbing' ontologist given an OWL ontology to extend and maintain. Therefore, participants were provided with an OWL file containing 13 subclasses of various potato varieties and another one with a small hierarchy of cropping times for potatoes, which also removed the burden of heavy editing.

Protégé4US was deployed onto a Windows 7 laptop and used to carry out the above-mentioned tasks. There was not a fixed time to complete the tasks although participants were free to stop their participation at any time. Participants filled out a post-test questionnaire about the perceived difficulty of each task using a 5-point Likert scale where 1 indicated 'easy' and 5 'difficult'.

5 Results

5.1 Performance Metrics

The median values for completion times indicate that it took 11.04 min for Task 1 ($m = 6.9, M = 18.05$), 11.83 min for Task 2 ($m = 7.36, M = 36.53$) and 17.87 min for Task 3 ($m = 10.13, M = 28.62$). These differences in completion time are significant as suggested by the Kruskal-Wallis test, $\chi^2 = 10.04, p < 0.01$. Figure 6 shows the completion times of each participant per task. All participants completed their task except for P7 and P15[2], who were not able to complete Task 2 and 3. While P7 gave up participating in the study, P15 finished all the tasks, but did not achieve the goals we established. The perceived difficulty of each task can be seen in Fig. 7, where the median value is 1 for Task 1, 2 for Task 2 and 2.5 for Task 3. A Kruskal-Wallis test indicates that these differences are significant, $\chi^2 = 10.79, p < 0.005$. This means that we succeeded in defining tasks with an increased level of difficulty.

[2] Participants are coded using the Pi notation, where i denotes the participant number $1 \leq i \leq 15$.

We found a moderate negative correlation between self-reported expertise with Protégé and the task completion time for Task 1, Spearman's $\rho = -0.51, p < 0.05$. This suggests that the more expert a participant was with Protégé, the faster Task 1 was completed. No correlation is found between expertise (either with Protégé or OWL) with the remaining task completion times. There is no correlation between the time taken to complete a task and its perceived difficulty, which suggests that the time taken was more an indicator of the number of authoring actions required to complete a task than an indicator of cognitive difficulty.

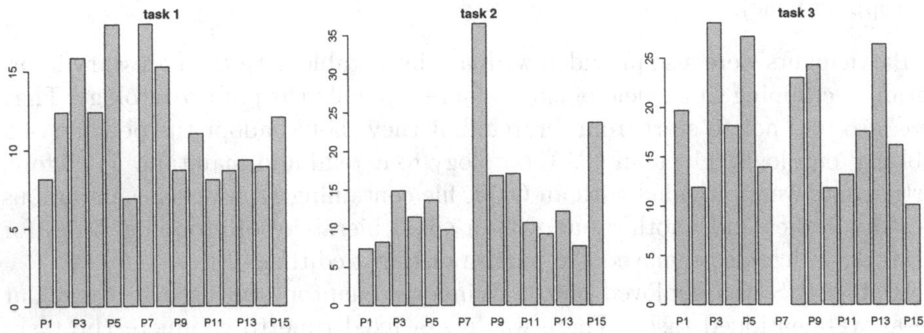

Fig. 6. Completion times for tasks; X-axis: participants; Y-axis: time in minutes

5.2 Usage Metrics

Figure 8 shows the number of events triggered by each participant at each Protégé tab (see Fig. 1). It can be observed that there are roughly 2 types of users when it comes to tab usage. On the one hand, those who stick to one tab: P1, P2, P14 and P15 use the *Classes* tab, while P3, P4, P5, P6, P9, P11 and P12 use mostly the *Entities* tab. On the other hand, P7, P10 and P13 use mostly two tabs, one of which is the *Classes* tab.

We selected a sample of the total events as they may be indicative of typical behaviours based on the findings of our previous study [6]. *Undoing*, *deleting*, *navigating back* and *renaming* are indicative of users trying to repair mistakes made. The invocation of the *reasoner* and *explanation handler* is often a way of testing the current ontology for the former and the user trying to know more about the source of problems for the latter. *Expanding* any hierarchy suggests that users are navigating the class or property hierarchy trying to find an entity. Table 4 shows the number of events triggered by each participant.

Considering the number of participants we can relax the α value and thus consider marginally significant those correlations with a *p value* between 0.05–0.1. When computing Spearman's correlation we find a strong correlation between

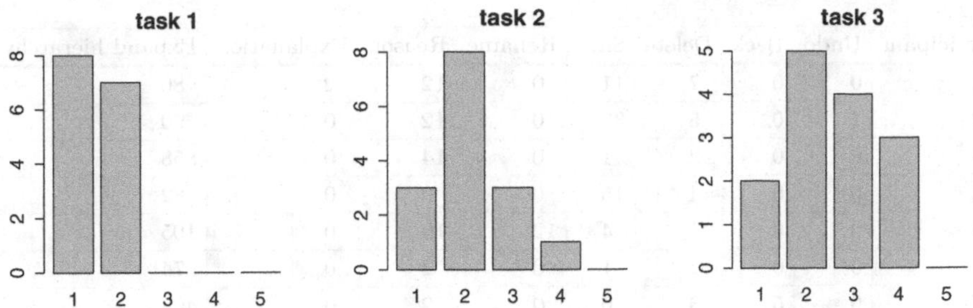

Fig. 7. Perceived difficulty of tasks: 1-easy, 5-difficult; X-axis: difficulty; Y-axis: frequency

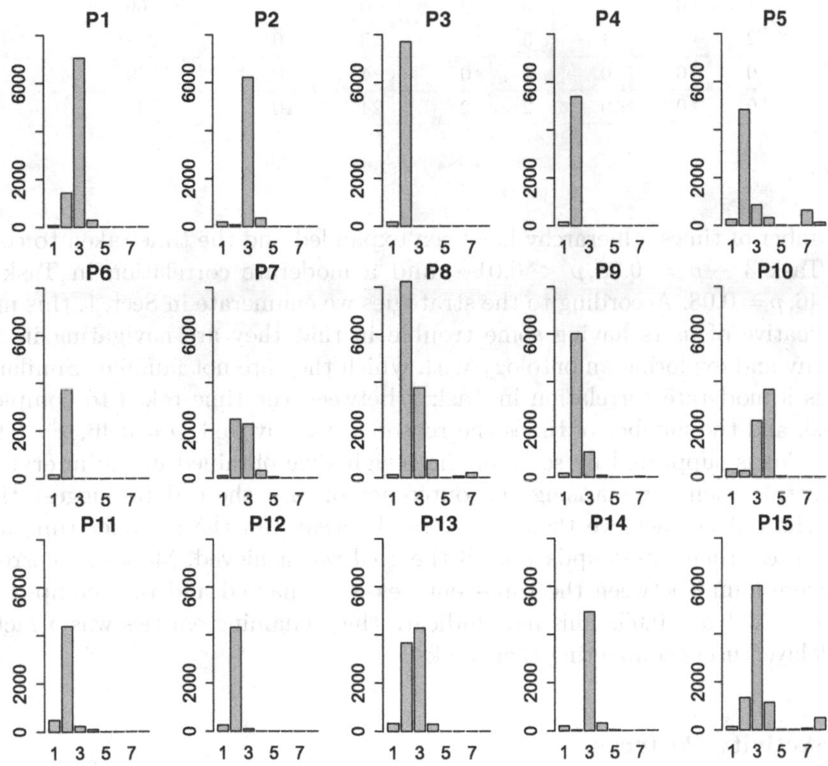

Fig. 8. Tab usage per user in Protégé 4.3; X-axis: 1: Active Ontology; 2: Entities; 3: Classes; 4: Object Properties; 5: Data Properties; 6: Annotation properties; 7: Individuals; 8: DL Query; Y-axis: number of events occurring in each tab

Table 4. Sample of the events triggered by each participant

Participant	Undo	Back	Delete	Save	Rename	Reason	Explanation	Expand hierarchy
P1	0	0	7	11	0	12	2	80
P2	1	0	5	33	0	12	0	90
P3	0	0	2	1	0	14	0	858
P4	0	0	4	15	0	9	0	82
P5	0	0	1	4	12	16	0	105
P6	0	0	1	1	0	2	0	74
P7	0	5	3	0	0	2	0	403
P8	2	0	3	15	3	36	1	316
P9	0	0	1	15	3	14	4	409
P10	0	0	2	11	0	0	1	80
P11	0	0	2	19	0	12	1	97
P12	7	0	2	5	2	0	0	69
P13	2	0	11	5	1	15	0	208
P14	0	0	0	1	0	4	0	279
P15	0	0	9	2	2	24	10	66

the number of times a hierarchy has been expanded and the time taken to complete Task 3 —$\rho = 0.68, p < 0.01$— and a moderate correlation in Task 1, $\rho = 0.46, p = 0.08$. According to the strategies we enumerate in Sect. 1, this may be indicative of users having some trouble in that they are navigating in the hierarchy and exploring an ontology with which they are not familiar. Similarly, there is a moderate correlation in Task 2 between the time taken to complete the task and the number of times the reasoner was invoked, $\rho = 0.46, p = 0.08$. Again, this is supported by some of the insights we obtained in the interviews (see Sect. 1 when summarising the outcomes of [6]): these data suggest that users who did not achieve their goal straight away ran the reasoner time and again to test their latest update until the goal was achieved. Moderate correlations were found between the times entities are renamed and task completion time, $\rho = 0.53, p = 0.05$. This may indicate that renaming entities was a factor that delayed users completing their tasks.

5.3 Activity Patterns

Since the sequence of events and their timestamps are collected, we are able to reconstruct the interaction and plot time diagrams such as the one shown in Fig. 9.

The blocks between events denote the time spent between events in which no other event (from the ones we sample) was triggered. These diagrams give visual hints on the strategies employed by participants to achieve their goals.

A preliminary visual analysis of 15 time diagrams allows us to uncover some activity patterns and regularities that may be shaped as a decision tree:

- The reasoner is invoked after,
  (a) A class is converted into a defined class.
  (b) An entity's modification is finished.
  (c) The ontology is saved.
  (d) An entity is selected.
- An ontology is saved after,
  (a) An entity's modification is finished.
- A tree is expanded after,
  (a) Reasoner finishes.
  (b) A tree is expanded.
  (c) Entity edition has been invoked.
- An entity is selected after,
  (a) Another entity is selected.

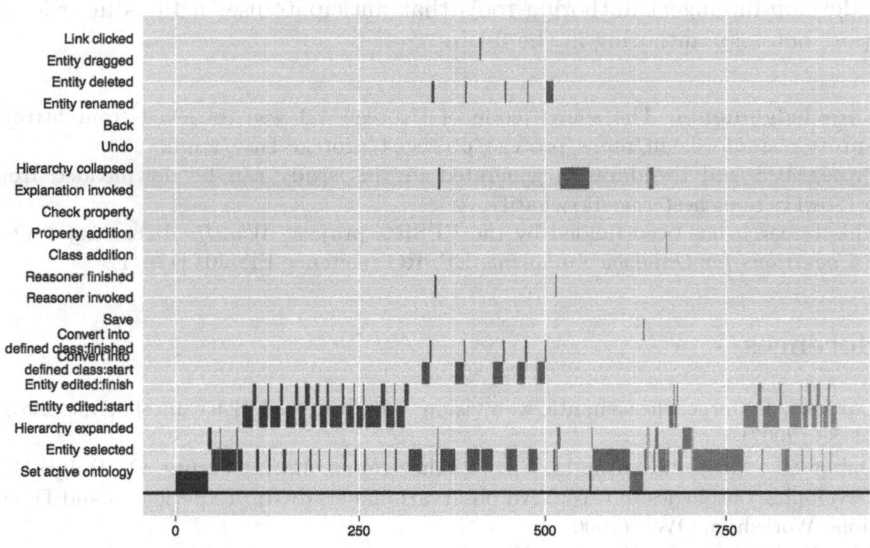

Fig. 9. The time diagram for the first 250 events of P13: the X-axis indicates the time elapsed in seconds, while the Y-axis shows the events triggered by the user.

In order to corroborate the information derived from the analysis of user interaction visualisations, future work will delve into analysing these data statistically. Consequently, we would be able to anticipate user behaviour and make Protégé adaptive. By implementing adaptive features we can address some of the limitations of current tools we list in Sect. 1. For instance, if we confirm that users invoke the reasoner after saving the ontology, the reasoner could be run as a background process right after saving, which would save time for the user.

6 Conclusion

We present Protégé4US, an instrument to carry out user tests of ontology authoring tasks. As a proof of concept we run a study in which 15 experts complete three tasks of different difficulty. The results show that it is feasible to collect objective and reliable performance metrics such as task completion time. Within the context established by these tasks we are able to: 1. identify two types of users based on how they use the tabs of Protégé; 2. find correlates between interaction events and performance metrics that corroborates our initial insights [6]: a higher number of times the reasoner is invoked indicates trouble and thus, longer completion times; 3. visualise emerging activity patterns: e.g. an ontology is saved before invoking the reasoner and after modifying an entity. This suggests that our instrument has an enormous potential to expand our knowledge about the ontology authoring process, identify its pitfalls, propose design guidelines and develop intelligent authoring tools that anticipate user actions in order to support ontology authoring in the future.

Acknowledgements. The source code of Protégé 4.3 was retrieved from http://smi-protege.stanford.edu/repos/protege/protege4/protege-base/trunk.

Protégé4US and the datasets generated in this study can be downloaded from http://owl.cs.manchester.ac.uk/whatif/.

This research has been funded by the EPSRC project: *WhatIf: Answering "What if... " questions for Ontology Authoring*. EPSRC reference EP/J014176/1.

References

1. Cardoso, J.: Jorge: the semantic web vision: where are we? IEEE Intell. Syst. **22**(5), 84–88 (2007)
2. Dzbor, M., Motta, E., Aranda, C.B., Gomez-Perez, J.M., Goerlitz, O., Holger, H.: Developing ontologies in OWL: An observational study. In: Experiences and Directions Workshop, OWL (2006)
3. Khalili, A., Auer, S.: User interfaces for semantic authoring of textual content: a systematic literature review. Web Semant. Sci. Serv. Agents World Wide Web **22**, 1–18 (2013)
4. Lambrix, P., Habbouche, M., Pérez, M.: Evaluation of ontology development tools for bioinformatics. Bioinformatics **19**(12), 1564–1571 (2003)
5. Tudorache, T., Vendetti, J., Noy, N.F.: Web-protege: a lightweight OWL ontology editor for the web. In: Proceedings of the 5th OWLED Workshop on OWL (2008)

6. Vigo, M., Jay, C., Stevens, R.: Design insights for the next wave ontology authoring tools. In: Proceedings of the SIGCHI Conference on Human Factors in Computing Systems, CHI' 14, pp. 1555–1558 (2014)
7. Wang, H., Tudorache, T., Dou, D., Noy, N.F., Musen, M.A.: Analysis of user editing patterns in ontology development projects. In: Meersman, R., Panetto, H., Dillon, T., Eder, J., Bellahsene, Z., Ritter, N., De Leenheer, P., Dou, D. (eds.) ODBASE 2013. LNCS, vol. 8185, pp. 470–487. Springer, Heidelberg (2013)

Survey of Semantic Media Annotation Tools for the Web: Towards New Media Applications with Linked Media

Lyndon Nixon[1](✉) and Raphaël Troncy[2]

[1] MODUL University, Vienna, Austria
lyndon.nixon@modul.ac.at
[2] EURECOM, Sophia Antipolis, France
raphael.troncy@eurecom.fr

Abstract. Semantic annotation of media resources has been a focus in research since many years, the closing of the "semantic gap" being seen as key to significant improvements in media retrieval and browsing and enabling new media applications and services. However, current tools and services exhibit varied approaches which do not easily integrate and act as a barrier to wider uptake of semantic annotation of online multimedia. In this paper, we outline the Linked Media principles which can help form a consensus on media annotation approaches, survey current media annotation tools against these principles and present two emerging toolsets which can support Linked Media conformant annotation, closing with a call to future semantic media annotation tools and services to follow the same principles and ensure the growth of a Linked Media layer of semantic descriptions of online media which can be an enabler to richer future online media services.

1 Introduction

The amount of non-textual content being shared via the Internet is growing at a massive scale, yet the original Web technology around hypertext is proving too limited for the needs of online users to find and re-use online media easily. Metadata has become a vital component of media retrieval but the vast majority of online media assets have very limited metadata attached to them, e.g. Google Image search works primarily on the text surrounding media embedded into web pages. Online media collections may expose some basic properties following the Dublin Core model, i.e. a title, a description or some keywords, while Social Web media sharing sites tend towards open tagging of their content (folksonomies). Some additional metadata is typically included in the creation process, such as digital cameras capturing date/time and location of a photo. However, this still proves far from ideal for supporting rich and innovative media-centric applications where there may be complex queries as well as a need for meaningful organisation of relevant media items for browsing or re-use. With the current emergence of the so-called *Visual Web* - image-centric web sites (e.g. Pinterest,

V. Presutti et al. (Eds.): ESWC Satellite Events 2014, LNCS 8798, pp. 100–114, 2014.
DOI: 10.1007/978-3-319-11955-7_9

Instagram, Tumblr) - and presumably the explosion very soon of an *Audiovisual Web* (Vine is a precursor of this but expect more professional content) the lack of actionable metadata is a major blocker to new innovation around retrieval and organisation of online media content.

On the other hand, the research community has been talking about semantic multimedia as a solution to richer media descriptions since over a decade - the basic idea being to move from basic metadata schemas to machine processable models with well defined properties and values, and provide sets of tools for manual or automatic creation of that metadata [3,8,11]. Research project showcases have repeatedly demonstrated improved media retrieval, faceted browsing or multimedia presentation as a result, e.g. [14]. However it has been typical of independent research activities to each choose different metadata models and vocabularies for the "semantic annotation" and build tools which were largely standalone and not connected to the rest of the media workflow. Furthermore, these models and tools for creating them have barely been applied to online media resources, and when they have been, separate approaches have not been well aligned meaning that semantic media demonstrators remain focused on individually annotated online collections instead of approaching online media retrieval and organisation at a truly Web scale. As a result, semantic media annotations remain at a small scale and in heterogenous formats today while the vast amounts of online media content remains unannotated or only attached to non-semantic metadata information.

In this paper, we want to address this situation. The authors believe we stand before a significant opportunity to make semantic annotations of online media a fundamental part of the Web fabric, enabling better Web media retrieval, reuse and re-mixing through new online services and applications able to leverage the semantic annotations. The timing is significant because the Visual Web is already here[1], and the Audiovisual Web (also driven by the shift of TV to digital and online) is only a matter of time. It needs to be driven by online tools and services which exhibit a consensus on interoperable input and output data formats, vocabularies and concept identifiers. Thus, in Sect. 2 we will propose a set of principles for Web-friendly semantic annotation of media which we call "Linked Media" and show how emerging Web specifications can address them. In Sect. 3, we look at currently available semantic multimedia annotation tools for the Web and compare these against those principles of "Linked Media", highlighting two recent developments for online annotation which conform to the Linked Media vision. Section 4 briefly outlines an example of new media applications potentially enabled by Linked Media. We conclude in Sect. 5 with a brief look into the future where significant amounts of online media are being semantically annotated and those annotations are being published on the Web, and call for future research work on semantic multimedia annotation to align itself with Linked Media.

[1] *The Triumph of the Visual Web*, http://readwrite.com/2013/12/18/visual-web-2013-trends.

2 Principles for Linked Media

Linked Media is a manifesto for a flexible, interoperable set of specifications for semantic media annotation, linking and presentation. It addresses metadata models, vocabularies for concepts, syntax for media fragments and Web based publication for subsequent retrieval and further processing. It has become possible now thanks to a consensual specification of how to refer to media fragments on the Web, annotate media and unambiguously refer to concepts and has become necessary with the scale of online media, making retrieval and re-use a pressing challenge.

Non-textual media such as audio-visual streams are not well integrated into the Web, where hypertext has traditionally been the baseline and thus links are made via textual anchors between Web pages which may embed non-textual media. The core problem is that there is not yet a Web-wide shared approach to annotating Web media such that the media metadata could consequently be found and used for linking across media collections, linking into and out of online documents, or also to generate links through the growing Web of Data. As such, we have identified core research issues around media on the Web today which are vital to be taken into account if, we believe, Web media is to be fully integrated into the Web of linked content and services in the future:

1. **Web media needs to be annotated in terms of its online parts, both along spatial and temporal dimensions**, since it is too imprecise to say that an atomic media item is about a concept X where that concept may only relate to a (small) part of the media. For a long time, we have lacked a standard means to refer to spatial or temporal segments of media on the Web.
2. **Web media needs to be annotated with terms which represent a shared understanding of a domain or identification of a thing.** When these terms are provided in a machine-understandable manner, we can say that they are drawn from an ontology. Providing ontologies and means to describe things using an ontology has been the activity of the Semantic Web community for many years.
3. **Web media needs to be annotated using a media ontology which supports the above two issues.** There is no agreed annotation schema for media on the Web, with the best known example MPEG-7 proving both to be too complex and not formally structured enough to be usable in this context. The W3C has proposed a Media Ontology, which seeks to capture common properties of different media annotation schemas and provide as a result a means to map between them [5]. However, we add an additional requirement for that ontology, which is that of capturing the type of the link between the media fragment and the represented thing. Current media annotations barely consider this aspect.
4. **The expressed representation of different concepts by different media fragments in different ways shall be the basis to interlink media across the Web.** By annotating media with concepts connected to

larger, shared domain models, we allow machines to choose and rank media resources on the Web by conceptual relevance and organize and present sets of media resources in a meaningful way based not just on the concepts but how those concepts relate to one another.

Linked Media is a reaction to the current heterogeneity of media descriptions on the Web [9]. Just as Web browsers could never have been successful without a core consensus on the Web page mark up (HTML), Web media can not fulfil its potential without a core consensus on the available descriptive metadata. While a W3C effort to define a common vocabulary for media description is laudable [5] the result is too generic for meaningfully annotating media to concepts, being restricted to a single, underspecified 'keyword' property. Both subject and object of the annotation also need clearer guidelines to ensure interoperability. The desire to open up multimedia annotations to the Web of Data, where they are understandable and sharable across systems, is shared by the creators of the Open Annotation Model (OAM) [13]. They also find that the subject of annotation is often a segment of a media item, and promote the re-use of fragment identification mechanisms already defined in the Web architecture [15].

Regarding the object of annotations, the Web of documents has long had the same problem in annotating its documents for better search and retrieval, since a shared understanding of the concepts the documents are annotated with was needed - neither free text annotation nor use of keywords or tags proved to be a solution immediately unless the differing usage of terms across systems and users could be aligned. Linked Data [4] is an emergent answer to this issue of Web-wide annotation by using the same principles as the Web itself with the concepts used in annotation: identify each concept by an URI, resolve these URIs to descriptions about those concepts, and create links between those URIs so that machines can browse concepts like humans browse Web pages. As noted in a paper outlining the design rationale for the OAM [2] it is the first Web media annotation model to embrace both Media Fragments as subject and Linked Data as object of Web media annotations, thus serving as a suitable starting point for Linked Media annotation.

In the next section, we will look at the currently available tools for semantic annotation of multimedia on the Web and compare their functionality to these Linked Media principles which find their realisation in the specifications mentioned above. We will show how work being done in two recent projects - ConnectME[2] and LinkedTV[3] - most closely follows these goals and outlines how this contributes to the wider vision of semantically annotated Web media.

3 Survey of Online Semantic Media Tools

Past and present research activities have also contributed to the implementation of tools for enabling the semantic annotation of media on the Web. An earlier

[2] http://www.connectme.at/

[3] http://www.linkedtv.eu/

survey made by Dasiopoulou *et al.* [1] is remarkable in that it is only a few years earlier and yet exhibits a lack of tools which work online (in the browser), not all can annotate media which is available at an URL rather than on the local machine, nor do any show any usage of Linked Data URIs or the set of W3C specifications referred in Sect. 2. The goal of semantic multimedia research on the Web must be to enable the publication online of interoperable and re-usable semantic descriptions which can support new online tools and services for media retrieval, re-use and re-mixing. Initial approaches to allow for images and video to be part of Linked Data has focused on natural language processing and clustering techniques across the free text tags attached to media on Web 2.0 sites like Flickr[4] and YouTube [7], but without re-publication of the extracted descriptions for subsequent re-use. We look at recent annotation tools which have emerged since the previous survey, are available online and create semantic descriptions of Web based media which could be published and re-used. We examine if they now more adequately address the below requirements, in line with our Linked Media principles, of:

- tool or service is online and allows to annotate media of different types via URL
- media can be annotated in terms of its parts and the media fragmentation follows a non-proprietary approach supported by other tools
- media can be annotated by concepts where a shared understanding is possible across systems
- media ontology used for the generated descriptions is interoperable across systems.

3.1 Review of Existing Semantic Multimedia Annotation Tools

We consider the following web-based[5] semantic multimedia annotation tools:

- Annomation[6]: this is a browser based tool for video annotation. It is currently restricted to educational material available within the Open University. Tags can be added at any point in the video timeline and given a duration. A number of vocabularies are supported for the tags, including DBPedia and GeoNames. The resulting video annotations re-use several ontologies, but seem to be saved back into the tool's own repository, i.e. they are only available again to the same tool.
- Annotorius[7]: this is an image annotation tool which is browser-based, implemented in JavaScript. It allows the attachment of free text descriptions to a spatial region. A Semantic Tagging plugin suggests named entities for the inserted text, which map to DBPedia resources. Annotations use their own JavaScript data objects for persistence and sharing.

---

[4] http://wifo5-03.informatik.uni-mannheim.de/flickrwrappr/

[5] We omit, on purpose, standalone softwares and plugins outside the context of a browser for performing the annotations.

[6] http://annomation.open.ac.uk/annomation

[7] http://annotorious.github.io/

- YUMA[8]: developed in the EuropeanaConnect project, it supports image, audio and video. Both DBPedia and Geonames resources can be annotation targets, and are suggested from free text or location references respectively. Annotations can be exported as RDF using a tool-specific vocabulary.
- SMAT[9] - Semantic Multimedia Annotation Tool - promises to allow the annotation using domain ontologies of fragments of content items within a rich internet application. Video can be accessed from any streaming server and annotated with spatial or temporal fragments connected to a term from a preloaded domain ontology. It is targeted to pedagogical usage and seems to be focused on demonstrating the act of media annotation rather than any wider re-use.
- SemTube[10] is a prototype for semantically annotating YouTube videos developed within the SemLib EU project. It allows attaching annotations to both spatial and temporal fragments, with annotations being free text, Freebase terms or full RDF triples. A faceted browser then allows users to explore their annotated videos. It appears functional but seems to be only enabled to save and retrieve annotations within a host server.
- Pundit[11] is an open source Web document annotation tool that has developed out of the SemLib EU project. It incorporates however only image annotation at the moment, allowing regions of the image to be annotated with LOD terms or freely chosen ontology URIs. A client can be downloaded and installed for local annotation of online Web pages which are saved to and retrieved from an instance of a Pundit server.
- IMAS[12] is a Web-based annotation tool developed within the SALERO EU project. Structured descriptions can be produced for media assets retrieved from a repository [16]. SALERO developed its own ontologies for annotating media and describing relationships between media according to the needs of the media production domain. The tool only allows global annotation of media resources and not annotating parts of them, and the output is specifically intended for the needs of producers (e.g. subsequent rediscovery of media) rather than for publication to the Web.
- ImageSnippets[13] enables to tag images using Linked Data resources. Interestingly, tagged images can then be published to the Web, both with descriptions embedded in the image data and included in the HTML file as RDFa metadata, on the fly. However, the tool does not yet support fragment-based annotation and it is restricted to the image medium. It is currently in beta but looks promising, except that its current open annotation approach could suffer from shared public image annotations not being interoperable due to a lack of a common annotation vocabulary among authors.

[8] http://dme.ait.ac.at/annotation/
[9] http://www.kp-lab.org/tools/semantic-multimedia-annotation-tool-smat
[10] http://www.semedia.dibet.univpm.it/semtube/
[11] http://thepund.it
[12] http://salero.joanneum.at/imas/
[13] http://www.imagesnippets.com/

- OpenVideoAnnotation[14] plans to offer a web-based tool to collaboratively annotate video on the web, at the fragment level and using the Open Annotation ontology. Annotations are free text comment and tag based, but it is not yet clear if Linked Data will be supported nor if spatial fragments will be included. This tool is clearly promising but this is still a work in progress with a soon to be launched beta program.

Having reviewed the most recent tools known to the authors, we highlight work of two projects the authors have been involved in which are continuing the task of supporting online semantic media annotation.

3.2 The ConnectME Toolset

In the ConnectME project, media fragment descriptions were generated out of industry partners existing media systems: in one case, a proprietary CMS and in the other case a Drupal installation. The Fig. 1a shows the extended proprietary CMS, where the legacy metadata fields filled in by the media channel owner (title, description, keywords for example) are complemented by a "Start Video Annotation Tool" button. When the button is pressed, the metadata in the CMS for this media asset is published to an API on the metadata repository using the mediaRSS format. An internal script maps the mediaRSS information into a new media asset description using a lightweight metadata model[15], re-using a subset of the W3C Media Ontology and the Open Annotation Model. The fragments are associated to concepts with specific properties (which can be extended) such as `explicitlyMentions` or `implicitlySeen`, allowing media systems processing these descriptions to make distinctions based on the concept being "represented" by the media fragment.

In the case of Drupal, a dedicated RDF Module is used to write Drupal node data into a RDF model and another dedicated module[16] is able to publish this RDF to the Linked Media Framework[17] (LMF) used as media metadata repository. Initial entity extraction for the media metadata is performed in the LMF using a trained Apache Stanbol instance over the media title, description and keywords, generating DBPedia resources. A Web based annotation tool has been developed[18] in which a media asset may be selected and its annotation inspected, using a timeline view (Fig. 1b) under the video frame to clearly show descriptions along the media's temporal fragments and allow editors intuitive editing of temporal fragment start/end times by drag & drop. Spatial fragments are also displayed for a selected annotation, if present, and can be changed by drag & drop of a spatial overlay over the video frame. The annotations are shown with their concept labels, with the addition/editing of annotations taking place in an easy-to-use wizard which allows plain text entry and suggests concepts to

[14] http://www.openvideoannotation.org/
[15] https://connect.me/ontology
[16] https://code.google.com/p/lmf/wiki/DrupalModule
[17] https://code.google.com/p/lmf/
[18] https://annotator.connectme.at

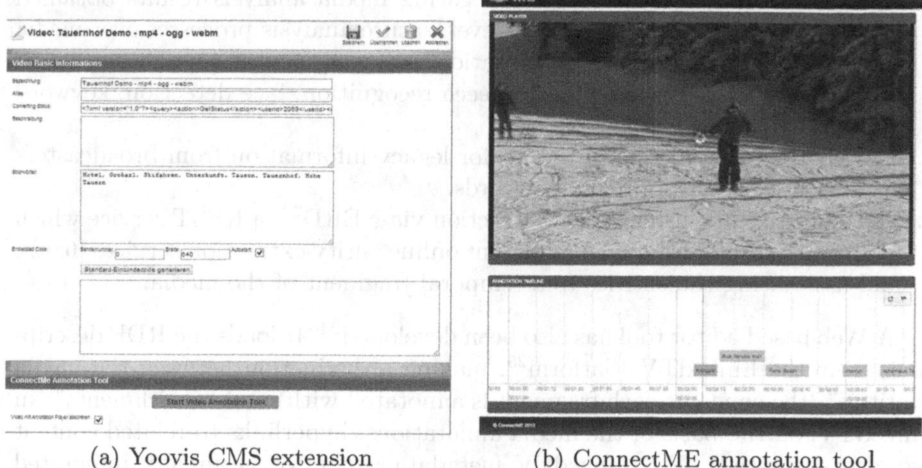

(a) Yoovis CMS extension (b) ConnectME annotation tool

Fig. 1. Export to semantic annotation integrated into CMS (courtesy Yoovis GmbH, http://www.yoovis.tv) (left) and online video annotation tool (right)

the annotator, providing a preview text to allow checking the correct concept is selected. Finished annotations are saved back to the repository, where they are used to enable automatic enrichment of video in a HTML5 based player[19].

3.3 The LinkedTV Toolset

In the LinkedTV project, a Web service is provided for ingesting various types of related information for a media asset and generating RDF descriptions according to the LinkedTV ontology[20] as a result. This combines several ontologies with a specific extension for its use case of modelling the (automated) annotation of media fragments and their association to related content (hyperlinking). It uses the idea of Media Fragments annotated (via the Open Annotation Model) with semantic concepts but can also model a wider range of information, including initial outputs from media analysis processes (which can subsequently be used for the semantic annotation), provenance information and different levels of granularity (fragments can correspond to `Shots`, `Scenes` or `Chapters`). The effect is that of enabling a fuller media fragment description which fits the full media lifecycle within a media management process, e.g. able to preserve information about where an annotation came from, which analysis results (e.g. entity extraction from subtitles) were used to create an annotation, or a series of edits to a fragment description via an annotation tool. The service aggregates the results of all the different input processing steps and a Web interface is available at http://linkedtv.eurecom.fr/tv2rdf/:

[19] https://player.connectme.at
[20] http://linkedtv.eu/ontology

1. EXMARaLDA[21], a format for aggregating media analysis results obtained after the execution of different low level feature analysis processes over media content. They include shot segmentation, scene segmentation, concept detection, object detection, automatic speech recognition, face detection, keyword extraction, etc.
2. TV Anytime[22], a metadata format for legacy information from broadcasters such as title, description and keywords.
3. SRT subtitles file, using entity extraction via NERD[23], a REST service which aggregates results from many different online entity extraction services [6,12], and associating the entities to a temporal fragment of the media.

A Web based editor tool has also been developed[24]. It loads the RDF descriptions from the LinkedTV Platform[25], making a distinction between the media "entities" (the concepts each fragment is annotated with) and "enrichments" (in LinkedTV, on the basis of the media annotations, hyperlinks to related content are also suggested). The LinkedTV metadata generator is already integrated within the LinkedTV platform so that generated descriptions of media assets are available to the Editor Tool. The tool allows an editor to select a specific chapter of the video, browse the existing annotations on the platform, and select them for the "media fragment description" or add new annotations. The manually selected annotations are saved back to the platform while attaching relevant provenance information (using the PROV ontology) which has the effect that - while the existing annotations are preserved and can be returned to - the manually selected annotations can also be selected out from the repository easily. The idea of the Editor Tool is to support content editors at TV broadcasters who will want to proof all automatically generated annotations and use, in the subsequent media workflow, only annotations they manually selected. Figure 2 shows the main interface of the Editor Tool:

Summarizing, two online media annotation UIs are available which can take results from prior analysis steps and store RDF data in dedicated platforms for which some front-end applications have already been developed for media enrichment. Furthermore, a REST service is available for producing semantic media descriptions for any online media making use of acquired analysis results, (TV Anytime) descriptive metadata and/or subtitling. If we consider the entire list of surveyed tools and services with respect to the requirements outlined at the beginning of the section, (Table 1) we observe that these ConnectME and LinkedTV implementations are closest to the vision and goal of publishing Linked Media for new media applications.

[21] http://www.exmaralda.org/

[22] http://www.tv-anytime.org/

[23] http://nerd.eurecom.fr/

[24] http://editortool.linkedtv.eu/

[25] http://api.linkedtv.eu/

Table 1. Survey of online semantic media annotation tools

Tool	Input Format	Fragment Support	Conceptual Annotation	Ontology
Annomation	Video only. URL loaded from local repository	Temporal fragments, proprietary syntax	DBPedia and GeoNames resources	Reuse of several vocabularies (FOAF, Dublin Core, Timeline, SKOS, Geo)
Annotorius	Image only. URL via JavaScript code	Spatial fragments, proprietary syntax	DBPedia resources	No ontology, proprietary JavaScript data model
YUMA	Audio, image or video. Reference by URL	Spatial and temporal fragments, using SVG	DBPedia and GeoNames resources	Own RDF-based vocabulary
SMAT	Flash video (FLV). Refer to a streaming server by URL	Spatial and temporal fragments, proprietary syntax	Terms selected from preloaded domain ontologies	Unclear, seems to not have any export option
SemTube	YouTube video by URL	Spatial and temporal fragments, presumed proprietary syntax	Freebase resources. Terms can be imported from other ontologies	Own RDF-based vocabulary
Pundit	Image only as part of a Web document	Spatial regions, presumed proprietary syntax	Freebase resources. Terms can be imported from other ontologies	Own RDF-based vocabulary
IMAS	Image and video from a media repository	No fragmentation of media	Assume ability to re-use any ontology term	SALERO ontologies, extensible
ImageSnippets	Image only, can be opened from URL	No fragmentation of media	Users are free to import terms from LOD or create their own	LIO ontology
Open Video Annotation tool	Video, unclear if access will be possible via URL	Only temporal fragments in the demo. Format unknown	Free text or tags, unclear if LOD will be supported	Open Annotation Model
ConnectME Annotation tool	Video, access via URL or from repository	Spatial and temporal fragments according to Media Fragment URI syntax	DBPedia and Geoname resource suggestion, extensible	ConnectME ontology, W3C Media Ontology and Open Annotation Model
TV2RDF service	Video, access via URL	Spatial and temporal fragments according to Media Fragment URI syntax	Depending on entity extraction service. Focus on using DBPedia	LinkedTV Ontology, W3C Media Ontology and Open Annotation Model
LinkedTV Editor Tool	Video, access via a media resource registered on LinkedTV Platform	Spatial and temporal fragments according to Media Fragment URI syntax	Any URI can be provided. Autocomplete available for suggesting DBPedia resources	LinkedTV Ontology, W3C Media Ontology and Open Annotation Model

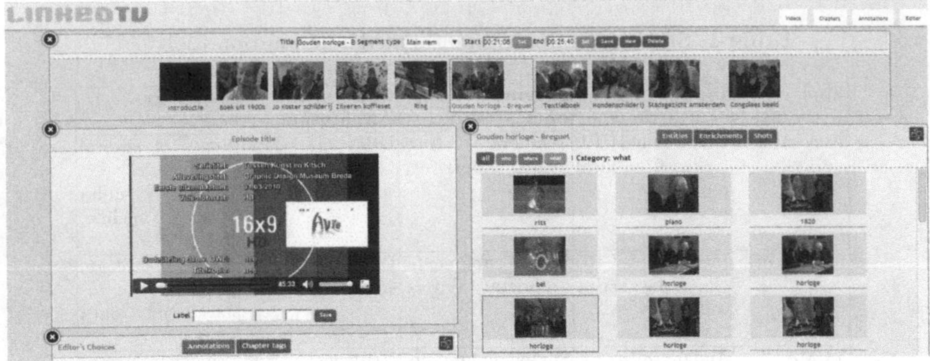

Fig. 2. LinkedTV editor tool

4 New Media Applications with Linked Media Systems

Future semantic media systems will incorporate analysis technology (for media fragment creation and classification) prior to (semi-automatic) semantic annotation of those fragments and subsequently copyright tools can support the attachment of licenses to the media fragments before the metadata is stored for use in new media applications. A number of such applications are being prototyped in the MediaMixer project[26] to highlight the value of semantic multimedia technology in the context of specific industry use cases, including dynamic video clip selection for newsrooms, license modeling for user generated content, and creating topical channels of online learning video content.

We briefly describe in this section the demonstrator prepared together with the VideoLectures.NET platform. VideoLectures.NET hosts more than 16 000 video lectures and it is currently challenging to find specific topics within those lectures as the current implementation relies on the indexing of basic top level metadata about each lecture (title and description). Media fragment and semantic technology has been introduced in a proof of concept with a selected subset of site materials. We focus here on the annotation, a fuller description of the implementation can be found at [10]. VideoLectures manages natively XML descriptions of lectures (title, description, category, keywords). We map this metadata into a TV Anytime like description using a XML template and simple script to perform the conversion. Analysis results are acquired from both shot segmentation algorithms run on the video itself and the slide transition XML documents, providing two different granularities of video temporal fragmentation. Using the TV2RDF service described in the Sect. 3.3, we can process these results as well as video transcripts created automatically by an ASR software[27] and acquire an aggregated semantic description of the lecture in terms of its salient fragments and Linked Data concepts attached to each fragment. In the resulting

[26] http://community.mediamixer.eu/demonstrators
[27] http://www.translectures.eu/tlk/

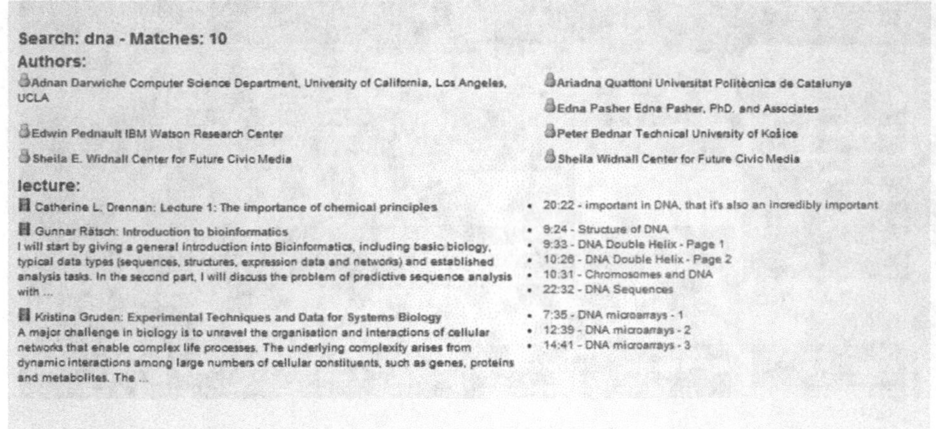

Fig. 3. VideoLecturesMashup: finding lecture snippets for a topic

demonstrator[28], a search on specific terms can now return video fragments from different lectures where the term has been extracted. For example `DNA` returns no results in the current Videolectures.NET site, while the MediaMixer demonstrator provides many matches across different video lectures (Fig. 3).

As a next step, since the fragment annotations use Linked Data resources (DBPedia), semantic search will be implemented so that search can also take into account synonyms, multilingualism, and topical relevance. We have taken technologies originally developed in the LinkedTV project developed to enrich TV programming with links to related content, and applied the same tools to enable fragment level search over lecture videos. It is an important contribution to have separate "building blocks" of what we call overall a Linked Media system (as it respects the principles of Linked Media outlined in Sect. 2) that can support different domains and end-user applications with the same data formats and approaches to semantic media annotation.

The experiences gained with demonstrators in different domains help validate the Linked Media vision and the technology, with annotation results being usable in a number of front end applications such as LinkedTV's interactive TV second screen application (Fig. 4, cf. http://linkedtv.eu/demos/linkednews). A full end-to-end workflow is being implemented within the server-side LinkedTV Platform with the goal to provide users with a simple means to ingest their video content and get access to the semantic annotation results via a SaaS model. As reflected in the survey of the previous section, it is these sort of tools which are preventing a wider uptake by media owners and enterprises of semantic annotating their media and re-use in new contexts.

---

28 http://mediamixer.videolectures.net

Fig. 4. LinkedTV second screen app displaying concepts annotated in a TV program

5 Conclusion

This paper began by acknowledging that, despite the benefits that semantic multimedia technology is perceived to offer - improved media management, retrieval and re-use - the amount of online media today having semantic annotations is desperately low. We have identified barriers to greater uptake of this technology in the unfortunate heterogeneity of approaches coming out of research and lack of integration with the Web itself as technology platform. We refer to principles for Linked Media which can connect online media descriptions more usefully into the Web of Data. A survey of current annotation tools reflected on a lack of consideration of these requirements in their implementation and has highlighted online tools and services from the ConnectME and LinkedTV projects which are closer to the vision and goal of eased, online publication of re-usable semantic descriptions of media. Demonstrators such as the VideoLecturesMashup point to the feasibility of following this Linked Media approach to ensure semantic media annotation can be integrated into media workflows and the resulting annotations re-used across different media applications.

Just as the Linked Data movement has worked hard to encourage data owners to embrace the value of online publication of their data in a structured, interlinkable manner, we must also address the challenge of encouraging media owners to publish semantic descriptions of their media online in a similarly structured and interlinkable manner. A growing body of semantic media annotations which follow interoperable data models, structures and concept vocabularies so that computer systems can search and link across them could support the creation of new media applications for search, re-use or re-mixing of online media. It should be noted that this is not insisting on the open publication of the media assets themselves: they may still be found behind paywalls or restricted by licenses, but through the publication of semantic descriptions they become more findable to applications which may need them for a re-use or re-mixing task.

If this is to become a true possibility in the soon to emerge Audiovisual Web, it is critical that current semantic multimedia research agrees to a consensus on how annotation is to be done: how it fits with outputs of prior media analysis, how it handles the different granularities of annotation on a single media asset, what metadata models, data formats and conceptual vocabularies it uses, how annotation output can be easily re-used by media management systems, in media retrieval, or for (multi)media presentation or re-purposing. This paper proposes to the semantic multimedia research community to embrace a consensus around the so-called Linked Media principles and has highlighted specifications which can provide for the necessary cross-system interoperability as well as validated this approach with first demonstrators building applications on top of Linked Media-conforming semantic media descriptions.

Acknowledgments. This work was partially supported by the European Union's 7th Framework Programme via the projects LinkedTV (GA 287911) and MediaMixer (GA 318101) as well as the Austrian FFG COIN programme through the project ConnectME.

References

1. Dasiopoulou, S., Giannakidou, E., Litos, G., Malasioti, P., Kompatsiaris, Y.: A survey of semantic image and video annotation tools. In: Paliouras, G., Spyropoulos, C.D., Tsatsaronis, G. (eds.) Multimedia Information Extraction. LNCS (LNAI), vol. 6050, pp. 196–239. Springer, Heidelberg (2011)
2. Haslhofer, B., Sanderson, R., Simon, R., Sompel, H.: Open annotations on multimedia Web resources. Multimedia Tools Appl. 1–21 (2012)
3. Hunter, J.: Adding multimedia to the semantic web - building an MPEG-7 ontology. In: 1st International Semantic Web Working Symposium (ISWC), pp. 261–281 (2001)
4. Lee, T.B.: Linked data principles. Des. Issues (2006)
5. Lee, W., Bailer, W., Bürger, T., Champin, P.-A., Evain, J.-P., Malaisé, V., Michel, T., Sasaki, F., Söderberg, J., Stegmaier, F., Strassner, J.: Ontology for Media Resources 1.0. W3C Recommendation (2012)
6. Li, Y., Rizzo, G., García, J.L.R., Troncy, R., Wald, M., Wills, G.: Enriching media fragments with named entities for video classification. In: 1st Worldwide Web Workshop on Linked Media (LiME'13), Rio de Janeiro, Brazil, pp. 469–476 (2013)
7. Li, Y., Rizzo, G., Troncy, R., Wald, M., Wills, G.: Creating enriched YouTube media fragments with NERD using timed-text. In: 11th International Semantic Web Conference (ISWC), Demo Session, Boston, USA (2012)
8. Nack, F., van Ossenbruggen, J., Hardman, L.: That obscure object of desire: multimedia metadata on the web (Part II). IEEE Multimedia **12**(1), 54–63 (2005)
9. Nixon, L.: The importance of linked media to the future web. In: 1st International Workshop on Linked Media (LiME), Rio de Janeiro, Brazil (2013)
10. Nixon, L., Zdolsek, T., Fabjan, A., Kese, P.: Video lectures mashup: remixing learning materials for topic-centred learning across collections. In: OCW Global Conference, Ljubljana, Slovenia (2014)
11. van Ossenbruggen, J., Nack, F., Hardman, L.: That obscure object of desire: multimedia metadata on the web (Part I). IEEE Multimedia **11**(4), 38–48 (2004)

12. Rizzo, G., Troncy, R.: NERD: a framework for unifying named entity recognition and disambiguation extraction tools. In: 13th Conference of the European Chapter of the Association for Computational Linguistics (EACL'12), Avignon, France (2012)
13. Sanderson, R., Ciccarese, P., Van de Sompel, H.: Open Annotation Data Model. W3C Community Draft (2013)
14. Schreiber, G., et al.: MultimediaN E-Culture demonstrator. In: Cruz, I., Decker, S., Allemang, D., Preist, C., Schwabe, D., Mika, P., Uschold, M., Aroyo, L.M. (eds.) ISWC 2006. LNCS, vol. 4273, pp. 951–958. Springer, Heidelberg (2006)
15. Troncy, R., Mannens, E., Pfeiffer, S., Van Deursen, D.: Media fragments URI 1.0 (basic). W3C Recommendation (2012)
16. Weiss, W., Bürger, T., Villa, R., Punitha, P., Halb, W.: Statement-based semantic annotation of media resources. In: Chua, T.-S., Kompatsiaris, Y., Mérialdo, B., Haas, W., Thallinger, G., Bailer, W. (eds.) SAMT 2009. LNCS, vol. 5887, pp. 52–64. Springer, Heidelberg (2009)

First Experiments in Cultural Alignment Repair (Extended Version)

Jérôme Euzenat(✉)

INRIA & LIG, Grenoble, France
Jerome.Euzenat@inria.fr

Abstract. Alignments between ontologies may be established through agents holding such ontologies attempting at communicating and taking appropriate action when communication fails. This approach, that we call cultural repair, has the advantage of not assuming that everything should be set correctly before trying to communicate and of being able to overcome failures. We test here the adaptation of this approach to alignment repair, i.e., the improvement of incorrect alignments. For that purpose, we perform a series of experiments in which agents react to mistakes in alignments. The agents only know about their ontologies and alignments with others and they act in a fully decentralised way. We show that cultural repair is able to converge towards successful communication through improving the objective correctness of alignments. The obtained results are on par with a baseline of a priori alignment repair algorithms.

Keywords: Ontology alignment · Alignment repair · Cultural knowledge evolution · Agent simulation · Coherence · Network of ontologies

1 Motivation

The work on cultural evolution applies, an idealised version of, the theory of evolution to culture. Culture is taken here as an intellectual artifact shared among a society. Cultural evolution experiments typically observe a society of agents evolving their culture through a precisely defined protocol. They perform repeatedly and randomly a task, called game, and their evolution is monitored. This protocol aims to experimentally discover the common state that agents may reach and its features. Luc Steels and colleagues have applied it convincingly to the particular artifact of natural language [11].

We aim at applying it to knowledge representation and at investigating some of its properties. A general motivation for this is that it is a plausible model of knowledge transmission. In ontology matching, it would help overcoming the limitations of current ontology matchers by having alignments evolving through their use [2], increasing the robustness of alignments by making them evolve if the environment evolves.

This paper is an extension of [6] with results of complementary experiments.

V. Presutti et al. (Eds.): ESWC Satellite Events 2014, LNCS 8798, pp. 115–130, 2014.
DOI: 10.1007/978-3-319-11955-7_10

In this paper, we report our very first experiments in that direction. They consider alignments between ontologies as a cultural artifact shared among agents. In the following, we call cultural repair the action of agents repairing these alignments while trying to communicate. We hypothesise that it is possible to perform meaningful ontology repair with agents acting locally. The experiments reported here aims at showing that, starting from a random set of ontology alignments, agents can, through a very simple and distributed mechanism, reach a state where (a) communication is always successful, (b) alignments are coherent, and (c) their quality, as measured by F-measure, has increased. We also compare the obtained result to those of state-of-the-art repair systems.

Related experiments have been made on emerging semantics (semantic gossiping [3,4]). They involve tracking the communication path and the involved correspondences. By contrast, we use only minimal games with no global knowledge and no knowledge of alignment consistency and coherence from the agents. Our goal is to investigate how agents with relatively little common knowledge (here instances and the interface to their ontologies) can manage to revise networks of ontologies and at what quality.

2 Experimental Framework

We present the experimental framework that is used in this paper. Its features have been driven by the wish that experiments be easily reproducible and as simple as possible. We first illustrate the proposed experiment through a simple example (Sect. 2.1), before defining precisely the experimental framework (Sect. 2.2) following [11].

2.1 Example

Consider an environment populated by objects characterised by three boolean features: color = {white|black}, shape = {triangle|square} and size = {small|large}. This characterises $2^3 = 8$ types of individuals: ■, ▲, □, △, ■, ▲, □, △.

Three agents have their own ontology of what is in the environment. These ontologies, shown in Fig. 1, identify the objects partially based on two of these features. Here they are a circular permutation of features: *FC* (shape, color), *CS* (color, size) and *SF* (size, shape).

In addition to their ontologies, agents have access to a set of shared alignments. These alignments comprise equivalence correspondences between their top (all) classes and other correspondences. Initially, these are randomly generated equivalence correspondences. For instance, they may contain the (incorrect) correspondence: SF:small $\equiv$ CS:black.

Agents play a very simple game: a pair of agents a and b is randomly drawn as well as an object of the environment o. Agent a asks agent b the class c (source) to which the object o belongs, then it uses an alignment to establish to which class c' (target) this corresponds in its own ontology. Depending on

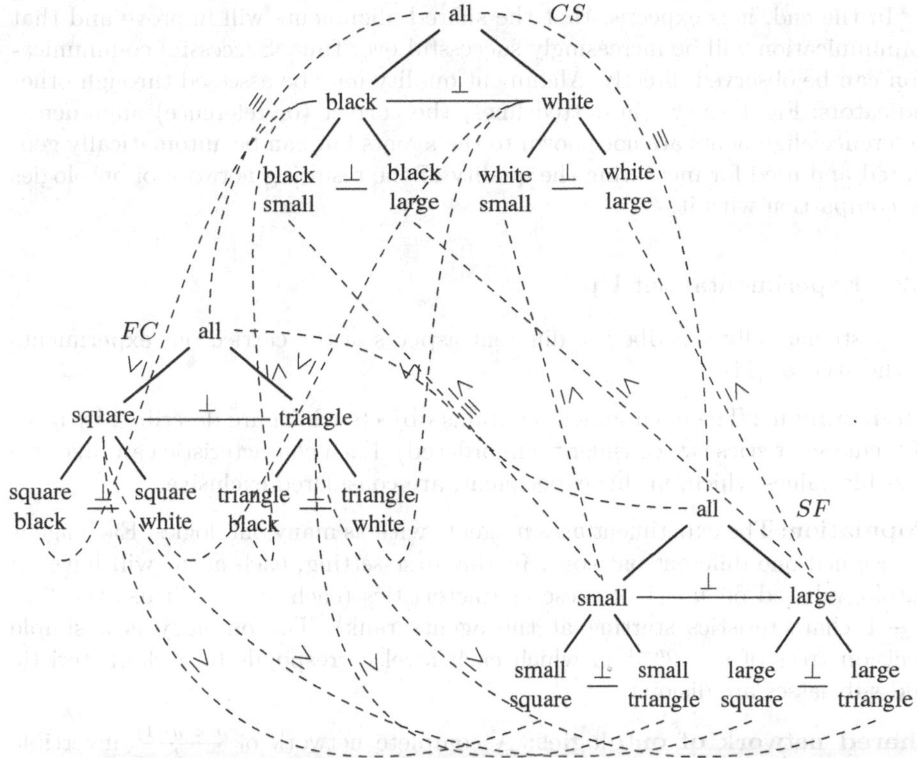

Fig. 1. Example of a generated network of ontologies with the exact reference alignments.

the respective relation between c and c', a may take the decision to change the alignment.

For instance, if agent CS draws the small-black-triangle (▲) and asks agent SF for its class, this one will answer: small-triangle. The correspondence SF:small $\equiv$ CS:black and the class of ▲ in CS is black-small which is a subclass of CS:black, the result is then a SUCCESS. The fact that the correspondence is not valid is not known to the agents, the only thing that counts is that the result is compatible with their own knowledge.

If, on the contrary, the drawn instance is small-white-triangle (△), SF would have made the same answer. This time, the result would be a FAILURE because △ belongs to class CS:white-small which is disjoint from CS:black-small.

How to deal with this failure is a matter of strategy:

delete SF:small $\equiv$ CS:black can be suppressed from the alignment;
replace SF:small $\equiv$ CS:black can be replaced by SF:small $\leq$ CS:black;
add in addition, the weaker correspondence SF:small $\geq$ CS:all can be added to the alignment (but this correspondence is subsumed by SF:all $\equiv$ CS:all).

In the end, it is expected that the shared alignments will improve and that communication will be increasingly successful over time. Successful communication can be observed directly. Alignment quality may be assessed through other indicators: Fig. 1 shows (in dotted lines) the correct (or reference) alignments. Reference alignments are not known to the agents but can be automatically generated and used for measuring the quality of the resulting network of ontologies by comparison with it.

2.2 Experimental Set Up

We systematically describe the different aspects of the carried out experiments in the style of [11].

Environment: The environment contains objects which are described by a set of n characteristics (we consider them ordered). Each characteristic can take two possible values which, in this experiment, are considered exclusive.

Population: The experiment uses n agents with as many ontologies. Each agent is assigned one different ontology. In this first setting, each agent will have an ontology based on $n-1$ of these characteristics (each agent will use the first $n-1$ characteristics starting at the agents rank). The ontology is a simple decision trees of size 2^{n-1} in which each level corresponds to a characteristic and subclasses are disjoint.

Shared network of ontologies: A complete network of $\frac{n\times(n-1)}{2}$ invertible alignments between the ontologies is shared among agents (public). The network is symmetric (the alignment between o and o' is the converse of the alignment between o' and o) and a class is in at most one correspondence per alignment.

Initialisation: In the initial state, each alignment contains equivalence correspondences between the most general classes of both ontologies, plus 2^{n-1} randomly generated equivalence ($\equiv$) correspondences.

Game: A pair of distinct agents $\langle a, b\rangle$ is randomly picked up as well as a set of characteristic values describing an individual (equiprobable). The first agent (a) asks the second one (b) the (most specific) class of its ontology to which the instance belongs (*source*). It uses the alignment between their respective ontologies for finding to which class this corresponds in its own ontology (*target*). This class is compared to the one the instance belongs to in the agent a ontology (*local*).

Success: Full success is obtained if the two classes (*target* and *local*) are the same. But there are other cases of success:

- *target* is a super-class of *local*: this is considered successful (this only means that the sets of alignments/ontologies are not precise enough);
- *target* is a sub-class of *local*: this is not possible here because for each instance, *local* will be a leaf.

Failure: Failure happens if the two classes are disjoint. In such a case, the agent a will proceed to repair.

Repair: Several types of actions (called modalities) may be undertaken in case of failure:

delete the correspondence is simply discarded from the alignment;

replace if the correspondence is an $\equiv$ correspondence it is replaced by the $\leq$ correspondence from the target class to the source class;

add in addition to the former a new $\leq$ correspondence from the source to a superclass of the target is added. This correspondence was entailed by the initial correspondence, but would not entail the failure.

These three strategies share two properties: (a) the resulting alignment would have avoided the uncovered mistake; (b) the resulting alignment is logically entailed by the initial one.

Success measure: The classical success measure is the rate of successful communication, i.e., communication without failure.

Secondary success measure: Several measures may be used for evaluating the quality of the reached state: consistency, redundancy, discriminability. We use two different measures: the averaged degree of incoherence [9] and the semantic F-measure [5]. Indeed, this setting allows for computing automatically the reference alignment in the network, so we can compute F-measure.

External validation: The obtained result can be compared with that of other repair strategies. We compare the results obtained with those of two directly available repair algorithms: Alcomo [8] and LogMap repair [7].

3 Experiments

We report four series of experiments designed to illustrate how such techniques may work and what are their capabilities. In addition to these experiments, which were reported in [6], we have added extra confirmatory experiments which test hypotheses stemming from the observations.

The tests are initially carried out on societies of at least 4 agents because, in the setting with 3 agents, the delete modality drives the convergence towards trivial alignments (containing only all $\equiv$ all) and the other modalities do it too often.

All experiments have been run in a dedicated framework that is available from http://lazylav.gforge.inria.fr.

3.1 Convergence

We first test that, in spite of mostly random modalities (random initial alignments, random agents and random instances in each games), the experiments converge towards a uniform success rate.

Four agents are used and the experiment is run 10 times over 2000 games. The evolution of the success rate is compared.

3.2 Modality Comparison

The second experiment tests the behaviour of the three repair modalities: **delete**, **replace**, **add**.

Four agents are used and the experiment is run 10 times over 2000 games with each modalities. The results are collected in terms of average success rate and F-measure.

3.3 Baseline Comparison

Then the results obtained by the best of these modalities are compared to baseline repairing algorithms in terms of F-measures, coherence and number of correspondences.

The baseline algorithms are Alcomo and LogMap repair. The comparison is made on the basis of success rate, F-measure and the number of correspondences.

LogMap and Alcomo are only taken as a baseline: on the one hand, such algorithms do not have the information that agents may use, on the other hand, agents have no global view of the ontologies and knowledge of consistency or coherence.

3.4 Scale Dimension

Finally we observe settings of increasing difficulty by taking the modality providing the best F-measure and applying it to settings with 3, 4, 5 and 6 ontologies.

This still uses 10 runs with the **add** modality over 10000 games. Results are reported as number of correspondences, F-measure and success rate and compared with the best F-measure of Alcomo and LogMap.

4 Results

Results of the four presented experiments are reported and discussed.

4.1 Convergence

Figure 2 shows the result of our first experiment: 10 runs with a random network as defined above with 4 ontologies. Each curve corresponds to one of the 10 runs over 2000 iterations.

Figure 2 shows a remarkable convergence between the runs. After the first 200 games dominated by randomness, they converge asymptotically and at the same pace towards 100 %. Indeed, as soon as the network of ontologies has been cleaned up (around 1200 iterations maximum), the rate only grows. It never reaches 1 because of the initial period which contains failures.

From now on, we will still consider 10 runs, but the results will be averaged over these runs.

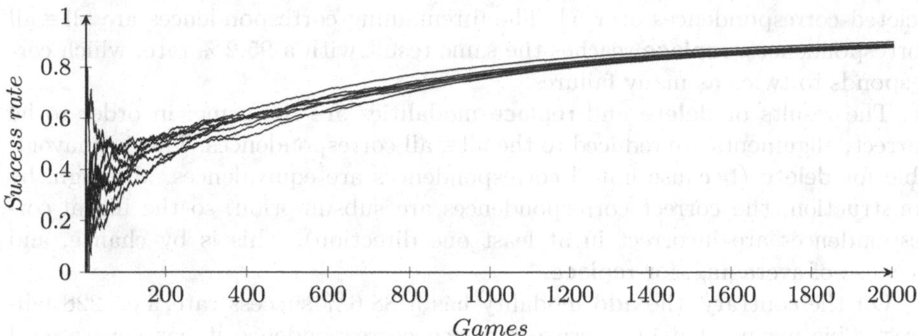

Fig. 2. Ten random runs and their overall success rate, i.e., the proportion of games which were successful so far [mod = **add**; #agents = 4; #games = 2000; #runs = 1].

4.2 Modality Comparison

Figure 3 shows the evolution over 2000 iterations of the success rate and F-measure of the three presented modalities.

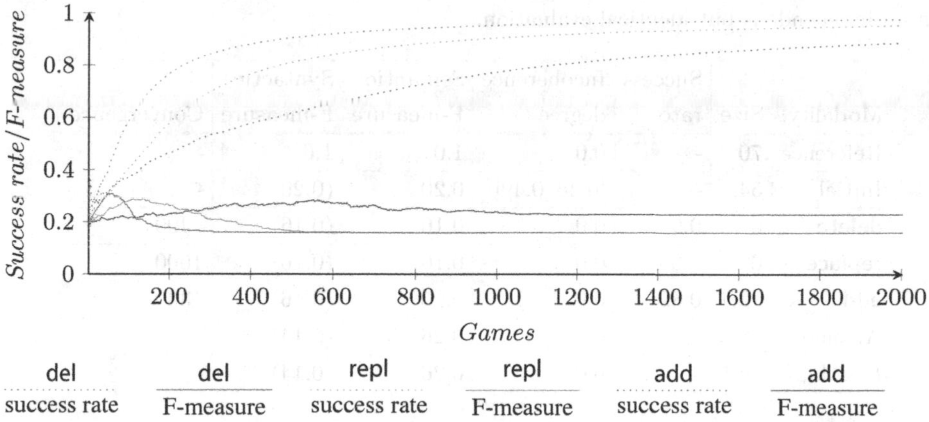

Fig. 3. The average F-measures (dashed) and success rate (plain) with the three different modalities: **delete** (red), **replace** (green) and **add** (blue) [mod = del,repl,add; #agents = 4; #games = 2000; #runs = 10] (Color figure online).

delete converges more quickly than **replace** which converges more quickly than **add**. This can easily be explained: **delete** suppresses a cause of problem, **replace** only suppresses half of it so it may need one further deletion for converging, while **add** replaces one incorrect correspondence by two correspondences which may be incorrect, so it requires more time to converge.

For the same reason, the success rate is consequently higher. Table 1 shows that for the **delete** modality, 97.6 % success rate corresponds to 48 failure, i.e. 48

deleted correspondences over 54. The 6 remaining correspondences are all ≡ all correspondences. **replace** reaches the same result with a 95.2 % rate, which corresponds to twice as many failures.

The results of **delete** and **replace** modalities are the same: in order to be correct, alignments are reduced to the all ≡ all correspondences. This is unavoidable for **delete** (because initial correspondences are equivalences, although, by construction, the correct correspondences are subsumption, so the initial correspondences are incorrect in at least one direction). This is by chance, and because of averaging, for **replace**.

On the contrary, the **add** modality has a 88.6 % success rate, i.e., 228 failures. This means that on average for each correspondence it has generated 4 alternative correspondences. This is only an average because after 2000 games (and even after 10000 games), there remain more than 12 correspondences.

Contrary to the other modalities, **add** improves over the initial F-measure.

Table 1 shows that all methods reach full consistency (incoherence rate = 0.) from a network of ontologies with 50 % incoherence, i.e., half of the correspondences are involved in an inconsistency (or incoherence).

Table 1. Results of the three different modalities compared with Alcomo and LogMap on 10 runs, 4 ontologies and 2000 iterations. Syntactic F-measure has been obtained in an independent but identical evaluation.

Modality	Size	Success rate	Incoherence degree	Semantic F-measure	Syntactic F-measure	Convergence
Reference	70	-	0.0	1.0	1.0	-
Initial	54	-	[0.46–0.49]	0.20	(0.20)	-
delete	6	0.98	0.0	0.16	(0.16)	400
replace	6	0.95	0.0	0.16	(0.16)	1000
add	12.7	0.89	0.0	0.23	(0.16)	1330
Alcomo	25.5	-	0.0	0.26	(0.14)	-
LogMap	36.5	-	0.0	0.26	(0.14)	-

Concerning F-measure, **add** converges towards a significantly higher value than the two other approaches. With four ontologies, it has a chance to find weaker but more correct correspondences. The **add** strategy is more costly but more effective than the two other strategies.

4.3 Baseline Comparison

This experiment exploits the same data as the previous one (Sect. 4.2); exploiting those of the next experiment (on 10000 iterations) provides similar results.

Table 1 shows that all three methods are able to restore full coherence and to slightly improve the initial F-measure. Their result is overall comparable but,

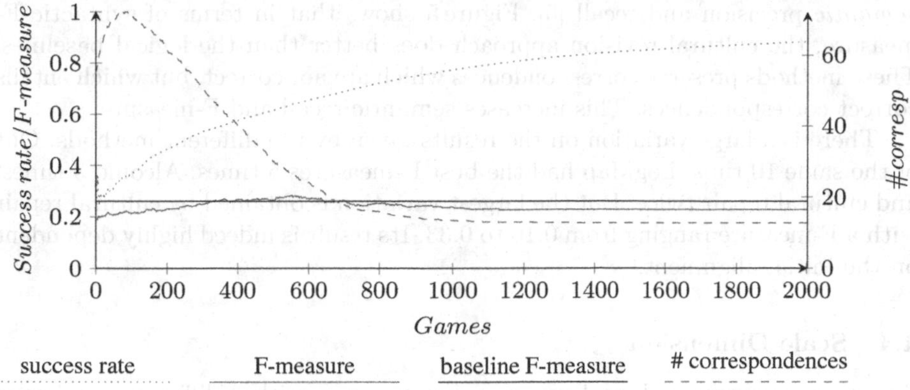

Fig. 4. Average success, semantic F-measure and number of correspondences for the **add** modality compared to the Alcomo and LogMap F-measure as a baseline [mod = **add**; #agents = 4; #games = 2000; #runs = 10].

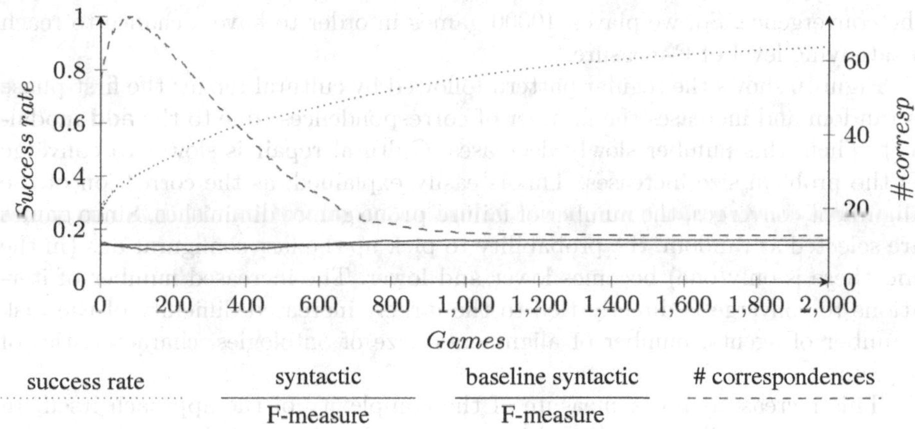

Fig. 5. Average success, syntactic F-measure and number of correspondences for the **add** modality compared to the Alcomo and LogMap F-measure as a baseline [mod = **add**; #agents = 4; #games = 2000; #runs = 10].

as can be seen in Fig. 4, cultural repair does not reach the F-measure of logical algorithms.

Cultural repair finds half of the correspondences of Alcomo and one third of those of LogMap. This is expected because Alcomo only discards the minimum number of correspondences which bring incoherence, while LogMap weaken them (like the **add** modality). The agents having more information on what is incorrect, discard more correspondences.

When looking at F-measures, it seems that logical repair strategies can find more than 6 new correspondences which are correct while the **add** strategy can only find more than 3. This is not true, as shown in Table 1, because we use *semantic* precision and recall [5]. Figure 5 shows that in terms of syntactic F-measure, the cultural revision approach does better than the logical baselines. These methods preserve correspondences which are not correct, but which entails correct correspondences. This increases semantic recall and F-measure.

There is a large variation on the results given by the different methods. Out of the same 10 runs, LogMap had the best F-measures 5 times, Alcomo 3 times, and cultural repair twice. But the largest variation is obtained by cultural repair with a F-measure ranging from 0.16 to 0.33. Its result is indeed highly dependent on the initial alignment.

4.4 Scale Dimension

So far, we concentrated on 4 agents, what happens with a different number of agents? The number of agents does not only determine the number of ontologies. It also determines the number of alignments (quadratic in the number of ontologies), the number of correspondences per alignments and the number of features per instances. This means that the more agents are used, the slower is the convergence. So, we played 10000 games in order to have a chance to reach a satisfying level of F-measure.

Figure 6 shows the regular pattern followed by cultural repair: the first phase is random and increases the number of correspondences (due to the **add** modality). Then, this number slowly decreases. Cultural repair is slower to converge as the problem size increases. This is easily explained: as the correction of the alignment converges, the number of failure-prone games diminishes. Since games are selected at random, the probability to pick up the last configurations (in the end there is only one) becomes lower and lower. The increased number of iterations to converge is directly tied to the largely increased difficulty of the task (number of agents, number of alignments, size of ontologies, characteristics of objects).

This increase is not a measure of the complexity of the approach itself. In fact, it is highly distributed, and it is supposed to be carried out while agents are achieving other tasks (trying to communicate). All the time spent between

Table 2. Number of correspondences, incoherence rate and F-measure over 10000 games.

# agents	# correpondences					Incoherence				F-measure				Convergence
	Reference	Initial	LogMap	Alcomo	Final	Initial	LogMap	Alcomo	Final	Initial	LogMap	Alcomo	Final	
3	15	15	12	10.3	3	0.31	0.	0.	0.	0.32	0.35	0.36	0.33	300
4	70	54	36.7	28.4	12.4	0.47	0.	0.	0.	0.20	0.24	0.25	0.21	1670
5	250	170	94.7	71.7	47.4	0.58	0.	0.	0.	0.11	0.18	0.17	0.24	5400
6	783	495	234	182	224	0.63	0.	0.	0.	0.06	0.12	0.11	0.14	10.000+

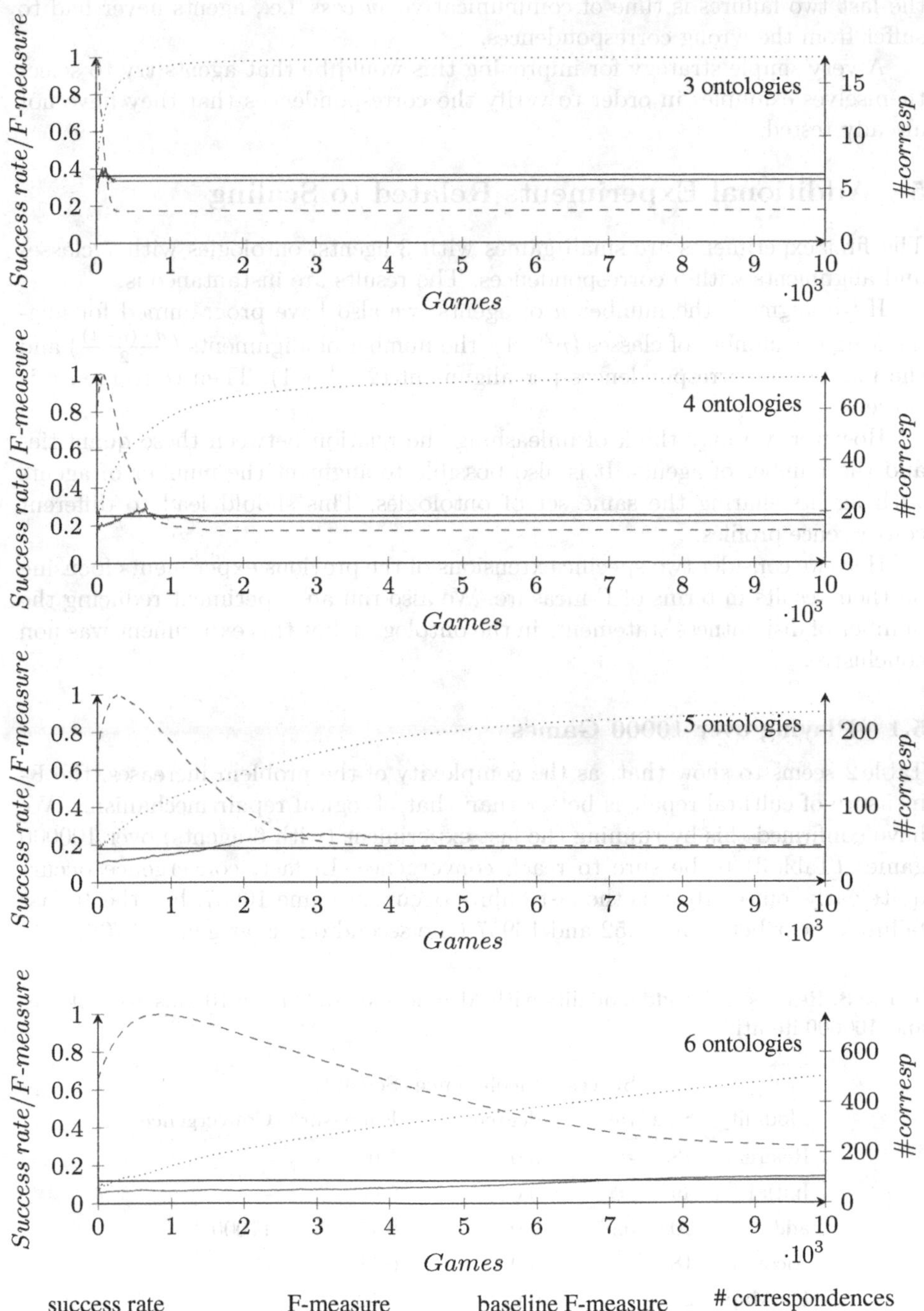

Fig. 6. 10.000 games with 3, 4, 5 and 6 ontologies [mod = **add**, #agents = 3, 4, 5, 6; #games = 10000; #runs = 10].

the last two failures is time of communicative *success*, i.e., agents never had to suffer from the wrong correspondences.

A very simple strategy for improving this would be that agents try to select themselves examples in order to verify the correspondences that they have not already tested.

5 Additional Experiments Related to Scaling

The first experiments are small games with 3 agents, ontologies with 7 classes and alignments with 5 correspondences. The results are instantaneous.

If we augment the number n of agents, we also have programmed for augmenting the number of classes (n^2-1), the number of alignments ($\frac{n\times(n-1)}{2}$) and the number of correspondences per alignment ($2^{n-1}+1$). Then convergence is slower.

However, we may think of unleashing the relation between these quantities and the number of agents. It is also possible to augment the number of agents with agents sharing the same set of ontologies. This should lead to different convergence profiles.

Here we consider two specific extensions of the previous experiments focusing on their results in terms of F-measure. We also run an experiment reducing the number of disjointness statements in the ontologies, but this experiment was non conclusive.

5.1 Playing over 10000 Games

Table 2 seems to show that, as the complexity of the problem increases, the F-measure of cultural repair is better than that of logical repair mechanisms. We have confirmed this by running the last experiment (with 6 agents) over 100000 games (Table 3) to be sure to reach convergence. In fact, convergence occurs quite early: out of 10 runs the last failure occurs at game 16957, but the 10 last failures occur between 11352 and 16957 (the second one is at game 13706).

Table 3. Results of the **add** modality with Alcomo and LogMap on 10 runs, 6 ontologies and 100000 iterations.

Modality	Size	Success rate	Incoherence degree	Semantic F-measure	Convergence
Reference	783	-	0.0	1.0	-
Initial	495	-	0.64	0.06	-
add	208	0.97	0.0	0.15	17000
Alcomo	180	-	0.0	0.11	-
LogMap	227	-	0.0	0.12	-

This experiment shows that at convergence, F-measure is better than the baseline.

5.2 Augmenting the Number of Correspondences in the Initial Alignments

The initial number of correspondences per alignments ($2^{n-1}+1$) had been chosen as an approximation of the number of correspondences in the reference alignment. As can be observed from Table 2, this approximation underestimates that number. We run additional experiments with the usual 4 agents to observe the effect of increased initial alignments.

From Fig. 7, we observe as expected that the success rate is lower to converge (there are more correspondences to invalidate), but F-measure grows to a higher level (the increased number of correspondences increases the chances to retain a correct correspondence).

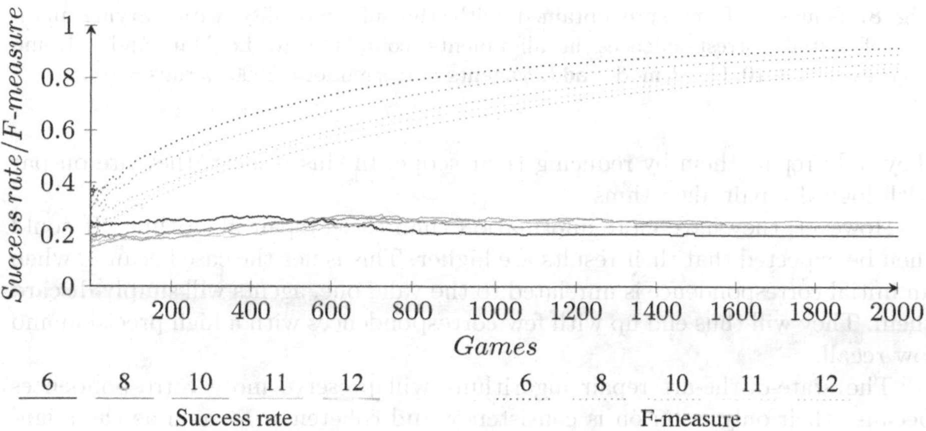

Fig. 7. Success rate and F-measure obtained with the **add** modality with varying number of initial correspondences in alignments [#coresp = 6, 8, 10, 11, 12, mod = **add**, #agents = 4; #games = 2000; #runs = 10].

Figure 8 shows that with an increased number of correspondences in initial alignments, the resulting F-measure is increased for cultural repair while it decreases in the baseline. The reason is that this increases the chances of the former to retain a correct correspondence, while this also increases the chances of the latter to retain an incorrect correspondence. Indeed, the former will in the end eliminate all incorrect correspondences while the latter tries to preserve as many correspondences as possible as long as the alignments are coherent.

6 Discussion

The relatively low F-measure rate is tied to the type of experiments: agents are constrained by the initial alignment. They do not invent any correspondences,

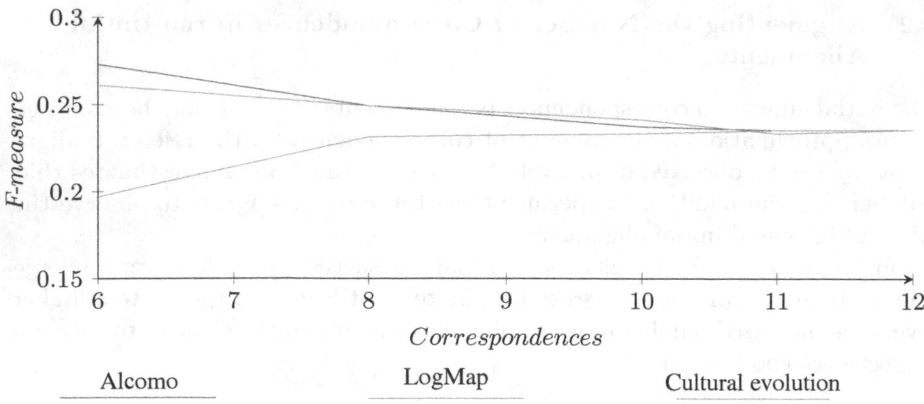

Fig. 8. Semantic F-measure obtained with the **add** modality with varying number of initial correspondences in alignments compared to LogMap and Alcomo [#coresp = 6, 8, 10, 11, 12, mod = **add**, #agents = 4; #games = 2000; #runs = 10].

they only repair them by reducing their scope. In this respect, they are on par with logical repair algorithms.

However, they have more information than these repair algorithms. It could then be expected that their results are higher. This is not the case because, when an initial correspondence is unrelated to the valid one, agents will simply discard them. They will thus end up with few correspondences with a high precision and low recall.

The state-of-the-art repair algorithms will preserve more correspondences because their only criterion is consistency and coherence: as soon as the alignment is coherent, such algorithms will stop. One could expect a lower precision, but not a higher recall since such algorithms are also tied to the initial alignment.

Because we use semantic precision and recall, it happens that among these erroneous correspondences, some of them entail some valid correspondences (and some invalid ones). This contributes to increase semantic recall.

7 Conclusion

We explored how mechanisms implemented as primitive cultural evolution can be applied to alignment repair. We measured:

- Converging success rate (towards 100 % success);
- Coherent alignments (100 % coherence);
- F-measures on par with logical repair systems;
- A number of games necessary to repair increasing very fast.

The advantage of this approach are:

- It is totally distributed: agents do not need to have the knowledge of what is an inconsistent or incoherent alignment (only an inconsistent ontology).

- The repair of the network of ontologies is not blind, i.e., restoring inconsistency without knowing if it is likely to be correct, so it also increases F-measure (which is not necessarily the case of other alignment repair strategies [10]).

Yet, this technique does not replace ontology matching nor alignment repair techniques.

8 Perspectives

We concentrated here on alignment repair. However, such a game can perfectly be adapted for matching (creating missing correspondences and revising them on the fly).

In the short term, we would like to adapt this technique in two directions:

- introducing probabilities and using such techniques in order to learn confidence on correspondences that may be used for reasoning [1],
- dealing with alignment composition by propagating instances across agents in the same perspective as the whispering games (propagating classes and see what comes back, setting weights to correspondences) [4].

In the longer term, such techniques do not have to be concentrated on one activity, such as alignment repair. Indeed, they are not problem solving techniques (solving the alignment repair problem). Instead, they are adaptive behaviours, not modifying anything as long as activities are carried out properly, and reacting to improper situations. So, cultural knowledge evolution techniques must be adapted to the lifetime of a society of agents which can generate alignments, react to environment change and encounter other societies.

Acknowledgements. Thanks to Christian Meilicke (Universität Mannheim) and Ernesto Jimenez Ruiz (Oxford university) for making Alcomo and LogMap available and usable. Thanks to an anonymous reviewer for useful suggestions.

References

1. Atencia, M., Borgida, A., Euzenat, J., Ghidini, C., Serafini, L.: A formal semantics for weighted ontology mappings. In: Cudré-Mauroux, P., Heflin, J., Sirin, E., Tudorache, T., Euzenat, J., Hauswirth, M., Parreira, J.X., Hendler, J., Schreiber, G., Bernstein, A., Blomqvist, E. (eds.) ISWC 2012, Part I. LNCS, vol. 7649, pp. 17–33. Springer, Heidelberg (2012)
2. Atencia, M., Schorlemmer, M.: An interaction-based approach to semantic alignment. J. Web Semant. **13**(1), 131–147 (2012)
3. Cerqueus, T., Cazalens, S., Lamarre, P.: Gossiping correspondences to reduce semantic heterogeneity of unstructured P2P systems. In: Hameurlain, A., Tjoa, A.M. (eds.) Globe 2011. LNCS, vol. 6864, pp. 37–48. Springer, Heidelberg (2011)
4. Cudré-Mauroux, P.: Emergent Semantics: Interoperability in Large-Scale Decentralized Information Systems. EPFL Press, Lausanne (2008)

5. Euzenat, J.: Semantic precision and recall for ontology alignment evaluation. In: Proceedings of the 20th International Joint Conference on Artificial Intelligence (IJCAI), Hyderabad, IN, pp. 348–353 (2007)
6. Euzenat, J.: First experiments in cultural alignment repair. In: Proceedings of the 3rd ESWC Workshop on Debugging Ontologies and Ontology Mappings (WoDOOM), Hersounisos, GR, pp. 3–14 (2014)
7. Jiménez-Ruiz, E., Meilicke, C., Cuenca Grau, B., Horrocks, I.: Evaluating mapping repair systems with large biomedical ontologies. In: Proceedings of the 26th Description Logics Workshop (2013)
8. Meilicke, C.: Alignment incoherence in ontology matching. Ph.D. thesis, Universität Mannheim (2011)
9. Meilicke, C., Stuckenschmidt, H.: Incoherence as a basis for measuring the quality of ontology mappings. In: Proceedings of the 3rd ISWC International Workshop on Ontology Matching, pp. 1–12 (2008)
10. Pesquita, C., Faria, D., Santos, E., Couto, F.: To repair or not to repair: reconciling correctness and coherence in ontology reference alignments. In: Proceedings of the 8th ISWC Ontology Matching Workshop (OM), Sydney, AU, pp. 13–24 (2013)
11. Steels, L. (ed.): Experiments in Cultural Language Evolution. John Benjamins, Amsterdam (2012)

Amending RDF Entities with New Facts

Ziawasch Abedjan(✉) and Felix Naumann

Hasso Plattner Institute, Potsdam, Germany
{ziawasch.abedjan,felix.naumann}@hpi.uni-potsdam.de

Abstract. Linked and other Open Data poses new challenges and opportunities for the data mining community. Unfortunately, the large volume and great heterogeneity of available open data requires significant integration steps before it can be used in applications. A promising technique to explore such data is the use of association rule mining. We introduce two algorithms for enriching RDF data. The first application is a suggestion engine that is based on mining RDF predicates and supports manual statement creation by suggesting new predicates for a given entity. The second application is knowledge creation: Based on mining both predicates and objects, we are able to generate entirely new statements for a given data set without any external resources.

1 Introduction

In the context of Linked Open Data (LOD), knowledge bases are usually incomplete or ontological structures are simply not available. Data inconsistencies and misusage of ontology axioms make it nearly impossible to infer new knowledge based on given axioms [6]. It is vital to achieve consistency within knowledge bases on the one hand by re-engineering ontology definitions [1] and to support the process of knowledge creation through value suggestions and auto-completion.

When creating new triples manually, one would hope that the creator exactly knows which properties and values should be created. However, regarding existing LOD data sets this is apparently not true. For instance, authors of Wikipedia infoboxes are often inexperienced and only infrequently edit such data. Such users might forget to use certain predicates or might use similar but not common predicates for a new entry (e.g., city instead of locationCity). Those heterogeneous entries make integration of the complete dataset difficult. Furthermore, a new user might be grateful for reasonable hints for creating a new entry. *Predicate suggestion* remedies the problem, providing users with a list of commonly used predicates. In case of Wikipedia infoboxes one could imagine to use the appropriate infobox-template for suggestions. However, reality is too complex to be covered by fixed static templates, and schema drift occurs[1] [1]. So, an instance-based approach is able to suggest predicates based on existing entities.

[1] While the template Infobox company asks for a name, the vast majority of company infoboxes uses companyName instead.

V. Presutti et al. (Eds.): ESWC Satellite Events 2014, LNCS 8798, pp. 131–143, 2014.
DOI: 10.1007/978-3-319-11955-7_11

Extending statistical reasoning to object values, we can create an approach to *amend* datasets with completely new facts.

We propose an approach that applies association rule mining at RDF statement level by using the concept of *mining configurations* [2,3]. Our approach is complementary to traditional reasoning approaches, as we do not use ontology logics but simple basket analysis adapted to the triple structure of RDF data. The benefit of a mining approach is that outliers and individual faulty facts do not affect the overall performance as long as the occurrence of a specific incorrect fact is not statistically relevant. To this end, we make the following contributions in extension to [3]:

1. We elaborate the algorithms for schema and value suggestion for new knowledge base entries. Unlike related approaches we do not rely on external knowledge, such as ontologies or textual information.
2. We introduce a new approach for auto-amendment of RDF data with new triples, based on high confidence rules among objects.

2 Related Work

Association rule mining on RDF data is an emerging topic with several new use cases [1,2,4,11,17,20]. Nebot et al. present a shopping basket analysis framework in medical RDF data to discover drug and disease correlations among patients [17]. We introduced mining configurations [2,3], a methodology to generate association rules in different contexts of an RDF statement. We further introduced association-rule-based applications to reconcile ontologies with underlying data [1] and to discover synonyms in knowledge bases [4]. Following a statistical methodology, Völker and others presented an association rule based approach for schema induction [11,20], based on given class membership relations. Our approach generate facts beyond this explicitly given ontology information.

Most related work on mining the semantic web concentrates on inductive logic programming (ILP) and machine learning approaches [9,14,16]. ILP concentrates on mining answer-sets of queries towards a knowledge base. Based on a general reference concept, additional logical relations are considered to refine the entries in an answer-set. This approach assumes a clean ontological knowledge base, which is most often not available. ALEPH, WARMR [9], and Sherlock [19] are known systems to mine such rules. ALEPH is an ILP system based on Muggleton's Inverse Entailment Algorithm [16]. WARMR uses a declarative language to mine association rules on small sets of conjunctive queries. Sherlock uses a probabilistic graphical model to infer first order clauses from a set of facts for a given relation [19]. A recent system for association rule mining in RDF data is AMIE [12]. It concentrates on horn rules among relations, such as $hasChild(p,c) \wedge isCitizenOf(p,s) \rightarrow isCitizenOf(c,s)$. Based on support and confidence thresholds on the instantiations of the variable subject and objects, the rule generates new relations $isCitizenOf(c,s)$. In a number of experiments AMIE showed to be the most efficient and effective approach to generate new facts compared to ALEPH and WARMR [12]. Therefore, we experimentally compare our system to AMIE.

Complementing the ILP method, many machine learning systems, such as similarity-based class-membership predictions, kernel-based methods, and multivariate prediction models, have been introduced [18]. D'Amato et al. propose approaches to enrich ontologies by applying ILP to heterogeneous sources, such as RDBMS and web sources [7,8]. Lisi et al. also present an approach to mine rules on ontologies and datalog programs [15]. Our approach does not rely on external data sources or structural information, such as ontologies or templates, but only the existing RDF statements of the current corpus.

3 Enriching RDF Data

To enrich RDF data, we distinguish two different scenarios: (1) *Suggestion* of predicates or object values for a given subject. (2) *Amendment* of RDF data with new triples. To this end, we only apply mining *configurations* in the context of subjects with predicates or objects as mining targets [2].

3.1 Association Rules and Triples

The concept of association rules has been widely studied in the context of market basket analysis [5], yet the formal definition is not restricted to any domain: Given a set of items $I = \{i_1, i_2, \ldots, i_m\}$, an association rule is an implication $X \rightarrow Y$ consisting of the *itemsets* $X, Y \subset I$ with $X \cap Y = \emptyset$. Given a set of transactions $T = \{t | t \subseteq I\}$, association rule mining aims at discovering rules holding two thresholds: minimum support and minimum confidence.

Support s of a rule $X \rightarrow Y$ denotes the fraction of transactions in T that include the union of the *antecedent* (left-hand side: itemset X) and *consequent* (right-hand side: itemset Y) of the rule, i.e., s% of the transactions in T contain $X \cup Y$. The confidence c of a rule denotes the statistical dependency of the *consequent* of a rule from the *antecedent*. The rule $X \rightarrow Y$ has confidence c if c% of the transactions T that contain X also contain Y.

To apply association rule mining to RDF data, it is necessary to identify the respective item set I as well as the transaction base T and its transactions. We follow the methodology of *mining configurations* [2], which is based on the subject-predicate-object (SPO) view of RDF data. Any part of the SPO statement can serve as a *context*, which is used for grouping one of the two remaining parts of the statement as the *target* for mining. So, a transaction is a set of target elements associated with one context element that represents the transaction id (TID). We call each of those *context* and *target* combinations a *configuration*.

3.2 Suggestion Step

Suggestion of predicates or objects aims at two goals: First, a user authoring new facts for a certain subject might be grateful for reasonable hints. Second, system feedback might prevent the user from using inappropriate synonyms for predicates as well as objects. Because the suggestion workflow for both predicates and objects is identical, we describe our approach referring to predicates. The suggestion workflow requires two preprocessing steps:

1. Generate all association rules between predicates.
2. Create a *rule matrix*, which is a two dimensional predicate-predicate matrix, where one index identifies the antecedents and the other index identifies the consequents of a rule. Each entry specifies the confidence of the rule involving the specific antecedent and consequent. For missing rules the entry is zero by default.

When the user is inserting or editing facts related to a specific subject, the system is aware of all predicates that have already been inserted for the current subject. We denote the initial set of these predicates with ${}^{s}P_0$, where the raised s refers to the subject at hand. We use a raised letter to denote that a statement part is fixed by known values, e.g., ${}^{s}p^{o}$ denotes a predicate connecting the subject s with the object o. The following formula describes the set of predicates ${}^{s}P_0'$ out of the set of all predicates P that are to be suggested for the current subject s:

$$ {}^{s}P_0' = \{p \in P | aConf({}^{s}P_0, p) \geq minConf\} $$

${}^{s}P_0'$ contains all predicates from P, for which the function *aConf* exceeds the minimum confidence threshold *minConf*. Here, *aConf* aggregates the confidence values of all available rules $conf(Q \rightarrow p)$ with $Q \subseteq {}^{s}P_0$ and creates one overall confidence value between 0 and 1. In our approach, we took the sum of all squared confidence values and normalized it by dividing by the number of schema elements in ${}^{s}P_0$:

$$ aConf({}^{s}P_0, p) = \frac{\sum_{Q \in {}^{s}P_0} conf(Q \rightarrow p)^2}{|{}^{s}P_0|} $$

This choice ensures that the occurrence of few high confidence rules has more impact than many low confidence rules. Having computed the set ${}^{s}P_0'$, the results can be sorted by their aggregated confidence values and presented to the user. When the user chooses the next predicate p to insert into the data set, ${}^{s}P_1'$ has to be computed based on the new schema set ${}^{s}P_1 = {}^{s}P_0 \cup \{p\}$. Table 1 illustrates some SPO facts extracted from DBpedia. Now, imagine we are to insert a record for *D. Cameron* by beginning with the statements *"Cameron birthPlace London."* and *"Cameron orderInOffice Prime Minister."* Then ${}^{s}P_0 = \{birthPlace, orderInOffice\}$ and the total set of remaining predicates would be $P = \{party, instrument\}$. Considering only rules of size 2, the set of predicate rules relevant for the next suggestion include $birthPlace \rightarrow party$ with 66.7 % confidence, $orderInOffice \rightarrow party$ with 100 % confidence, and $birthPlace \rightarrow instrument$ with 33.3 % confidence. Having $minConf = 50\,\%$, the predicate *party* would be added to P_0', because $aConf({}^{s}P_0, party)$ is above *minConf*.

Table 1. Some SPO facts

Subject	Predicate	Object
Obama	birthPlace	Hawaii
Obama	party	Democrats
Obama	orderInOffice	President
Merkel	birthPlace	Hamburg
Merkel	orderInOffice	Chancellor
Merkel	party	CDU
Lennon	birthPlace	Liverpool
Lennon	instrument	Guitar

Suggesting objects is technically equivalent to that of predicates, but the number of distinct objects is by magnitudes larger, resulting in weaker rules. For instance, the DBpedia 3.6 data set contains 1,100 distinct predicates but 3,980,642 distinct objects. Furthermore, for a user, authoring an object value for a suggested predicate is more convenient than vice versa. For example, a user might have created the entry *B. Obama birthPlace Honolulu.* Following the object suggestion, the system might contain an object-to-object rule with enough confidence saying *Honolulu* → *USA* and suggests to add a new fact with *USA* as its object. The user might not know how the subject and the proposed object are connected and which predicate (birthPlace, residence, etc.) to choose. In addition to the semantical fitting of the predicate, the user has also to consider its appropriateness with regard to consistency among similar entities. Previously reported experiments also showed the significant superiority of predicate suggestion to object suggestions [3].

3.3 Amending with New Statements

After we were able to suggest one missing part for a given subject, it is possible to also complete the remaining third part. For example, if the system decides to suggest the predicate *residence* for *B. Obama,* it is also able to choose the right object, e.g., *Washington D.C.* from the existing value range of *residence.* We call this method of creating new statements where the user decides which subject has to be amended with new triples *user-driven auto-amendment.* We described the user-driven auto-amendment in [3]. A different way of creating new statements is to let the system itself choose the subjects that should be amended with new triples. We call this approach *data-driven auto-amendment.*

In this data-driven approach the subject to be amended with a new fact is selected on the basis of existing high-confidence object rules. Our approach is based on the following intuitions:

1. For object rules $O' \to o$ with high confidence (above 90 %) and $O' \subseteq O$, the subjects $S^{O'}$ occurring with the objects O' are also likely to occur with the object o. However, up to 10 % of the subjects that occur with O' *violate* the rule by not occurring with o in any fact. Those facts may be absent, because of missing thoroughness during data creation.
2. A subject s should not be enriched with a fact containing object o if on the basis of the rules involving schema predicates ${}^{s}P$, no predicate can be chosen for the connection with o. This intuition allows a softening of the earlier intuition that expects all subjects that violate $O' \to o$ should be extended with a triple containing o.

One could adapt the intuitions based on high confidence rules also among predicates. However, the discovery of the appropriate object for a to-be-added predicate is much more cumbersome, because of the large number of available objects. Concerning the first intuition one could argue that some of these implicitly given facts can also be generated using ontological dependencies within the data. But, not all implicit dependencies in the real world are captured within an ontology. For example the high-confidence object rule *South Park* → *Trey Parker* among television episodes correctly suggests that Trey Parker is involved all episodes of South Park and should be added as the producer when absent. However, there can't be a general ontological rule that each episode of a series should have the same producer as listed for the complete series entity.
Algorithm overview. The algorithm for data-driven auto-amendment is divided into three steps:

1. Create predicate-predicate rule matrix as described in Sect. 3.2.
2. Generate high-confidence object rules $o_1, o_2, \ldots o_n \rightarrow o$ using FP-Growth [13].
3. Create statements for subjects that violate high-confidence object rules: For each rule $o_1, o_2, \ldots o_n \rightarrow o$ retrieve subjects S that violate the rule and for each $s \in S$ predict the predicate ${}^{s}p^{o}$ that connects s and the object o.

Statement creation. The third step is illustrated in Algorithm 1. For each object rule $O' \rightarrow o$ with $O' = o_1, o_2, \ldots o_n$, all subjects s that occur with the antecedent of the rule but not with its consequent ($s \in S^{O'} - S^{o}$) are retrieved in line 2. This set contains all subjects that may be amended with new facts having the current object rule consequent o as their value. The choice of 90 % as the high confidence threshold is arbitrary. We report evaluation results on this threshold in Sect. 4. As multiple object rules may contain the same consequent o, duplicate subject-object-pairs may be generated, which are naturally ignored. Further we exclude all rules $O' \rightarrow o$, with a more general rule $O'' \rightarrow o$, i.e., $O' \supset O''$, because $S^{O''} - S^{o}$ contains all subjects from $S^{O'} - S^{o}$. The rest of the algorithm is straightforward and starts with retrieving the candidate predicates P^{o} in line 5 and the schema predicates ${}^{s}P$ in line 6. The rating for each retrieved candidate predicate is computed in line 9. Given the set of schema elements ${}^{s}P$ and a candidate predicate $p \in {}^{o}P$, the confidence entries of the rule matrix are used to generate an overall rating for the specific candidate predicate p. The overall rating r_p for a candidate p is computed by $r_p = aConf({}^{s}P, p)$, the aggregated confidence of all rules with $Q \subseteq {}^{s}P$ as antecedent and p as consequent. After the candidate loop, the candidate with the highest rating is returned. Only if there is a predicate with a rating above a given threshold δ, e.g., 0 for any rating at all, the new fact *spo* consisting of the current subject s, the top rated predicate p, and current object rule consequent o is added to the set of new facts in line 14. Note, the number of new facts depends on the number of existent high-confidence rules and their corresponding set of violating subjects $S^{O'} - S^{o}$.

Algorithm 1. Statement Generation Algorithm

```
Data: objectRules /* with confidence above 90%*/
Result: newStatements
foreach objectRule ∈ objectRules do
    subjects ← getViolatingSubjects (objectRule);
    consequentObject ← objectRule.getConsequent ();
    foreach subject ∈ subjects do
        candidates ← getCandidatePredicates (consequentObject);
        schema ← getSchema (subject);
        topRating ← 0;
        foreach candidate ∈ candidates do
            currentRating←getRating (schema, candidate);
            if currentRating > topRating then
                topRating ← currentRating;
                predicate ← candidate;
        if topRating > δ then
            newStatements.add (subjects, predicate, consequentObject);
return newStatements
```

4 Experiments and Evaluation

To evaluate the accuracy and quality of our suggestion and auto-completion approaches we performed multiple experiments on multiple datasets. Table 2 shows sizes of the different data sets. The entities in each data set correspond to one or more of the 250 existing types, and so we are able to perform experiments not only over all entities, but also more fine-grained on entities of a certain type, resembling data of specific domains. The last three datasets in Table 2 are cleaned knowledge bases provided by the authors of AMIE[2] [12].

Table 2. Experimental data with distinct cardinalities

Data set	Triples	Subjects	Predicates	Objects
DBpedia 3.6	13,794,426	1,638,746	1,100	3,980,642
DBpedia 3.7	17,518,364	1,827,474	1,296	4,595,303
DBpedia 3.8	20,514,715	2,342,853	1,313	5,172,511
DBpedia 2.0 (see Footnote 2)	7,034,868	1,376,877	10,321	1,778,459
YAGO2 (see Footnote 2)	948,044	470,485	36	400,343
YAGO2s (see Footnote 2)	4,125,966	1,653,882	37	606,789

[2] http://www.mpi-inf.mpg.de/departments/ontologies/projects/amie/

We evaluate our amendment approach on multiple datasets. In particular, we adapt the scenario to compare the quality and efficiency of our approach with AMIE [12], using the implementation provided by the authors, and show that our system is competitive to AMIE achieving higher precision.

4.1 Comparing to AMIE

Our system as well as AMIE generates new facts based on evidence in knowledge bases. While we combine two mining configurations on statement level, AMIE mines horn rules between parameterized relations. We compared both systems with regard to prediction quality as well as efficiency.

Prediction quality. We used the same datasets and evaluation scenario as AMIE for a fair comparison [12]. That means we ran both approaches on YAGO2 and DBpedia 2.0 and compared the predictions to YAGO2s and DBpedia 3.8, respectively. According to the original experiments reported by the developers, AMIE generates up to 74 K hits in the YAGO2s dataset and 122 K hits in DBpedia 3.8. However, the ratio of hits to the number of total predictions is below 1‰, as no confidence threshold was defined. To make a fair comparison we chose the best rules generated by AMIE, that contribute the same number of predictions as our approach. To this end, we sort the horn rules generated by AMIE by their PCA (partial completeness assumption) confidence as proposed by the authors and iterate the list in descending order. We configured our approach with 90 % confidence threshold for object rules and 0.1 % support for both object as well as predicate rules.

The results in Table 3 show that our approach leads to a higher precision. Of course the results confirm only that some facts are true, but cannot confirm that any of the generated facts are false unless checked by a human expert. On the YAGO2 dataset we report the precision for all produced rules by AMIE as the best rule already produced ten times more predictions than our approach. That specific rule generated for each relation *isMarriedTo(a,b)* the missing symmetric relation *isMarriedTo(b,a)* resulting in 4,424 hits in DBpedia 3.8. Due to memory consumption restrictions (50 GB) we could not evaluate AMIE on the original DBpedia 3.6 dataset.

Table 3. Comparison to AMIE

Dataset	Approach	Facts	Hits	Precision
DBpedia 2.0	AMIE (63 rules)	2,359	55	2.3 %
	Mining conf.	2,335	146	**6.2 %**
YAGO2	AMIE	1.658 m	8.1 k	0.5 %
	Mining conf.	2,086	52	**2.5 %**
DBpedia 3.6	AMIE	-	-	-
	Mining conf.	26,660	8.2 k	**30.0 %**

Resource consumption. AMIE is a multithreaded approach where the knowledge base is kept and indexed in main memory to compute support and PCA confidence values in appropriate time. The drawback is clearly the high memory consumption that requires up to 22 GB to discover rules on the DBpedia 2.0 dataset and 3.4 GB for the YAGO2 dataset. Our mining configuration system needs only two FP-Trees in memory (one for discovering predicate rules and one for object rules), resulting in less than 600 MB when running on DBpedia 2.0 and about 200 MB for YAGO2. We perform both steps, mining predicates and objects, consecutively, which could just as well be done in parallel to improve runtime. The runtime of both approaches, AMIE as well as our mining configurations, on these datasets is under 1 min.

In general, both approaches are valid strategies to amend a knowledge base with new facts. While AMIE generates new facts based on closed rules considering entire fact patterns as rule atoms, our approach is more granular in considering predicate correlations and object correlations independently.

4.2 Amendment Quality on Large Datasets

To further analyze the capabilities of rule-based triple amendment we performed more experiments on the DBpedia 3.6 dataset. To identify strengths and weaknesses of the approach we also performed experiments on subsets of that dataset. Table 4 shows the number of generated facts and their inclusion ratio in the DBpedia 3.7 data set. The idea here is to automatically evaluate which percentage of generated triples is "validated" by a more up to date version of the same data source. The high precision of the results for Animals is caused by the fact that most of the newly added statements are Animal classification statements that have been missing in the older version because of the lack of thoroughness during data creation. Note, these classification statements do not correspond to the ontology class designators *rdfs:type*. Those statements were excluded to identify more interesting new facts.

While having 31 % precision for *minconf* = 90 %, experiments on the complete data set (all entities of type *Thing*) with thresholds of 95 % and 85 % resulted into 44.3 % precision having 5,866 new facts and 27.4 % precision having 39,589 new facts, respectively. These results confirm our assumption that the higher this threshold is set the more precision can be achieved but the fewer facts may be generated. Those facts that were not included in DBpedia 3.7 are not necessarily wrong facts. We manually evaluated a random set of 50 not-included facts and achieved 72 % precision.

Table 4. Generated statements on DBpedia v3.6 and their inclusion in v3.7

Type	Thing	Person	Album	Animal	Artist	Film	Organis.	Place	Species	Work
Facts	26,646	1,521	43	17,024	426	225	1,465	10,727	26,164	463
Included	8,237	278	25	8,753	219	27	187	1,140	9,448	67
Precision	30.9 %	18.9 %	58.1 %	51.4 %	51.5 %	12 %	18.1 %	10.6 %	36.1 %	14.5 %

Table 5. Percentage of true violations of a high-confidence rule

Type	Thing	Place	Person	Film
True positives	37	41	42	22
Percentage	74 %	82 %	84 %	44 %

How true is a high-confidence rule? Our intuition about high-confidence rules is that subjects that violate these rules are actually not intended to violate them. In other words, we assume that the number of those subjects that deliberately "violate" the rules is relatively low. We evaluated the quality of high-confidence rules $o_i \rightarrow o_j$ by manually verifying the relation of o_j to the violating subjects on 50 randomly selected violating subjects per data set.

Table 5 shows the results for four data sets (0.1 % support and 90 % confidence). Each data set corresponds to entities of the given type from DBpedia 3.6. We observe that the assumption holds for most objects rules in the domains *Person* and *Place*, such as *American Civil War* → *United States* for *Person* instances and *Vosges* → *Lorraine Region* for *Place* instances. High-confidence rules from movie data however are mostly the result of true exceptions. However, in movie data there are also interesting positive examples: the rule *Lon Chaney, Sr.* → *Silent Film* with 93 % confidence is a rule where the violating movies are in fact silent movies and can be updated with the object *Silent Film*.

Note that our algorithm creates a new fact with the presumably missing object only if there is a predicate that matches the subject and the object.

Completion with predicates. In previous experiments, we analyzed suggestion quality of predicates, where all top-10 recommendations had a success rate above 50 % [3]. As the results conform to other recommendation scenarios, such as the experiments given in [10], we can conclude that association rule mining is a reasonable strategy for predicate suggestion. In the following, we analyze the predicate completion, which is similar to predicate suggestion with the difference that the object value is known. Given a subject s, its schema ${}^{s}P$, and a related object ${}^{s}o$, the aim of predicate completion is to select the most appropriate predicate ${}^{s}p^{o}$ out of all predicates P^{o} that have o in their range. We evaluated this step by applying the leave-one-out strategy: For each high-confidence object rule $o_i \rightarrow o_j$ we considered all subjects s^{o_j} that do not violate this rule and removed the connecting predicate ${}^{s}p^{o_j}$ between the subject s and the consequence object o_j and tried to predict ${}^{s}p^{o_j}$ based on the predicate matrix and the predicate candidates P^{o}. Table 6 illustrates the results for experiments on the complete data set (*type:Thing*) as well as the eight types with the most instances. In comparison to the suggestion evaluation, we see that the choice of the correct predicate is very accurate when knowing also the object of the statement. We achieve lower precision on *Person*, because many object rules there refer to locations, such as *Buenos Aires* → *Argentina*, and the predicate selection confuses predicates, such as *nationality*, *deathPlace*, and *birthPlace*. But even though the

Table 6. Results for predicting removed predicates based on object rules

Type	Rules	Triples	Removed	Correct	Missing	Incorrect	Precision	Recall
Thing	189	13,794,426	1,019,785	919,815	1	99,969	90.2 %	90.2 %
Place	169	3,605,195	246,731	246,704	0	27	99.9 %	99.9 %
Person	37	3,618,525	30120	20440	0	9,680	67.9 %	67.9 %
Work	10	2,910,016	5725	5,669	0	56	99.0 %	99.0 %
Species	1,128	1,461,468	1,337,734	1,212,080	9	125645	90.6 %	90.6 %
Organisation	84	1,456,113	24,535	24,258	0	277	98.9 %	98.9 %
Animal	981	1,035,602	952,340	951,964	8	368	99.9 %	99.9 %
Album	6	934,005	782	683	0	99	87.3 %	87.3 %
Film	50	626,875	5,618	5,086	4	528	90.6 %	90.5 %

Table 7. Results for predicting 20,000 random predicates for each type

Type	Predictions	Correct	Missing	Incorrect	Precision	Recall
Thing	18,731	16,855	1,269	1,876	89.98 %	84.28 %
Place	19,775	18,359	225	1,416	92.84 %	91.80 %
Person	19,936	15,419	64	4,517	77.34 %	77.10 %
Work	19,865	17,291	135	2,574	87.04 %	86.55 %
Species	19,986	17,922	14	2,064	89.67 %	89.61 %
Organization	19,820	16,115	180	3,705	81.31 %	80.58 %
Animal	19,975	19,968	25	7	99.97 %	99.84 %
Album	19,861	19,121	239	640	96.27 %	95.61 %
Film	19,842	18,606	158	1,236	93.77 %	93.03 %

removed predicate is confused for these examples, the proposed predicate for the subject-object pair might still be a valid fact.

The column with the number of missing values represents the number of subject-object pairs, for which the algorithm does not select any predicate. For those pairs, the existing schema of the subject ${}^{s}P$ and the candidate predicates P^{o_j} are not related to each other. Because only few triples are concerned, the precision is always at least as high as the recall. One could assume that by increasing the minimum threshold for the selection decision (see Algorithm 1, line 13) incorrect selections can be avoided by being marked as undecidable. However, experiments showed that increasing the threshold yields more undecidable selections and fewer correctly selected predicates.

Finally, we evaluated the predicate selection based on randomly removed predicates. We wanted to examine whether the quality of the predicate selection depends on the choice of the objects and whether the fact that they are connected with consequences of high-confidence object rules influences the quality. Table 7 illustrates the results for predicting randomly removed predicates and shows that predicate selection does not depend on the choice of objects as there is no significant difference to the results in Table 6.

5 Conclusions

We showed how an association rule matrix can be used for suggesting both predicates as well as object values for a user who is inserting new statements for an entity. We proposed a user-driven and a data-driven approach for generating new facts without depending on external resources. We conclude that mining configurations is a reasonable approach to enrich RDF data. Comparing to state-of-the-art systems, we achieve higher precision allowing a manual verification step after generating new facts. In a real-world scenario, it is possible to drop object rules that denote weak hypotheses, as the predicate selection step works pretty accurate in turn. The generated facts and an online demonstration tool embedding our approach can be found on our website[3].

Further research includes joint reasoning on both RDF data using descriptive logic and statistical occurrences of statement parts, and reasoning and formalizing constraints and refinements that allow more complex configurations.

References

1. Abedjan, Z., Lorey, J., Naumann, F.: Reconciling ontologies and the web of data. In: CIKM, pp. 1532–1536 (2012)
2. Abedjan, Z., Naumann, F.: Context and target configurations for mining RDF data. In: SMER, pp. 23–24 (2011)
3. Abedjan, Z., Naumann, F.: Improving RDF data through association rule mining. Datenbank-Spektrum **13**(2), 111–120 (2013)
4. Abedjan, Z., Naumann, F.: Synonym analysis for predicate expansion. In: Cimiano, P., Corcho, O., Presutti, V., Hollink, L., Rudolph, S. (eds.) ESWC 2013. LNCS, vol. 7882, pp. 140–154. Springer, Heidelberg (2013)
5. Agrawal, R., Imieliński, T., Swami, A.: Mining association rules between sets of items in large databases. In: SIGMOD, pp. 207–216 (1993)
6. Bonatti, P.A., Hogan, A., Polleres, A., Sauro, L.: Robust and scalable linked data reasoning incorporating provenance and trust annotations. J. Web Semant. **9**(2), 165–201 (2011)
7. d'Amato, C., Bryl, V., Serafini, L.: Semantic knowledge discovery from heterogeneous data sources. In: ten Teije, A., Völker, J., Handschuh, S., Stuckenschmidt, H., d'Acquin, M., Nikolov, A., Aussenac-Gilles, N., Hernandez, N. (eds.) EKAW 2012. LNCS, vol. 7603, pp. 26–31. Springer, Heidelberg (2012)
8. d'Amato, C., Fanizzi, N., Esposito, F.: Inductive learning for the semantic web: what does it buy? Semant. Web J. **1**(1,2), 53–59 (2010)
9. Dehaspe, L., Toivonen, H.: Discovery of frequent datalog patterns. Data Min. Knowl. Dis. **3**(1), 7–36 (1999)
10. Deshpande, M., Karypis, G.: Item-based top-n recommendation algorithms. ACM Trans. Inf. Syst. **22**, 143–177 (2004)

[3] http://www.hpi.uni-potsdam.de/naumann/projekte/mining_rdf_data.html

11. Fleischhacker, D., Völker, J., Stuckenschmidt, H.: Mining RDF data for property axioms. In: Meersman, R., Panetto, H., Dillon, T., Rinderle-Ma, S., Dadam, P., Zhou, X., Pearson, S., Ferscha, A., Bergamaschi, S., Cruz, I.F. (eds.) OTM 2012, Part II. LNCS, vol. 7566, pp. 718–735. Springer, Heidelberg (2012)
12. Galárraga, L., Teflioudi, C., Hose, K., Suchanek, F.: AMIE: association rule mining under incomplete evidence in ontological knowledge bases. In: WWW (2013)
13. Han, J., Pei, J., Yin, Y.: Mining frequent patterns without candidate generation. In: SIGMOD, pp. 1–12 (2000)
14. Józefowska, J., Lawrynowicz, A., Lukaszewski, T.: The role of semantics in mining frequent patterns from knowledge bases in description logics with rules. Theor. Pract. Log. Program. **10**, 251–289 (2010)
15. Lisi, F.A., Esposito, F.: Mining the semantic web: a logic-based methodology. In: Hacid, M.-S., Murray, N.V., Raś, Z.W., Tsumoto, S. (eds.) ISMIS 2005. LNCS (LNAI), vol. 3488, pp. 102–111. Springer, Heidelberg (2005)
16. Muggleton, S.: Inverse entailment and progol. New Gener. Comput., Special issue on Inductive Log. Program. **13**(3–4), 245–286 (1995)
17. Nebot, V., Berlanga, R.: Mining association rules from semantic web data. In: García-Pedrajas, N., Herrera, F., Fyfe, C., Benítez, J.M., Ali, M. (eds.) IEA/AIE 2010, Part II. LNCS, vol. 6097, pp. 504–513. Springer, Heidelberg (2010)
18. Rettinger, A., Lösch, U., Tresp, V., d'Amato, C., Fanizzi, N.: Mining the semantic web - statistical learning for next generation knowledge bases. Data Min. Knowl. Discov. **24**(3), 613–662 (2012)
19. Schoenmackers, S., Etzioni, O., Weld, D.S., Davis, J.: Learning first-order horn clauses from web text. In: EMNLP, pp. 1088–1098 (2010)
20. Völker, J., Niepert, M.: Statistical schema induction. In: Antoniou, G., Grobelnik, M., Simperl, E., Parsia, B., Plexousakis, D., De Leenheer, P., Pan, J. (eds.) ESWC 2011, Part I. LNCS, vol. 6643, pp. 124–138. Springer, Heidelberg (2011)

Predicting the Impact of Central Bank Communications on Financial Market Investors' Interest Rate Expectations

Andy Moniz[1(✉)] and Franciska de Jong[1,2]

[1] Erasmus Studio, Erasmus University, Rotterdam, The Netherlands
moniz@rsm.nl

[2] Human Media Interaction, University of Twente, Enschede, The Netherlands
fdejong@eshcc.eur.nl
f.m.g.dejong@utwente.nl

Abstract. In this paper, we design an automated system that predicts the impact of central bank communications on investors' interest rate expectations. Our corpus is the Bank of England's '*Monetary Policy Committee Minutes*'. Prior studies suggest that effective communications can mitigate a financial crisis; ineffective communications may exacerbate one. The system described here works in four phases. First, the system employs background knowledge from Wikipedia to identify salient aspects for central bank policy associated with economic growth, prices, interest rates and bank lending. These *economic aspects* are detected using the *TextRank* link analysis algorithm. A multinomial Naive Bayesian model then classifies sentences from central bank documents to these aspects. The second phase measures sentiment using a count of terms from the *General Inquirer* dictionary. The third phase employs Latent Dirichlet Allocation (LDA) to infer topic clusters that may act as intensifiers/diminishers of sentiment associated with the economic aspects. Finally, an ensemble tree combines the phases to predict the impact of the communications on financial market interest rates.

Keywords: Sentiment analysis · Text mining · Link analysis · Financial markets

1 Introduction

Post the global financial crisis, there has been a dramatic change in the use of central bank communications as a central bank policy instrument [1, 2]. Central banks communicate qualitative information to the financial market through statements, minutes, speeches, and published reports [3]. Communication is an important tool that a central bank can use to avert a crisis, by providing investors with its assessment of the risks and the measures it views as necessary to reduce those risks within the economy [1, 4]. Previous studies suggest that effective central bank communications can mitigate and potentially prevent a financial crisis; ineffective communications may exacerbate one

V. Presutti et al. (Eds.): ESWC Satellite Events 2014, LNCS 8798, pp. 144–155, 2014.
DOI: 10.1007/978-3-319-11955-7_12

[1, 5]. In [4], the Swedish central bank, the Riksbank, is criticized because its communications were "not clear or strong enough" leading up to the global financial crisis, such that the bank's information went "unnoticed" [1]. In this paper, we design an automated system that predicts the impact of central bank communications on interest rate expectations as derived via financial market patterns. For the purposes of this study, we analyze economic sentiment, as expressed in the *'Monetary Policy Committee Minutes'* [2] published by the Bank of England, that details its monthly interest rate decisions.

Financial markets scrutinize central bank communications for *"clues and shades of meaning about its assessment of the economy and the direction of where economic policy may be heading"* [1]. As a prediction task, the measurement and evaluation of sentiment is challenging due to the complexities and subtleties of interpreting bank communications [1]. The formation of economic policy is a balancing act between achieving high economic growth and financial stability, while targeting low inflation [2]. The relative importance of these objectives is dynamic, and varies depending on prevailing economic conditions [2]. For example under benign economic conditions, high inflation may be construed by financial market investors as a negative signal for the direction of future interest rates. During the financial crisis of 2007–2009, high inflation was considered to be a positive signal by effectively lowering real interest rates[1] [6]. This motivates a need for fine-grained sentiment analysis, to automatically detect economic aspects and predict central bank sentiment expressed towards these aspects [7]. Such an approach would provide investors with an automated system to decipher the complexities and interactions of economic aspects, to interpret the consequences of these interactions for the future path of interest rates, and to incorporate the information into their investment decisions. For a central bank, such a system would provide it with the ability to predict the impact of its economic policies on the financial markets. The resulting 'price discovery' process [2] may promote a more efficient functioning of financial markets.

Our approach consists of four phases. First, the system detects salient references to economic aspects associated with economic growth, prices, interest rates and bank lending and employs a multinomial Naive Bayesian model to classify sentences within central bank documents. Economic aspects are identified in a pre-processing step, that employs a link analysis using the TextRank algorithm [8, 9] applied to background knowledge obtained from Wikipedia. The second phase measures sentiment expressed for the economic aspects, using a count of terms from the *General Inquirer* dictionary [17]. The third phase employs Latent Dirichlet Allocation (LDA) to infer intensifiers/ diminishers that may change the meaning of the economic aspects and economic sentiment [7, 10]. Specifically, the model categorizes whether the magnitude of the economic aspects has 'intensified' or 'diminished' over time [11, 12]. We refer to the resulting topic clusters as *directional topic clusters*. Finally, an ensemble tree combines the model components to predict the impact of the communications on financial market interest rates over the following day.

[1] The real interest rate is the rate of interest a borrower expects to pay on debt after allowing for inflation and is equal to the nominal interest rate (set by the central bank) minus the rate of inflation [2].

The rest of this paper is structured as follows. Section 2 draws on literature from the field of macroeconomics and discusses the implications for sentiment analysis and keyword detection. Section 3 models the individual components of the system. Section 4 outlines the corpus of central bank communications, provides an evaluation of the model components and then discusses the results. Section 5 concludes and suggests avenues for future research.

2 Related Work

2.1 Background: Central Bank Research

Post the financial crisis, several central banks have identified communications, particularly 'enhanced forward guidance', as an important policy instrument within their economic toolkit [1, 2]. Effective communications enhance a central bank's public transparency, accountability and credibility [13], which in turn aids its ability to implement economic policies [14]. To date, there has been little research into text mining of central bank communications. In [14], the impact of different types of communications (press releases, speeches, interviews, and news conferences) are analyzed to determine which media sources impact interest rate expectations. The analysis does not, however, classify the language used in the documents. In [3], a term counting approach is adopted to analyze the sentiment contained within the meeting minutes of the US central bank (the Federal Reserve). In [3, 15] Latent Semantic Analysis is employed to analyze the sentiment contained within the Bank of Canada's minutes. The intention of this study is to design a fine-grained sentiment analysis approach to analyze the impact of central bank communications on financial market investors. To our knowledge, this remains an unexplored avenue of research.

2.2 Background: Sentiment Analysis

Traditionally, fine-grained sentiment analysis has been researched for the classification of online user reviews of products and movies [16]. Readers are often not only interested in the general sentiment towards an aspect but also a detailed opinion analysis for each of these aspects [7]. Evaluation is conducted by comparing model classifications versus ratings provided by users. The evaluation of economic sentiment is arguably a harder task, due to the lack of a clearly defined outcome to assess model performance. For example, which economic variable should a model's predictions be evaluated against? The relative importance of the aspects (e.g. economic growth/inflation/interest rates) is subjective, may vary over time, and the measurement of the aspects is only known with significant time delay.

The traditional approach to text-mining within the field of finance is to count terms using the General Inquirer dictionary [17, 18]. The dictionary classifies words according to multiple categories, including 1,915 positive words and 2,291 negative words. The *General Inquirer* was developed for psychology and sociology research and while it is used for text mining within the field of finance, little research has been conducted as to its suitability within finance [19]. Aspects that are frequently mentioned in central bank communications, such as the terms 'employment', 'unemployment' and 'growth', are not classified by the *General Inquirer* dictionary. Adjectives are often needed before investors can interpret the patterns in the economy to form their interest rate expectations [3]. Furthermore, the terms 'inflation' and 'low' are classified as negative by the dictionary, yet 'low inflation' is a positive characteristic and indeed achieving this is a central bank's core objective [2]. The terms 'fall' and 'decline' are classified as negative terms in the *General Inquirer* dictionary, yet the opposite terms 'rise' and 'increase' are not classified at all.

2.3 Background: Keyword Detection

Graph-based algorithms have received much attention [8] as an approach to keyphrase extraction and are considered to be state-of-the-art unsupervised methods [20]. In a graph representation of a document, nodes are words or phrases, and edges represent co-occurrence or semantic relations. The underlying assumption is that all words in the text have some relationship to all other words in the text. Such an approach is statistical, because it links all co-occurring terms without considering their meaning or function in text. Centrality is often used to estimate the importance of a word in a document [22], and is a way of deciding on the importance of a vertex within a graph that takes into account global information recursively computed from the entire graph, rather than relying only on local vertex-specific information [23]. The main advantage of such a representation is that selected terms are independent of their language [21].

3 Model to Predict Changes in Investors' Expectations

In this section we describe the four phases of the system. First, the system detects salient references to economic aspects and employs a multinomial Naive Bayesian model to classify sentences within documents. The second phase measures sentiment expressed for the economic aspects, using a count of terms from the *General Inquirer* dictionary. The third phase employs a LDA model and categorizes whether the magnitude of the economic aspects has 'intensified' or 'diminished' [11, 12]. Finally, an ensemble tree combines the model components to predict the impact of the communications on financial market interest rates over the following day.

3.1 Aspect Detection

In [3] it is shown that *tf-idf* weighting selects infrequent terms that relate to major news events or economic shocks. By contrast, our approach is intended to detect the common economic themes that are discussed in central bank communications and are more likely to influence investors' interest rate expectations on a day-to-day basis [2]. To determine salient references, we employ a link analysis approach that detects the most frequently mentioned terms within two Wikipedia pages on Central Banking and Inflation. TextRank [8], a ranking algorithm based on the concept of eigenvector centrality, is employed to compute the importance of the nodes in the graph. Each vertex corresponds to a word. A weight, w_{ij}, is assigned to the edge connecting the two vertices, v_i and v_j. The goal is to compute the score of each vertex, which reflects its importance, and use the word types that correspond to the highest scored vertices to form keywords for the text [23]. The score for v_i, $S(v_i)$, is initialized with a default value and is computed in an iterative manner until convergence using recursive formula shown in Eq. (1).

$$S(v_i) = (1 - d) + d \times \sum_{v_j(v_i)} \frac{w_{ji}}{\sum_{v_k(v_j)} w_{jk}} s(v_j) \quad (1)$$

where $\mathrm{Adj}(v_i)$ denotes v_i's neighbors and d is the damping factor set to 0.85 [8]. Figure 1 displays the resulting clustering of terms. The size of each node is directly proportional to the TextRank score of the respective economic aspect.

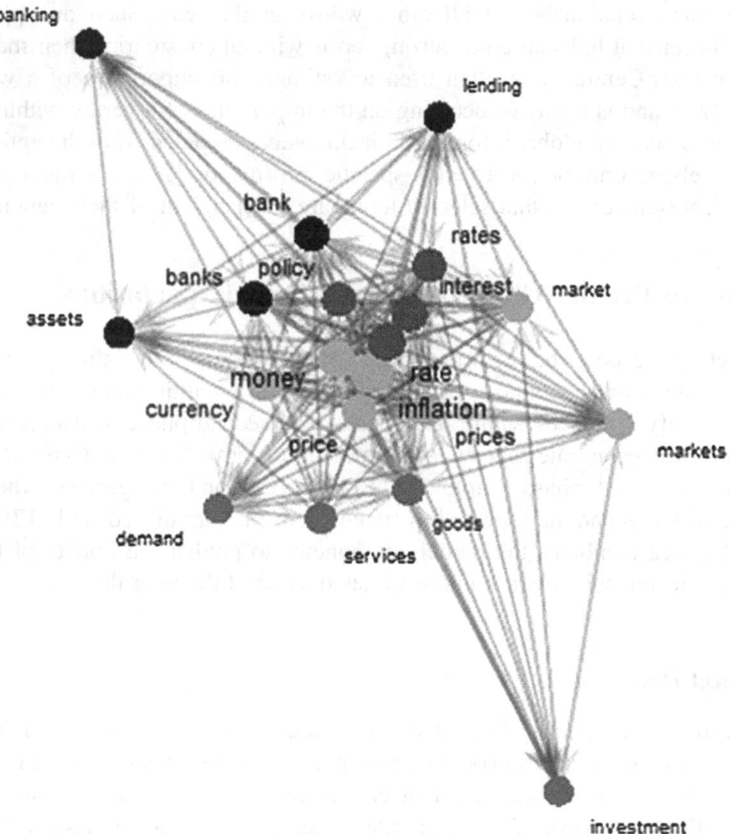

Fig. 1. Link analysis of frequently occurring terms. Different nodes colors reflect different communities identified using the Clauset-Newman-Moore algorithm.

A greedy algorithm is employed to detect communities of terms within the network [31]. The algorithm detects four communities which we label as economic aspects. The *economic growth aspect* detects the frequency of the terms: *'demand'*, *'goods'*, *'services'*, *'investment'*. The *prices aspect* detects the terms: *'inflation'*, *'prices'*, *'money'*, *'markets'*, *'currency'*. The *interest rate aspect* detects the occurrence of: *'interest'*, *'rates'*, *'policy'* and a *bank lending aspect* detects the terms: *'banks'*, *'lending'* and *'assets'*. It is not surprising to see these terms appear in the link analysis given a central bank's remit is to maintain price and financial stability. The choice of terms is consistent with the text mining research of [3] which identifies 'growth', 'price', 'rate', and 'econom' as the most frequently occurring terms for US central bank communications. Using the four economic aspects, the system next employs a multinomial Naive Bayesian model [24] to categorize sentences within each document. The resulting categorization labels form the basis upon which fine-grained sentiment analysis is applied.

3.2 Polarity Detection

In the second phase, the model computes a measure of economic sentiment associated with each of the four economic aspects. We measure polarity by counting the number of positive (P) versus negative (N) terms, $(P - N)/(P + N)$ identified using the *General Inquirer* dictionary [17]. In line with [16], our goal is not to show that a term counting method can perform as well as a Machine Learning method, but to provide a baseline methodology to measure central bank sentiment and to draw attention to the limitations of the approach that is widely adopted by text mining studies in the field of finance as indicated in Sect. 2.2. The sentiment metrics that are associated with the economic aspects: economic growth, prices, interest rate and bank lending are labelled $Tone_{growth}$, $Tone_{prices}$, $Tone_{interest\_rates}$ and $Tone_{bank\_lending}$ respectively. A fifth sentiment metric, $Tone_{overall}$, is computed to measure the polarity associated with the overall document, without conditioning upon the *economic aspects*. The five sentiment metrics are included as separate components within the ensemble tree.

3.3 Detection of LDA Directional Topic Clusters

Next we extend the baseline term-counting method by taking intensifiers and diminishers into account [11, 12]. These are terms that change the degree of the expressed sentiment in a document (see Sect. 2.2). In the case of central bank communications, the terms describe how economic aspects have changed over time. We employ an implementation of LDA [10], and represent each document as a probability distribution over latent topics, where each topic is modeled by a probability distribution of words. In [7], LDA is found to capture the global topics in documents, to the extent that topics do not represent ratable aspects associated with individual documents, but define clusterings of the documents into specific types. For the purposes of training the LDA model, we consider each sentence within each central bank communication to be a separate document. This increases the sample size of the dataset (see Sect. 4.1) and is intended to improve the robustness of the LDA model for statistical inference. We implement standard settings for LDA hyper-parameters, $\alpha = 50/K$ and $\beta = .01$, where the number of topics K is set to 20 [25]. We manually annotate two of the topic clusters that capture 'directional' information [1] and appear to act as intensifiers/diminishers of meaning. We label the clusters *directional topic clusters*. Table 1 identifies the top terms associated with the two clusters. Representative words are the highest probability document terms for each topic cluster.

Table 1. Representative document terms associated with the directional topic clusters

'intensifier cluster'		'diminisher cluster'	
word	**prob.**	**word**	**prob.**
increase	0.150	moderated	0.190
strong	0.107	lower	0.161
accelerate	0.081	downwards	0.123
strength	0.063	difficult	0.102
support	0.058	less	0.070

Next for each central bank communication the LDA model infers the probabilities associated with the 'intensifier' and 'diminisher' clusters within each of the four economic aspects detected by the Naïve Bayesian classifier. The output of the model is a vector of eight topic probabilities that proxy the central bank's assessment that the economic aspects are intensifying/diminishing. We label the model *directional LDA model* and the respective probability vectors: $\text{Topic}_{\text{growth}_\uparrow}$, $\text{Topic}_{\text{prices}_\uparrow}$, $\text{Topic}_{\text{interest\_rates}_\uparrow}$ and $\text{Topic}_{\text{bank\_lending}_\uparrow}$ if the economic aspects are increasing and $\text{Topic}_{\text{growth}_\downarrow}$, $\text{Topic}_{\text{prices}_\downarrow}$, $\text{Topic}_{\text{interest\_rate}_\downarrow}$ and $\text{Topic}_{\text{bank\_lending}_\downarrow}$ if the economic aspects are decreasing. We include the topic probabilities as components within the ensemble tree.

4 Experiments

In this section we discuss the corpus of central bank communications and describe the investor patterns data used to evaluate the impact of the central bank communications on investors' interest rate expectations. We then outline the evaluation of the ensemble classification tree, present the results and provide a discussion.

4.1 Data

We choose to analyze the interest rate minutes of the *Bank of England*. As cited in [3], central bank minutes are closely watched by investors to gauge the future direction of economic policies. Similar datasets for the US and Canadian central banks' minutes are examined in [3, 15]. The Bank of England announces the level of UK interest rates on the first Thursday of every month. The details that underpin this decision are only provided two weeks later and are published in the Bank of England's *'Monetary Policy*

Committee Minutes'. The communications are interesting to analyze because changes in investors' expectations on the day of the central bank communication may be attributed to the qualitative information contained within the meeting minutes rather than the interest rate decision announced two weeks before. Minutes typically include summaries of committee members' views on economic conditions and discuss the rationale for their interest rate decisions [26]. The central bank's minutes are, on average, 12 pages long (including a header page), and contain around 55 bullet points, typically with 5 sentences in each bullet. The documents are available from 1997, the year when Parliament voted to give the Bank of England operational independence from the UK government. We retrieve all meeting minutes available between July 1997–March 2014[2] to create a corpus that consists of 199 documents. For the purposes of aspect detection and to train the LDA model, we remove the header page and define a document as an individual sentence within each of the meeting minutes. This expands the corpus to a collection of 53,195 documents.

To evaluate the ensemble tree's predictions we utilize information obtained from financial market patterns. Interest rate futures contracts are financial instruments that enable investors to insure against or speculate on uncertainty about the future level of interest rates [27]. Changes in the price of the futures contracts therefore reflect changes in investors' views on the future direction in central bank interest rates. Investors' interest rate expectations for the following three, six and twelve months are derived and published daily by the Bank of England. We utilize investors' twelve month ahead forecasts. This data series has the greatest data coverage compared to the three and six month series. Furthermore, the twelve month forecast horizon is consistent with the time horizon over which that the Bank of England conducts its economic policies [2]. To isolate the effect of the central bank communication on investors' expectations, we compute the percentage change in the interest rate futures contract, as measured from the close of business on the day of the communication announcement until the close of business one day after. This narrow time window helps to minimize the influence on investors' interest rate expectations from other financial market factors that may occur at the same time [28].

4.2 Experiment Setup

We design the evaluation in stages in order to enhance our understanding of the system components. For a baseline, we evaluate the system's predictions by using only the tone of the overall document (see Sect. 3.2). The approach does not take into account individual economic aspects or diminishers/intensifiers [11, 12]. We label the model *naïve tone*. This approach is consistent with the methodology typically adopted by financial literature [18]. Next we compare the outcomes of an ensemble model that combines the tone associated with each of the economic aspects: economic growth, prices, interest rates and bank lending (see Sect. 3.2). We label this the *economic aspects model*. A third model compares the outcomes from an ensemble model that

[2] Central bank communications announced in August 1997 were excluded from the analysis because the communication document was not readily available in a machine readable format.

combines the intensifiers/diminishers associated with the four economic aspects (see Sect. 3.3). We label this the *directional LDA model*. Finally, we combine the components in a single ensemble tree and refer to the system as the *joint aspect-polarity model*.

Learning and prediction is performed using an ensemble tree. The goal of ensemble methods is to combine the predictions of several models built with a given learning algorithm in order to improve generalizability and robustness over a single model. We use the Random Forest algorithm [30] that employs a diverse set of classifiers by introducing randomness into the classifier construction. Experiments were validated using five-fold cross validation in which the dataset is broken into five equal sized sets; the classifier is trained on four datasets and tested on the remaining dataset. The process is repeated five times and we calculate the average across folds. For evaluation, we select Mean Absolute Error (MAE), Root Mean Squared Error and Spearman's rho (ρ). We also examine Spearman's rho since prediction may be considered to be a ranking task. The formulae are displayed in Eq. (2) below.

$$MAE = \frac{1}{n}\sum_{i=1}^{n}|O_i - E_i|, \quad RMSE = \left[\frac{1}{n}\sum_{i=1}^{n}|O_i - E_i|\right]^2, \quad \rho = 1 - \frac{6\sum(O_i - E_i)^2}{n(n^2-1)} \tag{2}$$

where E_i is the model's predicted value, O_i is the realized value, and n is the number of observations. MAE measures the average magnitude of the forecast errors without considering direction; RMSE penalizes errors and gives a relatively high weight to large errors. A smaller value of MAE or RMSE indicates a more accurate prediction. Spearman's rho is a non-parametric measure [29] of the degree of linear association between the predicted and realized values and is bound between the range −1 to +1. A positive Spearman's rho indicates the model's predictive ability; a negative value indicates a poor model fit.

4.3 Experiment Results

The evaluation metrics from the model components are shown in Table 2.

Table 2. Evaluation of the model components

Model	MAE	RMSE	ρ
Naive tone	0.022	0.016	−0.187***
Economic aspects	0.018	0.013	−0.044
Directional LDA	0.019	0.014	0.041
Joint polarity model	0.015	0.011	0.034

The asterisks provide the levels of significance where *** indicates that the model's predictions versus forecasts are statistically, negatively significant at the 0.1 % level.

The naïve tone model, which proxies the approach commonly adopted by text mining studies in the field of finance, shows the worst performance. It exhibits the highest MAE and RMSE. The rank correlation of the model's forecasts with realized changes in investors' interest rate expectations is highly statistically negative, implying that documents that are predicted to have a positive/negative impact on investors' interest rate expectations result in the reverse outcome. The economic aspects and directional LDA models exhibit monotonic decreases in MAE and RMSE, suggesting a slight improvement in the model fit. Finally, the joint aspect-polarity model, that includes all model components in the ensemble tree, displays the lowest MAE and RMSE. The mildly positive Spearman's rho is consistent with previous forecasting studies within the field of finance. As cited in [19], many factors influence the financial markets; a low, positive correlation provides sufficient comfort of the model's predictive power.

5 Discussion

One interpretation of the experiment results is that multiple aspects are needed to improve the accuracy of the prediction system. The existence of a positive Spearman's rho for the joint model versus a negative Spearman's rho for the naïve tone and economic aspects may be indicative of a non-linear relationship between the components that is only evident when the models are combined rather than considered in isolation. One of the strengths of a regression tree is that it does not assume a functional form, allowing it to detect interactions between model components. To aid our understanding of prediction in the joint model, Fig. 2 displays the decision tree results for one of the folds. The values in the grey boxes provide the predicted percentage change in investors' interest rate expectations associated with the sentiment contained within the central bank communication. A positive value indicates that the impact is expected to lead to an increase in investors' interest rate expectations, while a negative value indicates an expected decrease in interest rate expectations.

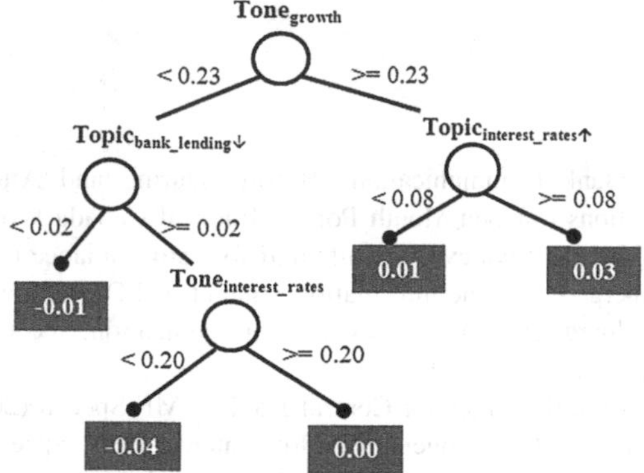

Fig. 2. Example decision tree from one of the folds

The regression tree identifies the interaction between the *directional topic clusters* and *Tone* measures. The primary decision in the decision tree is central bank sentiment towards economic growth. The right hand path indicates that if a central bank communication emphasizes positive economic growth and discusses interest rate increases, investors' expectations of future interest rates is predicted to rise by 3 %. The left hand path indicates that if a central bank tone towards economic growth is low, discussed declining bank lending and the tone towards interest rates is negative, investors are predicted to lower their expectations of future interest rates by 4 %.

6 Conclusion

The goal of central bank communication is to make messages as clear, simple and understandable as possible to a wide range of audiences [1]. In this study, we focus of one specific audience, namely financial market investors. The outcome of our study may feed the design of a system that can predict the impact of central bank communication on formation of investors' interest rate expectations. The results of the joint aspect-polarity model suggest that investors may benefit by incorporating a measure of central bank sentiment to forecast interest rates.

In this study we evaluate model performance using prices from financial market instruments. The market price of an interest rate contract implicitly measures the average investor's interest rate expectations [27]. It is also possible to compute an 'implied probability distribution' of those expectations [27]. In future work we plan to evaluate a range of metrics, including the dispersion of the expectations as a proxy of investor uncertainty. Post the 2007–2009 financial crisis, central banks have broadened the range of their communication, including the use of social media, live broadcasts, podcasts and blogs, to deliver their messages [1]. In future research, a wider range of central bank communications will be integrated into our study. We also intend to examine alternative approaches to select economic aspects, including dynamic approaches to detect salient terms as central bank communications change over time.

Acknowledgement. The research leading to these results has partially been supported by the Dutch national program COMMIT.

References

1. Vayid, I.: Central Bank Communications Before, During and After the Crisis: From Open-Market Operations to Open-Mouth Policy, Bank of Canada Working Paper (2013)
2. Bank of England. Monetary policy trade-offs and forward guidance (2013)
3. Boukus, E., Rosenberg, J., V. The information content of FOMC minutes (2006)
4. Meyersson, P., Karlberg, P.P, A Journey in Communication: the Case of the Sveriges Riksbank SNS Förlag (2012)
5. Viñals, J.: Lessons from the Crisis for Central Banks. IMF Speech (2010)
6. Danthine, J, P. Causes and consequences of low interest rates. Speech by Mr Jean-Pierre Danthine, Vice Chairman of the Governing Board of the Swiss National Bank, at the Swisscanto Market Outlook 2014, Lausanne (2013)

7. Titov, I, McDonald, R., T. Modeling online reviews with multi-grain topic models. In: Proceeding of the 17th WWW (2008)
8. Mihalcea, R., Tarau, P.: TextRank: Bringing order into texts. In: Proceedings of the 2004 Conference on Empirical Methods in Natural Language Processing (2004)
9. Brin, S., Page, L.: The anatomy of a large-scale hypertextual web search engine. Comput. Netw. ISDN Syst. **33**, 107–117 (1998)
10. Blei, D.: M., Ng, A., Jordan, M., I. Latent Dirichlet Allocation. J. Mach. Learn. Res. **3**, 993–1022 (2003)
11. Kennedy, A., Inkpen, D.: Sentiment classification of movie reviews using contextual valence shifters. Comput. Intell. **22**(2), 110–125 (2006)
12. Polanyi, L., Zaenen, A.: Contextual valence shifters. In: AAAI Spring Symposium on Exploring Attitude and Affect in Text: Theories and Applications (2004)
13. Carney, M.: Panel discussion comments to the BIS Conference on the Future of Central Banking under Post-Crisis Mandates (2010)
14. Fay, C., Gravelle, T.: Has the Inclusion of Forward-Looking Statements in Monetary Policy Communications Made the Bank of Canada More Transparent? Bank of Canada Discussion Paper (2010)
15. Hendry, S., Madeley, A.: Text Mining and the Information Content of Bank of Canada Communications, Bank of Canada Working Paper (2010)
16. Pang, B., Lee, L., Vaithyanathan, S. Thumbs up? Sentiment classification using machine learning techniques. In: Proceedings of EMNLP-02 (2002)
17. Stone, P., Dumphy, D.C., Smith, M.S., Ogilvie, D.M.: The General Inquirer: A Computer Approach to Content Analysis. The MIT Press, Cambridge (1966)
18. Tetlock, P., Saar-Tsechansky, M., Macskassy, S.: More than words: quantifying language to measure firms' fundamentals. J. Finan. **LXIII**(3), 1437–1467 (2008)
19. Loughran, T., McDonald, B.: When is a liability not a liability? Textual analysis, dictionaries and 10Ks. J. Finan. **66**, 35–65 (2010)
20. Liu, F., Pennell, D., Liu, F., Liu, Y. Unsupervised approaches for automatic keyword extraction using meeting transcripts. In: Proceedings of Human Language Technologies: The 2009 Annual Conference of the North American (2009)
21. Litvak, M., Last, M. Graph-based keyword extraction for single-document summarization. In: Proceedings of the 2nd Workshop on Multi-source, Multilingual Information Extraction and Summarization, Coling 2008, pp. 17–24. Association for Computational Linguistics (2008)
22. Opsahl, T., Agneessens, F., Skvoretz, J.: Node centrality in weighted networks: Generalizing degree and shortest paths (2010)
23. Boudin, F.: A Comparison of Centrality Measures for Graph-Based Keyphrase Extraction (2013)
24. McCallum, A., Nigam, K.: A comparison of event models for naive Bayes text classification. In: AAAI-98 Workshop on Learning for Text Categorization (1998)
25. Griffiths, T.L., Steyvers, M.: Finding scientific topics. Proc. Natl. Acad. Sci. **101**, 5228–5235 (2004)
26. Danker, D.J., Luecke, M.M.: Background on FOMC Meeting Minutes, Federal Reserve Bulletin, pp. 175–179 (2005)
27. Clews, R., Panigirtzoglou, N., Proudman, J.: Recent developments in extracting information from options markets. Q. Bull. **40**, 50–60 (2000). Bank of England
28. Mackinlay, A.C.: Event studies in economics and finance. J. Econ. Lit. **35**, 13–39 (1997)
29. Maritz, J.S.: Distribution-Free Statistical Methods. Chapman and Hall, London (1984)
30. Breiman, L.: Random forests. Mach. Learn. **26**(2), 123–140 (2001)
31. Clauset, A., Newman, M.E.J., Moore, C.: Finding community structure in very large networks. Phys. Rev. **69**, 066133 (2004)

AI MashUp Challenge

Enriching Live Event Participation with Social Network Content Analysis and Visualization

Marco Brambilla, Daniele Dell'Aglio[(✉)], Emanuele Della Valle, Andrea Mauri, and Riccardo Volonterio

Dipartimento di Elettronica, Informazione e Bioingegneria, Politecnico of Milano, P.za L. Da Vinci, 32, 20133 Milano, Italy
{marco.brambilla,daniele.dellaglio,emanuele.della.valle, andrea.mauri,riccardo.volonterio}@polimi.it

Abstract. During live events like conferences or exhibitions, people nowadays share their opinions, multimedia contents, suggestions, related materials, and reports through social networking platforms, such as Twitter. However, live events also feature inherent complexity, in the sense that they comprise multiple parallel sessions or happenings (e.g., in a conference you have several sessions in different rooms). The focus of this research is to improve the experience of (local or remote) attendees, by exploiting the contents shared on the social networks. The framework gathers in real time the tweets related to the event, analyses them and links them to the specific sub-events they refer to. Attendees have an holistic view on what is happening and where, so as to get help when deciding what sub-event to attend. To achieve its goal, the application consumes data from different data sources: Twitter, the official event schedule, plus domain specific content (for instance, in case of a computer science conference, DBLP and Google Scholar). Such data is analyzed through a combination of semantic web, crowdsourcing (e.g., by soliciting further inputs from attendees), and machine learning techniques (including NLP and NER) for building a rich content base for the event. The paradigm is shown at work on a Computer Science conference (WWW 2013)

1 Introduction

During live events like conferences, exhibitions, and sports or fashion happenings, it has become common practice to share opinions, recommendations, materials, and reports through social media. Usually, the shared content refers to specific occurrences or objects related to the event, such as talks, speakers, exhibition stands, discussions, and so on. However, the mapping to such elements is often shallow or partial. This makes the social networking content an input not so valuable for the audience, especially if the social stream is very crowded and thus one has to deal with a big information overloading problem.

The problem tackled by this work is to enrich and classify the social media content related to a live event, in a way that makes it valuable for (local or

V. Presutti et al. (Eds.): ESWC Satellite Events 2014, LNCS 8798, pp. 159–170, 2014.
DOI: 10.1007/978-3-319-11955-7_13

remote) attendees. In particular, we focus on determining which contents are associated to which sub-event, and on enriching those contents with links to relevant entities (speakers, sessions, papers, and so on) in a domain-specific knowledge base. We then provide appropriate visualization to the enriched content, in a way that makes people able to understand what are the hot topics or sub-events and thus get guidance on what to do while attending the event.

In our approach, we select Twitter as the main social source for event-specific content. Twitter is indeed one of the most adopted platforms for social sharing, especially in the context of professional events: it can easily reach a large amount of interested people, messages are very short and require only few seconds to be shared. Furthermore, typically participants share their thoughts through event-specific hashtags, which are more or less officially related to the event itself, which makes it easy to associate them to the event.

We implement our solution in framework called ECSTASYS (Event-Centered STream Analysis SYStem) which combines semantic web, crowdsourcing (e.g., by soliciting further inputs by the attendees through social network invitations), natural language processing, named entity recognition and machine learning techniques for building a rich content base for the event. The application works in real time, processing the tweets as soon as they are available: in this way, attendees can have an updated and holistic view on what is happening and where, so as to get help when deciding what sub-event to attend. The application consumes data from different data sources: in addition to the afore mentioned Twitter, inputs include the official event schedule, plus domain specific content (for instance, in case of a computer science conference, DBLP and Google Scholar). The data processing determines the relevant entities described in the tweets and, consequently, the sub-events they relate to. The result of the analysis is shown to the attendees by room/sub-event, thus highlighting the interest and engagement of each sub-event, by means of appropriate user interfaces. The work is validated against a set of past conferences in the computer science field (for instance the WWW conference).

The paper is organized as follows: Sect. 2 gives an holistic view of the proposed solution, describing how the micro posts are processed. Sections 3 and 4 describe in detail respectively the data sources and the components that perform the data processing. Finally, Sect. 5 closes with possible future extensions.

2 The ECSTASYS Processing Flow

This section delves into the processing flow of the ECSTASYS framework by a logical point of view. ECSTASYS aims at augmenting the participation experience to live events through social network content enrichment and linking. To illustrate the processing flow, and to have a running example to use along the paper, we consider an experiment we conducted using ECSTASYS and depicted in Fig. 1: the scenario is the one of scientific conferences in the computer science domain, and in particular, the World Wide Web conference (WWW) 2013[1]. Conferences

[1] Cf. http://www2013.org/

are interesting complex events, with several parallel sub-events located in different rooms, typically in the same building. It follows that the precision error in geo-location would let infer wrong associations between tweets and sub-events. Moreover, people could discuss what happens in other rooms, so the geo-location is not enough to create the correct links. Demo and videos are available at http://demo.search-computing.com/aimc-2014/home.

During computer science conferences, as the WWW, a high number of participants uses social networks, and in particular on Twitter, to post messages describing the conference, e.g., updates on the talks, considerations on the keynotes, positive and negative opinions on the sessions they were in. The first step of ECSTASYS (Fig. 1a) is the retrieval of those posts: Twitter offers an API to retrieve in real time the tweets according to different criteria (e.g., location and keywords).

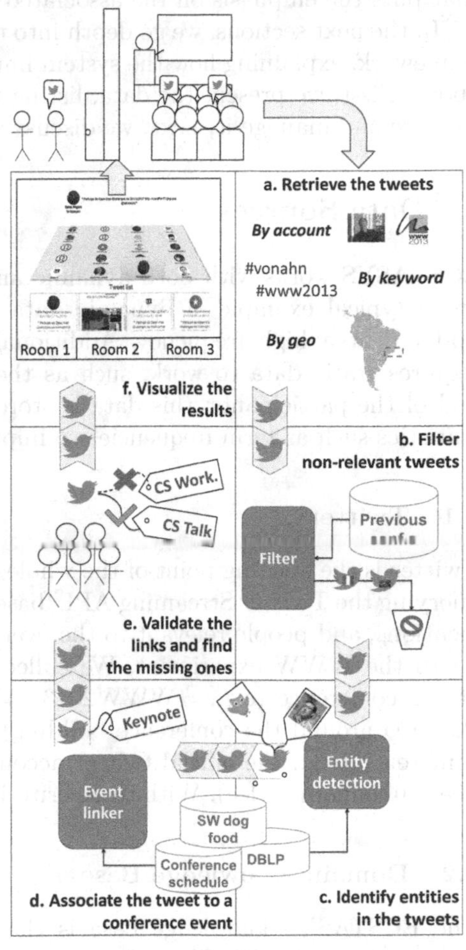

Fig. 1. ECSTASYS processing flow

In this step, it is important to capture the highest number of relevant tweets, and this is paid in precision: ECSTASYS retrieves more tweets than required, gathering also non-relevant tweets, e.g., tweets talking about the quality of the dishes at the social dinner. The precision issue is addressed in the second step, the filtering (Fig. 1b): messages that are non-relevant for ECSTASYS are detected and discarded. ECSTASYS is built in this way due to the fact that the Twitter APIs have limited support for complex criteria definition, and consequently is hard to assess both high precision and recall in the first step.

In the third step (Fig. 1c), the WWW-related concepts mentioned in the tweet messages are identified. Attendants, presentations and rooms are example of concepts that ECSTASYS aims at detecting. In fact, they are keys to determine the conference events the tweets refer to: a tweet that discusses an event usually cites the presenter, the article or the room.

The identification of those entities in the text is at the basis of the following step, where ECSTASYS infers the links between tweets and events. This task is performed in a semi-automated process: ECSTASYS makes an attempt to find the link automatically (Fig. 1d), and there are three possibilities: (1) a link is found with a confidence higher than a threshold; (2) there are more than one links with a high confidence; and (3) no links are found. In cases 2 and 3, additional manual tasks are executed, respectively a disambiguation and a link identification tasks (Fig. 1e). Finally, the tweets are visualised in a ad-hoc visualization that puts the emphasis on the associated event (Fig. 1f).

In the next sections, we go depth into the technical details of the ECSTASYS framework, explaining how the system implements the processing flow described above. First, we present the data, listing the sources and the componets we use to store and manage it; next, we discuss how it is processed.

3 Data Sources

ECSTASYS works with both dynamic and static data. Messages from Twitter are a typical example of dynamic data: a stream of time stamped messages updated at a high frequency. Additionally, as we see in Sect. 4, ECSTASYS requires static data to work, such as the description of the conference events and of the participants; this data is stored in a knowledge base, enriched with statistics such as term frequencies to improve the entity identification process.

3.1 Twitter

Twitter is the starting point of the whole approach: social feeds are retrieved by querying the Twitter Streaming API[2] based on hashtags, keywords, geographical locations, and people relevant to the event.

In the WWW experiment, We collected the tweets based on the hashtags of the conference (e.g., #WWW2013, #WWW, #vonahn), the location (i.e., the area around the conference building), and Twitter accounts related to the conference (e.g., the official twitter account – @www2013rio and Tim Berners-Lee – @timberners_lee). With these criteria, we collected more than 5000 tweets.

3.2 Domain Knowledge Base

The ECSTASYS knowledge base is the location on where the relevant data processed by the ECSTASYS components is stored. The knowledge base is exposed as a SPARQL endpoint and is built on the top of OpenRDF Sesame framework; as repository, we use OWLIM-Lite with the OWL 2 RL profile.

In our experiment, the knowledge base has been populated by: reusing some conference ontologies; importing the official data of the conference of interest; and importing bibliographic information about the people involved in the conference. We now report on this three aspects.

[2] Cf. https://dev.twitter.com/docs/api/streaming

Ontology. To design the ontology for ECSTASYS knowledge base, we reused existing ontologies: *(i)* the *Semantic Web Conference Ontology*[3], currently used to describe the data stored in the Semantic Web Dog Food repository[4] and describing conferences, related sub-events (e.g., keynotes, workshops, tutorials), talks and involved people with the different roles; and *(ii)* the BOTTARI ontology [5] for describing the tweets, an extension of the SIOC vocabulary to take into account the Twitter concepts (e.g., retweets, followers and followings). We also defined a set of custom concepts and properties to model the data produced by the ECSTASYS components that has to be stored: the mentions in the tweets, their relation with the entities and, consequently, the relations between the tweets and the events they relate to.

Conference Data. To describe the specific conference, we crawled the relevant information from the official Web site[5] and we performed the lifting from HTML/XML to RDF through XSPARQL [2] (information about the WWW 2013 conference is not available as linked data). This task required some manual work for setting up the crawler: in terms of effort, we spent one person day.

Bibliography. We use DBLP to enrich the ECSTASYS knowledge base with bibliographic information. We retrieved the list of the most recent papers written by each person involved in the conference (not only the authors, but also keynote speakers, organizers and chairs). As we describe in Sect. 4.4, this allows to enrich the keywords associated to each author and improve the precision of the entity detection step.

3.3 Domain Analytics

Analytics on the domain of interest are collected based on frequency of terms found in the social stream and of entities in the knowledge base. This aspect is important for reducing the impact of very frequent terms in the selected domain, which would not be considered as stop words in general sense but would actually generate noise in the specific domain. For instance, in our scenario terms such as *framework*, *solution*, *Web* are too frequent and their weight in the computation process is consequently lowered.

3.4 Crowd

The crowd is the source of input from human agents solicited by ECSTASYS. Typical collected information comprises confirmation of relevance of some entities for a tweet and selection of entities not automatically identified. In this case the crowd is compose by experts, since we target people attending the specific event. ECSTASYS builds the expert crowd by involving relevant tweets authors that are participating at the event.

[3] Cf. http://data.semanticweb.org/ns/swc/ontology

[4] Cf. http://data.semanticweb.org/

[5] Cf. http://www2013.org/

4 Processing Components

ECSTASYS puts together different techniques and tools to process and enrich the tweets. Figure 2 gives an overview of the framework, highlighting the data sources we presented above, and the components that implements the ECSTASYS processing flow. In the following, we present those components, explaining the technologies they use and how they work.

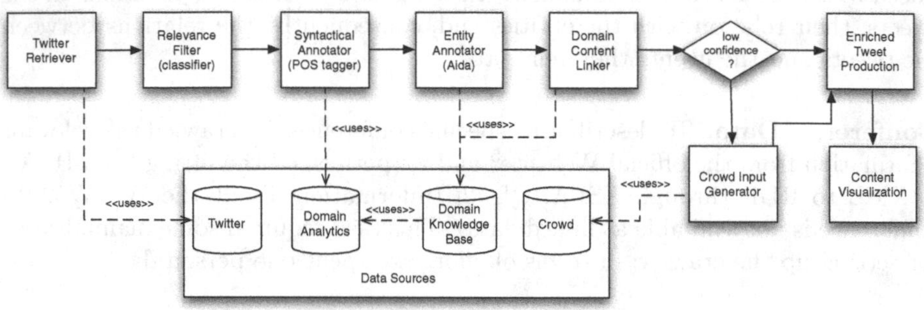

Fig. 2. Components of the ECSTASYS framework.

4.1 Twitter Retriever

The Twitter Retriever is the component that gathers the tweets that are relevant for the current event from Twitter. It uses the Twitter Stream APIs in order to connect itself to the public stream of tweets. This API allows to follow streams that match different predicates such as: users, keywords and location. All of these aspects are relevant for real world events, as they are typically identifiable by official hashtags, relevant people involved, and geographical coordinates of the venue.

4.2 Relevance Filter

The purpose of the Relevance Filter component is to filter out the non-relevant tweets that have been extracted by the Twitter Retriever but do not provide valuable information on the event. Typical examples include: tweets written in non-English language, tweets emitted in the prescribed geographical area or containing relevant keywords but not pertaining to the event, and so on.

The component immediately discards the tweets not written in English by looking at the *lang* field provided by Twitter as part of the tweet data structure. Furthermore, for selecting the relevant tweets we apply a classification approach, by exploiting a classifier based on Conditional Random Fields [10] trained on datasets coming from past events similar to the considered one. In particular we built a wrapper of the *CRF++* implementation[6] in NodeJS, and we released it as open-source project on GitHub[7].

4.3 Syntactical Annotator

Once the relevant tweets are selected, they are annotated through a Part Of Speech (POS) tagger. The component provides as output the annotated tweet, plus a customized set of syntactical elements extracted from the text which will be useful for the extraction of entities. Such elements consist in set of words that are good candidates for becoming named entities. On this we propose a set of heuristic solutions aimed at increasing the recall of candidate terms for the extraction of entities, as opposed to classical off-the-shelf Named Entity Extractors, which feature very high precision but also limited recall. Some examples of heuristics we apply include: generation of all the possible aggregation of contiguous nouns, contiguous nouns and adjectives, and so on.
For instance the tweet "Ingenious way to learn languages: duolingo #keynote #www2013" is tagged in the following way:

Ingenious'JJ way'NN to'TO learn'VB languages:'NN duolingo'NN #keynote'NN #www'NN 2013'CD

The two-letter annotations (e.g., NN, JJ) are the POS tags, which define the grammatical role of a word inside the sentence. For instance, *NN* indicates that the word is a noun, *VB* indicates a verb, and so on.

Finally the application of the heuristic algorithm on the list of nouns produces the following aggregation: ["way"]["languages","duolingo"]. The nouns "keynote" and "www" are not considered because they are too frequent by the Domain Analytics. Our preliminary evaluation shows that the trained classifier achieves 81 % precision and 97 % recall when applied to the WWW 2012 content and 71 % precision and 84 % recall when applied to the WWW 2013 content.

4.4 Entity Annotator

The Entity Annotator component processes the data produced by the Syntactical Annotator so as to determine which are the entities discussed in the text. Among the existing named entity recognition (NER) tools, we selected one based on the following requirements:

- capability of performing real-time processing of content;
- capability of linking the text items to entities in an ontology. In the recent years, several entity annotators were built on the top of open data and public knowledge bases (e.g., DBpedia and freebase) [6,7].
- support of customization of the reference knowledge base to be used by the tool.

[6] Cf. http://crfpp.googlecode.com/svn/trunk/doc/index.html

[7] Cf. https://github.com/janez87/node-crf

The last requirement is extremely critical in our setting because usually entity annotators are only able to process generic textual content and to extract the generic entities (e.g., entities described in Wikipedia). However, in our case every event typically focuses on a very specific setting or domain, for which generic knowledge bases would contain only generic terms and very famous entities, while they would miss most of the less famous people and subjects. As an example, Dr. Jong-Deok Choi, keynote speaker at the WWW 2014[8], does not have a page on Wikipedia (and consequently, does not appear in DBpedia).

To cope with those requirements, we decided to use AIDA [9], an open-source entity detector developed at the Max Planck Institute. It takes as input a text, it detects the set of mentions, i.e., relevant portions of the text, and associates each of them to an entity. To do it, it exploits an internal entity base and it performs two kinds of analyses: on the one hand, it selects the set of potential candidate entities for each mention; on the other hand, it performs entity-to-entity analysis to determine the coherence among the candidates. The default entity base of AIDA is built on the top of YAGO [8], but it can be customised (or replaced) with another one. To fit our needs, we built a custom entity base tailored on the domain specific knowledge base of the experimental scenario (as explained in Sect. 3.2).

The custom version of AIDA is wrapped in the Content Linker component: it takes as input a tweet, and enriches it with a set of couples ($mention - entity$). The resulting tweet is pushed to the Domain Content Linker. Continuing the example introduced above, one of the mentions identified by the Syntactical Annotator is *Duolingo*; when the Entity Annotator processes the tweet, it associates the mention with the paper "Duolingo: learn a language for free while helping to translate the web" of Luis Von Ahn at the IUI 2013. This annotation is an example of entity detection enabled by DBLP: the enrichment of the AIDA entity base with the list of recent papers of the people involved in the conference increase the probability to discover them.

4.5 Domain Content Linker

The Domain Content Linker aims at creating the relations between the tweets and the specific sub-events of the event, extracted from the official conference program (e.g., workshops, talks, sessions). As input, the component receives the tweets annotated by the Entity Annotator, i.e., a tweet with a list of related entities; as output, it enriches the tweets with the URI of the event it relates to.

This component infers two different relations: *discusses*, that indicates that a tweet talks about one of the sub-events (independently on the temporal relation between the two, i.e., the tweet could be talking about something that happened in the past or that will happen in the future); and *discusses during*, a sub-relation that states that the tweet talks about a sub-event while it is ongoing. This distinction is important for visualization purposes.

[8] Cf. http://www2014.kr/

The linkage among the tweets and the events is performed in two steps. First, the Linker retrieves the candidate events: this is done by combining the entities in the AIDA entity base that annotate the tweet, with the information in the ECSTASYS domain knowledge base. We encoded the rules that determine the candidates as continuous SPARQL queries [1] that are executed by the C-SPARQL engine; ECSTASYS runs a lifting operation on the tweet stream (from JSON to RDF) to process it. For example, let's consider the query q: select the *events* in which the creator of the work w is a participant, and w is an annotation of the tweet t. Let the input i be: "Ingenious way to learn languages: duolingo #keynote #www2013 #gwap", annotated with the mention–entity: (Duolingo, "Duolingo: learn a language for free while helping to translate the web"). The evaluation of q over i produces the list of events in which Luis Von Ahn participates.

If a tweet has more than one annotation, the first step produces a set of candidate events; the second step works on it in order to derive an ordered list of candidates, associating to each of them a confidence value. The score is determined by the number of repetitions of the events in the multiset, and by their *temporal distance* to the tweet, i.e., it is more probable that a tweet discusses an event occurring temporally near. For instance, among the events on which Luis Ahn participated at the WWW 2013, the tweet was posted during the keynote, so it is the event with the highest rank in the output.

The time stamp of the tweet and the event scheduled time are also used to determine if the event can be related to the tweet through a *discusses during* relation: if the tweet is posted within 30 min before/after the event, the *discusses during* relation can hold.

4.6 Crowd Input Generator

The Crowd Input Generator use crowd-sourcing techniques to improve the precision of the framework and solve the ambigous results of the Domain Content Linker. This component is based on the CrowdSearcher framework [3,4], which allows planning and control of crowdsourcing campaigns. The component is triggered by specific events (e.g., tweets that cannot be associated with any sub-event, or tweets for which the confidence of the association is low), and assigns them to the crowd for getting feedback. The invitation to respond is sent to people relevant to the event (e.g., the author of the tweet himself and people who twitted about the event).

Figure 3 shows the Web interface used by the crowd in order to provide the answer to the crowdsourcing tasks proposed by ECSTASYS. On the top of the form is shown one tweet, with a list of possible choices (determined by the Domain Content Linker). The crowd user has to choose the correct room/session from the list. Due to the fact that ECSTASYS is using an expert crowd (i.e., people attending the event), it considers a tweet as evaluated as soon as one performer provides an answer. In order to involve as many participants as possible ECSTASYS exposes a user interface compatible with both mobile and desktop devices.

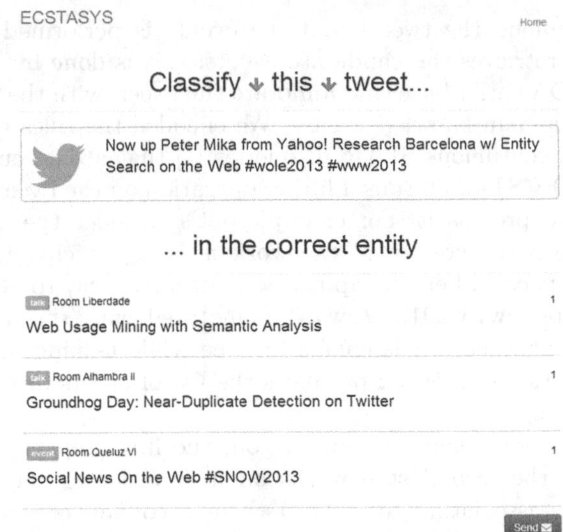

Fig. 3. Interface used by the crowd for providing the answers

4.7 Enriched Tweet Production

The Enriched Tweet Production component is in charge to create the tweet with the additional metadata generated by the ECSTASYS components, e.g., the information from the crowd, from the Domain Content Linker and so on. The output of the component is a stream of JSon tweets with additional ECSTASYS-related fields. Those tweets are then visible through the Content Visualization component, but in general they can also be used for further processing.

Listing 1. Example of an enriched tweet


```
{
 "created_at":"Mon May 06 15:01:02 +0000 2013",
 "id" : 331423366131101700,
                                        "...."
  "text":"don't miss the first ever #WWW2013 Linked Media w/s Monday
     @www2013rio promoting #semanticmedia and #mediafragments http://t.co/
     CWanSYwnj8",
 "names" : [ [ [ "t" ] ], [ [ "first" ] ], [ [ "Media" ] ], [ [ "/" ] ], [ [ "
     Monday" ] ], [ [ "rio" ] ] ],
  "taggedText":"don'VB''\" t'NN miss'VB the'DT first'NN ever'RB #WWW'NN 2013'
       CD Linked'VBN Media'NNP w'IN /'NN s'PRP Monday'NNP @www'NN 2013'CD rio'
       NN promoting'VBG #semanticmedia'NN and'CC #mediafragments'NNS http://t.
       co/CWanSYwnj8'URL",
 "relevant": true,
 "tweetAnnotations": [ {
   "mention":"WWW2013 Linked Media w/s",
   "entity":"http://www2013.org/program/first-worldwide-web-workshop-on-linked
        -media-lime2013/"
  } ],
 "relatedEvents": [ {
   "entity":"http://www2013.org/program/first-worldwide-web-workshop-on-linked
        -media-lime2013/",
   "prob" : 1
  } ]
}
```

Listing 1 shows an example of an enriched tweet. In bold (from Line 6) are highlighted the fields that are added by ECSTASYS. To make some examples, the *relevant* field (Line 8) contains the result of the Relevance Filter: it is a boolean that indicates if a tweet is relevant. The *taggedText* (Line 7) and *names* (Line 6) are the results generated by the Syntactic Generator: the former is the tweet message annotated with the POS tags, while the latter is the array with the relevant nouns sequences. The *tweetAnnotations* field (Line 9) contains the result of the Entity Annotator: the value is an array with the mentions found in the text message and the relative associated entity. Finally, the *relatedEvents* field (Line 13) contains the events related to the tweets found by the Domain Content Linker and the Crowd Input Generator, with the relative probability.

4.8 Content Visualization

ECSTASYS provides two types of visualizations for the enriched stream of tweets, as shown in Fig. 4. Both of them are web applications written in HTML5 and Javascript.

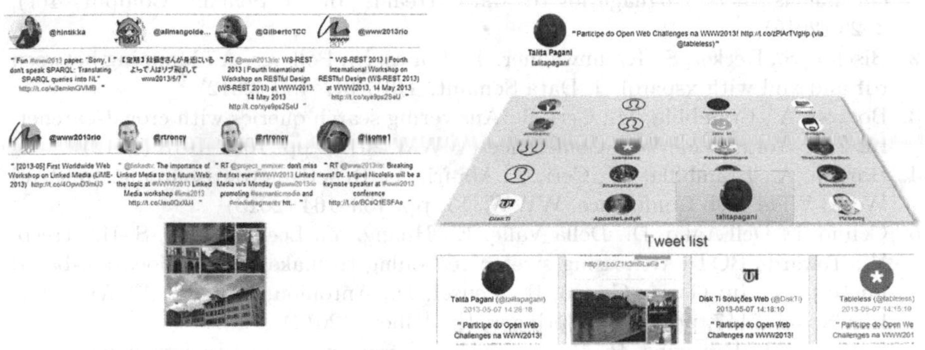

Fig. 4. *Wall* (left) and *Room* (right) visualizations of the enriched content.

The *Wall* visualization is meant to be used at the event venue on large panels (e.g., on screens or projectors in the lobby or outside the rooms of the sessions). It shows the tweets with highlighted author, mentions, hashtags and URLs. Rich media content linked by the tweets is shown separately at the bottom. The *Room* visualization instead aims at personal use (e.g., on desktop browsers) and mimics the layout of a room where a sub-event is happening. It shows a 3D view of the audience (i.e., people that twitted something related to the current sub-event) in the center, with the last relevant tweet on top. The author of the tweet flips up in the audience layout. At the bottom, a continuous slider shows the tweet stream. Each tweet appears with related media, highlighted URLs, mentions and hashtags.

5 Conclusions and Next Steps

In this paper we presented ECSTASYS, a framework for improving the experience of event attendees by exploiting and enriching the contents shared on the social networks. The prototype we developed prove the feasibility of the system, but additional work is required. First, we need to evaluate it: at the moment we have just some indicators about some components (e.g., the relevance filter), but we plan to evaluate the precision and recall of each separate components first, and of the whole system then. Additionally, we aims at improving the ECSTASYS components, e.g., design a more sophisticate heuristic algorithm for the extraction of syntactical elements and develop more precise crowd activation and control rules. Finally, we will investigate the generality of approach, deploying ECSTASYS during other conferences and more in general other kinds of events.

References

1. Barbieri, D.F., Braga, D., Ceri, S., Della Valle, E., Grossniklaus, M.: C-sparql: a continuous query language for rdf data streams. Int. J. Semant. Comput. **4**(1), 3–25 (2010)
2. Bischof, S., Decker, S., Krennwallner, T., Lopes, N., Polleres, A.: Mapping between rdf and xml with xsparql. J. Data Semant. **1**(3), 147–185 (2012)
3. Bozzon, A., Brambilla, M., Ceri, S.: Answering search queries with crowdsearcher. In: 21st World Wide Web Conference (WWW 2012), pp. 1009–1018 (2012)
4. Bozzon, A., Brambilla, M., Ceri, S., Mauri, A.: Reactive crowdsourcing. In: 22nd World Wide Web Conference, WWW '13, pp. 153–164 (2013)
5. Celino, I., Dell'Aglio, D., Della Valle, E., Huang, Y., Lee, T., Kim, S.-H., Tresp, V.: Towards BOTTARI: using stream reasoning to make sense of location-based micro-posts. In: García-Castro, R., Fensel, D., Antoniou, G. (eds.) ESWC 2011. LNCS, vol. 7117, pp. 80–87. Springer, Heidelberg (2012)
6. Cornolti, M., Ferragina, P., Ciaramita, M.: A framework for benchmarking entity-annotation systems. In: Proceedings of the 22nd International Conference on World Wide Web, WWW '13, pp. 249–260 (2013)
7. Gangemi, A.: A comparison of knowledge extraction tools for the semantic web. In: Cimiano, P., Corcho, O., Presutti, V., Hollink, L., Rudolph, S. (eds.) ESWC 2013. LNCS, vol. 7882, pp. 351–366. Springer, Heidelberg (2013)
8. Hoffart, J., Suchanek, F.M., Berberich, K., Weikum, G.: Yago2: a spatially and temporally enhanced knowledge base from wikipedia. Artif. Intell. **194**, 28–61 (2013)
9. Hoffart, J., Yosef, M.A., Bordino, I., Fürstenau, H., Pinkal, M., Spaniol, M., Taneva, B., Thater, S., Weikum, G.: Robust disambiguation of named entities in text. In: Proceedings of the 2011 Conference on Empirical Methods in Natural Language Processing (EMNLP2011), pp. 782–792 (2011)
10. Lafferty, J.D., McCallum, A., Pereira, F.C.N.: Conditional random fields: probabilistic models for segmenting and labeling sequence data. In: ICML '01: Proceedings of the 18th International Conference on Machine Learning, pp. 282–289 (2001)

Linked Widgets Platform: Lowering the Barrier for Open Data Exploration

Tuan-Dat Trinh(✉), Peter Wetz, Ba-Lam Do, Amin Anjomshoaa, Elmar Kiesling, and A Min Tjoa

Vienna University of Technology, Vienna, Austria
{tuan.trinh,peter.wetz,ba.do,amin.anjomshoaa, elmar.kiesling,a.tjoa}@tuwien.ac.at

Abstract. Despite a drastic increase in available Open and Linked Data, unmediated utilization of these data by end users is still relatively uncommon. Applications built on top of Open Data are typically domain-specific and discovering appropriate solutions that fit users' rapidly shifting needs is a cumbersome process. In line with the Linked Data paradigm, end user tools should be based on openness, foster reusability, and be flexible enough to handle arbitrary data sources. We develop an open platform based on Semantic Web technologies that encourages developers and users to access, process, integrate, and visualize Open Data sources. To help users overcome technological barriers of adoption and get in touch with Open Data, we introduce the concept of Linked Widgets. By connecting Linked Widgets from different developers, users without programming skills can compose and share ad-hoc applications that combine Open Data sources in a creative manner.

1 Introduction

In recent years, organizations and governments have made large volumes of useful Open Data available on the web. Publishers frequently release the data under a license that allow anyone to use, reuse and redistribute it. This allows interested stakeholders to analyze the data, put it in a new context, gain insights, and create innovative services. Using *Vienna Open Government*[1] data, for example, one can easily find Points of Interest (POI) such as public barbecue areas or bathing areas at the shores of the *Danube* River; from the *LinkedGeoData*[2] repository, a tourist can find POIs all over the world, accessible as Linked Data. Open Data, particularly if published as Linked Open Data (LOD) in an interlinked, structured and machine-understandable manner, has large potential to inform decisions and solve problems.

However, end users are not able to directly access, explore, and combine different sources to satisfy their information needs or support their everyday decision-making due to a number of technological barriers: (i) Users do not

[1] https://open.wien.at/site/

[2] http://linkedgeodata.org/

V. Presutti et al. (Eds.): ESWC Satellite Events 2014, LNCS 8798, pp. 171–182, 2014.
DOI: 10.1007/978-3-319-11955-7_14

know where to find the required data sources; (ii) provided that they are aware of appropriate sources, they frequently do not have the means and skills to access them; and (iii) if users are able of collecting raw data from various sources, they are typically not capable of performing the necessary data processing and data integration tasks manually.

Therefore, end users can not, as yet, tap the potential of Open Data, but rather have to rely on applications built by others. Research into End User Programming aims to emancipate users from this dependence upon programmers and allow them to satisfy their individual needs with limited up-front learning time investment [10]. In this research tradition, widget-based mashups were developed as a visual programming paradigm that allows end users to compose ad-hoc applications by combining available widgets. Such applications use "*content from more than one source to create a single new service displayed in a single graphical interface*" [3], thereby increasing the value of existing data.

Following a widget-based mashup approach, we have developed a Linked Widgets platform[3] that aims to (i) provide universal practical utility without restrictions on domain or data sources, (ii) allow users to combine multiple Open Data sources and leverage their joint value, and (iii) allow novice users to analyze, integrate and visualize data.

The platform is built upon Semantic Web technologies and its design follows three guiding principles: openness, connectedness, and reusability. Openness distinguishes the platform from similar approaches and is the key for achieving our first objective, i.e., the capability to deal with various data sources. This openness should encourage developers to implement and add new widgets to the platform. End users can reuse and connect these widgets to collect, integrate, and combine data from different sources in a dynamic and creative manner.

To achieve the second goal, we use a graph-based model to semantically describe the input and output of a widget. The platform uses the annotated models to provide semantic search, data model matching, and auto composition. *Semantic search* is a mechanism for the discovery of widgets that help solve a given information problem. *Data model matching* allows the platform to highlight compatible widgets (i.e., signal the user which widgets can be connected). *Auto composition* is an innovative approach to compose complete applications automatically from a set of widgets. Research on the latter is still in an early stage of development and beyond the scope of this paper.

The remainder of this paper is organized as follows. In Sect. 2, we introduce key terms and outline the Linked Widget life cycle. Section 3 illustrates the potential of the platform by means of a sample use case. Section 4 introduces the Linked Widget model, Sect. 5 outlines the widget development process, and Sect. 6 discusses how widgets from different developers are connected. Section 7 provides pointers to related work and we conclude in Sect. 8 with an outlook on future research.

[3] http://linkedwidgets.org/

2 Linked Widget Life Cycle

Before we define the Linked Widget life cycle, it is necessary to define a set of basic terms and concepts. A widget is an "*interactive single purpose application for displaying and updating local data or data on the Web, packaged in a way to allow a single download and installation on a user's machine or mobile device*".[4] Widgets can make use of web services or web Application Programming Interfaces (APIs). Furthermore, they can access existing Open Data sources such as Open Governmental Data (OGD) and Linked Data.

Linked Widgets [18] are the key concept that our platform is based upon. They extend standard widgets with a semantic model following Linked Data principles. The semantic model describes data input/output and metadata such as provenance and license. In particular, the model consists of four main components: (i) *input terminals*, (ii) *output terminals*, (iii) *options*, and (iv) *a processing function*. Input/output terminals are used to connect widgets in a mashup and represent the data flow. Options are HTML inputs inside a widget. They provide a mechanism for users to control a widget's behavior. Finally, the processing function defines how widgets receive input and return their output.

We distinguish three types of widgets: *data widget*, *process widget*, and *presentation widget*. A *data widget* retrieves data from a data source and provides the collected data to other widgets. Hence, it has no input terminals. A *process widget* takes input data from other widgets, applies operations on the data, and provides the result to other widgets. It has both input and output terminals. A *presentation widget* has at least one input terminal and presents the data from another widget in a particular manner (e.g., textually or visually). It has no output terminals.

A *Mashup* is an interconnected combination of widgets. It should contain at least one data widget providing the data and one presentation widget to display the final results.

Figure 1 illustrates the Linked Widgets life cycle. Developers first implement and deploy their widgets on arbitrary servers; then, they pass the Uniform Resource Locator (URL) of the widget to the *widget annotator* module. This module allows them to add semantic annotations to their widgets. Next, the platform manager checks whether (i) the widget is accessible via the annotated URL and (ii) whether the used vocabularies conform to existing widgets to enforce consistency throughout the platform. After this validation process, the created widget model is stored permanently as Linked Data and is accessible through a SPARQL endpoint. A published widget can be revoked if, for instance, its corresponding Open Data source is no longer available. The platform uses Pubby[5] to provide dereferenceable Uniform Resource Identifiers (URIs).

Once widgets are made available on the platform, users can use them in their mashups. To this end, because the number of widgets and related Open Data sources may be large, users may first need to search for appropriate widgets. By

[4] http://www.w3.org/TR/widgets/

[5] http://wifo5-03.informatik.uni-mannheim.de/pubby/

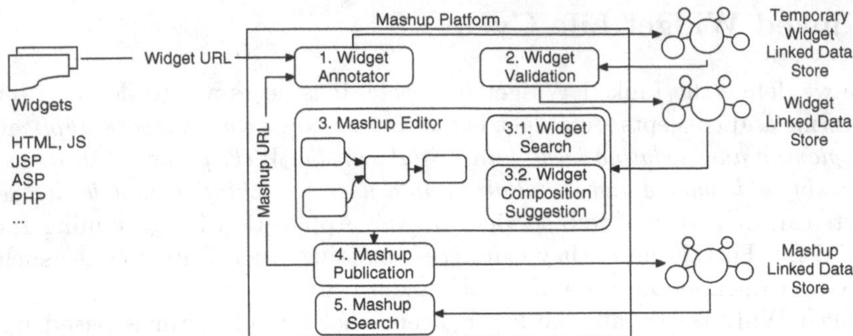

Fig. 1. Linked Widget life cycle

executing a SPARQL query over the semantic data repository of widget models in the background, the platform allows users to (i) search for widgets based on their input or output model, and (ii) for a selected terminal of a selected widget, find all terminals of other widgets that are compatible with it.

The final result of a mashup is directly displayed on the platform. Alternatively, it can also be shown via the *mashup publication* module and be shared and published on other websites. Users can also package a mashup as a new widget.

In conclusion, the platform is versatile, open and extensible. Maintaining this platform is economical since developers can store widgets externally and both the data retrieval and data processing tasks take place in either the client's browser or on the widget server. Finally, although widgets come from different developers and end users, they can be reused in an efficient manner: (i) users can creatively combine Linked Widgets from different developers to compose LOD applications, (ii) they can reuse LOD applications from others, but change the parameters of the constituent widgets, (iii) they can reuse a composed LOD application as a new widget, and (iv) based on available widgets, developers can implement new widgets to support new use cases.

3 Open Data Exploration

As the Open Data paradigm gains broad support, an increasingly relevant challenge is to provide means to utilize these data. The process of working with published Open Data sources should be as intuitive as possible, especially for users without a technical background. In this section we present a motivational scenario that illustrates how the platform allows users to handle Open Data sources in an innovative fashion and fosters (re)use of data.

We organize widgets into *widget collections* addressing different problem domains. Each collection might use various Open Data sources. For the example use case, consider a *tour guide* collection of seven widgets that combine data from *Google Maps*, *Last.fm*, *Flickr*, and *LinkedGeoData*.

- **Map Pointer:** Users can define a point on a map. The point's latitude and longitude is then returned as output.
- **Music Artist Search:** Via the last.fm API[6] this widget accepts an artist's name as an input and returns the corresponding URL.
- **Music Event by Artist:** Based on an artist URL this widget returns events this artist participates in while providing a time and event name filter. This is also done with the last.fm API.
- **Point of Interest Search:** This widget leverages the LinkedGeoData repository to find semantically encoded POIs. Users can influence the output by providing parameters. Users can select the type of POI and the radius of retrieved POIs with respect to the incoming location.
- **Flickr Geo Image Search:** By using the Flickr Image Search API[7] this widget enriches location data with images. Users may specify a radius and result limit.
- **Google Map:** This visualization widget displays points on a map. It is typically used to display the final results of a mashup.
- **Geo Merge:** This widget merges two lists of point data into a single list of pairs based on their distance. Users can specify a minimum and a maximum distance between points. The Geo Merge widget therefore serves two purposes, i.e., merging of two inputs into one output and filtering based on distance constraints.

Figure 2 shows one of the mashups in this collection. It covers the following scenario: *We are traveling to a city X and want to know whether our favorite*

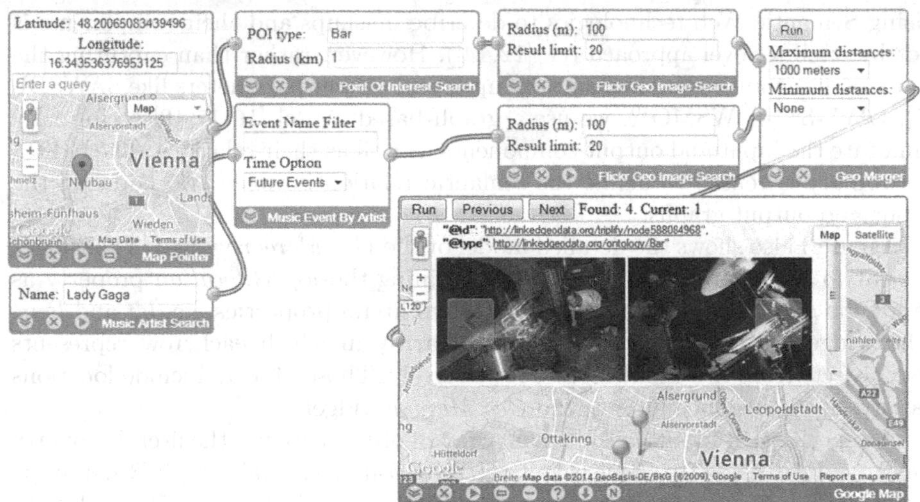

Fig. 2. A mashup example

[6] http://last.fm/api
[7] https://flickr.com/services/api/

music artist will give a concert there. After the concert, we want to go get a drink at a bar near the venue. Is there any combination of music events and bars which satisfy these conditions?

Google Map displays the enriched result. In our example, we get four pairings of a bar and a nearby music event that the artist is involved in. Each bar and music event combination is enriched with illustrative Flickr images and a URI pointing to the corresponding entities at LinkedGeoData and Last.fm.

Many other combinations of widgets are possible. The platform ensures the semantic validity of widget combinations. For example, we can find (i) all past or future music events for our artist on the map by wiring *Music Event By Artist* directly to *Google Map*, (ii) all POIs near a defined place by connecting *Point of Interest Search* to *Google Map* etc.

4 Linked Widget Model

We enrich the widget's input and output data with semantic models. These semantic I/O models are essential for the subsequent search and composition processes. Furthermore, they are crucial for the effective sharing of widgets. For example, even when the number of widgets available is limited (e.g. 43 for Yahoo! Pipes [15] and 300+ for Microsoft Popfly[8]), finding appropriate widgets needed to build a particular mashup solution is already a difficult task. Existing mashup platforms usually employ a text-based approach for widget search, which is not particularly helpful for advanced widget exploration and widget composition tasks.

Figure 3 presents a part of our ontology for the modeling of Linked Widgets. Using Semantic Web technologies to describe mashups and their components is not by itself a novel approach (cf. [12,14]). However, rather than capturing the functional semantics and focusing on input and output parameters like SAWSDL [7], OWL-S[9], or WSMO[10], we use a graph-based model [16,17,19] to formally annotate the input and output components as well as their relations. The *SWRL* vocabulary is reused to define the semantic relation between two nodes in the input and output graphs.

Figure 3 also shows the detailed model of the *Geo Merger* widget. The widget takes two arrays of arbitrary objects containing the *wgs84:location* property as input. Its domain is the *Point* class with two literal properties, i.e. *lat* and *long*. The widget output is a two-dimensional array in which each row represents two objects from two input arrays, respectively. Those objects include locations satisfying the distance filter of the *Geo Merger* widget.

To specify that input/output is an array of objects, we use the literal property *hasArrayDimension* (0: single element; $n > 0$: n-dimensional array). Because the input of *Geo Merger* is an "arbitrary" object, we apply the *owl:Thing* class to represent it in the data model.

[8] http://en.wikipedia.org/wiki/Microsoft_Popfly

[9] http://www.w3.org/Submission/OWL-S/

[10] http://www.w3.org/Submission/WSMO/

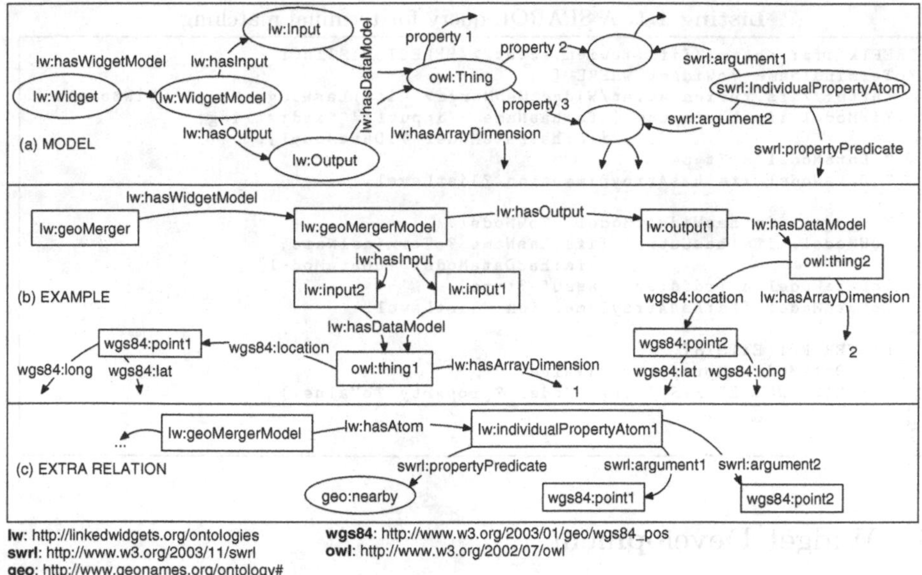

Fig. 3. General Linked Widget model and Geo Merger model

The *point*, *location*, *lat* and *long* terms are available in different vocabularies. However, since a well-established ontology facilitates data exchange between widgets, we chose *wgs84*. The *widget annotator* module interactively recommends frequently used terms of the most popular vocabularies to developers. This eases the annotation process and fosters consistency by diminishing the use of varying terms to describe the same concepts.

With SPARQL queries, we can find a widget that receives/outputs an object containing, for instance, geographic information. Moreover, based on an input terminal, e.g., the first input of *Geo Merger*, we can find all output terminals that can be connected (cf. Listing 1.1). Conditions that have to be satisfied for the terminals are: (i) matching type and array dimension; and (ii) matching attributes, i.e., the set of attributes required by the input terminal must be a subset of the attributes provided by the output terminal. In the *tour guide* collection, the outputs of *Map Pointer*, *Point of Interest Search*, *Flickr Geo Image Search*, and *Music Event by Artist* satisfy these conditions.

Similarly, we can model a more advanced widget. Its input and output have object attributes and there can be relations between those objects. For example, when modeling the *Geo Merger*, if required, we can present the *nearby* relation between the two input points as shown in Fig. 3. Due to the graph-based description, the platform can answer questions such as "find all widgets containing the *nearby* relation between two locations".

Listing 1.1. A SPARQL query for terminal matching

```
PREFIX ifs: <http://ifs.tuwien.ac.at/> SELECT DISTINCT
?oTerminalName ?oWidget WHERE {
  <http://ifs.tuwien.ac.at/WidgetGeoMerge>  ifs:hasWidgetModel  ?iWModel.
  ?iWModel ifs:hasInput  [ifs:hasName ''input1''^^xsd:string;
                          ifs:hasDataModel ?iDataModel].
  ?iDataModel a ?type.
  ?iDataModel ifs:hasArrayDimension ?listLevel.

  ?oWidget ifs:hasWidgetModel  ?oWModel.
  ?oWModel  ifs:hasOutput [ifs:hasName ?oTerminalName;
                           ifs:hasDataModel ?oDataModel]
  ?oDataModel a [rdfs:subClassOf ?type].
  ?oDataModel ifs:hasArrayDimension ?listLevel.

  FILTER NOT EXISTS{
    ?iDataModel ?property ?iValue.
    FILTER NOT EXISTS {?oDataModel ?property ?oValue.}
  }
}
```

5 Widget Development

Widgets may be created in two ways: either developers program them or end users create a mashup and save it as a new widget. In the former case, developers follow three steps: (i) inject a JavaScript file from the platform into the widget to equip it with the capability of cooperating with others, (ii) define the input and output configuration, and (iii) implement the JavaScript *run(data)* function which defines how the widget processes input data. If a widget has no input terminal, the corresponding *data* object is *null*. Otherwise, during runtime, the platform collects data from all relevant output terminals to build the *data* object and pass it to the *run* function as a parameter.

Developers can use arbitrary web languages. The *widget annotator* module can automatically generate a skeleton of the widget as well as sample data. Developers then only need to implement the *processing* function. We expect this simplicity of widget development will foster developers' productivity and creativity. Users hence have more means to explore and combine different Open Data sources.

6 Widget Cooperation

Technically, a Linked Widget is an HTML iframe wrapped in a widget skin. The platform automatically creates the skin to provide additional functionalities for the widget such as *create input and output terminals*, *run, cache, view output data*, and *resize widgets.*

Iframes can trigger events, which contain messages. These messages are then consumed by other iframes, which registered a listener for these events. Based on that, we implement a communication protocol that addresses the challenge of reusing and connecting different applications on top of Open Data. The protocol

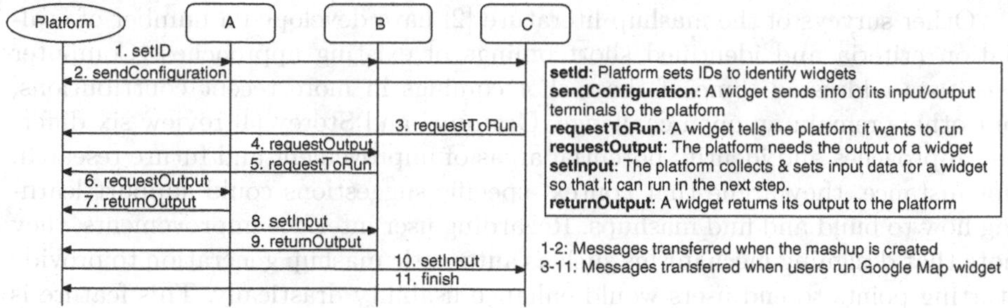

Fig. 4. An example of widget communication

is transparent to developers and can be easily extended to fit new use cases that require different types of data such as stream data or batch processed data.

As an example for how the protocol facilitates communication at runtime, consider a mashup with three widgets $A \rightarrow B \rightarrow C$. Typically, when a user triggers an action to run a widget, e.g., widget C, this action requires all widgets that provide input to this widget to run first. Because widget C requires the output from widget B, which in turn, requires output from widget A, widgets A and B need to run first. Figure 4 shows the messages transferred between the platform and the widgets. The first two messages are delivered when widgets are created for the mashup. The platform sets identifiers for all widgets and then receives their terminal configurations. The communication takes place entirely in the client's browser. After a user has created the mashup, the platform server is no longer needed because the browser and the widget's servers do the computation. This process reduces the platform-server load and improves performance and scalability.

7 Related Work

Researchers have been developing mashup-based tools for years. Many of them are geared towards end users and aim to allow them to efficiently create applications by connecting simple and lightweight entities.

Aghaee and Pautasso [1] provide a good overview of mashup approaches. They discuss open research challenges which we – at least partly – address with our platform. For instance, we address the *Simplicity* and *Expressive Power Tradeoff* challenges through a semantic model. They also evaluate Yahoo! Pipes [15], IBM Mashup Center[11], Presto Cloud[12], and ServFace [11]. A common limitation they identify for all these platforms is that the wiring paradigm is hard to grasp for non-expert end users. We aim to overcome this barrier, for instance, by recommending valid wiring options to the user.

[11] http://pic.dhe.ibm.com/infocenter/mashhelp/v3/index.jsp
[12] http://mdc.jackbe.com/enterprise-mashup

Other surveys of the mashup literature [2] have developed a number of evaluation criteria and identified shortcomings of existing approaches. Computer scientists addressed some of these shortcomings in more recent contributions, but others remain an open challenge. Grammel and Storey [4] review six different approaches and identify potential areas of improvement and future research. For instance, they argue that context-specific suggestions could support learning how to build and find mashups. Regarding user interface improvements, they note that designing mechanisms such as automatic mashup generation to provide starting points to end users would enhance usability drastically. This feature is also provided by the platform presented in this paper. However, detecting invalid mashups still remains a challenge that requires appropriate debugging mechanisms for non-programmers.

Super Stream Collider (SSC) [5], MashQL [6], and Deri Pipes [8] are three platforms aimed at semantic data processing. Whereas SSC consumes live stream data only, MashQL allows users to easily create a SPARQL query, using its custom query-by-diagram language. MashQL cannot aggregate data from different sources and its output visualization only supports text and table formats. Deri Pipes requires users to be familiar with Semantic Web technologies, SPARQL queries, and programming to perform semantic data processing tasks from different data sources. There are multiple other platforms which we only want to point at, such as Vegemite [9], Paggr [13], or Marmite [20]. They all follow a mashup-based approach to ease users' access to data sources, but unlike our approach, they do not make use of semantic models.

8 Conclusion and Future Work

This paper presents an overview of a extensible, generic, open, economical, and sharable mashup platform for the exploration of Open Data. The platform is aimed at end users without knowledge of Semantic Web technologies or programming skills. We encapsulate semantic, graph-based models inside Linked Widgets and provide mechanisms to annotate their inputs and outputs. Leveraging these annotations, the platform combines and searches widgets based on defined semantics.

Because we encourage developers to contribute their widgets to the platform and the widget development is language-independent, we expect to have a large number of versatile widgets in future. As a consequence, users can explore more Open Data sources and easily collect and combine desired information.

In the future, this system should serve as a universal data platform and bring together both mashup developers and mashup users. This will allow users to work with different kinds of data sources (e.g., governmental, financial, environmental data etc.) and types of data (e.g., open, linked, tabular data etc.), without technical barriers. From a data perspective, the vision is to support people in their everyday decision-making.

From a technical perspective, we aim to provide a mashup platform for the exploration of Open Data following Semantic Web design principles. We also want to push these ideas a step further by lifting non-semantic data on a semantic level and leverage its full potential.

Future research will focus on using the semantic models, especially for the widget auto-composition feature. We also need to improve the model-matching algorithm by utilizing ontology alignment techniques, since two models can use different resources from different ontologies. Another interesting direction for future research is the automatic creation of new widgets able to handle dynamic web data as an input source.

References

1. Aghaee, S., Pautasso, C.: End-user programming for web mashups: open research challenges. In: Harth, A., Koch, N. (eds.) ICWE 2011. LNCS, vol. 7059, pp. 347–351. Springer, Heidelberg (2012)
2. Aghaee, S., Pautasso, C.: An evaluation of mashup tools based on support for heterogeneous mashup components. In: Harth, A., Koch, N. (eds.) ICWE 2011. LNCS, vol. 7059, pp. 1–12. Springer, Heidelberg (2012)
3. Engard, N.C.: Library Mashups: Exploring New Ways to Deliver Library Data. Information Today, Medford (2009)
4. Grammel, L., Storey, M.-A.: A survey of mashup development environments. In: Chignell, M., Cordy, J., Ng, J., Yesha, Y. (eds.) The Smart Internet. LNCS, vol. 6400, pp. 137–151. Springer, Heidelberg (2010)
5. Nguyen Mau Quoc, H., Serrano, M., Le Phuoc, D., Hauswirth, M.: Super stream collider-linked stream mashups for everyone. In: Proceedings of the Semantic Web Challenge Co-located with ISWC2012, Nov 2012
6. Jarrar, M., Dikaiakos, M.D.: MashQL: a query-by-diagram topping SPARQL. In: Proceedings of the 2nd International Workshop on Ontologies and Information Systems for the Semantic Web. ONISW '08, pp. 89–96 (2008)
7. Kopecky, J., Vitvar, T., Bournez, C., Farrell, J.: SAWSDL: semantic annotations for WSDL and XML schema. IEEE Internet Comput. **11**(6), 60–67 (2007)
8. Le-Phuoc, D., Polleres, A., Hauswirth, M., Tummarello, G., Morbidoni, C.: Rapid prototyping of semantic mash-ups through semantic web pipes. In: Proceedings of the 18th International Conference on World Wide Web. WWW '09, pp. 581–590 (2009)
9. Lin, J., Wong, J., Nichols, J., Cypher, A., Lau, T.A.: End-user programming of mashups with vegemite. In: Proceedings of the 14th International Conference on Intelligent User Interfaces. IUI '09, pp. 97–106 (2009)
10. Nardi, B.A.: A Small Matter of Programming: Perspectives on End User Computing. MIT Press, Cambridge (1993)
11. Nestler, T., Feldmann, M., Hübsch, G., Preußner, A., Jugel, U.: The ServFace builder - a WYSIWYG approach for building service-based applications. In: Benatallah, B., Casati, F., Kappel, G., Rossi, G. (eds.) ICWE 2010. LNCS, vol. 6189, pp. 498–501. Springer, Heidelberg (2010)
12. Ngu, A.H.H., Carlson, M.P., Sheng, Q.Z., Paik, H.Y.: Semantic-based mashup of composite applications. IEEE Trans. Serv. Comput. **3**(1), 2–15 (2010)
13. Nowack, B.: Paggr: linked data widgets and dashboards. Web Semant. **7**(4), 272–277 (2009)

14. Pietschmann, S., Radeck, C., Meißner, K.: Semantics-based discovery, selection and mediation for presentation-oriented mashups. In: Proceedings of the 5th International Workshop on Web APIs and Service Mashups. Mashups '11, pp. 7:1–7:8 (2011)
15. Pruett, M.: Yahoo! Pipes, 1st edn. O'Reilly, Sebastopol (2007)
16. Taheriyan, M., Knoblock, C.A., Szekely, P., Ambite, J.L.: Rapidly integrating services into the linked data cloud. In: Cudré-Mauroux, P., et al. (eds.) ISWC 2012, Part I. LNCS, vol. 7649, pp. 559–574. Springer, Heidelberg (2012)
17. Taheriyan, M., Knoblock, C.A., Szekely, P., Ambite, J.L.: A graph-based approach to learn semantic descriptions of data sources. In: Alani, H., et al. (eds.) ISWC 2013, Part I. LNCS, vol. 8218, pp. 607–623. Springer, Heidelberg (2013)
18. Trinh, T.D., Do, B.L., Wetz, P., Anjomshoaa, A., Tjoa, A M.: Linked widgets: an approach to exploit open government data. In: Proceedings of International Conference on Information Integration and Web-Based Applications and Services. IIWAS '13, pp. 438–442 (2013)
19. Verborgh, R., Steiner, T., Van Deursen, D., Van de Walle, R., Gabarró Vallés, J.: Efficient runtime service discovery and consumption with hyperlinked RESTdesc. In: Proceedings of the 7th International Conference on Next Generation Web Services Practices, pp. 373–379, Oct 2011
20. Wong, J., Hong, J.I.: Making mashups with marmite: towards end-user programming for the web. In: Proceedings of the SIGCHI Conference on Human Factors in Computing Systems. CHI '07, pp. 1435–1444 (2007)

Poster Track

Annotating Ontologies with Descriptions of Vagueness

Panos Alexopoulos[1], Silvio Peroni[2,3](✉), Boris Villazon-Terrazas[1], and Jeff Z. Pan[4]

[1] ISOCO, Madrid, Spain
{palexopoulos,bvillazon}@isoco.com
[2] Department of Computer Science and Engineering, University of Bologna, Bologna, Italy
silvio.peroni@unibo.it
[3] STLab-ISTC, Consiglio Nazionale delle Ricerche, Rome, Italy
[4] Department of Computing Science, University of Aberdeen, Aberdeen, UK
jeff.z.pan@abdn.ac.uk

Abstract. Vagueness is a common linguistic phenomenon manifested by predicates that lack clear applicability conditions and boundaries such as *High*, *Expert* or *Bad*. The usage of vague terminology in ontology entities can hamper the latter's quality, primarily in terms of shareability and meaning explicitness. In this paper we present the Vagueness Ontology, a metaontology that enables the explicit identification and description of vague entities and their vagueness-related characteristics in ontologies, so as to make the latter's meaning more explicit.

1 Introduction

Ontologies are formal shareable conceptualizations of domains, describing the meaning of domain aspects in a common, machine-processable form by means of concepts and their interrelations [2]. As such, their role in the Semantic Web is very important as they enable the production and sharing of structured data that can be commonly understood among human and software agents. On the other hand, vagueness is a natural language phenomenon, demonstrated by concepts with blurred boundaries, like *tall*, *expert* etc., whose extensions is difficult to precisely determine (e.g. some people are borderline tall: neither clearly "*tall*" nor "*not tall*") [3]. When building ontologies, engineers and domain experts often use predicates that are vague. These, in turn, influence in a negative way the comprehension of these ontologies by other parties and limits their value as a reusable source of knowledge [1]. The reason is the subjective interpretation of vague definitions that can cause **disagreements** among the people who develop, maintain or use an ontology.

To reduce these disagreements we have put forward the notion of **vagueness-aware ontologies** [1], informally defined as *"ontologies whose vague elements are accompanied by comprehensive metainformation that describes the nature*

V. Presutti et al. (Eds.): ESWC Satellite Events 2014, LNCS 8798, pp. 185–189, 2014.
DOI: 10.1007/978-3-319-11955-7_15

and characteristics of their vagueness". An example of such metainformation is whether an ontology entity is vague or not; this is important as many ontology users may not immediately realize this. In this paper we show how vagueness-aware ontologies may be represented by means of the **Vagueness Ontology (VO)**, a metaontology that defines the necessary concepts, relations and attributes for creating explicit descriptions of vague ontology entities. VO is meant to be used by both producers and consumers of ontologies; the former will utilize it to **annotate** the vague part of their produced ontologies with relevant vagueness metainformation while the latter will **query** this metainformation and use it to make a better use of the vague ontologies.

2 The Vagueness Ontology

The Vagueness Ontology[1] enables the annotation of an ontological entity (class, relation or datatype) with a description of the nature and characteristic of its vagueness. A class is vague if, in the given domain, context or application scenario, it admits borderline cases, namely if there are (or could be) individuals for which it is indeterminate whether they instantiate the class (e.g., *"TallPerson"*, *"ExperiencedResearcher"*, etc.). Similarly, an object property (relation) is vague if there are (or could be) pairs of individuals for which it is indeterminate whether they stand in the relation (e.g., *"hasGenre"*, *"hasIdeology"*, etc.). The same applies for datatype properties and pairs of individuals and literal values. Finally, a vague datatype consists of a set of vague terms (e.g., *"RestaurantPriceRange"* with the terms *"cheap"*, *"moderate"* and *"expensive"*).

A vagueness description explicitly states whether the entity is vague or not. For example, the class *"StrategicClient"* defined as *"A client that has a high value for the company"* is vague while *"AmericanCompany"* as *"A company that has legal status in the Unites States"* is not. Moreover, it can often be the case that a seemingly vague entity can have a non-vague definition (e.g. *"TallPerson"* when defined as *"A person whose height is at least 180 cm"*). Then this element is not vague in the given ontology and that is something that needs to be explicitly stated. Also, vagueness can be quantitative or qualitative [3]. A predicate has quantitative vagueness if the existence of borderline cases stems from the lack of precise boundaries for the predicate along one or more dimensions (e.g. *"bald"* lacks sharp boundaries along the dimension of hair), and qualitative if there is a variety of conditions pertaining to the predicate, but it is not possible to make any crisp identification of those combinations which are sufficient for application (e.g., *"religion"*, *"strategic"*, etc.). Knowing the type of vagueness is important as elements with an intended (but not explicitly stated) quantitative vagueness can be considered by others as having qualitative one and vice versa. Also, when the entity has quantitative vagueness it is important to state explicitly its intended dimensions (e.g. the amount of R&D budget for the term *"strategic"*. Therefore, VO makes explicit the type of the entity's vagueness and the dimensions of the term's quantitative vagueness.

[1] Available at http://www.essepuntato.it/2013/10/vagueness.

Furthermore, vagueness is **subjective** and **context dependent**. The first has to do with the same vague entity being interpreted differently by different users. For example, two company executives might have different criteria for the entity *"StrategicClient"*, the one the amount of revenue this client has generated and the other the market in which it operates. Similarly, context dependence has to do with the same vague entity being interpreted differently in different contexts even by the same user; hiring a researcher in industry is different to hiring one in academia when it comes to judging his/her expertise and experience. Therefore, VO explicitly represents the **creator** of a vagueness annotation of a certain entity as well as the **applicability context** for which the entity is defined. Context-dependent can be (i) the description of vagueness of an entity (i.e. the same entity can be vague in one context and non-vague in another) and (ii) the dimensions related to a description of vagueness having quantitative type (i.e. the same entity can be vague in dimension A in one context and in dimension B in another).

Figure 1 depicts VO. To show how to use VO let us assume a scenario where the relation *ex:isExpertInResearchArea* is considered vague by John Doe in the context of researcher hiring and its vagueness is quantitative in the dimensions of the number of publications and the number of projects. The first dimension is related to the context of Academia while the second to the one of Industry. To represent this scenario we create an instance of the *VaguenessAnnotation* class and link it to its creator, the entity and a description of the entity's vagueness or non-vagueness:

```
ex:annotation a :VaguenessAnnotation ;
prov:wasAttributedTo ex:john-doe ;
  oa:hasBody ex:description-of-vagueness ;
  oa:hasTarget ex:isExpertInResearchArea .
ex:isExpertInResearchArea a owl:ObjectProperty .
ex:john-doe a prov:Agent .
```

Such a description is an instance of the class *DescriptionOfVagueness* or *DescriptionOfNonVagueness* respectively. Vagueness descriptions must specify a type and must provide at least one justification for considering the target ontological entity vague. Non-vagueness descriptions, instead, require only a justification and are used for entities that would typically be considered vague but which in the particular ontology are not (e.g. the *"TallPerson"* example mentioned above). Also, vagueness dimensions always refer to descriptions of quantitative vagueness and indicate some measurable characteristic of the annotated entity. Given this, the scenario's description of vagueness is represented as follows:

```
ex:description-of-vagueness a :DescriptionOfVagueness ;
  :hasJustification ex:justification ;
  :hasVaguenessType :quantitative-vagueness .
ex:justification a :Justification ;
  :hasNaturalLanguageText "It is not possible to define the exact minimum
      number of relevant publications and projects that make a researcher
      expert in a given area." ;
  :hasDimension ex:dimension-publications , ex:dimension-projects .
ex:dimension-publications a :Dimension ;
  :hasNaturalLanguageText "The number of relevant publications." .
ex:dimension-projects a :Dimension ;
  :hasNaturalLanguageText "The number of relevant projects." .
```

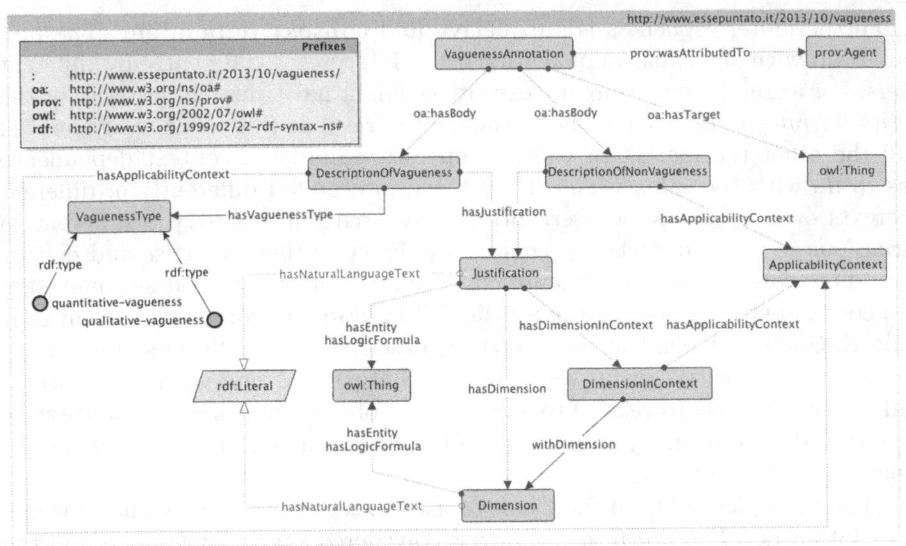

Fig. 1. Vagueness ontology structure.

Also, descriptions of vagueness/non-vagueness and related dimensions can be characterised by particular applicability contexts. This is facilitated by an assertion between the description and the related context through the object property *hasApplicabilityContext*. In the case of dimensions the context-dependent object is the *relation* between justifications and dimensions, therefore a reification of this relation is employed:

```
ex:description-of-vagueness
  :hasApplicabilityContext ex:researcher-hiring-context .
ex:researcher-hiring-context a :ApplicabilityContext .
ex:justification :hasDimensionInContext
  ex:dimension-publications-in-context , ex:dimension-projects-in-context .
ex:dimension-publications-in-context a :DimensionInContext ;
  :withDimension ex:dimension-publications ;
  :hasApplicabilityContext ex:academia-context .
ex:dimension-projects-in-context a :DimensionInContext ;
  :withDimension ex:dimension-projects ;
  :hasApplicabilityContext ex:industry-context .
ex:academia-context a :ApplicabilityContext .
ex:industry-context a :ApplicabilityContext .
```

3 Conclusions and Future Work

The Vagueness Ontology (VO) is a metaontology for annotating vague ontology entities with descriptions that describe the nature and characteristics of their vagueness in an explicit way. The idea is that even though the availability of the metainformation will not eliminate vagueness, it can help reduce the potentially high level of disagreement and low level of comprehensibility it may cause and achieve better shareability of vague semantic information. We are currently working towards facilitating the easier and more intuitive usage of VO for the production of vagueness-aware ontologies.

Acknowledgments. The research has been funded from the K-Drive project (FP7-286348).

References

1. Alexopoulos, P., Villazon-Terrazas, B., Pan, J.: Towards vagueness-aware semantic data. In: URSW. CEUR Workshop Proceedings, vol. 1073, pp. 40–45. CEUR-WS.org (2013)
2. Chandrasekaran, B., Josephson, J., Benjamins, R.: What are ontologies and why do we need them? IEEE Intell. Syst. **14**(1), 20–26 (1999)
3. Hyde, D.: Vagueness. Logic and Ontology, Ashgate New Critical Thinking in Philosophy (2008)

What Are the Important Properties of an Entity?

Comparing Users and Knowledge Graph Point of View

Ahmad Assaf[1](✉), Ghislain A. Atemezing[1], Raphaël Troncy[1], and Elena Cabrio[1,2]

[1] EURECOM, Sophia Antipolis, Nice, France
{ahmad.assaf,ghislain.atemezing,raphael.troncy}@eurecom.fr
[2] INRIA, Sophia Antipolis, Nice, France
elena.cabrio@inria.fr

Abstract. Entities play a key role in knowledge bases in general and in the Web of Data in particular. Entities are generally described with a lot of properties, this is the case for DBpedia. It is, however, difficult to assess which ones are more "important" than others for particular tasks such as visualizing the key facts of an entity or filtering out the ones which will yield better instance matching. In this paper, we perform a reverse engineering of the Google Knowledge graph panel to find out what are the most "important" properties for an entity according to Google. We compare these results with a survey we conducted on 152 users. We finally show how we can represent and explicit this knowledge using the Fresnel vocabulary.

Keywords: Entities · Google Knowledge graph · Visualization · Knowledge extraction

1 Introduction

In many knowledge bases, entities are described with numerous properties. However, not all properties have the same importance. Some properties are considered as keys for performing instance matching tasks while other properties are generally chosen for quickly providing a summary of the key facts attached to an entity. Our motivation is to provide a method enabling to select what properties should be used when depicting the summary of an entity, for example in a multimedia question answering system such as QakisMedia[1] or in a second screen application providing more information about a particular TV program[2].

Our approach consists in: (i) reverse engineering the Google Knowledge Panel by extracting the properties that Google considers as sufficiently important to

[1] http://qakis.org/
[2] http://www.linkedtv.eu/demos/linkednews/

V. Presutti et al. (Eds.): ESWC Satellite Events 2014, LNCS 8798, pp. 190–194, 2014.
DOI: 10.1007/978-3-319-11955-7_16

show (Sect. 2), and (ii) analyzing users' preferences by conducting a user survey and comparing the results (Sect. 3). We finally show how we can explicitly represent this knowledge of preferred properties to attach to an entity using the Fresnel vocabulary before concluding (Sect. 4).

2 Reverse Engineering the Google KG Panel

Web scraping is a technique for extracting data from Web pages. We aim at capturing the properties depicted in the Google Knowledge Panel (GKP) that are injected in search result pages [1]. We have developed a Node.js application that queries all DBpedia concepts that have at least one instance which is `owl:sameAs` with a Freebase resource in order to increase the probability that the search engine result page (SERP) for this resource will contain a GKP. We assume in our experiment that the properties displayed for an entity are "entity type dependent" and that context (country, query, time, etc.) can affect the results. Moreover, we filter out generic concepts by excluding those who are direct subclasses of `owl:Thing` since they will trigger ambiguous queries. We obtained a list of 352 concepts[3].

For each of these concepts, we retrieve n instances[4]. For each of these instances, we issue a search query to Google containing the instance label. Google does not serve the GKP for all user agents and we had to mimic a browser behavior by setting the $User-Agent$ to a particular browser. We use CSS selectors to extract data from a GKP. An example of a query selector is *_om* (all elements with class name *_om*) which returns the property DOM element(s) for the concept described in the GKP. From our experiments, we found out that we do not always get a GKP in a SERP. If this happens, we disambiguate the instance by issuing a new query with the concept type attached. However, if no GKP was found again, we capture that for manual inspection later on. Listing 1 gives the high level algorithm for extracting the GKP. The full implementation can be found at https://github.com/ahmadassaf/KBE.

3 Evaluation

We conducted a user survey in order to compare what users think should be the important properties to display for a particular entity and what the GKP shows.

User survey. We set up a survey[5] on February 25th, 2014 and for three weeks in order to collect the preferences of users in term of the properties they would like to be shown for a particular entity. We select one representative entity for nine classes: `TennisPlayer`, `Museum`, `Politician`, `Company`, `Country`, `City`, `Film`, `SoccerClub` and `Book`. 152 participants have provided answers, 72 % from

[3] SPARQL query: http://goo.gl/EYuGm1.

[4] In our experiment, n was equal to 100 random instances.

[5] The survey is at http://eSurv.org?u=entityviz.

Algorithm 1. Google Knowledge Panel reverse engineering Algorithm

```
INITIALIZE equivalentClasses(DBpedia, Freebase) AS vectorClasses
Upload vectorClasses for querying processing
Set n AS number-of-instances-to-query
for each conceptType ∈ vectorClasses do
    SELECT n instances
    listInstances ← SELECT-SPARQL(conceptType, n)
    for each instance ∈ listInstances do
        CALL http://www.google.com/search?q=instance
        if knowledgePanel exists then
            SCRAP GOOGLE KNOWLEDGE PANEL
        else
            CALL http://www.google.com/search?q=instance + conceptType
            SCRAP GOOGLE KNOWLEDGE PANEL
        end if
        gkpProperties ← GetData(DOM, EXIST(GKP))
    end for
    COMPUTE occurrence for each prop ∈ gkpProperties
end for
return gkpProperties
```

Table 1. Agreement on properties between the users and the Knowledge Graph Panel

Classes	TennisPlayer	Museum	Politician	Company	Country	City	Film	SoccerClub	Book
Agr.	20 %	66.97 %	50 %	40 %	60 %	60 %	60 %	50 %	60 %

academia, 20 % coming from the industry and 8 % having not declared their affiliation. 94 % of the respondents have heard about the Semantic Web while 35 % were not familiar with specific visualization tools. The detailed results[6] show the ranking of the top properties for each entity. We only keep the properties having received at least 10 % votes for comparing with the properties depicted in a KGP. Hence, users do not seem to be interested in the `INSEE code` identifying a French city while they expect to see the `population` or the `points of interest` of this city.

Comparison with the Knowledge Graphs. The results of the Google Knowledge Panel (GKP) extraction[7] clearly show a long tail distribution of the properties depicted by Google, with a top N properties (N being 4, 5 or 6 depending on the entity) counting for 98 % of the properties shown for this type. We compare those properties with the ones revealed by the user study. Table 1 shows the agreement between the users and the choices made by Google in the GKP for the 9 classes. The highest agreement concerns the type `Museum` (66.97 %) while the lowest one is for the `TennisPlayer` (20 %) concept. We think properties for museums or Books are more stable (no many variety) while for entities categories of Person/Agent, they change a lot according to the status, the function, etc. And so more subjective.

With this set of 9 concepts, we are covering 301, 189 DBpedia entities that have an existence in Freebase, and for each of them, we can now empirically

[6] https://github.com/ahmadassaf/KBE/blob/master/results/agreement-gkp-users.xls

[7] https://github.com/ahmadassaf/KBE/blob/master/results/survey.json

define the most important properties when there is an agreement between one of the biggest knowledge base (Google) and users preferences.

Modeling the preferred properties with Fresnel. Fresnel[8] is a presentation vocabulary for displaying RDF data. It specifies *what* information contained in an RDF graph should be presented with the core concept `fresnel:Lens` [2]. We use the Fresnel and PROV-O ontologies[9] to explicitly represent what properties should be depicted when displaying an entity.

```
:tennisPlayerGKPDefaultLens rdf:type fresnel:Lens ;
    fresnel:purpose fresnel:defaultLens ;
    fresnel:classLensDomain dbpedia-owl:TennisPlayer ;
    fresnel:group :tennisPlayerGroup ;
    fresnel:showProperties (dbpedia-owl:abstract dbpedia-owl:birthDate
         dbpedia-owl:birthPlace dbpprop:height dbpprop:weight
         dbpprop:turnedpro dbpprop:siblings) ;
    prov:wasDerivedFrom
      <http://www.google.com/insidesearch/features/search/knowledge.html> .
```

4 Conclusion and Future Work

We have shown that it is possible to reveal what are the "important" properties of entities by reverse engineering the choices made by Google when creating knowledge graph panels and by comparing users preferences obtained from a user survey. Our motivation is to represent this choice explicitly, using the Fresnel vocabulary, so that any application could read this configuration file for deciding which properties of an entity is worth to visualize. This is fundamentally different from the work in [4] where the authors created a generalizable approach to open up closed knowledge bases like Google's by means of crowd-sourcing the knowledge extraction task. We are aware that this knowledge is highly dynamic, the Google Knowledge Graph panel varies across geolocation and time. We have provided the code that enables to perform new calculation at run time and we aim to study the temporal evolution of what are important properties on a longer period. This knowledge which has been captured will be made available shortly in a SPARQL endpoint. We are also investigating the use of Mechanical Turk to perform a larger survey for the complete set of DBpedia classes.

Acknowledgments. This work has been partially supported by the ANR Datalift (ANR-10-CORD-009) and UCN (ANR-11-LABX-0031-01) projects.

References

1. Bergman, M.: Deconstructing the Google Knowledge Graph. http://www.mkbergman.com/1009/deconstructing-the-google-knowledge-graph

---

[8] http://www.w3.org/2005/04/fresnel-info/

[9] http://www.w3.org/TR/prov-o/

2. Pietriga, E., Bizer, C., Karger, D.R., Lee, R.: Fresnel: a browser-independent presentation vocabulary for RDF. In: Cruz, I., Decker, S., Allemang, D., Preist, C., Schwabe, D., Mika, P., Uschold, M., Aroyo, L.M. (eds.) ISWC 2006. LNCS, vol. 4273, pp. 158–171. Springer, Heidelberg (2006)
3. Shneiderman, B.: The eyes have it: a task by data type taxonomy for information visualizations. In: IEEE Symposium on Visual Languages, pp. 336–343 (1996)
4. Steiner, T., Mirea, S.: SEKI@home or crowdsourcing an open knowledge graph. In: 1st International Workshop on Knowledge Extraction and Consolidation from Social Media (KECSM'12), Boston, USA (2012)

RuQAR: Reasoning Framework for OWL 2 RL Ontologies

Jaroslaw Bak(✉), Maciej Nowak, and Czeslaw Jedrzejek

Institute of Control and Information Engineering, Poznan University of Technology,
M. Sklodowskiej-Curie Sqr. 5, 60-965 Poznan, Poland
{jaroslaw.bak,czeslaw.jedrzejek}@put.poznan.pl

Abstract. This paper addresses the first release of the Rule-based Query Answering and Reasoning framework (RuQAR). The tool provides the ABox reasoning and query answering with OWL 2 RL ontologies executed by forward chaining rule reasoners. We describe current implementation and an experimental evaluation of RuQAR by performing reasoning on the number of benchmark ontologies. Additionally, we compare obtained results with inferences provided by HermiT and Pellet. The evaluation shows that we can perform the ABox reasoning with considerably better performance than DL-based reasoners.

1 Introduction and Motivation

Ontologies in information systems are becoming more and more popular in various fields, such as web technologies, database integration, multi agent systems, natural language processing, etc. However, in order to utilize all features that an ontology provides we need to apply a reasoning engine. Moreover, we can use different engines with ontologies expressed in different OWL 2 Profiles[1] (as well as in different fragments of OWL 1.1[2], eg. Horn-$\mathcal{SHIQ}$). One of the most interesting profile is OWL 2 RL which enables the implementation of polynomial time reasoning algorithms in a standard rule engine. Nonetheless, a naive implementation of OWL 2 RL reasoner is known to perform poorly with large ABoxes [2]. Moreover, since the official list[3] of OWL 2 reasoners supporting OWL 2 RL is limited, we are motivated to provide such a tool. We intent to apply OWL 2 RL reasoning in a rule-based system in an efficient way. Description logic-based reasoners handle the TBox entailments better than the ABox ones. However, the ABox reasoning can be performed more efficiently by a rule engine [3]. Nevertheless, we do not limit ourselves to one particular engine or implementation. Instead, we aim at providing easy-to-use framework for performing the ABox reasoning with OWL 2 RL ontologies in any forward chaining rule engine which will be applicable in many rule-based applications. Thus, we

[1] http://www.w3.org/TR/owl2-profiles/

[2] http://www.w3.org/Submission/owl11-overview/

[3] http://www.w3.org/2001/sw/wiki/OWL/Implementations

V. Presutti et al. (Eds.): ESWC Satellite Events 2014, LNCS 8798, pp. 195–198, 2014.
DOI: 10.1007/978-3-319-11955-7_17

have developed the Abstract Syntax of Rules and Facts (ASRF) which can be easily applied in different rule engines. Moreover, since the interoperability with the widely-used Semantic Web Rule Language (SWRL) is desired in many practical applications, we included it in the ASRF syntax. Moreover, SWRL Built-ins are also supported.

In this paper, we describe the RuQAR (Rule-based Query Answering and Reasoning) framework. The main goal of the tool is to support query answering and reasoning with semantic data stored in a relational database. However, current implementation enables ontology-based reasoning using a standard forward chaining rule engine. We present the reasoning features that are already applicable in any application. Those features will be used in future development of RuQAR. Current implementation supports the OWL 2 RL Profile and DL-safe SWRL rules which are crucial in many Semantic Web applications.

2 The RuQAR Framework

Application of a rule engine to an ontology-based reasoning requires a transformation method of an ontology into a set of rules. According to this RuQAR implements a method of transforming an OWL 2 ontology into a set of rules and a set of facts expressed in ASRF. The transformation schema is presented in Fig. 1. Firstly, an OWL 2 ontology is loaded into the HermiT[4] engine. Then, the TBox reasoning is executed. Finally, the inferred ontology is transformed into two sets: one of rules and one of facts. Both are expressed in the ASRF notation which enables easy translation into the language of a rule engine.

In ontology-to-ASRF transformation we translate each logical ontology axiom into its equivalent rule. For example, if the *prp-symp* axiom of OWL 2 RL defines a symmetric property P, then the axiom can be expressed as the following rule: $triple(?x, P, ?y) \rightarrow triple(?y, P, ?x)$, where $?x$ and $?y$ are variables. Such a rule operates on the ABox part only. As a result the transformation materializes the semantics of a given ontology in the set of Datalog-like rules (we consider it as a non-naive translation).

The reasoning process is divided into two sub-processes: for the TBox reasoning and for the ABox reasoning. The TBox reasoning is performed by HermiT during the transformation, while the ABox reasoning is performed by a rule engine. By loading a translated and inferred ontology, produced by HermiT, into the rule engine we can produce more entailments during the ABox reasoning than those supported by OWL 2 RL. However, it depends on an applied

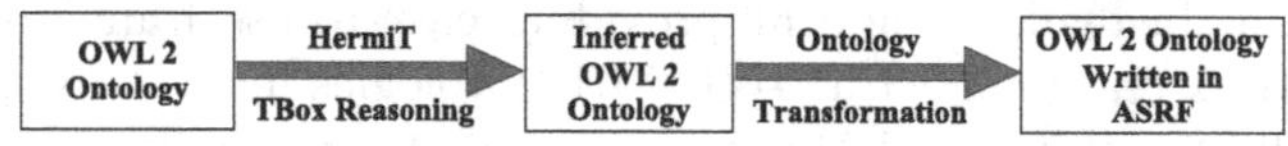

Fig. 1. OWL 2 ontology transformation schema.

[4] http://www.hermit-reasoner.com/

ontology (whether or not it uses constructs that are beyond the OWL 2 RL Profile).

Using ASRF sets produced by RuQAR one can apply it in any forward chaining rule engine by implementing mappings between ASRF and the language of the engine. Nevertheless, RuQAR implements translation into two rule engines: Jess[5] and Drools[6]. Both translations can be performed automatically. Moreover, ASRF is similar to syntaxes of well-known rule engines like Jess or Clips. More information about RuQAR and ASRF can be found at RuQAR's web page[7].

3 Evaluation

We evaluated RuQAR using test ontologies taken from the KAON2 website[8]: Vicodi - an ontology about European history, Semintec - an ontology about financial domain and LUBM - an ontology benchmark about organizational structures of universities. We used different datasets of each ontology (Semintec_0, Semintec_1, etc.) where the higher number means bigger ABox set. Our tests were performed on a Windows 7 desktop machine with Java 1.7 update 25 while the maximum heap space was set to 1 GB.

Evaluation schema for each ontology was the following. Firstly, we performed the TBox reasoning using HermiT. Then, an inferred ontology was loaded into each tested engine and the ABox reasoning was executed. In each case we recorded the reasoning time and counted the size of the resulting ABox. We performed the ABox reasoning with the following engines: Jess, Drools, HermiT

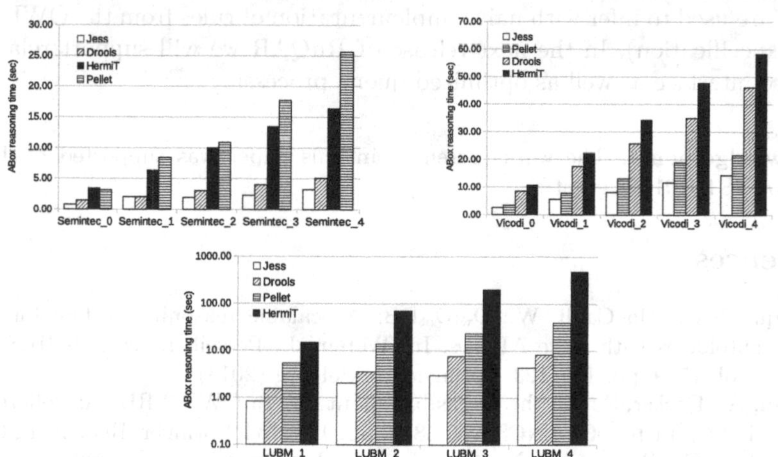

Fig. 2. The ABox reasoning times of the tested ontologies.

[5] http://jessrules.com/

[6] http://www.jboss.org/drools/

[7] http://etacar.put.poznan.pl/jaroslaw.bak/RuQAR.php

[8] http://kaon2.semanticweb.org/

and Pellet[9]. We verified that the reasoners produced identical results (a similar empirical approach is applied in [1,4] in order to compare their OWL 2 RL reasoners with Pellet/RacerPro and HermiT, respectively). However, HermiT and Pellet provided more reasoning results in the LUBM case. It is correct, since only Vicodi is within the OWL 2 RL Profile. Nevertheless, all results inferred by Jess and Drools were among the results produced by HermiT/Pellet. Generally, we obtained better performance in the ABox reasoning with Jess/Drools than with HermiT or Pellet (see Fig. 2). However, in the Vicodi case Pellet was on the second place. The reason for that is that Vicodi contains large number of classes - which means that the reasoning produces many new triples. Drools performs slower than Jess in creating new triples (or checking if a triple exists in the working memory) since it uses pure Java classes (while Jess uses its own classes). Nevertheless, the obtained results confirm that RuQAR increases the performance of the ABox reasoning in comparison to the DL-based reasoners.

4 Conclusions and Future Work

In this paper we presented RuQAR which is the first release of a reasoning framework for OWL 2 RL ontologies. This tool enables ontology transformation into rules and facts expressed in the ASRF syntax. The translation from ASRF into Jess and Drools is also provided. Moreover, we described the reasoning schema, preliminary implementation as well as performed experiments. To the best of our knowledge presented work is the first not-naive implementation of the OWL 2 RL reasoning in Drools and Jess which can be applied in any application requiring efficient ABox reasoning (except the work presented in [4], where these engines are used to infer with naive implementation of rules from the OWL 2 RL Profile specification). In the next release of RuQAR we will support relational database interface as well as optimized query processing.

Acknowledgements. The work presented in this paper was supported by UMO-2011/03/N/ST6/01602 grant.

References

1. Faruqui, R.U., MacCaull, W.: $\mathsf{O_{wl}O_{nt}DB}$: A scalable reasoning system for OWL 2 RL ontologies with large ABoxes. In: Weber, J., Perseil, I. (eds.) FHIES 2012. LNCS, vol. 7789, pp. 105–123. Springer, Heidelberg (2013)
2. Hogan, A., Decker, S.: On the ostensibly silent 'W' in OWL 2 RL. In: Polleres, A., Swift, T. (eds.) RR 2009. LNCS, vol. 5837, pp. 118–134. Springer, Heidelberg (2009)
3. Meditskos, G., Bassiliades, N.: Combining a DL reasoner and a rule engine for improving entailment-based OWL reasoning. In: Sheth, A.P., Staab, S., Dean, M., Paolucci, M., Maynard, D., Finin, T., Thirunarayan, K. (eds.) ISWC 2008. LNCS, vol. 5318, pp. 277–292. Springer, Heidelberg (2008)
4. O'Connor, M.J., Das, A.: A pair of OWL 2 RL reasoners. In: Klinov, P., Horridge, M. (eds.) OWLED. CEUR Workshop Proceedings, vol. 849. CEUR-WS.org (2012)

[9] http://clarkparsia.com/pellet/

An Investigation of HTTP Header Information for Detecting Changes of Linked Open Data Sources

Renata Dividino, André Kramer, and Thomas Gottron(✉)

WeST – Institute for Web Science and Technologies,
University of Koblenz-Landau, Koblenz, Germany
{dividino,akramer,gottron}@uni-koblenz.de

Abstract. Data on the Linked Open Data (LOD) cloud changes frequently. Applications that operate on local caches of Linked Data need to be aware of these changes. In this way they can update their cache to ensure operating on the most recent version of the data. Given the HTTP basis recommended in the Linked Data guidelines, the native way of detecting changes would be to use HTTP header information, such as the *Last-Modified* field. However, it is uncertain to which degree this field is currently supported on the LOD cloud and how reliable the provided information is. In this paper, we analyse a large-scale dataset obtained from the LOD cloud by weekly crawls over almost two years. On these weekly snapshots, we observed that for only 15 % of the Linked Data resources the HTTP header field *Last-Modified* is actually available and that the date provided for the last modification aligns in only 8 % with the observed changes of the data itself.

1 Introduction and Background

The Linked Open Data (LOD) cloud is a global information space to structurally represent and connect data items. The LOD principles provide a flexible publishing paradigm to integrate and interlink any kind of data from arbitrary datasets, published by various data providers on the Web. The distributed, Web-based nature of the data motivates many applications to keep local copies of the data. Data is fetched live from the Web only in those cases where the data is missing or known to be highly dynamic [5]. However, given the rate of changes of Linked Data [3] also local caches need to be updated from time to time [2]. Thus, the question is when to perform such an update.

A intuitive approach to this task is to exploit the way Linked Data is provided on the Web. According to the Linked Data guidelines resources should be modelled using dereferenceable HTTP Uniform Resource Identifiers (URIs). Whenever a client application invokes an HTTP request to a server for a particular URI on the LOD cloud, the server should respond by providing useful information about the entity represented by this URI. Naturally, this response will make use of the HTTP protocol itself. The HTTP header of this response

V. Presutti et al. (Eds.): ESWC Satellite Events 2014, LNCS 8798, pp. 199–203, 2014.
DOI: 10.1007/978-3-319-11955-7_18

can contain metadata about the resource (e.g. owner, creation date, etc.) [1]. Among these metadata there is a field which can denote when the resource behind this URI has been changed last. In combination with an HTTP HEAD request this *Last-Modified* field is intended for probing a resource for whether or not it has been changed since its inclusion in the cache of a Web or Linked Data application.

Nevertheless, even with existing W3C specifications which define rules and conditions to be followed by the LOD servers, the information contained in the HTTP headers may in practice be inaccurate or wrong [4]. Therefore, applications relying on such information are susceptible to draw wrong conclusions. In this paper, we empirically evaluate the conformance of time related HTTP header metadata information on the LOD cloud. In particularly, we check for the conformance of the *Last-Modified* field. Knowledge about the reliability of this field is important for applications which intend to make use of it.

To this end, we analyse a large-scale dataset that is obtained from the LOD cloud by weekly crawls from the period between May, 2012 and January, 2014. The dataset contains 84 snapshots. For each pair of subsequent snapshots, we check for changes in the data and compare the observations to the information provided by the *Last-Modified* HTTP header field. Using the results of our experiments, we discuss the benefits of the availability and conformance of the HTTP header fields in real world scenarios.

2 Linked Data Metadata: The HTTP Header

The LOD cloud is composed by various data servers which enable data access via the HTTP protocol. A client application invokes an HTTP request to a server by, for instance, sending a HTTP GET message for a particular URI. The Linked Data server responds via HTTP by sending meaningful information for the represented resource, ideally using RDF as data format. The HTTP response header is mainly composed by:

1. The status code information about the request. For instance, a status code of 200 is the standard response for successful HTTP requests. This means that information about the resource is successfully returned. A code of 303 indicates a reference to another URI which can actually provide the requested resource. Also this response is encountered frequently on the LOD cloud, as it implements a technical solution to differentiate between the URI representing a real world entity and the URL providing the description about it. Finally, a response code in the range of 400 or 500 indicates errors on the client or server side.
2. Metadata about the resource. Some of the standard response header fields are: (1) *Content-Language* which indicates the language of the content, (2) *Content-Length*, the length of the response body in octets, (3) *Content-Type*, the MIME type of this content, (4) *Date*, the date and time that the message was sent, and (5) *Server*, indicating the name for the server.

In this work we focus on the analysis of the header field *Last-Modified*. HTTP/1.1 servers should send a *Last-Modified* value whenever feasible. This field is intended for a date when the requested object has been modified last. In the context of Linked Data, this corresponds to the most recent date at which (some part of) the resources' RDF description has changed. Following the HTTP/1.1 specification [1], the *Last-Modified* value must not be later than the time of the server's response message. In such cases, where the resource's last modification would indicate some time in the future it is to be considered invalid. Furthermore, the server should obtain the *Last-Modified* value as close as possible to the time that it generates the *Date* value of its response. This allows a recipient to make an accurate assessment of the entity's modification time.

3 Empirical Evaluation of the Conformance of the *Last-Modified* HTTP Header Field

The main goal of our experiments is to measure the degree of how often the *Last-Modified* field in HTTP header of LOD resources is available and how often it is used correctly. We consider the use to be correct if the fields returns a date and time which does not violate the observations of when the data for a resource has changed last. For this purpose, we work with data from the Dynamic Linked Data Observatory (DyLDO) [3]. The DyLDO dataset has been created to monitor a fixed set of Linked Data documents (and their neighborhood) on a weekly basis. For the sake of consistency, we use only the kernel seed documents of DyLDO. Our test dataset is composed of 84 snapshots corresponding to a period of almost two years (from May, 2012 until January, 2014). Furthermore, the DyLDO dataset contains (parts of) various well known and large LOD sources, e.g., dbpedia.org, musicbrainz.com, and bbc.co.uk. For more detailed information about the DyLDO dataset, we refer the reader to [3].

Each version of the DyLDO dataset consists of a set of RDF triples retrieved from different LOD sources. Furthermore, the data provides also information about the HTTP headers received when retrieving the data. From the 84 snapshots available in the dataset, we took each pair of subsequent snapshots from the same data source and computed the set difference over their set of triples. If we observe a difference we consider the data to have changed, otherwise we treat it as unchanged. A change should be reflected by a *Last-Modified* date which lies in the time range between the two snapshots of the data.

Figure 1(a) illustrates that on average only 15 % of the resources actually do provide some value for the *Last-Modified* field in the HTTP Header. Subsequently, we checked for those resources which provide a value for the *Last-Modified* field, how many of them return a correct or an incorrect value (see Fig. 1(b)). As mentioned above, correct values are the ones where the last modified data aligns with actual changes in the RDF data. Incorrect values includes (1) values that indicate changes but no change has been observed, (2) values

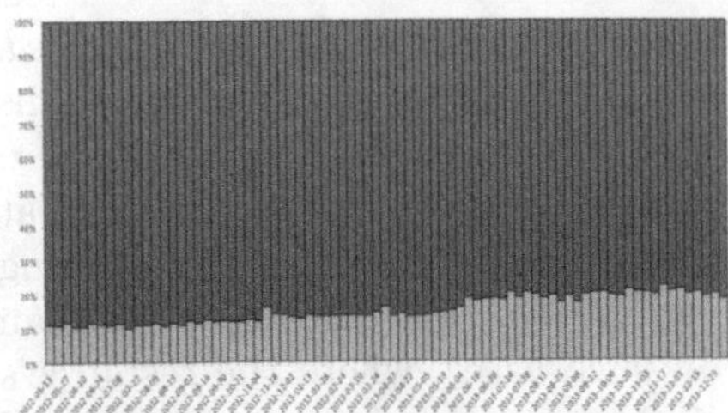

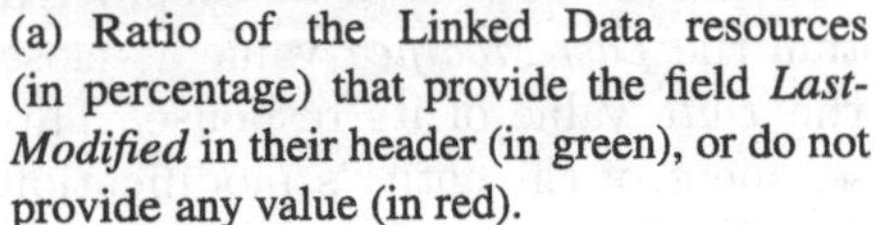

(a) Ratio of the Linked Data resources (in percentage) that provide the field *Last-Modified* in their header (in green), or do not provide any value (in red).

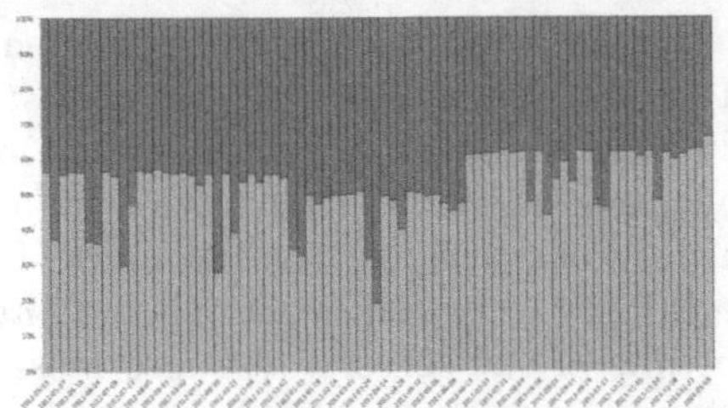

(b) Ratio of the resources (in percentage) providing a *Last-Modified* that is correct (in green), or incorrect or invalid (in red).

Fig. 1. Availability and correctness of the *Last-Modified* HTTP header field

that indicate no changes but changes have been observed and (3) invalid values. Invalid values are the ones which indicate a time in the future relative to the time of the HTTP response or which indicate a time of last modification which actually precedes the time at which the resource was created. On average, we observe that only 52 % of the resources which provide a value for the *Last-Modified* field provide also a correct value for it. The slight growth of both ratios in Fig. 1 towards the end of the time period covered by the dataset is an artefact caused by data sources going offline, i.e. not responding or providing a 400 or 500 status code as response. It seems that more data sources providing no or wrong *Last-Modified* went offline during the covered time span.

4 Summary and Discussion

In this paper we evaluated the conformance of LOD data source to provide a valid and correct *Last-Modified* HTTP header field, which indicates the date and time at which the resource was last modified. Our experiment shows that overall and on average only 8 % of the resources in the datasets provide correct values for this field. This number is far too low to be of use for any practical application. It is, however, not clear why LOD sources do not provide valid information. We conjecture that some default configuration of LOD servers leads to this misbehaviour.

The reliable provision of meta data in the context of the established HTTP protocol would be beneficial to the entire Web of Data. Many base technologies such as Linked Data caches and indexes may benefit of this information since a simple check on this metadata could support their decision process of determining which sources need to be updated. In conclusion, with this work we point out the dimension of the problem of erroneous and missing information of the HTTP header for Linked Data. Thereby, we motivate LOD sources to publish correct and valid values to support application needs. We believe that publishing correct the HTTP Header information is a step towards quality-oriented data usage in the LOD cloud.

Acknowledgements. The research leading to these results has received funding from the European Community's Seventh Framework Programme (FP7/2007–2013), REVEAL (Grant agree number 610928).

References

1. Fielding, R., Gettys, J., Mogul, J., Frystyk, H., Masinter, L., Leach, P., Berners-Lee, T.: Hypertext transfer protocol-http/1.1 (1999)
2. Gottron, T., Gottron, C.: Perplexity of index models over evolving linked data. In: Presutti, V., d'Amato, C., Gandon, F., d'Aquin, M., Staab, S., Tordai, A. (eds.) ESWC 2014. LNCS, vol. 8465, pp. 161–175. Springer, Heidelberg (2014)
3. Käfer, T., Abdelrahman, A., Umbrich, J., O'Byrne, P., Hogan, A.: Observing linked data dynamics. In: Cimiano, P., Corcho, O., Presutti, V., Hollink, L., Rudolph, S. (eds.) ESWC 2013. LNCS, vol. 7882, pp. 213–227. Springer, Heidelberg (2013)
4. Stadtmüller, S., Maurino, A., Rula, A., Palmonari, M., Harth, A.: On the diversity and availability of temporal information in linked open data. In: Cudré-Mauroux, P., et al. (eds.) ISWC 2012, Part I. LNCS, vol. 7649, pp. 492–507. Springer, Heidelberg (2012)
5. Umbrich, J., Hausenblas, M., Hogan, A., Polleres, A., Decker, S.: Towards dataset dynamics: change frequency of linked open data sources. In: LDOW (2010)

A Semantic Approach to Support Cross Border e-Justice

Enrico Francesconi[1(✉)], Ginevra Peruginelli[1], Ernst Steigenga[2], and Daniela Tiscornia[1]

[1] ITTIG-CNR, via de' Barucci 20, Florence, Italy
francesconi@ittig.cnr.it
[2] Ministry of Security and Justice, The Hague, The Netherlands

Abstract. The possibility to file and exchange legal procedures between European Member States is essential to increase cross-border relations in a pan-European e-Justice area. In this paper an overview of the e-Delivery platform developed within the e-CODEX project, as well as the semantic solution conceived to transmit business documents within a scenario characterized by different languages and different legal systems, are described.

Keywords: e-Justice · Semantic interoperability · Knowledge representation · e-Delivery · Domain model · Document model

1 Introduction

The e-CODEX[1] project is a Large Scale Pilot in the domain of e-Justice aiming to implement building blocks for a system supporting cross border judicial procedures between European Member States and to provide citizens, enterprises and legal professionals with easier access to platforms that support transnational judicial issues. In this paper the main features of the e-CODEX system, based on semantic technologies and Web services, are presented. In particular the e-CODEX e-Delivery platform (Sect. 2) is briefly described. Moreover an approach, based on document standards and semantic models, able to provide a semantic interoperability layer for message exchange is shown (Sects. 3 and 4). Finally some conclusions and future developments are discussed (Sect. 5).

2 The Architecture of the e-CODEX e-Delivery Solution

The e-CODEX platform provides facilities for cross border communication via gateways, behind which national domains are unchanged. Reliable messaging and non-repudiation between the actual endpoints located within the national

[1] e-Justice Communication via Online Data EXchange (http://www.e-codex.eu) (Retrieved: 25/04/2014).

V. Presutti et al. (Eds.): ESWC Satellite Events 2014, LNCS 8798, pp. 204–208, 2014.
DOI: 10.1007/978-3-319-11955-7_19

domains are guaranteed by a so called "circle of trust", based on legal agreements, and by evidences based on ETSI REM specifications, respectively [1]. Gateways[2] are endowed with routing capabilities able to resolve gateway physical addresses and national competent courts. Connectors, developed by each Member State, act as interface between national and European e-Delivery systems, facilitating message routing and document semantics management. For the piloting phase two use-cases have been foreseen: application forms exchange within Small Claims and European Payment Order procedures, as ruled by the corresponding EU regulations [2]. The way document semantics is managed is discussed in the next sections with respect to the foreseen use cases.

3 Semantic Interoperability

For document exchange between member states, having different legal systems and traditions, a semantic interoperability layer is essential for sharing and harmonizing the meaning, as well as highlighting nuances of national jurisdiction-dependent concepts. e-CODEX uses three knowledge models for facing semantic interoperability. The *Conceptual Model* is the model for communication and concept harmonization. The *Logical Model* is the set of data types and code lists ensuring data reusability[3]. The *Physical Model* is the syntax and data formats (XML and PDF for e-CODEX documents) ensuring mutual understanding between information systems. Within such a framework, domain and document modeling has been conceived: the *Domain Model* is the model of the addressed scenario and the *Document Model* is the model of a document instance pertaining to that scenario. Each of them can be further distinguished as follows (Fig. 1 as reference). The Document Model can be viewed in terms of *Document Physical Model*, collection of document objects viewed on the basis of their domain independent function (input fields, check boxes, etc.), and *Document Logical Model* [3], collection of document objects viewed on the basis of the human-perceptible meaning of their content (Claimant, Claimant name, Court name, etc.). Similarly, the Domain Model can be viewed in terms of a *Domain Logical Model*, as a set of building blocks (data types, code lists, etc.) to describe documents of a particular domain, and a *Domain Conceptual Model*, as semantic description of a specific domain. The Domain Model gives semantic interpretation to the document elements (physical objects) in terms of logical objects.

From a technical point of view two strategies for implementing the proposed knowledge modeling are given. In a short term strategy the Document Physical Model is the view of an HTML or PDF form in terms of physical objects, while the Document Logical Model is the view of such objects as logical components, described in XML, compliant to an XML Schema representing the Domain Model including elements and relations (Domain Conceptual Model), as well as

[2] http://holodeck-b2b.sourceforge.net (Retrieved: 25/04/2014).

[3] CCTSUN/CEFACT Core Components Technical Specification. Version 3.0. Second Public Review. 16-April-2007.

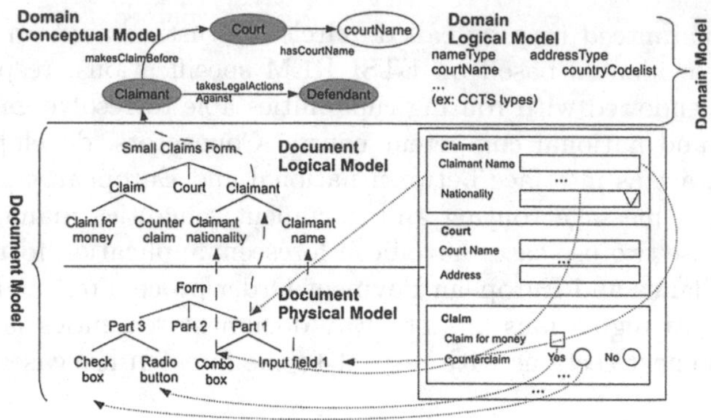

Fig. 1. Relations between domain and document models

datatypes (Domain Logical Model). In a long term strategy, the Document Physical Model is the view of an HTML or PDF form in terms of physical objects, while the Document Logical Model is the logical view of such objects, described in RDF. The meaning of such entities and relations can be given by an ontology (Domain Model) composed by classes and relations (Domain Conceptual Model) as well as datatypes and codelists (Domain Logical Model). In a long term strategy the Domain Model is expressed using RDFS/OWL technologies, following the methodology used by the European Commission DIGIT's ISA Program[4]. In Table 1 implementations of the short and long term strategies are summed up.

Table 1. e-CODEX short and long term implementations

Knowledge Modeling	Short Term Implementation	Long Term Implementation
Domain Model		
a) Domain Conceptual Model	XMLSchema	RDFS/OWL model (ontology)
b) Domain Logical Model	Data types, code lists (ex. CCTS or specific e-CODEX proprietary datatypes)	Data types, code lists (ex. CCTS or specific e-CODEX proprietary datatypes)
Document Model		
a) Document Logical Model	XML	RDF
b) Document Physical Model	HTML or PDF forms	HTML or PDF forms

4 e-CODEX Knowledge Modeling Deployed on Example

A narrative example, concerning a dispute leading litigants to start a European Small Claim procedure, is used as example to show our semantic approach:

[4] DIGIT: Directorate-General for Informatics; ISA: Interoperability Solutions for European Public Administration. http://ec.europa.eu/isa/ (Retrieved: 25/04/2014).

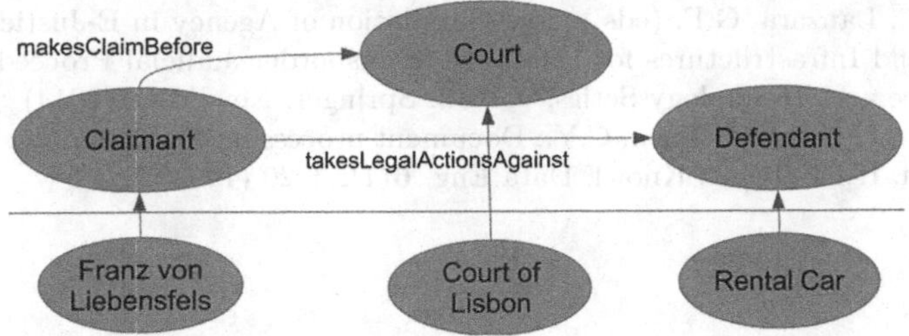

Fig. 2. Relation between Document Logical Model and Domain Model representations (lower and upper part, respectively) of a small claim scenario.

Franz von Liebensfels from Klagenfurt rented a car on the Internet for use in Portugal. Due to the existence of damage to the vehicle he decided to go to the company's office and the employee agreed to the change. The employee discovered damage to the windscreen. Mr. Liebensfels assured this was already there when he had collected the vehicle. Then he saw that his credit card had been charged with 400 Euro. He decides to file a claim against Rental Car at the court of Lisbon using the European Small Claim Procedure.

This narrative can be generalized into a more abstract form as follows:

A claimant from a Member State files a claim against a defendant in another Member State. The claimant filed the claim at a court in the other Member State demanding reimbursement of the money taking form his credit card by the defendant.

In e-CODEX the real case extensional description is represented by a Document Logical Model generated by a document template (Document Physical Model) which, in our narrative case, is a Small Claim procedure form. The connection between the extensional (Document Logical Model) and intensional (Domain Model) representations of a small claim scenario stemming from our example is shown in Fig. 2.

5 Conclusions

e-CODEX aims to represent an effective implementation of the current e-Justice policies of the EU. Legal contents representation and content transport infrastructure are the key activities currently under implementation in a scenario characterized by language and legal systems diversity. In the next phases of the project particular attention will be payed to the implementation of a secure and reliable data exchanged system, as well as an e-Payment system for a complete on-line finalization of judicial proceedings.

References

1. ETSI. Electronic signatures and infrastructures (esi); registered electronic mail (rem); part 2: Data requirements, formats and signatures for rem. Technical Report ETSI TS 102 640–2, ETSI, v. 2.1.1 (2010)

2. Contini, F., Lanzara, G.F. (eds.): The Circulation of Agency in E-Justice. Interoperability and Infrastructures for European Transborder Judicial Proceedings. Law, Governance and Technology Series, vol. 13. Springer, New York (2014)
3. Tang, Y.Y., De Yan, C., Suen, C.Y.: Document processing for automatic knowledge acquisition. IEEE Trans. Knowl. Data Eng. **6**(1), 3–20 (1994)

Rapid Deployment of a RESTful Service for Data Collected by Oceanographic Research Cruises

Linyun Fu[1(✉)] and Robert A. Arko[2]

[1] Tetherless World Constellation,
Rensselaer Polytechnic Institute, Troy, NY, USA
ful2@rpi.edu
[2] Lamont-Doherty Earth Observatory,
Columbia University, Palisades, NY, USA
arko@ldeo.columbia.edu

Abstract. The Rolling Deck to Repository (R2R) program has the mission to capture, catalog, and describe the underway environmental sensor data from US oceanographic research vessels and submit the data to public long-term archives. Information about vessels, sensors, cruises, datasets, people, organizations, funding awards, logs, reports, etc. is published online as Linked Open Data, accessible through a SPARQL endpoint. In response to user feedback, we are developing a RESTful service based on the Elda open-source Java package to facilitate data access. Our experience shows that constructing a simple portal with limited schema elements in this way can significantly reduce development time and maintenance complexity compared to PHP or Servlet based approaches.

Introduction. The Rolling Deck to Repository (R2R) program addresses the need for consistent preservation and dissemination of environmental sensor data routinely acquired by oceanographic research vessels in the U.S. academic fleet. R2R collects information about each expedition that includes vessel identifier and operator; cruise identifier, project title, and research program; port stops and dates; science party names, institutions, and roles; funding agency and award identifier; sensor identifier, classification, manufacturer, and model; cruise reports and event logs; and file manifests.

R2R publishes content as Linked Data [1] using the D2RQ[1] software package, which transforms content from a SQL database to RDF resources in a virtual triple store. Content is mapped to community-standard controlled vocabularies where these are available online as RDF with stable URIs, such as the NERC Vocabulary Server.[2]

For example, one vessel called "Atlantis" is assigned the identifier `<http://data.rvdata.us/id/vessel/33AT>` and is described with the following triples, encoded in Turtle format for the sake of simplicity.

[1] D2RQ. http://d2rq.org/d2r-server.
[2] NERC Vocabulary Server (NVS), Version 2.0. http://vocab.nerc.ac.uk/.

V. Presutti et al. (Eds.): ESWC Satellite Events 2014, LNCS 8798, pp. 209–212, 2014.
DOI: 10.1007/978-3-319-11955-7_20

```
<http://data.rvdata.us/id/vessel/33AT>
  rdf:type <http://data.rvdata.us/vocab/id/class/Vessel> ;
  dcterms:identifier "33AT" ;
  rdfs:label "Atlantis" ;
  r2r:Operator <http://data.rvdata.us/id/organization/edu.whoi> ;
  r2r:Owner <http://data.rvdata.us/id/organization/mil.navy> ;
  skos:exactMatch <http://vocab.nerc.ac.uk/collection/C17/current/33AT/> .
```

The Linked Data API[3] was developed in response to a requirement from Web developers that Linked Data in the RDF data structure should be accessible in a way that is familiar to them, namely through RESTful services [2], in addition to through SPARQL endpoints. The Linked Data API achieves this goal by defining a proxy layer on top of existing SPARQL endpoints that (1) translates HTTP requests into SPARQL queries, and (2) renders the returned results as required by the request sender using content negotiation, suffixes and parameters.

The first part, HTTP-request-to-SPARQL-query translation, is done by modules called *selectors*, whereas the second part, rendering, is done by *viewers* and *formatters*. Selectors, viewers and formatters are usually grouped together to form *endpoints*. Unlike SPARQL endpoints which accept SPARQL queries, Linked Data API endpoints accept HTTP requests. Figure 1 shows some important classes along with relationships among them in Linked Data API, created with COE [3].

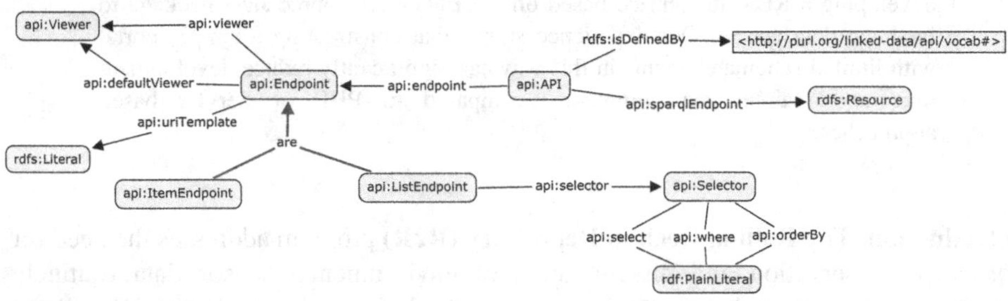

Fig. 1. Part of Linked Data API ontology (The full ontology is online at http://purl.org/linked-data/api/vocab#). Prefixes used: rdfs: http://www.w3.org/2000/01/rdf-schema# api: http://purl.org/linked-data/api/vocab#

Note that only part of the whole Linked Data API ontology is shown in Fig. 1 for the sake of simplicity. For example, we do not show the formatter class in the Figure because it deals with the detailed representation of the returned Web page in response to an HTTP request and is not the focus of this paper. We also omit the `rdfs:Literal` valued `api:base` property of the `api:API` class here because it is best illustrated, and will be shown through a detailed example in the next section.

The HTTP request pattern that an endpoint accepts is encoded in its `api:uriTemplate` field, and specification for selecting resources is encoded in terms of `api:select`, `api:where`, `api:orderBy`, etc.

[3] Linked Data API Specification. https://code.google.com/p/linked-data-api/wiki/Specification.

Once implemented as a software package, this API enables Linked Data publishers or proxy builders to create their RESTful service by writing a configuration file containing only the definition of an `api:API` instance. The `api:API` instance is recognized upon invocation of the HTTP request, and the RESTful service backed by the software performs the translation and rendering jobs according to the `api:API` instance definition. We will show in the next section how we define this instance along with one of its associated endpoints and the endpoint's selector to create our RESTful service for the R2R dataset.

Configuration of the RESTful Service. Figure 2 shows how the `api:API` instance is defined in our application. It talks to the SPARQL endpoint located at `http://data.rvdata.us/sparql`, as its `api:sparqlEndpoint` value indicates. Here we just show one Linked Data API endpoint of this instance, namely `spec:listVesselsByLabelContains`. This endpoint is responsible for listing all the resources in the dataset that have a certain substring in their `rdfs:label` fields.

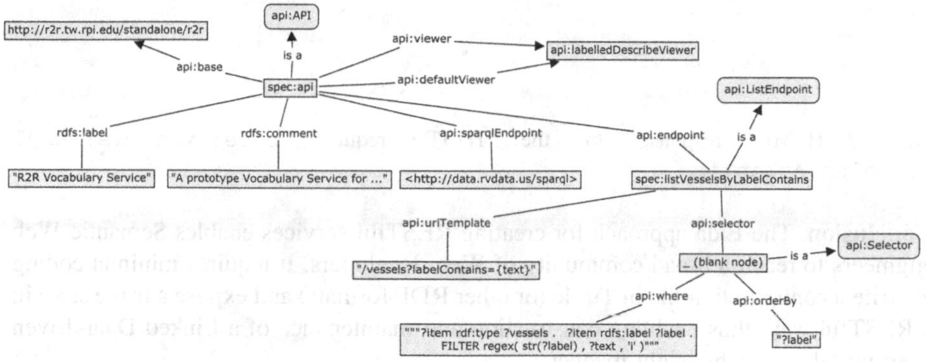

Fig. 2. Part of R2R Linked Data API Configuration. In addition to the prefixes used in Fig. 1, we have: spec: http://r2r.tw.rpi.edu/spec/r2r#

The `spec:listVesselsByLabelContains` endpoint deals with HTTP requests matching the pattern `base:/vessels?labelContains={text}`, as its `api:uriTemplate` field indicates. The `base` prefix is the `api:base` value of the `spec:api`, so this endpoint responds to requests such as `http://r2r.tw.rpi.edu/standalone/r2r/vessels?labelContains=Atlantis`. This endpoint uses a selector to fulfill its duty in a way that is encoded as `api:where` and `api:orderBy` values. These values are simply the `WHERE` clause and the `ORDER BY` clause in a SPARQL query. The actual query submitted to the SPARQL endpoint is as follows.

```
PREFIX rdf: <http://www.w3.org/1999/02/22-rdf-syntax-ns#>
PREFIX rdfs: <http://www.w3.org/2000/01/rdf-schema#>
SELECT DISTINCT ?item
WHERE { ?item rdf:type <http://data.rvdata.us/vocab/id/class/Vessel> .
        ?item rdfs:label ?label .
        FILTER regex( str(?label) , "Atlantis" , 'i' ) }  ORDER BY ?label
```

The endpoint received a result for this SPARQL query, and creates a view with the `api:labelledDescribeViewer`, as indicated by the `api:defaultViewer` value of the `spec:api`. The viewer returns the graph created from a DESCRIBE query for each query result, supplemented by labels for linked resources. The final Web page rendered by Elda,[4] which is one implementation of the Linked Data API, is shown in Fig. 3.

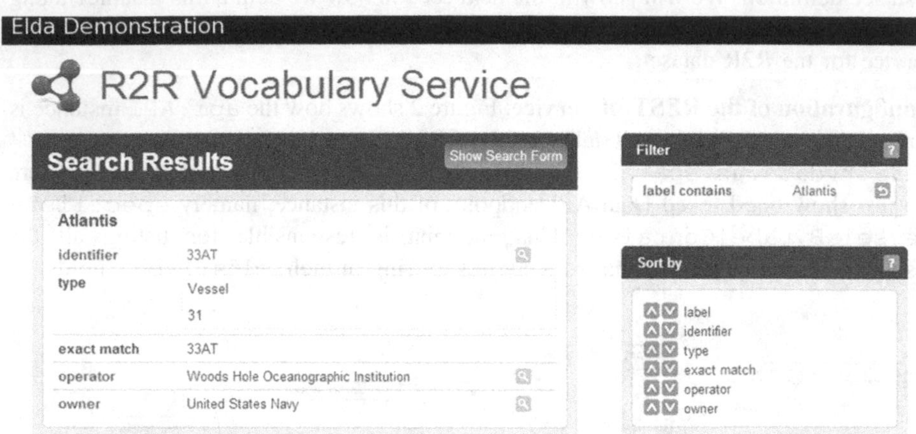

Fig. 3. HTML response to the HTTP request `base:/vessels?labelContains=Atlantis`

Conclusion. The Elda approach for creating RESTful services enables Semantic Web engineers to reach a broad community of Web developers. It requires minimal coding to write a configuration file in Turtle (or other RDF formats) and expose a triple store in a RESTful way, thus enabling construction and maintenance of a Linked Data-driven Web portal in a lightweight manner.

Acknowledgements. This research is funded by the U.S. National Science Foundation via the Rolling Deck to Repository (R2R) program and the Ocean Data Interoperability Platform (ODIP), working collaboratively with the U.S. University-National Oceanographic Laboratory System (UNOLS) Office.

References

1. Bizer, Christian, Heath, Tom, Berners-Lee, Tim: Linked data - the story so far. Int. J. Semant. Web Inf. Syst. **5**(3), 1–22 (2009)
2. Richardson, L., Ruby, S.: RESTful Web Services. O'Reilly, Sebastopol (2007). ISBN 978-0-596-52926-0
3. Hayes, P., Eskridge, T.C., Mehrotra, M., Bobrovnikoff, D., Reichherzer, T., Saavedra, R.: COE: tools for collaborative ontology development and reuse. In: Knowledge Capture Conference (KCAP) (2005)

[4] Elda: the linked-data API in Java. http://www.epimorphics.com/web/tools/elda.html.

TMR: A Semantic Recommender System Using Topic Maps on the Items' Descriptions

Angel Luis Garrido(✉) and Sergio Ilarri(✉)

IIS Department, University of Zaragoza, Zaragoza, Spain
{garrido,silarri}@unizar.es

Abstract. Recommendation systems have become increasingly popular these days. Their utility has been proved to filter and to suggest items archived at web sites to the users. Even though recommendation systems have been developed for the past two decades, existing recommenders are still inadequate to achieve their objectives and must be enhanced to generate appealing personalized recommendations effectively. In this paper we present TMR, a context-independent tool based on topic maps that works with item's descriptions and reviews to provide suitable recommendations to users. TMR takes advantage of lexical and semantic resources to infer users' preferences and thus the recommender is not restricted by the syntactic constraints imposed on some existing recommenders. We have verified the correctness of TMR using a popular benchmark dataset.

Keywords: Topic maps · Recommendation systems · NLP · Semantics

1 Introduction

Machine learning, information retrieval, data mining, natural language processing, and probabilistic models have been adopted for developing systems that recommend items like books, songs, and movies, for example. Our proposed system, TMR (Topic Map Recommender), is a semantic, ontological, and linguistic enhanced recommendation system, which takes advantage of natural language processing (NLP) and semantic tools to provide personalized item suggestions tailored to the preferences of individual users. Unlike its counterparts, TMR examines the "meaning" of textual item metadata, such as content descriptions and reviews on items to be recommended, considered during the recommendation process, as opposed to simply syntactically analyse the words in the texts.

There are already some semantic and ontological approaches such as [1,2]. TMR differs from them in the way the system generates abstractions of themes and subject areas from items and user profiles. For this purpose, the system uses topic maps, a kind of diagram that shows relationships between concepts within a context. As a representation of a conceptualization corresponds to the definition of an ontology [3], we can use techniques and methodologies from ontological engineering to model these representations and work with them. Furthermore, unlike its ontology-based counterparts, TMR does not depend on the availability

V. Presutti et al. (Eds.): ESWC Satellite Events 2014, LNCS 8798, pp. 213–217, 2014.
DOI: 10.1007/978-3-319-11955-7_21

of a domain ontology, since it is not domain-dependent: ontologies in the form of topic maps are automatically built by the system.

2 Our Proposed Methodology

The main idea is to represent both the user's likes and dislikes and the items. We will use topic maps to represent all this information, and we will compare the corresponding topic maps in order to evaluate the degree of similarity between the likes/dislikes of the user and the items. The more similar the representation of an element is with respect to the representation of the profile of what a user likes/disklikes, the more likely we are to recommend it/not to recommend it.

We use text descriptions of the items (the items that can be recommended to the user, as well as the items that the user valued positively –likes– and negatively –dislikes–) and other user's reviews. All this information is contained in natural language texts, so we need an information extraction tool to exploit it. To obtain the relevant data in order to build the topic maps from text, TMR adopts TM-Gen [4], which is a tool that extracts information from any number of texts and represents them in a topic map format.

TM-Gen scans the texts to find the most important keywords and the main named entities [5]. It divides the text into sentences and assigns them a relevance score, in order to find those that are most important in the text. Afterwards, TM-Gen analyzes syntactically the sentences to find the best candidates to be a topic, and then it establishes associations between them, creating the relations. We have adapted this method to analyse the items' descriptions in TMR.

TMR examines the descriptions using Freeling[1], an NLP tool. The system then proceeds to extract concepts and the corresponding relationships among them using the aforementioned techniques from TM-Gen. The different topic maps obtained are merged into a single one using SIM (Subject Identity Measure) [6], an existing approach that describes the relationships among two subjects or topics. As part of the topic map generation process, TMR performs a semantic analysis of the topic map and simplifies it if the system finds redundancies, incompatible associations, or ambiguities, using for this purpose lexical databases (i.e., WordNet), Linked Data resources like DBPedia, and a disambiguation engine [7] (similar to that used in [8]).

TMR analyzes also each item review to find relevant information, which is used to enrich the topic map of the item. As the language used in the reviews is usually much less formal than the one employed in item descriptions, it is more difficult to use parsers to extract information. For this reason, TMR lemmatizes the texts in the reviews and extracts the most frequent keywords and named entities using the well-known TF-IDF algorithm [9]. These extracted keywords and named entities are incorporated into the topic map as new elements either as topics or as relationships, by using Freeling's morphological analyzer.

The next step in the TMR's recommendation process is to construct a profile of the user which captures his/her preferences, by examining the ratings that

[1] http://nlp.lsi.upc.edu/freeling/

he/she has previously assigned to other items. In doing so, TMR generates two different topic maps: one for the likes *(TMlikes)*, and another one for the dislikes *(TMdislikes)*. The texts used to build those topic maps are the ones describing the corresponding data items.

The last step applied by TMR in making suggestions involves predicting the degree to which a user will like (or not) a new item. TMR evaluates the degree of similarity between the topic map of an item and each of the topic maps that capture the likes and dislikes of the user. To calculate the similarity between topic maps, TMR employs an algorithm we developed that evaluates the resemblance between the topics of any two topic maps. This algorithm is based on two measures introduced in [10]: *lexical similarity* and *relation overlap*; while the first measure calculates the lexical overlap between strings, the second one quantifies the degree to which the relations of two concepts in an ontology match. Using Eq. 1, TMR yields a score for an item on a [1, 10] range.

$$Rate(Item) = Norm[(Sim(TMlikes) - Sim(TMdislikes))] \quad (1)$$

where *Sim* captures the degree of similarity between the corresponding topic map of likes and dislikes and the one corresponding to the item, and *Norm* is a function that maps the differences in similarity scores from a [−1, 1] range to a [1, 10] range.

3 Experiments

To evaluate the performance of TMR, we have used the BookCrossing dataset as a test case. BookCrossing is a popular benchmark dataset commonly-used to assess the performance of book recommendation systems. We apply the popular five-fold cross validation protocol. For each one of the five repetitions, 85 % of the books rated by a user U in a set of users BX were used to model U's likes/dislikes (i.e., U_{train}) and the remaining 15 % (U_{test}) were used for actual testing.

In our empirical study, we quantified the performance of a recommender system R using the Root Mean Squared Error (RMSE), as shown in Eq. 2, which is a de facto metric for evaluating predictive recommendation systems.

$$RMSE(R) = \frac{\sum_{U \in BX} \sqrt{\frac{\sum_{b \in U_{test}} |R_{U,b} - r_{U,b}|}{|U_{test}|}}}{|BX|} \quad (2)$$

where $R_{U,b}$ denotes the rating *predicted* by R for a book b ($\in U_{test}$) given the corresponding user U, and $r_{U,b}$ is the *actual* rating given to b by U.

We executed each experiment five times, and the overall RMSE score is the average of the RMSE scores computed for each repetition. In our experiments, the RMSE score generated using TMR is 1.25. Its performance, in terms of RMSE, is much higher than some baseline recommenders like SVD++ [11] (4.67) and Bias-SVD [11] (3.94). If we compare TMR with other state-of-the-art recommenders like fLDA [12] (1.31), RLMF [12] (1.32), and uLDA [12] (1.35), we find that our results are very promising, given the significant difference obtained with respect to its counterparts.

4 Conlusions and Future Work

In this paper we have presented TMR, a domain-independent recommender that combines semantic and ontological techniques with NLP tools and lexical resources to made recommendations suitable to the preferences/interests of each individual user. In principle, TMR can work in any context where a textual description and textual reviews of the data items are available. We conducted an empirical study with the BookCrossing dataset and obtained positive results.

Our intention now is to verify the generality of our solution. For this purpose, we will evaluate the performance of TMR using other datasets to prove that our system is indeed context-independent. Comparing the proposal with other domain-specific recommenders in different contexts is also a relevant task of future work, as we can expect a trade-off between the generality of the proposal and its performance, that needs to be quantified.

Acknowledgment. Supported by CICYT project TIN2010-21387-C02-02 and DGA-FSE. Thank you to Maria Soledad Pera, Maria G. Buey, Sandra Escudero and Alvaro Peiro.

References

1. Cantador, I., Bellogin, A., Castells, P.: A multilayer ontology-based hybrid recommendation model. AI Commun. **21**(2–3), 203–210 (2008)
2. IJntema, W., Goossen, F., Frasincar, F., Hogenboom, F.: Ontology-based News Recommendation. In: ACM EDBT/ICDT Workshops, Article 16, 6p (2010)
3. Gruber, T.: A translation approach to portable ontology specifications. Knowl. Acquis. **5**(2), 199–220 (1993). (Academic Press Ltd.)
4. Garrido, A.L., Buey, M.G., Escudero, S., Ilarri, S., Mena, E., Silveira, S.: TM-Gen: a topic map generator from text documents. In: IEEE ICTAI, pp. 735–740 (2013)
5. Sekine, S., Ranchhod, E.: Named Entities: Recognition, Classification and Use. John Benjamins, Amsterdam (2009)
6. Maicher, L., Witschel, H.: Merging of distributed topic maps based on the subject identity measure (SIM) approach. Berliner XML-Tage **4**, 301–307 (2004)
7. Navigli, R.: Word sense disambiguation: a survey. ACM Comput. Surv. **41**(2), 1–69 (2009)
8. Granados Buey, M., Luis Garrido, Á., Escudero, S., Trillo, R., Ilarri, S., Mena, E.: SQX-Lib: developing a semantic query expansion system in a media group. In: de Rijke, M., Kenter, T., de Vries, A.P., Zhai, C.X., de Jong, F., Radinsky, K., Hofmann, K. (eds.) ECIR 2014. LNCS, vol. 8416, pp. 780–783. Springer, Heidelberg (2014)
9. Salton, G., Buckley, C.: Term-weighting approaches in automatic text retrieval. Inf. Process. Manage. **24**(5), 513–523 (1988)

10. Maedche, A., Staab, S.: Measuring similarity between ontologies. In: Gómez-Pérez, A., Benjamins, V.R. (eds.) EKAW 2002. LNCS (LNAI), vol. 2473, p. 251. Springer, Heidelberg (2002)
11. Koren, Y.: Factorization meets the neighborhood: a multifaceted collaborative filtering model. In: ACM SIGKDD, pp. 426–434 (2008)
12. Agarwal, D., Chen, B.: fLDA: matrix factorization through latent dirichlet allocation. In: ACM WSDM, pp. 91–100 (2010)

The Normalized Freebase Distance

Fréderic Godin[1(✉)], Tom De Nies[1], Christian Beecks[2], Laurens De Vocht[1], Wesley De Neve[1,3], Erik Mannens[1], Thomas Seidl[2], and Rik Van de Walle[1]

[1] Multimedia Lab, Ghent University - iMinds, Ghent, Belgium
{frederic.godin,tom.denies,laurens.devocht,wesley.deneve, erik.mannens,rik.vandewalle}@ugent.be

[2] Data Management and Data Exploration Group, RWTH Aachen University, Aachen, Germany
{seidl,beecks}@informatik.rwth-aachen.de

[3] IVY Lab, KAIST, Daejeon, Republic of Korea

Abstract. In this paper, we propose the Normalized Freebase Distance (NFD), a new measure for determing semantic concept relatedness that is based on similar principles as the Normalized Web Distance (NWD). We illustrate that the NFD is more effective when comparing ambiguous concepts.

1 Introduction

In the last decade, the *Normalized Web Distance* (NWD) [2] has proven to be a simple, yet powerful measure of the semantic relatedness between two concepts. The NWD measures the semantic relatedness between two concepts in terms of their frequency of single and mutual occurrence in web pages. Essentially, two concepts appearing together on a web page reduces their NWD.

One of the most prominent instantiations of the NWD is the *Normalized Google Distance* (NGD) [1], which is based on the Google search engine. The NGD epitomizes the utilization of the NWD to web search engines, such as Google, Bing, and Yahoo. While these web search engines have the advantage that nearly all concepts can be found, they suffer from the issue of concept ambiguity: a concept that is issued as a query to the search engine can be interpreted in different ways. For example, the concept "Washington" can either refer to the state, the capital or the former president. This disambiguation is partially or completely lost when using traditional web search engines.

In this paper, we investigate how we can keep the powerful idea behind the NWD, while disambiguating the semantic meaning of concepts. Instead of textual indexes and search engines, we rely on semantic graph-structured data stores, such as DBpedia or Freebase, which can be queried unambiguously.

2 Related Work

Measuring the semantic relatedness between single language units or phrases in terms of similarity or distance has been an active research area for a long

V. Presutti et al. (Eds.): ESWC Satellite Events 2014, LNCS 8798, pp. 218–221, 2014.
DOI: 10.1007/978-3-319-11955-7_22

time. Many similarity measures [3,5,7] are based on static semantic networks such as *WordNet*. More recent similarity metrics such as the NGD [1] and *Flickr Distance* [9] are based on dynamic repositories of user-generated content.

The idea of using graph-structured knowledge bases such as DBpedia or Freebase to calculate the distance between two disambiguated concepts has already been proposed in literature [4,6]. However, these distance measures rely on the direct or indirect connections between two resources, and can only be calculated by using a potentially computationally expensive algorithm, such as finding the shortest path in a graph [6], or recursively calculating similarity [4].

3 The Normalized Freebase Distance

Our approach is based on the Normalized Web Distance, which is defined as:

$$NWD(x,y) = \frac{max\{logf(x), logf(y)\} - logf(x,y)}{logN - min\{logf(x), logf(y)\}},$$

where $f(x)$ and $f(y)$ are the numbers of web pages containing either concept x or y, $f(x,y)$ is the number of web pages containing both concepts x and y, and N is the total number of web pages. The function f thus depends on a specific search engine. As mentioned above, the best-known implementation of the NWD is the NGD. However, since recent updates by Google resulted in the removal of the + and AND operators, the implementation and thus computation of the NGD becomes infeasible. We therefore make use of the *Normalized Bing Distance* (NBD) as a representative baseline during our evaluation, since Microsoft Bing still offers this query capability.

Our approach uses the graph-structured knowledge base Freebase to calculate these values instead of a conventional web search engine. Freebase currently contains about two billion links between concepts. Consequently, a more complex approach such as searching the shortest path between two concepts would be a computationally expensive task. Therefore, we propose to make use of a similar principle as the NWD, only making use of the incoming links to a certain concept.

For two concepts x and y, we can compare the number of concepts in the dataset with links pointing to x or y separately, to the number of concepts with links pointing to both. This is similar to the page counts provided by web search engines, where a link can be seen as an occurrence on a web page. By substituting the functions $f(x)$, $f(y)$, and $f(x,y)$ as follows:

$$f(x) = number\,of\,concepts\,linking\,to\,x,$$

$$f(y) = number\,of\,concepts\,linking\,to\,y,$$

$$f(x,y) = number\,of\,concepts\,linking\,to\,x\,AND\,y,$$

we define the Normalized Freebase Distance (NFD) in a similar manner as the NWD. For our approach, we set N to the total number of concepts in Freebase.

4 Preliminary Experiments

To verify the effectiveness of the NFD, we analyze the distance matrix of a number of ambiguous examples and compare the output with the NBD. To calculate the NFD, we set up a Virtuoso SPARQL endpoint and used the Freebase RDF dump of March 16, 2014 containing over 1.9 billion triples.

The function $f(x)$ is defined as (the function $f(y)$ is defined similarly):

```
SELECT COUNT(DISTINCT ?s) WHERE { ?s ?p <x> }
```

The function $f(x, y)$ is defined as:

```
SELECT COUNT(DISTINCT ?s) WHERE { ?s ?p1 <x> . ?s ?p2 <y> }
```

The returned triples were filtered on duplicates by removing triples that used the predicates `rdf:type` and `rdfs:label`, and forced the subject to be an URI.

To evaluate the NFD, we were particularly interested in concepts that would confuse traditional search engines. To that end, we have calculated the distance between three types of fish, and the word *bass guitar*. We were particularly interested in how search engines will deal with the fish species *bass* that is contained in the word *bass guitar*.

Table 1. Distance matrices of four concepts, using the NBD (left) and the NFD (right). For Freebase entities, their unique identifier is used as label.

	Salmon	**Trout**	**Bass**	**Bass guitar**
Salmon	0	0.072	0.133	0.283
Trout	0.072	0	0.123	0.247
Bass	0.133	0.123	0	0.086
Bass g.	0.283	0.247	0.086	0

	09777	**0cqpb**	**0cqvj**	**018vs**
09777	0	0.070	0.087	0.274
0cqpb	0.070	0	0.070	0.269
0cqvj	0.087	0.070	0	0.276
018vs	0.274	0.269	0.276	0

As can be seen in Table 1, distances between the different concepts are of the same magnitude. The NBD between *salmon* and *trout* is 0.072, while the NFB between these two concepts is 0.070. Similarly, the NBD between *salmon* and *bass guitar* and the NBD between *trout* and *bass guitar* is of the same magnitude as the NFD between the aforementioned concept pairs. However, the NBD between *bass* and the three other concepts is much more different compared to the NFD. In fact, the NBD between *bass* and *trout* and the NBD between *bass* and *salmon* is much higher than the NFB between *bass* and *trout* and the NFB between *bass* and *salmon*. Likewise, the distances between *bass guitar* and the other three concepts (last row) are of the same magnitude, except for the NBD with *bass*. There, we can observe a big drop in distance, bringing *bass guitar* to the same magnitude level as the other fish. Here, the NFD captures the distances much better than NBD. We can attribute this to the fact that the NBD only relies on the occurrence of certain words and that the NBD does not take into account that concepts may consist of multiple words that can be concepts on their own.

5 Conclusions and Outlook

We have illustrated that the Normalized Freebase Distance (NFD) allows for more effective measurement of semantic concept relatedness than the Normalized Bing Distance. Additionally, the calculation of the NFD does not require to execute computationally expensive algorithms on the Freebase data set such as the shortest path algorithm.

In future research, we plan to conduct more extensive experiments, paying more detailed attention to both the effectiveness and efficiency of the proposed distance metric in a variety of use cases.

Whereas our preliminary experiments focus on the use of Freebase, one could imagine applying this principle on the scale of the entire Web. New developments in the field of Web-scale querying could make this possible in the near future [8]. That way, we could expand our NFD to a Normalized Semantic Web Distance, which would share much of the flexibility and power of the NWD, with the added benefit of semantic awareness.

Acknowledgments. The research activities in this paper were funded by Ghent University, iMinds (by the Flemish Government), the IWT Flanders, the FWO-Flanders, the European Union, and the Excellence Initiative of the German federal and state governments.

References

1. Cilibrasi, R.L., Vitanyi, P.M.B.: The google similarity distance. IEEE Trans. Knowl. Data Eng. **19**(3), 370–383 (2007)
2. Cilibrasi, R., Vitányi, P.M.B.: Normalized web distance and word similarity. CoRR abs/0905.4039 (2009)
3. Hirst, G., St-Onge, D.: Lexical chains as representations of context for the detection and correction of malapropisms. In: WordNet: An Electronic Lexical Database, pp. 305–332. MIT Press, Cambridge (1998)
4. Jeh, G., Widom, J.: Simrank: a measure of structural-context similarity. In: Proceedings of the Eighth ACM SIGKDD International Conference on Knowledge Discovery and Data Mining, pp. 538–543. ACM (2002)
5. Jiang, J.J., Conrath, D.W.: Semantic similarity based on corpus statistics and lexical taxonomy. arXiv preprint cmp-lg/9709008 (1997)
6. Passant, A.: Measuring semantic distance on linking data and using it for resources recommendations. In: AAAI Spring Symposium: Linked Data Meets Artificial Intelligence (2010)
7. Resnik, P.: Using information content to evaluate semantic similarity in a taxonomy. arXiv preprint cmp-lg/9511007 (1995)
8. Verborgh, R., Vander Sande, M., Colpaert, P., Coppens, S., Mannens, E., Van de Walle, R.: Web-scale querying through linked data fragments. In: Proceedings of the 7th Workshop on Linked Data on the Web (2014)
9. Wu, L., Hua, X.S., Yu, N., Ma, W.Y., Li, S.: Flickr distance: a relationship measure for visual concepts. IEEE Trans. Pattern Anal. Mach. Intell. **34**(5), 863–875 (2012)

Predicting SPARQL Query Performance

Rakebul Hasan(✉) and Fabien Gandon

INRIA Sophia Antipolis, Wimmics, 2004 Route des Lucioles, B.P. 93, 06902 Sophia-Antipolis Cedex, France
{hasan.rakebul,fabien.gandon}@inria.fr

Abstract. We address the problem of predicting SPARQL query performance. We use machine learning techniques to learn SPARQL query performance from previously executed queries. We show how to model SPARQL queries as feature vectors, and use k-nearest neighbors regression and Support Vector Machine with the nu-SVR kernel to accurately (R^2 value of 0.98526) predict SPARQL query execution time.

1 Query Performance Prediction

The emerging dataspace of Linked Data presents tremendous potential for large-scale data integration over cross domain data to support a new generation of intelligent application. In this context, it increasingly important to develop efficient ways of querying Linked Data. Central to this problem is knowing how a query would behave prior to executing the query. Current generation of SPARQL query cost estimation approaches are based on data statistics and heuristics. Statistics-based approaches have two major drawbacks in the context of Linked Data [9]. First, the statistics (e.g. histograms) about the data are often missing in the Linked Data scenario because they are expensive to generate and maintain. Second, due to the graph-based data model and schema-less nature of RDF data, what makes effective statistics for query cost estimation is unclear. Heuristics-based approaches generally do not require any knowledge of underlying data statistics. However, they are based on strong assumptions such as considering queries of certain structure less expensive than others. These assumptions may hold for some RDF datasets and may not hold for others. We take a rather pragmatic approach to SPARQL query cost estimation. We learn SPARQL query performance metrics from already executed queries. Recent work [1,3,4] in database research shows that database query performance metrics can be accurately predicted without any knowledge of data statistics by applying machine learning techniques on the query logs of already executed queries. Similarly, we apply machine learning techniques to learn SPARQL query performance metrics from already executed queries. We consider query execution time as the query performance metric in this paper.

2 Modeling SPARQL Query Execution

We predict SPARQL query performance metrics by applying machine learning techniques on previously executed queries. This approach does not require any

V. Presutti et al. (Eds.): ESWC Satellite Events 2014, LNCS 8798, pp. 222–225, 2014.
DOI: 10.1007/978-3-319-11955-7_23

statistics of the underlying RDF data, which makes it ideal for the Linked Data scenario. We use two types of query features: SPARQL algebra features and graph pattern features. We use frequencies and cardinalities of the SPARQL algebra operators[1], and depth of the algebra expression tree as SPARQL algebra features. Regarding graph patterns features, transforming graph patterns to vector space is not trivial because the space is infinite. To address this, we create a query pattern vector representation relative to the query patterns appearing in the training data. First, we cluster the structurally similar query patterns in the training data into K_{gp} number of clusters. The query pattern in the center of a cluster is the representative of query patterns in that cluster. Second, we represent a query pattern as a K_{gp} dimensional vector where the value of a dimension is the structural similarity between that query pattern and the corresponding cluster center query pattern. To compute the structural similarity between two query patterns, we first construct two graphs from the two query patterns, then compute the approximate graph edit distance – using a suboptimal algorithm [7] with $O\left(n^3\right)$ computational complexity – between these two graphs. The structural similarity is the inverse of the approximate edit distance. We use the k-mediods [5] clustering algorithm to cluster the query patterns of training data. We use k-mediods because it chooses data points as cluster centers and allows using an arbitrary distance function. We use the same suboptimal graph edit distance algorithm as the distance function for k-mediods. Figure 1 shows an example of extracting SPARQL algebra features (left) and graph pattern features (right) from SPARQL query string.

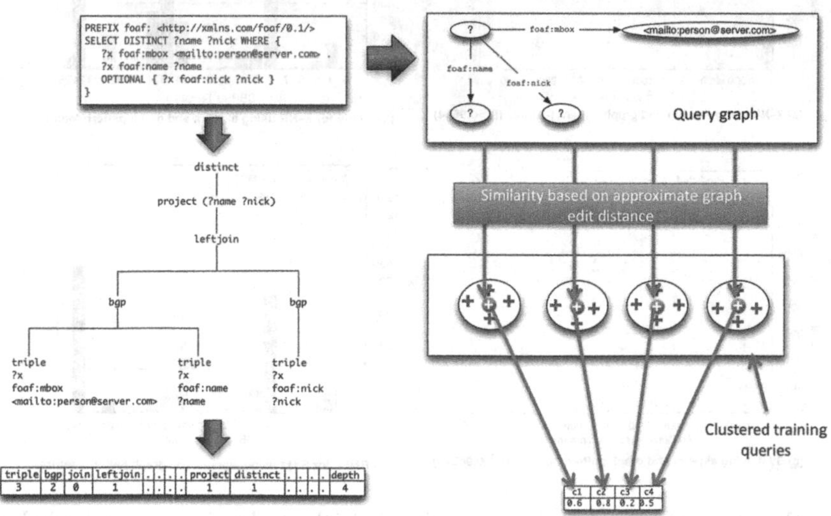

Fig. 1. Example of extracting SPARQL feature vector from a SPARQL query.

[1] Algebra operators: http://www.w3.org/TR/sparql11-query/#sparqlAlgebra

3 Experiments and Results

We generate 1260 training, 420 validation, and 420 test queries from the 25 DBPSB benchmark query templates [6]. To generate queries, we assign randomly selected RDF terms from the DBpedia 3.5.1 dataset to the placeholders in the query templates. We run the queries on a Jena-TDB 1.0.0 triple store loaded with DBpedia 3.5.1 and record their query execution time. We exclude queries which do not return any result (queries from template 2, 16, and 21) and run more than 300 seconds (queries from template 20). We experiment with k-nearest neighbors (k-NN) regression [2] and Support Vector Machine (SVM) with the nu-SVR kernel for regression [8] to predict query execution time. We achieve an R^2 value of 0.9654 (Fig. 2(a)) and a root mean squared error (RMSE) value of 401.7018 (Fig. 2(b)) on the test dataset using k-NN (with $K_{gp} = 10$ and $k = 2$ selected by cross validation). We achieve an improved R^2 value of 0.98526 (Fig. 2(c)) and a lower RMSE value of 262.1869 (Fig. 2(d)) using SVM (with $K_{gp} = 25$ selected by cross validation). This shows that our approach can accurately predict SPARQL query execution time.

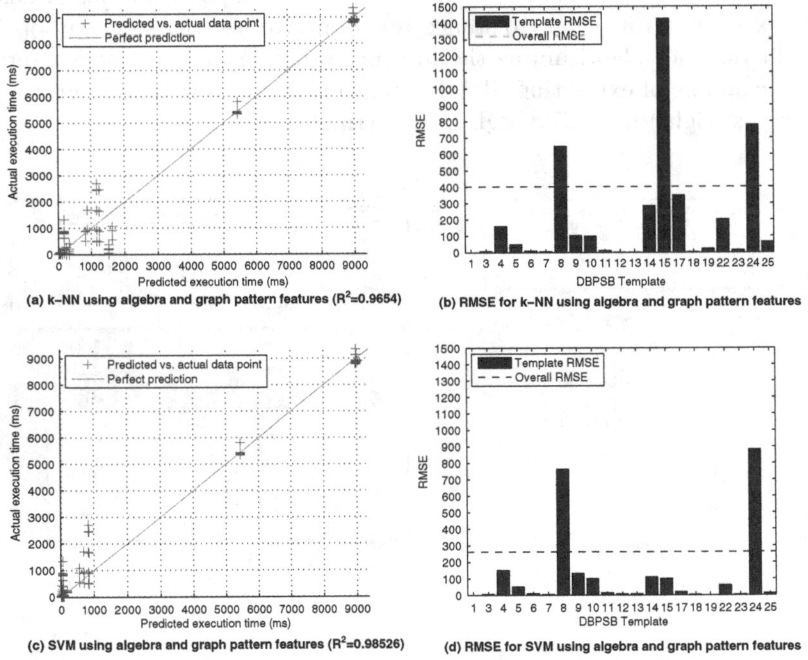

(a) k-NN using algebra and graph pattern features (R^2=0.9654)

(b) RMSE for k-NN using algebra and graph pattern features

(c) SVM using algebra and graph pattern features (R^2=0.98526)

(d) RMSE for SVM using algebra and graph pattern features

Fig. 2. Predictions for the test dataset with SPARQL algebra features and graph pattern features using k-NN ($K_{gp} = 10$ and $k = 2$) and SVM ($K_{gp} = 25$).

4 Conclusion and Future Work

We present an approach to predict SPARQL query execution time using machine learning techniques. We learn query execution times from already executed queries. This approach can be useful where statistics about the underlying data are unavailable We discuss how to model SPARQL queries as feature vectors, and show highly accurate results. In future, we would like to compare our approach to the existing SPARQL query cost estimation approaches in the context of Linked Data query processing.

Acknowledgments. This work is supported by the ANR CONTINT program under the Kolflow project (ANR-2010-CORD-021-02).

References

1. Akdere, M., Cetintemel, U., Riondato, M., Upfal, E., Zdonik, S.: Learning-based query performance modeling and prediction. In: 2012 IEEE 28th International Conference on Data Engineering (ICDE), pp. 390–401 (2012)
2. Altman, N.: An introduction to kernel and nearest-neighbor nonparametric regression. Am. Stat. **46**(3), 175–185 (1992)
3. Ganapathi, A., Kuno, H., Dayal, U., Wiener, J.L., Fox, A., Jordan, M., Patterson, D.: Predicting multiple metrics for queries: better decisions enabled by machine learning. In: Proceedings of the 2009 IEEE International Conference on Data Engineering. ICDE '09, pp. 592–603. IEEE Computer Society, Washington, DC, USA (2009)
4. Gupta, C., Mehta, A., Dayal, U.: PQR: predicting query execution times for autonomous workload management. In: Proceedings of the 2008 International Conference on Autonomic Computing. ICAC '08, pp. 13–22. IEEE Computer Society, Washington, DC, USA (2008)
5. Kaufman, L., Rousseeuw, P.: Clustering by means of medoids. In: Dodge, Y. (ed.) Statistical Data Analysis Based on the L1-Norm and Related Methods, pp. 405–416. North Holland Publishing, New York (1987)
6. Morsey, M., Lehmann, J., Auer, S., Ngonga Ngomo, A.-C.: DBpedia SPARQL benchmark – performance assessment with real queries on real data. In: Aroyo, L., Welty, C., Alani, H., Taylor, J., Bernstein, A., Kagal, L., Noy, N., Blomqvist, E. (eds.) ISWC 2011, Part I. LNCS, vol. 7031, pp. 454–469. Springer, Heidelberg (2011)
7. Riesen, K., Bunke, H.: Approximate graph edit distance computation by means of bipartite graph matching. Image Vision Comput. **27**(7), 950–959 (2009)
8. Shevade, S.K., Keerthi, S.S., Bhattacharyya, C., Murthy, K.R.K.: Improvements to the SMO algorithm for SVM regression. IEEE Trans. Neural Netw. **11**(5), 1188–1193 (2000)
9. Tsialiamanis, P., Sidirourgos, L., Fundulaki, I., Christophides, V., Boncz, P.: Heuristics-based query optimisation for SPARQL. In: Proceedings of the 15th International Conference on Extending Database Technology. EDBT '12, pp. 324–335. ACM, New York, NY, USA (2012)

Linked Data Finland: A 7-star Model and Platform for Publishing and Re-using Linked Datasets

Eero Hyvönen(✉), Jouni Tuominen, Miika Alonen, and Eetu Mäkelä

Semantic Computing Research Group (SeCo),
Department of Media Technology, Aalto University, Espoo, Finland
{eero.hyvonen,jouni.tuominen,miika.alonen,eetu.makela}@aalto.fi
http://www.seco.tkk.fi/

Abstract. The idea of Linked Data is to aggregate, harmonize, integrate, enrich, and publish data for re-use on the Web in a cost-efficient way using Semantic Web technologies. We concern two major hindrances for re-using Linked Data: It is often difficult for a re-user to (1) understand the characteristics of the dataset and (2) evaluate the quality the data for the intended purpose. This paper introduces the "Linked Data Finland" platform LDF.fi addressing these issues. We extend the famous 5-star model of Tim Berners-Lee, with the sixth star for providing the dataset with a schema that explains the dataset, and the seventh star for validating the data against the schema. LDF.fi also automates data publishing and provides data curation tools. The first prototype of the platform is available on the web as a service, hosting tens of datasets and supporting several applications.

1 Publishing Linked Data

Lots of Linked Data (LD) platforms have emerged on the Web since the publication of the four Linked Data publication principles and the 5-star model[1]. For example, in Life Sciences alone there are LinkedLifeData[2], NeuroCommons[3], Chem2Bio2RDF[4], HCLSIG/LODD[5], BioLOD[6], and Bio2RDF[7].

LDF.fi[8] contributes to the current state-of-the-art of Linked Data publishing [2] as follows: (1) We propose extending the 5-star model[9] into a 7-star model,

[1] http://www.w3.org/DesignIssues/LinkedData.html
[2] http://linkedlifedata.com/
[3] http://neurocommons.org/
[4] http://chem2bio2rdf.wikispaces.com/
[5] http://www.w3.org/wiki/HCLSIG/LODD
[6] http://biolod.org/
[7] http://bio2rdf.org/
[8] Our work is funded by Tekes and a consortium of 20 public organizations and companies.
[9] http://5stardata.info/

V. Presutti et al. (Eds.): ESWC Satellite Events 2014, LNCS 8798, pp. 226–230, 2014.
DOI: 10.1007/978-3-319-11955-7_24

with the goal of encouraging data publishers to provide their data with explicit metadata schemas and to validate their data for better quality. (2) LDF.fi automates the data publishing process so that not only a SPARQL endpoint but also a rich set of additional data services are generated automatically based on the metadata about the dataset and its graphs. (3) LDF.fi provides end users with additional tools and documentation for publishing, curating, and re-using the datasets. This paper first explains these ideas, and then presents the actual service available online[10].

2 7-star Linked Data

A major hindrance of re-using a dataset is the difficulty to evaluate how suitable the data is for the application purpose at hand. Datasets often use schemas (vocabularies) for which definitions or descriptions are not available, but are embedded in the data itself. This makes it difficult to figure out the characteristics of the data. Furthermore, given the data and its schema it may be difficult to say how well the data actually matches the schema; there are lots of data quality problems on the Semantic Web[11].

To address these issues, we encourage data publishers by two extra stars:

- The 6th star is given if the schemas (vocabularies) used in the dataset are explicitly described and published alongside the dataset, unless the schemas are already available somewhere on the Web.
- For the 7th star, the quality of the dataset against the schemas used in it must be explicated, so that the user can evaluate whether the data quality matches her needs.

LDF.fi provides supporting tools related to these issues: First, schemas are documented automatically for the human reader by using a schema documentation generator. In our case, the LODE[12] online service is employed. (Other possible tools for schema documentation include SpecGen, Neologism[13], dowl[14], Parrot[15], OWLDoc[16], and OntologyBrowser[17].) Second, in order to find out how schemas are actually used in a dataset, we created a new service http://vocab.at [1]. It analyses a dataset, creates an HTML report that explains vocabulary usage in the data, and reports issues of undefined properties or unresolvable namespaces. The input for vocab.at is either an RDF file, a SPARQL endpoint, or an HTML page with embedded RDFa markup.

10 http://www.ldf.fi/
11 http://pedantic-web.org/
12 http://www.essepuntato.it/lode
13 http://neologism.deri.ie/
14 https://github.com/ldodds/dowl
15 http://ontorule-project.eu/parrot/parrot
16 http://code.google.com/p/co-ode-owl-plugins/wiki/OWLDoc
17 http://code.google.com/p/ontology-browser/

3 Automatic Service Generation

LDF.fi tries to automate the process of publishing datasets as far as possible in the following way: The publisher is expected to create an RDF dataset with minimal metadata about it and its schemas. Here an extended version of the new W3C Service Description recommendation[18] and the VoID vocabulary[19] can be used, and the data is stored into the SPARQL endpoint. Alternatively, a simple JSON object listing the dataset and graph names, human readable labels, and a description of the data can be provided. In the metadata, it is also possible to give an example URI pointing into the dataset, a SPARQL query example for querying the data, and optionally a link to possible visualizations of the dataset. Based on such metadata, LDF.fi generates for each dataset a home page on which the following functionalities are available for re-users:

1. Links for downloading datasets and graphs are provided (if licensing permits it).
2. Schemas can be downloaded if provided with the data, and links to their documentation are provided (when available).
3. Following forms are created for inspecting the dataset in more detail: (1) Given a URI the corresponding RDF description can be read in various formats (Turtle, RDF/XML, RDF/JSON, N3, N-triples) for human consumption in a browser. The example URI is used as a first choice to try out. (2) Given a URI, Linked Data browsing can be started from it, with the example URI as a starting point.
4. There is a SPARQL query form for querying the service with the given query used as a first example.
5. Links providing Vocab.at analysis reports of the graphs in the dataset are provided. They tell the end-user what schemas (vocabularies) are used in the data, and how they have been used. Issues on data quality are pointed out.
6. SPARQL Service Descriptions of the datasets are provided, if available. LDF uses W3C SPARQL Service Description recommendation for this.
7. Links to visualizations of the data that may give the re-user more insight on how the dataset can be used in applications.
8. Licensing conditions of the dataset are provided as well as a label of 1–7 stars.

4 Data Curation Tools

Data curation refers to activities and processes done to create, manage, maintain, and validate data. In LDF.fi several data curation services are available for analyzing textual data and for creating semantic annotations (semi-)automatically from them:

1. SeCo Lexical Analysis Services[20] can be used for language recognition, lemmatization, morphological analysis, inflected form generation, and hyphenation.

[18] http://www.w3.org/TR/sparql11-service-description/
[19] http://rdfs.org/ns/void
[20] http://demo.seco.tkk.fi/las/

2. ARPA Automatic Text Annotation System[21] can be used for extracting Linked Data from unstructured texts.
3. SAHA[22] tool can be used for investigating and editing LDF.fi datasets interactively in real time. In LDF.fi we modified and extended SAHA to work on top of any standard SPARQL endpoint. SAHA is now used as a Linked Data Browser in LDF.fi in the same vein as, e.g., URIBurner[23]. Using SAHA as an editor service for a dataset requires permission from the LDF.fi team.

In our work, we are also using some external tools, such as the SILK Framework[24] for linking data.

5 The Service

In addition to dataset home pages, the LDF.fi portal includes the following pages available through menu links: *Project* page describes the underlying national Linked Data Finland initiative; *Datasets* lists the datasets in the system and links to their home pages; *Schemas* lists the schemas in the system; *Services* explains what kind of services LDF.fi provides; *Policies* documents URI minting and licensing policies in use; *Documentation* explains dataset documentation features of the portal; *Validation* explains dataset validation features of the portal; *Applications* lists application examples of the portal datasets; *Your Data?* tells how external users can get their data published in LDF.fi.

The first datasets available in LDF.fi include: Finnish DBpedia as a service; various Cultural Heritage datasets including, e.g., BookSampo, whose deployed end-user application[25] has 65,000 monthly users; history datasets Semantic National Biography (6,300 biographies as Linked Data) and events of World War I (in collaboration with University of Colorado Boulder); Finnish Law first time as Linked Open Data; Aalto University Linked Open Data[26]; two Linked Science datasets about ornithological observations and weather data; various ontologies used by the ONKI Ontology Service[27]; a linked news dataset. The LDF.fi service is implemented using a combination of the Fuseki SPARQL server[28] for serving primary data, and the Varnish web application accelerator[29] for routing URIs to pertinent applications as well as content negotiation.

21 http://www.seco.tkk.fi/services/arpa/
22 http://www.seco.tkk.fi/tools/saha
23 http://linkeddata.uriburner.com/
24 http://wifo5-03.informatik.uni-mannheim.de/bizer/silk/
25 http://www.kirjasampo.fi/
26 The service http://data.aalto.fi/ is based on LDF.fi.
27 http://www.onki.fi
28 http://jena.apache.org/documentation/serving_data/
29 https://www.varnish-cache.org/

6 Evaluation in a Living Lab Environment

LDF.fi was opened officially in January 2014. The platform is being evaluated by providing the service in an open Living Laboratory environment for data publishers and application developers. References to first data applications can be found in the applications page of the portal[30].

References

1. Alonen, M., Kauppinen, T., Hyvönen, E.: Vocab.at - automatic linked data documentation and vocabulary usage analysis, manuscript (2013). http://www.seco.tkk.fi/publications/submitted/alonen-et-al-vocab.pdf
2. Heath, T., Bizer, C.: Linked Data Evolving the Web into a Global Data Space, 1st edn. Morgan & Claypool, Palo Alto (2011). http://linkeddatabook.com/editions/1.0/

[30] http://www.ldf.fi/applications/

Data Cleansing Consolidation with PatchR

Magnus Knuth(✉) and Harald Sack(✉)

Hasso Plattner Institute for Software Systems Engineering,
Prof.-Dr.-Helmert-Str. 2–3,
14482 Potsdam, Germany
{magnus.knuth,harald.sack}@hpi.uni-potsdam.de
http://www.hpi.uni-potsdam.de

1 Introduction

The Linking Open Data (LOD) initiative is turning large resources of publicly available structured data from various domains into interlinked RDF(S) facts to constitute the so-called "Web of Data". But, this Web of Data is by no means a perfect world of consistent and valid facts. Linked Data has multiple dimensions of shortcomings ranging from simple syntactical errors over logical inconsistencies to complex semantic errors and wrong facts. Multiple efforts target data quality assessment or aim to detect and to resolve such shortcomings in Linked Data datasets, such as crowdsourcing based, statistical, or heuristical approaches. These approaches rather address particular problems or datasets than to be generalizable for any kind of error. Moreover, results are published in various forms, which makes it hard to combine their results.

In this paper we propose the aggregation of heterogeneous Linked Data cleansing efforts by using the Patch Request ontology [1]. This allows to include less assured outcomes in order to reach a higher coverage.

2 Linked Data Cleansing Approaches

SDtype [2] deduces new entity types based on statistics about the usage of properties with entities of known type, e.g. for the *DBpedia Type Completion Service*[1]. Due to the statistical character of this approach, the results are somewhat vague and in order to achieve a high precision only the most probable type mappings are applied. That means the published dataset[2] still contains incorrect mappings while on the other hand valid mappings have been omitted due to their potential vagueness.

[1] http://wifo5-21.informatik.uni-mannheim.de:8080/DBpediaTypeCompletionService/

[2] http://dbpedia.org/Downloads39#mapping-based-types-heuristic

V. Presutti et al. (Eds.): ESWC Satellite Events 2014, LNCS 8798, pp. 231–235, 2014.
DOI: 10.1007/978-3-319-11955-7_25

RDFUnit (a.k.a. Databugger) [3] allows to unit test RDF(S) datasets. Therefore, tests in form of SPARQL queries are derived from the set of schemas applied in the dataset according to predefined patterns, which detect failing resources. These tests are generally applicable and the introduction of restrictions to the schema leads to higher test coverage. Currently, these tests indicate erroneous RDF(S) triples in the dataset but do not provide solutions. Though for some patterns equally generic solutions can easily be found. Likewise, *Inconsistency Checker* [4] detects logical inconsistencies in DBpedia using a reasoner based on an enriched ontology model with strict type constraints. A default solution proposal could be the deletion of triples involved in failed tests.

Crowdsourcing is a valuable (and high quality) mean to detect inconsistency of data to the real world. *TripleCheckMate* [5] have collected erroneous triples in DBpedia. Games with a purpose (GWAP), such as *WhoKnows?* [6], aim to identify errors and inconsistencies on various levels of semantic expressivity.

3 The Patch Request Ontology

The PatchR ontology[3] [1] allows to describe patches, i.e. the removal or insertion of particular RDF(S) triples (or if necessary, wider spanning subgraphs) within a dataset in conjunction with provenance information of how this patch has been detected. Patch description may also include confidence values that express the self-determined reliability of this patch. This confidence must be expressed as a numerical value in the range of $(0, 1]$, whereas a high value means higher confidence and a value of 1 signifies absolute certainty.

Some of the referenced approaches, e.g. *SDtype*, deliver a confidence by default. For other approaches either a ranking could be determined depending on the origin of the patch or a manually provided default value can be applied. As for this experiment we have assumed the confidence of patches from the crowdsourcing approaches *WhoKnows?* and *TripleCheckMate* as relatively high (0.8), and for *RDFUnit* the confidence value depends on the applied pattern. Nevertheless, any agent may be wrong and can not be genuinely trusted. Therefore, each agent obtains a trust value, which might compile from the validation of previous statements.

Such descriptions will allow the aggregation and comparison of multiple efforts' results.

4 Examples

SDtype excludes results of low reliability in the provided dataset. If these results are fostered by other approaches they should likely enter the DBpedia dataset as well. As e. g., the assignment of type `dbo:Artist` to the resource `dbp:Maria_Callas` is omitted since it has received a relatively low score of ≈ 0.18:

[3] http://purl.org/hpi/patchr

```
:patch-1 a pat:Patch ;
    pat:advocate :SDtype ;
    pat:appliesTo <http://dbpedia.org> ;
    pat:status"active" ;
    pat:update [
        guo:target_subject dbp:Maria_Callas ;
        guo:insert [
            a dbo:Artist
    ] ]
    prov:wasGeneratedBy [
        prov:wasAssociatedWith :SDtype ;
        pat:confidence "0.17729138"^^xsd:double
    ] .
```

The *RDFUnit* INVFUNC pattern instantiated with the property dbo:keyPerson, and a player of *WhoKnows?* have identified the same triple to be incorrect in DBpedia. Both patch requests can be aggregated as follows:

```
:patch-2 a pat:Patch ;
    pat:advocate :RDFUnit/INVFUNC , :WhoKnows/Player-1 ;
    pat:appliesTo <http://dbpedia.org> ;
    pat:status "active" ;
    pat:update [
        guo:target_subject dbp:Vimeo ;
        guo:delete [
            dbo:keyPerson dbp:President
    ] ]
    prov:wasGeneratedBy [
        prov:wasAssociatedWith :RDFUnit/INVFUNC ;
        pat:confidence "0.9"^^xsd:double
    ] , [
        prov:wasAssociatedWith :WhoKnows/Player-1 ;
        pat:confidence "0.7"^^xsd:double
    ] .
```

4.1 Combining Confidence Values

In case multiple agents propose the same patch, the confidence grows that this change is valid and should be applied to the dataset. To combine multiple confidences ($c_{p|a}$ and $c_{p|b}$) for the same patch p, the following associative, commutative, uniformely continuous operation $\oplus$ can be applied:

$$\begin{aligned} c_{p|a,b} = c_{p|a} \oplus c_{p|b} &= 1 - ((1 - c_{p|a}) * (1 - c_{p|b})) \\ &= c_{p|a} + c_{p|b} - (c_{p|a} * c_{p|b}) \end{aligned} \tag{1}$$

To achieve the reliability of a patch, we multiply the confidence with the trust in the respective agent. To combine reliabilities we apply again the operation $\oplus$.

$$\begin{aligned} r_{p|a,b} = r_{p|a} \oplus r_{p|b} &= r_{p|a} + r_{p|b} - (r_{p|a} * r_{p|b}) \\ &= t_a c_{p|a} + t_b c_{p|b} - (t_a c_{p|a} * t_b c_{p|b}) \end{aligned} \tag{2}$$

The combined confidence value of `:patch-2` proposed by *RDFUnit* (R) and *WhoKnows?* (W) from the listing above calculates to 0.97. Assuming a trust of 0.75 in both agents the reliability of the patch is ≈ 0.85.

$$\begin{aligned} c_{p2|R,W} &= c_{p2|R} + c_{p2|W} - (c_{p2|R} * c_{p2|W}) \\ &= 0.9 + 0.7 - (0.9 * 0.7) = \underline{0.97} \end{aligned} \tag{3}$$

$$\begin{aligned} r_{p2|R,W} &= t_R c_{p2|R} + t_W c_{p2|W} - (t_R c_{p2|R} * t_W c_{p2|W}) \\ &= 0.75 \cdot 0.9 + 0.75 \cdot 0.7 - (0.75 \cdot 0.9 * 0.75 \cdot 0.7) = \underline{0.845625} \end{aligned} \tag{4}$$

5 Conclusion and Outlook

We described a simple way to collect and aggregate patch descriptions from multiple heterogeneous agents. Aggregating patch descriptions allows to increase the coverage of incorrect and missing RDF(S) triples, whereas the accuracy might decrease.

Further processing of these patches could be the direct application of patches to datasets in order to achieve higher quality. Since the actual sources of errors can be diverse, we plan to identify classes of errors. Therefore, a larger collection of patches can be helpful. We currently generate the patch descriptions for the named approaches using the PatchR API[4]. Many datasets are derived from external sources, such as DBpedia is derived from Wikipedia, it might be necessary or appropriate to fix errors in the original version of the data. On the other hand, the extraction process itself might be imperfect in a way that it produces incorrect triples. In case of DBpedia this includes the extraction framework as well as the mappings that are used to create the triples.

References

1. Knuth, M., Hercher, J., Sack, H.: Collaboratively patching linked data. In: Proceedings of 2nd International Workshop on Usage Analysis and the Web of Data (USEWOD 2012), Co-located with the 21st International World Wide Web Conference 2012 (WWW 2012), Lyon, France, April 2012
2. Paulheim, H., Bizer, C.: Type inference on noisy RDF data. In: Alani, H., Kagal, L., Fokoue, A., Groth, P., Biemann, C., Parreira, J.X., Aroyo, L., Noy, N., Welty, C., Janowicz, K. (eds.) ISWC 2013, Part I. LNCS, vol. 8218, pp. 510–525. Springer, Heidelberg (2013)
3. Kontokostas, D., Westphal, P., Auer, S., Hellmann, S., Lehmann, J., Cornelissen, R., Zaveri, A.J.: Test-driven evaluation of linked data quality. In: Proceedings of the 23rd International Conference on World Wide Web (2014)
4. Töpper, G., Knuth, M., Sack, H.: DBpedia ontology enrichment for inconsistency detection. In: 2012 Proceedings of the 8th International Conference on Semantic Systems (I-SEMANTICS 2012), September 5–7, Graz, Austria, ACM International Conference Proceedings, Graz, Austria, ACM, pp. 33–40, September 2012

[4] https://github.com/mgns/patchr

5. Kontokostas, D., Zaveri, A., Auer, S., Lehmann, J.: Triplecheckmate: a tool for crowdsourcing the quality assessment of linked data. In: Proceedings of the 4th Conference on Knowledge Engineering and Semantic Web (2013)
6. Waitelonis, J., Ludwig, N., Knuth, M., Sack, H.: WhoKnows? - Evaluating linked data heuristics with a quiz that cleans up DBpedia. Int. J. Interact. Technol. Smart Educ. (ITSE) **8**(3), 236–248 (2011)

SPARQL-MM - Extending SPARQL to Media Fragments

Thomas Kurz[1(✉)], Sebastian Schaffert[1], Kai Schlegel[2], Florian Stegmaier[2], and Harald Kosch[2]

[1] Salzburg Research, Salzburg, Austria
thomas.kurz@salzburgresearch.at
http://www.salzburgresearch.at
[2] University of Passau, Passau, Germany
http://www.dimis.fmi.uni-passau.de

Abstract. Interconnecting machine readable data with multimedia assets and fragments has recently become a common practice. But specific retrieval techniques for the so called Semantic Multimedia data are still lacking. On our poster we present SPARQL-MM, a function set that extends SPARQL to Media Fragment facilities by introducing spatio-temporal filter and aggregation functions.

Keywords: SPARQL · Semantic Web · Media fragments

1 Introduction

In the recent past Multimedia and the Semantic Web have moved closer together, reflected in many efforts like W3C recommendations for Media Annotations [2] and Fragment URIs [7], which are also taken up by industry like described e.g. in [4,5]. These efforts mainly focus on a standardized representation of multimedia metadata and the connection to knowledge using Semantic Web technologies, but currently do not consider multimedia specific query functionalities. On our poster we present SPARQL-MM, an extension for SPARQL that introduces spatio-temporal filter and aggregation functions to the de-facto standard query language in the Semantic Web. In the following we give an example, how media is currently represented in the Semantic Web and which functions are missing for current SPARQL.

2 The Hidden Knowledge of Fragment Annotations

Figure 1 outlines an example of an annotated video showing the winners ceremony of an extreme sports event. We use Media Fragment URIs to link annotations to specific spatio-temporal parts of the video. The specification provides a media-format independent, standard means of addressing media fragments on the Web using Uniform Resource Identifiers. It supports particular name-value pairs,

V. Presutti et al. (Eds.): ESWC Satellite Events 2014, LNCS 8798, pp. 236–240, 2014.
DOI: 10.1007/978-3-319-11955-7_26

e.g. `('t='start','end)` for temporal and `('xywh=',x','y','width','height)` for regional fragments. In our example *Connor Macfarlane* appears from second 194 to 198 on the left side, while *Lewis Jones* is marked from second 193 to 198 on the right side. If a user wants to retrieve the (spatio-temporal) snippet, that covers exactly these both person, she may issue a query like: "Give me the spatio-temporal snippet that shows *Lewis Jones* right beside *Connor Macfarlane*". Currently SPARQL does not support such queries, because some necessary information is not explicitly expressed in RDF, but hidden within the Media Fragment URIs. Neither does SPARQL support filter functions like *rightBeside* or *temporalOverlap*, nor aggregation functions like *boundingBox*.

`<http://example.org/person/Connor_Macfarlane>`

↑ `dct:subject`

`<http://example.org/v1#xywh=percent:26,20,22,80&t=194,198>`

`<http://example.org/v1#xywh=percent:71,0,29,100&t=193,198>`

↓ `dct:subject`

`<http://example.org/person/Lewis_Jones>`

Fig. 1. A sample for an annotated video

3 SPARQL Multimedia Functions

Table 1 lists all functions that we took into account for our extension. We follow well known standards like DE-9IM [3] for topological and [1] for temporal relations. The parameters `r1`, `r2` are of type media fragment resource, the boolean `flag` decides, if equal ranges are included or not (whereby `false` is default). A detailed description of all functions in human and machine readable format (following the sparql-service-description extension for describing SPARQL extensions and function libraries[1]) can be found on the source repository of our reference implementation[2]. Each function is identified by a unique

[1] http://www.ldodds.com/schemas/sparql-extension-description/

[2] http://github.com/tkurz/sparql-mm/

URI but all together share the same base URI mm:<http://linkedmultimedia.org/sparql-mm/functions#>. Currently the implementation uses the OpenRDF Sesame[3] API and its extension interfaces, which makes it backend agnostic but requires expensive and inefficient in-memory calculations. We plan to improve this by a backend specific implementation for KiWi Triplestore[4] in combination with SQL/MM [6].

Table 1. SPARQL-MM functions

	Relation function	Aggregation function
Spatial	mm:spatialCovers(r1,r2[,flag])	mm:spatialBoundingBox(r1,r2)
	mm:spatialDisjoint(r1,r2)	mm:spatialIntersection(r1,r2)
	mm:spatialEqual(r1,r2)	
	mm:spatialIntersects(r1,r2[,flag])	
	mm:spatialTouches(r1,r2)	
	mm:bottom(r1)	
	mm:isAbove(r1,r2)	
	mm:isBelow(r1,r2)	
	mm:left(r1)	
	mm:leftBeside(r1,r2)	
	mm:right(r1)	
	mm:rightBeside(r1,r2)	
	mm:top(r1)	
Temporal	mm:after(r1,r2)	mm:temporalIntersection(r1 r2)
	mm:before(r1,r2)	mm:temporalBoundingBox(r1,r2)
	mm:temporalContains(r1,r2[,flag])	mm:temporalIntermediate(r1,r2)
	mm:temporalEqual(r1,r2)	
	mm:finishes(r1,r2[,flag])	
	mm:temporalMeets(r1,r2)	
	mm:temporalOverlaps(r1,r2[,flag])	
	mm:starts(r1,r2)	
Combined		mm:boundingBox(r1,r2)
		mm:intersection(r1,r2)

Using SPARQL-MM functions we can now formulate the users need from Sect. 2 ("Give me the spatio-temporal snippet that shows *Lewis Jones* right beside *Connor Macfarlane*"), as a SPARQL query like in Listing 1.1. We use *mm:temporalOverlaps* to get fragments that appear in the identical temporal sequence. *mm:rightBeside* handles the spatial relation and *mm:boundingBox*

[3] http://www.openrdf.org/

[4] http://marmotta.apache.org/kiwi/triplestore.html

merges every two fragments that match the filters. You can test the query by selecting the example from the samples menu in the demo page[5].

```
PREFIX foaf: <http://xmlns.com/foaf/0.1/>
PREFIX mm: <http://linkedmultimedia.org/sparql-mm/functions#>
PREFIX ma: <http://www.w3.org/ns/ma-ont#>
PREFIX dct: <http://purl.org/dc/terms/>

SELECT (mm:boundingBox(?l1,?l2) AS ?two_guys) WHERE {
    ?f1 a ma:MediaFragment; ma:locator ?l1; dct:subject ?p1.
    ?p1 foaf:name "Lewis Jones".
    ?f2 a ma:MediaFragment; ma:locator ?l2; dct:subject ?p2.
    ?p2 foaf:name "Connor Macfarlane".
    FILTER mm:rightBeside(?l1,?l2)
    FILTER mm:temporalOverlaps(?l1,?l2)
}
```

Listing 1.1. A SPARQL-MM query

4 Conclusion and Further Work

In this paper we presented SPARQL-MM, a function set that adds spatio-temporal filters and aggregators to SPARQL. In further steps we will extend the function set to fragment feature extractors (e.g. *getDuration*) that can for example be used for sorting. We also try to include more complex spatial structures like polygons, e.g. by extending the MediaFragments URIs with a `rel` attribute that points to SVG shapes.

SPARQL-MM is implemented as Open Source project hosted on GitHub.

Acknowledgments. SPARQL-MM is developed within MICO, a research project partially funded by the European Commission 7th FP (grant agreement no: 610480).

References

1. Allen, J.F.: Maintaining knowledge about temporal intervals. Commun. ACM **26**(11), 832–843 (1983)
2. Bailer, W., et al.: Ontology for media resources 1.0. W3C recommendation, W3C, February 2012. http://www.w3.org/TR/2012/REC-mediaont-10-20120209/
3. Clementini, E., di Felice, P., van Oosterom, P.: A small set of formal topological relationships suitable for end-user interaction. In: Abel, D.J., Ooi, B.-C. (eds.) SSD 1993. LNCS, vol. 692, pp. 277–295. Springer, Heidelberg (1993)
4. Kurz, T., et al.: Semantic enhancement for media asset management systems. Multimedia Tools Appl. 1–27 (2012). doi:10.1007/s11042-012-1197-7
5. Lyndon J.B.N.. et al.: Connectme: semantic tools for enriching online video with web content. In: I-SEMANTICS (Posters & Demos). vol. 932, CEUR Workshop Proceedings, pp. 55–62 (2012)

[5] http://demos.mico-project.eu/sparql-mm/sparql-mm/demo/index.html

6. Stolze, K.: SQL/MM spatial - the standard to manage spatial data in a relational database system. In: BTW, pp. 247–264 (2003)
7. Troncy, R., et al.: Media fragments URI 1.0 (basic). W3C recommendation, W3C, September 2012. http://www.w3.org/TR/2012/REC-media-frags-20120925/

A Companion Screen Application for TV Broadcasts Annotated with Linked Open Data

Lyndon Nixon[1(✉)], Lotte Belice Baltussen[2], Lilia Perez Romero[3], and Lynda Hardman[3]

[1] MODUL University, Vienna, Austria
lyndon.nixon@modul.ac.at
[2] Sound and Vision, Hilversum, Holland
[3] CWI, Amsterdam, Holland

Abstract. Increasingly, European citizens consume television content together with devices connected to the Internet where they can look up related information. In parallel, growing amounts of Linked Open Data are being published on the Web, including rich metadata about its cultural heritage. Linked Data and semantic technologies could enable broadcasters to achieve added value for their content at low cost through the re-use of existing and extracted metadata. We present on-going work in the LinkedTV project, whose goal is to achieve seamless interlinking between TV and Web content on the basis of semantic annotations: two scenarios validated by user trials - Linked News and the Hyperlinked Documentary - and a companion screen application which provides related information for those programs during viewing.

1 Introduction

More and more consumers will have SmartTVs at home[1], complemented by laptops or tablets which can function as second screens, e.g. to explore related content (from broadcaster's archives and other online resources) alongside a TV programme. Multitasking while watching TV is a significant consumer trend, with 88 % of TV viewers going online in parallel, and 40 % using their second screen to get more information on what they are watching [1]. Broadcast companies want to provide their viewers with richer interactive television experiences, and are becoming increasingly interested in enriching television content with hyperlinks to data sources that could enhance the attractiveness of watching their content and keep viewers from switching to other content sources online. The European project LinkedTV (http://www.linkedtv.eu) believes that a "true TV ecosystem must functionally integrate the apps with the television programming"[2]. Thus it develops an end-to-end workflow that automates the process

[1] 54 million SmartTVs sold in 2012 will grow to 170 million in 2017, by then 64 'SmartTV device forecasts', Informa Telecoms & Media. https://commerce.informatm.com/reports/smart-tv-device-forecasts.html.

[2] TVs can't be smart. Stop trying to make it happen - WIRED Opinion, Gary Myer, Oct 2013.

V. Presutti et al. (Eds.): ESWC Satellite Events 2014, LNCS 8798, pp. 241–244, 2014.
DOI: 10.1007/978-3-319-11955-7_27

of enriching TV programmes with content, which significantly enhances the user experience. For this, semantic technologies and Linked Open Data (LOD) datasets are used to lower the cost of annotation, which is not scalable in a completely human curated enrichment. In order to get an insight into what potential end-users want to see and do, we conducted user studies. Based on this, a companion screen application was developed that allows viewers to get extra information on the topics in their favourite TV programmes while watching, which they can bookmark and share. In our submission we will talk about (1) the technical process, (2) the LinkedTV use cases (Interactive News, Hyperlinked Documentary) validated by user trials, and (3) the companion screen application.

2 Technical Process and Workflow

The end-to-end server-side workflow of LinkedTV starts with automatic analysis of the audiovisual material and its metadata, applying shot and scene segmentation, visual analysis for concept detection [2], and entity extraction from subtitles [3]. Media Fragments[3] are generated which refer to specific temporal and spatial parts within the analysed television show that present a particular topic or object. For example: an art expert mentions the Greek goddess Hebe, and a Media Fragment corresponding to the utterance is created, e.g. using subtitle information. These Media Fragments are annotated with named entities extracted from the text or visual classifiers. For this, LinkedTV has developed a dedicated ontology[4] and re-uses Linked Data URIs for the entity identifiers. For example, the concept Hebe (ancient Greek goddess) can be found in DBpedia with the URI http://dbpedia.org/resource/Hebe_(mythology). LinkedTV uses "white lists" of Web content sources trusted by the media owner to contain high-quality links that can be used for enrichments. Distinct Web services provide link matches in these "white list" sources for entities, e.g. recent media shared via social Web channels, structured databases of media resources such as the European digital library Europeana, and HTML-based Web sites via a dedicated crawler for embedded media items. A programme editor has access to a dedicated Editor Tool[5] to curate which of these links they want to show to their end users, since usually many more potential targets are found than are reasonable to show. Finally, the LinkedTV Player displays the curated results using HTML5 technology on the companion screen.

3 Use Cases and User Studies

Two scenarios were used to inspire the LinkedTV work: Linked News and the Hyperlinked Documentary. The Linked News scenario is based on the local news

[3] http://www.w3.org/TR/media-frags/
[4] http://linkedtv.eu/ontology
[5] http://editortool.linkedtv.eu

show RBB Aktuell by Rundfunk Berlin Brandenburg; the Hyperlinked Documentary scenario is based on Tussen Kunst en Kitsch (similar to the BBC's Antiques Roadshow, henceforth TKK) of Dutch public broadcaster AVRO[6]. Both programmes contain distinct chapters about specific topics, e.g. Obama's Berlin visit in June 2013 or a 19th century gold watch by famous watch maker Breguet. These specific topics, being linked to open data from the Web, can be enriched with further Web content which offers more information and context about the topics in these chapters. For example, the watch chapter is supplemented with links to the Wikipedia article and Europeana images relating to the figure inside the watch - the Greek goddess Hebe - thanks to the DBpedia URI in the video annotation and the ability to SPARQL query Europeana. To understand what news and TKK viewers really want, we conducted user studies with representative audiences in a living room environment[7]. The results of the user trials led us to adapt our scenarios to highlight topics and objects in the TV programmes which were more of interest to typical viewers, and to link them to Web content which they would have liked to search for (Fig. 1).

4 Enabling Companion Screens for Enriched Television Content

To support viewer access to LinkedTV enrichments via companion screen applications, we developed the Springfield Multiscreen Toolkit (SMT). It supports application developers by abstracting away the low-level details of the synchronization and distribution of content between screens. Developers can create a

(a) User interface highlighting concepts currently active in the TV programme

(b) Living room setting for the Linked News scenario

Fig. 1. LinkedTV companion screen application

[6] http://avro.nl

[7] LinkedTV D3.5 'Requirements Document for LinkedTV User Interfaces (Version 2)' (http://www.linkedTV.eu/wp/wp-content/uploads/2013/12/LinkedTV_D3.5.pdf).

single application that is independent of how many screens are involved and such an application can dynamically react to changes in the amount and types of screens attached to it. Applications are developed using standard technologies, such as HTML5 and Java. The first prototype allows companion screens to control video playback on the main screen and synchronise the associated LinkedTV enrichments to the main screen video.

5 Conclusion

LinkedTV is continually refining the annotation and hyperlinking workflow, expanding the LOD sources it uses and how the available metadata from those sources can be increasingly used in guiding the system to select more relevant links to enrich TV programming. A new, larger cycle of user trials using the scenario demonstrators will help validate further the usefulness of the selected enrichments for viewers, acceptance of personalisation functionality when it requires modelling of user preferences or tracking viewer behaviour, as well as the intuitiveness of the user interface. Furthermore, the cognitive load for end users that a dual screen set-up demands will be explored. The results of the evaluations will be used to improve the added value of using Linked Open Data in the enrichment process for our broadcast partners, namely: greater automation leading to lower costs for providing added value services around their content, which in turn helps keep viewers connected.

Acknowledgments. This work is supported by the Integrated Project LinkedTV (www.linkedTV.eu) funded by the European Commission through the 7th Framework Programme (FP7-287911). LinkedTV would like to thank the AVRO for allowing us to reuse Tussen Kunst & Kitsch content for our research.

References

1. Abreu, J., Almeida, P., Teles, B., Reis, M.: Viewer behaviors and practices in the (new) Television Environment, In: EuroITV 2013, Como, Italy, June 2013. http://socialitv.web.ua.pt
2. Stein, D., et al.: From raw data to semantically enriched hyperlinks: recent advances in the LinkedTV analysis workflow. In: NEM Summit 2013, Nantes, France, October 2013
3. Li, Y., Troncy, R., et al.: Enriching media fragments with named entities for video classification. In: The Linked Media (LiME) Workshop, WWW 2013, Rio de Janeiro, Brazil, May 2013

A Semantic Web Based Core Engine to Efficiently Perform Sentiment Analysis

Diego Reforgiato Recupero[1(✉)], Sergio Consoli[1], Aldo Gangemi[1,2], Andrea Giovanni Nuzzolese[1,3], and Daria Spampinato[1]

[1] STLab-ISTC Consiglio Nazionale delle Ricerche, Rome, Italy
{diego.reforgiato,sergio.consoli,aldo.gangemi,andrea.nuzzolese, daria.spampinato}@istc.cnr.it

[2] LIPN, University Paris 13, Sorbone Cit'e, UMR CNRS, Paris, France

[3] Department of Computer Science and Engineering, University of Bologna, Bologna, Italy

Abstract. In this paper we present a domain-independent framework that creates a sentiment analysis model by mixing Semantic Web technologies with natural language processing approaches (This work is supported by the project PRISMA SMART CITIES, funded by the Italian Ministry of Research and Education under the program PON.). Our system, called Sentilo, provides a core sentiment analysis engine which fully exploits semantics. It identifies the holder of an opinion, topics and sub-topics the opinion is referred to, and assesses the opinion trigger. Sentilo uses an OWL opinion ontology to represent all this information with an RDF graph where holders and topics are resolved on Linked Data. Anyone can plug its own opinion scoring algorithm to compute scores of opinion expressing words and come up with a combined scoring algorithm for each identified entities and the overall sentence.

Keywords: Sentic computing · Sentiment analysis · Semantic features

1 Introduction

Sentiment Analysis is a research area that involves the analysis of people's sentiments, opinions, emotions towards entities such as products, movies, services, etc. It is one of the hottest problems which belongs to the Natural Language Processing field which has been investigated only starting from the year 2000. So far, Sentiment Analysis approaches have used statistical classifiers, natural language processing techniques, data mining and lexical resources to identify the tone of a given sentence respect to a certain topic. For example, given the following opinion: *"Joy Ride is not an interesting film but the director John Dahl made a perfect work for his audience"*; an ideal system would be able to identify several topics referred to by such opinionated sentence. *"Joy Ride"* is certainly one, the *"work of John Dahl"* associated with this movie is another one, and finally *"John Dahl"*. Additionally, such ideal system would be able to analyze that the

V. Presutti et al. (Eds.): ESWC Satellite Events 2014, LNCS 8798, pp. 245–248, 2014.
DOI: 10.1007/978-3-319-11955-7_28

sentiment expressed on *"Joy Ride"* is negative, while the sentiment expressed on the work of *"John Dahl"*, and on *"John Dahl"* himself is slightly positive, and that the whole sentence carries both positive and negative sentiments.

The goal of Sentiment Analysis is to detect quintuples $(e_j, a_{jk}, so_{ijkl}, h_i, t_l)$ from unstructured text where e_j is the topic, $\mathrm{a_{jk}}$ is the aspect/feature of the topic e_j, so_{ijkl} is the sentiment value of the opinion from the opinion holder h_i on aspect a_jk at time t_l. Structure the unstructured data extracted from raw text is still a challenging task [1].

Semantics has been used only recently for Sentiment Analysis [10] where the authors provide evidence that the inclusion of semantics features in sentiment analysis algorithms improves the overall performance.

Semantic sentiment analysis can take advantage from linked data, ontologies, controlled vocabularies, and lexical resources (e.g. DBpedia, YAGO, ConceptNet [9], SenticNet [4], Nell[1], OIE[2], etc.), which help aggregating the conceptual and affective information associated with natural language opinions.

In this paper we describe Sentilo, a sentic computing system introduced in [8] that can be used as a sentiment analysis core engine to structure text and detect sentiment quintuples according to an ontology defined ad-hoc for the sentiment analysis tasks. Sentilo produces a RDF representation of an opinion sentence that allows the identification of holders, topics (resolved on Linked data to allow aggregation of sentiments on the same topic in different contexts/sources) and opinion triggers with high accuracy. With the use of semantics, we can extend the current state of the art in sentiment analysis to track, correlate, and compare sentiment of specific entities or group of related entities over time and across different contexts. Sentilo core engine prototype can be accessed through its REST API[3] and extended with sentiment scoring modules focusing on the features/domain that researchers want to target.

2 Sentilo Semantic Model

Sentilo consists of a set of components connected in a pipeline [8]. Given a sentence, the syntactic constructs are provided by C&C [6], a highly efficient linguistically parser using a tightly-integrated supertagger, which assigns combinatory categorial grammar lexical categories to words in a sentence. On top of that, the data are processed by Boxer [2], an open-domain software component for semantic analysis of text. It is compatible with first-order logic and builds upon the combinatory categorial grammar and discourse representation theory (DRT). DRT uses an explicit semantic structured language called Discourse Representation Structure (DRS). In Boxer, DRS are enriched with the VerbNet[4] inventory of thematic roles. Output of Boxer is then processed by FRED[5], a tool that uses

[1] http://rtw.ml.cmu.edu/rtw/
[2] http://ai.cs.washington.edu/projects/open-information-extraction
[3] http://wit.istc.cnr.it/stlab-tools/sentilo/service
[4] http://verbs.colorado.edu/~mpalmer/projects/verbnet.html
[5] http://wit.istc.cnr.it/stlab-tools/fred

frame-based design and a set of heuristics in order to produce correct terminology and structure according to Semantic Web design practices. FRED transforms the logical output of Boxer with frames into RDF/OWL in compliance with linked data principles as existing vocabularies are re-used whenever possible, named entities are resolved over resources existing in RDF datasets of the linked data cloud and, terms are disambiguated against WordNet and foundational ontologies. FRED is inspired by Davidson's view [5]: events and situations are primary objects for the representation of a domain. Based on this view of the world, sentences are represented as linked events or situations, with participating objects. We use DOLCE+DnS [7][6] as a vocabulary for events and situations, and VerbNet as reference for thematic roles of events. On top of FRED, we have developed an *opinion model annotator* (see [8] for the new and re-used components employed in Sentilo), a component that implements a set of heuristics that extract, from the FRED's graph of a given sentence, information about holders of an opinion sentence, its topics, and its opinion expressing words (i.e., opinion features). To the best of our knowledge, only a few of semantic models have been provided for sentiment analysis. One of the most relevant includes the MARL model which has been adopted in [3] to represent languages resources for sentiment analysis in a Linked Data conform way enabling leveraging of existing Semantic Web technologies. Sentilo enriches the RDF/OWL semantic representation of an opinion sentence with annotation triples based on *OntoSentilo*, an ontology for opinion sentences that we have defined in [8]. OntoSentilo represents concepts and relations existing between entities composing an opinion sentence. Figure 1 shows a fragment of the RDF graph that represents the sentence *You may think that the summer weather provides the perfect backdrop to a big day.* The use of the prefix `sentilo:` is intended for the local namespaces of concepts and relations added by Sentilo. Sentilo formally represents the holder of the opinion, i.e. person, the main topic of the sentence, i.e. the event occurrence `fred:think_1`, and its subtopics, i.e. the event occurrence `fred:backdrop_1`. Opinion features are identified as values of the relation `dul:hasQuality`, in this case `fred:perfect1`

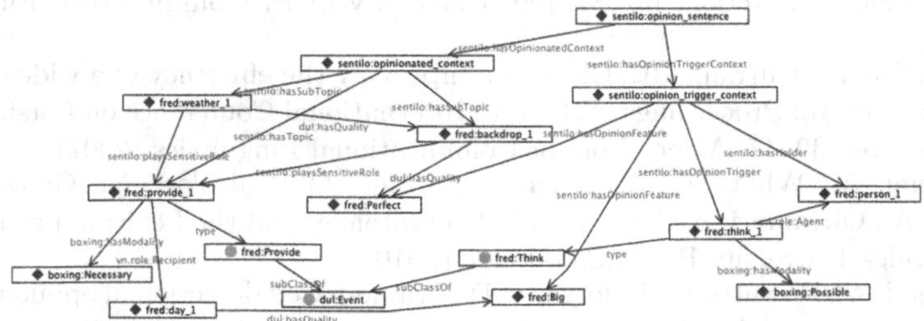

Fig. 1. An extract of the semantic representation for *"You may think that the summer weather provides the perfect backdrop to a big day"*. Note all the semantic relations provided by the framework that can be used for different purposes.

[6] http://ontologydesignpatterns.org/ont/dul/DUL.owl

is a quality of the subtopic `fred:backdrop_1`. As an example of scoring, let us assume that `perfect` is assigned a score of 0.8. Then we can easily associate that score to the entity `backdrop` whose holder is already provided by the framework. The scores to assign to words in the model depends on the domain to focus and on the kind of feelings that want to be extracted. For example, one may want to extract feelings related to fear/bravery and provide scoring for words in that domain. Sentilo performances have been computed in [8] for time and accuracy of topic and sub-topic detection. A deep evaluation on the use of semantics to improve the sentiment analysis tasks (and comparisons) has to be done yet.

3 Conclusions

In this paper we have shown Sentilo, a semantic sentiment analysis core engine able to identify holders, topics, subtopics, opinion triggers, semantic sentiment relationships between terms. Anyone can use the information structured by Sentilo according to a sentiment analysis ontology and design his own sentiment analysis scoring algorithms to build on top of our framework in order to provide entity and sentence level sentiment scores.

References

1. Bing, L.: Sentiment analysis and subjectivity. In: Invited Chapter for the Handbook of Natural Language Processing (2010)
2. Bos, J.: Wide-coverage semantic analysis with boxer. In: Bos, J., Delmonte, R. (eds.) STEP 2008 Conference Proceedings on Semantics in Text Processing. vol. 1. Research in Computational Semantics, pp. 277–286. College Publications (2008)
3. Buitelaar, P., Arcan, M., Iglesias, C.A., Sanchez, J.F., Strapparava, C.: D3.1 - language resource model. Specification for semantic interoperability. In: EUROSENTIMENT Project FP7, pp. 1–21 (2013)
4. Cambria, E., Havasi, C., Hussain, A.: SenticNet 2: a semantic and affective resource for opinion mining and sentiment analysis. In: Youngblood, G.M., McCarthy, P.M. (eds.) FLAIRS Conference, pp. 202–207. AAAI Press (2012)
5. Davidson, D.: The logical form of action sentences. In: Rescher, N. (ed.) The Logic of Decision and Action, pp. 81–120. University of Pittsburgh Press, Pittsburgh (1967)
6. Djordjevic, B., Curran, J.R., Clark, S.: Improving the efficiency of a wide-coverage CCG parser. In: Proceedings of the 10th International Conference on Parsing Technologies, pp. 39–47. Association for Computational Linguistics (2007)
7. Gangemi, A.: What's in a schema? In: Huang, C., Calzolari, N., Gangemi, A., Lenci, A., Oltramari, A., Prevot, L. (eds.) Ontology and the Lexicon, pp. 144–182. Cambridge University Press, Cambridge (2010)
8. Gangemi, A., Presutti, V., Reforgiato, D.: Frame-based detection of opinion holders and topics: a model and a tool. IEEE Comput. Intell. Mag. **9**(1), 31–43 (2014)
9. Liu, H., Singh, P.: ConceptNet: a practical commonsense reasoning toolkit. BT Technol. J. **22**(4), 211–226 (2004)
10. Saif, H., He, Y., Alani, H.: Semantic sentiment analysis of twitter. In: Cudré-Mauroux, P., Heflin, J., Sirin, E., Tudorache, T., Euzenat, J., Hauswirth, M., Parreira, J.X., Hendler, J., Schreiber, G., Bernstein, A., Blomqvist, E. (eds.) ISWC 2012, Part I. LNCS, vol. 7649, pp. 508–524. Springer, Heidelberg (2012)

Balloon Synopsis: A Modern Node-Centric RDF Viewer and Browser for the Web

Kai Schlegel(✉), Thomas Weißgerber, Florian Stegmaier, Christin Seifert, Michael Granitzer, and Harald Kosch

University of Passau, Innstrasse 41, 94032 Passau, Germany
{kai.schlegel,thomas.weibgerber,florian.stegmaier,christin.seifert, michael.granitzer,harald.kosch}@uni-passau.de

Abstract. Nowadays, the RDF data model is a crucial part of the Semantic Web. Especially web developers favour RDF serialization formats like RDFa and JSON-LD. However, the visualization of large portions of RDF data in an appealing way is still a cumbersome task. RDF visualizers in general are not targeting the Web as usage scenario or simply display the complex RDF graph directly rather than applying a human friendly facade. *Balloon Synopsis* tries to overcome these issues by providing an easy-to-use RDF visualizer based on HTML and JavaScript. For an ease integration, it is implemented as jQuery-plugin offering a node-centric RDF viewer and browser with automatic Linked Data enhancement in a modern tile design.

1 RDF Data Is Online - Most RDF Visualizations Are Not

Linked Data and the Semantic Web increase in volume leading to huge amounts of RDF data. Today, even non-experts manage open data, extract semantic information from text and integrate these sources easily in their information system [1]. However, displaying graph-based RDF data in a human-friendly way is challenging.

This paper demonstrates a modern tile-based visualization of RDF data. While there are many tools available to present RDF data to an user [2–4], most of them are not available in web-browsers and use tree- or graph-based layouts. RDF visualizations should support the user to conceive information from the data quickly. Furthermore, aggregation of different knowledge sources should be possible to enable a simplified view. However, the common node-link layouts can be very space consuming and may show node or edge overlappings. As a result, even simple RDF graphs can look confusingly complex to humans. Additionally, a RDF visualization can exploit the fact, that RDF data is interlinked with other online resources. Browsing a RDF graph can be automatically extended by

The presented work was developed within the CODE and MICO project partially funded by the EU Seventh Framework Programme, grant agreement number 296150 and 610480.

V. Presutti et al. (Eds.): ESWC Satellite Events 2014, LNCS 8798, pp. 249–253, 2014.
DOI: 10.1007/978-3-319-11955-7_29

considering Linked Data resources. *Balloon Synopsis* was developed to allow Web developers an easy-to-use and embeddable RDF visualization for their website, enabling simple access and re-use of Linked Data. The key-highlights of this approach are as follows:

- Human friendly presentation of RDF utilizing a *node-centric view* and *ontology templating.*
- *Automatic enrichment* using SPARQL endpoints or automatic query federation over Linked Data.
- *HTML and JavaScript based*, to ensure a simple integration and extension by web developers.

The remaining paper discusses these in more detail.

2 Node-Centric and Human Friendly RDF Visualization

The user interface of *balloon Synopsis* is inspired by modern operation systems and design trends. A main principle is to focus on the content and direct relationship between semantic entities rather than showing a global and complex context. Semantic entities (graph nodes) are considered as autonomous tiles, containing information about the entity itself. Clicking on a tile gives the user the possibility to view the represented resource in detail, leading to a new node-centric overlay. Figure 1 shows a screenshot of a detail view. All related information or entities are again arranged as clickable tiles, allowing an iteratively browsing trough the data.

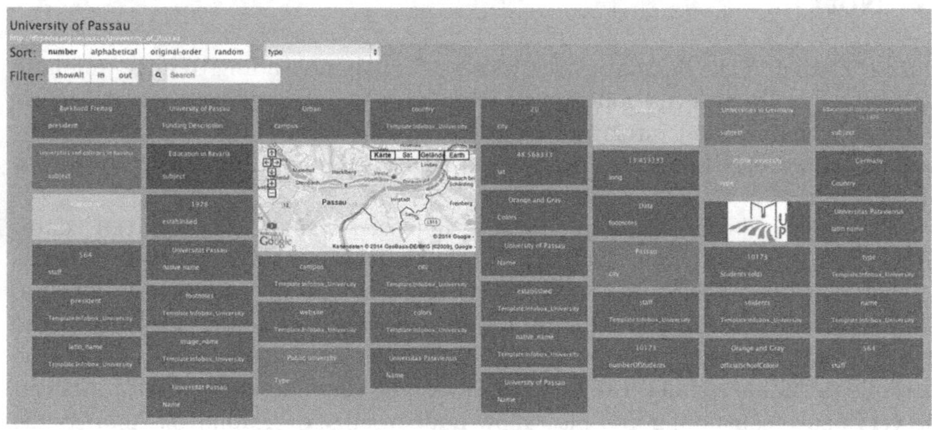

Fig. 1. Viewing an example entity with enriched information and ontology templating

At any time, the user has the possibility to sort, filter and search (using keywords and regular expressions) the displayed tiles to gather information, according to the need of an users. Typically a tile represents low-end information like resource, blank node or literal. This could result in overloaded visualizations, because a specific entity can be included in many different triples. To overcome this issue, *balloon Synopsis* implements customizable filters. These filters, for example, combine equal predicates and nodes in a common tile or remove irrelevant nodes (blacklist) to simplify the view. Furthermore, developers can easily configure ontology templates to transform data to a human friendly representation. As an example, Fig. 1 shows an instance of ontology templating by viewing a map instead of longitude and latitude coordinates.

Based on its configuration, *balloon Synopsis* can either work with imported data alone or can make use of an automatic enrichment of the data at runtime. In the second case configured knowledge bases are queried in the background to enhance current tile views successively. All filters are then applied on the resulting data consequently. While browsing the data, a history is saved to allow jumping back to already shown view layers and to track an users behavior.

3 Prototypic Open Source Implementation

Balloon Synopsis features a HTML and JavaScript implementation and is available as jQuery-plugin. To give more detailed information, Fig. 2 highlights essential internal components. At its core, balloon Synopsis uses a **local SPARQL capable RDF store**[1]. To import data into the local store, a set of different possibilities are offered. Besides common RDF serializations like Turtle, N3 or

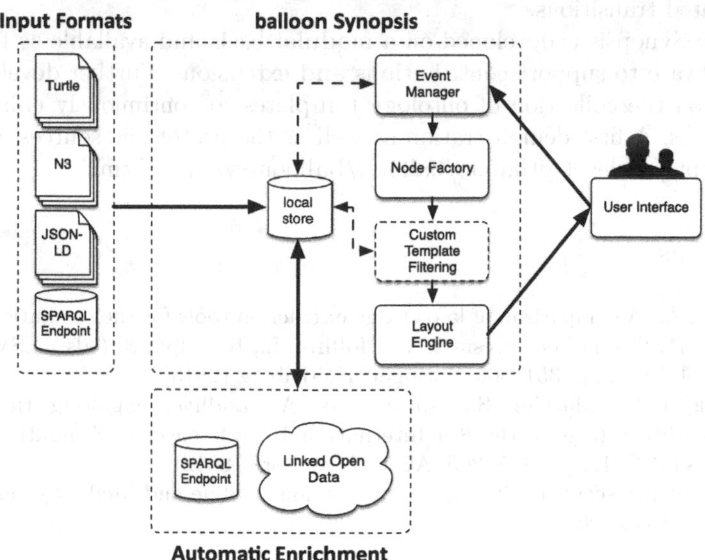

Fig. 2. Conceptual overview of internal processing steps

[1] https://github.com/antoniogarrote/rdfstore-js

JSON-LD, *balloon Synopsis* offers to specify a SPARQL endpoint and SPARQL query to load remote RDF data portions. In the whole project, cross domain problems are circumvented by using YQL[2], to facilitate remote data querying. The initial view can be configured by an arbitrary initialization query to the local store or an automatic arrangement of all entities.

By clicking on a tile, the **user interface** invokes the **event manager** to show a specific detail view. The event manager is supposed to query the local store for information about the desired entity. As described above, *balloon Synopsis* offers an **automatic enrichment** of the local RDF data by querying (i) remote SPARQL endpoints or (ii) do an query federation over Linked Data endpoints utilizing the recently introduced *balloon Fusion* service [5]. The selection of proper remote endpoints is significant for a fast browsing performance. The event manager transmits all results to the **node factory**, which transforms the RDF data to corresponding JavaScript components to represent the content of a basic tile. These components are then forwarded to a **(custom) template filtering**. Besides aforementioned pre-packed filters to simplify the view, a developer can easily integrate custom ontology templates by means of a JavaScript function and a HTML snippet using handlebars syntax[3]. The custom filter also has access to the local store to load additional informations or alter existing tiles. The final layout is then computed by the **layout engine**, which can influence, for example, the ranking, scale and color of tiles based on importance or similarity. In addition, the user interface itself can affect the layout due to searching, sorting or responsive design events (e.g. resizing or panning). Integrated layouting mechanisms, building upon isotope[4], enable flexible reordering of the view and animated transitions.

Balloon Synopsis is developed on a modular basis and available as free open source software to support contributions and extensions. Further developments will focus on the collection of ontology templates to continuously enhance the visualizations. A first demonstration as well as the prototypic sources are available at http://schlegel.github.io/balloon/balloon-synopsis.html.

References

1. Gangemi, A.: A comparison of knowledge extraction tools for the semantic Web. In: Cimiano, P., Corcho, O., Presutti, V., Hollink, L., Rudolph, S. (eds.) ESWC 2013. LNCS, vol. 7882, pp. 351–366. Springer, Heidelberg (2013)
2. Camarda, D.V., Mazzini, S., Antonuccio, A.: Lodlive, exploring the web of data. In: Proceedings of the 8th International Conference on Semantic Systems, I-SEMANTICS '12, pp. 197–200. ACM, New York (2012)
3. Sayers, C.: Node-centric rdf graph visualization. Mobile and Media Systems Laboratory, HP Labs (2004)

[2] http://developer.yahoo.com/yql/
[3] http://handlebarsjs.com/
[4] http://isotope.metafizzy.co/

4. Pietriga, E.: Isaviz: a visual environment for browsing and authoring RDF models. In: Eleventh International World Wide Web Conference Developers Day (2002)
5. Schlegel, K., Stegmaier, F., Bayerl, S., Granitzer, M., Kosch, H.: Balloon fusion: SPARQL rewriting based on unified co-reference information. In: 5th International Workshop on Data Engineering Meets the Semantic Web, Co-Located with the 30th IEEE International Conference on Data Engineering (2014)

Ranking Entities in a Large Semantic Network

Michael Schuhmacher(✉) and Simone Paolo Ponzetto

Research Group Data and Web Science, University of Mannheim, Mannheim, Germany
{michael,simone}@informatik.uni-mannheim.de

Abstract. We present two knowledge-rich methods for ranking entities in a semantic network. Our approach relies on the DBpedia knowledge base for acquiring fine-grained information about entities and their semantic relations. Experiments on a benchmarking dataset show the viability of our approach.

1 Introduction

Entity ranking [2] is the task of ordering a given set of entities on the basis of their relevance with respect to a reference entity. As an example, "Apple Inc." can have different degrees of association with other entities, ranging from highly related ones ("Steve Jobs") to mildly ("NeXT") or marginally relevant ones ("Ford Motor Company") – see Fig. 1. Entity ranking can be produced automatically by computing the degree of semantic relatedness between the reference entity, and each of the other entities of interest. Much work in the field of Natural Language Processing has focused on knowledge-rich approaches to semantic relatedness [5]. However, almost all approaches using knowledge resources rely on the hierarchical structure of a taxonomy, typically WordNet, as opposed to full-fledged semantic networks – like, for instance, DBpedia [1] – containing fine-grained, explicit semantic relations, and whose taxonomic backbone represents only a fraction of the semantic information they encode.

2 Knowledge-Based Entity Ranking

We study two knowledge-rich methods to rank entities in a semantic network.

Path-Based Method. We compute relatedness directly on the basis of the cheapest path between two entities. This leverages information from the knowledge base by means of a weighting method that takes into account the explicit semantic relations found within the resource (see [4] for details):

(1) We build from the set of input entities a labeled, directed graph containing the entities themselves and all intermediate entities and relations in the knowledge base.

V. Presutti et al. (Eds.): ESWC Satellite Events 2014, LNCS 8798, pp. 254–258, 2014.
DOI: 10.1007/978-3-319-11955-7_30

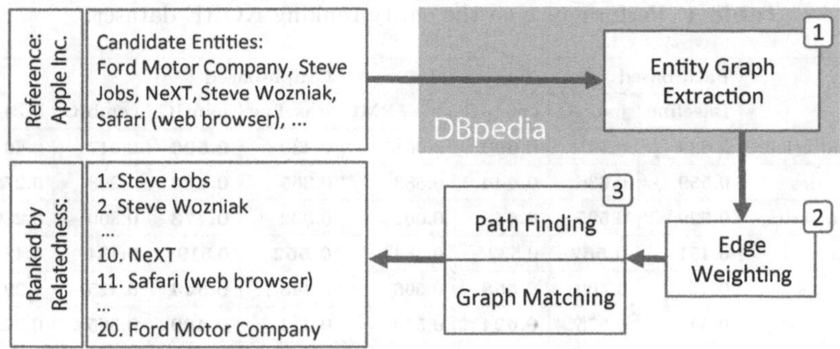

Fig. 1. Entity ranking workflow.

(2) We weight graph edges by edge cost, where weights capture the degree of associativity between the source and target nodes. We use the information-theoretic measures of [4] to capture different degrees of associations between entities in the semantic network on the basis of their specificity.
(3) We compute semantic distances between entity pairs – i.e., the reference entity and each of the entities of interest – as the minimum path cost between them in our weighted graph. Finally, we rank the entity pairs increasingly by semantic distance.

Graph-Matching Method. The approach described so far relies on entities being connected by meaningful semantic relations in the reference resource. However, this requirement could be too strict for some entities, namely those for which very few or no informative semantic relations exist in the underlying ontology (e.g., technical terms like "Oxygen fluoride" or "Manifold"). Even more problematic, this method cannot be applied to entities that are not found in the knowledge base – e.g., how much related is "Simone Ponzetto" with "I-SEMANTICS"? For this reason, we explore a second, alternative approach:

(1) We represent each entity using the set of entities linked within the abstract of the corresponding (English) Wikipedia article. For example, "Manifold" links to "Topological Space", "Lemniscate", "Klein bottle", and so on.
(2) For each set of entities, we build a weighted semantic graph following the previously described graph construction method, in order to identify the sub-graph of DBpedia covered by each definition.
(3) Given that each entity is now represented as a subgraph, we view computing relatedness as a graph comparison problem, and compute relatedness using a Graph Edit Distance based measure, which finds the optimal matching between two entity-based graphs using the Hungarian method [3].

Our hunch here is to use a knowledge-rich text similarity method applied to the entities' textual descriptions in order to overcome the limited availability of semantic relations for some entities in the knowledge base. Crucially, this

Table 1. Performance on the entity ranking KORE dataset.

	Path-based				Graph-based			
	Baseline	jointIC	combIC	IC + PMI	Baseline	jointIC	combIC	IC + PMI
Hollywood celebr.	0.639	0.541	**0.690**	0.661	0.439	**0.506**	0.417	0.401
IT companies	0.559	0.636	**0.644**	0.583	0.355	**0.446**	0.298	0.278
Television series	0.529	0.595	**0.643**	0.602	0.302	**0.473**	0.300	0.280
Video games	0.451	**0.562**	0.532	0.484	**0.552**	0.519	0.434	0.424
Chuck norris	0.458	0.409	**0.558**	0.506	0.448	**0.544**	0.425	0.291
All	0.541	0.575	**0.624**	0.579	0.414	**0.489**	0.365	0.343

method enables knowledge-rich entity ranking even for those entities which are not in the knowledge base, provided they can be associated with a semantified textual description. To this end, we build upon the work from [4] who present a structure-based method to compute semantic similarity between documents, here applied to compute entity relatedness instead.

3 Experiments

Experimental Setting. We use the KORE entity ranking dataset [2], consisting of 21 different reference entities from four different domains. Relatedness assessments were obtained using a crowd-sourcing approach. We evaluate using Spearman's rank correlation (ρ) and DBpedia 3.8 as knowledge base.

Results and Discussion. The results in Table 1 indicate that weighing paths based on their information content (as introduced in [4]) consistently outperforms a baseline approach that simply computes entity relatedness as a function of distance in the network. In the case of the path-based approach, the best weighting schema is combIC, which achieves an average increase of 15.5 % (statistically significant for each task at $p \leq .001$ level with paired t-test).

The graph-matching approach always performs lower than the cheapest path based method. Error analysis revealed that this is due to the fact that, although the Wikipedia abstracts from which entity graphs are built provide us with an enriched context, they also introduce noise deriving from generic entities – especially in the case of popular (and hence, highly hyperlinked) entities. For instance, in the abstract for "Apple Inc." we found hyperlinks to "Coca-Cola" and "Fortune 500". While a context-based approach could still help with those poorly connected entities, we opt here for evaluation on benchmarking data (i.e., KORE) and leave further experimental analysis for future work.

Path-based Method with Top-K Paths. Our path-based method achieves competitive performance – when compared against [2], our methods achieves a performance only slightly lower than their original proposal (ρ = 0.673), while outperforming all its approximations (ρ = 0.621 and 0.425). However, our approach relies only on the single cheapest path connecting two entities.

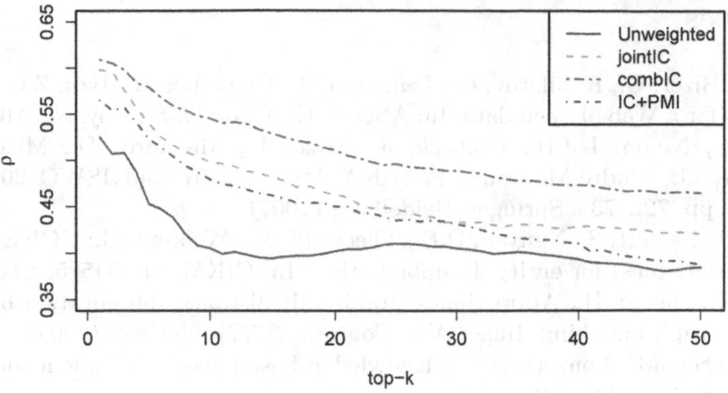

Fig. 2. Results using top-k average path costs.

Consequently, we analyze the impact of taking multiple paths between a pair of entities, and aggregating evidence by averaging their costs to compute the final relatedness score. We show the results in Fig. 2. For all three weighting schemes the performance of our method monotonically decreases with the number of top-k paths used for computing relatedness. The best results are obtained for $k = 1$, namely the cheapest path only, thus indicating that robust performance on this task relies on finding specific, highly informative paths – and thus meaningful semantic relations – between entities. Again, the best results are obtained using the combIC weighting, which outperforms all other measures for any k.

Path-Based Method with Different Knowledge Base. We next perform a diachronic evaluation by evaluating the path-based method using the latest DBpedia Version (3.9), which contains more entities (+6.2 %) and semantic relations (+23.9 %)[1]. Results for all three weighting approaches show minimal variations ($\rho = 0.592$, 0.620 and 0.580 for jointIC, combIC and IC + PMI, respectively), as opposed to the unweighted baseline, which, in contrast decreases by more than 6 points (−11.3 %). Manual inspection revealed that the increased amount of new relations causes the unweighted approach more often to choose noisy, i.e., low-informative paths. In contrast, thanks to our weighting, we are able to maintain a stable performance, regardless of the continuous growth of the network.

4 Conclusions

We presented a knowledge-rich approach to entity ranking. Results indicate that fine-grained semantic information from a wide-coverage knowledge base can be effectively used for this task when combined with robust weighting and path search techniques. Future work will explore multilinguality, and exploit relatedness scores of unknown entities for knowledge base population.

[1] http://wiki.dbpedia.org/Datasets39/DatasetStatistics

References

1. Auer, S., Bizer, C., Kobilarov, G., Lehmann, J., Cyganiak, R., Ives, Z.G.: DBpedia: a nucleus for a Web of open data. In: Aberer, K., Choi, K.-S., Noy, N., Allemang, D., Lee, K.-I., Nixon, L.J.B., Golbeck, J., Mika, P., Maynard, D., Mizoguchi, R., Schreiber, G., Cudré-Mauroux, P. (eds.) ASWC 2007 and ISWC 2007. LNCS, vol. 4825, pp. 722–735. Springer, Heidelberg (2007)
2. Hoffart, J., Seufert, S., Nguyen, D.B., Theobald, M., Weikum, G.: KORE: keyphrase overlap relatedness for entity disambiguation. In: CIKM, pp. 545–554 (2012)
3. Riesen, K., Bunke, H.: Approximate graph edit distance computation by means of bipartite graph matching. Image Vis. Comput. **27**(7), 950–959 (2009)
4. Schuhmacher, M., Ponzetto, S.P.: Knowledge-based graph document modeling. In: WSDM, pp. 543–552 (2014)
5. Zhang, Z., Gentile, A.L., Ciravegna, F.: Recent advances in methods of lexical semantic relatedness - a survey. Nat. Lang. Eng. **1**(1), 1–69 (2012)

Improving the Online Visibility of Touristic Service Providers by Using Semantic Annotations

Ioan Toma(✉), Corneliu Stanciu, Anna Fensel, Ioannis Stavrakantonakis, and Dieter Fensel

Semantic Technology Institute (STI) - Innsbruck, ICT Technologiepark, Technikerstrasse 21a, 6020 Innsbruck, Austria
{ioan.toma,corneliu.stanciu,anna.fensel,ioannis.stavrakantonakis, dieter.fensel}@sti2.at

Abstract. The vast majority of people use the Internet to search for various products and services including those touristic. Now more than ever it becomes critical for touristic businesses to have a strong online presence. In order to achieve this goal it is however essential that multiple communication channels and technologies are properly used. In particular having semantic annotations on the website that can be understood by search engines is extremely important. In this paper we present our ongoing effort on using Linked Data technologies to improve the online visibility of touristic service providers from Innsbruck and its surroundings. We show which technologies are relevant, how they can be applied in our real world pilot and we measure the impact of using such technologies.

1 Introduction

Having a good online marketing strategy results into higher online visibility and ultimately into increased sales. In order to achieve this goal it is however essential that multiple communication channels (e.g. social media channels, website, blog, etc.) and technologies are properly used. In particular having semantic annotations on the website that can be understood by search engines is extremely important as it boosts the online visibility and increases the chances that the website is in the search engines' results to a relevant query. In one of our recent studies [1], we analyzed more than 2000 touristic service providers, namely hotels and hotels chains in Austria, on how they use Web technologies, including Linked Data and semantic annotations. Our study shows that most touristic service providers nearly fail completely to use such technologies, either by not using them at all or by using them only minimally and mostly inappropriately. In contrast, intermediaries such as booking engines (e.g. booking.com, hrs.de) are using these technologies nearly perfectly. As part of our project pilot with Tourismusverband Innsbruck (TVb)[1], the touristic association of touristic

[1] http://www.innsbruck.info/

V. Presutti et al. (Eds.): ESWC Satellite Events 2014, LNCS 8798, pp. 259–262, 2014.
DOI: 10.1007/978-3-319-11955-7_31

service providers located in the city of Innsbruck and its surroundings, we are showing that using multiple communication channels and the latest Web technologies, including Linked Data and semantic annotations, brings concrete, measurable benefits in terms on online visibility. In this paper we present our ongoing effort on using these technologies to improve the TVb online visibility. In the pilot we are annotating the content of the TVb website using schema.org annotations. We provide annotations for hotels, restaurants, cafes and events, and we are also building a Linked Open Data dataset which includes and integrates these annotations. The remainder of this paper is structured as follows: Sect. 2 presents more details about our approach, in terms of overall architecture and technologies used. Finally, Sect. 3 provides preliminary results on how the usage of our proposed solution has impacted the TVB online visibility, discusses future work and concludes the paper.

2 Approach

In our approach we use schema.org to create annotations. schema.org is an approach supported by the main search engines i.e. Bing, Google, Yahoo!, Yandex. schema.org is the major initiative that webmasters can use to markup their pages in ways recognized by major search providers. schema.org is a very large vocabulary counting hundreds of terms from multiple domains (the full specification of schema.org is available at https://schema.org/docs/full.html). Of course not all of the schema.org terms are relevant for the tourism domain. For the TVb website in particular the relevant schema.org terms are those that belong to the categories Hotels, Food and Drink Establishments, Events, Trips, Place of Interest and News. Most of the content on the TVb website is pulled from an external data source provider, namely feratel media technologies AG[2]. More precisely this includes: Hotels, Apartments, Camping, Restaurants, Bars or Pubs, Cafes, Events and Sightseeing. Table 1 shows the mappings between content types coming from feratel to those in schema.org.

In terms of implementation, in order to inject the semantic annotations into the TVb website, we have extended the integration of the TVb website and the feratel system. The integration is implemented as a Typo3[3] extension plugin, referred as seo_feratel in Fig. 1. TVb web site is built using the Typo3 content management system, and the Typo3 extensions seo_feratel is responsible for periodically getting content from feratel and shown it into the Typo3 website.

The plugin is actually using a html template to structure the content - Hotels, Restaurants, etc. In order to insert annotations according to schema.org into the TVb website we extended the HTML template as shown in Fig. 1. Using the modified HTML template, we insert annotations inside the HTML tags for the following types:

1. Hotels, Apartments and Campings using the following properties: Name, Email, URL, Map, PostalAddress (including streetAddress, addressCountry, postalCode, addressLocality, telephone and faxNumber).

[2] http://www.feratel.at/
[3] http://typo3.org/

Table 1. Mapping feratel content to schema.org for the TVb website

No.	Concept in feratel	Type in schema.org
1	Hotel	schema:Hotel (rdfs:subClassOf schema:LodgingBusiness)
2	Apartment	schema:LodgingBusiness (rdfs:subClassOf schema:LocalBusiness)
3	Camping	schema:LodgingBusiness (rdfs:subClassOf schema:LocalBusiness)
4	Restaurant	schema:Restaurant (rdfs:subClassOf schema:FoodEstablishment)
5	Bar, Pub	schema:BarOrPub (rdfs:subClassOf schema:FoodEstablishment)
6	Cafe	schema:CafeOrCoffeeShop (rdfs:subClassOf schema:FoodEstablishment)
7	Event	schema:Event (rdfs:subClassOf schema:Thing)
8	Sightseeing	schema:TouristAttraction (rdfs:subClassOf schema:Place)

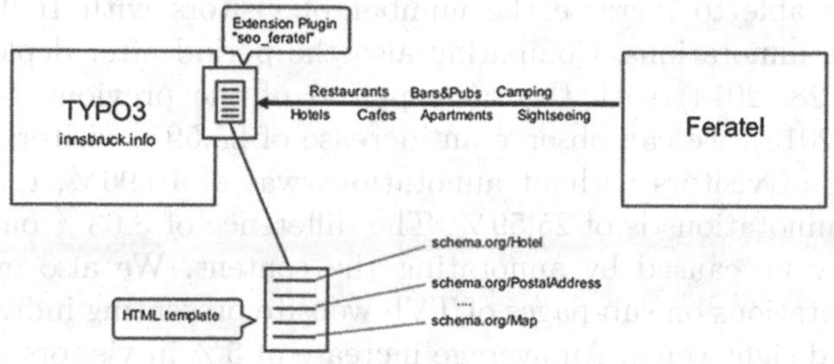

Fig. 1. TVb website feratel integration - HTML template modified to insert schema.org annotations

2. Restaurants, Cafes, Bars and Pubs, and Sightseeing using the following properties: Name, Map, PostalAddress (including streetAddress, addressCountry, postalCode, addressLocality, telephone and faxNumber).

The automatic creation of semantic annotations, on the fly according to schema.org, is complemented by a knowledge engineering effort we are carrying on in order to improve the quality of annotations. We are creating Linked Open Data dataset which includes and integrates annotations of touristic service providers such Hotels, Restaurants, Cafes, etc. The dataset is available at http://loi.sti2.at/openrdf-workbench/repositories/STI/summary and contains annotations of about 100 touristic service providers in Innsbruck and its surroundings.

3 Evaluation, Conclusions and Future Work

We have performed a preliminary evaluation in order to measure the impact of having deployed semantic annotations according to schema.org on the TVb

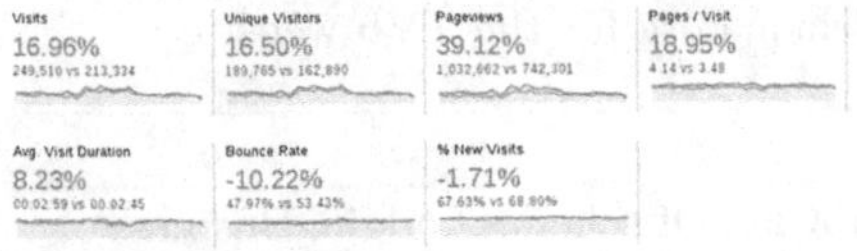

Fig. 2. Comparison of visitors before deployment and the same period of previous year.

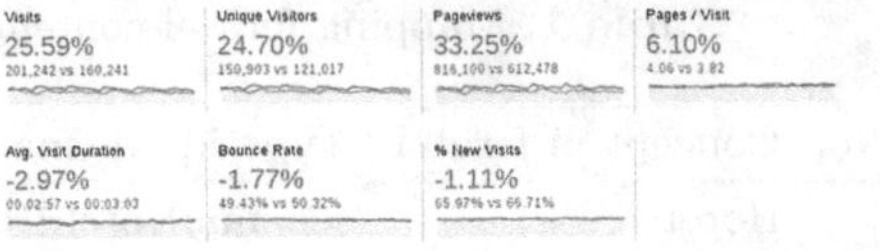

Fig. 3. Comparison of visitors after deployment and the same period of previous year.

website. As evaluation criteria we use the number of the website visitors for a period of 40 days before and after deployment of the annotations i.e. Jan 20, 2014. We compare the number of visitors in this time interval with the numbers of visitors during the same time interval a year ago. We use Google Analytics to obtain these numbers.

First we compare the period before the deployment of annotations (Dec 11, 2013–Jan 19, 2014) with the same period of the previous year (Dec 11, 2012 Jan 19, 2013). As is shown in Fig. 2, there is an increase of 16.96 % visitors, meaning that TVb was able to increase the number of visitors with 16.96 % without using semantic annotations. Comparing also the period after deployment (Jan 20, 2014–Feb 28, 2014) with the same period of the previous year (Jan 20, 2013–Feb 28, 2013), we can observe an increase of 25.59 % visitors (see Fig. 3). If the increase of visitors without annotations was of 16.96 %, the increase of visitors with annotations is of 25.59 %. The difference of 8.63 % on the number of visitors may be caused by annotating the content. We also evaluated the impact of annotations on sub-pages of TVb website presenting individual hotels, restaurants and sightseeing. An average increase of 5 % in visitors was observed on the sub-pages after the deployment of the annotations.

As part of our current and future work we are developing a schema.org annotations plugin which is able to insert annotations not at the destination (e.g. the TVb website or other touristic service providers websites) but rather at the source (e.g. feratel). We are also in the process of extending the loi.sti2.at LOD dataset by curating and including annotated content about more touristic service providers.

Acknowledgments. The work presented in this paper is partly funded by FP7 projects PlanetData, MSEE, Prelida and LDBC. We would like to thank all the members of the Online Communication (http://oc.sti2.at/) working group for their valuable feedback and suggestions.

Reference

1. Stavrakantonakis, I., Toma, I., Fensel, A., Fensel, D.: Hotel websites, web 2.0, web 3.0 and online direct marketing: the case of austria. In: 21th International Conference on Information and Communication Technologies in Travel and Tourism (ENTER2014). Springer, Heidelberg (2014)

LiFR: A Lightweight Fuzzy DL Reasoner

Dorothea Tsatsou[1](✉), Stamatia Dasiopoulou[2], Ioannis Kompatsiaris[1], and Vasileios Mezaris[1]

[1] Centre for Research and Technology Hellas, Information Technologies Institute, Athens, Greece
{dorothea,ikom,bmezaris}@iti.gr
[2] Department of Information and Communication Technologies, Pompeu Fabra University, Barcelona, Spain
stamatia.dasiopoulou@upf.edu

Abstract. In this paper we present LiFR, a lightweight DL reasoner capable of performing in resource-constrained devices, that implements a fuzzy extension of Description Logic Programs. Preliminary evaluation against two existing fuzzy DL reasoners and within a real-world use case has shown promising results.

1 Introduction

Managing vague and imprecise knowledge is a common requirement in many real-world application domains. For this purpose, several fuzzy DLs extensions to classical DLs [1] have been proposed [9,10] and alongside, a number of reasoners for very expressive fuzzy DLs have been implemented, including FiRE[1] [13], FuzzyDL[2] [4] and DeLorean [3]). Furthermore, a number of optimisation techniques have been proposed recently for improving reasoning efficiency for very expressive fuzzy DLs [5,12]. However, many applications require less expressive DLs and would benefit from trading the full expressivity of the language for reasoning efficiency. For instance in location- and context-aware applications that run in resource-constrained devices, like smartphones, tablets, set-top boxes etc., computational efficiency and scalability would enable decision-making to take place either on the server-side or on the end-device, thereby also enhancing privacy preservation.

To this scope, this paper presents LiFR (Sect. 2), a lightweight fuzzy DL reasoner that supports a subset of fuzzy Description Logics Programs (*f-DLP*) [15]. Section 3 discusses preliminary evaluation results, while future directions are given in Sect. 4.

2 LiFR Semantics, Syntax and Reasoning Services

LiFR[3] is a lightweight fuzzy DL reasoner that supports *f-DLP*. It extends Pocket KRHyper [6], a (crisp) first order model generator for last-generation mobile

[1] http://www.image.ece.ntua.gr/~nsimou/FiRE/
[2] http://nemis.isti.cnr.it/~straccia/software/fuzzyDL/fuzzyDL.html
[3] Maintained at http://mklab.iti.gr/project/lifr

V. Presutti et al. (Eds.): ESWC Satellite Events 2014, LNCS 8798, pp. 263–267, 2014.
DOI: 10.1007/978-3-319-11955-7_32

devices that performs DL reasoning by translating DL axioms to first order clauses and by using the hyper-tableaux calculus [2]. Fuzzy DLs extend classical DLs by interpreting concepts and roles as fuzzy sets of individuals and binary relations respectively. The crisp set operations intersection, union and implication, are extended to fuzzy sets and performed by t-norm, t-conorm and implication functions respectively [7], providing corresponding semantics.

LiFR implements the operators of Zadeh fuzzy logic (Table 1), namely the minimum t-norm, the maximum t-conorm and the Kleene-Dienes implication ($\Rightarrow_{KD}$), and provides in addition support for weighted concept modifiers as introduced in [4]. Currently fuzzy assertions are restricted to concepts only and role assertions are treated as crisp with an imposed membership degree of $\geq$1.0. Its syntax (Table 2) is a variant of the Knowledge Representation System Specification (KRSS) proposal [11], rendering it significantly more lightweight compared to other specifications (e.g. RDF/XML serialisation), thus enhancing the capability of performing in resource-constrained devices.

Table 1. LiFR semantics.

Syntax	Semantics
$C \sqsubseteq D$	$C^I(x) \Rightarrow_{KD} D^I(x)$
$C \sqcap D$	$\min(C^I(x), D^I(x))$
$C \sqcup D$	$\max(C^I(x), D^I(x))$
$\exists$ R.C	$\sup_{y \in \Delta^I}\{min(R^I(x,y), C^I(y))\}$
$\forall$ R.D	$\inf_{y \in \Delta^I}\{R^I(x,y) \Rightarrow_{KD} C^I(y)\}$
$w \cdot C$	$C^I(x) \cdot w$
$\langle \alpha : C \geq d \rangle$	$C^I(\alpha^I) \geq d$
$\langle \alpha, \beta \rangle$:R	$R^I(\alpha^I, \beta^I) \geq 1.0$

Table 2. LiFR syntax.

DL syntax	LiFR syntax
$\top$	TOP
$\bot$	BOTTOM
$C \sqsubseteq D$	(IMPLIES C D)
$C \equiv D$	(EQUIVALENT C D)
$C \sqcap D$	(AND C D)
$C \sqcup D$	(OR C D)
$C \sqcap D \sqsubseteq \bot$	(DISJOINT C D)
$\exists R.C$	(SOME R C)
$\forall R.D$	(ALL R C)
$w \cdot C$	(WEIGHT C w)
$S \sqsubseteq R$	(ROLE R :PARENT S)
$R^- \equiv S$	(ROLE R :INVERSE S)
R^+	(ROLE R :TRANSITIVE)
$\langle \alpha : C \geq d \rangle$	(INSTANCE a C $\geq$ d)
$\langle \alpha, b : R \rangle$	(RELATED a b R)

Given a fuzzy DL knowledge base Σ, LiFR currently supports the following reasoning services: (i) *satisfiability checking*, i.e. whether there exists a fuzzy interpretation I that satisfies all axioms in Σ, (ii) *fuzzy entailment*, i.e. whether every model of Σ satisfies τ, where τ is an axiom of the form $C(\alpha) \geq d$, (iii) *concept subsumption*, i.e. whether every model of Σ satisfies $C^I(x) \leq D^I(x)$ $\forall x \in \Delta^I$, and (iv) *greatest lower bound* (GLB), defined as the $\sup\{\ \alpha : \Sigma \models \langle \tau \geq \alpha \rangle\ \}$ where τ is an axiom of the form $C(\alpha) \geq d$. GLB is one of the most important and interesting reasoning services in fuzzy DLs, as it enables to determine which is the greatest degree that Σ entails an individual α to participate in a concept C. Extending Pocket KRHyper, LiFR's default reasoning service consists in the generation of all models that satisfy the input fuzzy knowledge base, thereby providing native support for the computation of the *global GLB*, i.e. the GLB for all combinations of individuals and concepts.

3 Evaluation

LiFR's performance was evaluated against fuzzyDL and FiRE on several sets of randomly generated assertions using the LinkedTV User Model Ontology (LUMO)[4][14], as demonstrated in Table 3[5].

Table 3. Time performance and memory consumption of LiFR, FiRE and FuzzyDL on *global GLB* calculation.

Individuals	Time (ms)			Memory (MB)		
	LiFR	*FuzzyDL*	*FiRE*	*LiFR*	*FuzzyDL*	*FiRE*
20	189	38458	47538	10.00	59.07	67.95
50	192	169875	318228	92.42	181.19	252.80
100	332	596292	665721	137.28	206.36	274.27
250	923	4955568	3137765	169.26	268.23	386.82
500	2015	23239036	6316162	191.64	294.75	474.02
1000	4208	>12 h	12260563	239.93	N/A	515.12

LiFR's reasoning services are currently employed within the LinkedTV EU project[6], primarily for personalized content and concept filtering and for mappings retrieval among ontologies, while supplementary it is used in several tasks, such as topic detection within content and user preferences. To this scope, as part of an evaluation experiment, it was called to label a dataset of 970 media content items with topics from the reference LUMO ontology, ranked by the membership degree of each topic belonging to a media item.

The content items were annotated with ~500–2500 DBPedia [8] entities (individuals) along with their types (concepts) from the DBpedia ontology. In most cases these types represented agents, events, locations and objects, of which existing counterparts in LUMO are related to certain topics by axioms of the sort $Type \sqsubseteq \forall has(Sub)Topic.Topic$, where $Type$ is the concept in the annotation and $Topic$ is subsumed by the $Topics$ concept/category of LUMO. The process involved running three distinct reasoning services per content item: (1)*entailment* based on the LUMO mappings[7] TBox, in order to map DBPedia types

[4] http://data.linkedtv.eu/ontologies/lumo/: 804 atomic concepts, 6 roles, >200 complex concepts.

[5] Due to time restrictions, FuzzyDL was terminated for the 1000 instances case after it exceeded 12 h of processing without rendering results.

[6] http://www.linkedtv.eu/

[7] http://data.linkedtv.eu/ontologies/lumo_mappings/: 1309 concepts.

to LUMO concepts; (2) *global GLB* calculation within the LUMO TBox, based on the assertions retrieved in the previous step as the ABox per content item (main task); (3) Iterative *subsumption* check for each of the predicates in the produced model against the LUMO *Topics* concept, to retrieve from the entirety of the predicates in the produced model, the ones that are subsumed by *Topics*, thus are actually topics. The time performance of LiFR for this experiment is portrayed in Fig. 1.

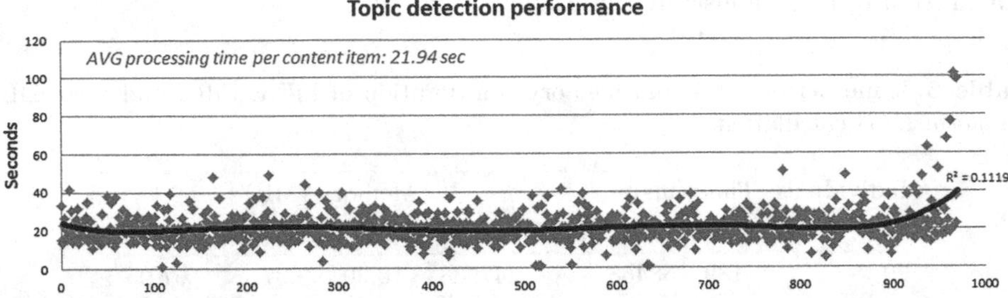

Fig. 1. LiFR's time performance for topic detection. Points denote each content item's processing time. The line shows the polynomial trendline (order of 6) of the data points.

4 Conclusions and Future Work

In this paper, we presented LiFR, a lightweight fuzzy DL reasoner that implements a fuzzy extension of DLP. A preliminary evaluation shows that LiFR is capable of performing in limited-resource devices. In future work, we plan to extend LiFR to support the OWL 2 RL profile and develop a benchmark for a more detailed evaluation and comparison with other fuzzy DLs reasoners.

Acknowledgments. This work has been supported by the European Commission under Contract FP7-287911 LinkedTV.

References

1. Baader, F., Calvanese, D., McGuinness, D.L., Nardi, D., Patel-Schneider, P.F. (eds.): The Description Logic Handbook: Theory, Implementation, and Applications. Cambridge University Press, New York (2003)
2. Baumgartner, P.: Hyper tableau – the next generation. In: de Swart, H. (ed.) TABLEAUX 1998. LNCS (LNAI), vol. 1397, pp. 60–70. Springer, Heidelberg (1998)
3. Bobillo, F., Delgado, M., Gómez-Romero, J.: Reasoning in fuzzy OWL 2 with DeLorean. In: Bobillo, F., Costa, P.C.G., d'Amato, C., Fanizzi, N., Laskey, K.B., Laskey, K.J., Lukasiewicz, T., Nickles, M., Pool, M. (eds.) URSW 2008-2010/UniDL 2010. LNCS, vol. 7123, pp. 119–138. Springer, Heidelberg (2013)
4. Bobillo, F., Straccia, U.: FuzzyDL: an expressive fuzzy description logic reasoner. In: FUZZ-IEEE, pp. 923–930 (2008)

5. Bobillo, F., Straccia, U.: General concept inclusion absorptions for fuzzy description logics: a first step. In: Description Logics, pp. 513–525 (2013)
6. Kleemann, T.: Towards mobile reasoning. In: Description Logics (2006)
7. Klir, G.J., Yuan, B.: Fuzzy Sets and Fuzzy Logic - Theory and Applications. Prentice Hall, Upper Saddle River (1995)
8. Lehmann, J., Isele, R., Jakob, M., Jentzsch, A., Kontokostas, D., Mendes, P.N., Hellmann, S., Morsey, M., van Kleef, P., Auer, S., Bizer, C.: DBpedia - a large-scale, multilingual knowledge base extracted from wikipedia. Semant. Web J. (2014)
9. Lukasiewicz, T., Straccia, U.: Managing uncertainty and vagueness in description logics for the semantic Web. J. Web Sem. **6**(4), 291–308 (2008)
10. Ma, Z.M., Zhang, F., Wang, H., Yan, L.: An overview of fuzzy description logics for the semantic Web. Knowl. Eng. Rev. **28**(1), 1–34 (2013)
11. Schneider, P.P., Swartout, B.: Description-Logic Knowledge Representation System Specification from the KRSS Group of the ARPA Knowledge Sharing Effort (1993). http://www.bell-labs.com/user/pfps/papers/krss-spec.ps
12. Simou, N., Mailis, T.P., Stoilos, G., Stamou, G.B.: Optimization techniques for fuzzy description logics. In: Description Logics (2010)
13. Stoilos, G., Simou, N., Stamou, G.B., Kollias, S.D.: Uncertainty and the semantic Web. IEEE Intell. Syst. **21**(5), 84–87 (2006)
14. Tsatsou, D., Mezaris, V.: LUMO: the LinkedTV user model ontology. In: ESWC 2014 (Satellite Events) (2014)
15. Venetis, T., Stoilos, G., Stamou, G.B., Kollias, S.D.: f-DLPs: extending description logic programs with fuzzy sets and fuzzy logic. In: FUZZ-IEEE, pp. 1–6 (2007)

LUMO: The LinkedTV User Model Ontology

Dorothea Tsatsou(✉) and Vasileios Mezaris

Centre for Research and Technology Hellas, Information Technologies Institute, Athens, Greece
{dorothea,bmezaris}@iti.gr

Abstract. This paper introduces the LinkedTV User Model Ontology (LUMO), developed within the LinkedTV EU project. LUMO aims to semantically represent user-pertinent information in the networked media domain and to enable personalization and contextualization of concepts and content via semantic reasoning. The design principles of LUMO and its connection to relevant ontologies and known vocabularies is described.

1 Introduction

Networked Media, i.e. the convergence of traditional media interfaces with Web content, is the focal point of the Television Linked To The Web (LinkedTV)[1] EU project. However, the convergence of voluminous multimedia content avails to a traditional problem of the Web: information overload. Personalization is a key factor that can alleviate this problem. A holistic vocabulary to classify user-pertinent information under would enable efficient elicitation of user preferences and context. An ontology, comprising of a shared, explicit model of domain conceptualizations and their relations can be used as the reference vocabulary for predictive inferencing of user preferences and for targeted content recommendations.

The use of Linked Open Data (LOD) [1] vocabularies for this purpose, like DBPedia [7], YAGO [8], schema.org[2], is still hampered by the large volume of data [5] and the shallow, malformed structure, as well as the lack of important user-pertinent semantics or inclusion of semantics not relevant to a user [9]. This poses scalability, coverage and inconsistency problems, while the data volume restricts their use to the server-side, thus compromising user privacy. Conversely, as also argued in [9], upper formal ontologies consist of too abstract conceptualisations to meaningfully describe user preferences, while assembling specific, granular domain ontologies to represent a general domain again elevates the concept space to an unmanageable size.

The lack of an expressive ontology that adequately describes the broad networked media domain from the users' perspective but at the same time is not too abstract or too specific, in order to scale well and maintain the decidability of reasoning algorithms has urged us to engineer LUMO (Sect. 2), and means to

[1] www.linkedtv.eu
[2] http://schema.org/

V. Presutti et al. (Eds.): ESWC Satellite Events 2014, LNCS 8798, pp. 268–272, 2014.
DOI: 10.1007/978-3-319-11955-7_33

render it inter-usable with prominent LOD vocabularies (Sect. 3). Future work is presented in Sect. 4.

2 LUMO: A Lightweight Reference Ontology

LUMO's modelling objective is to represent user preferences and contextual features regarding networked media content in order to enable intelligent recommendations over concepts and content via semantic inferencing.

Design Principles. LUMO aims to provide a comprehensive coverage of the domain through a uniform, finite and expressive vocabulary which considers the user's perspective of the domain, while at the same time remains as lightweight as possible so that it can enable user models' storage and the recommendation process to be performed on the user client, even if that consists of a limited-resource device. The latter aims to alleviate scalability issues but, most prominently, to safeguard user privacy by limiting the need to communicate sensitive user information to remote servers. The design methodology used bares resemblance to Methontology [2], with an emphasis on inspection of similar ontologies and vocabularies for knowledge acquisition.

Description of LUMO. LUMO[3] is designed as an OWL 2 RL [3] ontology, combining ontologies and rules. This profile limitation offers a tradeoff between expressivity and reasoning efficiency in order to reduce computational cost. LUMO is currently accompanied by a separate ontology[4], modelling mappings of LUMO to several existing vocabularies. Both[5] were developed using Protégé[6].

The current version of LUMO includes 804 classes and 6 object properties. It addresses four major user-pertinent facets: *Context Dimensions*, *Domain-dependent dimensions*, *Agents* and *Spatio-Temporal* aspects (Fig. 1). The two latter facets may regard both contextual and domain-dependent aspects of the user and as so are modelled independently at the top of the hierarchy.

Apart from the taxonomy, LUMO incorporates roughly 200 universal restriction axioms, relating concepts via non-taxonomical object properties. In the current version, such axioms are mostly of the type $Type \sqsubseteq \forall has(Sub)Topic.Topic$

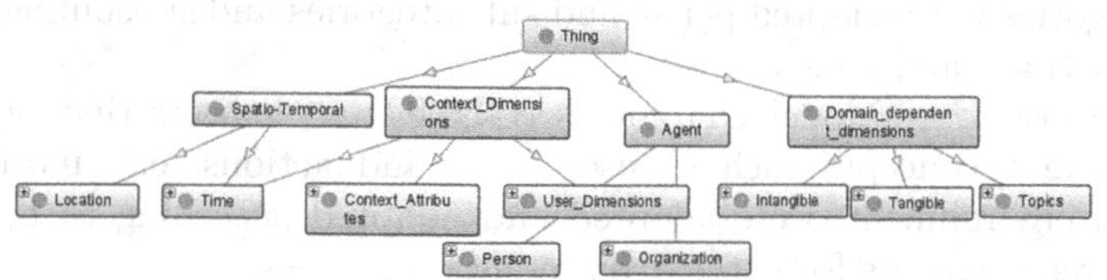

Fig. 1. Graphical representation of the top level LUMO hierarchy

3 http://data.linkedtv.eu/ontologies/lumo
4 http://data.linkedtv.eu/ontologies/lumo_mappings
5 Also available at http://mklab.iti.gr/project/lumo.
6 http://protege.stanford.edu/

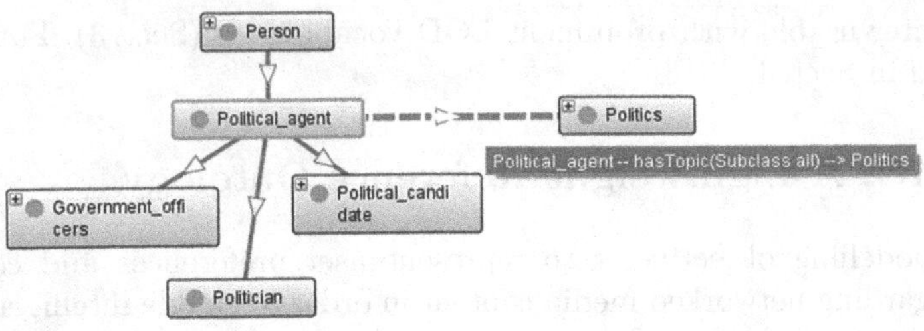

Fig. 2. An illustration of the relation of concept *Political_Agent* to the topic *Politics* via the *hasTopic* property

and enable inference of topics in both the content's annotation and in the user profile, since content annotation in LinkedTV does not provide this information. *Type* corresponds to the type of an entity in the annotation (usually an agent, event, location or object), *Topic* is subsumed by the *Topics* concept/category and *hasSubTopic*, *hasTopic* are object properties. An example can be seen in Fig. 2.

Influences from Existing Vocabularies. A key modelling objective was to adopt the most relevant entities and semantics from open vocabularies, discard user-extraneous information and adapt them to the requirements of the LinkedTV users and scenarios[7]. This included redefining semantics, with respect to leveraging LOD inconsistencies and enhancing coherency and completeness.

Within LinkedTV, multimedia content is annotated with entities from a plurality of LOD vocabularies describing *what a fragment is about.* Representing user-relevant information from consumed content heavily relied on the vocabularies used in the annotations. To this end, schema.org, the DBPedia ontology[8] and the NERD ontology[9] influenced the modelling of the *Agent*, *Location*, *Intangible* and *Tangible* subhierarchies, while better structuring, adding new information and selecting the parts that complied with the desired granularity was pursued.

The IPTC newscodes[10] is widely used by news agents to categorize news content, thus relevant to the LinkedTV news scenario, therefore it consisted of the main influence in modelling the LUMO *Topics* subhierarchy. Most upper IPTC categories were adopted per se and subcategories and subsuming concepts were restructured and added.

The General User Model Ontology's (GUMO) [4] subsets that depict user context-relevant concepts such as user state and actions, e.g. motion, location, social environment, were adopted and adapted according to the specific LinkedTV requirements for context representation.

---

[7] News, artistic artifacts and a general artistic scenario: http://www.linkedtv.eu/scenarios/.

[8] http://dbpedia.org/ontology/

[9] http://nerd.eurecom.fr/ontology/

[10] https://www.iptc.org/site/NewsCodes/

3 Mappings to Existing Vocabularies

LUMO's mappings serve (a) for interpretation of content annotation to the LUMO vocabulary and (b) as the means to facilitate re-use of LUMO by the Semantic Web. The mappings were generated automatically via the LogMap ontology alignment tool [6] and were further evaluated and revised manually.

Currently, mappings are available to the main vocabularies that influenced the engineering of LUMO: *(a)* the DBpedia ontology, *(b)* schema.org, *(c)* the NERD ontology, *(d)* IPTC news codes[11] and (e) the GUMO ontology[12]. 524 LUMO classes are mapped to 785 classes from these vocabularies through equivalence axioms.

4 Conclusions and Future Work

This paper presented LUMO and its mappings to existing vocabularies. Future work will focus on evaluating and enriching LUMO's coverage over the generic networked media domain and also expand across the arts subdomain as a requisite of LinkedTV scenarios. We will also endeavour to engineer more non-taxonomical axioms (such as connection of objects/events to genres) and extend to more object properties. Lastly, extending the mappings to more prominent vocabularies is a major objective. Already under way are mappings to respective parts of YAGO and to a dedicated set of entities within DBPedia resources which are deemed semantically high-level enough to consist of concepts at the schema level and are not in the DBPedia ontology.

Acknowledgments. This work has been supported by the European Commission under Contract FP7-287911 LinkedTV.

References

1. Bizer, C., Heath, T., Berners-Lee, T.: Linked data - the story so far. Int. J. Semant. Web Inf. Syst. **5**(3), 1–22 (2009)
2. Fernández-López, M., Gómez-Pérez, A., Juristo, N.: Methontology: from ontological art towards ontological engineering. In: AAAI97 (1997)
3. Grau, B.C., Horrocks, I., Motik, B., Parsia, B., Patel-Schneider, P.F., Sattler, U.: OWL 2: the next step for OWL. J. Web Sem. **6**(4), 309–322 (2008)
4. Heckmann, D., Schwartz, T., Brandherm, B., Schmitz, M., von Wilamowitz-Moellendorff, M.: GUMO – the general user model ontology. In: Ardissono, L., Brna, P., Mitrović, A. (eds.) UM 2005. LNCS (LNAI), vol. 3538, pp. 428–432. Springer, Heidelberg (2005)
5. Jain, P., Hitzler, P., Yeh, P.Z., Verma, K., Sheth, A.P.: Linked data is merely more data. In: AAAI Spring Symposium: Linked Data Meets Artificial Intelligence (2010)

[11] As owl-fied by the WebTLab (http://webtlab.it.uc3m.es/): http://webtlab.it.uc3m.es/results/NEWS/subjectcodes.owl

[12] http://www.ubisworld.org/ubisworld/documents/gumo/2.0/gumo.owl

6. Jiménez-Ruiz, E., Cuenca Grau, B.: LogMap: logic-based and scalable ontology matching. In: Aroyo, L., Welty, C., Alani, H., Taylor, J., Bernstein, A., Kagal, L., Noy, N., Blomqvist, E. (eds.) ISWC 2011, Part I. LNCS, vol. 7031, pp. 273–288. Springer, Heidelberg (2011)
7. Lehmann, J., Isele, R., Jakob, M., Jentzsch, A., Kontokostas, D., Mendes, P.N., Hellmann, S., Morsey, M., van Kleef, P., Auer, S., Bizer, C.: DBpedia - a large-scale, multilingual knowledge base extracted from wikipedia. Semant. Web J. (2014)
8. Suchanek, F.M., Kasneci, G., Weikum, G.: Yago: a core of semantic knowledge. In: Proceedings of the 16th International Conference on World Wide Web, WWW '07, pp. 697–706. ACM, New York (2007)
9. Tsatsou, D., Mezaris, V., Kompatsiaris, I.: Semantic personalisation in networked media: Determining the background knowledge. In: SMAP, pp. 101–106 (2012)

Demo Track

Making Use of Linked Data for Generating Enhanced Snippets

Mazen Alsarem[1], Pierre-Édouard Portier[1(✉)], Sylvie Calabretto[1], and Harald Kosch[2]

[1] Université de Lyon, CNRS, INSA-Lyon, LIRIS, UMR5205, 69621 Lyon, France
{mazen.alsarem,pierre-edouard.portier,sylvie.calabretto}@insa-lyon.fr
[2] Universität Passau, Innstr. 43, 94032 Passau, Germany
harald.kosch@uni-passau.de

Abstract. We enhance an existing search engine's snippet (i.e. excerpt from a web page determined at query-time in order to efficiently express how the web page may be relevant to the query) with linked data (LD) in order to highlight non trivial relationships between the information need of the user and LD resources related to the result page. To do this, we introduce a multi-step unsupervised co-clustering algorithm so as to use the textual data associated with the resources for discovering additional relationships. Next, we use a 3-way tensor to mix these new relationships with the ones available from the LD graph. Then, we apply a first PARAFAC tensor decomposition [5] in order to (i) select the most promising nodes for a 1-hop extension, and (ii) build the enhanced snippet. A video demonstration is available online (http://liris.cnrs.fr/drim/projects/ensen/).

Keywords: Linked data · Information retrieval · Snippets · Co-Clustering · Tensor decomposition

1 Introduction

In this work, we show that the LOD (Linking Open Data) graph can be combined with analysis of the original textual content of a search engine's results to create efficient enhanced snippets. Contrary to other approaches (such as [4]), we don't rely exclusively on explicit semantic annotations (e.g. RDFa, ...) but we are able to enhance any result even if the corresponding web page doesn't contain annotations.

The paper is organized as follows: we start with a brief state of the art for the domains of snippets' enhancement, and snippet generation for corpus of RDF documents (Sect. 2). Then we describe our approach (Sect. 3) before concluding (Sect. 4).

V. Presutti et al. (Eds.): ESWC Satellite Events 2014, LNCS 8798, pp. 275–279, 2014.
DOI: 10.1007/978-3-319-11955-7_34

2 Related Works

Many approaches tried to enhance the Search Engine Result Page (SERP) snippets, but none of them seem to have used the LoD graph. First, Haas *et al.* [4] employed structured metadata to enhance the SERP with multimedia elements, key-value pairs and interactive features. They chose not to use the LoD graph to avoid the problem of the transfer of trust between the Web of documents and the Web of Data. Also Google Rich Snippet (GRS) [10] is a similar initiative that relies exclusively on structured metadata authored by the web pages' publishers.

We should also mention the works of Ge *et al.* [3], and Penin *et al.* [9] focused on the generation of snippets for ontology search, and also the work of Bai *et al.* [1] about the generation of snippets for native RDF documents.

In summation, we agree with Ge *et al.* [3] that the main benefit of possessing highly structured data from an RDF graph is the possibility to find non-trivial relations among the query terms themselves, and also between the query terms and the main concepts of the document. Moreover, we agree with Penin *et al.* [9] and Bai *et al.* [1] about the necessity to design a ranking algorithm for RDF statements that considers both the structure of the RDF graph and lexical properties of the textual data. However, we find ourselves in an inverted situation with genuine textual data from classical web pages, and RDF graphs generated from these web pages by using the LoD graph.

3 Proposal

Our main purpose is to highlight on a practical and convincing use case the benefits of a conjoint use of the web of documents and the web of data. Thus, for each result of the SERP, we want to build a RDF graph and combine this graph with a textual analysis of the document in order to obtain features from which to build an enhanced snippet. Meanwhile, our main concern is to limit the amount of noise introduced by this process.

In a first step, we use DBpedia Spotlight [6] to extract LoD resources from the content of the SERP result. Next, we use a SPARQL endpoint connected to the DBpedia dataset to introduce RDF statements between the resources we just found. At that time we have a first graph associated to the SERP result.

3.1 Multi-step Unsupervised Co-clustering

We need to build a more informed graph in order to efficiently select, in a subsequent step, a relevant subset of nodes to extend. Thus, our main objective is to highlight relevant relations between the resources based on an analysis of the textual data associated to the resources. Therefore, to discover more diverse relationships than the ones obtained from a naive lexical approach (e.g. cosine distance between the abstracts...), we introduce a new multi-step unsupervised co-clustering algorithm. At the core of our algorithm, lies a classical co-clustering algorithm based on SVD [7] that we adapted for the X-means [8] algorithm so as to avoid having to estimate the number of clusters. We use a co-clustering approach because the relation between resources of a given cluster will be qualified by the terms present in this cluster. First, we remove the stop-words from the texts associated to each node of the graph and we build a resource-term matrix on which we apply a co-clustering.

However, the first time the co-clustering algorithm is executed, the internal quality of the found clusters is very poor — with a mean silhouette index close to zero. Our approach is to decrease the size of the features' space (i.e. the number of terms and resources) until we find clusters of a good enough quality. When we find clusters of good internal quality and containing only terms we remove those terms and repeat the co-clustering. The underlying rationale for this strategy is that the terms that lie well in their own clusters but do not associate with resources will not help to discover and explain relationships between resources. However, we observed that this dimension reduction mechanism is insufficient since there can be clusterings with a poor average silhouette and with no clusters only made of terms. Therefore we also remove from the features' space the terms and the resources of the small clusters with a weak silhouette. Furthermore, when we can find no clusters only made of terms, no small clusters with a low silhouette, and when the average silhouette remains low, we heuristically re-apply this recursive algorithm on the clusters with a poor silhouette. A more detailed presentation of the algorithm is available online in the form of a technical report[1].

3.2 Graph Extension by Tensor Decomposition

We would not benefit much from the LoD if we didn't extend the graph in order to find facts not present in the original document. However, we must be careful not to introduce noise during the extension. To do this, we propose to guide this process with the knowledge obtained from the previous multi-step co-clustering. Therefore, we have to combine the connectivity information of the graph with the labeled clusters. We propose to represent these two kinds of information in one structure: a 3-way tensor (denoted $\mathcal{T}$).

As in [2], the three modes of the tensor are associated respectively to the subject, the object and the predicate of the triples that constitute the graph. Thus, for each predicate, there is one horizontal slice that represents the adjacency matrix of the subgraph only made of the triples that link resources thanks to that predicate. We propose to add a horizontal slice for each cluster returned by the multi-step co-clustering algorithm. Such a slice represents the clique of all the resources present in the cluster. To each edge of the clique, we assign a weight linearly proportional to the silhouette index of the cluster. This coefficient of proportionality is chosen so as to make all the slices of the tensor comparable.

In order to select the nodes to extend, we start by applying a PARAFAC [5] tensor decomposition algorithm to the tensor. This decomposition computes a

[1] http://liris.cnrs.fr/drim/projects/ensen/

representation of the tensor as a sum of rank-one tensor (a rank-one three-way tensor is the outer product of three vectors), i.e.,

$$\mathcal{T} = \sum_{r=1}^{R} \mathbf{s}_r \circ \mathbf{o}_r \circ \mathbf{p}_r. \tag{1}$$

If there are n_r resources and n_p predicates, the lengths of each $\mathbf{s}_r$, $\mathbf{o}_r$ and $\mathbf{p}_r$ vectors are respectively n_r, n_r and n_p. The components of the vectors $\mathbf{s}_r$ and $\mathbf{o}_r$ represent, for the number r factor, the importance of each resource as it plays respectively the part of subject and object in relations involving the high-scored predicates of $\mathbf{p}_r$. Our strategy is to select for each factor r, with at least one high-scored predicate found in $\mathbf{p}_r$, the high scored resources of $\mathbf{s}_r$ and $\mathbf{o}_r$ as the nodes to extend (i.e. we query a DBpedia SPARQL endpoint to find new triples for which these nodes are subject).

3.3 Snippet Construction

We apply a new tensor decomposition on the extended graph and we select only the factors for which there are values in $\mathbf{p}_r$ larger than an experimentally fixed threshold (in our case 0.1). For those factors, we then select the resources of $\mathbf{s}_r$ and $\mathbf{o}_r$ with a weight greater than this same threshold. Thus, for each factor that describes an important sub-graph (i.e. for which there exist high-scored predicates) we isolate the main-resources that act either as hubs or authorities.

To each main-resource we associate a set of explanatory triples and we select a sentence of the SERP's result for its capacity to contextualize the main-resource. The triples associated to a main-resource are trivially derived from the factors where this resource appears either as an important subject or as an important object. The sentence associated to a main-resource is found by ranking the sentences of the document according to seven factors: (1) the presence of a DBpedia Spotlight annotation for the main-resource, (2) the presence of a DBpedia Spotlight annotation for a resource that appears with a high score in a group where the main-resource also has an high score, (3) the presence in the text of the local name of a predicate that belongs to one of the main-resource's groups, (4) the presence of query's terms, (5) the presence in the text of the local name of the resource, (6) the presence of a DBpedia Spotlight annotation for a resource that appears in the query, and (7) the presence of a DBpedia Spotlight annotation for a resource adjacent to the main-resource in the graph.

Finally, we apply a similar ranking strategy to find a sentence that is both close to the query and a place of co-occurrence for as many main-resources as possible. This sentence is shown in addition to the original excerpt chosen by the search engine.

4 Conclusion

We proposed a way of enhancing a traditional snippet with structured data coming from the LoD. Our intention was firstly to identify relationships between the main concepts of a document relevant to the user's information need, and secondly to link these concepts with either relevant concepts not present in the document, or facts about them. Our main challenge was to succeed in this task while introducing as little noise as possible. In this respect, we identified the keystone as the graph extension step for which more relational information was needed in order to efficiently choose the resources that would benefit most from an extension. Thus, we proposed a multi-step unsupervised co-clustering algorithm in order to discover additional relationships between the resources by taking into account textual data associated to them. Next, we represented both the structures coming from the LoD and those added by our co-clustering process with a 3-way tensor before running a tensor decomposition so as to identify the main resources we should extend. Our proposal has been implemented — a more detailed version of this work, screenshots and a demonstration are available online[2] — and we are now in the process of thoroughly evaluating the end-user satisfaction.

References

1. Bai, X., Delbru, R., Tummarello, G.: RDF snippets for semantic web search engines. In: Meersman, R., Tari, Z. (eds.) OTM 2008, Part II. LNCS, vol. 5332, pp. 1304–1318. Springer, Heidelberg (2008)
2. Franz, T., Schultz, A., Sizov, S., Staab, S.: TripleRank: ranking semantic web data by tensor decomposition. In: Bernstein, A., Karger, D.R., Heath, T., Feigenbaum, L., Maynard, D., Motta, E., Thirunarayan, K. (eds.) ISWC 2009. LNCS, vol. 5823, pp. 213–228. Springer, Heidelberg (2009)
3. Ge, W., Cheng, G., Li, H., Qu, Y.: Incorporating compactness to generate term-association view snippets for ontology search. Inf. Process. Manage. **49**(2), 513–528 (2012)
4. Haas, K., Mika, P., Tarjan, P., Blanco, R.: Enhanced results for web search. In: Proceedings of the 34th International ACM SIGIR Conference on Research and Development in Information Retrieval, pp. 725–734. ACM (2011)
5. Kolda, T.G., Bader, B.W.: Tensor decompositions and applications. SIAM Rev. **51**(3), 455–500 (2009)
6. Mendes, P.N., Jakob, M., García-Silva, A., Bizer, C.: Dbpedia spotlight: shedding light on the web of documents. In: Proceedings of the 7th International Conference on Semantic Systems, I-Semantics '11, pp. 1–8. ACM (2011)
7. Park, L.A.F., Leckie, C.A., Ramamohanarao, K., Bezdek, J.C.: Adapting spectral co-clustering to documents and terms using latent semantic analysis. In: Nicholson, A., Li, X. (eds.) AI 2009. LNCS, vol. 5866, pp. 301–311. Springer, Heidelberg (2009)
8. Pelleg, D., Moore, A.W., et al.: X-means: extending k-means with efficient estimation of the number of clusters. In: ICML, pp. 727–734 (2000)
9. Penin, T., Wang, H., Tran, T., Yu, Y.: Snippet generation for semantic web search engines. In: Domingue, J., Anutariya, C. (eds.) ASWC 2008. LNCS, vol. 5367, pp. 493–507. Springer, Heidelberg (2008)
10. Steiner, T., Troncy, R., Hausenblas, M.: How google is using linked data today and vision for tomorrow. In: Proceedings of Linked Data in the Future Internet 700 (2010)

[2] http://liris.cnrs.fr/drim/projects/ensen/

Durchblick - A Conference Assistance System for Augmented Reality Devices

Anas Alzoghbi[1], Peter M. Fischer[1], Anna Gossen[2], Peter Haase[2(✉)], Thomas Hornung[1], Beibei Hu[2], Georg Lausen[1], Christoph Pinkel[2], and Michael Schmidt[2]

[1] Albert-Ludwigs-Universität, Freiburg, Germany
{alzoghba,peter.fischer,hornungt,lausen}@informatik.uni-freiburg.de
[2] FluidOps AG, Walldorf, Germany
{anna.gossen,peter.haase,beibei.hu,christoph.pinkel,
michael.schmidt}@fluidops.com

Abstract. We present Durchblick, a conference assistance system for Augmented Reality devices. We demonstrate a prototype which can deliver context-sensitive event information and recommendations via Google Glass. This prototype incorporates semantic data from user-specific and public sources to build user profiles, maintains rich context information and employs event processing as well as recommender systems to proactively select and present relevant information.

Keywords: Augmented reality · Semantic data · Context adaptation

1 Introduction

Augmented reality (AR) applications have recently drawn a considerable interest, triggered by the announcement and public discussion of devices like Google Glass[1]. While this discussion is mostly centered around the hardware aspects of AR, the far more interesting questions arise in the area of applications. These applications are driven by novel interaction models, going beyond the explicit approaches used on computers and smartphones, since such interaction is very cumbersome on AR devices. Instead, information has to be delivered proactively in a contextualized way, necessitating a different approach to data management and presentation. In this demo, we show such an application and its accompanying software in the form of an interactive conference guide. The AR device provides the participants of a conference with relevant background information about presenters, events or topics around the conference based on the current context, e.g., publications of a presenter who shares the same research interests with a participant. This application is developed within the Durchblick project[2], which extends an already proven conference information system

[1] http://google.com/glass
[2] http://www.fluidops.com/projects/durchblick/

V. Presutti et al. (Eds.): ESWC Satellite Events 2014, LNCS 8798, pp. 280–285, 2014.
DOI: 10.1007/978-3-319-11955-7_35

(conference explorer[3]) based on semantic technology. It relies on personal information such as social networks or public data such as conference schedules or publications collected there, combines it with contextual information and applies state-of-the-art recommendation and event processing techniques to tailor the information presented on the AR device in a rapid fashion.

Existing conference support applications like Conference4Me[4] are smartphone-based and provide a static display of conference information with limited personalization, thus requiring explicit user action. Utilizing context information to tailor information has been studied extensively, e.g. for digital libraries [2] or information streams [1], but has rarely been developed to full systems. Employing semantic technology in AR settings has only recently gained attention, such as the semantic event processing in the ARTSENSE project [4].

2 Demonstration Scenario

In the following we present a scenario as it will be demonstrated based on actual conference metadata at the conference[5]: Consider a researcher (called 'Sarah') who plans to attend the ESWC'14 conference. Like most other attendants, her goals for a conference visit are twofold: (1) learning more about relevant advancement in the fields and (2) connecting to other researchers in her domain. For this purpose, she will get support from the context-aware conference support system in Durchblick. This system employs Google Glass to deliver its services enabling Sarah to gain the maximum benefit from her visit in various ways, combining user profiles and contextual knowledge: According to her research interests obtained explicitly from her LinkedIn profile and implicitly from the publication registry, Durchblick recommends an initial program for Sarah's visit to the conference. The program is tailored towards conference events that match her preferences and interests. Additionally, she can build her own personal schedule by directly selecting available events, rejecting or accepting the recommended events, initially or during the conference. Such interactions (feedback) on the recommended events along with user's activities on the conference are employed to enhance the recommended program over time and provide more personalized recommendations. Figure 1 shows an example of a notification of an upcoming event and possible interactions. While attending talks and meetings, 'Sarah' is able to see the background information of the presenter such as previous publications or research topics and learn more information about the presentation topic on her AR devices. Durchblick explores the background information from social network and publication registries and uses context information such as schedules or location to automatically select the relevant parts. Once 'Sarah' takes a picture and shares it via the Glass, Durchblick provides annotation information related to the picture and shares it with other participants who may want to

[3] http://conference-explorer.fluidops.net

[4] http://conference4me.psnc.pl

[5] A Web-based frontend including Google Glass screenshots of the demonstration is accessible at http://conference-explorer.fluidops.net/resource/Durchblick.

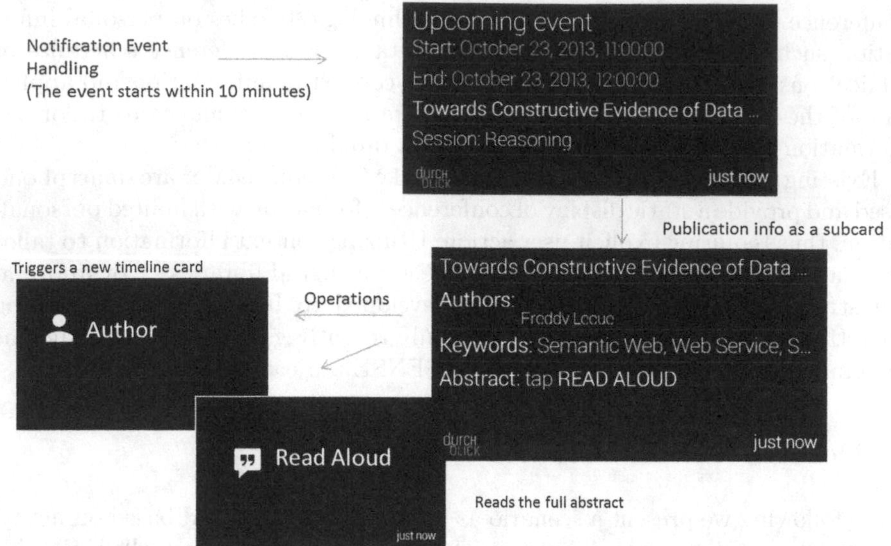

Fig. 1. Use Case Scenario: UI flow and screen shots

search for photos related to the conference or its specific sessions. Finally, Sarah gets all important announcements made by conference organizers via Durchblick, like rescheduling events or announcing a delay on the plan for the conference dinner.

3 Architecture

Durchblick tackles the challenges of AR applications in two ways: first, it perceives and models the user context for a better understanding of her needs, and second, it utilizes the linked data integrated from different resources: social networks; publication registries; and conference meta data. Both aspects help providing a rich platform for delivering the suitable information proactively. As shown in Fig. 2, the user interface layer (the top layer) with the AR device, plays the main role not only in delivering the requested information to the user, but also in capturing the user context. The second layer (Durchblick application server) however, takes care of modelling that context properly. On the other hand, Durchblick business logic is depicted in this layer through the collaboration of different components appearing here (Recommender, Event processing, and context-based query processing components). Integrated linked data is made available by the means of the two layers at the bottom of the hierarchy. Those layers are responsible for collecting data from the original sources in various formats and integrating them in the form of a unified RDF data graph. In this section we will present the user context and delve deeper into the second layer giving more details about its components.

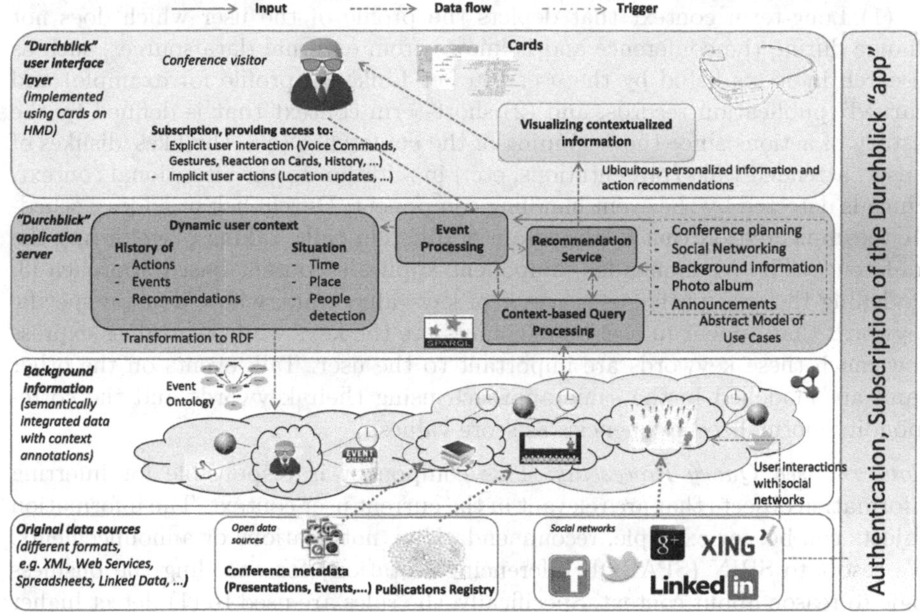

Fig. 2. Durchblick architecture

User context: In Durchblick we define two categories that characterize the user context: Situational context and historical context. The situational context covers user location, current time, social context, and user preferences. The history includes previous actions, events attended, and recommendations reacted to.

In order to model the user context, we reused several vocabularies from different ontologies. The situation pattern from the DUL ontology[6] is employed as a context holder that models user's time, location, and the current attended event. For representing user preferences, we resort to the weighted interests ontology[7].

Event Processing: The Event processing component handles events delegated by the user interface layer up on different user actions. Those actions may be explicitly triggered by the user as a request for a specific service (background information, recommended events,...) or derived implicitly upon a detected change in the user context. The event processing component models those events and forwards a contextualized user object to the responsible component. Specifically, in the case of Google Glass, events are received via the Mirror API, which provides a subscription mechanism for events detected on the device, such as change in location or a particular user action.

Recommender: Recommendations are based on the context model of the user. Here, two different kinds of context for the user profile are distinguished:

[6] http://www.ontologydesignpatterns.org/ont/dul/DUL.owl
[7] http://smiy.sourceforge.net/wi/spec/weightedinterests.html

(1) Long-term context that depicts the profile of the user which does not change during the conference and is known from external data sources, such as research interests listed by the user (on her LinkedIn profile for example) and learned[8] publication records, and (2) short-term context that is defined by the history of actions since the beginning of the conference (e.g. the likes/dislikes of a user, attended talks/presentations, etc.) in addition to the situational context, which is detected by the event handling component. Durchblick provides a schedule recommendation that is a program of different talks taking place during the conference. The recommender component applies a content based approach [3] modelling the user profile as a vector of key-value pairs, where domain specific keywords that appear in user's preferences are the keys while the values express how much these keywords are important to the user. Talk events on the other hand are modelled in the same approach using their keywords and the corresponding normalized frequencies as score values.

Context-based Query Processing: This component is responsible for inferring information objects that are relevant in the current user context. The information objects can be, for example, recommendations, notifications or announcements. We resort to SPIN (SPARQL Inferencing Notation) for encoding the business logic to reason about context. Specifically, the rules are used to (1) detect higher level situation descriptions (e.g. attending a session, interacting with a person) based on low level events, (2) inferring relevant information objects based on the current situation, and (3) establishing relationships between objects in a particular situation (e.g. to annotate a shared picture with the current user context). Upon context changes, the rules are evaluated and the inferred relevant information objects are sent pro-actively to the user. In the case of Glass, we again make use of the Mirror API to display timeline cards for the information objects.

4 Conclusion

In this demo, we provide insights how upcoming AR devices greatly benefit from semantic data management. We build an architecture that puts contextualized query processing, event processing and recommendations on top of semantic data and delivers relevant information proactively. Currently, we employ early prototypes of these components; we plan to improve them in many aspects: The interaction context and recommendations needs further investigation, both from the conceptual side (recommendations under constraints, parametrized recommendations) and the system design side (realtime results vs. context flexibility). Similarly, the interaction of visualization and context-based query processing needs to be studied in more detail.

Acknowledgements. The Durchblick project has received funding by the German Federal Ministry of Economics and Technology (BMWi) (KF2067905BZ).

[8] Long-term profiles are learned using a linear regression approach [3] utilizing the users' previous publications as training data sets.

References

1. Dittrich, J.-P., Fischer, P.M., Kossmann, D.: Agile: adaptive indexing for context-aware information filters. In: ACM SIGMOD (2005)
2. Haase, P.: Situation aware mobile access to digital libraries. In: Jensen, C.S., Jeffery, K., Pokorný, J., Šaltenis, S., Bertino, E., Böhm, K., Jarke, M. (eds.) EDBT 2002. LNCS, vol. 2287, pp. 772–774. Springer, Heidelberg (2002)
3. Pazzani, M.J., Billsus, D.: Content-based recommendation systems. In: Brusilovsky, P., Kobsa, A., Nejdl, W. (eds.) Adaptive Web 2007. LNCS, vol. 4321, pp. 325–341. Springer, Heidelberg (2007)
4. Xu, Y., et al.: Demo: efficient human attention detection in museums based on semantics and complex event processing. In: ISWC (2012)

Publication of RDF Streams with Ztreamy

Jesús Arias Fisteus(✉), Norberto Fernández García, Luis Sánchez Fernández, and Damaris Fuentes-Lorenzo

Dpto. Ing. Telemática, Universidad Carlos III de Madrid,
Avda. Universidad 30, 28911 Leganés, Madrid, Spain
{jaf,berto,luiss,dfuentes}@it.uc3m.es

Abstract. There is currently an interest in the Semantic Web community for the development of tools and techniques to process RDF streams. Implementing an effective RDF stream processing system requires to address several aspects including stream generation, querying, reasoning, etc. In this work we focus on one of them: the distribution of RDF streams through the Web. In order to address this issue, we have developed Ztreamy, a scalable middleware which allows to publish and consume RDF streams through HTTP. The goal of this demo is to show the functionality of Ztreamy in two different scenarios with actual, heterogeneous streaming data.

1 Introduction

Nowadays there are many practical applications (like social or sensor networks) where the information to be processed takes the form of a stream, that is, *a real-time, continuous, ordered, sequence of items* [5], where each item describes an application event (social network post, sensor measurement, etc.).

The popularization of streaming data applications has fostered the interest of the Semantic Web community for this kind of data. As a result of this interest, a W3C community group on RDF Stream Processing[1] has recently started.

There are several aspects that need to be taken into account when implementing an effective RDF stream processing system. For instance, querying the RDF streams (with proposals like C-SPARQL [2] and $\text{SPARQL}_{\text{Stream}}$ [3]), reasoning on streams [9], scaling the stream processing [7], etc.

Another aspect to be taken into account is the scalable publication of RDF streams on the Web. To address this issue, we have developed Ztreamy [1], a middleware for large-scale distribution of RDF streams on top of HTTP. As shown in [1], Ztreamy, is able to publish a real-time stream to tens of thousands of simultaneous clients with delays of a few seconds, outperforming in this aspect the mechanisms for stream publication integrated in alternative platforms such as DataTurbine [8] and Linked Stream Middleware [6]. To achieve these results, Ztreamy relies on the use of buffering strategies, stream compression and a single-threaded non-blocking input/output paradigm at the server.

1 http://www.w3.org/community/rsp/ (March 12th, 2014)

V. Presutti et al. (Eds.): ESWC Satellite Events 2014, LNCS 8798, pp. 286–291, 2014.
DOI: 10.1007/978-3-319-11955-7_36

```
Event-Id: a360bdd8-695b-4e5b-b74e-bdaaec3eeafe
Source-Id: wikipedia-changes-002
Application-Id: wikipedia-changes
Syntax: text/n3
Timestamp: 2014-03-12T18:30:58+01:00
Body-Length: 296

@prefix dc: <http://purl.org/dc/elements/1.1/> .
@prefix webtlab: <http://webtlab.it.uc3m.es/> .

webtlab:_642529540 dc:date "2014-03-12T17:30:28Z" ;
    webtlab:pageid "16866376" ;
    webtlab:title "Persona (satellite)" .
```

Fig. 1. An example of item in a Ztreamy stream.

The main goal of this demo is to show the functionality of Ztreamy. In particular, we demonstrate how applications can publish their own RDF streams and how these streams can be consumed by other applications. The demonstration involves actual, heterogeneous streaming data coming from two different sources: (i) physical sensors placed in a room; and, (ii) information obtained by monitoring the activities of Wikipedia editors.

2 A Brief Introduction to Ztreamy

Ztreamy is a scalable middleware platform for the distribution of RDF streams on the Web. Its main objective is serving RDF streams on top of HTTP to as many clients as possible with minimal delays.

A stream in Ztreamy is a sequence of data items, where each item is composed by a RDF graph and metadata about it, such as its creation timestamp and the identifier of its source entity. Figure 1 shows an example of a data item.

Stream servers are the core of Ztreamy. They aggregate the items they receive from data producers (e.g. physical sensors) into streams, and provide those streams to consumers with a publish-subscribe paradigm. The platform is flexible with respect to how streams are served an manipulated. For example, a stream can easily be filtered, split into separate streams, joined with other streams in order to form aggregate streams, etc. Streams can be served from just one server or replicated from many servers.

Like the Web, the Ztreamy platform is intended to be open. It allows any entity to publish its own streams just by installing a server. It is also possible to mirror any stream that can be consumed or publish derivative streams.

Data producers and consumers communicate with Ztreamy servers through HTTP. Therefore, producers and consumers can be programmed with almost any programming language and run on almost any platform. This includes fully-fledged servers for stream processing, desktop applications, JavaScript applications that run on Web browsers, mobile applications and embedded systems.

Ideally, consumers subscribe to a stream with long-lived HTTP requests. With this mechanism the server sends the response in chunks as new data is available, but never finishes the response neither closes the connection. This way of communication is efficient because just one underlying TCP connection is used and just one HTTP request needs to be processed for a possibly long period of time. Some HTTP client libraries and HTTP proxies may not be compatible with long-lived requests, as they expect responses to be complete before retransmitting them. In that case, consumers can use long-polling instead, in which the server finishes the response as soon as all the available data has been sent, and the consumer sends a new HTTP request immediately after that.

The Ztreamy platform provides some basic built-in services ready to use by applications, such as some simple semantics-based filters. However, it does not aim at being a complete platform for RDF stream processing. Applications that need more complex services such as a stream query engine can integrate them on top of Ztreamy, or use other systems for the data processing tasks and leave Ztreamy just for publishing the streams.

The main focus of our work was on scalable publication of streams to large amounts of simultaneous consumers. Therefore, we carried out a performance evaluation of Ztreamy in which we show that it outperforms other existing solutions in that task [1]. Our experiments show that the main factors that contribute to achieving that level of performance are:

- Buffering data at the server: Instead of sending new data to consumers as soon as it is available, it is buffered and sent periodically. The experiments show that even with very small periods (e.g. 0.5 s), which barely delay the delivery of data, there are big gains in the use of CPU of the servers. Thus, the servers are able to handle more simultaneous clients.
- Compressing the streams: Streams in Ztreamy can be compressed with the Deflate stream compression protocol. In combination with the server buffering mechanism, our experiments show not only a reduction of about 85 % in network traffic but also additional gains in the use of CPU in the server, which allows it to handle more clients.
- Use of single-threaded non-blocking input/output: Ztreamy servers are built on top of the Tornado Web server, which was designed to handle large amounts of simultaneous clients. To do so, Tornado uses a single-threaded non-blocking input/output paradigm based on the new asynchronous facilities of modern operating systems. Many servers are recently switching from the multi-threaded to the non-blocking paradigm because of its performance advantages when handling many simultaneous network connections.

We have published the current prototype of Ztreamy, which is implemented with the Python programming language, under the free software GNU GPL license. More information about the platform is available at [1] and at its website[2].

[2] http://www.it.uc3m.es/jaf/ztreamy (March 12th, 2014)

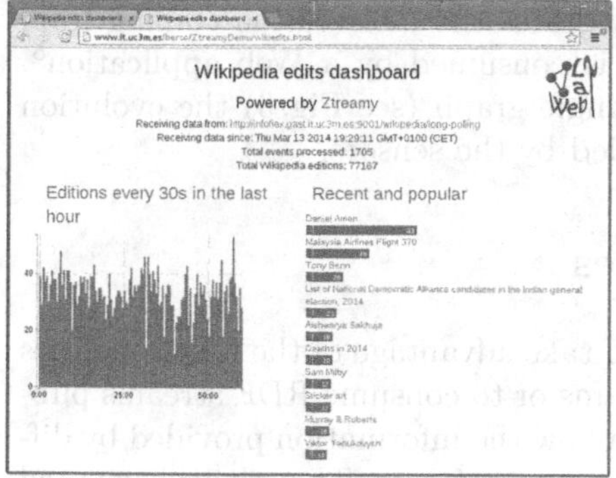

Fig. 2. Wikipedia edits demo interface.

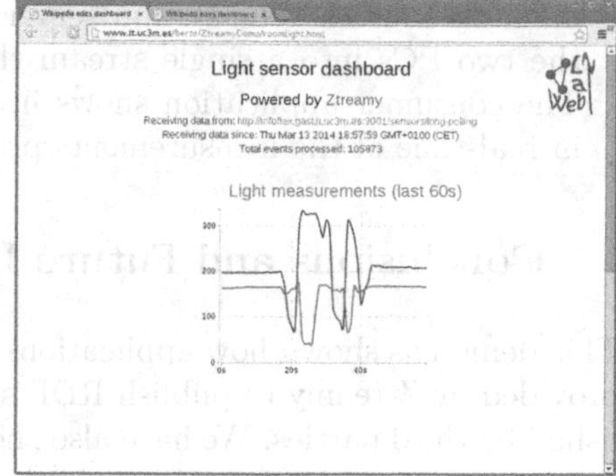

Fig. 3. Light sensor demo interface.

3 Ztreamy Demo

The main goal of the demo is to show how applications can publish their own RDF streams using Ztreamy and how can these streams be consumed by other applications. In particular, we center our demo in two different scenarios:

- **Wikipedia edits**: In this scenario, a Python application acts as information source. It uses the Wikipedia API[3] to monitor the activity of Wikipedia editors. Every 30 s, this applications generates a new data item (similar to that in Fig. 1) with metadata about the edits recently carried out in the encyclopedia (including the timestamp and the title of the modified page). Then, using HTTP, the application sends the item to a Ztreamy stream server that publishes it in a stream. A second application connects to this server to consume the stream. It is a Web application[4] implemented in JavaScript that runs in the Web browser of the user. It uses the *ztreamy.js* library in order to interact with the stream server. The interface of the application (depicted in Fig. 2) includes two graphs: one graph shows the number of edits every 30 s in the last hour, and a second graph shows a ranking with the top 10 Wikipedia pages by number of edits (from a list containing the last 2000 edited pages). Both graphs are dynamic: they are updated every time a new item in the stream is received at the browser.
- **Physical sensors**: In this scenario two information sources publish items to the same stream. In particular, each information source consists of a PC connected to an Arduino and a TSL235R light sensor. Every second, a Python application installed in each of the PCs, reads the measurements provided by the local sensor through an USB port and generates a Ztreamy stream item. Then, it publishes the item into a single stream server shared between the

[3] http://en.wikipedia.org/w/api.php (March 12th, 2014)

[4] Available at: http://www.it.uc3m.es/berto/ZtreamyDemo/wikiedits.html

different sources. The stream server integrates the information coming from the two PCs into a single stream that is consumed by a Web application[5]. The consumer application shows in a single graph (see Fig. 3) the evolution in real-time of the measurements provided by the sensors.

4 Conclusions and Future Lines

This demo has shown how applications can take advantage of the functionalities provided by Ztreamy to publish RDF streams or to consume RDF streams published by third parties. We have also shown how the information provided by different sources can be easily integrated into a single stream. Though we have used Python to implement the information providers and JavaScript to implement the consumers, given that Ztreamy relies on HTTP as communication protocol, it is possible to use other alternatives. Thus, implementing libraries to interact with Ztreamy from other languages, like Java or Ruby, is a work to be developed in the near future. At the moment Ztreamy relies on the general-purpose Zlib stream compressor, which implements Deflate. However, we are considering as a future line the possibility of integrating RDF stream compression algorithms like [4] into the system.

Acknowledgements. This work has been partially funded by the Spanish Government through the project HERMES-SMARTDRIVER (TIN2013-46801-C4-2-R).

References

1. Arias, J., Fernández, N., Sánchez, L., Fuentes-Lorenzo, D.: Ztreamy: a middleware for publishing semantic streams on the Web. Web Semant. Sci. Serv. Agents World Wide Web **25**, 16–23 (2014). doi:10.1016/j.websem.2013.11.002
2. Barbieri, D.F., Braga, D., Ceri, S., Grossniklaus, M.: An execution environment for C-SPARQL queries. In: Proceedings of the 13th International Conference on Extending Database Technology, EDBT '10, pp. 441–452 (2010)
3. Calbimonte, J.-P., Corcho, O., Gray, A.J.G.: Enabling ontology-based access to streaming data sources. In: Patel-Schneider, P.F., Pan, Y., Hitzler, P., Mika, P., Zhang, L., Pan, J.Z., Horrocks, I., Glimm, B. (eds.) ISWC 2010, Part I. LNCS, vol. 6496, pp. 96–111. Springer, Heidelberg (2010)
4. Fernández, N., Arias, J., Sánchez, L., Fuentes-Lorenzo, D., Corcho, Ó.: RDSZ: an approach for lossless RDF stream compression. In: Presutti, V., d'Amato, C., Gandon, F., d'Aquin, M., Staab, S., Tordai, A. (eds.) ESWC 2014. LNCS, vol. 8465, pp. 52–67. Springer, Heidelberg (2014)
5. Golab, L., Özsu, M.T.: Issues in data stream management. SIGMOD Rec. **32**, 5–14 (2003)
6. Le-Phuoc, D., Nguyen-Mau, H.Q., Parreira, J.X., Hauswirth, M.: A middleware framework for scalable management of linked streams. Web Semant. Sci. Serv. Agents World Wide Web **16**(5), 42–51 (2012)

[5] Available at: http://www.it.uc3m.es/berto/ZtreamyDemo/roomlight.html

7. Le-Phuoc, D., Nguyen Mau Quoc, H., Le Van, C., Hauswirth, M.: Elastic and scalable processing of linked stream data in the cloud. In: Alani, H., et al. (eds.) ISWC 2013, Part I. LNCS, vol. 8218, pp. 280–297. Springer, Heidelberg (2013)
8. Tilak, S., Hubbard, P., Miller, M., Fountain, T.: The ring buffer network bus (RBNB) dataturbine streaming data middleware for environmental observing systems. In: IEEE International Conference on e-Science and Grid Computing, pp. 125–133, December 2007
9. Valle, E.D., Ceri, S., Harmelen, Fv, Fensel, D.: It's a streaming world! reasoning upon rapidly changing information. IEEE Intell. Syst. **24**(6), 83–89 (2009)

rdf:SynopsViz – A Framework for Hierarchical Linked Data Visual Exploration and Analysis

Nikos Bikakis[1,2(✉)], Melina Skourla[1], and George Papastefanatos[2]

[1] National Technical University of Athens, Athens, Greece
bikakis@dblab.ntua.gr
[2] IMIS, ATHENA Research Center, Athena, Greece

Abstract. The purpose of data visualization is to offer intuitive ways for information perception and manipulation, especially for non-expert users. The Web of Data has realized the availability of a huge amount of datasets. However, the volume and heterogeneity of available information make it difficult for humans to manually explore and analyse large datasets. In this paper, we present rdf:SynopsViz, a tool for hierarchical charting and visual exploration of Linked Open Data (LOD). Hierarchical LOD exploration is based on the creation of multiple levels of hierarchically related groups of resources based on the values of one or more properties. The adopted hierarchical model provides effective information abstraction and summarization. Also, it allows efficient -on the fly- statistic computations, using aggregations over the hierarchy levels.

Keywords: Visual analytics · Semantic web · LOD · RDF visualization · Data exploration · RDF statistics · RDF charts · Faceted search · RDF facets

1 Introduction

The purpose of data visualization is to offer intuitive ways for information perception and manipulation that essentially amplify, especially for non-expert users, the overall cognitive performance of information processing. This is of great importance in the Web of Data, where the volume and heterogeneity of available information make difficult for humans to manually explore and analyse large datasets. An important challenge is that visualization techniques must offer scalability and efficient processing for on the fly visualization of large datasets. They must also employ appropriate data abstractions and aggregations for avoiding information overloading due to the size and diversity of the data presented to the user. Finally, they must be generic and provide uniform and intuitive visualization results across multiple domains.

In this work, we present rdf:SynopsViz, a framework for hierarchical charting and exploration of Linked Open Data (LOD). Hierarchical LOD exploration realized through the creation of multiple levels of hierarchically related groups of

V. Presutti et al. (Eds.): ESWC Satellite Events 2014, LNCS 8798, pp. 292–297, 2014.
DOI: 10.1007/978-3-319-11955-7_37

resources based on the values of one or more properties. For example, a numerical group, characterized by a numerical range, comprises all resources with a property value within the range of this group. Hierarchical browsing can address the problem of information overloading as it provides information abstraction and summarization [1]. It can also offer rich insights on the underlying data when combined with rich statistical information on the groups and their contents.

The key features of rdf:SynopsViz framework are summarized as follows: (1) It adopts a *hierarchical model* for RDF data visualization, browsing and analysis. (2) It offers *automatic* on-the-fly hierarchy construction based on data distribution, as well as *user-defined* hierarchy construction based on user's preferences. (3) Provides *faceted* browsing and filtering over classes and properties. (4) Integrates *statistics with visualization*; visualizations have been enriched with useful statistics and data information. (5) Offers several visualizations techniques (e.g., timeline, chart, treemap). (6) Provides a large number of dataset's *statistics* regarding the: data-level (e.g., number of sameAs triples), schema-level (e.g., most common classes/properties), and structure level (e.g., entities with the larger in-degree). (7) Provides numerous *metadata* related to the dataset: licensing, provenance, linking, availability, undesirability, etc. The latter are useful for assessing data quality [13].

2 Framework Overview

The architecture of rdf:SynopsViz is presented in Fig. 1. Our scenario involves three main parts: the Client GUI, the rdf:SynopsViz framework, and the input data. The *Client* part, corresponds to the framework's front-end offering several functionalities to the end-users (e.g., statistical analysis, facet search, etc.). rdf:SynopsViz consumes RDF data as *Input data*; optionally, OWL-RDF/S vocabularies/ontologies describing the input data can be loaded. Next, we describe the basic components of the rdf:SynopsViz framework.

In the preprocessing phase, the *Data and Schema Handler* parses the input data and inferes schema information (e.g., properties domain(s)/range(s), class/property hierarchy, type of instances, type of properties, etc.). *Facets Generator* generates class and property facets over input data. *Statistics Generator* computes several statistics regarding the schema, instances and graph structure of

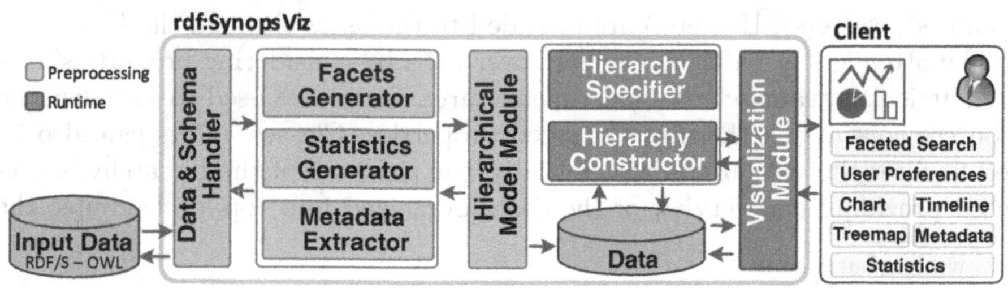

Fig. 1. System architecture

the input dataset, such as the number of different types of classes and properties, or the number of sameAs triples, or finally the average in/out degree of the RDF graph, respectively. *Metadata Extractor* collects dataset metadata which can be used for data quality assessment. *Hierarchical Model Module* adopts our hierarchy model and stores the initial data enriched with the information computed during the preprocessing phase.

During runtime the following components are involved. *Hierarchy Specifier* is responsible for managing the configuration parameters of our hierarchy model, e.g., the number of hierarchy levels, the number of nodes per level, and providing this information to the Hierarchy Constructor. *Hierarchy Constructor* implements the hierarchy model. Based on the selected facets, and the hierarchy configuration: it determines the hierarchy of groups and the contained triples, and computes the statistics about their contents (e.g., range, variance, mean, number of triples contained, etc.). *Visualization Module* allows the interaction between the user and the framework, allowing several operations (e.g., navigation, filtering, hierarchy specification) over the visualized data.

3 Implementation and Demonstration Outline

Implementation. rdf:SynopsViz is implemented on top of several open source tools and libraries. Regarding visualization libraries, we use Highcharts[1], for the area and timeline charts and Google Charts[2] for treemap and pie charts. Additionally, it uses Jena framework[3] for RDF data handing and Jena TDB for RDF storing.

The web-based prototype of rdf:SynopsViz is available at http://synopsviz.imis.athena-innovation.gr. Also a video demonstrating the scenario presented below is available at http://youtu.be/8v-He1U4oxs.

Demonstration scenario. First, the attenders will be able to select a dataset from a number of offered real-word datasets (e.g., dbpedia, Eurostat, World Bank, U.S. Census, etc.) or upload their own. Then, for the selected dataset, the attendees are able to examine several of the dataset's *metadata*, and explore several datasets's *statistics*.

Using the facets panel, the attenders are able to navigate and filter data based on classes, numeric and date properties. In addition, through facets navigation several information about the classes and properties (e.g., number of instances, domain(s), range(s), IRI, etc.) are provided to the users through the UI.

The attenders are able to navigate over data by considering properties' values. Particularly, area charts and timeline-area charts are used to visualize the resources considering the user's selected properties. Classes' facets can also be used to filter the visualized data. Initially, the top level of the hierarchy is presented providing an overview of the data, organized into top-level groups; the

[1] www.highcharts.com
[2] developers.google.com/chart
[3] jena.apache.org

user can interactively zoom in and out the group of interest, up to the actual values of the raw input data. At the same time, statistical information concerning the hierarchy groups as well as their contents (e.g., mean value, variance, sample data, etc.) are presented.

In addition, the attenders are able to navigate over data, through class hierarchy. Selecting one or more classes, the attenders can interactively navigate over the class hierarchy using treemaps. In rdf:SynopsViz the treemap visualization has been enriched with schema and statistical information. For each class, schema metadata (e.g., number of instances, subclasses, datatype/object properties) and statistical information (e.g., the cardinality of each property, min, max value for datatype properties' ranges, etc.) are provided.

Finally, the attenders can interactively modify the hierarchy specifications. Particularly, they are able to increase or decrease the level of abstraction/detail presented, by modifying both the number of hierarchy levels, and number of nodes per level.

4 Related Work

A large number of works studying issues related to RDF or LOD visualization and analysis have been proposed in the literature [2–5]. Additionally, numerous tools offering RDF or Linked Open Data visualization have been developed, e.g., *Sgvizler* [6], *LODWheel* [7], *Payola* [8], *CubeViz* [9], *KC-Viz* [10], *RelFinde*[4], *Welkin*[5], *IsaViz*[6], *RDF-Gravity*[7], etc.

In the context of RDF and Linked Open Data statistics, *RDFStats* [12] calculates statistical information about RDF datasets. *LODstats* [11] is an extensible framework, offering scalable statistical analysis of Linked Open Data datasets.

Regarding the quality assessment issues, [13] studies the criteria which can be used in Linked Data quality assessment. Reference [14] review millions of RDF documents to analyse Linked Data conformance. Finally, several frameworks for the quality assessment in the Web of Data, have been proposed *LINK-QA* [15], *Sieve* [16], *WIQA* [17]. In contrast to existing approaches, we provide hierarchical RDF data visualization enriched with data statistics. The hierarchical model solves the visualization overload issues, offering efficient, on the fly statistical computations over hierarchy levels. Finally, due to hierarchical model our tool can efficiently handle and analyse very large datasets.

5 Conclusions

In this paper we have presented rdf:SynopsViz, a framework for hierarchical charting and exploration of Linked Open Data. The hierarchical model adopted by

[4] www.visualdataweb.org/relfinder.php
[5] simile.mit.edu/welkin
[6] www.w3.org/2001/11/IsaViz
[7] semweb.salzburgresearch.at/apps/rdf-gravity

our framework can address the problem of information overloading, offering an effective mechanism for information abstraction and summarization. Additionally, the adopted model allows the efficient statistic computations, using aggregations over the hierarchy levels.

Some future extensions of our tool include the application of more sophisticated filtering techniques (e.g., SPARQL-enabled browsing over the data), as well as the addition of more visual techniques and libraries.

Acknowledgement. This research has been co-financed by the European Union (European Social Fund - ESF) and Greek national funds through the Operational Program "Education and Lifelong Learning" of the National Strategic Reference Framework (NSRF) - Research Funding Program: THALIS and KRIPIS - Investing in knowledge society through the European Social Fund.

References

1. Elmqvist, N., Fekete, J.-D.: Hierarchical aggregation for information visualization: overview, techniques, and design guidelines. IEEE Trans. Vis. Comput. Graph. **16**(3), 927–934 (2010)
2. Dadzie, A., Rowe, M.: Approaches to visualising Linked Data: a survey. Seman. Web **2**(2), 89–124 (2011)
3. Brunetti, J., Auer, S., Garcia, R.: The linked data visualization model. In: ISWC 2012 (2012)
4. Dadzie, A.-S., Rowe, M., Petrelli, D.: *Hide the Stack*: toward usable linked data. In: Antoniou, G., Grobelnik, M., Simperl, E., Parsia, B., Plexousakis, D., De Leenheer, P., Pan, J. (eds.) ESWC 2011, Part I. LNCS, vol. 6643, pp. 93–107. Springer, Heidelberg (2011)
5. Alonen, M., Kauppinen, T., Suominen, O., Hyvönen, E.: Exploring the linked university data with visualization tools. In: Cimiano, P., Fernández, M., Lopez, V., Schlobach, S., Völker, J. (eds.) ESWC 2013. LNCS, vol. 7955, pp. 204–208. Springer, Heidelberg (2013)
6. Skjveland M.: Sgvizler: a JavaScript wrapper for easy visualization of SPARQL result sets. In: ESWC 2012 (2012)
7. Stuhr, M., Dumitru, R., Norheim, D.: LODWheel - JavaScript-based visualization of RDF data. In: Workshop on Consuming Linked Data 2011 (2011)
8. Klímek, J., Helmich, J., Nečaský, M.: *Payola*: collaborative linked data analysis and visualization framework. In: Cimiano, P., Fernández, M., Lopez, V., Schlobach, S., Völker, J. (eds.) ESWC 2013. LNCS, vol. 7955, pp. 147–151. Springer, Heidelberg (2013)
9. Salas, P., Mota, F., Breitman, K., Casanova, M., Martin, M., Auer, S.: Publishing statistical data on the web. In: IEEE Semantic Computing 2012 (2012)
10. Motta, E., Mulholland, P., Peroni, S., d'Aquin, M., Gomez-Perez, J.M., Mendez, V., Zablith, F.: A novel approach to visualizing and navigating ontologies. In: Aroyo, L., Welty, C., Alani, H., Taylor, J., Bernstein, A., Kagal, L., Noy, N., Blomqvist, E. (eds.) ISWC 2011, Part I. LNCS, vol. 7031, pp. 470–486. Springer, Heidelberg (2011)

11. Auer, S., Demter, J., Martin, M., Lehmann, J.: LODStats – an extensible framework for high-performance dataset analytics. In: Aussenac-Gilles, N., d'Acquin, M., Handschuh, S., Hernandez, N., Nikolov, A., Stuckenschmidt, H., Teije, A., Völker, J. (eds.) EKAW 2012. LNCS, vol. 7603, pp. 353–362. Springer, Heidelberg (2012)
12. Langegger, A., Wöß, W.: RDFStats - an Extensible RDF Statistics Generator and Library. In: Workshop on Web Semantics 2009 (2009)
13. Zaveri, A., Rula, A., Maurino, A., Pietrobon, R., Lehmann, J., Auer, S.: Quality assessment methodologies for linked open data. Under review, available at Semantic Web Journal site
14. Hogan, A., Umbrich, J., Harth, A., Cyganiak, R., Polleres, A., Decker, S.: An empirical survey of Linked Data conformance. J. Web Sem. **14**, 14–44 (2012)
15. Guéret, C., Groth, P., Stadler, C., Lehmann, J.: Assessing linked data mappings using network measures. In: Simperl, E., Cimiano, P., Polleres, A., Corcho, O., Presutti, V. (eds.) ESWC 2012. LNCS, vol. 7295, pp. 87–102. Springer, Heidelberg (2012)
16. Mendes, P., Mühleisen, H., Bizer, C.: Sieve: linked data quality assessment and fusion. In: Workshop on Linked Web Data Management 2012 (2012)
17. Bizer, C., Cyganiak, R.: Quality-driven information filtering using the WIQA policy framework. J. Web Sem. **7**(1), 1–10 (2009)

Boosting QAKiS with Multimedia Answer Visualization

Elena Cabrio[1,2](✉), Vivek Sachidananda[2], and Raphaël Troncy[2]

[1] INRIA Sophia Antipolis, Valbonne, France
elena.cabrio@inria.fr
[2] EURECOM, Biot, France
{vivek.sachidananda,raphael.troncy}@eurecom.fr

Abstract. We present an extension of QAKiS, a system for Question Answering over DBpedia language specific chapters, that allows to complement textual answers with multimedia content from the linked data, to provide a richer and more complete answer to the user. For the demo, English, French and German DBpedia chapters are the RDF data sets to be queried using a natural language interface. Beside the textual answer, QAKiS output embeds (i) pictures from Wikipedia Infoboxes, (ii) OpenStreetMap, to visualize maps for questions asking about a place, and (iii) YouTube, to visualize pertinent videos (e.g. movie trailers).

1 Multimedia Question Answering

The goal of a Question Answering (QA) system is to return precise answers to users' natural language questions, extracting information from both documentary text and advanced media content. The research area on QA, and especially on scaling up QA to the linked data, is a wide and emergent research area that still needs an in-depth study to benefit from the rich linked data resources on the web. Up to now, QA research has largely focused on text, mainly targeting factual and list questions (for an overview on ontology-based Question Answering systems, see [5]).[1] However, a huge amount of increasingly multimedia contents are now available on the web on almost any topic, and it would be extremely interesting to consider them in the QA scenario, in which the best answers may be a combination of text and other media answers [4].

This demonstration presents an extension of QAKiS [2], a Question Answering system over DBpedia [1], that allows to exploit the structured data and metadata describing multimedia content on the linked data to provide a richer and more complete answer to the user, combining textual information with other media content. A first step in this direction consists in determining the best sources and media (image, audio, video, or a hybrid) to answer a query. For this reason, we have carried out an analysis of the questions provided by the Question Answering over Linked Data (QALD) challenge, and we have categorized them

[1] See the Question Answering over Linked Data (QALD) challenges http://greententacle.techfak.uni-bielefeld.de/~cunger/qald/.

V. Presutti et al. (Eds.): ESWC Satellite Events 2014, LNCS 8798, pp. 298–303, 2014.
DOI: 10.1007/978-3-319-11955-7_38

according to the possible improved multimedia answer visualization. Then, we have extended QAKiS output to include (i) pictures from Wikipedia Infoboxes, for instance to visualize images of people or places (for questions as *Who is the President of the United States?*); (ii) OpenStreetMap, to visualize maps for questions asking about a place (e.g. *What is the largest city in Australia?*) and (iii) YouTube, to visualize videos related to the answer (e.g. a trailer of a movie, for questions like *Which films starring Clint Eastwood did he direct himself?*).

2 Extending QAKiS to Visualize Multimedia Answers

QAKiS system description. QAKiS (Question Answering wiKiFramework-based System) [2] addresses the task of QA over structured knowledge-bases (e.g. DBpedia) [3], where the relevant information is expressed also in unstructured forms (e.g. Wikipedia pages). It implements a relation-based match for question interpretation, to convert the user question into a query language (e.g. SPARQL). More specifically, it makes use of relational patterns (automatically extracted from Wikipedia and collected in the WikiFramework repository [2]), that capture different ways to express a certain relation in a given language. QAKiS is composed of four main modules (Fig. 1): (i) the *query generator* takes the user question as input, generates the typed questions, and then generates the SPARQL queries from the retrieved patterns; (ii) the *pattern matcher* takes as input a typed question, and retrieves the patterns (among those in the repository) matching it with the highest similarity; (iii) the *sparql package* handles the queries to DBpedia; and (iv) a *Named Entity (NE) Recognizer*.

The actual version of QAKiS targets questions containing a Named Entity related to the answer through one property of the ontology, as *Which river does the Brooklyn Bridge cross?*. Such questions match a single pattern (i.e. one relation).

Before running the *pattern matcher* component, the question target is identified combining the output of Stanford NE Recognizer, with a set of strategies

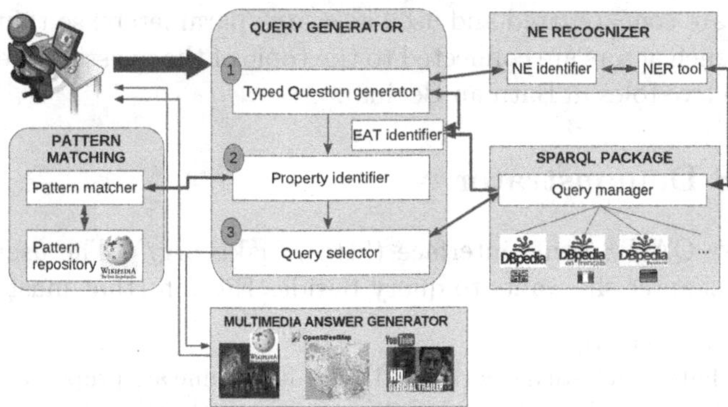

Fig. 1. QAKiS workflow [2]

that compare it with the instances labels in the DBpedia ontology. Then a *typed question* is generated by replacing the question keywords (e.g. who, where) and the NE by the types and supertypes. A Word Overlap algorithm is then applied to match such typed questions with the patterns for each relation. A similarity score is provided for each match: the highest represents the most likely relation. A set of patterns is retrieved by the pattern matcher component for each typed question, and sorted by decreasing matching score. For each of them, a set of SPARQL queries is generated and then sent to the endpoints of language specific DBpedia chapters that the user has selected. If no results are found the next pattern is considered, and so on. Currently, the results of a SPARQL query on the different language specific DBpedia chapters are aggregated by the set union.

QAKiS multimedia. While providing the textual answer to the user, the *multimedia answer generator module* queries again DBpedia to retrieve additional information about the entity contained in the answer. To display the images, it extracts the properties `foaf:depiction` and `dbpedia-owl:thumbnail`, and their value (i.e. the image) is shown as output. To display the maps (e.g. when the answer is a place), it retrieves the GPS co-ordinates from DBpedia (properties `geo:geometry`, `geo:lat` and `geo:long`), and it injects them dynamically into OpenStreetMap[2] to display the map. Given the fact that DBpedia data can be inconsistent or incomplete, we define a set of heuristics to extract the co-ordinates: in case there are several values for the latitude and longitude, (i) we give priorities to negative values (indicating the southern hemisphere[3]), and (ii) we take the value with the highest number of decimal values, assuming it is the most precise. Finally, to embed YouTube[4] videos, first the Freebase[5] ID of the entity is retrieved through the DBpedia property `owl:sameAs`. Then, such ID is used via YouTube search API (v3) (i.e. it is included in the embed code style `<iframe>`, that allows users to view the embedded video in either Flash or HTML5 players, depending on their viewing environment and preferences). Moreover, since we want to have pertinent videos (i.e. showing content related to the answer in the context of the question only), we remove stopwords from the input question, and we send the remaining words as search parameters. For instance, for the question *Give me the actors starring in Batman Begins*, the words "actors", "starring", "Batman Begins" are concatenated and used as search parameters, so that the videos extracted for such actors are connected to the topic of the question (i.e. the actors in their respective roles in Batman Begins).

3 QAKiS Demonstrator

Figure 2 shows QAKiS demo interface (http://qakis.org/). The user can select the DBpedia chapter she wants to query besides English (that must be selected

[2] www.openstreetmap.org

[3] We verified that when both a positive and a negative value are proposed, the negative is the correct one (the letter S, i.e. South, is not correctly processed).

[4] www.youtube.com/

[5] www.freebase.com

Fig. 2. QAKiS demo interface

as it is needed for NER), i.e. French or German DBpedia. Then the user can either write a question or select among a list of examples, and click on *Get Answers!*. As output, in the tab *Results* QAKiS provides: (i) the textual answer (linked to its DBpedia page), (ii) the DBpedia source, (iii) the associate image in Wikipedia Infobox, (iv) a *more details* button. Clicking on that button, both the entity abstract in Wikipedia, the map and the retrieved videos (if pertinent) are shown. In the tab *Technical details*, QAKiS provides (i) the user question (the recognized NE is linked to its DBpedia page), (ii) the generated typed question, (iii) the pattern matched, and (iv) the SPARQL query sent to the DBpedia SPARQL endpoint. The demo we will present follows these stages for a variety of queries, described in the next section.

3.1 Queries and Datasets for Demonstration

In order to determine the best sources and media (image, audio, video, or a hybrid) to answer a query, we have carried out an analysis on a subset of the questions provided by the QALD-3 challenge.[6] The goal was to categorize them according to the possible improved multimedia answer visualization, and to extract some heuristics to be exploited by QAKiS to provide the most complete answer to a certain question. In this analysis, we discarded the questions for which no additional multimedia content would be pertinent, e.g. questions whose answer is a number (e.g. *How many students does the Free University in Amsterdam have?*), or boolean questions (e.g. *Did Tesla win a nobel prize in physics?*). In future work we could provide multimedia content on the entity in the question, but in the current work we are focusing on boosting the answer visualization only. Table 1 shows the categories of multimedia content for answer visualization on which we are focusing, together with an example of question for which such kind of multimedia content would be appropriate.

[6] http://doi.org/10.4119/unibi/citec.2013.6

Table 1. QALD-3 questions improved answer visualization

Multimedia	Example question
Picture	Give me all female Russian astronauts
Picture + video	Give me all movies directed by Francis Ford Coppola
Picture + map	In which country does the Nile start?
Map + barchart	Give me all world heritage sites designated within the past 5 years.
Statcharts	What is the total amount of men and women serving in the FDNY?
Timelines	When was Alberta admitted as province?

4 Future Perspectives

The work we present in this demonstration is ongoing, and represents a first step in the direction of dealing with the huge potential amount of available multimedia data. As a short-term improvement, we are planning to add other sources of images. For instance, Ookaboo RDF Data contains pictures with topics derived from Freebase and DBpedia, and can therefore be coupled with the output of QAKiS, to provide additional images describing the answer. For other available datasets, metadata could be RDF-ized (e.g. MIRFLICKR, IMAGENET[7]) and the interlinking of such structured sources with DBpedia can be explored to provide to the user semantically enriched multimedia presentations. As a long-term improvement, we plan to address types of questions that have been less investigated in the literature (e.g. how to and why questions), and for which multimedia answers seem to be more intuitive and appropriate [4]. Moreover, a natural language answer should be generated and presented to the user in a narrative form for an easy consumption, supported by multimedia elements [6].

Acknowledgements. The work of E. Cabrio is funded by the ANR-11-LABX-0031-01 Program. We thank Amine Hallili for contributing to images extraction.

References

1. Bizer, C., et al.: DBpedia - a crystallization point for the web of data. Web Semant. **7**(3), 154–165 (2009)
2. Cabrio, E., Cojan, J., Aprosio, A.P., Magnini, B., Lavelli, A., Gandon, F.: QAKiS: an open domain QA system based on relational patterns. In: Proceedings of the ISWC 2012 Posters and Demonstrations Track, Boston, US, November 2012
3. Cabrio, E., Cojan, J., Gandon, F., Hallili, A.: Querying multilingual DBpedia with QAKiS. In: Cimiano, P., Fernández, M., Lopez, V., Schlobach, S., Völker, J. (eds.) ESWC 2013. LNCS, vol. 7955, pp. 194–198. Springer, Heidelberg (2013)
4. Hong, R., Wang, M., Li, G., Nie, L., Zha, Z.-J., Chua, T.-S.: Multimedia question answering. IEEE MultiMed. **19**(4), 72–78 (2012)

[7] http://press.liacs.nl/mirflickr/; https://www.image.net/

5. Lopez, V., Uren, V.S., Sabou, M., Motta, E.: Is question answering fit for the semantic web?: A survey. Semant. Web **2**(2), 125–155 (2011)
6. Vocht, L.D., Coppens, S., Verborgh, R., Sande, M.V., Mannens, E., de Walle, R.V.: Discovering meaningful connections between resources in the web of data. In: LDOW (2013)

Painless URI Dereferencing Using the DataTank

Pieter Colpaert(✉), Ruben Verborgh, Erik Mannens, and Rik Van de Walle

Department of Electronics and Information Systems, Multimedia Lab,
Ghent University - iMinds, Gaston Crommenlaan 8 Bus 201,
9050 Ledeberg, Ghent, Belgium
pieter@irail.be, {ruben.verborgh,erik.mannens}@ugent.be

Abstract. If we want a broad adoption of Linked Data, the barrier to conform to the Linked Data principles need to be as low as possible. One of the Linked Data principles is that URIs should be dereferenceable. This demonstrator shows how to set up The DataTank and configure a Linked Data repository, such as a turtle file or SPARQL endpoint, in it. Different content-types are acceptable and the response in the right format is generated.

Keywords: Linked data · Semantic web · Dereferencing · Linked data fragments

1 Introduction

Following the trend towards Open Data, Linked Data and the Semantic Web, more and more organizations are publishing their data to the Web. The academic world and standardization bodies have defined various frameworks and principles in order to do so: e.g., the Linked Data (LD) principles [2], hypermedia and REST principles [3], Linked Data Fragments (LDF) principles [6] or the RDF framework[1]. In our lab at Ghent University we are involved in projects on Linked Data which request often to do the same over and over again, adhering to the same set of principles. In this paper we are introducing *tdt/triples*, a project which takes away the pain of having to implement these principles for publishing data over and over again.

First we are going to describe how the perfect triple looks like according to principles. In the related work, we are discussing what projects already take care of these principles and why we believe *tdt/triples* will be a great benefit to a lot of tools. In the next section, we introduce the *tdt/triples* project. Next, the live demo is described and, finally, a conclusion is formulated.

2 The Perfect Triple

For each concept identifier within a triple – a fact described using RDF – a URI is used. In the design issues with Linked Data[2] Tim Berners-Lee, inventor

[1] A primer on RDF: http://www.w3.org/TR/rdf11-concepts/.
[2] http://www.w3.org/DesignIssues/LinkedData.html

V. Presutti et al. (Eds.): ESWC Satellite Events 2014, LNCS 8798, pp. 304–309, 2014.
DOI: 10.1007/978-3-319-11955-7_39

of the World-Wide Web, introduces dereferencing: "When someone looks up a URI, provide useful information". According to the W3C's note on dereferencing HTTP URIs[3], the act of retrieving a representation of a resource identified by a URI is known as dereferencing that URI. This way, user agents can retrieve facts about the concept the URI is identifying.

Different kinds of user agents are surfing the Web. For a URI about a certain government service, a user agent may be for example looking for news facts. The user agent is going to prefer an *application/rss+xml* representation over a *text/html* representation. The server which serves the representations of the URI may also have its preferences: it may prefer to send *text/html* over *application/rss+xml* as the latter has for instance a slow implementation on the server. The HTTP protocol supports this *content negotiation* using its *Accept* headers. RDF also has different serializations in which triples can be defined. Using content negotiation, different representations of the data should be provided.

These URIs also need to be discoverable. Using DCAT, a W3C vocabulary to describe data catalogs, and VoID, the W3C Vocabulary of Interlinked Datasets, dataset can be made discoverable.

LDF [6] makes the Web of Data Web-scale by allowing clients to query datasets. A basic LDF server has to provide 3 things: data that corresponds to a basic triple pattern, meta-data that consists of the (approximate) total triple count and controls that lead to all other fragments of the same dataset.

The perfect triple is a triple whom's URIs are dereferenced through the HTTP protocol. According to REST principles, the responses to requests towards these URIs have to be cacheable. Furthermore, different serializations and representations of the data have to be provided through content negotiation in order to make the data easy to consume for all machines. Hypermedia controls are needed when dereferencing the URI which provide affordances to the URIs in the triple. Finally, meta-data has to be provided in order to query the data according to the LDF principles and meta-data about the the dataset needs to be given using the DCAT and VoID ontologies.

3 Related Work

Pubby[4] is a Java project written by Richard Cyganiak and Chris Bizer in order to dereference URIs in a triple store with a SPARQL endpoint that supports *DESCRIBE* queries. It supports content negotiation[5] and it follows the REST and hypermedia principles. Pubby does not provide meta-data through the hypermedia interface using DCAT or VoID. Known limitations are that it only supports SPARQL endpoints which support *DESCRIBE*, multiple datasets may not work as expected and hash URIs are not supported. Furthermore, the visualization of the triples in the HTML representation are not extensible[6].

[3] http://www.w3.org/2001/tag/doc/httpRange-14/2007-05-31/HttpRange-14

[4] http://wifo5-03.informatik.uni-mannheim.de/pubby/

[5] https://github.com/cygri/pubby/blob/master/src/main/java/de/fuberlin/wiwiss/pubby/negotiation/ContentTypeNegotiator.java

[6] https://github.com/cygri/pubby/issues/20

Amongst all limitations, only supporting SPARQL endpoints is a problem as for instance ontologies are commonly written by hand in a turtle file and uploaded on a server without triple store, or some data are not stored in a triple store at all and needs to be accessed in another way.

Triplify[7] [1] is a light-weight Data Publication platform. It is a small plugin for Web applications, which reveals the semantic structures encoded in relational databases. Triplify is focused on converting unstructured data from Web applications, stored in a relational database, to RDF. While the project also lowers the barrier for adoption of the Linked Data technology, it does not provide any solution to derefercing new URIs.

Virtuoso[8], a triple store built by OpenLink, provides optional URI dereferencing on top of their triple store software. In a document[9], they describe their implementation details exposing RDF data and bridging the "Linked Data Web" and the traditional "Document Web". While it is an interesting project, it only works on top of Virtuoso.

Another project is the DBpedia viewer [4] and is used by the, at the time of writing, beta version of DBpedia live. The main drawback for reusing this project, is that the code[10] is written specifically for DBpedia's Virtuoso instance.

4 Demo

For this demonstrator, we have chosen a URI namespace, http://triples.demo.thedatatank.com/, further referred to with the prefix *triples:*. On this namespace, it is our goal to provide a hypermedia interface which dereferences URIs defined in an RDF file. For public transit stop points, we want two LDP[11] containers: one describing the stoppoints of the Belgian railway company NMBS, *triples:NMBS* and one describing the stoppoints of the Dutch railway company NS, *triples:NS*. In these containers, the locations and names of these stop points are given.

The *tdt/triples*[12] project can be installed over *tdt/core*[13] instance. After installation using the composer[14] command on a (apache, mysql, PHP5.4+) stack, the instance can be configured using the API at the relative path */api/triples*. POSTing a new resource to this collection can be done by providing the type of the reader and its parameters. Self-documentation on the sources and their parameters can be found in the discovery document, which in this case can be found at *triples:discovery*.

In the beginning of our example project, our turtle file is small and only contains two transit agencies. In order to dereference the URIs in it, we configure The

[7] http://triplify.org/

[8] http://virtuoso.openlinksw.com/

[9] http://virtuoso.openlinksw.com/whitepapers/deploying%20linked%20data.html

[10] https://github.com/lukovnikov/dbpedia-vad-i18n

[11] The Linked Data Platform (LDP) is a vocabulary to describe read-write Linked Data resources based on HTTP access: http://www.w3.org/TR/ldp/.

[12] http://github.com/tdt/triples

[13] http://github.com/tdt/core

[14] A dependency manager for PHP: http://getcomposer.org.

DataTank to dereference our file by POSTing its location to *triples:api/triples*, thus, no need to set up a triple store and SPARQL endpoint. The turtle file used in this demo can be found at *triples:demo.ttl*. When going to the specific URIs, only the triples mentioning this URI as a subject are returned and visualized. The visualization within the HTML uses a javascript library called rdf2html[15]. It is an extensible library which creates a certain type of visualization for an, or a couple of, ontologies. Through content-negotiation, the same data can be requested through different formats: *text/html*, *application/json*, *application/ld+json*, *application/rdf+xml*, *text/turtle*...

A basic LDF server has to be able to solve triple patterns. The DataTank solves this using this template: *{URI}?subject={subject}&predicate={predicate}&object={object}*. This way, we have also introduced URIs for triples and triple patterns. By dereferencing these, we can provide more information: the answer to the triple pattern can be given, but also the (approximation of the) count, provenance and extra hypermedia handles can be given. The basic LDF server is advertised in the data catalog feed on the server accessible at *triples:api/dcat*.

When in the course of the project, a triple store is set up, an extra source can be configured on */api/triples*. This new SPARQL endpoint source can work in parallel to the turtle file, until the turtle file is not needed any longer.

5 Getting Started

tdt/triples is an extension of *tdt/core*. Both repositories are available at *github.com*. The only requirement is a standard Apache – MySQL – PHP stack. Composer[16], a dependency manager for PHP, can be used in order to set up The DataTank on your namespace. First, fill out *app/config/database.php* after downloading *tdt/core*. Next, run *composer require tdt/triples* followed by a *composer install*. If all goes well, your namespace should now return an empty The DataTank.

By using the interface at *api/admin* you can configure tdt/core resources. At the time of writing, supported sources are: a CSV file, a SHP file, an XML file, a JSON file, an XLS file, a JSON-LD file, an N3 file, a SPARQL endpoint and custom written PHP code to fetch and transform data. With the added *tdt/triples* functionalities, you can now configure extra sources at *api/triples*. Posting Listing 1 to *api/triples* will result in all the configured file's triples to be added to your namespace. The result, with this particular file, can be seen at for example *triples:NMBS*, which will now return the relevant triples, including VoID, Hydra[17] and DCAT metadata.

---

[15] http://github.com/tdt/rdf2html

[16] http://getcomposer.org

[17] A vocabulary to describe hypermedia APIs used by LDF: http://www.hydra-cg.com/.

```
{
  type:"Turtle",
  uri: "http://triples.demo.thedatatank.com/demo.ttl"
}
```

Listing 1. An example of a tdt/triples source configuration.

Up to date documentation can be found at http://docs.thedatatank.com.

6 Conclusion

This demonstrator introduces *tdt/triples*, a new project which lowers the bar to start dereferencing URIs on a certain namespace. Several principles to publish data on the Web were discussed and applied to the project, amongst others: the Linked Data principles, the hypermedia and REST principles and the Linked Data Fragments principles. The readers or visitors of the demonstrator are able to set up *tdt/triples* and can add their RDF file or SPARQL endpoint to the configuration. They are able to see an automatically generated representation requested through content-negotiation, see the rdf2html view and follow links. All processing is done on the fly: when the file or store changes, the URI representation does too.

We hope that *tdt/triples* and *rdf2html* will get a broad uptake amongst ontology maintainers, dataset owners and other people that have to dereference URIs as part of their Linked Data project. Future work lies in enabling the read/write Web within *tdt/triples* using distributed versioning techniques. This work has already started in our lab with R&Wbase [5]: distributed version control for triples.

Acknowledgments. We would like to thank Jan Vansteenlandt and Michiel Vancoillie of the Open Knowledge Foundation Belgium for the close collaboration on the implementation of tdt/triples. The research activities described in this paper were funded by Ghent University, iMinds, the Flemish department of Economics, Science and Innovation (EWI), the Institute for the Promotion of Innovation by Science and Technology in Flanders (IWT) and the European Union.

References

1. Auer, S., Dietzold, S., Lehmann, J., Hellmann, S., Aumueller, D.: Triplify: lightweight linked data publication from relational databases. In: Proceedings of the 18th international conference on World Wide Web, pp. 621–630. ACM (2009)
2. Bizer, C., Heath, T., Berners-Lee, T.: Linked data-the story so far. Int. J. Semant. Web Inf. Syst. **5**(3), 1–22 (2009)
3. Fielding, R.T., Taylor, R.N.: Principled design of the modern web architecture. ACM Trans. Internet Technol. (TOIT) **2**(2), 115–150 (2002)
4. Lukovnikov, D., Kontokostas, D., Stadler, C., Hellmann, S., Lehmann, J.: DBpedia viewer - An integrative interface for DBpedia leveraging the DBpedia service eco system. In: Proceedings of the 7th Workshop on Linked Data on the Web (2014)

5. Vander Sande, M., Colpaert, P., Verborgh, R., Coppens, S., Mannens, E., Van de Walle, R.: R&Wbase: Git for triples. In: Proceedings of the 6th Workshop on Linked Data on the Web (2013)
6. Verborgh, R., Vander Sande, M., Colpaert, P., Mannens, E., Van de Walle, R.: Web-scale querying through linked data fragments. In: Proceedings of the 7th Workshop on Linked Data on the Web (2014)

CORNER: A Completeness Reasoner for SPARQL Queries Over RDF Data Sources

Fariz Darari(✉), Radityo Eko Prasojo, and Werner Nutt

Faculty of Computer Science, Free University of Bozen-Bolzano, Bolzano, Italy
{fariz.darari,radityoeko.prasojo}@stud-inf.unibz.it, nutt@inf.unibz.it

Abstract. With the increased availability of data on the Semantic Web, the question whether data sources offer data of appropriate quality for a given purpose becomes an issue. With CORNER, we specifically address the data quality aspect of completeness. CORNER supports SPARQL BGP queries and can take RDFS ontologies into account in its analysis. If a query can only be answered completely by a combination of sources, CORNER rewrites the original query into one with SPARQL `SERVICE` calls, which assigns each query part to a suitable source, and executes it over those sources. CORNER builds upon previous work by Darari et al. [1] and is implemented using standard Semantic Web frameworks.

Keywords: Data quality · Data completeness · Query completeness · SPARQL

1 Introduction

In recent years, large amounts of data have been made available on the Semantic Web, which can be accessed by posing queries to SPARQL endpoints. As more data become available, quality of data becomes an issue since data in different sources may be suitable for different usages. In particular, *data completeness* may vary among data sources. Consequently, users who pose a query to different sources may get answers with different degrees of completeness. The question is how to support users in choosing sources over which their queries can retrieve complete answers.

For relational databases, Levy [2] proposed a format for statements about data completeness and studied how to assess the completeness of a query in the presence of such statements. Razniewski and Nutt [3] introduced a general reasoning technique for this problem and provided a comprehensive complexity analysis. Darari et al. [1] developed a framework for completeness reasoning techniques on the Semantic Web. The framework enables one to provide descriptions as to which parts of a data source are complete, called *completeness statements*, and to perform checks whether a given query over such a data source returns a complete result, called *query completeness* checks. The framework supports basic graph pattern (BGP) queries [4] and can take into account RDFS ontologies featuring `subclass`, `subproperty`, `domain` and `range`. Moreover, if a query can be

V. Presutti et al. (Eds.): ESWC Satellite Events 2014, LNCS 8798, pp. 310–314, 2014.
DOI: 10.1007/978-3-319-11955-7_40

ensured to be complete over a combination of data sources, the framework tells one how to produce a federated rewriting of the query that contains `SERVICE` calls [4], with query parts that are to be sent to the relevant data sources.

We have implemented the reasoning techniques of Darari et al. [1] using standard Semantic Web frameworks that can process RDF data and SPARQL queries, and reason with RDFS ontologies in a system called CORNER. Moreover, we have built a Web-based demo to show the functionalities of CORNER, which can be accessed at http://corner.inf.unibz.it/. While our implementation is based on Apache Jena[1], the approach would also be applicable to other Semantic Web frameworks like OpenRDF Sesame[2]. As a demo for our system, we show various aspects of completeness reasoning in the domain of movies, using the LinkedMDB[3] and DBpedia[4] data sources, which are RDF versions of IMDb and Wikipedia, respectively. Interestingly, IMDb already contains assertions in English about the completeness of cast and crew of movies[5], which are currently still not reflected in its RDF counterpart, LinkedMDB.

2 Motivating Examples

Suppose a moviegoer is interested in finding all movies starring Quentin Tarantino. This information need can be expressed by the SPARQL BGP query:[6]

```
SELECT * WHERE { ?m actor Tarantino }
```

In our demo, CORNER has meta-information about parts of LinkedMDB and DBpedia that are complete. Completeness statements can be represented in two ways: a human-readable abstract syntax, or an RDF syntax, which implements the abstract syntax. Both were developed in [1] and are accepted by CORNER. Abstract completeness statements have the form $Compl(P_1|P_2)$, consisting of two parts: the *pattern* P_1 and the *condition* P_2. The completeness statement specifies that the source contains all data with the pattern shape, provided that in addition they satisfy the condition. To express that a source is complete for "all movies starring Tarantino", we write in the abstract syntax

```
Compl(?m actor Tarantino | true).
```

We attach this statement to LinkedMDB but not to DBpedia, since some information that Tarantino was starred in some movies is actually missing in DBpedia. CORNER then analyzes the query and the statement, and concludes that the query over LinkedMDB can be answered completely, while it cannot give such a guarantee for DBpedia.

We imagine that such statements could be part of the meta-information about a data source like the ones provided by VoID descriptions[7]. In fact, completeness

---

1 http://jena.apache.org/

2 http://www.openrdf.org/

3 http://linkedmdb.org/

4 http://dbpedia.org/

5 As an instance, the page at http://www.imdb.com/title/tt0105236/fullcredits about Reservoir Dogs is stated to contain all cast and crew of the movie.

6 For simplicity, we omit namespaces.

7 http://www.w3.org/TR/void/

statements in RDF syntax can be embedded into VoID descriptions. Alternatively, there could be query hubs that contain such metadata about sources, propose sources suitable for a given query and execute the query over those sources. CORNER demonstrates the second possibility.

Suppose now our moviegoer would also like to see the budget and box-office gross of the movies. This is expressed by the SPARQL BGP query:

```
SELECT *
WHERE { ?m actor Tarantino . ?m budget ?b . ?m gross ?g }
```

Suppose we also have a statement asserting that DBpedia is complete for "the budget and gross of movies starring Tarantino", or in the abstract syntax:

```
Compl(?m budget ?b . ?m gross ?g | ?m actor Tarantino )
```

Note that by the condition, we can express that DBpedia has complete data about budget and box-office gross of movies starring Tarantino, even if in DBpedia Tarantino may not be listed as actor of all such movies. Now, none of the two sources alone is sufficient to answer this new query completely. Suppose as well that we have mappings using the RDFS predicates `subclass` and `subproperty` that associate terms in DBpedia to their LinkedMDB counterparts, if they exist, and vice versa. In this situation, CORNER can rewrite the original query in such a way, using SPARQL `SERVICE` calls, that each source contributes parts of a query for which they are complete. In our example, CORNER sends the subquery asking for movies starring Tarantino to LinkedMDB and the subquery asking for the budget and box-office gross to DBpedia:

```
SELECT *
WHERE {
  SERVICE <http://linkedmdb.org/sparql> { ?m actor Tarantino }
  SERVICE <http://dbpedia.org/sparql> { ?m budget ?b . ?m gross ?g } }
```

3 System Architecture

As shown in Fig. 1, CORNER consists of two main components, built on top of the Linked Data layer.

The first component is the user interface (UI), which is developed using the Google Web Toolkit (GWT)[8]. The UI provides users with the possibility to specify what queries they want to check for completeness as well as which completeness statements over which data sources and which RDFS ontologies they want to use for the checking. The second component is the reasoner, the backend of CORNER. The reasoner is implemented using Apache Jena[9]. The backend performs the completeness reasoning, that is, the query completeness checking based on the inputs. The RDFS reasoner is needed since CORNER takes into account RDFS ontologies. If a query can be ensured to be complete, CORNER rewrites the query into a complete federated version and executes it over Linked Data. For this, the SPARQL engine is necessary. The query results along with the completeness information are given back to the users via the UI.

[8] http://www.gwtproject.org/

[9] http://jena.apache.org/

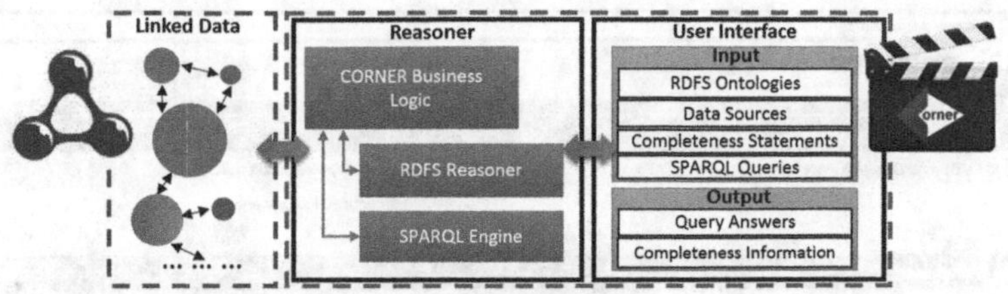

Fig. 1. CORNER Architecture

The processes inside the backend are controlled by the CORNER business logic, which implements the completeness reasoning technique in [1] consisting of the following steps. From the query Q, CORNER generates an initial RDF graph G^i_Q that represents the information needed for answering the query. Moreover, every completeness statement C is translated into a SPARQL `CONSTRUCT` query Q_C. Application of all the queries Q_C to the graph G^i_Q results in a graph G^a_Q, which is a subgraph of G^i_Q and represents the parts of the query for which data are complete. By evaluating Q over G^a_Q, CORNER tests whether the complete data are sufficient to answer Q. Finally, if Q can be answered completely, based on the data sources information of the completeness statements that contribute to generate G^a_Q, CORNER distributes the query parts of Q to their suitable, complete data sources.

4 Demo Description

From the CORNER homepage, users may add RDFS ontologies, data sources, completeness statements of a specific data source, and queries, in addition to those already there. There is a panel in CORNER for each type of information. There are also the options to upload and download CORNER completeness statements in RDF in order to embed them into VoID descriptions of data sources. When adding a new completeness statement, users see a pop-up window where they can specify patterns, conditions, the data source where the statement holds, the author and a description of the completeness statement. When checking the completeness of a query, CORNER displays a pop-up window comprising completeness information about the query, the query results, the debugging information, the ontologies used in the reasoning, a federated rewriting of the query, and the author information for each completeness statement.

Figure 2 shows the example of the query about budget and box-office gross of movies starring Quentin Tarantino, mentioned above. We first specify the SPARQL query in the query panel of the Web UI. Then, in the ontology panel, we specify which ontologies we want to use. In this case, we only need to activate the mapping ontology for LinkedMDB and DBpedia. After that, in the completeness statements panel, we select the statements about data sources to be used for query completeness checking. The figure shows the two completeness statements we mentioned above.

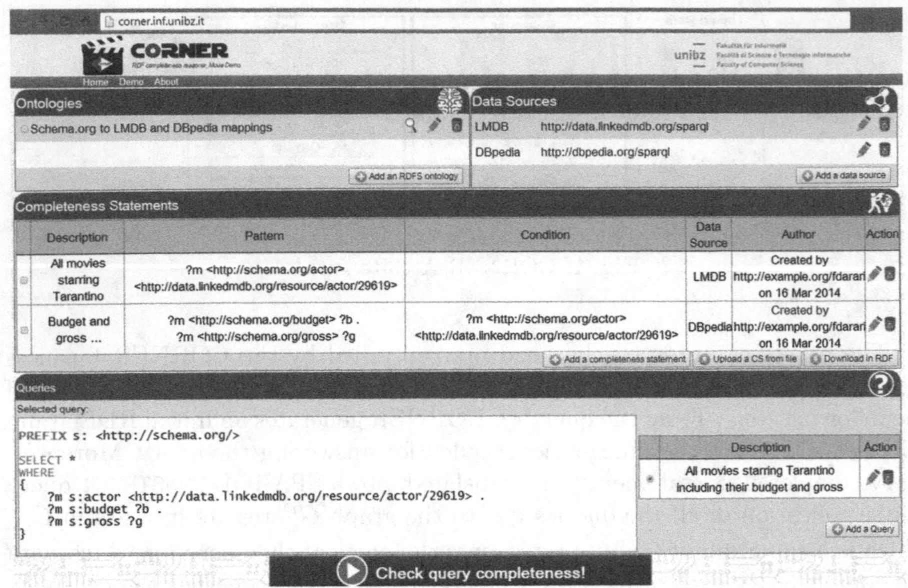

Fig. 2. CORNER Homepage

To start completeness reasoning, the user has to click the execution button at the bottom of the UI. Now, CORNER returns to the user the query results and information stating that the completeness of the query can be guaranteed. CORNER also provides debugging information about the completeness reasoning and the federated rewriting of the query that was executed over the data sources.

Acknowledgments. This work has been partially supported by the project "MAGIC: Managing Completeness of Data" funded by the province of Bozen-Bolzano, and the European Master's Program in Computational Logic (EMCL).

References

1. Darari, F., Nutt, W., Pirrò, G., Razniewski, S.: Completeness statements about RDF data sources and their use for query answering. In: Alani, H., et al. (eds.) ISWC 2013, Part I. LNCS, vol. 8218, pp. 66–83. Springer, Heidelberg (2013)
2. Levy, A.Y.: Obtaining complete answers from incomplete databases. In: PVLDB (1996)
3. Razniewski, S., Nutt, W.: Completeness of queries over incomplete databases. In: PVLDB (2011)
4. Harris, S., Seaborne, A.: SPARQL 1.1 query language. Technical report, W3C (2013)

AnnoMarket – Multilingual Text Analytics at Scale on the Cloud

Marin Dimitrov[1(✉)], Hamish Cunningham[2], Ian Roberts[2], Petar Kostov[1], Alex Simov[1], Philippe Rigaux[3], and Helen Lippell[4]

[1] Ontotext AD, Sofia, Bulgaria
{marin.dimitrov,petar.kostov,alex.simov}@ontotext.com

[2] Department of Computer Science, University of Sheffield, Sheffield, UK
{h.cunningham,i.roberts}@dcs.shef.ac.uk

[3] Internet Memory Research SAS, Montreuil, France
philippe.rigaux@internetmemory.net

[4] The Press Association Ltd, London, UK
helen.lippell@pressassociation.com

Abstract. AnnoMarket is an open platform for cloud-based text analytics services and language resources acquisition. Providers of text analytics services and language resources can deploy and monetize their components via the platform, while users can utilize such available resources in multiple languages and in various domains in an on-demand, pay-as-you-go manner. The AnnoMarket platform is deployed on the Amazon Web Services cloud and it provides free text analytics and language acquisition services to the general public.

Keywords: Text mining · Cloud computing · Software-as-a-service · Linked data

1 Introduction

AnnoMarket[1] is an FP7[2] project that aims to revolutionise the text analytics market, by delivering an open marketplace for pay-as-you-go, cloud-based text mining resources and services, in multiple languages. The current services available on the AnnoMarket marketplace[3] are applicable to a wide set of business cases, e.g. large-volume multilingual information management, business intelligence, social media monitoring, customer relations management.

The Software-as-a-Service delivery model adopted by AnnoMarket reduces the complexity of deployment, maintenance, customisation and sharing of text processing resources and services by SMEs and developers. Additional beneficiaries of AnnoMarket are SME providers of text analytics services or language resources, who are able to deploy their custom components, applications, datasets or corpora, and receive revenue via the AnnoMarket marketplace. The marketplace currently provides various

[1] https://annomarket.eu/

[2] The AnnoMarket project is funded by the European Commission under the 7th Framework Programme, Project No. 296322.

[3] https://annomarket.com/

V. Presutti et al. (Eds.): ESWC Satellite Events 2014, LNCS 8798, pp. 315–319, 2014.
DOI: 10.1007/978-3-319-11955-7_41

services for multilingual information extraction and semantic annotation, sentiment detection, as well as multilingual corpora and LOD datasets.

2 AnnoMarket Platform

The AnnoMarket platform is based on the *GATE* [1] and *GateCloud.net* [2] platforms with various new components related to language resource acquisition, scalable and elastic processing of large volumes of data, usage monitoring and quota enforcement, as well as billing and online payments.

2.1 Language Resource Acquisition

The language resource acquisition component of the platform is based on the large scale web crawling infrastructure by IMR comprised of three main components:

- *MemoryBot*, a scalable web crawler which provides user-defined, on-demand crawls at a large scale.
- An integrated annotation mechanism, which provides means for pre-processing of the crawled corpora (feature extraction, statistical information, etc.) and generates various metadata that is utilized for indexing and searching.
- A distributed language resource repository, based on HBase, which stores the original crawled content and the metadata from the pre-processing step.

In addition to corpora crawled on-demand from the web, the language resource acquisition component provides integration with the Common Crawl[4] dataset.

2.2 Multilingual Text Mining Services

Various multilingual text mining services are currently deployed and ready to use via the AnnoMarket platform. The current set of services includes more than 30 different text processing pipelines covering 17 languages: Arabic, Bulgarian, Danish, Dutch, English, Finnish, French, German, Hungarian, Italian, Norwegian, Portuguese, Romanian, Russian, Spanish, Swedish, and Turkish.

The text processing pipelines vary from low level ones (stemmers, part-of-speech taggers, noun phrase chunkers and parsers), to general purpose pipelines (named entity recognisers) and domain specific pipelines (for the bio-medical domain, news publishing domain, or sentiment analysis over social media).

2.3 Marketplace

The marketplace provides an eShop[5] where customers can explore the catalogue of available text analytics services, language resources and datasets as well as additional

---

[4] http://commoncrawl.org/

[5] https://annomarket.com/shopfront

processing resources available on-demand via the platform (e.g. an LOD server hosting Freebase, DBpedia and GeoNames datasets which can be used to populate various gazetteers for text mining pipelines). All products deployed on the marketplace provide information about their functionality and the associated usage and pricing terms. Text analytics services may also show a simple web form where customers can supply sample input data and test the functionality of the service. Customers can also post public ratings and comments regarding the performance and quality of service of any product they have used via the AnnoMarket platform[6].

2.4 Cloud Platform

The AnnoMarket platform is currently deployed on the Amazon Web Services[7] (AWS) public cloud and it utilizes various cloud services for storage (S3, EBS and SimpleDB), computing (EC2), and scalability (Simple Queue Service, Auto Scaling and CloudWatch), and a design for a multi-datacenter deployment for improved availability.

AnnoMarket customers can utilize the various services on the platform via two delivery channels

- platform-as-a-service, where customers configure, start and stop various processing and storage components on demand and customers are billed for the duration of using the components (per hour);
- software-as-a-service (Fig. 1), where multiple customers can access the text analytics components in a multi-tenant manner via predefined RESTful service interfaces. Customers in this case are billed based on usage metrics (number of documents processed, input data size, number of SPARQL queries, etc.)

2.5 Workflow

The interaction with the AnnoMarket platform when using text analytics components in a platform-as-service manner includes the following steps:

1. Users specify the input data to be processed. This may include user data already residing on Amazon S3, language resources and datasets available on the platform, or a new on-demand focused crawl from the web.
2. Users choose and configure various processing and indexing services, which are automatically deployed and started on Amazon EC2, or access the RESTful services in a software-as-a-service manner.
3. After the processing is complete, the results are available to the customer via S3 and can be downloaded at any time.

---

[6] See for example https://annomarket.com/shopfront/displayItem/2 information available for the particular pipeline: developer's documentation and instructions, a "Test This Pipeline" component and a user comments section.

[7] https://aws.amazon.com/

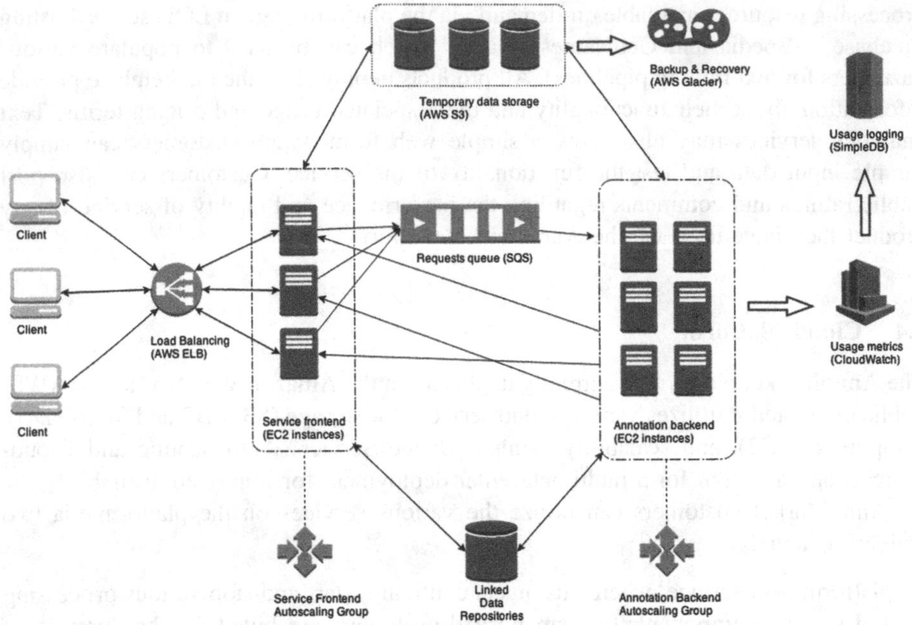

Fig. 1. AnnoMarket AWS-based architecture

When using the text analytics components of the platform in a software-as-service manner users directly submit documents to the RESTful services, together with various specifications (requested output format, processing pipeline, etc.). The results of the processing are immediately available as part of the service response and do not require additional downloading.

2.6 Client APIs and Browser Plugins

For the purpose of making first interactions with the AnnoMarket platform easier, we have developed a Client API and a browser plugin for Firefox and Chrome.

The Client API[8] provides a set of high-level APIs in Java, C#, Groovy and Python, which make interaction with the platform easier for developers (as opposed to directly making RESTful invocations).

3 AnnoMarket Demo

The AnnoMarket team will demonstrate the platform via various scenarios targeting different users:

[8] https://github.com/annomarket/online-clients

1. For developers – a demonstration on (1) how to configure the MemoryBot crawler and to perform focussed crawling over a large number of websites; (2) how to access the real-time text analytics service via the Client API or directly via the RESTful service interface; and (3) how to configure a long-running text analytics jobs, provide input data, and run various text processing or indexing components.
2. For text analytics providers – how to package their own text analytics pipelines, so that they can be deployed on the AnnoMarket platform and available for use to 3rd parties via the Marketplace.

The AnnoMarket platform is currently open to the general public and its functionality can be accessed via:

- The marketplace[9], providing entry points to the various text analytics services deployed on the platform
- The real-time text processing RESTful services[10]
- The RESTful services[11] for configuring and starting long-running text annotation jobs
- The Client APIs[12] in various programming languages

4 Related Work

There exist various platforms for text analytics as-a-service, such as: *OpenCalais*, *Alechemy*, *OpenAmplify*, *Semantria*, *TextWise*, *Saplo*, etc., or on-demand crawling such as *80Legs*, *Spinn3R* and *PromptCloud*. *Mashape* is a somewhat similar platform and marketplace for 3rd party APIs. The main differentiation of AnnoMarket is a combination of the following aspects: (1) extensive list of text analytics components covering 17 languages; (2) ability of 3rd party text analytics providers to deploy and monetize their components via the platform; (3) a combination of on-demand crawling and text analytics capabilities.

The AnnoMarket platform is currently undergoing an evaluation by a 3rd party focus group of various performance, usability, and availability aspects.

References

1. Cunningham, H., Tablan, V., Roberts, A., Bontcheva, K.: Getting more out of biomedical documents with GATE's full lifecycle open source text analytics. PLoS Comput. Biol. **9**(2), e1002854 (2013)
2. Tablan, V., Roberts, I., Cunningham, H., Bontcheva, K.: GATECloud.net: a platform for large-scale, open-source text processing on the cloud. Philos. Trans. Roy. Soc. Math. Phys. Eng. Sci. 371(1983) (2012)

[9] https://annomarket.com/shopfront

[10] https://api.annomarket.com/online-processing/item/<pipeline-number>

[11] https://annomarket.com/api/shop/item/<pipeline-number>

[12] https://github.com/annomarket/online-clients

Modelling OWL Ontologies with Graffoo

Riccardo Falco[1], Aldo Gangemi[2,3], Silvio Peroni[1,2(✉)], David Shotton[4], and Fabio Vitali[1]

[1] Department of Computer Science and Engineering, University of Bologna, Bologna, Italy
riccardo.falco@studio.unibo.it, silvio.peroni@unibo.it, fabio@cs.unibo.it
[2] STLab-ISTC, Consiglio Nazionale delle Ricerche, Rome, Italy
aldo.gangemi@cnr.it
[3] Laboratoire d'Informatique de Paris Nord, Université Paris 13, Villetaneuse, France
[4] Oxford e-Research Centre, University of Oxford, Oxford, UK
david.shotton@oerc.ox.ac.uk

Abstract. In this paper we introduce *Graffoo*, i.e., a graphical notation to develop OWL ontologies by means of *yEd*, a free editor for diagrams.

Keywords: DiTTO · Graffoo · OWL · yEd · Graphical notation

1 Introduction

In many contexts where the use of formal languages is needed (e.g., software development, GUI implementation, ontology engineering), the adoption of an appropriate graphical notation simplifies the design and property checking of a system since it enables an overview of the system that is difficult to have using textual syntaxes. Within the Semantic Web domain, this seems to be particularly true when developing ontologies: graphical languages, among the others, seem to support ontology modelling and understanding as well as the discussion between all the involved actors (i.e., domain experts, knowledge engineers and final users). Designing a graphical notation specific for OWL requires to consider what are the appropriate requirements that such notation should address according to different kinds of players coming from several academic and industrial contexts. At various SW conferences and workshops, we started brainstorming informally about the ideal features of a graphical notation for OWL ontologies, and we identified the following requirements:

1. *Oriented to OWL.* The notation should address all the capabilities of OWL.
2. *Graphical elements to make modelling and understanding easy.* It should facilitate users in dealing with *modelling* and *understanding* of ontologies.
3. *Colours are a complementary aid, not a fundamental discriminant.* Although the use of different colours helps to reduce the cognitive effort of users [1] in the aforementioned activities, each graphical element of the notation should be clearly recognisable even when it is presented in a grey scale.

V. Presutti et al. (Eds.): ESWC Satellite Events 2014, LNCS 8798, pp. 320–325, 2014.
DOI: 10.1007/978-3-319-11955-7_42

4. *Invent the notation, not the editor.* The effort of creators of a notation should concern the development of the notation itself, since diagram applications usually provide mechanisms to extend them with additional notations easily.

Existing tools and notations developed to deal with modelling and understanding activities seem to be hardly appropriate to address all the aforementioned features – either because they do not address all OWL 2 capabilities [5], or because they were developed to address modelling tasks (e.g., ontology editors [3]) or understanding tasks (e.g., documentation generators [6]) but never both.

The aim of this demonstration is to show how to create OWL-aware ontology diagrams by using *Graffoo* (Sect. 2), a graphical notation for OWL ontologies that tries to address the aforementioned requirements. We accompany the discussion of Graffoo with preliminary outcomes of a comparative user testing session, and we briefly present the extension of DiTTO [2] (i.e., an online service that converts diagrams into OWL ontologies) we developed to convert Graffoo diagrams into proper OWL sources in Manchester Syntax. Finally, in Sect. 3, we conclude the paper sketching out some future works.

2 A Graphical Framework for OWL Ontologies

The *Graphical Framework For OWL Ontologies*, a.k.a. *Graffoo*[1], is a graphical notation that addresses all the requirements introduced in Sect. 1. All the graphical elements of Graffoo, summarised in Fig. 1, have been developed using the standard library of *yEd*[2], i.e., a free diagram editor running on Windows, Mac and Linux. The Graffoo graphical elements are available online and can be loaded as a proper section in the yEd palette, as shown in Fig. 2. To add the Graffoo graphical elements to yEd one needs to download the Graffoo *.graphml* file[3], and then to import it as a palette – by selecting that file in the window that appears clicking on "Edit / Manage Palette / Import Section" in the yEd tool bar, and then by adding and including it in the available palettes.

Graphical Elements. All the ontological entities (i.e., ontologies, classes, properties, datatypes, and individuals) can be defined either as an *IRI* surrounded by angular brackets (e.g., <http://xmlns.com/foaf/0.1/Person>) or as a *CURIE* with a *prefix* (e.g., `foaf:Person`). All the prefixes can be defined within a particular box (entitled "Prefixes") as a list of prefix-IRI pairs (e.g., `foaf:` <http://xmlns.com/foaf/0.1/>). In Graffoo there are two different kinds of graphical elements, i.e., *blocks* (or nodes) and *arcs*. Blocks are used to define classes and class restrictions (yellow rectangles with solid and dotted borders respectively), datatypes and datatype restrictions (green rhomboids with solid and dotted borders respectively), individuals (pink circles with solid black border), ontologies (boxes with light-blue heading and dotted black border), additional axioms in Manchester Syntax for all those constructs that are

1 Available at http://www.essepuntato.it/graffoo
2 Available at http://www.yworks.com/en/products_yed_about.html
3 Available at http://www.essepuntato.it/graffoo/sources

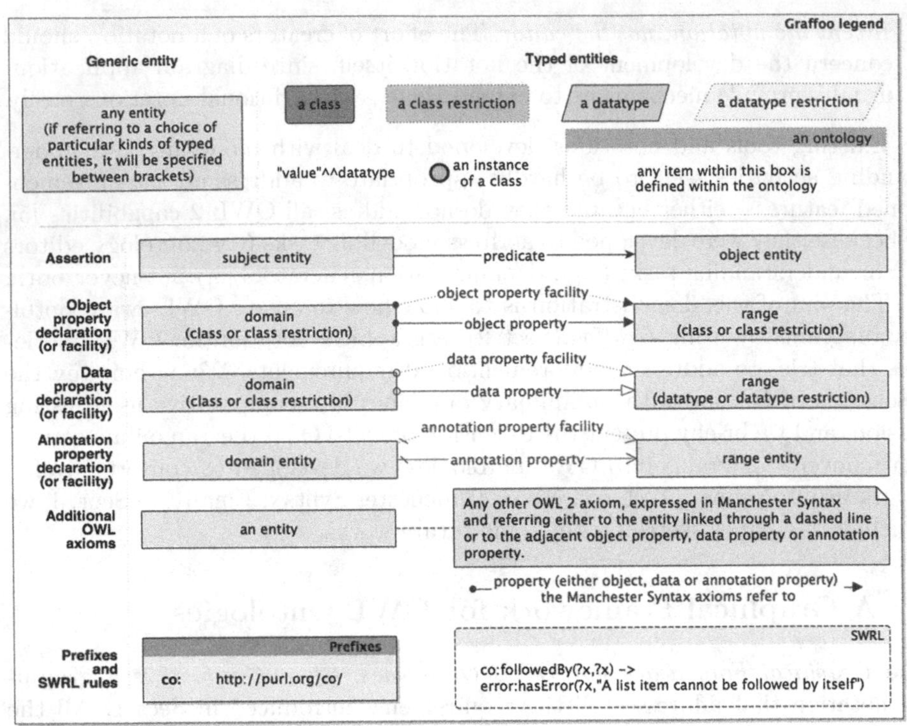

Fig. 1. The full set of graphical elements of Graffoo.

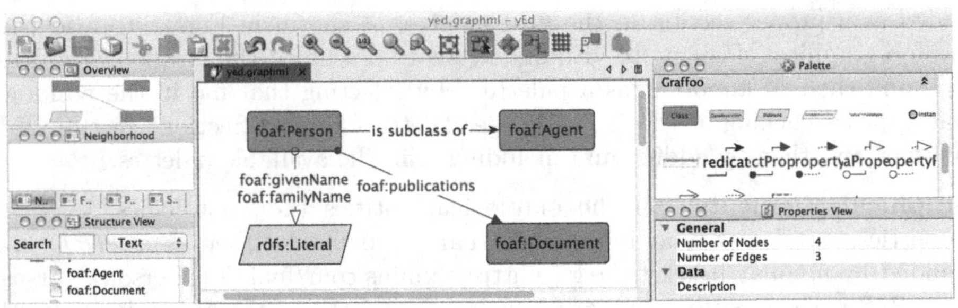

Fig. 2. The Graffoo palette in yEd.

not directly supported by a particular graphical element (light-blue and folded boxes), and rules (boxes with light-grey heading and black dashed border). Arcs are used to define assertions (black lines ending with a solid arrow[4]),

[4] All the assertions defining typical OWL axioms, such as sub-class axioms, equivalent axioms, etc., can be expressed by natural language names in Graffoo (e.g., by using "is subclass of" instead of "rdfs:subClassOf", "is equivalent to" instead of "owl:equivalentClass" and "owl:equivalentProperty", etc.).

annotation properties (orange lines beginning with backslash and ending with a dashed arrow), data properties (green lines beginning with an empty circle and ending with an empty arrow), and object properties (blue lines beginning with a solid circle and ending with a solid arrow). In addition to these graphical elements, there is a particular kind of graphical elements (named *property facilities*, i.e., arcs having dotted border and referring to data, object and annotation properties), that were studied to decrease the cognitive effort of users when understanding an ontology. For instance, they allow one to say explicitly that a certain property can be used in the context of two classes without declaring them as domain and range. The full specification of Graffoo graphical elements is available at http://www.essepuntato.it/graffoo/specification/current.html.

Usability. As a preliminary study, we performed a comparative user testing session so as to gather some evidences on the usability of Graffoo when modelling OWL ontologies. We asked eleven PhD students in Computer Science and Law (with no expertise in ontologies and Semantic Web technologies) to use four different tools – i.e., the Manchester Syntax, Protégé, E/R as introduced in [2], and Graffoo – for modelling small OWL ontologies (with 5–15 entities). All the four tools were appropriately introduced to PhD students during six lectures of two hours each and, at the end of the last lecture, we asked them to answer a questionary containing ten likert questions according to the *System Usability Scale* (*SUS*)[5] – sub-scales of pure *Usability* and pure *Learnability* were considered as well [4]. As shown in Table 1, the SUS score for Graffoo was the highest (58.9, in a 0–100 range), meaning that it was perceived more usable than the others – even if none of the differences between SUS scores was statistically significant.

Table 1. SUS (mean) scores of all the notations/tools involved.

Tool	SUS	Learnability	Usability
Manchester Syntax	45.9 (s.d. 15.9)	45.4 (s.d. 21.1)	46.0 (s.d. 16.0)
Protégé	50.9 (s.d. 15.5)	45.4 (s.d. 20.4)	52.3 (s.d. 15.2)
E/R	50.4 (s.d. 17.6)	51.1 (s.d. 22.7)	50.3 (s.d. 17.7)
Graffoo	58.9 (s.d. 16.0)	54.4 (s.d. 23.2)	59.1 (s.d. 15.3)

DiTTO extension. *DiTTO* [2] is a Web service available at http://www.essepuntato.it/ditto developed, originally, to transform E/R diagrams into OWL ontologies according to three distinct conversion strategies. The core of DiTTO – i.e., a set XSLT 2.0 documents included in a Java Web Application Archive (i.e., a WAR file) served as a Tomcat application – has been recently extended with additional XSLT documents that apply several rewriting templates to the source file of the Graffoo diagram created through yEd, and return the converted OWL ontology in Manchester Syntax. This extension allows one to use some features available in yEd to simplify the work of ontology engineers.

[5] All data are available at http://www.essepuntato.it/graffoo/preliminary-test.

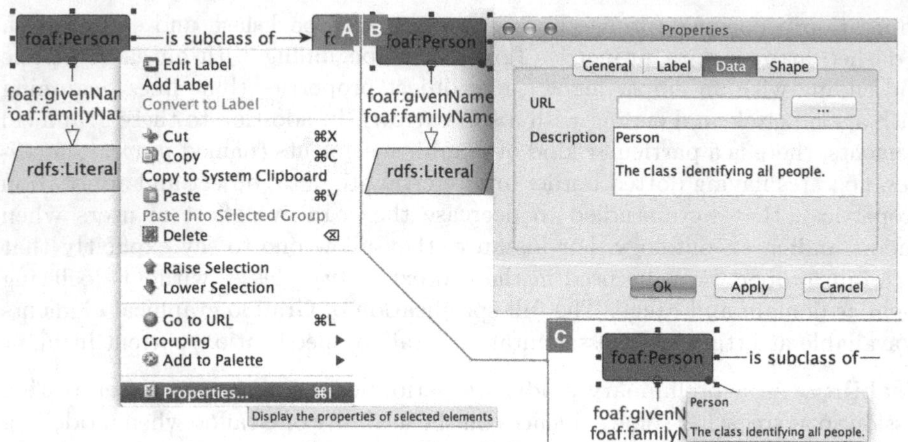

Fig. 3. The steps to add *rdfs:label* and *rdfs:comment* annotations to ontological entities. A: right-click on the entity to access its properties; B: add label (first line) and comment (following lines) as free text in the "Description" field of the "Data" panel. C: hover the pointer on the entity to show the annotations.

In particular, it is possible to add annotations to ontological entities by using the preference panel (as shown in Fig. 3), avoiding the use of the graphical element for additional axioms to specify such annotations as common axioms.

3 Conclusions and Future Works

In this paper we have introduced Graffoo, a graphical notation to model OWL ontologies. We have shown Graffoo graphical elements, we have described preliminary outcomes of a user testing session, and we have presented an extension of DiTTO for transforming Graffoo diagrams into OWL. We plan to extend Graffoo (and the related DiTTO extension) with a new compact syntax (in order to create, for instance, subclass axioms involving class restrictions when declaring properties), to generate Graffoo diagrams from OWL ontologies, and to perform additional usability evaluations to confirm the results sketched out herein.

References

1. Chalmers, P.A.: The role of cognitive theory in human-computer interface. Comput. Hum. Behav. **19**(5), 593–607 (2003). doi:10.1016/S0747-5632(02)00086-9
2. Gangemi, A., Peroni, S.: DiTTO: diagrams transformation into OWL. In: Proceedings of the ISWC 2013 Posters & Demonstrations Track (2013). http://ceur-ws.org/Vol-1035/iswc2013_demo_2.pdf
3. García-Barriocanal, E., Sicilia, M.A., Sánchez-Alonso, S.: Usability evaluation of ontology editors. Knowl. Organ. **32**(1), 1–9 (2005)

4. Lewis, J.R., Sauro, J.: The factor structure of the system usability scale. In: Proceedings of HCSE 2009, pp. 94–103 (2009). doi:10.1007/978-3-642-02806-9_12
5. Negru, S., Haag, F., Lohmann, S.: Towards a unified visual notation for OWL ontologies: insights from a comparative user study. In: Proceedings of i-Semantics 2013, pp. 73–80 (2013). doi:10.1145/2506182.2506192
6. Peroni, S., Shotton, D., Vitali, F.: Tools for the automatic generation of ontology documentation: a task-based evaluation. Int. J. Semant. Web Inf. Syst. **9**(1), 21–44 (2013). doi:10.4018/jswis.2013010102

Graphium Chrysalis: Exploiting Graph Database Engines to Analyze RDF Graphs

Alejandro Flores(✉), Maria-Esther Vidal, and Guillermo Palma

Universidad Simón Bolívar, Caracas, Venezuela
{aflores,mvidal,gpalma}@ldc.usb.ve

Abstract. We present Graphium Chrysalis, a tool to visualize the main graph invariants that characterize RDF graphs, i.e., graph properties that are independent of the graph representation such as, vertex and edge counts, in- and out-degree distribution, and in-coming and out-going h-index. Graph invariants characterize a graph and impact on the cost of the core graph-based tasks, e.g., graph traversal and sub-graph pattern matching, affecting time and space complexity of main RDF reasoning and query processing tasks. During the demonstration of Graphium Chrysalis, attendees will be able to observe and analyze the invariants that describe graphs of existing RDF benchmarks. Additionally, we will show the expressiveness power of state-of-the-art graph database engine APIs (e.g., Neo4j or Sparksee) (Sparksee was previously known as DEX), when main graph invariants are computed against RDF graphs.

1 Introduction

Graph invariants are properties that remain the same under two isomorphic graphs and any representation of the graph. These graph measures not only characterize bound complexity of some core graph-based tasks, but also some of them provide remarkable information on the graph topology, which allows to uncover hidden properties of the relationships modeled in the graph. For example, vertex and edge counts, adjacency distribution, in- and out-degree distributions, treewidth, betweenness centrality, reciprocity, and h-index are well-known invariants. Based on these invariants, complexity and graph topology properties can be formally described [1]. Computing graph invariants requires to traverse the whole graph to aggregate vertex and edge statistics as well as to identify certain patterns between these objects. Although some RDF query and reasoning complexity problems have been defined in terms of graph invariants [3], because existing RDF triple stores rely on tailored data structures to manage sub-graph pattern matching queries, they usually do not offer support to implement the computation of these measures efficiently. Different engines have been developed to manage, store and query graph databases (e.g., Neo4j [4] or Sparksee [2]). Each graph database engine implements general data structures and usually relies on indices to speed up execution time; additionally, some engines make available APIs comprised of methods to solve core graph-based tasks that facilitate the implementation of graph invariants. We present Graphium Chrysalis,

V. Presutti et al. (Eds.): ESWC Satellite Events 2014, LNCS 8798, pp. 326–331, 2014.
DOI: 10.1007/978-3-319-11955-7_43

a visualization tool that exploits different graphical representations to report on the results of evaluating a variety of RDF graphs, and graph invariants implemented on top of Neo4j and Sparksee. Visualization techniques used in Graphium Chrysalis facilitate the understanding of graph invariants and the structure of RDF graphs generated by state-of-the-art benchmarks, e.g., the Berlin Benchmark. During the demonstration attendees will go through the visualization of different patterns in the measurements of the studied RDF graphs that will allow them to uncover the properties of existing benchmarks, as well as to identify the impact that these properties may have on the complexity of typical RDF data management tasks. Graphium Chrysalis is part of the Graphium project which has the goal of defining benchmarks for graph database engines. The demo is available at http://graphium.ldc.usb.ve/chrysalis/.

2 The Graphium Chrysalis Architecture

Graphium Chrysalis is built on top of existing graph database engine APIs to compute graph invariants on-the-fly efficiently; additionally, Graphium Chrysalis exploits visualization services implemented in JavaScript, to identify patterns between the values of different graph properties and the impact that they may have on main core graph-based tasks. Furthermore, we publish a Java library at the Graphium project website[1], thus, users will be able compute graph invariants locally. Figure 1 shows the Graphium Chrysalis GUI. In the area enclosed in red rectangle number 1, users can select different RDF graphs, and upload other graph results computed with our tool. This will allow users to understand: (i) characteristics of a graph that impact on the values of the invariants; (ii) time and space required to load a graph; and (iii) time and space complexity of main core graph-based tasks, e.g., k-hops or shortest paths. Results are visualized in the area enclosed by the blue rectangle number 2; additionally, we plot the distributions of invariants such as in- and out-degree, and vertex and edge counts. Graphium Chrysalis exploits visualization capabilities of the HeatMaps[2] to compare in- and out-degree distributions and the cost of core graph-based tasks. Thus, attendees will be able to observe the relationships between the cost and the invariant measurements of an RDF graph.

3 Demonstration of Use Cases

We consider different RDF graphs generated by the Berlin SPARQL Benchmark[3]; additionally, attendees will be able to upload any other graph results during the demonstration. The goal of the demonstration is to visualize patterns that can be found in the invariants of these RDF graphs and the relationships between these measures and the cost of core graph-based tasks, e.g., graph adjacency, sub-graph pattern matching, graph traversals, and query processing.

[1] http://www.graphium.ldc.usb.ve
[2] http://bl.ocks.org/tjdecke/5558084
[3] http://wifo5-03.informatik.uni-mannheim.de/bizer/berlinsparqlbenchmark/

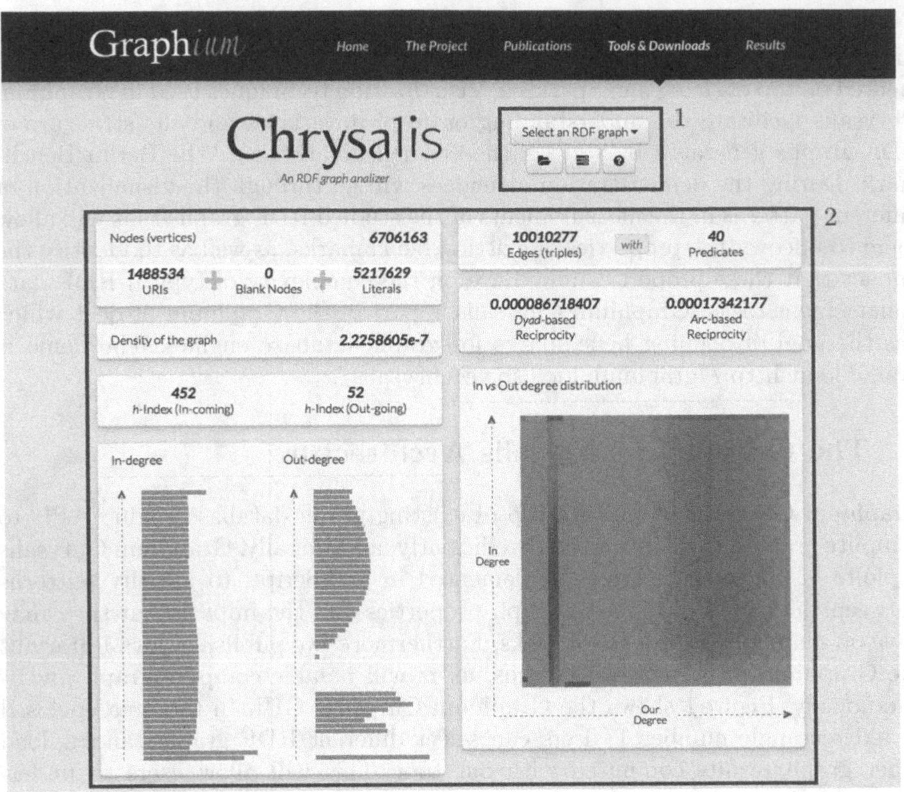

Fig. 1. The Graphium Chrysalis GUI. 1-Selection Area: RDF Graphs can be selected. 2-Visualization Area: Report of Graph Invariant Measurements: Node and Edge Count, In- and Out-Degree Distributions, In-coming and Out-going h-index, Graph Density, and Dyad- and Arc-based Reciprocity. Reported measurements for Berlin10M.

3.1 Graph Invariants and Property Statistics

Among the graph invariants to be considered are the following:

Vertex and Edge Counts: outputs the number of vertices (i.e., graph order) and number of edges (i.e., graph size) of each RDF graph; vertices are categorized as URIs, BlankNodes, or Literals. Edges are also discriminated in terms of different predicates.

Graph Density: corresponds to the number of edges in the graph divided by the number of possible edges in a complete digraph. Highly dense RDF graphs are comprised of a small number of resources (i.e., vertices) versus the number of triples (i.e., edges).

Reciprocity (Dyad-based): reciprocity measures the extend to which a triple that relates resources A and B is reciprocated by a another triple that relates B with A too. In general, graphs with high values of reciprocity are highly dense.

A value of dyadic reciprocity reflects the proportion of dyads (pairs) with reciprocated triples among all possible adjacent dyads, i.e., a dyadic reciprocity of an RDF graph G corresponds to the number of mutual triples in G divided by the number of mutual triples plus the number of asymmetric triples. A triple *t=(A p B)* in G is mutual if there is another triple *t'=(B p' A)* in G, while t is asymmetric if there is no such triple t' in G. The number of mutual triples corresponds to the number of dyads, i.e., if t and t' exist in G, then they comprise only one dyad. A value of dyadic reciprocity close to 1.0 indicates that a large number of triples are mutual, and this impacts on the cost of reasoning services such as instance reasoning and query answering.

Reciprocity (Arc-Based): reciprocity can also be measured in terms of the number of reciprocated triples among all the triples in a graph, i.e., arc-based reciprocity corresponds to the number of symmetric triples divided by the number of triples in G, where the number of symmetric triples corresponds to the double of the number of dyads.

In- and Out-degree Distribution: distribution of the number of in-coming and out-going edges of the vertices of a graph. These distributions allow to visualize if vertices with small degrees are more or less frequent. Looking at the logarithmic plots is useful to explain the low selectivity (resp., high selectivity) of the queries than involve the highly connected vertices (resp., low connected vertices).

In-coming and Out-going h-index of a Graph: h is the maximum number, such that h vertices have each at least h in-coming neighbors (resp., out-going neighbors). An RDF graph with a high value of in-coming h-index indicates that at least a large number h of vertices play the role of objects in h-stars, while a small value of out-going h-index represents that at least a small number of h resources play the role of subjects in h-stars. High values of h-index impact on the cost of reasoning and query processing tasks, as well as on the query selectivity.

3.2 Use Cases

We will demonstrate the following use cases:

Patterns and Effects of Vertex and Edge Counts. Attendees will be able to choose between diverse RDF graphs, and analyze different counts of edges and vertices as well as the ones that are resources, literals, or predicates. In the area enclosed by the blue rectangle number 2 in Fig. 1, we can observe the relationships between the number of resources, literals, and predicates in a Berlin Benchmark RDF graph of 10 million-triples (Berlin10M). Additionally, attendees will be able to observe that these counts monotonically impact on the cost of core graph-based tasks and query processing; thus these statistics can be used during query optimization to identify good query plans.

Patterns and Effects of In-and Out-Degree Distributions. Attendees will observe distributions of both in-coming and out-going edges in RDF graphs, i.e., a distribution of the frequency of a resource playing the role of subject (out-degree), and the number of times a resource or literal is an object (in-degree). Additionally, comparison of both distributions can be analyzed. Blue rectangle in Fig. 1 encloses the distributions of in-, out-degree, and the correlation of both distributions for Berlin10M. We exploit the properties of the HeatMaps to represent these correlations. In Fig. 1, an entry (x, y) in the HeatMap represents the number of resources or literals that appear x times as subjects and y times as objects. Entries colored from yellow to red correspond to resources or literals with low to high frequency of appearance. We notice that there is one red point located at $(0, 1)$ which encloses all the literals of the RDF graph. Another interesting pattern that can be observed is that there is a clear difference between the resources that are highly or lowly connected. Based on these statistics, we could conclude the queries where triple patterns are instantiated to vertices colored in red are low selective, while those that refer to resources colored in light yellow are very selective.

Patterns and Effects of In-coming and Out-going h-index. We demonstrate the values of h-index for both in-coming and out-going edges, and distributions of different values of the vertices that comprise the studied graphs. Attendees will observe that in Berlin graphs, values of h-index increase as the size of the graphs. Furthermore, resources that represent products, and literals are part of the set of vertices that meet the condition of the h-index, i.e., they have at least h in-coming neighbors (resp., out-going neighbors). Thus, queries composed of triple patterns where a product is instantiated and the predicate is unbound will be low selective. On the other hand, queries with triple patterns bound to resources with low values of h-index will be highly selective. Additionally, traversal tasks in graphs with high values of h-index will be more expensive in time and space than in graphs with low values of this property. Finally, attendees will explore the resources which are in the set of the vertices that meet the h-index condition, and they will also observe the structural patterns that characterize these vertices.

Patterns and Effects of Reciprocity Values. We illustrate values of reciprocity that characterize the studied RDF graphs, and the distribution of both dyad- and arc-based reciprocity. Attendees will observe that values of reciprocity of the Berlin Benchmark graphs are very low, and remain almost the same as the size of the graphs increase.

4 Conclusions

Graphium Chrysalis allows to visualize patterns in the invariants of the RDF graphs, and the impact that the distributions of these values have on core graph-based tasks and reasoning services. Different configurations of RDF graphs will be analyzed, allowing the attendees to understand the graph invariants that characterize graphs generated by existing benchmarks. Attendees will learn the different characteristics of the resources that exhibit high values of the studied measures and what are the effects of using these resources in the different described graph tasks.

References

1. Lin, M.C., Soulignac, F.J., Szwarcfiter, J.L.: Arboricity, h-index, and dynamic algorithms. Theor. Comput. Sci. **426**, 75–90 (2012)
2. Martínez-Bazan, N., Muntés-Mulero, V., Gómez-Villamor, S., Nin, J., Sánchez-Martínez, M.-A., Larriba-Pey, J.-L.: Dex: high-performance exploration on large graphs for information retrieval. In: CIKM, pp. 573–582 (2007)
3. Pichler, R., Polleres, A., Wei, F., Woltran, S.: dRDF: entailment for domain-restricted RDF. In: Bechhofer, S., Hauswirth, M., Hoffmann, J., Koubarakis, M. (eds.) ESWC 2008. LNCS, vol. 5021, pp. 200–214. Springer, Heidelberg (2008)
4. Robinson, I., Webber, J., Eifrem, E.: Graph Databases. O'Reilly Media (2013)

SemLAV: Querying Deep Web and Linked Open Data with SPARQL

Pauline Folz[1,2(✉)], Gabriela Montoya[1,3], Hala Skaf-Molli[1], Pascal Molli[1], and Maria-Esther Vidal[4]

[1] LINA – Nantes University, Nantes, France
{pauline.folz,gabriela.montoya,hala.skaf,pascal.molli}@univ-nantes.fr
[2] Nantes Métropole - Direction Recherche, Innovation Et Enseignement Supérieur, Nantes, France
[3] Unit UMR6241 of the Centre National de la Recherche Scientifique (CNRS), Paris, France
[4] Universidad Simón Bolívar, Caracas, Venezuela
mvidal@ldc.usb.ve

Abstract. SemLAV allows to execute SPARQL queries against the Deep Web and Linked Open Data data sources. It implements the mediator-wrapper architecture based on view definitions over remote data sources. SPARQL queries are expressed using a mediator schema vocabulary, and SemLAV selects relevant data sources and *rank* them. The ranking strategy is designed to deliver results quickly based only on view definitions, *i.e.*, no statistics, nor probing on sources are required. In this demonstration, we validate the effectiveness of SemLAV approach with real data sources from social networks and Linked Open Data. We show in different setups that materializing only a subset of ranked relevant views is enough to deliver significant part of expected results.

1 Introduction

The Deep Web is constituted from data that are not indexed by traditional search engines, and may not have static URL links; it is around 500 times the size of the Surface Web [2]. Performing SPARQL queries without considering the Deep Web can deliver poor results. For example, the execution of the SPARQL query: *Which members of the Semantic Web community are interested in* Dalai Lama, Barack Obama, *or* Rihanna*?* (cf Fig. 1) without the Deep Web support, will deliver no answer. Some semantic data-warehouses such as Virtuoso with SPONGER [1] address this issue by declaring wrappers able to query unsemantified data including web service calls, CSV files, and so on. Such approach is relevant if the number of sources used to answer the query remains low. However, the time for first answers can be very high because the query engine has to contact all the declared wrappers for a query.

Contrary, SemLAV [3] is able to deliver answers quickly for this query. It follows the mediator-wrapper approach where the Deep Web data can be retrieved through view definitions and wrappers. A view constitutes a data source for

V. Presutti et al. (Eds.): ESWC Satellite Events 2014, LNCS 8798, pp. 332–337, 2014.
DOI: 10.1007/978-3-319-11955-7_44

```
SELECT DISTINCT *
WHERE {
  ?P foaf:member ?C .
  ?C rdfs:label "Semantic Web" .
  ?P foaf:knows ?WKP .
  ?WKP foaf:name ?N .
   FILTER (?N="Dalai Lama" || ?N="Barack Obama" || ?N="Rihanna")
}
```

Fig. 1. Which members of the Semantic Web community are interested in *Dalai Lama, Barack Obama*, or *Rihanna*?

the mediator. Given a SPARQL query, SemLAV selects relevant views and most importantly, it *ranks* them without requiring costly statistics. SemLAV uses wrappers to semantify data of the selected data sources on-demand during query execution. It retrieves data from the ranked sources in a smart order that gives a high probability of delivering results. Consequently, even in the presence of a large number of relevant views, SemLAV is able to deliver results in a reasonable time. In this paper, we demonstrate how SemLAV is able to quickly deliver results for SPARQL queries mixing Deep Web data sources and Linked Open Data defined using around 250 views. A video of the demo is available at https://www.youtube.com/channel/UCMQO5QVq5UcztE8kkkRRXKQ/videos.

2 SemLAV Overview

Given a query and a set of views, SemLAV computes a ranked set of relevant views for answering the query. Ranking is computed using the number of equivalent covered rewritings detailed in [3]. Views are materialized by calling traditional wrappers such as those defined in SPONGER [1] in sequence or in parallel. Each time a new view is fully materialized, the original query is executed to deliver results as fast as possible. Views used in SemLAV could be also generated by tools like Karma [4]. To illustrate the benefits of SemLAV, consider the query defined in Fig. 1, and the following five views:

```
v1(P,A,I,C,L):-made(P,A),affiliation(P,I),member(P,C),label(C,L)
v2(A,T,P,N,C):-title(A,T),made(P,A),name(P,N),member(P,C)
v3(P,N,R,M):-name(P,N),name(R,M),knows(P,R)
v4(P,N,G,R,C):-name(P,N),gender(P,G),knows(P,R),member(P,C)
v5(P,N,R,C,L):-name(P,N),knows(P,R),member(P,C),label(C,L)
```

SemLAV will compute the following sorted bucked for each query subgoal:

member(P, C)	label(C, L)	knows(P, WKP)	name(WKP, N)
v5(P,N,R,C,L)	v5(P,N,R,C,L)	v5(P,N,R,C,L)	v5(P,N,R,C,L)
v4(P,N,G,R,C)	v1(P,A,I,C,L)	v4(P,N,G,R,C)	v4(P,N,G,R,C)
v1(P,A,I,C,L)		v3(P,N,R,M)	v2(A,T,P,N,C)
v2(A,T,P,N,C)			v3(P,N,R,M)

```
SELECT DISTINCT *
WHERE {
  ?follower <http://xmlns.com/foaf/0.1/name> ?name .
  ?follower <http://xmlns.com/foaf/0.1/knows> ?followed .
  ?follower <http://xmlns.com/foaf/0.1/member> ?community .
  ?community <http://www.w3.org/2000/01/rdf-schema#label> "Semantic Web"
}
```

Fig. 2. Description of the followers of ESWC Conferences Twitter account

The execution of all possible combinations produces the complete answers for the query. To deliver answers quickly, SemLAV ranks the relevant views according to their contribution to cover the query subgoals, *i.e.,* first ranked views are those that cover maximum number of subgoals. Therefore, the number of covered combinations grows as fast as possible.

# Included	SemLAV ranking		Random order	
views (k)	Included views (V_k)	# Covered rewritings	Included views (V_k)	# Covered rewritings
1	v5	$1 \times 1 \times 1 \times 1 = 1$	v1	$1 \times 1 \times 0 \times 0 = 0$
2	v5, v4	$2 \times 1 \times 2 \times 2 = 8$	v1, v2	$2 \times 1 \times 0 \times 1 = 0$
3	v5, v4, v1	$3 \times 2 \times 2 \times 2 = 24$	v1, v2, v3	$2 \times 1 \times 1 \times 2 = 4$
4	v5, v4, v1, v3	$3 \times 2 \times 3 \times 3 = 54$	v1, v2, v3, v4	$3 \times 1 \times 2 \times 3 = 18$
5	v5, v4, v1, v3, v2	$4 \times 2 \times 3 \times 4 = 96$	v1, v2, v3, v4, v5	$4 \times 2 \times 3 \times 4 = 96$

3 Demonstration Setup

In this demonstration, we use well known Deep Web sites such as social networks Twitter and Facebook, and Linked Open Data sources such as DBLP, Semantic Web Dog Food, and DBpedia. We define 253 views data sources (views) over Twitter, Facebook, DBLP, Semantic Web Dog Food, and DBpedia. We use several RDF vocabularies to describe the members of a community, and the links between them and the Linked Open Data cloud. The following are our assumptions: (i) a person is member of a community if there is a link between the person and the community. This link is represented with the `foaf:member` predicate. Links of this type are established, for example, when someone follows a community conference Twitter account, or someone is member of a community group in Facebook, or someone has published a paper in a community conference. (ii) A person knows another person if there exists a link between them. This link is represented with the `foaf:knows` predicate. Links of this type are established, for example, when: a user is following someone in Twitter, two persons are co-authors of a paper. Sources are described by SPARQL queries, e.g., query in Fig. 2 describes data extracted from the Twitter account of *ESWC Conferences.*

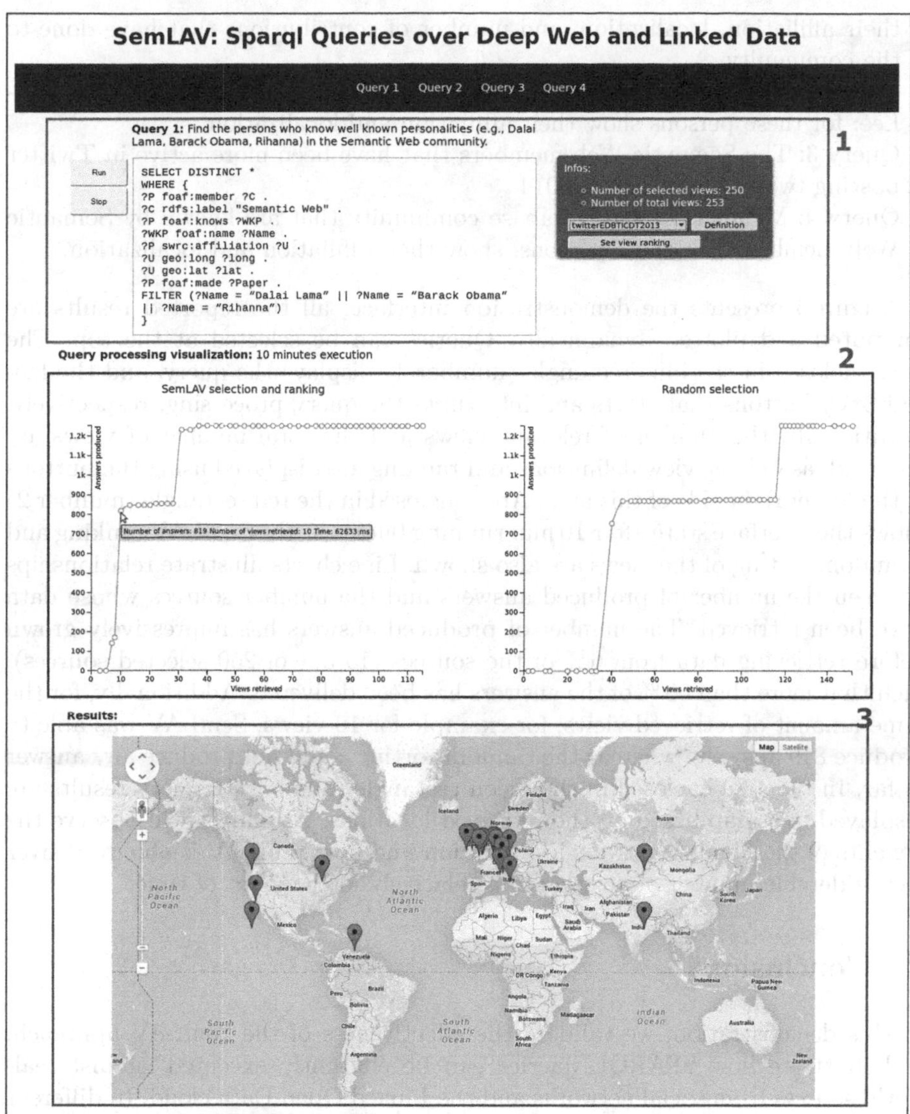

Fig. 3. Snapshots for Query 1 execution. During the demonstration all the reported results will be computed on-the-fly.

3.1 Queries

We will demonstrate the behavior of SemLAV with the following four queries:

- Query 1: Semantic Web community members who know well-known personalities (e.g., Dalai Lama, Barack Obama, or Rihanna); for these persons show

their affiliation, localization, and number of contributions that have done to the community.
- Query 2: Members of different scientific communities that know Tim Berners-Lee; for these persons show their affiliation and localization.
- Query 3: The Semantic Web members that have been more active in Twitter posting tweets about ESWC2014.
- Query 4: Members of the Database community that are known by Semantic Web members. For these persons, show their affiliation and localization.

Figure 3 presents the demonstration interface; all the reported results are computed and plotted dynamically. Queries can be selected at the top. The area enclosed in the blue rectangle (number 1) displays the query, and the `Run` and `Stop` buttons that starts and interrupts the query processing, respectively. Additionally, the number of relevant views and the total number of views are reported, as well as, view definitions and ranking are displayed using the buttons in the upper right side of this area. Area enclosed in the red rectangle (number 2) shows the interface state after 10 min running `Query 1`; the SemLAV ranking and a random sorting of the views are also shown. Line charts illustrate relationships between the number of produced answers and the number sources whose data have been retrieved. The number of produced answers has impressively grown before retrieving data from 6 % of the sources (15 out of 250 selected sources), such that more than 50 % of the answers has been delivered. Additionally, for the same amount of retrieved views, for example for 10 views, SemLAV was able to produce 819 answers, whereas the random sorting could not produce any answer so far. In the area enclosed in the green rectangle (number 3), query results are displayed in a map based on the retrieved locations. Attendees will observe the benefits of the SemLAV strategies in action and how SemLAV is able to deliver a considerable number of answers in a relatively low amount of time.

4 Conclusions

In this demonstration, we validate the effectiveness of the SemLAV approach, and illustrate how SPARQL queries can be efficiently executed against real-world sources from social networks and the Linked Open Data cloud. In different setups, sources are selected and ranked by SemLAV in a way that it benefits the incremental delivery of answers, while only a small number of views are retrieved.

References

1. Virtuoso sponger. White paper, OpenLink Software
2. He, B., Patel, M., Zhang, Z., Chang, K.C.-C.: Accessing the deep web. Commun. ACM **50**(5), 94–101 (2007)

3. Montoya, G., Ibáñez, L.-D., Skaf-Molli, H., Molli, P., Vidal, M.-E.: SemLAV: local-as-view mediation for SPARQL queries. In: Hameurlain, A., Küng, J., Wagner, R. (eds.) TLDKS XIII 2014. LNCS, vol. 8420, pp. 31–56. Springer, Heidelberg (2014)
4. Taheriyan, M., Knoblock, C.A., Szekely, P., Ambite, J.L.: Rapidly integrating services into the linked data cloud. In: Cudré-Mauroux, P., Heflin, J., Sirin, E., Tudorache, T., Euzenat, J., Hauswirth, M., Parreira, J.X., Hendler, J., Schreiber, G., Bernstein, A., Blomqvist, E. (eds.) ISWC 2012, Part I. LNCS, vol. 7649, pp. 559–574. Springer, Heidelberg (2012)

Towards a Semantic Web Platform for Finite Element Simulations

André Freitas[1(✉)], Kartik Asooja[1], Swapnil Soni[1,2], Marggie Jones[1], Panagiotis Hasapis[3], and Ratnesh Sahay[1]

[1] Insight Centre for Data Analytics, National University of Ireland, Galway, Ireland
andre.freitas@deri.org

[2] Kno.e.sis Center, Wright State University, Dayton, OH 45435, USA

[3] Intrasoft International, Lëtzebuerg, Luxembourg

Abstract. Finite Element (FE) simulations are present in many different branches of science. The growth in the complexity of FE models and their associated costs bring the demand to facilitate the construction, reuse and reproducibility of FE models. This work demonstrates how Semantic Web technologies can be used to represent FE simulation data, improving the reproducibility and automation of FE simulations.

1 Motivation

Scientific investigation practice is evolving in the direction of the creation of large-scale, highly complex, multi-domain and multi-scale scientific models and theories [1]. The complexity intrinsic to these models, brings barriers for interpreting, reproducing and reusing third-party scientific results. The lack of *reproducibility* in science and the effort necessary for *reusing* and *adapting* existing scientific models are major problems in contemporary scientific *praxis*.

Finite Element (FE) methods are numerical techniques for finding approximate solutions for differential equations, and are examples of computational models which are present in different branches of science, including Biology, Physics and Engineering. The construction of FE models is a high complexity task which depends on multiple steps, including the definition of a discretized geometrical model (a mesh), the definition of a physical model, the selection of numerical methods, the visualization and interpretation of the results and the experimental validation of the model. Building a consistent and realistic FE model is an empirical and time consuming process, depending on the composition and fine-tuning of different parameters. This complexity is expressed in the difficulty of building and validating FE Models and in reproducing and reusing third-party FE models. Previous works in the area have concentrated on the representation of FE elements in the mechanical engineering design domain [2]. This work targets the FE modeling problem from an eScience perspective.

This work describes the SIFEM[1] platform, a semantic infrastructure to support the construction, validation, reproducibility and reuse of Finite Element

[1] Acronym for Semantic Infostructure for Finite Element Methods.

V. Presutti et al. (Eds.): ESWC Satellite Events 2014, LNCS 8798, pp. 338–342, 2014.
DOI: 10.1007/978-3-319-11955-7_45

models. The next sections provide a brief description and demonstration of the SIFEM system.

2 Semantic Infrastructure

The motivation for the construction of a semantic infrastructure for FE simulations is twofold: (i) *facilitating the construction and validation of multi-scale FE models* and (ii) *increasing the reuse and reproducibility of scientific models based on FE simulations.* Both motivations are dependent on a *standards-based representation* model for FE data. In the first case, existing experimental and simulation data can be used to validate input parameters for simulations. A FE model consists of the specification of a geometrical model, material properties, boundary conditions, a physical model, numerical methods and reference experimental data. A standards-based representation supports the collaborative construction of a reference FE knowledge base, which can be reused across different simulations, facilitating the validation of existing models against previous simulations and real world experimental data, and also the selective exploration of the simulation parameter space (by the elimination of unrealistic models previously explored). With the growth of the knowledge base, the exploration of the input parameter space can be partially automated, where domain experts specify a range of values and non-realistic or inconsistent parameters are automatically eliminated.

Additionally, the SIFEM platform allow users to specify *data analysis rules*, which support the semi-automated analysis of the results of different simulation scenarios. The simulation numerical results are lifted to a *qualitative/symbolic level*, through a feature extraction process. The features allow users to specify the expected behaviour of an output variable as a *qualitative data analysis rule* (Fig. 1).

In this work, the standardized Semantic Web data model (RDF(S)) and the reuse of existing vocabularies are used to maximize the interoperability of the

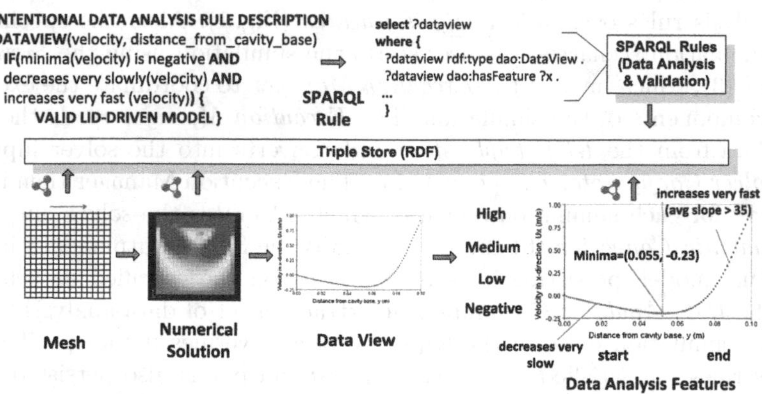

Fig. 1. Finite element data at different steps in the simulation workflow.

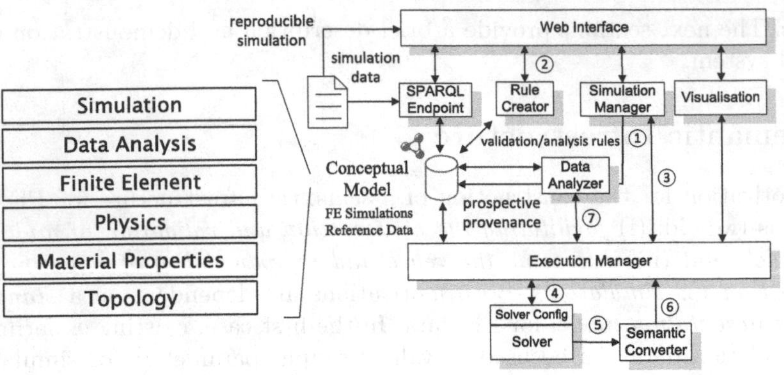

Fig. 2. High-level components of the SIFEM system and conceptual model.

generated simulation data. The standards-based representation also facilitates the composition of multi-scale FE models, i.e. models in which interacting but distinct physical systems at different scales are combined into a complex FE model. From the reproducibility perspective, a standardized data and conceptual model, in combination with the SIFEM web interface, allows the publication of simulation data and code artefacts directly linked from its paper description. While the combination of RDF(S) and vocabularies provides a well-known pattern for maximizing data interoperability, the main contribution of this work concentrates on the use of Semantic Web technologies in the automation of FE experiments.

Figure 2 shows the high-level components of the SIFEM platform and a typical usage workflow of the platform (represented by the number sequence). The workflow starts with the specification of the simulation parameters and of different simulation scenarios on the *Simulation Manager* component (1). This specification of the simulation is stored in the RDF triple store using a *prospective provenance representation*. The user then specifies the expected qualitative behavior of output variables through the *Rule Creator* component (2), using data analysis rules over *data analysis features* (Fig. 1). After the specification of the simulation scenarios, the user starts the simulation using the *Simulation Manager* (3), which invokes the *Execution Manager* to coordinate the execution of the components of the simulation. The *Execution Manager* reads the solver input data from the *RDF triple store* and converts into the solver input format (*Solver Configurator* component) (4). The Execution Manager then invokes the solver for each simulation scenario, which generates the solver output (5). The *Semantic Converter* (6) component maps the Solver output data into the conceptual model, persisting it as RDF. Based on the specified data analysis rules, the *Data Analyzer* (7) component extracts a set of data analysis features from the simulation data on the triple store, and verifies if the specified data analysis rules are satisfied. The *Data Analysis* output is also persisted on the triple store. After the data is persisted, users can access the data using the *Data Visualization* and the *SPARQL Endpoint* components.

A FE simulation in SIFEM is represented using a *multi-layered conceptual model*. The conceptual model layers are depicted on Fig. 2 and consist of the following domains: *simulation*, *data analysis*, *finite element*, *physics*, *material properties* and *topology*. Figure 2 also depicts the main ontologies which are reused and extended in the SIFEM system. Additional details on the SIFEM conceptual model can be found in [1].

3 Demonstration

The demonstration[2] shows the use of the SIFEM platform for specifying, executing and analysing a set of FE simulations based on the lid-driven cavity flow (LDCF) model. The LDCF is a benchmark model for FE simulations and consists of box filled with a fluid with a moving lid. The user starts by uploading the *geometric discretized model (mesh)* into the platform. Based on the mesh model, the geometric patches are loaded and the user specifies the *boundary conditions* for different simulation scenarios. The user then specifies the *material properties*, the *solver* and the *numerical method* for the simulation. In the demonstration example, the user specified five different scenarios with varying lid velocities. Input parameters such as *kinematic viscosity* are validated against a reference model, by using validation rules (encoded as SPARQL Rules). The specification of the simulation scenarios is loaded into a triple store, following the conceptual model (Fig. 2).

From the simulation specification, through the execution manager, the platform instantiates different simulation scenarios in the RDF triple store. The RDF simulation specification data for each scenario is loaded into the solver, which executes the simulation. For this example, the solver is solving the Navier-Stokes equation by using the PCG Finite Differences numerical method to calculate the fluid velocity and pressure at each mesh element. The solver outputs the velocity and pressure fields for each element in the mesh, at different points in time. After the simulation is finished and the data is loaded in the triple store, different data visualizations can be selected by users. In the example demonstration, the velocity and pressure fields over the mesh, and the graphs *velocity(x) vs. distance from cavity base* and *pressure vs. distance from cavity base* are shown.

Different simulation scenarios from the experiment can be analysed by the specification of data analysis rules. This mechanism allows users to verify which simulation results match an expected output behavior. The demonstration uses the data analysis rule in Fig. 1. In the demonstration, all the scenarios satisfy the rule, i.e. a vortex was generated above the center of the box.

The triple store data is accessible through a SPARQL Endpoint and as Linked Data through dereferenceable URIs. In the SPARQL Endpoint users can retrieve simulations with specific properties and compare different simulations. Examples of queries are: (i) *What are the maximum fluid pressures for each scenario?*, (ii) *Which simulations are using the PCG numerical method?* and (iii) *Which kinematic viscosity values are used?*.

[2] The demonstration video can be found in http://bit.ly/1j4nVup.

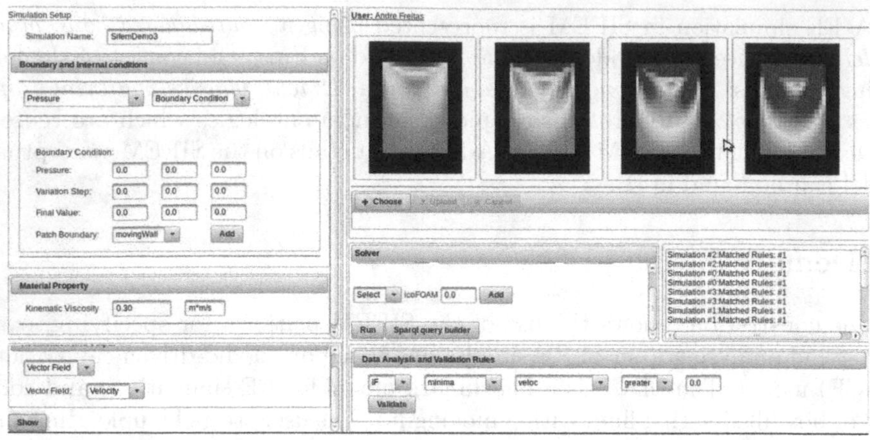

Fig. 3. Screenshot of the SIFEM platform for the Lid-driven cavity flow simulation.

In the demonstration, the simulation and the associated Linked Data are directly linked from an example publication: a user clicks on a graph in an article and the associated simulation specification is opened on the SIFEM web interface. This allows the reader (who now becomes an interactive user) to re-run the simulations described in the paper, thereby supporting reproducibility and verifiability. The user is also enabled to run their own 'what if' scenarios using their choice of input parameters, facilitating further experimentation (possibly exploring scenarios not envisaged by the original model creators) (Fig. 3).

4 Conclusions and Future Work

This work demonstrated the SIFEM platform, which uses Semantic Web technologies to increase the reproducibility, reusability and automation of Finite Element (FE) simulations. Future work includes the generalisation of the platform to cope with more complex FE simulations.

Acknowledgments. This work is supported by the EU: Grant No. 600933 (SIFEM).

References

1. Freitas, A., et al.: Towards a semantic representation for multi-scale finite element biosimulation experiments. In: 13th IEEE International Conference on BioInformatics and BioEngineering (BIBE) (2013)
2. Sun, W., Ma, Q., Chen, S.: A Framework for automated finite element analysis with an ontology-based approach. J. Mech. Sci. Technol. **23**(12), 3209–3220 (2009)

A Demonstration of a Natural Language Query Interface to an Event-Based Semantic Web Triplestore

Richard A. Frost[1(✉)], Jonathon Donais[1], Eric Mathews[1], Wale Agboola[1], and Rob Stewart[2]

[1] School of Computer Science, University of Windsor, Windsor, ON N9B 3P4, Canada
rfrost@cogeco.ca

[2] Department of Computer Science, Heriot-Watt University, Edinburgh, UK

Abstract. Natural language semantic-web queries can be treated as expressions of the lambda calculus and evaluated directly with respect to an event-based triplestore using only basic triple retrieval operations. This facilitates the accommodation of complex NL constructs.

1 Introduction

Most semantic-web data sources contain sets of "entity-based" triples, e.g.:

`<dbpedia:Al_Capone> <dbpedia_owl:spouse> <dbpedia:Mae_Capone>.`

Many methods have been developed for querying entity-based triplestores, including: [2,3,5,6,9,11,12,14,15,17]. A good survey of work up to 2011 is given in [13]. Most of these methods convert the query to the SPARQL query language and then run the SPARQL query against the triplestore.

There are two difficulties with this approach. Firstly, consider a query with a simple prepositional phrase "in 1918":

```
"Who married Al Capone in 1918?"
```

Adding the following triple is insufficient as Capone could have married twice:

`<..Al_Capone> <..marriage_year> <..1918>.`

There are solutions to this problem which involve various forms of reification. However, most of these solutions appear to complicate translation of the NL query to SPARQL.

Another problem is the apparent difficulty of translating complex NL queries to SPARQL. Consider the following query:

```
"Who joined every gang that was joined by a person who stole a car
in 1899 or 1908 in Brooklyn?"
```

We are not aware of any approach, other than ours, that can accommodate such NL queries, which contain chained complex prepositional phrases containing arbitrarily-nested quantifiers (e.g. "a" and "every").

V. Presutti et al. (Eds.): ESWC Satellite Events 2014, LNCS 8798, pp. 343–348, 2014.
DOI: 10.1007/978-3-319-11955-7_46

2 Event-Based Triplestores

Our proposed solution, called DEV-NLQ, is to represent data using a form of reification involving event-based triples, and to treat NL queries as expressions of the lambda calculus which are evaluated directly with respect to event-based triplestores. For example, in the following, `event1030` ties the data together:

```
<...event1030>   <...type>      <...marriage_ev>.
<...event1030>   <...subject>   <...Al_Capone>.
<...event1030>   <...object>    <...Mae_Capone".
<...event1030>   <...year>      <..."1918">.
```

The event-based triplestore that we use in our demo can be accessed at: http://speechweb2.cs.uwindsor.ca/ESWC/demo.html.

3 Direct Evaluation of NL Queries

In [7] we describe a denotational semantics for natural-language query interfaces to event-based triplestores. Our semantics is based on an efficient version of Montague Semantics [4]. Our semantics accommodates proper and common nouns, adjectives, intransitive and transitive verbs, negation, and chained complex prepositional phrases containing arbitrarily-nested quantifiers.

The idea is that every word in English (after disambiguation by the parser) denotes a function. For example, in the following, `person`, `capone`, `a` etc. are functions defined in the Haskell programming language. The functions `getts_1` and `getts_3` are basic triple retrieval functions. See [7] for explanations. Note that `e => r` means that `r` is the result of evaluating `e`. Note also that we ignore URIs in the following, but address them in Sect. 4.

```
e.g. getts_1 ("?","subject","torrio")    => ["event1009","event1011"],
     getts_3 ("event1009","type","?")    => ["join_ev"]

get members set               = defined in terms of getts_1
get_subjs_of_event_type et = defined in terms of getts_1 and getts_3

gang     = get_members"gang"
           e.g.   gang             => ["fpg","bowery"]

smoke    = get_subjs_of_event_type"smoke_ev"
           e.g.   smoke            => ["capone"]

capone     setofents   = member"capone"setofents
           e.g.   capone smoke  => True

a        nph vbph       = length (intersect  nph vbph) /= 0
every    nph vbph       = subset nph vbph
no       nph vbph       = length (intersect  nph vbph) = 0
```

```
nounand s t          = intersect s t
that                 = nounand
nounor  s t          = mkset (s ++ t)

-- termand is a higher-order function which creates a new function from
the two functions given as input
termand tmph1 tmph2 = f  where
                      f setofents = (tmph1 setofents) && (tmph2 setofents)
        e.g.   (capone 'termand'torrio) person => True

-- steal is a complex function (see Frost et al. 2014 for the definition)
steal tmph preps = defined in terms of getts_1 and getts_3
        e.g. steal (a car) [("year", year_1899 'termor'year_1908),
                             ("location", brooklyn)]  => ["capone"]
```

Note that we can define the meaning of words in terms of others, e.g.

```
gangster = join (a gang)
```

4 Interfacing the Query Processor to the Semantic Web

We use the Haskell package `hsparql` [1] to interface our query processor to an external SPARQL endpoint containing our data. The functions `getts_1` and `getts_3` above are re-defined in terms of `hsparql` functions in a module called `Getts_4V`. All strings, such as `"capone"` in the definitions exemplified in Sect. 3 are modified by a function `gts` to include a URI prefix. The Haskell code is available at the following URL:

http://speechweb2.cs.uwindsor.ca/ESWC/src1

Note that we do not translate the *whole* NL query to SPARQL. The `hsparql` functions only issue two types of basic SPARQL SELECT requests:

```
SELECT ?first WHERE {?first, <given_second>, <given-third>} .
SELECT ?third WHERE {<given_first>, <given_second>, ?third} .
```

Note that our semantics could be used with other non-SPARQL-endpoint interfaces to triplestores.

5 The Demonstration

Readers can access our query interface as follows: (1) go to the Welcome page `http://speechweb2.cs.uwindsor.ca/ESWC/` which has three links: "Live Demo", "Source Code", and "Haskell Code ..", (2) -> "Live Demo"-> "List of triples in the Graph" to see how we represent data such as "Capone stole car_1 in 1908 in Brooklyn", (3) -> Welcome page -> "Source Code" -> `gangster_v4.hs` which contains the Haskell definitions of the denotations of different words,

(4) -> Welcome page -> "Source Code"-> `Getts_v4.hs` which contains the code that links our semantics program to our external tripestore using the `h_sparql` module, (5) -> Welcome page -> "Live Demo" -> "Click here for more examples" which shows how brackets are placed in the queries according to their syntactic structure. Readers can copy and paste some of the examples into the "query" box on the "Live Demo" page and hit the "run query" button. Readers can also experiment with their own bracketed queries.

Queries are evaluated by our Haskell program in the same way as the expression `3 + (2 * 4)`. For example the query "Which gangster who stole a car in 1899 or 1908 in Brooklyn, joined a gang that was joined by Torrio?" can be entered into the query box as the following bracketed expression (note that you cannot cut and paste the expression from this .pdf document as the quotes are different in pdf).

```
which (gangster 'that'(steal'(a car)
                              [(gts"year",year_1899 'termor'year_1908),
                               (gts"location", brooklyn)]))
      (join (a (gang 'that'(joined_by torrio))))
```

the following result is returned by our query interface:

```
["http://richard.myweb.cs.uwindsor.ca/ESWC/gangster_triplestore#capone"]
```

6 Concluding Comments

We are currently integrating the semantics with our NL parser [8] which will introduce the brackets according to the syntactic structure of the query.

Our approach assumes that the full URIs are known (and used in the definitions of the denotations of words). We intend to investigate the integration of the method of Walter et al. [16] for mapping query words to appropriate URIs and building the denotations of words in real-time when the query is parsed.

Our approach assumes the existence of event-based triplestores. We are currently investigating how to extract sets of event-based triples from conventional triplestores as required. However, we also note that triplestores are being developed to accommodate "richer" contextual data. YAGO2 is an example [10] which uses a simple form of reification to represent temporal and spatial properties. We are developing another denotational semantics so that NL queries can be evaluated directly with respect to YAGO2 data.

Because there is no need to translate NL queries to a formal query language such as SPARQL, F-Logic or SPOTLX, we can concentrate solely on linguistic issues and develop semantics to accommodate highly-complex NL constructs.

Acknowledgments. The authors acknowledge the Natural Science and Engineering Council of Canada (NSERC), and the reviewers who provided very useful constructive criticism.

References

1. Wheeler, J.: The hsparql package. http://hackage.haskell.org/package/hsparql-0.1.2. Maintained by: Rob Stewart
2. Damljanovic, D., Agatonovic, M., Cunningham, H.: FREyA: an interactive way of querying linked data using natural language. In: García-Castro, R., Fensel, D., Antoniou, G. (eds.) ESWC 2011. LNCS, vol. 7117, pp. 125–138. Springer, Heidelberg (2012)
3. Damova, M., Dannelles, D., Enache, R., Mateva, M., Ranta, A.: Natural language interaction with semantic web knowledge bases and LOD. In: Buitelaar, P., Cimiano, P. (eds.) Towards the Multilingual Semantic Web. Springer, Berlin (2013)
4. Dowty, D., Wall, R., Peters, S.: Introduction to Montague Semantics. D. Reidel Publishing Company, Dordrecht, Boston, Lancaster, Tokyo (1981)
5. Ferré, S.: SQUALL: a controlled natural language for querying and updating RDF graphs. In: Kuhn, T., Fuchs, N.E. (eds.) CNL 2012. LNCS, vol. 7427, pp. 11–25. Springer, Heidelberg (2012)
6. Freitas, A., de Faria, F.F., O'Riain, S., Curry, E.: Answering natural language queries over linked data graphs: a distributional semantics approach. In: Proceedings of the 36th International ACM SIGIR Conference on Research and Development in Information Retrieval, pp. 1107–1108. ACM (2013)
7. Frost, R.A., Agboola, W., Matthews, E.: Querying graph-structured data using natural language. In: Proceedings of the GraphQ Workshop EDBT/ICDT 2104, pp. 192–199 (2014)
8. Hafiz, R., Frost, R.A.: Lazy combinators for executable specifications of general attribute grammars. In: Carro, M., Peña, R. (eds.) PADL 2010. LNCS, vol. 5937, pp. 167–182. Springer, Heidelberg (2010)
9. Hakimov, S., Tunc, H., Akimaliev, M., Dogdu, E.: Semantic question answering system over linked data using relational patterns. In: Proceedings of the Joint EDBT/ICDT 2013 Workshops, pp. 83–88. ACM (2013)
10. Hoffart, J., Suchanek, F.M., Berberich, K., Weikum, G.: Yago2: a spatially and temporally enhanced knowledge base from wikipedia. Artif. Intell. **194**, 28–61 (2013)
11. Kaufmann, E., Bernstein, A.: Evaluating the usibility of natural language query languages and interfaces to semantic web knowledge bases. Web Semant. Sci. Serv. Agents World Wide Web **8**(4), 377–393 (2009)
12. Lopez, V., Fernández, M., Motta, E., Stieler, N.: Poweraqua: supporting users in querying and exploring the semantic web. Semant. Web **3**(3), 249–265 (2012)
13. Lopez, V., Uren, V., Sabou, M., Motta, E.: Is question answering fit for the semantic web?: a survey. Semant. Web **2**(2), 125–155 (2011)
14. Ran, A., Lencevicius, R.: Natural language query system for RDF repositories. In: Proceedings of the 7th International Symposium on Natural Language Processing, SNLP, pp. 1–6 (2007)
15. Unger, C., Cimiano, P.: Pythia: compositional meaning construction for ontology-based question answering on the semantic web. In: Muñoz, R., Montoyo, A., Métais, E. (eds.) NLDB 2011. LNCS, vol. 6716, pp. 153–160. Springer, Heidelberg (2011)

16. Walter, S., Unger, C., Cimiano, P., Bär, D.: Evaluation of a layered approach to question answering over linked data. In: Cudré-Mauroux, P., Heflin, J., Sirin, E., Tudorache, T., Euzenat, J., Hauswirth, M., Parreira, J.X., Hendler, J., Schreiber, G., Bernstein, A., Blomqvist, E. (eds.) ISWC 2012, Part II. LNCS, vol. 7650, pp. 362–374. Springer, Heidelberg (2012)
17. Yahya, M., Berberich, K., Elbassuoni, S., Ramanath, M., Tresp, V., Weikum, G.: Natural language questions for the web of data. In: The 2012 Joint Conference on Empirical Methods in Natural Language Processing and Computational Natural Language Learning, July 2012, pp. 379–390. ACL (2012)

Kuphi – an Investigation Tool for Searching for and via Semantic Relations

Michael Färber(✉), Lei Zhang, and Achim Rettinger

Karlsruhe Institute of Technology (KIT), 76131 Karlsruhe, Germany
{michael.faerber,l.zhang,rettinger}@kit.edu

Abstract. In this work, we present a new process-oriented approach for information retrieval called *Kuphi*. It is intended for investigating entities and their semantic relations to other entities in text documents. We extend the traditional search capabilities which are based on the bag-of-words model in the following way: Starting with a keyword search for a specific entity, the user can not only search for appearances of this entity in the text documents; she can also search via user-specified relations of the queried entity to other entities for these associated entitites in the text. The user has the possibility to search indirectly for manifestations of these relations. Due to cross-lingual annotation, we allow the query language to be different from the language of the documents. We demonstrate our approach with DBpedia as knowledge base and news texts gathered from RSS feeds.

Keywords: Semantic search · Document ranking · Cross-lingual annotation

1 Introduction

The idea of annotation-based document retrieval is that queries and documents with additional annotations enhance document search. A study [1] showed that the quality of information extraction and, therefore, annotation, has a high impact on the semantic search performance.

Kandogan et al. [2] present an approach called *Avatar Semantic Search* where keyword queries are transformed into one or more queries over the used structured data set. They limit themselves to a specific domain with a few concepts such as email. In [3] an ontology-based scheme for a semi-automatic annotation of documents and a retrieval system is presented. The ranking is based on an adaptation of the traditional vector space model taking into account weights for annotations.

This work is supported by the German Federal Ministry of Education and Research (BMBF) under grant 02PJ1002 SyncTech).
The authors acknowledge the support of the European Community's Seventh Framework Programme FP7-ICT-2011-7 (XLike, Grant 288342).

V. Presutti et al. (Eds.): ESWC Satellite Events 2014, LNCS 8798, pp. 349–354, 2014.
DOI: 10.1007/978-3-319-11955-7_47

The work we present here can be dedicated to research in this area. It provides a significant new search paradigm. It is intended for investigating entitites and their relations written in documents. On the one hand it is based on the observation that keyword search has proven to be the most intuitive way for end users to satisfy their information needs. On the other hand it is based on the fact that nowadays there are many news portals which provide a vast amount of textual information which needs to become accessible by end users via *targeted search. Targeted search* means the user can (i) search for specific entitites occurring in text documents; (ii) she can search for relations of these entities to other entities (expressed in prose text); and (iii) she can search via these specified relations for other entities which stand in relation to the search entity in a specific way.

From a technical point of view, we make the following contributions: (1) *Kuphi*[1,2] exploits the knowledge base (KB) semantics during the document retrieval process, which includes the steps *text annotation*, *keyword matching*, *query refinement* and *document ranking*. The rich semantics of DBpedia as used KB are firstly used to obtain a semantic representation of the documents. During the online search process, the KB is also used to infer the semantics of queries. Based on the various semantic interpretations that can be found for the ambiguous query, users can choose the refinement that match the intent. (2) The main difference to existing works is our strong emphasize on semantic relations during the ranking of documents. One the one hand, we use them to capture the semantic focus of documents and to rank them according to how well the query matches the focus. Also, they are used for manual weighting, a mechanism we introduce for the users to influence the ranking during the search process. (3) Our semantic search system is designed for cross-lingual search. The user can select the query language and also the language of the documents to search for. This is enabled by using the huge cross-lingual lexica called xLiD [4]. This feature is especially interesting in case documents about a topic are only available in other languages than the query language. For instance, breaking news are at the beginning often written in the local language.

2 Document Search with *Kuphi*

We present a process-oriented approach to document search, which can start with a rather vague information need that becomes more concrete during the process. It assists users in specifying and addressing their information needs through several steps of a search process, as shown in Fig. 1.

In the following, we first discuss the preprocessing step, namely *text annotation*, before we focus on the on-line steps where the user is involved in.

Text Annotation. This preprocessing step is performed to enrich documents with contexts that are linked to KBs to help to bridge the ambiguity of natural

[1] *Kuphi* means "Where?" in Zulu language.

[2] The demo is available at http://km.aifb.kit.edu/services/kuphi/.

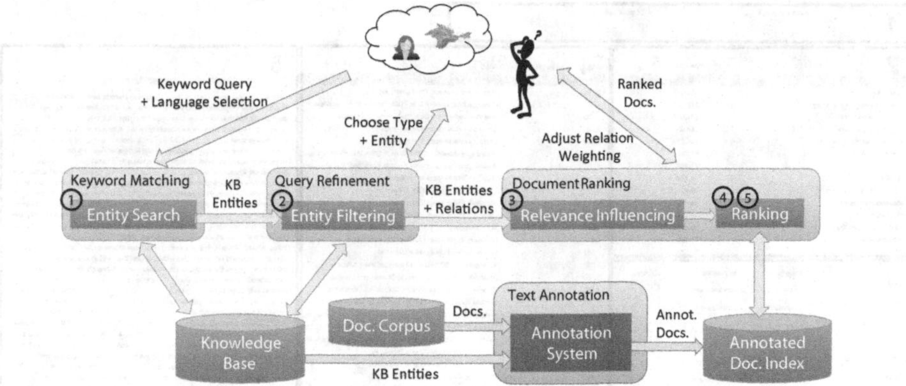

Fig. 1. The document search process with *Kuphi*. The numbers represent the different UI components as shown in Fig. 2.

language text and precise formal semantics captured by KBs. For our demonstration, we use DBpedia as formal KB containing entities and semantic relations between them.

For linking textual mentions – also called *surface forms* – to KB entities, we apply a huge lexica data set called xLiD [4]. In this data set, for all DBpedia entites we provide a list of potential textual mentions. For the used data set we retrieved this mention list by extracting anchor texts from an English Wikipedia dump of July 2013.

An example of an annotated sentence in a document is the following:

```
[[John McCain|Senator John McCain]] was one of several senior
[[Republican Party (United States)|Republicans]] opposed to the
[[International Monetary Fund|IMF]] measures.
```

Here wiki-syntax was used to separate each surface form from its actual KB representation, the entity. For instance, the mention "IMF" was correctly disambiguated and linked to the entity "International Monetary Fund". Note that in other document languages than English we also use our xLiD data set, but link directly to the English DBpedia entities. The canonicalized DBpedia, hence, is used as hub for all provided languages.

Given the documents and their linked entities stored in the index, we now discuss the online steps involved in our search process. We will use the query "Krim"(German for the Crimea) as an example throughout the search process. Our user wants to investigate about the current Crimea crises and is especially interested in documents in English which adress the capital and the ethnical groups of the Crimea.

Keyword Matching. While keyword queries are simple and intuitive, they can be highly ambiguous. Even the phrase "Krim" could stand for the Crimea, the peninsula, or other entities such as Mathilde Krim, a medical researcher. Using the bag-of-words model that relies on term information only, semantic

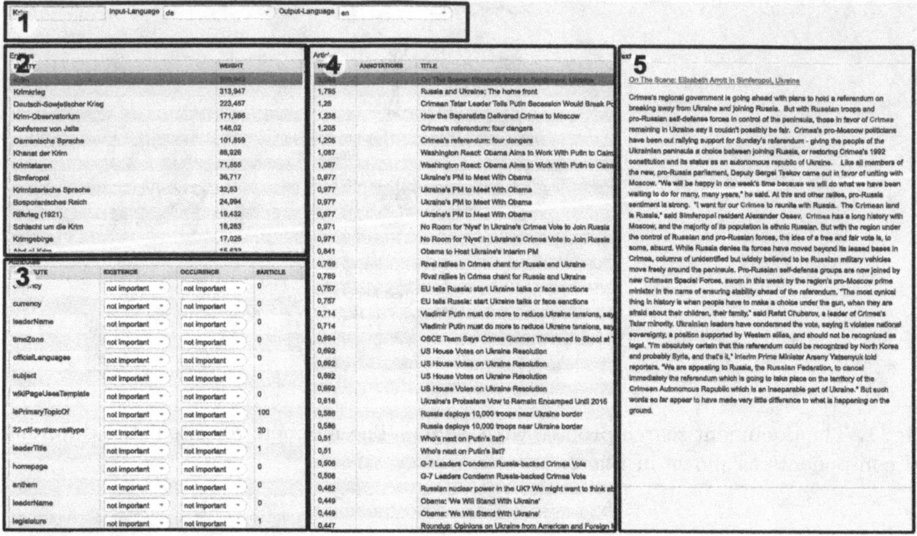

Fig. 2. Screenshot of our semantic search system *Kuphi* with frames indicating the different steps in the search process.

ambiguities of these kind are difficult to address. Thus, even when the precise query intent is given, e.g., "Krim", it is difficult to tell which of the retrieved documents are actually relevant.

Our online search process starts with a possibly ambiguous keyword query (see Frame 1 in Fig. 2). The ambiguity is resolved with the help of the user. Instead of retrieving documents, our approach first finds entities from the KB with labels matching the query keywords. These entities represent different semantic interpretations of the query and are, thus, employed in the following steps to help the user to refine the search and influence document ranking according to the intent. The ranking of the entities is performed by means of pre-computed DBpedia PageRank values and the prior probabilities of the surface forms.

Query Refinement. By displaying all possible interpretations of the query (cf. Frame 2 in Fig. 2), the user selects the intended entity she wants to search for in the documents.

Document Ranking. Afterwards, the documents containing the queried entity are retrieved from the index[3] (cf. Frame 4 and 5 in Fig. 2). We observe that while annotated documents have different links to the KB, they generally share the following structure pattern: Every document is linked to a set of entities. A subset of these entities are connected via relations in the KB, forming a graph. Based on these entities and relations, a document can also be conceived as a graph containing several connected components. The largest connected component represents

[3] We use Apache Lucene to index the documents together with their annotations.

the main focus of the document. For instance, the example document (written in English) contains the entity *Crimea* and other entities such as *Crimean Tatars*, *Ukrainians*, *Russians*, and *Simferopol*. From the KB we can infer the relations between these entities. In our concrete example we have the relations *ethnic group* and *capital* of the entity *Crimea*.

Focus-Based Ranking. Leveraging this structure pattern, we incorporate the following intuition into our ranking scheme: Given two documents d_1 and d_2 retrieved for the entity / query intent e, d_1 is more relevant than d_2 if it focuses more on e than d_2 does, i.e., when the largest connected component of d_1 containing e is larger than the largest connected component of d_2 containing e. For example, the document containing the connected entities *Crimea*, *Simferopol* and *Tatars* is more relevant than the document containing *Crimea* only.

Relation-Based Weighting. We enable the user to influence the document ranking by adjusting the weights of entity relations to obtain a personalized document ranking (see Frame 3 in Fig. 2). For this, the chosen entity is shown and extended with relations to other entities retrieved from the KB. For instance, if a user would like to obtain information about the *Crimea* and its capital, she would increase the weight of the *capital* relation and give no weight to other relations, so that the latter are not considered for ranking. This relation-based search capability is especially useful when the user does not know the capital by its name. Furthermore, the user can weight both the existence of a relation and the number of its occurrences in the document[4]. This differentiation separates the one scenario where the user is interested in obtaining more detailed information about the relation itself from the other, where users are interested in the quantity of relations. In this way, varying intents, such as "the number of different ethnical groups on the Crimea" and "one ethnical group of the Crimea", can be distinguished.

3 Conclusions

We presented a process-oriented approach called *Kuphi* for searching for entities and relations in documents. We discussed that the semantics captured by the KBs, especially semantic relations, can be exploited in this process to allow the information needs of the user to be specified and addressed on the semantic level. Based on DBpedia as KB and on news texts gathered from RSS feeds in different languages we demonstrated the practical benefit. In the future, we will advance the query capability of *Kuphi* to support information needs involving several entities.

References

1. Chu-Carroll, J., Prager, J.: An experimental study of the impact of information extraction accuracy on semantic search performance. In: Proceedings of the CIKM '07, New York, NY, USA, pp. 505–514. ACM (2007)

[4] Technically, not the number of the relations, but the number of the objects of the relations is weighted.

2. Kandogan, E., Krishnamurthy, R., Raghavan, S., Vaithyanathan, S., Zhu, H.: Avatar semantic search: a database approach to information retrieval. In: Proceedings of SIGMOD '06, New York, NY, USA, pp. 790–792. ACM (2006)
3. Castells, P., Fernandez, M., Vallet, D.: An Adaptation of the vector-space model for ontology-based information retrieval. IEEE Trans. Knowl. Data Eng. **19**(2), 261–272 (2007)
4. Zhang, L., Färber, M., Rettinger, A.: xLiD-Lexica: cross-lingual linked data lexica. In: Proceedings of the 9th Edition of the Language Resources and Evaluation Conference (LREC 2014) (May 2014) (To appear)

FAGI-tr: A Tool for Aligning Geospatial RDF Vocabularies

Giorgos Giannopoulos[1(✉)], Thomas Maroulis [2], Dimitrios Skoutas [1], Nikos Karagiannakis[1], and Spiros Athanasiou[1]

[1] IMIS Institute, "Athena" Research Center, Marousi, Greece
giann@imis.athena-innovation.gr
[2] Imperial College, London, UK

Abstract. In this paper, we present FAGI-tr, a tool for aligning RDF vocabularies with respect to their geospatial aspect. The tool provides a framework for (a) loading a source and a target geospatial RDF dataset, (b) identifying vocabularies for representing geospatial RDF data, (c) selecting, from both datasets, the representations to be considered for processing, (d) selecting a target vocabulary and transforming all geospatial triples from both datasets into the respective format and (e) outputting the two datasets for further processing. The outcome of the process is datasets that follow exactly the same vocabulary and, also, are cleansed from possible duplicate triples containing geospatial metadata, which is the case when an RDF dataset adopts more than one vocabularies to describe spatial data. The tool is tested with DBpedia data and performs rather efficiently.

1 Introduction

The Semantic Web and Linked Data practices have been gaining increasing interest the last years. More and better technologies and tools are becoming available for producing RDF datasets that adhere to common, widely adopted schemata and vocabularies, so that the contained information can be searched and integrated in a more automated and principled manner. However, it is rarely the case that there exists a single, commonly used schema or ontology for a given domain. Often, several overlapping or complementary schemata may have evolved in parallel and be used by different communities. Moreover, users may be unaware of or unwilling to use an existing schema, resorting instead to custom schemas and vocabularies when producing RDF data. This is also the case in the geospatial data domain, where several vocabularies have been proposed and utilized for describing geospatial features in RDF, such as Basic Geo or GeoRSS [4], although GeoSPARQL [8] is lately becoming a more widely accepted standard.

In addition, it is often the case that different data sources, although describing the same real world entities, provide different views of them, either by providing information on different subsets of attributes or even by providing different values on the same attributes. Typical reasons for this is that some sources may be outdated or may serve a different purpose and have different focus. As a result,

V. Presutti et al. (Eds.): ESWC Satellite Events 2014, LNCS 8798, pp. 355–361, 2014.
DOI: 10.1007/978-3-319-11955-7_48

information for the same real world entities is often spread across several heterogeneous datasets, each one providing partial and/or contradicting views of it, which then need to be fused in order to acquire a richer, cleaner and universal dataset.

In this paper, we focus on fusion of geospatial RDF data and specifically, the first necessary step of the process: the alignment of RDF vocabularies. FAGI-tr, the first component of our envisioned framework for *Fusion and Aggregation of Geospatial Information*, allows the configuration of matching rules that identify different geospatial RDF vocabularies, the efficient application of such rules on RDF datasets and the transformation of the data from one vocabulary to another.

2 Related Work

There are several approaches for transforming conventional data to RDF. Indicatively, some approaches are presented next. However, to the best of our knowledge, this work is the first one addressing RDF-to-RDF transformations on geospatial RDF vocabularies.

In [10], the authors present SPARQL2XQuery, a framework that provides a mapping model for the expression of OWL-RDF/S to XML Schema mappings as well as a method for SPARQL to XQuery translation. Through the framework, XML datasets can be turned into SPARQL endpoints. Sparqlify [3] is a SPARQL-SQL query rewriter that allows the definition of RDF views using a *Sparqlification Mapping Language*. This way, it enables SPARQL queries on relational databases, emphasizing on the LinkedGeoData framework [11] which utilizes Sparqlify to provide access to OpenStreetMap data in RDF form, through SPARQL endpoints and dowloadable data dumps. Finally, TripleGeo [12] is an ETL utility that can extract geospatial features from various sources (shapefiles and DBMSs) and transform them into Basic Geo or GeoSPARQL compatible RDF triples for subsequent loading into RDF stores.

3 Vocabulary Transformations in FAGI

In this Section, we present FAGI-tr (FAGI for transformations) the module of FAGI that handles the recognition of different RDF representations of spatial features in RDF, i.e. different vocabularies, literal (feature values) formats and coordinate reference systems, as well as the transformation of these representations from one to another.

FAGI-tr is implemented in Java, as a desktop application, and provides a graphical user interface. It takes as input SPARQL endpoints from where source and target datasets are loaded and stored into the underlying RDF store. For the latter, we have used Virtuoso[1]. Next, the two datasets are parsed, and preconfigured regular expressions that recognize different RDF representations of

[1] http://virtuoso.openlinksw.com/

triples involving geospatial data are applied. The regular expressions are organized in distinct configuration files, that, currently, need to be manually editer by the user in order to create new matching rules. For each dataset, the identified vocabularies are presented to the user in order to select the types of triples (i.e., the respective vocabularies) that are to be processed further. At the final step, the user selects a target vocabulary (from all the available/defined vocabulary matching rules) and all selected geospatial triples from both datasets are transformed into the respective vocabulary. The output is written either on the same datasets or new datasets can be created, so that the original ones are kept for future use. The source code of FAGI-tr is publicly available, and also available as a jar file for execution [2]. In what follows, we describe in more detail the tool components, the rule matching configuration, and we demonstrate the usage of the tool.

3.1 Components

FAGI-tr consists of four basic components, described next:

- *GUI component.* It consists of three parts, implementing the user interfaces.
- *CORE component.* This component is responsible for fetching both conventional (non-spatial) triples and identified spatial triples from a source dataset and storing them into Virtuoso. It also handles vocabulary rule matching and provides matching metadata (e.g. number of matched geospatial triples to a specific vocabulary rule).
- *GEOMETRY component.* This component implements all the necessary geospatial functionality. It provides parsing and transformation functions for handling geometry serializations and coordinate reference systems.
- *RULES component.* This component handles the synthesis of vocabulary matching rules in the form of regular expressions and their translation into SPARQL queries to be applied on the RDF datasets both for matching vocabularies and for transforming from one vocabulary to another.

3.2 Supported data sources and formats

Currently, FAGI-tr supports loading data from SPARQL endpoints where the actual endpoint and the graph URI of the dataset are required. The supported RDF triples format is N-triples. The output of the tool is written into the underlying Virtuoso RDF store. As far as RDF vocabularies for geospatial features representation are concerned, we currently have defined rules for three vocabularies: GeoRSS [7], Basic Geo Vocabulary [6], and GeoSPARQL. Implementation of support of RDF files as input/output sources, other RDF triple formats (RDF/XML, Turtle, etc.) and definition of additional vocabulary matching rules are part of ongoing work. We note that, defining new rules is possible by defining proper regular expressions into the configuration files of the tool.

3.3 Configuration rules

Rules for matching and transforming triples are expressed in the form of triple restrictions and are defined in five separate configuration files. We define four types of rules. The first three rule types (property, class, object) are helper rules intended to improve the readability and formulation of full triple rules. The only rules that will be matched are the full triple rules. The values of any helper rule will be substituted into the full triple rule internally by the rule parser. Due to lack of space, we briefly present the four rule types and provide an example of a full configuration rule. Detailed description of the rules syntax can be found in [5].

- *property*: Configuration file 'property' is used for the definition of rules that match RDF properties.
- *class*: Configuration file 'class' is used for the definition of rules that match classes.
- *object*: Configuration file 'object' is used for the definition of rules that match object literals.
- *full triple rules*: Configuration files 'triple_default' and 'triple_user' are used for the definition of the full triple rules that will be used for matching. These rules reference property, object and class rules. The former contains predefined rules, while the latter contains user added rules. Both files use the same syntax and are handled the same way internally.

An example rule is given below. In the first line, the rule *id*, *description* and *number of triples* are given. Next, the three triple expressions comprising the rule are provided, referring property and object rule ids (corresponding to the respective regular expressions) from the rest configuration files.

```
<k_w3c_loc2> "WGS84 identification rule" 3
?x <p_wgs84_loc> _:a
_:a <p_wgs84_lat> <o_lat>
_:a <p_wgs84_long> <o_long> .
```

3.4 Tool demonstration

In the first step, the user specifies the datasets to be processed and where the results are to be stored. For both source and target datasets, the SPARQL endpoint and the graph URI of the dataset are required. Then, the rule matching process is executed on both datasets. This is illustrated in Figure 1. The left panel displays all available rules. Upon selecting one of them, the user can see whether the rule was matched and, if so, with how many triples. Also, information for the matched rule is presented, including its description, the structure of the rule, and a sample matching set of triples from the dataset. The user is able to select which kind of triples to retain for further processing, e.g. to retain only the triples matching a specific vocabulary rule. This allows the user to keep only certain vocabulary versions of the geospatial triples, saving processing effort for the next steps, as well as clearing out possible erroneously contained triples.

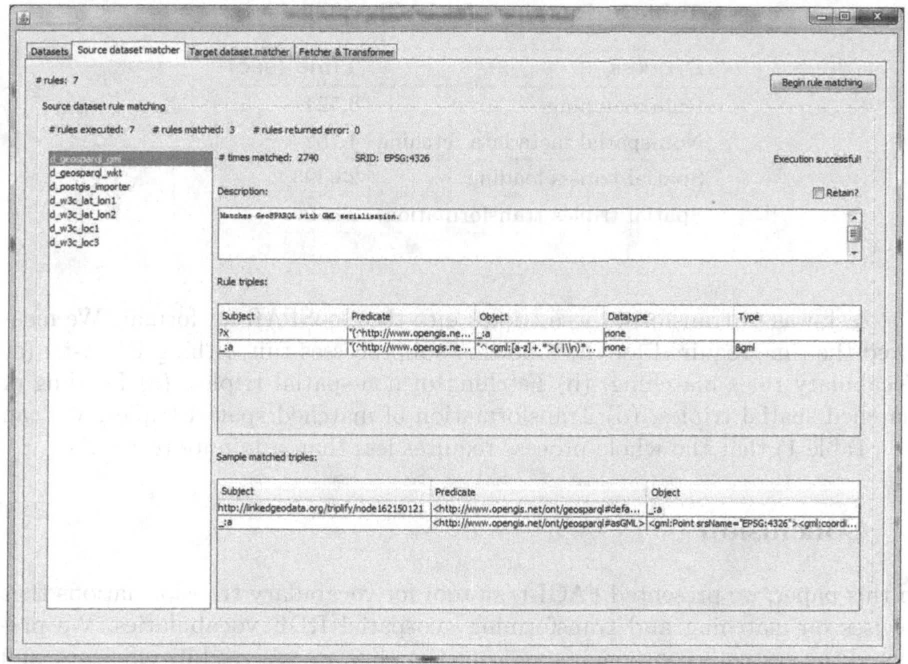

Fig. 1. Rulo matching panel

Rule matching statistics for the source and target datasets are presented in a separate panel, the fetching and transforming panel. This allows to choose a target vocabulary rule, so that all retained geospatial triples from both datasets are transformed according to the vocabulary specified by the rule. The transformed triples, along with the unmodified non-spatial triples are then written into the RDF store, in different output graphs, depending on the user selection on the dataset loading panel. There is also limited support for changing the CRS, which will be extended in the future. A video that demonstrates FAGI-tr is provided in the link below (copy-paste the link to your browser).

http://web.imis.athena-innovation.gr/%7egiann/FAGI-tr.mp4

3.5 Evaluation

The correctness of the transformation process has been verified by examining all possible vocabulary transformations and the triples produced. Thus, our evaluation focused on assessing the efficiency of the tool, that is, the total time required to match geospatial vocabularies, as well as to transform triples from one vocabulariy to another. We used a DBpedia dataset[2] containing 2M triples, of which 1M triples corresponded to 500K geometries in Basic Geo vocabulary.

---

[2] http://www.downloads.dbpedia.org/3.9/en/geo_coordinates_en.nt.bz2

Table 1. Run times for FAGI-tr functions.

Process	Time (sec)
Rule matching	3.524
Non-spatial metadata fetching	4.782
Spatial triples loading	23.393
Spatial triples transformation	23.596

The task was to transform these triples into the GeoSPARQL format. We measured the time required for the following subprocesses run withing FAGI-tr: (a) Vocabulary rules matching, (b) Fetching of non-spatial triples, (c) Loading of matched spatial triples, (d) Transformation of matched spatial triples. We can see (Table 1) that the whole process requires less than a minute to run.

4 Conclusion

In this paper, we presented FAGI-tr, a tool for vocabulary transformations that focuses on matching and transforming geospatial RDF vocabularies. We presented the system's components and functionality, we assessed its efficiency and showcased its usage. To the best of our knowledge this is the first tool that specializes on aligning geospatial RDF vocabularies. Our next steps involve enriching the input and output formats of the tool, as well as increasing the tool's scalability and efficiency.

Acknowledgments. This work was supported by a grant from the EU's 7th Framework Programme (2007-2013) provided for the project GeoKnow (GA no. 318159).

References

1. Bleiholder, J., Naumann, F.: Declarative data fusion – syntax, semantics, and implementation. In: Eder, J., Haav, H.-M., Kalja, A., Penjam, J. (eds.) ADBIS 2005. LNCS, vol. 3631, pp. 58–73. Springer, Heidelberg (2005)
2. FAGI-tr. https://www.github.com/GeoKnow/FAGI-tr
3. Sparqlify. https://www.github.com/AKSW/Sparqlify
4. GeoKnow EU/FP7 project. Market and Research Overview. http://svn.aksw.org/projects/GeoKnow/Public/D2.1.1_Market_and_Research_Overview.pdf
5. GeoKnow EU/FP7 project. Fusing of geographic features. http://www.svn.aksw.org/projects/GeoKnow/Public/D3.2.1_Fusing_of_geographic_features.pdf
6. Basic Geo (WGS84 lat/long) Vocabulary. http://www.w3.org/2003/01/geo/
7. Open Geospatial Consortium. An Introduction to GeoRSS. Whitepaper (2006)
8. Open Geospatial Consortium Inc. OGC GeoSPARQL standard - A geographic query language for RDF data. https://www.portal.opengeospatial.org/files/?artifact_id=47664
9. PostGIS - Spatial and Geographic objects for PostgreSQL. http://www.postgis.net/

10. Bikakis, N., Tsinaraki, C., Stavrakantonakis, I., Gioldasis, N., Christodoulakis, S.: The SPARQL2XQuery interoperability framework. World Wide Web J. 1–88 (2014)
11. Stadler, C., Lehmann, J., Höffner, K., Auer, S.: LinkedGeoData: a core for a web of spatial open data. Seman. Web J. **3**(4), 333–354 (2012)
12. Patroumpas, K., Alexakis, M., Giannopoulos, G., Athanasiou, S.: TripleGeo: an ETL Tool for Transforming Geospatial Data into RDF Triples. In Proceedings of LWDM'14, EDBT/ICDT Workshops (2014) (To appear). http://www.dblab.ece.ntua.gr/pubs/uploads/TR-2014-2.pdf

SparqlFilterFlow: SPARQL Query Composition for Everyone

Florian Haag, Steffen Lohmann(✉), and Thomas Ertl

Institute for Visualization and Interactive Systems (VIS), University of Stuttgart, Universitätsstr. 38, 70569 Stuttgart, Germany
{florian.haag,steffen.lohmann,thomas.ertl}@vis.uni-stuttgart.de

Abstract. SparqlFilterFlow provides a visual interface for the composition of SPARQL queries, in particular SELECT and ASK queries. It is based on the intuitive and empirically well-founded filter/flow model that has been extended to address the unique specifics of SPARQL and RDF. In contrast to related work, no structured text input is required but the queries can be created entirely with graphical elements. This allows even users without expertise in Semantic Web technologies to create complex SPARQL queries with only little training. SparqlFilterFlow is implemented in C#, supports a large number of SPARQL constructs and can be applied to any SPARQL endpoint.

Keywords: SPARQL · RDF · Visual querying · Filter/flow · Semantic web · Linked data · Triplestore · Query language · Visualization · Faceted search

1 Introduction

SPARQL is currently the de facto standard for querying RDF data. It is supported by most triplestores, and many RDF datasets provide SPARQL endpoints [4,8]. However, writing SPARQL queries is not an easy task and requires knowledge about Semantic Web concepts and technologies. Since average users cannot be expected to have the necessary skills, visual interfaces are needed that hide the SPARQL syntax and provide graphical support for query building.

We present SparqlFilterFlow, a novel approach for visual SPARQL querying based on the filter/flow model.[1] It is implemented in C# and uses the Windows Presentation Foundation (WPF) for the graphical user interface. In contrast to related work, no structured text input is required. Instead, the queries can be created entirely with graphical elements. SparqlFilterFlow considers most features of SPARQL and can hence also be used for the construction of complex query expressions. In particular, it enables the creation of SELECT and ASK queries,

[1] While this demo paper presents the interactive implementation, the concept of applying the filter/flow model to SPARQL querying is described more in-depth in [10].

V. Presutti et al. (Eds.): ESWC Satellite Events 2014, LNCS 8798, pp. 362–367, 2014.
DOI: 10.1007/978-3-319-11955-7_49

though it may also be used for other query forms (i.e. `CONSTRUCT` and `DESCRIBE` queries) with only little variation.[2]

2 Related Work

Several attempts to assist in the creation of SPARQL queries have been presented in the last couple of years. For instance, SPARQLViz [9] provides a form-based wizard that guides the user through the query building process. Other form-based approaches are the Graph Pattern Builder of the DBpedia project [6] or Konduit VQB [5]. However, these tools represent the queries in a way that is closely related to the triple syntax of RDF and SPARQL. They do not relieve the users from the need to know how SPARQL queries are structured.

An alternative is the use of visual query languages that provide graphical representations for the different SPARQL elements and combine them to node-link diagrams. NITELIGHT [16], iSPARQL [2], and RDF-GL [13] are examples of tools based on visual query languages. A slightly higher degree of abstraction is provided by approaches that use UML-like diagrams to compose SPARQL queries [7]. While these attempts help to lower the barrier for creating correct queries, they still require knowledge of the structure and syntax of SPARQL.

SparqlFilterFlow is more related to the idea of using visual pipes to process RDF data. This approach is implemented in the tools DERI pipes [15] and MashQL [14], both of which are inspired by the mashup framework Yahoo! Pipes [3]. However, these attempts focus on rearranging, sorting and transforming data and not on the composition of SPARQL queries.

3 Filter/Flow Model

SparqlFilterFlow is based on the filter/flow model originally introduced by Young and Shneiderman in the context of relational databases and SQL querying [17]. The filter/flow model provides an intuitive representation of Boolean expressions that can be used for data filtering. The expressions are visualized as directed acyclic graphs, where the nodes define the filter criteria and the edges depict the flow of data. The thickness of the edges indicates the number of data items contained in the flow. Conjunctions are modeled as sequential paths and disjunctions as parallel paths.

Several improvements to the original filter/flow idea have been proposed over the years. We developed an extended filter/flow model that incorporates the most common ones [11]. In that model, flows are linked to explicit connection points on the filter nodes called *receptors* and *emitters*. This allows the filter nodes to receive data from several inbound flows that can be processed in different ways. Likewise, there can be several outbound flows, each representing another filter function. Along with these changes, filter nodes in the extended model are

[2] A screencast of SparqlFilterFlow and a lightweight web demo with limited functionality are publicly available at http://www.sparql.visualdataweb.org.

not restricted to atomic operations but can consider several filtering parameters. Finally, the extended model defines special nodes that display the result of filtering and can be placed at arbitrary positions in the graph, like any other filter node. This way, not only the final result set but also intermediate results can be shown.

Overall, the filter/flow graphs of the extended model have a smaller size and complexity, with positive effects on their readability, as we found in a comparative user study [12].

4 SparqlFilterFlow

SparqlFilterFlow implements our approach of applying the extended filter/flow model to SPARQL querying [10]. Users can visually compose queries by adding filter nodes and using drag-and-drop to connect them with flows.

Example. Figure 1 shows a screenshot of a filter/flow graph created with SparqlFilterFlow on the RDF dataset of Faceted DBLP [1]. Examples like this one can be created for different RDF datasets and will be shown in the ESWC demo.

The filtering starts in the initial nodes of the graph, which are the ones without inbound flows, in this case the two *type* nodes selecting all authors (`foaf:Agent`) and proceedings papers (`swrc:InProceedings`). Both sets are then gradually reduced by the subsequent filter nodes. Following the filter/flow metaphor, the thickness of the flows indicates the relative size of the sets. This helps users determine whether a given filter node has a significant effect on the data—which is the case if the thickness of the outbound flows is visibly reduced compared to the inbound flows—or even blocks the whole set.

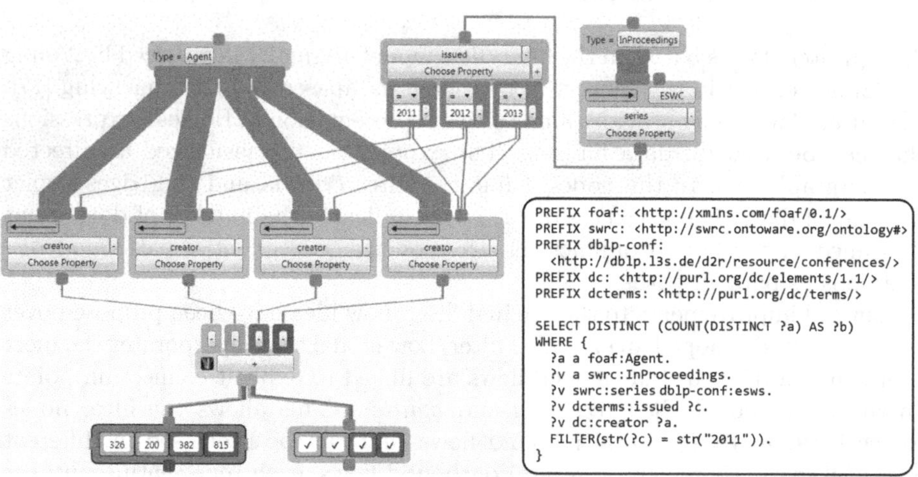

Fig. 1. Screenshot of SparqlFilterFlow: This graph counts authors of papers presented at ESWC in the years 2011 to 2013, using RDF data of Faceted DBLP [1]. One of the SPARQL queries generated by the graph is shown in the box on the right.

In the example of Fig. 1, only papers presented at ESWC (`dblp-conf:esws`) in the years 2011 to 2013 (`dcterms:issued`) are considered. This set of papers is then used to filter the set of authors by selecting only those people that co-authored one of the papers (`dc:creator`). The data stream is additionally split up into four sets, with the first three containing the ESWC authors from the individual years, and the fourth containing the ESWC authors from all three years. Finally, the four sets of authors are bundled with a corresponding node.

Filter Nodes. The example illustrates some of the filter nodes provided by SparqlFilterFlow. Their settings can be directly manipulated by users. The basic group of filters compares IRIs or literals, such as strings, numbers or dates, with operators like equality, greater or less than. Certain attributes of a literal can also be restricted in these filters, such as its language tag or its length in characters. Another group of filters examines the RDF graph structure, for instance the existence of a given property. There are also filters that help organize the structure of the filter/flow graph, including filters that bundle different sets to run in a single flow. Finally, there are specializations of general filter nodes that predefine frequently applied restrictions to ease query composition. An example is the *type* filter in Fig. 1, which is a specialization of a comparison filter.

Result Nodes. Once the desired restrictions have been defined by the combination of filter nodes, users can add result nodes that apply the restrictions in `SELECT` or `ASK` queries and display the result. In Fig. 1, two result nodes have been inserted—one showing the number of authors in each of the sets (by using a SPARQL `COUNT` function along with the `SELECT` query), and one showing whether there are any results at all (by applying a SPARQL `ASK` query).[3]

The results reveal that the total number of ESWC authors was lower in the year 2012 than in the other two years. In addition, it gets apparent that the total number of authors throughout the three considered years is barely lower than the sum of the author counts per year, indicating that many of the authors contributed only in one of the years.

SPARQL Queries. Several SPARQL queries are generated and processed during the composition of the graph. Most obviously, the result nodes issue one or more SPARQL queries when they are inserted into the graph to retrieve the values to be displayed. As an example, the SPARQL query generated to get the number of ESWC authors for the year 2011, as given by the first value in the left result node, is shown in Fig. 1.

However, SPARQL queries are also generated at other points in the graph, in particular for every emitter to determine the thickness of the outbound flows. The query expression generator of SparqlFilterFlow traverses the graph in upstream direction, starting at the emitter that issued the SPARQL query. It gradually constructs the query that comprises of the conjunctions, disjunctions and filter functions defined by the partial graph reachable upstream, usually but

[3] The result node for the `ASK` query is only added for illustration purposes in this case, as it is somewhat redundant to the result node applying the `COUNT` function.

not exclusively by adding statements to the WHERE clause of the query. Whenever any part of the graph structure or filter node settings changes, all nodes reachable downstream from the changed graph part may be affected and are thus notified, whereupon they reissue their SPARQL queries.

5 Conclusion and Future Work

SparqlFilterFlow enables the composition of SPARQL queries using exclusively graphical elements and simple text strings, while avoiding any structured text input. It requires no knowledge of Semantic Web concepts beyond a basic understanding of the RDF idea. It can be applied to any SPARQL endpoint and allows for creating complex SPARQL queries with only little training. Results from a qualitative user study indicate that the approach is comparatively usable and easy to learn [10].

Future work includes support for the creation of DESCRIBE and CONSTRUCT queries besides SELECT and ASK queries. This will require the integration of additional visualization and interaction concepts, such as an intuitive way to specify the graph structure for the result of the CONSTRUCT query. Another goal of future work is the development of features that suggest appropriate filter nodes and values based on the schema information available in the RDF data.

References

1. Faceted DBLP. http://www.dblp.l3s.de
2. OpenLink iSPARQL. http://www.oat.openlinksw.com/isparql/
3. Pipes: Rewire the web. http://www.pipes.yahoo.com/pipes/
4. SPARQL endpoints status. http://www.sparqles.okfn.org
5. Ambrus, O., Möller, K., Handschuh. S.: Konduit VQB: a visual query builder for SPARQL on the social semantic desktop. In: Proceedings of VISSW '10, CEUR-WS, vol. 565 (2010)
6. Auer, S., Bizer, C., Kobilarov, G., Lehmann, J., Cyganiak, R., Ives, Z.G.: DBpedia: a nucleus for a web of open data. In: Aberer, K., Choi, K.-S., Noy, N., Allemang, D., Lee, K.-I., Nixon, L.J.B., Golbeck, J., Mika, P., Maynard, D., Mizoguchi, R., Schreiber, G., Cudré-Mauroux, P. (eds.) ASWC 2007 and ISWC 2007. LNCS, vol. 4825, pp. 722–735. Springer, Heidelberg (2007)
7. Barzdins, G., Rikacovs, S., Zviedris, M.: Graphical query language as SPARQL frontend. In: Proceedings of 13th East-European Conference (ABDIS '09), pp. 93–107 (2009)
8. Bizer, C., Heath, T., Berners-Lee, T.: Linked data - the story so far. Int. J. Semant. Web. Inf. Syst. **5**(3), 1–22 (2009)
9. Borsje, J., Embregts, H.: Graphical query composition and natural language processing in an RDF visualization interface. Bachelor thesis, EUR (2006)
10. Haag, F., Lohmann, S., Bold, S., Ertl, T.: Visual SPARQL querying based onextended filter/flow graphs. In: Proceedings of AVI '14 (To appear)
11. Haag, F., Lohmann, S., Ertl, T.: Simplifying filter/flow graphs by subgraph substitution. In: Proceedings of VL/HCC '12, pp. 145–148. IEEE (2012)

12. Haag, F., Lohmann, S., Ertl, T.: Evaluating the readability of extended filter/flow graphs. In: GI '13, pp. 33–36. CIPS (2013)
13. Hogenboom, F., Milea, V., Frasinca, F., Kaymak, U.: RDF-GL: A SPARQL-based graphical query language for RDF. Emergent Web Intelligence: Advanced Information Retrieval, pp. 87–116. Springer, Heidelberg (2010)
14. Jarrar, M., Dikaiakos, M.D.: MashQL: A query-by-diagram topping SPARQL. In: Proceedings of ONISW '08, pp. 89–96. ACM (2008)
15. Morbidoni, C., Polleres, A., Phuoc, D.L., Tummarello, G.: Semantic web pipes. Technical report 2007-11-07, DERI (2007)
16. Russell, A., Smart, P., Braines, D., Shadbolt, N.: NITELIGHT: A graphical tool for semantic query construction. In Proceedings of SWUI '08, CEUR-WS, vol. 543 (2008)
17. Young, D., Shneiderman, B.: A graphical filter/flow representation of boolean queries: a prototype implementation and evaluation. J. Am. Soc. Inf. Sci. **44**(6), 327–339 (1993)

Visualizing RDF Data Cubes Using the Linked Data Visualization Model

Jiří Helmich[1,2(✉)], Jakub Klímek[2,3], and Martin Nečaský[1]

[1] Faculty of Mathematics and Physics, Charles University in Prague, Malostranské nám. 25, 118 00 Praha 1, Prague, Czech Republic
{helmich,necasky}@ksi.mff.cuni.cz

[2] University of Economics, Prague, Nám. W. Churchilla 4, 130 67 Praha 3, Prague, Czech Republic

[3] Faculty of Information Technology, Czech Technical University in Prague, Thákurova 9, 160 00 Praha 6, Prague, Czech Republic
klimek@fit.cvut.cz

Abstract. Data Cube represents one of the basic means for storing, processing and analyzing statistical data. Recently, the RDF Data Cube Vocabulary became a W3C recommendation and at the same time interesting datasets using it started to appear. Along with them appeared the need for compatible visualization tools. The Linked Data Visualisation Model is a formalism focused on this area and is implemented by Payola, a framework for analysis and visualization of Linked Data. In this paper, we present capabilities of LDVM and Payola to visualize RDF Data Cubes as well as other statistical datasets not yet compatible with the Data Cube Vocabulary. We also compare our approach to CubeViz, which is a visualization tool specialized on RDF Data Cube visualizations.

Keywords: Linked data · RDF · Visualization · Data cube

1 Introduction

Data analysts are accustomed to making projections from multi-dimensional datasets to low-dimensional ones using aggregations, slicing and dicing known from OLAP [3]. Those can be easily visualized by well-known and widely implemented techniques like charts, timelines, map visualizations, etc. More and more stakeholders including governments and scientific groups are publishing their datasets in a form of Linked Data[1]. Our goal is to apply the well-known visualization techniques which are understandable by non-expert users and use the Data Cube Vocabulary (DCV)[2] W3C Recommendation to achieve it. An expert

The research is supported in part by the EU ICT FP7 under No.257943, LOD2 project and in part by project SVV-2014-260100.

[1] http://wiki.planet-data.eu/web/Datasets

[2] http://www.w3.org/TR/2014/REC-vocab-data-cube-20140116/

V. Presutti et al. (Eds.): ESWC Satellite Events 2014, LNCS 8798, pp. 368–373, 2014.
DOI: 10.1007/978-3-319-11955-7_50

user prepares a data cube and a non-expert one is provided with an easy way of exploring the cube with simple faceted visualization tools. In this paper, we demonstrate that our Linked Data Visualization Model enables us to create a flexible solution for RDF Data Cube visualizations that fit into a bigger, more general framework.

2 Linked Data Visualization Model

In our previous work we defined the Linked Data Visualization Model (LDVM) [1], an abstract visualization process customized for the specifics of Linked Data. LDVM allows users to create data visualization pipelines that consist of four stages: Source Data, Analytical Abstraction, Visualization Abstraction and View.

Source Data allows a user to define a custom transformation to prepare an arbitrary dataset for further stages, which require their input to be RDF. In this paper we only consider RDF data sources such as RDF files or SPARQL endpoints, e.g. DBPedia.

The *Analytical Abstraction* enables the user to specify analytical operators that extract data to be processed from a data source and then transform it to create the desired analysis. The transformation can also compute additional characteristics or even generate a new multi-dimensional dataset. For example, we can create a statistical dataset from DBPedia by querying for resources of type `dbpedia-owl:City` and using data from their properties such as `dbpedia-owl:populationAsOf` for a dimension and `dbpedia-owl:population Total` for a measure. Further analytical steps could be performed within this stage, e.g. filtering cities from a specific country.

In the *Visualization Abstraction* stage of LDVM we need to prepare the analytical data to be compatible with our Data Cube visualizer. In the case of the analytical data already being described by DCV, this stage can be skipped. Otherwise, we would have to use a LDVM transformer to convert non-DCV statistical data to DCV as it is the format required by our visualizer. This stage is what allows users to reuse statistical analyses with results in various formats without rewriting them simply by appending an appropriate transformer.

In *View Stage*, DCV-compliant data is passed to a visualizer which creates a user-friendly data cube visualization. Based on dimension links to SDMX and SKOS concepts, a visualizer can generate more sophisticated facets in order to let the user to slice and dice the data cube. A proper visualizer should contain the well-known data cube visualization techniques and in Payola, our LDVM implementation, we have such a visualizer.

3 Mapping Non-Data Cube Data to Data Cube

While experimenting with statistical data, we have encountered Linked Data datasets which contain statistical data, but do not use DCV. Since we have a visualizer using DCV, we implemented a tool, which is capable of mapping RDF non-cube data to a form compliant with DCV as a plugin usable in LDVM

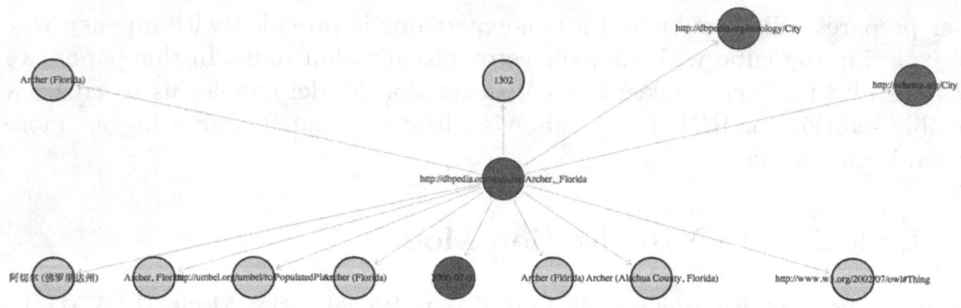

Fig. 1. User inputs a mapping pattern

analyzers. While creating a new LDVM analyzer in Payola, a user is able to create a new instance of the DCV analytical plugin. On its input the plugin receives arbitrary RDF data and based on a user-defined pattern, it maps the data to a specified DCV data structure definition. A user is asked to supply a URL containing at least one DCV data structure definition (DSD) in RDF. The user is presented with a list of available DSDs and after selecting one, a new analytical plugin is created for this DSD. This plugin can then be used by other Payola users without the need for specifying the URL with DSD and becomes a part of our extensible library of reusable DCV analyzers.

To be able to map an arbitrary dataset into a form compliant with DCV, the plugin needs the user to specify the data mapping. Based on DCV, this could be partially automated in the future. As can be seen in Fig. 1 the process is based on the *query-by-example* principle. The plugin shows the user a generic graph visualization based on a preview of the input which will be processed by the DCV analytical plugin. It lets them to select a pattern: step by step, they are asked by the application to mark a vertex, which represents one of dimensions/measures/attributes of the chosen DSD (red vertices). To narrow down the volume of the results or to be able to specify more sophisticated patterns, the user is also able to mark vertices (green ones), which refine the pattern, but do not represent any DSD component. Based on the given example, the plugin produces a SPARQL query. When executed against a SPARQL endpoint, it creates new links between existing resources and components of the DSD.

The resulting plugin can be used in various ways in an LDVM analyzer. Connected directly to a data source it works as a filter and transformer which selects only data related to the specified DSD and maps it to DCV at the same time. It could also be beneficial for a user to use the plugin as an inner analytical operator to filter and map processed data since using DCV it becomes snowflake-shaped and can be easier to work with in further analytical steps. Or, as a final plugin of an analyzer, it can transform results of a non-DCV analysis into DCV in the same way a visualization transformation does.

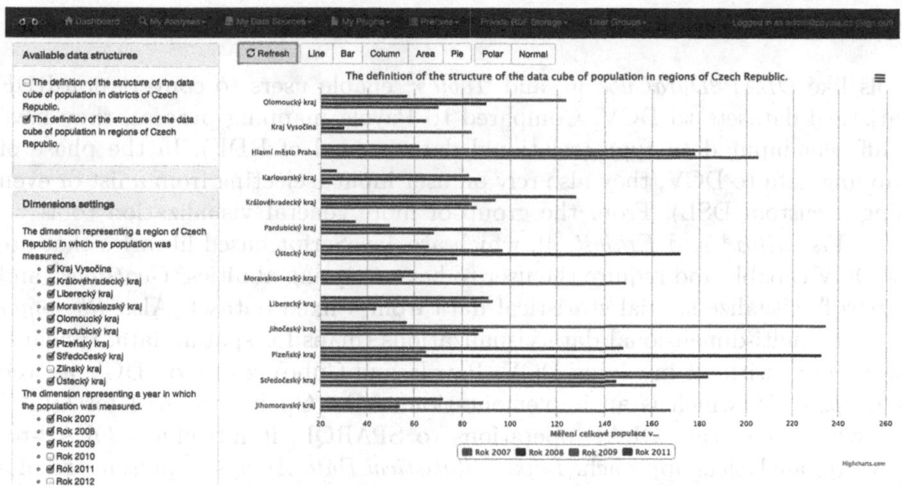

Fig. 2. An example of a visualization prepared in Payola. The four-dimensional cube is based on Czech Statistical Office data

4 Payola and CubeViz

Payola and *CubeViz* represent visualization tools that use DCV. Both of them use the Highcharts library to deliver user-friendly visualizations (line, bar, column, area and pie charts) (see Fig. 2) and enable users to obtain a permanent link to a created visualization. When sent to a non-expert user, the link enables them to view a DCV-based visualization without any knowledge of Linked Data or DCV in an environment of a faceted browser. In addition, CubeViz provides a packing layout visualization of SKOS hierarchies using the d3js library. Such a visualizer is, however, also present in Payola but not as a part of the DCV visualizer as it can be also used in a more general way for non-DCV data.

Faceted capabilities of the two tools enable a user to slice a DCV cube, which means that they are enabled to select multiple values of two dimensions, one value from the rest of dimensions and choose a single measure. Configuring facets in such a way makes the tools load a 2-dimensional table, which is visualized by the aforementioned techniques. Both tools are technically capable of dicing (produces sub-cubes), but do not offer a way of visualizing more than 2 dimensions at a time.

A DCV-based dataset could be visualized in both Payola and CubeViz with no additional transformations involved. The difference is that in Payola, any statistical RDF data can be transformed and visualized using the same data cube visualizer. In theory, CubeViz could even be used as an instance of a LDVM visualizer proving that LDVM is a more general and reusable framework. This could be achieved by supplying it with a DCV compatible LDVM visualization abstraction produced by a data cube LDVM pipeline. However, at the time of writing this paper, CubeViz was unstable and was crashing when loading data from our SPARQL endpoints so we could not finish evaluating this possibility.

5 Related Work

Tools like *OLAP2DataCube* [6] and *Tables*[3] enable users to convert non-RDF statistical datasets to DCV. Compared to Payola mapping process, they have a different input data type (relational data instead of RDF). In the phase of mapping data to DCV, they also rely on user input (selecting from a list or even using a custom DSL). From the group of more general visualization tools we name *VisualBox*[4] and *Exhibit* [4], which are JavaScript based libraries that are not DCV capable and require the user to have scripting abilities. *GeoGlobe*[5] and map4rdf[6] visualize spatial statistical data from a fixed dataset. Also *Rhizomer* [2] offers multi-dimensional data visualizations (maps for spatial data, timeline, charts, etc.) without involving DCV. Payola and CubeViz rely on DCV as well as *Olap4ld* [5], which is an implementation of the Open Java API for OLAP and while converting OLAP operations to SPARQL, it introduces OLAP-to-SPARQL analytical approach. *Linked Statistical Data Analysis*[7] presents results of SDMX-ML transformations into DCV. It enables a user to visualize correlations over a fixed statistical datasets prepared by a set of custom analytical and transformation scripts[8].

6 Conclusions

In this demo we present the Payola Data Cube Vocabulary mapping plugin that demonstrates how DCV can be utilized throughout the stages of LDVM. For the View Stage of LDVM we implemented a DCV visualizer in Payola that is capable of visualizing DCV datasets and provides a user with facets with slicing and dicing of data cubes. A sample DCV visualization is located at http://vis.payola.cz/dcv_czso. Compared to CubeViz, which is another tool for RDF Data Cube visualization, Payola, thanks to being a LDVM implementation, offers a wider range of usage scenarios. One of those scenarios is visualizing statistical data that is not described by DCV simply by mapping it to DCV as a part of a standard LDVM pipeline.

References

1. Brunetti, J.M., Auer, S., García, R., Klímek, J., Nečaský, M.: Formal linked data visualization model. In: Proceedings of the 15th International Conference on Information Integration and Web-based Applications & Services (IIWAS'13), pp. 309–318 (2013)

[3] http://idi.fundacionctic.org/tabels/
[4] https://github.com/alangrafu/visualbox
[5] http://data.i2g.pl/insigos/hz-geo/globe/
[6] http://oegdev.dia.fi.upm.es/map4rdf/
[7] http://stats.270a.info/
[8] https://github.com/csarven/publishing-statistical-linked-data/blob/master/csarven.publishing-statistical-linked-data.pdf?raw=true

2. Brunetti, J.M., García, R., Auer, S.: From overview to FACETs and pivoting for interactive exploration of semantic web data. Int. J. Seman. Web Inf. Syst. **9**(1), 1–20 (2013)
3. Chaudhuri, S., Dayal, U.: An overview of data warehousing and OLAP technology. SIGMOD Record **26**(1), 65–74 (1997)
4. Huynh, D.F., Karger, D.R., Miller, R.C.: Exhibit: lightweight structured data publishing. In: Proceedings of the 16th International Conference on World Wide Web, WWW '07, New York, NY, USA, pp. 737–746. ACM (2007)
5. Kämpgen, B., Harth, A.: No Size fits all – running the star schema benchmark with SPARQL and RDF aggregate views. In: Cimiano, P., Corcho, O., Presutti, V., Hollink, L., Rudolph, S. (eds.) ESWC 2013. LNCS, vol. 7882, pp. 290–304. Springer, Heidelberg (2013)
6. Salas, P.E., Martin, M., Mota, F.M.D., Breitman, K., Auer, S., Casanova, M.A.: Olap2datacube: an ontowiki plugin for statistical data publishing. In: Proceedings of the 2nd Workshop on Developing Tools as Plug-ins, TOPI 2012, New York, NY, USA. ACM (2012)

Prod-Trees: Semantic Search for Earth Observation Products

M. Karpathiotaki[1(✉)], K. Dogani[1], M. Koubarakis[1], B. Valentin[2], P. Mazzetti[3], M. Santoro[3], and S. Di Franco[3]

[1] National and Kapodistrian University of Athens, Athens, Greece
{mkarpat,koubarak}@di.uoa.gr
[2] Space Applications Services, Zaventem, Belgium
[3] Institute of Atmospheric Pollution Research - National Research Council, Rome, Italy

Abstract. Access to Earth Observation products remains difficult for end users in most domains. Although various search engines have been developed, they neither satisfy the needs of scientific communities for advanced search of EO products, nor they use standardized vocabularies reusable from other organizations. To address this, we present the Prod-Trees platform, a semantically-enabled search engine for EO products enhanced with EO-netCDF, a new standard for accessing Earth Observation products.

1 Introduction and Motivation

The demand for aerial and satellite imagery, and products derived from them has been increasing over the years, in parallel with technological advances that allow producing a bigger variety of data with an increasing quality and accuracy. As a consequence of these advances, and the multiplication of deployed sensors, the amount of Earth Observation (EO) data collected and stored has exploded.

However, access to EO products remains difficult for end users in most scientific domains. Various search engines for EO products, generally accessible through Web portals, have been developed. For example, see the interfaces offered by the European Space Agency portal for accessing data of Copernicus, the new satellite programme of the European Union[1] or the EOWEB portal of the German Aerospace Center (DLR)[2]. Typically these search engines allow searching for EO products by selecting some high level categories (e.g., the mission from which the product was generated, the satellite instrument that was used etc.) and specifying basic geographical and temporal filtering criteria. Although this might suit the needs of very advanced users that know exactly what dataset they are looking for, other scientific communities or the general public require more application-oriented means to find EO products.

This work was supported by the Prod-Trees project funded by ESA ESRIN.

[1] http://gmesdata.esa.int/web/gsc/home

[2] https://centaurus.caf.dlr.de:8443/eoweb-ng/template/default/welcome/entryPage.vm

V. Presutti et al. (Eds.): ESWC Satellite Events 2014, LNCS 8798, pp. 374–378, 2014.
DOI: 10.1007/978-3-319-11955-7_51

In this demo paper, we present a semantically-enabled search engine for EO-products currently under development by the project Prod-Trees funded by the European Space Agency. The system uses semantic technologies to allow users to search for EO products in an application-oriented way using free-text keywords (as in search engines like Google), their own domain terms or both, in conjuction with the well-known interfaces already available for expert users. A specific innovation of the presented system is the use of a new standard called EO-netCDF, currently under development in Prod-Trees and expected to be submitted to OGC, for accessing EO products annotated with netCDF. netCDF is a well-known standard consisting of set of self-describing, machine-independent data formats and software libraries that support the creation, access, and sharing of array-oriented scientific data.[3]

The Prod-Trees system has been developed using state of the art semantic technologies developed by the partners of the project: the company Space Applications Services, the National and Kapodistrian University of Athens and the research institute CNR.

2 The Prod-Trees Platform

The Prod-Trees platform is a semantically-enabled EO products search engine. It allows end-users to search for EO products using filtering criteria provided by the EO-netCDF specification and the EO vocabulary designed and implemented in the Prod-Trees project[4]. Figure 1 depicts the architecture of the platform, which partially re-uses components from the RARE platform[5].

The web interface of the Prod-Trees platform allows the users to submit free-text queries, navigate to the ontology browser, select applications terms defined in the supported ontologies and finally, search for EO product by specifing EO-netCDF parameters and controlled (bounding box, time, range) search criteria.

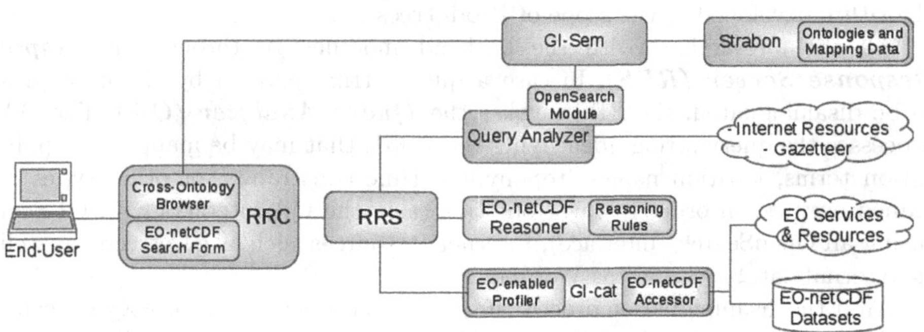

Fig. 1. The Prod-Trees platform architecture

[3] http://www.unidata.ucar.edu/software/netcdf/

[4] http://deepenandlearn.esa.int/tiki-index.php?page=Prod-Trees+Project

[5] http://deepenandlearn.esa.int/tiki-index.php?page=RARE%20Project

When the user has filled the search form, the Query Analyzer is responsible for displaying a number of different interprentations for the inserted free-text. After the user has selected the semantics she wants to be used for the search, the backend service is called, generates one or more queries and sends them to GI-cat through its EO-netCDF Profiler. GI-cat searches for the matching EO products and returns back the metadata. Depending on the nature of each product (JPG, XML, HDF, etc.), this may be either visualized on-line or downloaded on the local system. The following paragraphs describe in more detail the components of the Prod-Trees architecture and their interaction.

The ***Rapid Response***[6] ***Client (RRC)*** provides the user interface to the Prod-Trees platform and communicates with several backend services. It displays a search form, where a user can give as input EO-specific search criteria or free text and can navigate to the supported ontologies through the ***Cross-Ontology Browser***. This component is a browser for ontologies expressed in SKOS that allows the users to exploit the knowledge contained in the supported ontologies. It provides relevant information for each concept and highlights the connections between different (but related) concepts belonging to the same or other ontologies. Its role is to support the user in the query creation phase, as a disambiguation and discovery tool. The browser is accessed via the RRC search page.

GI-Sem [4] is a middleware which is in charge of interconnecting heterogeneous and distributed components. Its main role in the Prod-Trees platform is to create a connection between the Cross-Ontology Browser and the supported ontologies. GI-Sem performs remote queries to Strabon and returns the results to the Cross-Ontology Browser. It can also be omitted from the system by using a version of the Cross Ontology Browser that calls Strabon directly.

Strabon [3] is a well-known spatiotemporal RDF store. It holds the supported ontologies and the cross-ontology mappings appropriately encoded in RDF. The supported SKOS ontologies are the GSCDA, GEOSS, GEMET and NASA GCMD. The mappings between these ontologies were created using an algorithm developed in the scope of Prod-Trees [2].

All the interactions with the backend modules go through the ***Rapid Response Server (RRS)***. In case a query string entered by the user need to be disambiguated, the RRS invokes the ***Query Analyzer (QA)***. The QA processes the query string, identifying the words that may be mapped to application terms, location names (toponyms), time constraints, or other types of named entities. In order to carry out this task, the QA interacts with GI-Sem (using an OpenSearch[7] interface), Internet Resources such as gazetteers, as well as external databases such as Wordnet.

After the disambiguation process, if the user has selected an ontology concept, the RRS interacts with the ***EO-netCDF Reasoner*** to obtain the filter criteria

[6] The name "Rapid Response" comes from project RARE where the main application of the developed system was rapid response for various emergencies (e.g., humanitarian or environmental). Similarly, for the Rapid Response Server mentioned below.

[7] http://www.opensearch.org/Home

for the search. The reasoner uses reasoning rules to map an ontology concept to EO-netCDF search criteria. These rules have been built manually with the consultation of experts in the context of the project Prod-Trees and the previous project RARE. RSS uses the returned results to build an appropriate query that is sent to GI-cat.

GI-cat [1] is an implementation of a catalogue service, which can be used to access various distributed sources of Earth Observation products. In Prod-Trees, it has been extended to support products compliant with the EO-netCDF convention. Thus, it provides an EO-netCDF enabled discovery and access engine, so that products annotated with EO-netCDF are searchable and accessible to the users.

3 Demonstration Overview

We will now present the core scenarios that we plan to demonstrate at ESWC.

In the first scenario the user inserts a free-text query, for example "water". The system replies by presenting a number of different interpretations for the inserted text, which are provided by the Query Analyzer during the disambiguation phase. This way it is clear for the user what are the semantics of the text on which the search will be based. The default interpretation for "water" maps this text to the concept "water" of GSCDA ontology. In case the user is not satisfied with this interpretantion, she can select another one from a proposed list, for example "water use", "water temperature", "ocean level" and more. Another option is to use the inserted text without any specific interpretation. In this case, a simple text-based search will be performed. The EO-netCDF reasoner is used to map the concept "water" of GSCDA to EO-netCDF parameters with specific values. This is done using appropriate mapping rules which allow us to connect concepts of an ontology (in this case water of GSCDA) to EO-netCDF parameters with specific values (in this case combinations of satellite sensor type, resolution, polarization etc.). As a result, GI-cat returns only the EO products that include EO-netCDF parameters with these values. Figure 2 displays the first two results of the keyword search for "water".

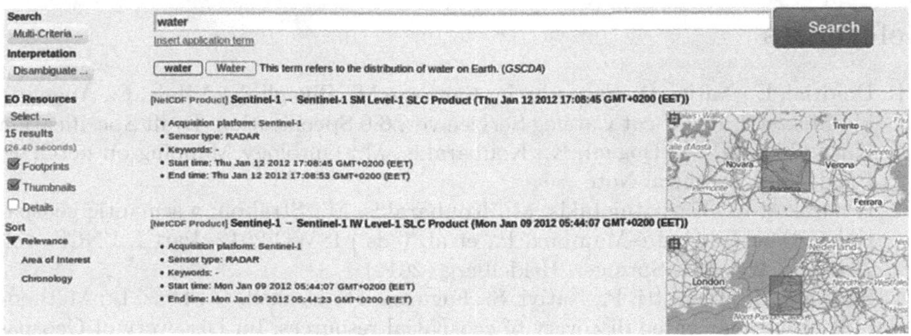

Fig. 2. Search results for the keyword "water"

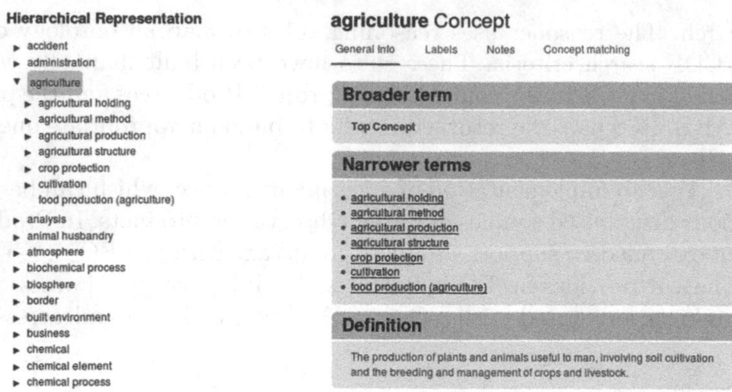

Fig. 3. The Cross-Ontology Browser displaying the GEMET ontology

Instead of the text queries, the user can also use the ontology browser to select terms he wants to search for. Figure 3 displays the interface of the browser. The selected concept is copied back to the initial text area. Assuming the user has selected the concept "agriculture" of GEOSS ontology, she can add then more keywords (toponyms, date etc.) to the text area in order to restrict the search, for example "agriculture Bahamas 2010". Keywords with toponyms are also disambiguated using the Geonames gazetteer. Afterwards, the workflow is similar to the one described above.

Finally, the third scenario will show how to search using EO-related search criteria. This option might be more appropriate for expert users. In particular, the user can search using specific metadata attributes such as sensor type, bounding box, time, etc. and by specifying one or more EO-netCDF parameters. The search will be based on these attributes and will return only EO products that satisfy them. For example, selecting the parameter "Sensor Type" an optional value would be "optical" or "radar". As the EO-netCDF parameter is provided directly by the user, the EO-netCDF reasoner is bypassed and only the GI-cat component is invoked to return the relevant resources.

A video demonstrating the above functionality is available at http://bit.ly/ProdTreesPlatform.

References

1. Boldrini, E., Nativi, S., Papeschi, F., Santoro, M., Bigagli, L., Vitale, F., Angelini, V., Mazzetti, P.: GI-cat Catalog Service ver. 6.0 Specification. Draft Specification
2. Karpathiotaki, M., Dogani, K., Koubarakis, M.: Ontology Mapping on netCDF. Prod-Trees Technical Note
3. Kyzirakos, K., Karpathiotakis, M., Koubarakis, M.: Strabon: a semantic geospatial DBMS. In: Cudré-Mauroux, P., et al. (eds.) ISWC 2012, Part I. LNCS, vol. 7649, pp. 295–311. Springer, Heidelberg (2012)
4. Santoro, M., Mazzetti, P., Nativi, S., Fugazza, C., Granell, C., Diaz, L.: Methodologies for augmented discovery of geospatial resources. In: Discovery of Geospatial Resources: Methodologies, Technologies and Emergent Applications, chap. 9

UnifiedViews: An ETL Framework for Sustainable RDF Data Processing

Tomáš Knap[1,2](✉), Maria Kukhar[1], Bohuslav Macháč[1], Petr Škoda[1], Jiří Tomeš[1], and Ján Vojt[1]

[1] Department of Software Engineering, Faculty of Mathematics and Physics, Charles University in Prague, Malostranské nám. 25, 118 00 Prague, Czech Republic
[2] EEA s.r.o, Vlašská 349/15, 118 00 Prague, Czech Republic
tomas.knap@mff.cuni.cz

Abstract. We present UnifiedViews, an Extract-Transform-Load (ETL) framework that allows users to define, execute, monitor, debug, schedule, and share ETL data processing tasks, which may employ custom plugins created by users. UnifiedViews differs from other ETL frameworks by natively supporting RDF data and ontologies. We are persuaded that UnifiedViews helps RDF/Linked Data consumers to address the problem of sustainable RDF data processing; we support such statement by introducing list of projects and other activities where UnifiedViews is successfully exploited.

1 Introduction and Basic Concepts of UnifiedViews

The advent of Linked Data [1] accelerates the evolution of the Web into an exponentially growing information space where the unprecedented volume of data offers information consumers a level of information integration that has up to now not been possible.

Suppose a consumer building a data mart integrating information from various RDF and non-RDF sources. There are lots of tools used by the RDF/Linked Data community[1], which may support various phases of the data processing; e.g., a consumer may use *any23*[2] for extraction of non-RDF data and its conversion to RDF data, *Virtuoso*[3] database for storing RDF data and executing SPARQL (Update) queries [2,3], *Silk* [5] for RDF data linkage, or *Cr-batch*[4] for RDF data fusion. Nevertheless, the consumer who is preparing a *data processing task* producing the desired data mart typically has to (1) configure every such tool properly (using a different configuration for every tool), (2) implement

This work was supported by Seventh Framework Programme of the European Union under Grant Agreement number 611358 and by Specific Research Project at Charles University in Prague under number SVV-2014-260100.

[1] http://semanticweb.org/wiki/Tools
[2] https://any23.apache.org/
[3] http://virtuoso.openlinksw.com/
[4] https://github.com/mifeet/cr-batch

V. Presutti et al. (Eds.): ESWC Satellite Events 2014, LNCS 8798, pp. 379–383, 2014.
DOI: 10.1007/978-3-319-11955-7_52

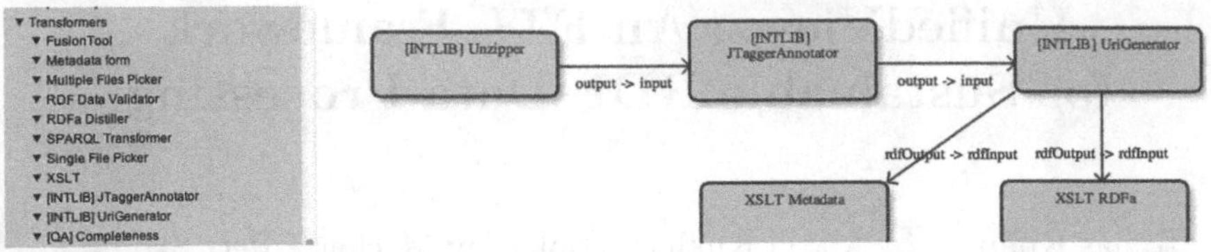

Fig. 1. UnifiedViews framework – definition of a data processing task

a script for downloading and unpacking certain source data, (3) write his own script holding the set of SPARQL Update queries refining the data, (4) implement custom transformers which, e.g., enrich processed data with the data in his knowledge base, (5) write his own script executing the tools in the required order, so that every tool has all desired inputs when being launched, (6) prepare a scheduling script, which ensures that the task is executed regularly, and (7) extend his script with notification capabilities, such as sending an email in case of an error during task execution.

Maintenance of such data processing tasks is challenging. Suppose for example that a consumer defines tens of data processing tasks, which should run every week. Further, suppose that certain data processing task does not work as expected. To find the problem, the consumer typically has to browse/query the RDF data outputted by certain tool; to realise that, he has to manually launch the required tool with the problematic configuration and load the outputted RDF data to the store, such as Virtuoso, supporting browse/query capabilities. Furthermore, when other consumers prepare similar data processing tasks, they cannot use the already prepared scripts, they cannot use the tools' configurations already prepared by the consumer.

The general problem RDF/Linked Data consumers are facing is that they have to write most of the logic to define, execute, monitor, schedule, and share the data processing tasks themselves. Furthermore, consumers do not get any support regarding the debugging of the tasks. To address these problems, we developed UnifiedViews, an Extract-Transform-Load (ETL) framework, where the concept of data processing task is a central concept. Another central concept is the native support for RDF data format and ontologies.

A *data processing task* (or simply task) consists of one or more data processing units. A *data processing unit* (DPU) encapsulates certain business logic needed when processing data (e.g., one DPU may extract data from a SPARQL endpoint or apply a SPARQL query). Every DPU must define its required/optional inputs and produced outputs. UnifiedViews supports exchange of RDF data between DPUs. Every tool produced by RDF/Linked Data community can be used in UnifiedViews as a DPU, if a simple wrapper is provided[5].

UnifiedViews allows users to define and adjust data processing tasks, using graphical user interface (an excerpt is depicted in Fig. 1). Every consumer may also define their custom DPUs, or share DPUs provided by others together with

[5] https://grips.semantic-web.at/display/UDDOC/Creation+of+Plugins

their configurations. DPUs may be drag&dropped on the canvas where the data processing task is constructed. Data flow between two DPUs is denoted as an edge on the canvas (see Fig. 1); a label on the edge clarifies which outputs of a DPU are mapped to which inputs of another DPU. UnifiedViews natively supports exchange of RDF data between DPUs; apart from that, files and folders may be exchanged between DPUs.

UnifiedViews takes care of task schedulling, a user may configure UnifiedViews to get notifications about errors in the tasks' executions; user may also get daily summaries about the tasks executed. UnifiedViews ensures that DPUs are executed in the proper order, so that all DPUs have proper required inputs when being launched. UnifiedViews provides users with the debugging capabilities – a user may browse and query (using SPARQL query language) the RDF inputs to and RDF outputs from any DPU. UnifiedViews allows users to share DPUs and tasks as needed.

The code of UnifiedViews is available at https://github.com/UnifiedViews/Core under a combination of GPLv3 and LGPLv3 license[6]. The demo of the tool is available at http://odcs.xrg.cz:8080/uv-demo. You can use the account eswc/eswc to work with the framework.

2 Related Work

There are plenty of ETL frameworks for preparing tabular data to be loaded to data warehouses, some of them are also opensource[7] – for example Clover ETL (community edition)[8]. In all these frameworks custom DPUs may be created in some way, but the disadvantage of these non-RDF ETL frameworks is that there is no support for RDF data format and ontologies in the framework itself. As a result, these non-RDF ETL frameworks are, e.g., not prepared to suggest ontological terms in DPU configurations, a feature important when preparing SPARQL queries or mappings of the table columns to RDF predicates. Furthermore, these frameworks do not have a native support for exchanging RDF data between DPUs; also the existing DPUs do not support RDF data format, URIs for identifying things according to Linked Data principles. Therefore, further, we discuss the related work in the area of RDF ETL frameworks.

ODCleanStore (Version 1)[9], was the original Linked data management framework, which was used as an inspiration for ODCleanStore (Version 2)[10], the student's project implemented at Charles University in Prague and defended in March 2014. UnifiedViews is based on ODCleanStore (Version 2). Linked Data Manager (LDM)[11] is a Java based Linked (Open) Data Management suite to

[6] http://www.gnu.org/licenses/gpl.txt, http://www.gnu.org/licenses/lgpl.txt

[7] http://sourceforge.net/directory/business-enterprise/enterprise/data-warehousing/etl/

[8] http://www.cloveretl.com/products/community-edition

[9] http://sourceforge.net/projects/odcleanstore/

[10] https://github.com/mff-uk/ODCS/

[11] https://github.com/lodms/lodms-core

schedule and monitor required ETL tasks for web-based Linked Open Data portals and data integration scenarios. LDM was developed by Semantic Web Company in Austria[12]. They currently decided to replace LDM, used by their clients, with UnifiedViews and further continue to maintain UnifiedViews together with the Czech Linked Data company, Semantica.cz[13].

DERI Pipes[14] is an engine and graphical environment for general Web Data transformations. DERI Pipes supports creation of custom DPUs; however, an adjustment of the core is needed when new DPU is added, which is not acceptable; in UnifiedViews, it is possible to reload DPUs as the framework is running. DERI Pipes also does not provide any solution for library version clashes; on the other hand, in UnifiedViews, DPUs are loaded as OSGi bundles, thus, it is possible to use two DPUs requiring two different versions of the same dependency (library) and no clashes arise. In DERI pipes, it is not possible to debug inputs and outputs of DPUs.

Linked Data Integration Framework (LDIF) [4] is an open-source Linked Data integration framework that can be used to transform Web data. The framework consists of a predefined set of DPUs, which may be influenced by their configuration; however, new DPUs cannot be easily added[15]. LDIF provides user interface to monitor results of executed tasks.; however, when compared with UnifiedVicws, LDIF does not provide any graphical user interface for defining and scheduling tasks, managing DPUs, browsing and querying inputs from and output to the DPUs, and managing users and their roles in the framework. LDIF also does not provide any possibility to share pipelines/DPUs among users. On the other hand, LDIF provides possibility to run tasks using Hadoop[16].

3 Impact of the UnifiedViews Framework

The goal of the *OpenData.cz initiative*[17] is to extract, transform and publish Czech open data in the form of Linked Data, so that the initiative contributes to the Czech Linked (Open) Data cloud. For this effort, UnifiedViews framework is successfully used since September 2013.

Project INTLIB[18] aims at extracting (1) references between legislation documents, such as decisions and acts, (2) entities (e.g., a citizen, a president) defined by these documents and (3) the rights and obligations of these extracted entities. UnifiedViews is used in INTLIB to extract data from selected sources of legislation documents, convert it to RDF data, and provide it as Linked Data.

[12] http://www.semantic-web.at
[13] http://semantica.cz/en/
[14] http://pipes.deri.org/
[15] http://ldif.wbsg.de/
[16] http://hadoop.apache.org/
[17] http://opendata.cz
[18] http://www.isvav.cz/projectDetail.do?rowId=TA02010182

COMSODE FP7 project[19] has the goal to create a publication platform for publishing (linked) open data. UnifiedViews is used there as the core tool for converting hundreds of original datasets to RDF/Linked Data.

UnifiedViews framework is being integrated to the stack of tools produced by the *LOD2 project*[20]. As a result, anybody using tools from LOD2 stack, such as Virtuoso and Silk, has also the possibility to use UnifiedViews. UnifiedViews framework is intended to be used for commercial purposes by companies Semantica.cz, Czech Republic, and Semantic Web Company, Austria, to help their customers to prepare and process RDF data.

4 Conclusions

We presented UnifiedViews, an ETL framework with a native support for processing RDF data. The framework allows to define, execute, monitor, debug, schedule, and share data processing tasks. UnifiedViews also allows users to create custom plugins - data processing units. We are persuaded that UnifiedViews is a matured tool, which addresses the major problem of RDF/Linked Data consumers – the problem of sustainable RDF data processing; we support such statement by introducing list of projects where UnifiedViews is successfully used and mention two commercial exploitations of the tool.

The practical demonstration of UnifiedViews at the conference will clearly demonstrate how UnifiedViews can help RDF/Linked Data consumers and show the real instance of UnifiedViews with tens of data processing tasks and DPUs motivated by real use cases.

References

1. Bizer, C., Heath, T., Berners-Lee, T.: Linked data - the story so far. Int. J. Seman. Web Inf. Syst. **5**(3), 1–22 (2009)
2. Garlik, S.H., Seaborne, A., Prud'hommeaux, E.: SPARQL 1.1 Query Language. W3C Recommendation (2013). http://www.w3.org/TR/2013/REC-sparql11-query-20130321/. Accessed 20 March 2014
3. Gearon, P., Passant, A., Polleres, A.: SPARQL 1.1 Update. Technical report, W3C. 21 March 2013. http://www.w3.org/TR/2013/REC-sparql11-update-20130321/. Accessed 20 March 2014
4. Schultz, A., Matteini, A., Isele, R., Bizer, C., Becker, C.: LDIF: linked data integration framework. In: Proceedings of the Second International Workshop on Consuming Linked Data (COLD), Bonn, Germany. CEUR-WS.org (2011)
5. Volz, J., Bizer, C., Gaedke, M., Kobilarov, G.: Silk - A link discovery framework for the web of data. In: Proceedings of the WWW2009 Workshop on Linked Data on the Web (LDOW), Madrid, Spain. CEUR-WS.org (2009)

[19] http://www.comsode.eu/

[20] http://lod2.eu/

SmarT INsiGhts (STING) - An Intelligence Application for Querying Heterogeneous Databases

Vikash Kumar(✉), Ganesh Selvaraj, Andy Shin, and Paulo Gottgtroy

Inland Revenue, Auckland, New Zealand
{vikash.kumar,ganesh.selvaraj,andy.shin,paulo.gottgtroy}@ird.govt.nz

Abstract. This paper presents an application implemented at Inland Revenue, New Zealand that enables users to access data seamlessly from different types of databases. It was developed to provide our investigators the ability to get comprehensive information about a business entity or a group of entities. The solution presented so far has been implemented using relational, semantic and document databases. It allows its users to pose fairly complex queries on the mentioned databases and retrieve results without having to know the specific query languages. Up to this point, it supports the presentation of results in graph and tabular formats.

Keywords: Semantic database · Enterprise semantics · Heterogeneous database access · Semantic intelligence

1 Introduction

One of the advantages of semantic technologies has been to bridge the silos of data in a typical enterprise architecture. Many enterprises are, for various reasons, still uncomfortable with the idea of completely wrapping their data via a semantic access layer. Some of their concerns arise from having to re-engineer or completely lose out on the host of functionalities already developed upon traditional relational databases. In this paper, we present a real example of how we successfully implemented an application that queries relational, semantic and document databases seamlessly depending on the nature of the query. This implementation does not replace the existing relational database but extends it by pairing it with the semantic and document databases. The resulting application paved the way to make use of the best features of each type of database enabling efficient key, pattern and text based queries on the available data. The presented application called SmarT INsiGhts (STING)[1] is meant for investigators of Inland Revenue, New Zealand (IR-NZ) for analyzing transactions (events) received from an entity (company) or a group of entities. The main goal of STING is to provide a simple way of accessing a variety of

[1] Demonstration video of the Application: http://youtu.be/enVGpQTwusE.

V. Presutti et al. (Eds.): ESWC Satellite Events 2014, LNCS 8798, pp. 384–388, 2014.
DOI: 10.1007/978-3-319-11955-7_53

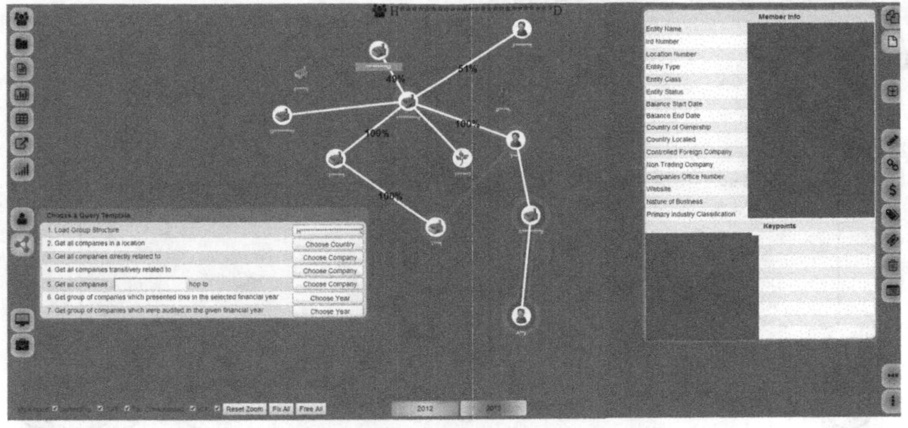

Fig. 1. The STING application

information about these entities. It is achieved by enabling the investigators to answer simple or complex queries through a single interface.

2 The STING Application

In this section, we describe the STING application and its use in our business along with the details about its architecture and the underlying technologies.

2.1 Motivation

When receiving any transaction from customers, IR-NZ needs to assess the level of risk associated with the transaction. Understanding how companies and group of companies are organized for tax purposes is one of the critical pieces of information that IR-NZ needs to have. The application presented in this paper (Fig. 1[2]) helps in visualizing such comprehensive information gathered from multiple sources in interactive graph and tabular representations.

2.2 Architecture

A high level conceptual architecture of STING is presented in Fig. 2. The importance of this architecture lies in its model-driven hybrid backend that consists of the following modules:

Common Domain Model. This is a java based abstraction layer for all the underlying databases. The main purpose of this layer is to help software developers in building applications based on the data abstraction without worrying about the underlying knowledge representation and implementation database.

[2] For privacy and security considerations, actual data has been masked in this figure and in the demo video.

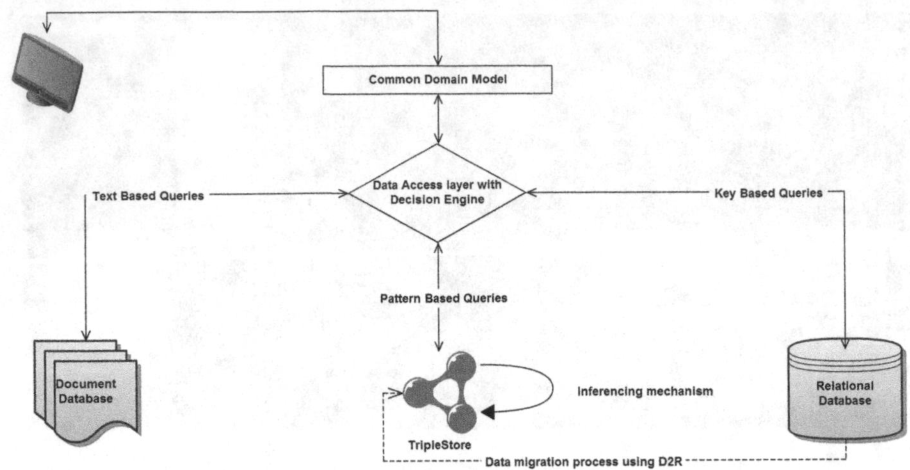

Fig. 2. High level conceptual architecture of the system

The Data Access Layer (DAL) and Decision Engine. DAL helps in performing CRUD (Create, Read, Update, Delete) operations on the databases. Since there are several database implementations, this layer is powered by a decision engine that decides on which database a query should be executed. The decision engine is currently working based on several predefined static criteria. The reason for using the static predefined criteria was because of our fixed and well defined business domain. The key features and operations of each database are mentioned in Table 1. The additional advantage of this architecture is its ability to integrate diverse sources of data while maintaining a good performance as seen in this application.

Table 1. Key features of the used databases

	Relational database	Semantic database	Document database
Query type	Key based queries *Example: Get companies with Name = "XX"*	Pattern based queries *Example: Get companies which have risk patterns similar to company "XX"*	Text based queries *Example: Get all documents which has a text containing "XX"*
Schema	Schema constrained data	Uses Ontology but not constrained. Anyone can say Anything on Any topic (AAA)	Flexible Schema
Usage	Existing applications keep working on this.	Data gets migrated in a batch. Reasoning & pattern search is done here.	Data gets migrated in a batch. Text search is done here.

STING's Query Approach. The application is developed based on a "Single Page" concept where modules are used to allow not only customization of the application but also the usage of "docks" that allow access to the application's functionalities without impacting on its usability aspect. The query functionality follows this principle by allowing users to pose semi-customized queries in natural language to the system through the selection of a dock icon.

Based on past experiences, we compiled a list of most common queries that an investigator might be interested in and presented them in natural language through the querying interface. In some cases, a user may make slight changes in a query by clicking on its highlighted area, which provides them with alternative variables as options. Some queries are also adapted based on the context of the user, such as user's location, level of authentication, etc. [1]. Behind the natural language presentation, we have a SPARQL serialization of the query that is posed to the semantic triple store. Parametrized SPARQL 1.1 queries are used for binding the variable parameters chosen by the user.

Semantic queries can therefore be posed using a natural language template or predefined "function buttons" on the user interface. The output from these queries is represented as interactive graph structure (single or overlaid graphs) or in tabular format where the users can expand or contract the entities spawning out of a certain node. Examples of few of our pattern based queries in natural language is shown in Table 2.

The whole system uses an adapted version of the Organization ontology[3], which in turn is mapped to the IR-NZ upper ontology. The IR-NZ upper ontology is a lightweight adaptation of Proton[4] and DOLCE+DnS Ultralite (DUL) ontologies[5]. One of the prime considerations in design of ontology was to be able to record provenance information and to query the 'situation' at a certain point of time in past. The reasoning is limited to answering pattern based queries over entity structure using SPARQL 1.1 features. In future, we plan to integrate more detailed information from external open data sources.

Tools and Technologies. The User Interface is a single page web application built using Angular.js[6]. D3.js[7] is used to visualize information as graph in Scalar

Table 2. Some of our sample semantic queries

Query ID	Query text
Query 1	*Get all entities which are transitively related to a particular entity.*
Query 2	*Get the group structure for a given group of companies.*
Query 3	*Filter companies of a certain group by Location.*
Query 4	*Find relationships between a chosen set of entities.*

[3] http://www.w3.org/TR/2014/REC-vocab-org-20140116/
[4] http://www.ontotext.com/proton-ontology
[5] http://www.loa.istc.cnr.it/ontologies/DUL.owl
[6] http://www.angularjs.org
[7] http://www.d3js.org

Vector Graphics. The graph is formatted using a customized force layout method based on Barnes-Hut Algorithm [2]. Node.Js[8] is a JavaScript framework that is used as web server enabling asynchronous calls from the I/O to the databases. OWLIM Lite (version 5.4) [3] is used as our triplestore and Sesame (version 2.7.3) API is used to access information from OWLIM Lite. D2RQ[9] (version 0.8.1) is used to generate RDF dump from an existing relational database. We are still evaluating the document database. Our choice would be mongoDb for its powerful features and wide community support. For this application, we used spring data for mongoDb[10] and pymongo[11] libraries to load and query the mongoDb.

3 Conclusions

In this paper, we presented an application intended to help investigators in assessing risk profiles of entities by answering their queries from different databases. SQL, SPARQL and text-based queries are posed asynchronously on the respective databases depending on the nature of a query. The architecture allows for an unhindered user experience bereft of any noticeable latency issues. We showed how a specific application can use best of different worlds in answering queries without compromising its existing infrastructure. During the demo, we will also share our lessons learned in using different technologies along with the semantic technology.

Acknowledgements. This work has been supported by Information, Intelligence and Communications unit of Inland Revenue. We would like to thank the team members of Analytics and Insight for their valuable inputs towards finalization of this Application.

References

1. Kumar, V., Fensel, A., Fröhlich, P.: Context based adaptation of semantic rules in smart buildings. In: The 15th ACM International Conference on Information Integration and Web-based Applications & Services (iiWAS2013), Vienna, Austria, December 2013
2. Barnes, J., Hut, P.: A hierarchical O(N log N) force-calculation algorithm. Nature **324**(4), 446–449 (1986)
3. Bishop, B., Kiryakov, A., Ognyanoff, D., Peikov, I., Tashev, Z., Velkov, R.: OWLIM: a family of scalable semantic repositories. Semant. Web **2**(1), 33–42 (2011)

[8] http://www.nodejs.org
[9] http://www.d2rq.org
[10] http://projects.spring.io/spring-data-mongodb/
[11] https://pypi.python.org/pypi/pymongo/

OLAP4LD – A Framework for Building Analysis Applications Over Governmental Statistics

Benedikt Kämpgen(✉) and Andreas Harth

Institute AIFB, Karlsruhe Institute of Technology, Karlsruhe, Germany
{benedikt.kaempgen,harth}@kit.edu

Abstract. Although useful governmental statistics have been published as Linked Data, there are query processing and data pre-processing challenges to allow citizens exploring such multidimensional datasets in pivot tables. In this demo paper we present OLAP4LD, a framework for developers of applications over Linked Data sources reusing the RDF Data Cube Vocabulary. Our demonstration will let visiting developers and dataset publishers explore European statistics with the Linked Data Cubes Explorer (LDCX), will explain how LDCX makes use of OLAP4LD, and will show common dataset modelling errors.

1 Introduction

According to the G8 Open Data Charter and Technical Annex[1] governmental statistics provide data of high value for improving transparency and encouraging innovative re-use of data. In frontends such as Microsoft Excel, pivot tables have proved intuitive to build and easy to understand for exploring statistics. If published using Linked Data, statistics become easier to integrate with other data, e.g., the GDP of a country in one and the population in another dataset with linked country identifiers allow to compute the GDP per capita.

We have published more than 5,000 datasets from Eurostat[2] as Linked Data, yet, there are challenges to allow citizens to explore such datasets in pivot tables: Eurostat datasets exhibit varying number of dimensions, e.g., geo, time, gender and age for the population dataset, which makes visualisations, such as in two-dimensional line diagrams, and comparisons difficult. How to translate analytical operations to queries over Linked Data sources? How to reduce the dimensionality of datasets? Eurostat statistics are originally published using SDMX and re-published as Linked Data in a Google App Engine; other statistics such as from the World Bank are published differently. How to ensure that necessary data is extracted from distributed sources and properly modelled? How to pre-process and integrate heterogeneously modelled datasets?

Current systems [1,2,4,5] do not help developers to build pivot analysis applications over general datasets. This demo paper provides the following contributions:

[1] https://www.gov.uk/government/publications/open-data-charter/g8-open-data-charter-and-technical-annex

[2] http://estatwrap.ontologycentral.com/table_of_contents.html

V. Presutti et al. (Eds.): ESWC Satellite Events 2014, LNCS 8798, pp. 389–394, 2014.
DOI: 10.1007/978-3-319-11955-7_54

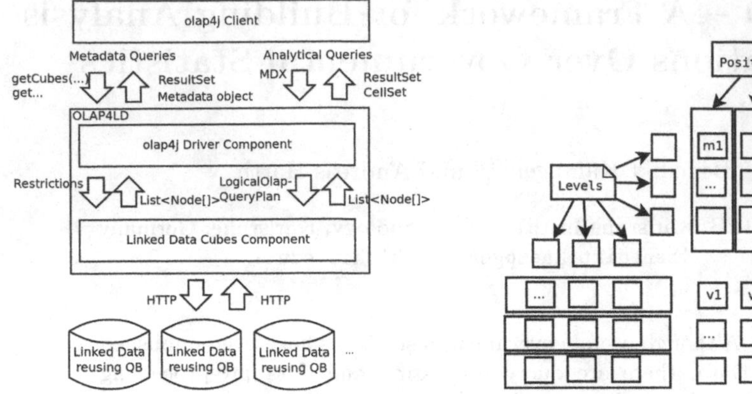

Fig. 1. Components of OLAP4LD.

Fig. 2. Pivot table schema from a typical MDX query.

(1) In Sect. 2, we present OLAP4LD, a development framework for applications over Linked Data sources reusing the RDF Data Cube Vocabulary.
(2) In Sect. 3, we present the Linked Data Cubes Explorer (LDCX) that is based on OLAP4LD and allows the exploration of governmental statistics.

After describing related work in Sect. 4, we conclude in Sect. 5.

2 OLAP4LD Integration and Analysis Framework

OLAP4LD[3] is an Open Source Java framework for building analysis applications over statistics published as Linked Data. As illustrated at the top of Fig. 1, OLAP4LD implements olap4j, a standard interface between OLAP frontends and backends. Application developers can make use of a common abstraction of datasets as data cubes, the quasi-standard analytical query language MDX, and existing olap4j clients such a Saiku and JPivot. As illustrated at the bottom of the architecture, OLAP4LD provides access to multidimensional datasets published as Linked Data reusing the W3C-standardised RDF Data Cube Vocabulary (QB). QB allows to represent general datasets such as statistics or from sensors and is widely-adopted.

OLAP4LD roughly consists of two components. The *olap4j Driver Component* translates queries from an olap4j client to queries more suitable for processing over Linked Data sources in the *Linked Data Cubes Component*. Vice-versa, the olap4j component translates results from Linked Data sources to representations understandable by the client.

Metadata queries are methods such as `getCubes(...)` and `getMeasures (...)` that return multidimensional elements, i.e., data cubes containing facts with members for a pre-defined set of dimensions (independent variables) that

[3] http://linked-data-cubes.org/index.php/Olap4ld

determine the value of one or more measures (dependent variables). In Linked Data, multidimensional elements are identified and described using sets of RDF terms; OLAP4LD represents RDF terms using `Nodes` from the *NxParser* library. The schema of multidimensional elements from Linked Data, i.e., the name and types of columns of `List<Node[]>` is adopted from the olap4j specification.

Analytical (MDX) queries return data from a data cube to be displayed in a two-dimensional pivot table as illustrated in Fig. 2: one or more queried data cubes, lists of member combinations (positions) from a fixed set of levels for rows and columns, and member combinations from a fixed set of levels as filter conditions. For instance, from a Eurostat dataset "Employment Rate", we may query for a pivot table containing sex as dimension on columns (e.g., position `F`), time and place as dimensions on rows (e.g., position `2005`, `AT`). Results of analytical queries fill the cells of the pivot table, e.g., that 64.9 % of women in Austria in 2005 have been employed.

OLAP4LD defines an analytical query as a nested set of common operators from an OLAP algebra: For every queried data cube, `Base-Cube` loads the relevant data defined by the dataset URI; for the chosen measures or if no measure is chosen the first measure, `Projection` removes not selected measures; for every possible member combination on axes, `Dice` removes filtered dimension members; `Slice` removes every dimension not mentioned in either column or row axis (i.e., aggregates over with aggregation function of measures); and for any higher level selected on columns or rows axes, `Roll-Up` aggregates dimensions to higher levels. Finally, all resulting data cubes are joined via `Drill-Across`. Note, the drill-across operator requires as input equally-structured data cubes. For more information about the definition of analytical queries, see the documentation and previous work [3].

In the *Linked Data Cubes Component*, for metadata queries, any instance of `qb:DataSet` is mapped to a data cube. Similarly, other resources represented in QB are mapped to multidimensional elements. For analytical queries, OLAP operators are executed over instances of `qb:DataSet`.

Queries can be executed in different ways, e.g., reusing a common OLAP engine over relations or in-memory, and directly with an RDF store; aggregated values from the data cube may be computed on demand or views selected and maintained; similarly, data pre-processing and integration can be done differently, e.g., a database may be pre-filled with all relevant data in advance or populated dynamically; also, there are various ways with which information can be provided, e.g., packed in data dumps or queryable from several SPARQL endpoints. For executing metadata and analytical queries, an OLAP4LD application has to implement a *Linked Data Cubes Engine.* Developers can reuse existing engines and concentrate on the challenges of query execution and integration over Linked Data sources.

3 OLAP4LD for the Linked Data Cubes Explorer

The Linked Data Cubes Explorer (LDCX)[4] is based on OLAP4LD and allows citizens to explore governmental statistics. In our demonstration, we will let visitors try the three-step user interface of LDCX: (1) a user selects one or more comma-separated URIs of *qb:DataSets*. With "Explore Dataset...", metadata queries are issued to populate the user interface; (2) the user selects measures to be displayed in the pivot table cells; (3) the user selects dimensions to add member combinations to rows and columns of the pivot table and clicks "Update Table...". Note LDCX automatically queries every dimension on the most granular level since multi-level hierarchies are rarely used and users can still slice dimensions to view datasets on a higher aggregation level. In our demonstration we will show how changes in modelling are propagated to LDCX by live modifying a published QB dataset. Also, we show common modelling errors in existing QB datasets such as missing dimension `rdfs:range` or `qb:CodeList` and observations not adhering to data structure definitions.

LDCX implements an *EmbeddedSesameEngine* as Linked Data Cubes Engine that evaluates metadata queries using SPARQL templates filled with *Node* parameters. For each multidimensional element, there are several SPARQL templates for different ways of modelling, e.g., measures can define their own aggregation functions or *AVG* and *COUNT* are used by default. To evaluate analytical queries, the logical query plan is translated to a physical query plan; for each separate drill-across sub-query plan, we execute our *OLAP-to-SPARQL* algorithm [3] and join the results. Before executing a metadata or analytical query with SPARQL, the EmbeddedSesameEngine automatically loads necessary data into an embedded Sesame RDF store. EmbeddedSesameEngine first resolves all queried dataset URIs, then in turn asks SPARQL queries to its store for additional URIs to resolve and load; EmbeddedSesameEngine resolves all instances of concepts defined in the QB specification in the order they can be reached from the dataset URI, from `qb:DataStructureDefinitions` over `qb:ComponentProperty` to single `qb:Concepts`. Since there is no standard way to publish QB observations, the engine assumes that the observations are represented as blank nodes and stored at the location of the dataset URI. Such "directed crawling" of the data cube has the advantage that necessary data is found quickly and not all information has to be given in one location, but can be distributed and reused, e.g., the range for the *ical:dtstart* dimension is provided by its URI. EmbeddedSesameEngine ensures that the entire QB dataset is loaded and well-formed according to the QB specification; SPARQL queries materialise implicit information and check integrity constraints.

For an online questionnaire not considering drill-across, 8 of 20 asked business engineering students at KIT used LDCX in 11 tasks, e.g., to find "the average GDP for Germany" in example and real datasets and rated the system according to 13 statements with average 2.5 from 1 (strongly agree) to 10 (strongly disagree), e.g., regarding usability. LDCX seems usable and robust;

[4] http://ldcx.linked-data-cubes.org/projects/ldcx/

improvements are possible regarding slow performance, counter-intuitive error messages and cumbersome selection of datasets. For a workload of 5 drill-down and 5 slice queries over datasets with 10 to 1000 observations we observed that elapsed query time was mainly spent for loading the datasets and much less for query plan generation and execution.

4 Related Work

The most common format to share datasets is XML. Other representations such as the Google *Dataset Publishing Language*, *SDMX* and *XBRL* require specific tools or focus on specific domains and provide few possibilities to link, and less-widely adopted mechanisms to access data over the Web.

Applications are available that, similar to LDCX, try to hide most RDF-specificities from the user to analyse a QB dataset. In the *stats.270a.info* analysis platform [1] users can select two datasets from a fixed set for integration on the time and location dimension and for finding correlations in a scatter plot. McCusker et al. [4] present *qb.js* to analyse the effect of tobacco policies on consumption. Though presenting useful systems to analyse QB datasets in specific data integration scenarios, it is unclear how well such approaches can be applied to more general use cases. Other systems provide more general analyses: Salas et al. [5] present *CubeViz* that offers faceted-browsing and visualizations of QB datasets. Hoefler [2] present the *CODE Visual Analytics Wizard* that automatically suggests appropriate chart types for QB datasets. LDCX automatically loads and checks the modelling of datasets and allows exploration of general datasets in pivot tables. Although the interface of LDCX is not as nice as of other systems, we argue that OLAP4LD reduces the costs of building analysis applications since UIs and backends are separated and can be reused.

5 Conclusions

In this demo paper, we have presented OLAP4LD, a framework for building analysis applications with Linked Data reusing the RDF Data Cube Vocabulary. In a demonstration of OLAP4LD we allow visitors to validate and explore governmental statistics with the Linked Data Cubes Explorer (LDCX).

References

1. Capadisli, S., Auer, S., Riedl, R.: Linked statistical data analysis. In: Semantic Web Challenge 2013 (2013)
2. Hoefler, P.: Linked data interfaces for non-expert users. In: Cimiano, P., Corcho, O., Presutti, V., Hollink, L., Rudolph, S. (eds.) ESWC 2013. LNCS, vol. 7882, pp. 702–706. Springer, Heidelberg (2013)
3. Kämpgen, B., Harth, A.: No size fits all – running the star schema benchmark with SPARQL and RDF aggregate views. In: Cimiano, P., Corcho, O., Presutti, V., Hollink, L., Rudolph, S. (eds.) ESWC 2013. LNCS, vol. 7882, pp. 290–304. Springer, Heidelberg (2013)

4. McCusker, J.P., McGuinness, D.L., Lee, J., Thomas, C., Courtney, P., Tatalovich, Z., Contractor, N., Morgan, G., Shaikh, A.: Towards next generation health data exploration: a data cube-based investigation into population statistics for tobacco. In: Proceedings of the 2013 46th Hawaii International Conference on System Sciences (2013)
5. Salas, P.E.R., Martin, M., Mota, F.M.D., Auer, S., Breitman, K., Casanova, M.A.: Publishing statistical data on the web. In: Proceedings of the 2012 IEEE Sixth International Conference on Semantic Computing (2012)

The ProtégéVOWL Plugin: Ontology Visualization for Everyone

Steffen Lohmann[1(✉)], Stefan Negru[2], and David Bold[1]

[1] Institute for Visualization and Interactive Systems (VIS), University of Stuttgart, Universitätsstr. 38, 70569 Stuttgart, Germany
steffen.lohmann@vis.uni-stuttgart.de

[2] Faculty of Computer Science, Alexandru Ioan Cuza University, Strada General Henri Mathias Berthelot 16, Iasi, Romania
stefan.negru@info.uaic.ro

Abstract. The Visual Notation for OWL Ontologies (VOWL) provides a visual language for the representation of ontologies. In contrast to related work, VOWL aims at an intuitive and interactive visualization that is also understandable to users less familiar with ontologies. This paper presents ProtégéVOWL, a first implementation of VOWL realized as a plugin for the ontology editor Protégé. It accesses the internal ontology representation provided by the OWL API and defines graphical mappings according to the VOWL specification. The information visualization toolkit Prefuse is used to render the visual elements and to combine them into a force-directed graph layout. Results from a preliminary user study indicate that ProtégéVOWL does indeed provide a comparatively intuitive and usable ontology visualization.

1 Introduction

Ontologies are not only the backbone of the Semantic Web but increasingly used in many different contexts. More and more people in modern knowledge societies get in contact with ontologies as a means to structure and organize information. This requires a new generation of tools that enable not only experts but also non-experts to work with ontologies. Visualizations play a key role in this context, as they can assist users in reading and understanding ontologies.

While several visualizations for ontologies have been developed in the last couple of years, they either focus on specific ontology aspects or are hard to interpret for non-expert users. The silver bullet would be an ontology visualization that is equally comprehensive and comprehensible. It must be easy to read and printable but also provide intuitive means to interactively explore ontologies.

Having these goals in mind, we developed the Visual Notation for OWL Ontologies (VOWL) that provides a well-specified visual language for the user-oriented representation of ontologies. It defines graphical depictions for a large part of the Web Ontology Language (OWL) that are combined to a graph visualization representing the ontology. This paper presents ProtégéVOWL, a first implementation of VOWL realized as a plugin for the ontology editor Protégé.

V. Presutti et al. (Eds.): ESWC Satellite Events 2014, LNCS 8798, pp. 395–400, 2014.
DOI: 10.1007/978-3-319-11955-7_55

2 Related Work

Many ontology visualizations focus on the representation of certain aspects of ontologies. Examples are OWLViz[1], OntoGraf[2], KC-Viz [10], OWLPropViz[3], and the RelFinder [7] that visualize either the class hierarchy of ontologies or selected property relations. This is similar in approaches that use special types of diagrams to depict ontologies, such as treemaps [5,12], nested graphs [12], or cluster maps [4]. While these visualizations are partly very usable, they are limited to ontology aspects that can be expressed with the respective diagram types.

A very powerful type of diagram related to OWL and often reused to visualize ontologies is the class diagram of the Unified Modeling Language (UML). Examples of OWL tools that make use of UML class diagrams are the Visual Ontology Modeler (VOM)[4] or OWLGrEd [2]. Mappings between OWL elements and UML class diagrams are precisely defined in the Ontology Definition Metamodel (ODM) published by OMG[5]. However, while class diagrams are well-known to many people working in IT, they are less familiar to people from other domains who usually find it difficult to interpret these diagrams [11].

Most closely related to VOWL are works that use graph visualizations to represent ontologies. Examples are TGViz [1], NavigOWL [8], GrOWL [9], and SOVA[6]. All these tools provide force-directed graph layouts resulting in appealing visualizations. TGViz, OntoGraf, and NavigOWL use simple notations with little visual variation, making the different OWL elements hardly distinguishable. In contrast, GrOWL and SOVA define more elaborated notations consisting of various symbols, colors, and node shapes. However, they are designed for users with expertise in description logic and related formalizations.

3 Visual Notation for OWL Ontologies (VOWL)

The main goal of VOWL is to provide a visual language that can also be understood by users less familiar with ontologies. We therefore avoided to use formal symbols to represent OWL constructs, like in GrOWL or SOVA. Instead, we designed visual elements that are more intuitive and easy to use. They are based on only a handful graphical primitives forming the alphabet of the visual language: Classes are depicted as circles that are connected by lines representing the property relations, while property labels and datatypes are shown in rectangles. The visual elements are combined into a graph visualization representing the ontology and being arranged in a force-directed layout.

---

1 http://protegewiki.stanford.edu/wiki/OWLViz
2 http://protegewiki.stanford.edu/wiki/OntoGraf
3 http://protegewiki.stanford.edu/wiki/OWLPropViz
4 http://thematix.com/tools/vom/
5 http://www.omg.org/spec/ODM/
6 http://protegewiki.stanford.edu/wiki/SOVA

Some OWL elements are treated in a special way to increase the readability of the visualization. For instance, the predefined classes `owl:Thing` and `rdfs:Resource` usually do not carry domain information. They are multiplied and depicted in smaller size in order to give them less prominence in the visualization. Similarly, `rdfs:datatype` and `rdfs:literal` are shown multiple times so that datatype properties are arranged radially around the classes they are connected with.

In addition, VOWL defines a color scheme for a better distinction of the different elements. The colors are described in an abstract way leaving room for customization, while concrete colors and color codes are recommended by VOWL. However, colors are not required in order to use the visualization but it is also understandable when printed in black and white or read by color-blind people. Details that rely on color, such as the subtle distinction of `owl:Class` and `rdfs:Class` may be added as text information in these cases. The complete VOWL specification is publicly available at the persistent URL http://purl.org/vowl/spec.

4 ProtégéVOWL

ProtégéVOWL implements version 2.0 of the VOWL specification to a large extent. Like the specification, it focuses on the visualization of the ontology schema (i.e. the classes, properties and datatypes, sometimes called TBox), while it does not consider individuals and data values (the ABox) for the time being. ProtégéVOWL is based on Java and deployed as a JAR file that has to be copied to the *plugins* folder of the Protégé installation. It is released under the MIT license and available for download at http://vowl.visualdataweb.org.

Figure 1 shows a screenshot of ProtégéVOWL depicting revision 1.35 of the SIOC Core Ontology[7]. The user interface consists of three parts: The *VOWL Viewer* displaying the ontology visualization, the *VOWL Sidebar* listing details about the selected element, and the *VOWL Controls* allowing to adapt the force-directed graph layout.

VOWL Viewer: ProtégéVOWL uses the visualization toolkit Prefuse [6] to render the visual elements and to arrange them in a force-directed graph layout. It accesses the internal ontology representation provided by the OWL API of Protégé and transforms it into the data model required by Prefuse. The OWL elements are then mapped to the graphical representations as specified by VOWL and combined to a graph. Prefuse uses a physics simulation to generate the force-directed graph layout, consisting of three different forces: edges act as springs, while nodes repel each other and drag forces ensure that nodes settle [6]. The forces are iteratively applied resulting in an animation that dynamically places the nodes. Users can smoothly zoom in to explore certain ontology parts in detail or zoom out to analyze the global structure of the ontology. They can pan the

[7] http://rdfs.org/sioc/spec/

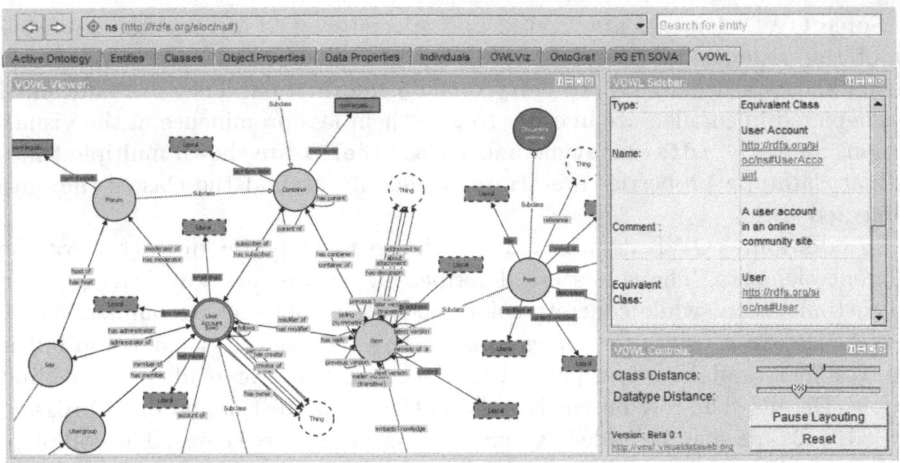

Fig. 1. ProtégéVOWL consists of the ontology visualization, a sidebar and control panel.

background and move elements around, which results in a repositioning of the nodes by animated transitions according to the force-directed layout.

VOWL Sidebar: If an element is selected in the visualization, details about it are shown in the sidebar, such as for the selected class `sioc:UserAccount` in Fig. 1. The details are provided by the OWL API and include the URI of the element and comments added to it, among others. URIs are displayed as hyperlinks that can be opened with a web browser or other tools for further exploration.

VOWL Controls: The repelling forces of classes and datatypes are adaptable with the two sliders in the VOWL Controls. This allows to fine-tune the force-directed layout in accordance with the size and structure of the visualized ontology. Since datatypes have a separate repelling force, they can be placed in close proximity to the classes they are connected with—to emphasize their radial arrangement and further increase readability. In addition, the layout animation can be paused via the VOWL Controls. This does not only reduce processor load but can also be useful to manually adapt, copy, and print the visualization.

5 Evaluation and Future Work

We conducted a small user study in which we compared ProtégéVOWL with the SOVA plugin for Protégé, which is conceptually and technically most closely related to ProtégéVOWL (see Sect. 2). We recruited six participants that were familiar with the idea of ontologies but would not consider themselves ontology experts. We presented them both ProtégéVOWL and SOVA in alternating order. They had to solve 16 different tasks with the tools (eight with each) using two ontologies of different size (MUTO[8] and FOAF[9]). The tasks were related to different aspects of ontologies, such as the approximate number of classes or whether any class is equivalent to a given one. Finally, the participants had to rate both tools with regard to the perceived intuitiveness and ease-of-use.

All six participants preferred ProtégéVOWL over SOVA. They considered the VOWL notation to be more clear and liked the clean layout of the visualization. They also found it easier to distinguish different OWL elements and to understand how they are related. Overall, the results suggest that ProtégéVOWL does provide a comparatively intuitive and usable ontology visualization that can also be understood by users without much expertise in ontologies. However, this needs to be further validated in a more comprehensive user study in the future.

Apart from that, we plan to integrate more features into ProtégéVOWL. In particular, we would like to enable the representation of individuals and find more compact visualizations for very large ontologies. Furthermore, we are currently working on a web implementation of VOWL based on JavaScript and SVG and using the visualization library D3 [3]. A first prototype is available along with ProtégéVOWL at http://vowl.visualdataweb.org.

References

1. Alani, H.: TGVizTab: an ontology visualisation extension for Protégé. In: Proceedings of the VIKE '04 (2004)
2. Bärzdiņš, J., Bärzdiņš, G., Čerāns, K., Liepiņš, R., Sproģis, A.: OWLGrEd: a uml style graphical notation and editor for OWL 2. In: Proceedings of the OWLED '10. CEUR, vol. 614 (2010)
3. Bostock, M., Ogievetsky, V., Heer, J.: D3 data-driven documents. IEEE Trans. Vis. Comput. Graph. **17**(12), 2301–2309 (2011)
4. Fluit, C., Sabou, M., van Harmelen, F.: Ontology-based information visualization. In: Visualizing the Semantic Web, pp. 36–48. Springer, London (2002)
5. García-Palacios, F.J., Colomo-Palacios, R., García, J., Therón, R.: Towards an ontology modeling tool. a validation in software engineering scenarios. Expert Syst. Appl. 39(13), 11468–11478 (2012)
6. Heer, J., Card, S., Landay, J.: Prefuse: a toolkit for interactive information visualization. In: Proceedings of the CHI '05, pp. 421–430. ACM (2005)
7. Heim, P., Lohmann, S., Stegemann, T.: Interactive Relationship Discovery via the Semantic Web. In: Aroyo, L., Antoniou, G., Hyvönen, E., ten Teije, A., Stuckenschmidt, H., Cabral, L., Tudorache, T. (eds.) ESWC 2010, Part I. LNCS, vol. 6088, pp. 303–317. Springer, Heidelberg (2010)
8. Hussain, A., Latif, K., Rextin, A., Hayat, A., Alam, M.: Scalable visualization of semantic nets using power-law graphs. Appl. Math. Inf. Sci. **8**(1), 355–367 (2014)
9. Krivov, S., Villa, F., Williams, R., Wu, X.: On visualization of OWL ontologies. In: Semantic Web, pp. 205–221. Springer, New York (2007)

[8] http://purl.org/muto/core#

[9] http://xmlns.com/foaf/spec/

10. Motta, E., Mulholland, P., Peroni, S., d'Aquin, M., Gomez-Perez, J.M., Mendez, V., Zablith, F.: A novel approach to visualizing and navigating ontologies. In: Aroyo, L., Welty, C., Alani, H., Taylor, J., Bernstein, A., Kagal, L., Noy, N., Blomqvist, E. (eds.) ISWC 2011, Part I. LNCS, vol. 7031, pp. 470–486. Springer, Heidelberg (2011)
11. Negru, S., Haag, F., Lohmann, S.: Towards a unified visual notation for OWL ontologies: Insights from a comparative user study. In: Proceedings of the I-SEMANTICS '13, pp. 73–80. ACM (2013)
12. Storey, M.-A., Noy, N., Musen, M., Best, C., Fergerson, R., Ernst, N.: Jambalaya: An interactive environment for exploring ontologies. In: Proceedings of the IUI '02, pp. 239–239. ACM (2002)

A Rule-Based System for Monitoring of Microblogging Disease Reports

Wojciech Lukasiewicz(✉), Kia Teymourian, and Adrian Paschke

AG Corporate Semantic Web, Institute for Computer Science,
Freie Universität Berlin, Berlin, Germany
{wojlukas,kia,paschke}@inf.fu-berlin.de

Abstract. Real-time microblogging messages are an interesting data source for the realization of early warning systems that track the outbreaks of epidemic diseases. Microblogging monitoring systems might be able to detect disease outbreaks in communities faster than the traditional public health services. The realization of such systems requires a message classification approach that can distinguish the messages which concern diseases from other unrelated messages. The existing machine learning classification approaches have some difficulties due to the lack of a longer history-based learning curve and the short length of the messages. In this paper, we present a demonstration of our rule-based approach for classification of disease reports. Our system is built based on the extraction of disease-related named entities. The type identification of the recognized named entities using the existing knowledge bases helps our system to classify a message as a disease report. We combine our approach with further text processing approaches like term frequency calculation. Our experimental results show that the presented approach is capable of classifying the disease report messages with acceptable precision and recall.

1 Motivation

People from all around the world use microblogging services on a daily basis and send messages, among others, about their current health condition. Those behaviors and tools on the Web provide us with the perfect technological-sociological background to develop a real-time disease and epidemic outbreak surveillance system. It would monitor the Twitter message data stream, decide if certain posts can be considered disease reports and cluster the appropriate ones based on the sender's geographic whereabouts.

To motivate the underlying problem which we address, we present a couple of example messages which come from a Twitter data stream:

This work has been partially supported by the "InnoProfile-Transfer Corporate Smart Content" project funded by the German Federal Ministry of Education and Research (BMBF) and the BMBF Innovation Initiative for the New German Länder-Entrepreneurial Regions. Special thanks to Gary Ng for the implementation of the demonstration GUI.

V. Presutti et al. (Eds.): ESWC Satellite Events 2014, LNCS 8798, pp. 401–406, 2014.
DOI: 10.1007/978-3-319-11955-7_56

"This feeling sick is starting to bore me now. #headaches #fever piss right off"
"Ew I think I have the worst fever in the book of fevers"

are messages that should be considered disease reports, whereas

"I have bieber fever. justinbieber #BELIEVEtour"
"my parents are arguing about saturday night fever is before or after grease um"

are messages that definitely should not be considered disease reports.

In this paper, we present a demonstration[1] of our rule-based approach that can distinguish the disease reports from other microblogging messages containing the disease-related keywords.

Typical obstacles for classifiers of microblogging messages using standard machine learning approaches are:

Short Text Messages: Due to the length of the microblogging messages, the established text classification approaches, such as *Naïve Bayes*, turn out not to be very effective. Given the fact that the microblogging messages are rather short (140 characters is the Twitter limit), the training data set would have to be enormous for the algorithm to be able to distinguish the messages properly.

Term Frequency Equals Document Frequency: Again because of the length limit the terms are most often used only once in the messages which might make this numerical statistic not very meaningful.

Lack of the Learning Curve: The microblogging messages are not per default labelled regarding their disease relevance and the classifier does not get any feedback during its lifetime unless the messages would be marked manually – in the contrary to, e.g., spam filters, where the users help the system to learn and improve it by saying that this email is or is not spam. As a result there is no relation between experience of the classifier and its performance.

Specific Language: The colloquial Internet and microblogging diction differs from high language standards. This slang is often influenced by current offline events and thus constantly evolves requiring re-training the classifier.

The above mentioned problems clearly show that the existing text classification approaches cannot achieve high precision in the classification of the microblogging messages. Therefore we propose a new, content-based approach which performs the analysis and classification of short, specific text messages.

2 Rule-Based Content Analysis of Microblogging Messages

A classifier is required that can assign the microblogging messages to one of three classes: disease report (***DR***), no disease report (***NDR***) and possible disease report (***PDR***, which means that the poster's intentions were not clear).

We propose a rule-based classification that can classify each message by triggering multiple rules which are applied in a sequential order. A specific score

[1] Our demonstrator is hosted at: http://www.mi.fu-berlin.de/en/inf/groups/ag-csw/Research/Demos/.

is assigned to each rule and in case that it matches when analyzing a message m, we add the rule score to the overall score of m. At the end, we compare the calculated score to the fix *thresholds* and decide which class should a message belong to. The thresholds, a pair (t_n, t_p), should be interpreted as follows:

$$\boldsymbol{DR} = \{m \mid score(m) \in (-\infty, t_n)\}$$
$$\boldsymbol{PDR} = \{m \mid score(m) \in [t_n, t_p]\}$$
$$\boldsymbol{NDR} = \{m \mid score(m) \in (t_p, \infty)\}$$

Our rules are grouped in several categories. Provided that a message contains a disease-related keyword, it is processed by the following content analysis rules:

Category-1: Rules Based on Frequent Words: In the first step, we analyze the messages considering the most common words appearing in the disease report candidates.

We have set up a service which filters the Twitter stream based on the set of predefined keywords and stores the messages locally. We collected over 300 million candidates for disease reports between Jan 16th, 2013 and Aug 17th, 2013 and created taxonomies for each keyword by summing up the term frequencies of all words occurring in the messages containing this keyword. The stop words are removed and the remaining tokens are stemmed.

We analysed the lists of frequent words and manually assigned a classification sentiment for every *keyword* $\rightarrow$ *word* collocation. For this we used the Twitter search engine to obtain sample messages containing both words and, based on the context, assigned values from the range $[-5, \ldots, 5]$, with -5 meaning a definitely disease-related and 5 a definitely not disease-related collocation. Having that, we find all keywords in an analysed message and look for sentiments in the corresponding taxonomies. This way we calculate the *disease score* of a single message.

Category-2: Rules Based on the Types of Detected Named Entities: We use DBPedia Spotlight [8] for the extraction of semantic resources from the text. Other existing public services like AlchemyAPI, OpenCalais and Zemanta cannot be used because of heavy processing load of the message stream. We use an internal mirror of the DBpedia and the DBpedia spotlight on a cluster of hosts. After the identification of the semantic sources, we query their types, like *rdf:type* (dbpedia-owl:Disease), *dbpedia-owl:type* to check the type of the recognized semantic concepts. This approach lets us derive more meaning from the tweets, e.g., take disease-related words from outside our taxonomies or the synonyms into account. Let us consider the following tweet: *"found out that I need surgery on the first week of holidays and I had glandular fever and Ross river fever in the past 6 months. Not happy"* In this example the message that would not be classified as disease report without the help of semantic concepts. The word *happy* would be the only match in the sentiments list (see **Category-3**) and no collocation from the taxonomy of *fever* would be found. DBPedia Spotlight however annotates *"glandular fever"* (dbpedia:Infectious_mononucleosis) and *"Ross river fever"* (dbpedia:Ross_River_fever) as diseases.

Category-3: Rules Based on General Mood of Messages: To improve the classification precision, we apply further rules to extract the sentiment of the message.

We use the word list by Hansen et al. [3] to look up the message's tokens and thus calculate its *general mood*. Unfortunately, the disease report candidates generally tend to have a negative score calculated by this rule because of the diction that consists mainly of words with negative sentiment.

Category-4: Other Rules: The microblogging messages are often enriched with *emoticons* (also called *smileys*, conventional symbols for expressing emotions) to put emphasis on the author's mood. For that reason we check the tweet for the presence of smileys.

Furthermore, when people tell about their illness when having a fever, they sometimes mention its height. We could assume that a number found in a message (restricted to ranges which correspond to fever temperatures, both in Fahrenheit and Celsius scale) means with high probability that it concerns a disease.

3 Related Work

The studies by Signorini [10] and Chew [2] exemplarily explain how massively the Twitter data stream is influenced by current real life events. Among many other triggers, like for example the American Idol contest, the authors of these publications took a look at the 2009 *Swine Flu* (H1N1) outbreak.

Stewart and Diaz [11] present different approaches of health-related Twitter surveillance. Discussing Early Warning, as well as Outbreak Control and Analysis Systems, they introduce several biosurveillance algorithms and techniques (Khan [6]; Hutwagner et al. [5]; Basseville and Nikiforov [1]) and use them to analyse the crowd's behavior during the 2011 *enterohemorrhagic Escherichia coli* (EHEC) outbreak in Germany. Their main focus was to detect aberration patterns when the observed variable (here: tweets containing the "EHEC" keyword but more generally: the number of tweets regarding diseases that do not reveal seasonal patterns) exceeds an expected threshold value. They used four different biosurveillance algorithms for early detection, each one of which proved to be at least one day faster than well-established early warning systems, like e.g. The Early Warning and Response System of the European Union[2], MedISys[3] or ProMED-mail[4].

Lampos and Cristianini [7] investigate the 2009 *Swine Flu* outbreak. Hu et al. [4] aim to cluster Twitter messages by topic and extract meaningful human-readable labels for each cluster. They decompose the unstructured text using NLP and then transform the syntactic feature space (parse [sub]trees) into semantic feature space using WordNet and Wikipedia. Saif et al. [9] propose

---

[2] **EWRS**: https://ewrs.ecdc.europa.eu/

[3] **MedISys**: http://medusa.jrc.it/

[4] **ProMED-mail**: http://promedmail.org/

to add the semantic concepts of extracted entities as additional features for sentiment analysis.

Hansen et al. [3] analysed which tweets attract the biggest attention and are most likely to be retweeted. As a part of this publication one of the authors, Finn Årup Nielsen, prepared a list of 2477 English words rated for valence with an integer between minus five (negative) and plus five (positive).

The main difference of our approach with the existing approaches are that our approach is based on the collected heuristics, manually added sentiment scores and the semantic types of the extracted entities in the messages. Its advantage is that it does not require to have a learning loop (only an update of the keyword list / taxonomies) and has no shortcomings when applied to the very short messages.

4 Conclusion

On this basis, we demonstrate a real-time system for classification of disease messages from mass of microblogging messages. Our system is a live service connected to the Twitter stream that receives messages and visualizes the disease reports on a map provided that they were enriched with the geographic whereabouts of the sender (sent from a mobile device).

Given that our system could receive a complete data stream, after some time it could extract anomalies based on the daily/weekly number of messages originating from a certain area. Such a tool could be a great complement to the well-established health surveillance systems.

References

1. Basseville, M., Nikiforov, I.V.: Detection of Abrupt Changes: Theory and Application. Prentice-Hall Inc, Upper Saddle River (1993)
2. Chew, C.M.: Pandemics in the age of Twitter: a content analysis of the 2009 h1n1 outbreak. Master's thesis, University of Toronto (2010)
3. Hansen, L.K., Arvidsson, A., Nielsen, F.A., Colleoni, E., Etter, M.: Good friends, bad news - affect and virality in Twitter. CoRR, abs/1101.0510 (2011)
4. Hu, X., Tang, L., Liu, H.: Enhancing accessibility of microblogging messages using semantic knowledge. In: Proceedings of the 20th ACM International Conference on Information and Knowledge Management, CIKM '11, pp. 2465–2468. ACM, New York, NY, USA (2011)
5. Hutwagner, L., Thompson, W., Seeman, G.M., Treadwell, T.: The bioterrorism preparedness and response early aberration reporting system (EARS). J. Urban Health **80**(2 Suppl 1), i89–i96 (2003)
6. Khan, S.A.: Handbook of biosurveillance, M.M. Wagner, A.W. Moore, R.M. Aryel (eds.) Elsevier Inc. ISBN-13: 978-0-12-369378-5. J. Biomed. Inf. **40**, 380–381 (2007)
7. Lampos, V., Cristianini, N.: Tracking the flu pandemic by monitoring the social web. In: 2nd IAPR Workshop on Cognitive Information Processing (CIP 2010), pp. 411–416. IEEE Press, June 2010

8. Mendes, P.N., Jakob, M., García-Silva, A., Bizer, C.: Dbpedia spotlight: shedding light on the web of documents. In: Proceedings of the 7th International Conference on Semantic Systems, I-Semantics '11, pp. 1–8. ACM, New York, NY, USA (2011)
9. Saif, H., He, Y., Alani, H.: Semantic sentiment analysis of Twitter. In: Cudré-Mauroux, P., et al. (eds.) ISWC 2012, Part I. LNCS, vol. 7649, pp. 508–524. Springer, Heidelberg (2012)
10. Signorini, A.: Social web information monitoring for health (2009)
11. Stewart, A., Diaz, E.: Epidemic intelligence: for the crowd, by the crowd. In: Brambilla, M., Tokuda, T., Tolksdorf, R. (eds.) ICWE 2012. LNCS, vol. 7387, pp. 504–505. Springer, Heidelberg (2012)

LinkZoo: A Linked Data Platform for Collaborative Management of Heterogeneous Resources

Marios Meimaris(✉), George Alexiou, and George Papastefanatos

Research Center "Athena", Institute for the Management of Information Systems, Athens, Greece
{m.meimaris, galexiou, gpapas}
@imis.athena-innovation.gr

Abstract. Modern collaborations rely on sharing and reusing heterogeneous resources. The ability to combine different types of information objects in semantically meaningful ways becomes a necessity for the information-intensive requirements of collaborative environments. In this paper we present LinkZoo, a web-based, linked data enabled platform that allows users to create, manage, discover and search heterogeneous resources such as files, web documents, people and events, interlink them, annotate them, exploit their inherent structures, enrich them with semantics and make them available as linked data. LinkZoo easily and intuitively allows for dynamic communities that enable web-based collaboration through resource sharing and annotating, exposing objects on the Linked Data Web under controlled vocabularies and permissions.

Keywords: Linked data · Semantic web · Collaborative environments · Resource management · Personal information management

1 Introduction

The semantic web is being manifested in a large way through the linked data (LD) paradigm, focusing on either the provision of semantic representations of singular entities through web documents or on large datasets created through domain-dependent, often complex publishing workflows. In this sense, the process of creating and publishing linked data has proven to be non-trivial as technical and conceptual expertise is required in order to build tailored LD publishing frameworks, more so when exposing or consuming personal resources in dynamically created collaborative environments.

The co-existence and collaborative management of heterogeneous objects in rich information spaces is a requirement that has not been successfully met. Providing a common representation model for different types of resources, such as files, web documents, persons and events enables their organization under shared contexts and the creation of complex, artefact-oriented aggregations. The reuse of common ontologies and vocabularies provides a rich semantic layer that helps organize, interlink and explore these resources in a multitude of dimensions. LD provides the way for exposing them, publicly or privately, for external reference and processing.

V. Presutti et al. (Eds.): ESWC Satellite Events 2014, LNCS 8798, pp. 407–412, 2014.
DOI: 10.1007/978-3-319-11955-7_57

There are several tools in the fields of collaborative semantic editing [2, 6], tag-based file systems [1] and semantic desktops [3–5]. Most of these either target the editing of resource properties or the semantic representation of physical files; however they do not address adequately the need of non-expert users to be able to leverage LD technology for creating, organizing and exploiting collaborative information spaces containing diverse resources found on the Data Web.

In this paper, we present LinkZoo; a collaborative linked data platform that enables users to reuse established ontologies as well as semantics created on-the-fly in order to annotate and share heterogeneous resources over dynamically defined usage contexts. It provides cloud-based functionality, where users can upload, link and manage various different types of resources, i.e., more than plain files, in collaborative workspaces. It offers the sharing and collaborative authoring of resources, enrichment with properties manually or via external services and their publishing as linked data for citing and machine-based consuming. LinkZoo enables users to create views that organize their resources under very different perspectives and make them available to others. Finally, it offers an intuitive way of searching over private or public resources and exploring them via a faceted browsing functionality.

This paper is organized as follows: in Sect. 2 the main features are presented, in Sect. 3 the design and architecture is described, Sect. 4 deals with the system's implementation and demo and Sect. 5 concludes and discusses future directions.

2 LinkZoo Features

Linked Data Publishing and Sharing. LinkZoo seamlessly integrates the processes of creating and publishing heterogeneous resources as RDF linked data, and offers a toolkit of common actions for their appropriate management. Four resource types are handled at the moment, namely files, web documents (i.e., URLs), persons and directories. Directories are special types of resources that organize into contexts sets of resources and can be enriched and linked with knowledge in the same way as other resources. Extending the list of resource types is a trivial procedure, as we intend to do so with calendar events in the near future. The available user actions include creation of a new resource (file upload, URL import or custom definition via JavaScript), creation of new directories, move, rename and delete resources, sharing of resources and editing/enriching of resource properties, either manually or in an automatic way. A SPARQL RESTful endpoint is deployed in order to be accessed programmatically with the appropriate user credentials.

Collaborative Resource Management. The created resources can be processed, annotated, enriched and shared by their editors, independently of their type. Currently two user roles are implemented, owner and editor. Owners and editors practically have the same rights, but help keep track of provenance. In the future, the viewer role will be introduced. Furthermore, resources can be private (when their discoverability is defined by the sharing process) or public (when they can be openly discovered and annotated). Shared directories bequeath their sharing status to their contents. Resources can be given properties by any shared editor.

Non-structured, Loosely-Controlled Annotations. Users can assert facts about resources as RDF triples. Some well-known ontologies have been imported in the platform for ease of access (auto-complete mechanism), but users can define their own properties on the fly under their custom namespace or use external ontologies and vocabularies at will. Furthermore, collections of resources in different directories can be aggregated in a drop-zone and assigned with properties in a bulk manner. Enrichment with properties and interlinking with other resources and external LD can be done manually by the users or automatically using external web service APIs.

Keyword Search and Exploration. LinkZoo offers advanced resource exploration by combining keyword search functionality over resource descriptions with property based filtering. Keyword search is implemented in a close-to-natural-language way, based on the characteristics of a user's available resources. Property filtering is implemented in the form of facets over the list of available properties of the search results. The two methods can be combined and applied in an exploratory "find-as-you-go" manner and ongoing results can be stored in multiple views.

View-Centric Organization. Resource descriptions provide multiple dimensions of organization due to their properties. The default way of browsing resources is based on an intuitive directory-like manner; still our platform exploits resources' semantics for offering multiple ways for organizing, exploring and searching resources. Users have the ability to organize resources (public or private), based on their characteristics and store the results as linked views. Views can be static or dynamic, where the latter store their search parameters thus enabling the user to refresh the contents of the view based on its definition. Views leverage semantic web by offering intuitive means to users for organizing, searching and discovering new resources either within the platform or the entire LOD cloud.

3 Model and Architecture

LinkZoo uses its own data model implemented as a linked data vocabulary. The model has three parts; the first contains the resources along with their metadata, such as types, titles, descriptions, identifiers, dates and related users, the second contains the set of constructs for user administration and privileges over resources and the third contains the definitions of views and the participation of resources in them.

The main architectural components are shown in Fig. 1. LinkZoo employs a quad store for data manipulation; profile manager is used for managing the profile data of each user, resource manager implements all actions applied on resources, view manager is used for defining and update of static and dynamic views whereas the search and exploration module provides keyword search and property filtering. Furthermore, the interlinking and enrichment module uses external APIs in order to retrieve and enrich resources with facts. Currently, Wikipedia, DBPedia and AlchemyAPI are used for knowledge enrichment, and the FalconsAPI for searching external ontologies. Permissions and user privileges are managed separately, as most actions require user authentication.

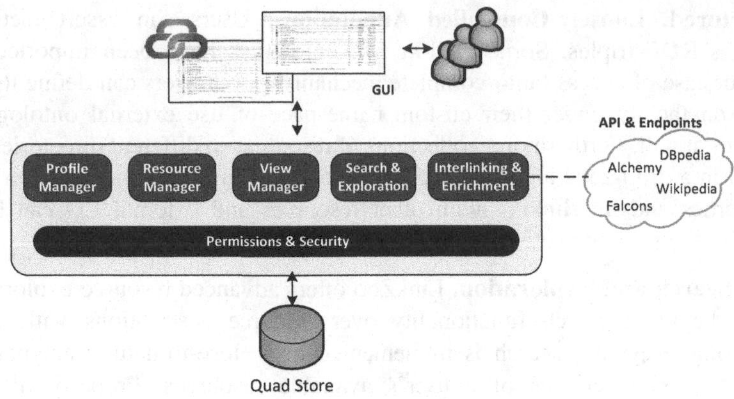

Fig. 1. LinkZoo architecture

4 Implementation and Demonstrator

LinkZoo is implemented using open source technologies. Virtuoso 7 open source edition is used as a quad store. The web GUI and application server are deployed on an Apache web server, using PHP for the main functionality.

Resources are given URIs upon creation based on a simple timestamp mechanism. Upon registration, each user is given a dedicated named graph, used in order to store the resources created by each user. When a resource is shared there is no replication of its description, thus allowing users to be able to collaborate on the same data object when manipulating a resource. Hence, the sharing procedure creates two triples on the shared users' graphs, one f their role and one to declare the resource's source graph.

Searching is implemented using auto-complete suggestions over resource types and property values, in combination with a faceted property filtering mechanism. The resulting query strings are visualized as natural-language phrases (e.g. '*find URLs with rdfs:seeAlso dbpedia:Youtube and linkZoo:owner 'John''*). Search can be limited on a directory, a view or a user's privately shared resources, but can also be done publicly. Public resources are stored in a publicly shared – anonymous - graph.

Views are also named graphs containing references to resource URIs and they can be static or dynamic. A static view is manually created and the user can explicitly add one or more resources to it. A dynamic view is created based on a search operation and the search parameters (SPARQL query) are kept along with the retrieved resources. The user can refresh the view's contents by revaluating the query on the available public or private resources. Views act as workspaces allowing the same resources to be found in many collections at the same time.

Demonstration Scenario. Our demo involves a Human Resources Management scenario. The scenario assumes that companies publish job openings in various formats (documents and websites) and independent recruiters (users of the demo) collaborate in order to find and match candidates to openings, along with related resources such as LinkedIn profiles, CVs, referrals, publications, etc. Each recruiter owns his own portfolio (user graph) with resources and has access to candidate profiles shared to him as well as to public resources.

First, the recruiter discovers available job openings by performing a search on the public workspace for resources posted by certain companies. The results are then explored based on the skills attributed to each job description. Then, the user searches over his personal portfolio for possible candidates and resources that exhibit some of the required skills. The results contain persons, CV documents, user and web pages, which are properly organized into a view per candidate. These are further linked with interview minutes, referrals, and cover letters. Some of the enriched profiles are then shared with other recruiters. Finally, the recruiter filters out candidates based on their skills and save the results as a dynamic view that he refreshes when new possible candidates are found in the shared with him portfolios.

Our platform prototype along with the demo is available at http://snf-80575.vm.okeanos.grnet.gr/encode2/index.php and the video presenting the aforementioned scenario is at http://youtu.be/bwQFOr80cZM.

5 Conclusions and Future Work

We have presented LinkZoo, a LD platform for collaborative management of heterogeneous resources. LinkZoo's social and semantic aspects can be used to facilitate collaboration between non-expert users over diverse domains and scenarios. In the future we intend to extend the coverage of resource types and incorporate data from social networks, such as LinkedIn, g^+ and youtube in order to build thorough social user profiles. We also intend to study scalability and performance issues concerning large userbases and greedy annotation. Finally, we intend to use the platform as a test-bed for automated integration of information resources on the Data Web.

Acknowledgement. This work has been co-financed by the EU and Greek national funds through the Operational Program "Education and Lifelong Learning" of the National Strategic Reference Framework (NSRF) - Research Funding Program: ARISTEIA. Investing in knowledge society through the European Social Fund.

References

1. Schandl, B., Popitsch, N.: Lifting file systems into the linked data cloud with TripFS. In: LDOW (2010)
2. Auer, S., Dietzold, S., Riechert, T.: OntoWiki – a tool for social, semantic collaboration. In: Cruz, I., Decker, S., Allemang, D., Preist, C., Schwabe, D., Mika, P., Uschold, M., Aroyo, L.M. (eds.) ISWC 2006. LNCS, vol. 4273, pp. 736–749. Springer, Heidelberg (2006)
3. Bernardi, A., Grimnes, G.A., Groza, T., Scerri, S.: The NEPOMUK semantic desktop. In: Warren, P., et al. (eds.) Context and Semantics for Knowledge Management, pp. 255–273. Springer, Heidelberg (2011)
4. Franz, T., Staab, S., Arndt, R.: The X-COSIM integration framework for a seamless semantic desktop. In: K-CAP (2007)

5. Sauermann, L.: The Gnowsis semantic desktop for information integration. In: Wissensmanagement (2005)
6. Quan, D., Huynh, D.F., Karger, D.R.: Haystack: a platform for authoring end user semantic web applications. In: Fensel, D., Sycara, K., Mylopoulos, J. (eds.) ISWC 2003. LNCS, vol. 2870, pp. 738–753. Springer, Heidelberg (2003)

TRTML - A Tripleset Recommendation Tool Based on Supervised Learning Algorithms

Alexander Arturo Mera Caraballo[1(✉)], Narciso Moura Arruda Jr.[2], Bernardo Pereira Nunes[1], Giseli Rabello Lopes[1], and Marco Antonio Casanova[1]

[1] Department of Informatics, PUC-Rio, Rio de Janeiro, RJ, Brazil
{acaraballo,bnunes,grlopes,casanova}@inf.puc-rio.br
[2] Computer Science Department, UFC, Fortaleza, CE, Brazil
narciso@lia.ufc.br

Abstract. The Linked Data initiative promotes the publication of interlinked RDF triplesets, thereby creating a global scale data space. However, to enable the creation of such data space, the publisher of a tripleset t must be aware of other triplesets that he can interlink with t. Towards this end, this paper describes a Web-based application, called *TRTML*, that explores metadata available in Linked Data catalogs to provide data publishers with recommendations of related triplesets. *TRTML* combines supervised learning algorithms and link prediction measures to provide recommendations. The evaluation of the tool adopted as ground truth a set of links obtained from metadata stored in the DataHub catalog. The high precision and recall results demonstrate the usefulness of *TRTML*.

Keywords: Linked Data · Recommender systems · Link prediction · Machine learning

1 Introduction

Over the past years, data publishers have been encouraged to publish their data following the Linked Data principles to facilitate data sharing, data reuse and enhance (semantic) interoperability on the Web [1,2]. The main idea behind Linked Data is to connect resources across triplesets and, thereby, facilitate the discovery of related resources [3], the integration of data sources [4] and the enrichment of datasets [5].

However, with the steady growth of the number of triplesets published on the Web and the lack of tools to recommend and interlink related triplesets, most data publishers rely on a few reference data sources, such as DBpedia, Freebase and Geonames, to interlink their triplesets, leaving out other potentially related triplesets. As an attempt to assist data publishers in the process of tripleset interlinking, the Linked Data community created metadata catalogs describing triplesets (e.g. DataHub). Despite the existence of such catalogs, the arduous and laborious task of searching for related triplesets remains. Furthermore, a recent research [6] shows that metadata catalogs are often outdated and miss relevant information, further hindering the process of tripleset interlinking.

V. Presutti et al. (Eds.): ESWC Satellite Events 2014, LNCS 8798, pp. 413–417, 2014.
DOI: 10.1007/978-3-319-11955-7_58

Thus, in this paper, we describe a Web-based application, called *TRTML*, that provides recommendations of triplesets related to a given tripleset. *TRTML* relies on supervised algorithms (such as Multilayer Perceptron, Decision Trees - J48 and Support Vector Machines) and link prediction measures (such as Common Neighbors, Jaccard coefficient, Preferential Attachment and Resource Allocation) that explore a set of features (e.g. vocabularies, classes and properties) available for the triplesets in data catalogs. In particular, the supervised learning algorithms are responsible for determining the best set of features for the recommendation task.

To evaluate the tool, we adopted as ground truth a set L of links obtained from metadata stored in the DataHub catalog. Briefly, we removed some of the links in L and evaluated, in terms of precision, recall and F-measure, how many of the removed links the *TRTML* tool was able to find. The experiments show that *TRTML* achieves an F-measure of 78 %.

The rest of this paper is organized as follows. Section 2 presents an overview of the TRTML tool along with the supervised learning algorithms, link prediction measures and features used. Section 3 describes the evaluation setup and the results achieved. Finally, Sect. 4 summarizes the contributions and results.

2 Tripleset Recommendation Approach

Let $D = \{d_1, ..., d_n\}$ be a set of triplesets considered in the recommendation process and t be the tripleset one wants to receive recommendations for interlinking. Instead of providing a restricted list of recommendations, we define the task of recommending triplesets to be interlinked with t as a task of ranking triplesets d_i in D according to the estimated probability that one can define links between resources of t and d_i. To generate the rankings, we explore an approach that combines link prediction measures and machine learning techniques.

Link prediction measures. The approach uses link prediction measures to estimate the likelihood of the existence of a link between triplesets. To estimate the measures, we construct a bipartite graph $G = (D, F, E)$ consisting of two disjoints sets of nodes representing triplesets D and features F. The set of edges E represents the association between the triplesets and their features. The set of features of a tripleset t, F_t, correspond to the vocabularies, classes or properties extracted from the VoID descriptions defined in t. The tool implements four of the traditional link prediction measures, summarized in Table 1, which demonstrated good performance in previous works [7,8].

Supervised learning algorithms. The approach uses supervised learning algorithms to learn if a pair of triplesets can be interlinked, using as training set the existing links between triplesets. Specifically, we build a J48 decision tree (Quinlan's C4.5 implementation), where the nodes represent the measures reported in Table 1, estimated using different feature sets (vocabularies, classes or properties). The leaf nodes represent the values of a binary class such that, given two triplesets (t, d_i), 1 represents that d_i can be recommended to t and 0 denotes

Table 1. Link prediction measures

Measure	Equation
Common Neighbors	$CN_{t,d_i} = \|F_t \cap F_{d_i}\|$
Jaccard coefficient	$Jaccard_{t,d_i} = \frac{\|F_t \cap F_{d_i}\|}{\|F_t \cup F_{d_i}\|}$
Preferential Attachment	$PA_{t,d_i} = \|F_t\| . \|F_{d_i}\|$
Resource Allocation	$RA_{t,d_i} = \sum_{f_j \in F_t \cap F_{d_i}} \frac{1}{\|D_{f_j}\|}$

Where:

- F_{d_i} is the feature set of tripleset d_i (direct neighbors of d_i in G);
- D_{f_j} is the set of triplesets having feature f_j (direct neighbors of f_j in G).

that d_i is not a good candidate to be recommended to t. The advantage of decision tree classifiers over other supervised learning algorithms is that they produce an interpretable model that allows users to understand how to classify new instances.

TRTML Overview. Suppose that a user is working on a tripleset t and that he wants to discover one or more triplesets d_i such that t can be interlinked with d_i. He then uses the tool to obtain tripleset recommendations. First, the tool builds a classifier over the set of VoID descriptions, obtained from the DataHub catalog. Then, the user defines the rest of the input data the tool requires: (i) he selects the serialization format of the VoID descriptor (TURTLE, RDF/XML or N-TRIPLE N3); and (ii) uploads a VoID descriptor V_t for t from which the tool extracts the feature set F_t by analyzing the `void:vocabulary`, `void:class` and `void:property` occurring in V_t. Finally, the tool applies the classifier, using F_t, and outputs a ranked list of triplesets, sorted by the estimated probability of creating links with t.

The tool is available at http://web.ccead.puc-rio.br:8080/Uncover/ml/.

3 Experimental Evaluation

Triplesets. We based the experiments on the VoID descriptions stored in the DataHub catalog. We obtained a set D of 293 triplesets whose VoID descriptions indicated the vocabularies, classes and properties the tripleset used. Out of the 42,778 possible links, we uncovered a set L of 410 links connecting such triplesets by analyzing the `void:linkset` property.

Ground truth. Due to the lack of benchmarks for validating the creation of links between triplesets, we adopted as ground truth the set L of links defined above. Furthermore, we separated the tripleset pairs in $D \times D$ into two classes: (i) *(ground truth) linked tripleset pairs* that are connected by a link in L, and (ii) *(ground truth) unlinked tripleset pairs* that are not connected by a link in L.

Performance measures. To validate the recommendation algorithms, we adopted the standard metrics **R**ecall, **P**recision and **F**-measure, defined based on true positives (TP), true negatives (TN), false positives (FP) and false negatives

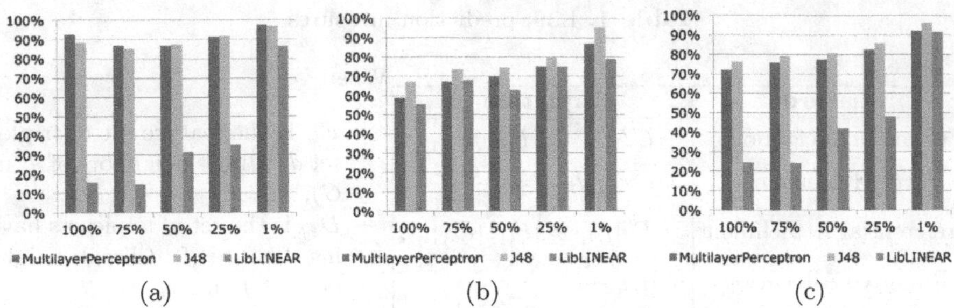

(a) (b) (c)

Fig. 1. (a) Precision, (b) Recall and (c) F-measure of the supervised classifiers by the percentage of (ground truth) unlinked tripleset pairs considered (100 %, 75 %, 50 %, 25 % and 1 %)

(FN) links between triplesets. Briefly, the *positive* and *negative* terms refer to link prediction, while *true* and *false* refer to the links in L. Thus, precision, recall and F-measure are defined as: $\mathbf{P} = \frac{TP}{TP+FP}$; $\mathbf{R} = \frac{TP}{TP+FN}$; and $\mathbf{F} = 2 \times \frac{\mathbf{P}\times\mathbf{R}}{\mathbf{P}+\mathbf{R}}$.

Baselines. As baselines for the experiments, we used two standard supervised learning algorithms: Support Vector Machines - SVM (LibLINEAR implementation) and Multilayer Perceptron. Similarly to the J48 decision tree, we used both SVM and Multilayer Perceptron to classify pairs of triplesets into (ground truth) linked tripleset pairs and (ground truth) unlinked tripleset pairs, based on link prediction measures values estimated considering different features sets.

Results. Before discussing the results, we observe that a pair of triplesets may not be in L, the set of links obtained from the DataHub catalog, because of a lack of metadata information or because they were never interlinked, but they might be. This indeterminacy might contaminate the learning algorithms. Hence, we vary the percentage of (ground truth) unlinked tripleset pairs considered when analyzing the performance of the various algorithms.

Figure 1 shows the precision, recall and F-measure achieved when the percentage of (ground truth) unlinked tripleset pairs varies (100 %, 75 %, 50 %, 25 % and 1 %), while maintaining the number of (ground truth) linked tripleset pairs constant:

- Figure 1(a) shows that both the Multilayer Perceptron and the J48 implementations achieved a precision greater than 85 %, independently of the percentage of (ground truth) unlinked tripleset pairs considered.
- Figure 1(b) indicates that the recall of the supervised classifiers increases when the percentage of (ground truth) unlinked tripleset pairs is reduced.
- Figure 1(c) shows that the J48 algorithm obtained the best overall performance, independently of the percentage of (ground truth) unlinked tripleset pairs considered.

To conclude, the J48 implementation achieved higher recall and F-measure, independently of the percentage of (ground truth) unlinked tripleset pairs considered.

4 Conclusions

In this paper, we presented a tool for tripleset recommendation, called *TRTML*, which reduces the effort of searching for related triplesets in large data repositories. *TRTML* is based on link prediction measures and supervised learning algorithms. The crucial role of the supervised learning algorithms is to automatically select a set of features, extracted from the VoID vocabulary, and a set of link prediction measures that, when combined, lead to effective tripleset interlinking recommendations. After a comprehensive evaluation of the supervised learning algorithms, the results show that the implementation based on the J48 decision tree (Quinlan's C4.5 implementation) achieved the best overall performance, when compared with the Multilayer Perceptron and the SVM algorithms.

Acknowledgments. This work was partly supported by CNPq, under grants 160326/2012-5, 303332-2013-1 and 557128/2009-9, by FAPERJ, under grants E-26/170028/2008 and E-26/103.070/2011.

References

1. Berners-Lee, T.: Linked Data - Design Issues, W3C (2009). http://www.w3.org/DesignIssues/LinkedData.html. Accessed March 2013
2. Bizer, C., Heath, T., Berners-Lee, T.: Linked data - the story so far. Int. J. Semant. Web Inf. Syst. **5**, 1–22 (2009)
3. Nunes, B.P., Kawase, R., Fetahu, B., Dietze, S., Casanova, M.A., Maynard, D.: Interlinking documents based on semantic graphs. In: KES. Procedia Computer Science, vol. 22, pp. 231–240. Elsevier (2013)
4. Nunes, B.P., Mera, A., Casanova, M.A., Fetahu, B., Leme, L.A.P.P., Dietze, S.: Complex matching of RDF datatype properties. In: Decker, H., Lhotská, L., Link, S., Basl, J., Tjoa, A.M. (eds.) DEXA 2013, Part I. LNCS, vol. 8055, pp. 195–208. Springer, Heidelberg (2013)
5. Nunes, B.P., Dietze, S., Casanova, M.A., Kawase, R., Fetahu, B., Nejdl, W.: Combining a co-occurrence-based and a semantic measure for entity linking. In: Cimiano, P., Corcho, O., Presutti, V., Hollink, L., Rudolph, S. (eds.) ESWC 2013. LNCS, vol. 7882, pp. 548–562. Springer, Heidelberg (2013)
6. Fetahu, B., Dietze, S., Nunes, B.P., Casanova, M.A., Taibi, D., Nejdl, W.: A scalable approach for efficiently generating structured dataset topic profiles. In: Presutti, V., d'Amato, C., Gandon, F., d'Aquin, M., Staab, S., Tordai, A. (eds.) ESWC 2014. LNCS, vol. 8465, pp. 519–534. Springer, Heidelberg (2014)
7. Caraballo, A.A.M., Nunes, B.P., Lopes, G.R., Leme, L.A.P.P., Casanova, M.A., Dietze, S.: Trt-a tripleset recommendation tool. In: ISWC (Posters & Demos), pp. 105–108 (2013)
8. Lopes, G.R., Leme, L.A.P.P., Nunes, B.P., Casanova, M.A., Dietze, S.: Recommending tripleset interlinking through a social network approach. In: Lin, X., Manolopoulos, Y., Srivastava, D., Huang, G. (eds.) WISE 2013, Part I. LNCS, vol. 8180, pp. 149–161. Springer, Heidelberg (2013)

morph-LDP: An R2RML-Based Linked Data Platform Implementation

Nandana Mihindukulasooriya[1,2(✉)], Freddy Priyatna[2], Oscar Corcho[2], Raúl García-Castro[1,2], and Miguel Esteban-Gutiérrez[1,2]

[1] Center for Open Middleware, Universidad Politécnica de Madrid, Madrid, Spain
[2] Ontology Engineering Group, Facultad de Informática, Universidad Politécnica de Madrid, Madrid, Spain
{nmihindu,fpriyatna,ocorcho,rgarcia,mesteban}@fi.upm.es

Abstract. The W3C Linked Data Platform (LDP) candidate recommendation defines a standard HTTP-based protocol for read/write Linked Data. The W3C R2RML recommendation defines a language to map relational databases (RDBs) and RDF. This paper presents morph-LDP, a novel system that combines these two W3C standardization initiatives to expose relational data as read/write Linked Data for LDP-aware applications, whilst allowing legacy applications to continue using their relational databases.

1 Introduction

The W3C Linked Data Platform (LDP) candidate recommendation is focused on supporting read/write Linked Data by providing a standard HTTP-based RESTful protocol. An obvious way of generating an LDP implementation is by storing RDF data in a triple store and internally doing SPARQL SELECT and UPDATE queries. However, there are contexts in which organizations are interested in continuing with their existing relational databases instead of transforming data into an RDF format and managing it from a triple store. Hence, the work that has been done in the past at W3C on the definition of the R2RML language, as well as the implementations available that support such language (e.g., Ontop [1], morph-RDB [2], D2R [3]), may be useful as an alternative implementation for LDP, as shown in Fig. 1.

In this demo we show how we can make use of the W3C R2RML recommendation as the underlying support for providing read/write Linked Data access to relational databases. Database administrators only need to generate a R2RML mapping document and morph-LDP exposes the relational data as Linked Data. Such Linked Data is not only dereferenceable and available through the HTTP GET operation, but can also be updated using write operations such as PUT, POST, PATCH, and DELETE.

V. Presutti et al. (Eds.): ESWC Satellite Events 2014, LNCS 8798, pp. 418–423, 2014.
DOI: 10.1007/978-3-319-11955-7_59

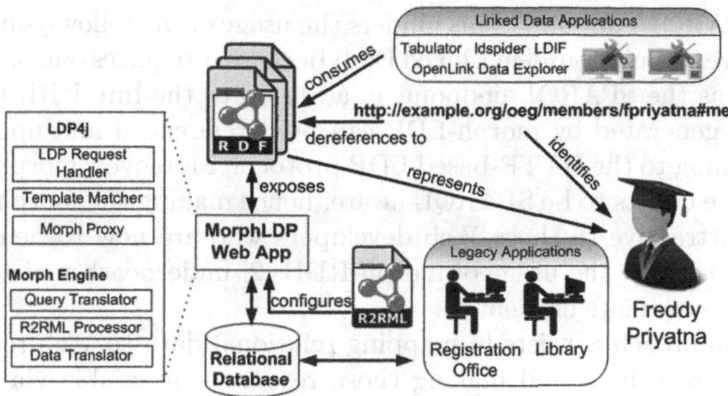

Fig. 1. The morph-LDP use case

2 Background

The Linked Data Platform (LDP) [4] is an initiative by the W3C LDP WG to provide a standard protocol and a set of best practices enabling read/write Linked Data scenarios. The LDP specification extends the HTTP protocol with a set of new constraints, HTTP headers, and Link headers that are useful for read/write Linked Data applications. The two main types of concepts defined in LDP include:

- A Linked Data Platform Resource (LDPR) which is any HTTP resource that conforms to additional constraints defined in the LDP specification.
- A Linked Data Platform Container (LDPC) which is a specialization of an LDPR that acts as a collection resource that helps organizing LDPRs and creating new LDPRs as its members.

R2RML [5] is a W3C recommendation for the definition of a mapping language from relational databases to RDF. An R2RML mapping document contains a set of TriplesMap, used to specify the rules to generate RDF triples from database rows/values. A TriplesMap consists of a LogicalTable (either a base table or a SQL view), a SubjectMap (to generate the subject component of RDF triples), and a set of PredicateObjectMaps. A PredicateObjectMap is composed of a set of PredicateMaps and ObjectMaps (to generate the predicate and object components of RDF triples, respectively).

3 Related Works

There is some previous work on the provision of update functionalities to R2RML-based systems (e.g., [6]). However, so far Linked Data generated by such an approach cannot be dereferenced using HTTP GET but rather have to be queried through a SPARQL endpoint. This hinders the usage of the follow-your-nose approach[1] to traverse links found in Linked Data because it requires out-of-band information such as the SPARQL endpoint in addition to the link URI. In contrast, Linked Data generated by morph-LDP can be dereferenced and updated using URIs conforming to the HTTP-based LDP protocol. Moreover, morph-LDP does not require the clients to be SPARQL-aware, hence making the morph-LDP approach more attractive to those Web developers who are new to Semantic Web technologies. Finally, the usage of morph-RDB [2] underneath makes the query evaluation process more efficient.

Another approach consists in mapping relational data to Web resources following REST principles and making those resources accessible via the HTTP protocol. Some systems that follow this approach are: HTTP database connector (HDBC) [7], sqlREST[2], and restSQL[3]. Nevertheless, none of those systems provides RDF representations. HDBC generates data according to the Atom format, while both sqlREST and restSQL generate XML outputs using W3C XLink and custom SQL Resources. While following the same approach, morph-LDP provides RDF representations (Turtle, RDF/XML, N-Triples and JSON-LD utilizing HTTP content negotiation). In addition, another advantage of morph-LDP is the use of a standard mapping language.

4 Morph-LDP

4.1 Mapping LDP Components with R2RML

In this section, we explain how the concepts of LDP are mapped to R2RML so that the two standards can be combined to provide read/write Linked Data access to relational data.

The second Linked Data principle[4] mandates the use of HTTP URIs so that people can look up those names. By inspecting the rules specified in SubjectMaps, these URIs can be mapped to Linked Data resources (LDPR) enabling read/write access through the LDP protocol.

PredicateObjectMaps allow generating the information about a specific resource, so that *when someone looks up a URI*, morph-LDP can *provide useful information using RDF* following the third Linked Data principle. LDP not only allows to lookup those resources but also to update them using HTTP write operations.

In R2RML, TriplesMaps are used to generate RDF triples out of the rows of logical tables. In LDP, LDP Containers are used as collection resources to organize LDPRs. Thus logical tables and their corresponding TripleMaps can be mapped to LDP Containers.

---

[1] http://patterns.dataincubator.org/book/follow-your-nose.html
[2] http://sqlrest.sourceforge.net/
[3] http://restsql.org/
[4] http://www.w3.org/DesignIssues/LinkedData.html

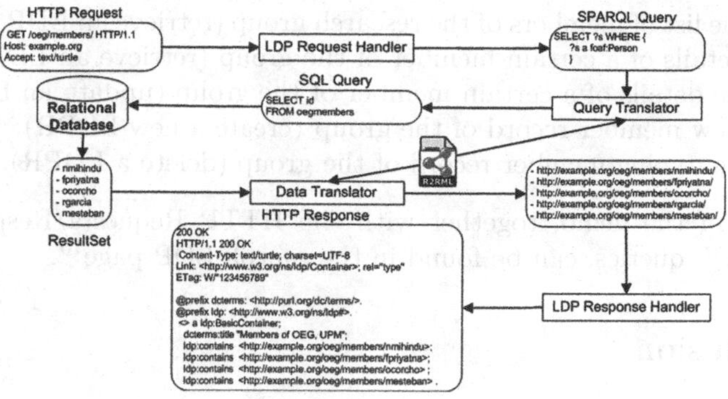

Fig. 2. An example of morph-LDP in action, using the SPARQL query mode.

4.2 Implementation

Our implementation[5] is based on the result of two existing projects: **morph-RDB** and **LDP4j**. morph-RDB [2][6] is a Scala-based RDB2RDF engine that complies with the R2RML specification. Its query translator component is based on the algorithm defined in [8] with some optimizations, such as self-join, left-outer join, and subquery elimination. morph-RDB has been successfully applied in several projects: Répener [9], BizkaiSense[7], and Integrate[8]. LDP4j[9] is a Java-based middleware for the development of LDP-aware applications. LDP4j is being developed in the context of the ALM iStack project, where the LDP middleware is used to integrate Application Lifecycle Management tools [10].

morph-LDP extends morph-RDB with an LDP layer provided by LDP4j. The LDP layer extracts the metadata from the HTTP request and send it as an input for morph-RDB. morph-RDB has two modes of operation: API mode and SPARQL query mode and handles the transformation between RDF and relational data. Figure 2 illustrates the process when morph-LDP receives an HTTP Request when using the SPARQL query mode.

5 An Example Scenario

Our demo scenario uses a relational database which manages information of members of a research group. morph-LDP exposes this data as Linked Data that can be managed using the LDP protocol. In the demo, we showcase the following user stories:

As a Linked Data application developer, I want to:

---

5 https://github.com/fpriyatna/morph-LDP

6 https://github.com/fpriyatna/morph

7 http://www.tecnologico.deusto.es/projects/bizkaisense/

8 http://www.fp7-integrate.eu

9 http://ldp4j.org

- retrieve the list of members of the research group (retrieve an LDP Container).
- retrieve details of a certain member of the group (retrieve an LDPR).
- update the details of a certain member of the group (update an LDPR).
- create a new member record of the group (create a new LDPR).
- delete an outgoing member record of the group (delete a LDPR).

A video of the demo, together with the HTTP Requests/Responses, and SPARQL/SQL queries, can be found in the morph-LDP page[10].

6 Conclusion

W3C LDP is in the final stages of the standardization process and we believe that integrating it with relational databases using W3C R2RML will help a wider adoption in the industry. In this paper, we presented how LDP and R2RML can be combined to expose relational data as read/write Linked Data. Nevertheless, there is still some work to be done on providing support for Quality-of-Service requirements such as secure access and transactions. In addition to that, currently morph-LDP supports only simple R2RML mappings (no SQL view, no multiple mappings to a class/property) and we are working on giving support for more complex mappings.

Acknowledgments. The authors have been supported by the PlanetData (FP7-257641), myBigData (TIN2010-17060), and ALM iStack (Center for Open Middleware) projects.

References

1. Rodríguez-Muro, M., Kontchakov, R., Zakharyaschev, M.: Ontop at work. In: Proceedings of the 10th OWL: Experiences and Directions Workshop (OWLED 2013) (2013)
2. Priyatna, F., Corcho, O., Sequeda, J.F.: Formalisation and experiences of R2RML-based SPARQL to SQL query translation using morph. In: Proceedings of the 23rd International World Wide Web Conference (2014)
3. Bizer, C., Cyganiak, R.: D2R server-publishing relational databases on the semantic web. In: Poster at the 5th International Semantic Web Conference (2006)
4. Speicher, S., Arwe, J., Malhotra, A.: Linked Data Platform 1.0 (2014) W3C Last Call Draft. http://www.w3.org/TR/ldp/
5. Das, S., Sundara, S., Cyganiak, R.: R2RML: RDB to RDF mapping language W3C Recommendation. http://www.w3.org/TR/r2rml/
6. Garrote, A., García, M.: Restful writable APIs for the web of linked data using relational storage solutions. In: WWW 2011 Workshop: Linked Data on the Web (LDOW2011) (2011)
7. Marinos, A., Wilde, E., Lu, J.: HTTP database connector (HDBC): RESTful access to relational databases. In: Proceedings of the 19th International Conference on World Wide Web, pp. 1157–1158. ACM (2010)

[10] http://oeg-dev.dia.fi.upm.es/morph-ldp/

8. Chebotko, A., Lu, S., Fotouhi, F.: Semantics preserving SPARQL-to-SQL translation. Data Knowl. Eng. **68**(10), 973–1000 (2009)
9. Sicilia, A., Nemirovskij, G., Massetti, M., Madrazo, L.: RÉPENER's linked dataset (in revision). Semantic Web Journal (2013)
10. Mihindukulasooriya, N., García-Castro, R., Esteban-Gutiérrez, M.: Linked Data Platform as a novel approach for Enterprise Application Integration. In: Proceedings of the 4th International Workshop on Consuming Linked Data (COLD2013) (2013)

Combining a REST Lexical Analysis Web Service with SPARQL for Mashup Semantic Annotation from Text

Eetu Mäkelä(✉)

Semantic Computing Research Group (SeCo), Aalto University, Espoo, Finland
eetu.makela@aalto.fi
http://www.seco.tkk.fi/

Abstract. Current automatic annotation systems are often monolithic, holding internal copies of both machine-learned annotation models and the reference vocabularies they use. This is problematic particularly for frequently changing references such as person and place registries, as the information in the copy quickly grows stale. In this paper, arguments and experiments are presented on the notion that sufficient accuracy and recall can both be obtained simply by combining a sufficiently capable lexical analysis web service with querying a primary SPARQL store, even in the case of often problematic highly inflected languages.

1 Introduction

The context of the current work is that as part of a national Semantic Web infrastructure for Finland [1], a service for extracting automatic semantic annotations from texts was desired. There are already many tools for such, falling into different categories based on which languages they support, the types of entitities they recognize and if they are bound to a particular reference vocabulary, or even use any vocabulary at all[1]. Unfortunately, the requirements for our service ruled out all of the existing candidates. First, the service would have to support at least Finland's two official languages of Finnish and Swedish. Second, it should allow for picking keywords from any of the many general keyword vocabularies [3] used in Finland, as well as the larger national person, place and event instance registries currently being created.

To solve this problem, a first iteration of a novel automatic indexing service ARPA was created [4], based on the Maui indexing tool [5], which could combine an arbitrary language processor, vocabulary and training corpus into a human-competitive automated indexer web service. This worked well, but caused problems in maintenance, because any update to the vocabulary, training data or lemmatizer needed a new manual packaging of the service. While this was

[1] For the purposes of this paper, a good overview of the field is given in the related work section of [2].

V. Presutti et al. (Eds.): ESWC Satellite Events 2014, LNCS 8798, pp. 424–428, 2014.
DOI: 10.1007/978-3-319-11955-7_60

sufferable for the seldom-changing keyword vocabularies, it created insurmountable problems for the much larger instance registries, which constantly update to add new people, places and events.

To counteract the problem, sights were set on modularizing the system, of which good results had been previously obtained on other parts of the national infrastructure stack [6]. A particular goal was for the system to not have to maintain a local, stale copy of the vocabulary used, but to be able to e.g. query the master SPARQL endpoint of the instance registries for matches.

2 Requirements for Modular Semantic Annotation

Generally, semantic annotation can be thought of as being composed of two phases [2,5]. First, in a phrase spotting or candidate selection phase, possible annotations are extracted from the text. Then, in a disambiguation and selection phase, the candidates are compared and some are selected, others discarded.

For disambiguation, it turns out that the simple algorithm of *always selecting the concept that already appears most often in annotations* nearly matches the accuracy of more complex methods. In [7] for example, differences in accuracy ranged only from 0.002 to 0.024 for 7 different languages tested. Thus, there didn't seem to be enough added benefit in teaching and re-teaching the naive Bayes -based Maui classifier for concept selection. Instead, as this is such an easy to implement measure and benefits from access to an up-to-date version of the dataset being added to, it was decided that this functionality would not be implemented at all, with the task given over to the end user system.

As for the candidation selection phase, what is required depends on the language. For weakly inflected languages such as English, Swedish or Dutch, where word forms are seldom modified to respond to grammatical structure, even a completely language ignorant naive approach functions well. As an example for Dutch, merely *selecting any exact phrase matching a concept in the vocabulary* resulted in virtually equivalent recall to an implementation utilizing NLP processing (55.01 % vs 55.53 % in [7]). Thus, for automatic indexing of Swedish, adequate functionality could have been obtained merely by enumerating all n-grams in the incoming text, and then issuing label match queries to the master up-to-date SPARQL endpoints of the vocabularies and instance registries.

However, for highly inflected languages such as Russian or Hungarian, language ignorant recall in phrase spotting is considerable lower (30.62 % and 34.07 % respectively in [7]). Unfortunately, Finnish is a highly inflected language, where e.g. the noun for shop, "kauppa", can appear in a total of 2,253 different forms depending on the sentence[2]. For good recall in such languages it is essential to utilize lemmatization, whereby each word is transformed into its base form [4].

Thus it was decided that our new automatic indexing service would be composed of two components: first, a lexical analysis service would lemmatize the

[2] http://www.ling.helsinki.fi/~fkarlsso/genkau2.html

text into baseforms, and then a simple querying component would use the resulting n-grams to query a (SPARQL) web service for matching concepts.

3 The Need for Morphological Analysis and Inflected Form Generation

Decoupling the vocabulary from the lemmatization service caused some new problems, however. In the earlier Maui implementation, where the vocabularies were loaded into an internal model, the indexer could also lemmatize the terms in the vocabulary for easy matching. With the vocabulary outside the indexer, this was no longer possible.

While in most cases, words in the reference vocabularies to be used are already in their nominal base form, there are still enough notable exceptions to cause problems. First, the most important Finnish vocabulary, the National Finnish General Thesaurus YSA, contains nouns in their plural form instead of singular (e.g. "presidentit" [presidents] instead of "presidentti" [president]). Second, for applications needing to index also verbs, they are often in their nominative form (e.g. both YSA and Wikipedia contain "lentäminen" [flying] instead of "lentä" [to fly]). Finally and most importantly for compound phrases, not all words turn into their baseforms. For example, the Foreign ministry of Finland has a base form (and a Wikipedia page) of "Suomen ulkoministeriö" instead of the form "Suomi ulkoministeriö", which a naive lemmatization algorithm would turn out.

Because of this, it was deemed that the lexical analysis service should also (1) support deeper morphological analysis of the text in order to be able to flexibly handle compound phrases and (2) support the generation of any inflected form instead of just the baseform to handle any quirks of the target vocabularies.

Luckily, there existed ready tools for this, in the form of the Helsinki Finite State Transducer toolkit [8] and accompanying transducers for multiple languages interesting from the Finnish standpoint (including for example the Finnish minority language of Sami). All that was needed was to package these tools together in the form of an easy to use web service.

4 The SeCo Lexical Analysis Service

The end result produced by the packaging is the SeCo Lexical Analysis Web Service at http://demo.seco.tkk.fi/las/, with source code available at http://github.com/jiemakel/seco-lexicalanalysis-play. All in all, the service is comprised of five functionalities:

1. Language recognition for a total of 95 languages, based on three sources: (1) the langdetect library [9], (2) own custom code and (3) finite state transducers from the HFST [8], Omorfi [10] and Giellatekno [11] projects.
2. Lemmatization for a total of 20 languages, utilizing again the finite state transducers from the HFST, Omorfi and Giellatekno projects, with a fallback to Snowball [12] stemmers.

3. More complete morphological analysis is available for the 14 languages fully supported by the finite state transducers.
4. Inflected form generation is likewise available for the same 14 languages.
5. Hyphenation based on finite state transducers is available for 46 languages.

All functionalities are available as RPC-style web services, supporting both the HTTP and WebSocket protocols. All services are additionally CORS-enabled and return results in JSON for easy integration into HTML5 web applications. Further details as well as live examples are available at the service itself.

5 ARPA Automatic Annotation Service

As after the lexical processing the actual querying for semantic annotations is relatively simple, a demonstration of this was implemented as a static HTML5 Javascript application at http://demo.seco.tkk.fi/sarpa/.

The application is comprised of a text field and a series of controls by which it is possible to change parameters of the lexical analysis process, as well as specify an arbitrary SPARQL endpoint and query for fetching candidate annotations. There are also four different complete pre-configured examples to select from demonstrating the various options and functionalities. One targets the Finnish edition of DBPedia while another targets the YSA thesaurus. The remaining two target the public SPARQL endpoint of DBPedia with different query restrictions.

As a complete example, consider the analysis[3] of the Finnish sentence "Erkki Tuomiojan mukaan Suomen ulkoministeriön tietomurtoa käsiteltiin tasavallan presidentin Sauli Niinistön kanssa heti tämän lennettyä Helsinkiin" (According to Erkki Tuomioja, the data system break-in at the Ministry for Foreign Affairs of Finland was talked over with president Sauli Niinistö as soon as he had flown to Helsinki). Run with a configuration targeting the SPARQL endpoint of the Finnish edition of DBPedia, this results in finding the pages for "Erkki Tuomioja", "Suomen ulkoministeriö" (the Ministry of Foreign Affairs of Finland), "tietomurto" (data system break-in), "presidentti" (president), "Sauli Niinistö", "lentäminen" (flying) and "Helsinki". Notable here is that first part of the compound word "Suomen ulkoministeriö" is still inflected, and the verb "lentäminen" is in its nominative form, not the base form. On the other hand, against the General Finnish Thesaurus, the concepts "tietomurto", "presidentit" (notice the plural form version of the word) and "lentäminen" (again notice the nominative form of the verb) are found.

6 Conclusions

Based on the analysis and experience presented here, it is easily possible to create lightweight automatic semantic annotation systems just by combining a lexical analysis service with a standard vocabulary query interface. In addition,

[3] http://j.mp/1cBiBvL

from analysis and prior experiments it seems that such systems can approach the accuracy and recall levels provided by more complex annotators, although this requires further experimentation to conclusively decide.

In addition to proving the basic premise, this work also highlighted some dirty details that must be taken into account when attempting the creation of such a system for highly inflected languages. In this work, these were surmounted for the automatic indexing of Finnish material by making use of more thorough morphological analysis of the text, as well as inflected form generation.

References

1. Hyvänen, E.: Developing and using a national cross-domain semantic web infrastructure. Semantic Computing, pp. 421–438. Wiley, New York (2010)
2. Mendes, P.N., Jakob, M., García-Silva, A., Bizer, C.: Dbpedia spotlight: shedding light on the web of documents. In: Ghidini, C., Ngomo, A.C.N., Lindstaedt, S.N., Pellegrini, T. (eds.) I-SEMANTICS. ACM International Conference Proceeding Series, pp. 1–8. ACM (2011)
3. Frosterus, M., Tuominen, J., Pessala, S., Seppälä, K., Hyvönen, E.: Linked open ontology cloud KOKO—managing a system of cross-domain lightweight ontologies. In: Cimiano, P., Fernández, M., Lopez, V., Schlobach, S., Völker, J. (eds.) ESWC 2013. LNCS, vol. 7955, pp. 296–297. Springer, Heidelberg (2013)
4. Sinkkilä, R., Suominen, O., Hyvönen, E.: Automatic semantic subject indexing of web documents in highly inflected languages. In: Antoniou, G., Grobelnik, M., Simperl, E., Parsia, B., Plexousakis, D., De Leenheer, P., Pan, J. (eds.) ESWC 2011, Part I. LNCS, vol. 6643, pp. 215–229. Springer, Heidelberg (2011)
5. Medelyan, O.: Human-competitive automatic topic indexing. Ph.D. thesis, The University of Waikato (2009)
6. Mäkelä, E., Viljanen, K., Alm, O., Tuominen, J., Valkeapää, O., Kauppinen, T., Kurki, J., Sinkkilä, R., Kansala, T., Lindroos, R., Suominen, O., Ruotsalo, T., Hyvönen, E.: Enabling the semantic web with ready-to-use web widgets. In: Nixon, L.J.B., Cuel, R., Bergamini, C. (eds.) FIRST. CEUR Workshop Proceedings, vol. 293, pp. 56–69. CEUR-WS.org (2007)
7. Daiber, J., Jakob, M., Hokamp, C., Mendes, P.N.: Improving efficiency and accuracy in multilingual entity extraction. In: Sabou, M., Blomqvist, E., Noia, T.D., Sack, H., Pellegrini, T. (eds.) I-SEMANTICS, pp. 121–124. ACM (2013)
8. Lindén, K., Axelson, E., Hardwick, S., Pirinen, T.A., Silfverberg, M.: HFST—framework for compiling and applying morphologies. In: Mahlow, C., Piotrowski, M. (eds.) SFCM 2011. CCIS, vol. 100, pp. 67–85. Springer, Heidelberg (2011)
9. Shuyo, N.: Language detection library for java (2010). http://code.google.com/p/language-detection/
10. Pirinen, T.A.: Modularisation of finnish finite-state language description - towards wide collaboration in open source development of morphological analyser. In: Proceedings of Nodalida. NEALT proceedings, vol. 18 (2011)
11. Moshagen, S.N., Pirinen, T.A., Trosterud, T.: Building an open-source development infrastructure for language technology projects. In: Proceedings of the 19th Nordic Conference of Computational Linguistics (NODALIDA 2013). NEALT Proceedings Series, vol. 16, 22–24 May 2013
12. Porter, M.F.: Snowball: a language for stemming algorithms, October 2001. http://snowball.tartarus.org/texts/introduction.html

Aether – Generating and Viewing Extended VoID Statistical Descriptions of RDF Datasets

Eetu Mäkelä(✉)

Semantic Computing Research Group (SeCo), Aalto University, Espoo, Finland
eetu.makela@aalto.fi
http://www.seco.tkk.fi/

Abstract. This paper presents the Aether web application for generating, viewing and comparing extended VoID statistical descriptions of RDF datasets. The tool is useful for example in getting to know a newly encountered dataset, in comparing datasets between versions and in detecting outliers and errors. Examples are given on how the tool has been used to shed light on multiple important datasets.

1 Introduction

Dataset descriptions, of which VoID descriptions [1] are the current norm, are RDF descriptions of the contents of RDF datasets. They contain for example information about the licensing and access endpoints of the dataset, as well as statistical spreads about its content and interlinking. Use cases for such descriptions [2,3] include improving discovery and selection of datasets for a particular task [4], as well as query optimization, particularly in federared querying [5,6].

However, only 14 % of the 438 endpoints catalogued by the SPARQL endpoint status tool Sparqles[1] currently present a VoID description of their contents. Further, many of those that do lack the statistic spreads of the contents. Finally, some descriptions, most notably the official one of DBPedia[2], are heavily outdated and/or still follow an older, incompatible version of the VoID specification.

This may be a chicken-and-egg problem in the sense that despite the availability of automated tools [3,6] for offline dataset description creation, they are still not easy enough to use. Neither are there many tools that would make use of such data if it were available. The Aether web application presented here[3] aims to tackle both sides of this problem, by being able to automatically generate extended VoID statistical spreads from a SPARQL 1.1 endpoint, as well as by allowing such spreads to be viewed in a graphical interface.

More specifically, the original goal of the Aether tool was to be able to generate and visualize such descriptions of a dataset that a user encountering the

[1] http://sparqles.okfn.org/discoverability

[2] At http://dbpedia.org/void/Dataset

[3] online at http://demo.seco.tkk.fi/aether/, with code available at http://github.com/jiemakel/aether/

V. Presutti et al. (Eds.): ESWC Satellite Events 2014, LNCS 8798, pp. 429–433, 2014.
DOI: 10.1007/978-3-319-11955-7_61

dataset for the first time would be able to make sense of its content and general outlook. In addition, the tool also has features for comparing datasets, particularly useful for seeing how they change between versions. It has also become apparent that the tool can aid in detecting outliers and errors in a dataset, by e.g. highlighting subjects and objects with disproportionate amounts of references.

In the following, first some extensions and clarifications to the VoID vocabulary that were necessary for attaining the goals set for the tool are discussed. Then, the Aether tool itself is presented, along with example use cases.

2 Extended VoID Description

The VoID vocabulary [1] defines statistics properties for disclosing the number of triples, entities and classes in a dataset, as well as the number of distinct properties, subjects and objects. In addition, the vocabulary defines properties whereby a dataset may be split into class- or property-based partitions. Combining these, one is able to for example state that there are a certain number of triples with the property "foaf:name". In the Aether viewer interface, these combinations are grouped into bar charts by partition type, intuitively visualizing e.g. the top 50 properties with the most triples, as seen in Fig. 1.

For answering the goals set forth for Aether, the two partitions and six statistics defined in VoID are however insufficient. Indeed before, first the RDFStats tool [6] and later the LODStats project [3] have defined further dimensions and statistics for datasets. Particularly the LODStats extended set of 32 statistical criteria[4], deriving from (1) a survey of VoID and RDFStats statistics, (2) analysis

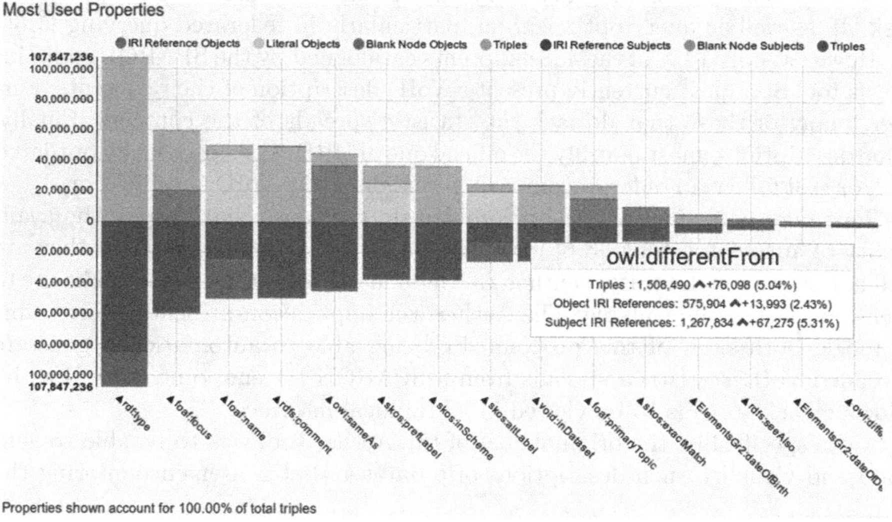

Fig. 1. Part of the Aether visualization interface showing property-related statistics compared between two different versions of the VIAF dataset

[4] https://github.com/AKSW/LODStats/wiki/Statistical-Criteria

of RDF data model elements and (3) expert interviews, seems to naturally serve as a great starting point for a comprehensive description of a dataset.

Upon further inspection however, it seems that while the criteria themselves are good, their formal serialization is problematic. First, the namespace IRIs do not resolve. Then, by looking at the SPARQL endpoint which does contain definitions, it seems that those definitions do not match the spirit of the RDF Data Cube vocabulary [7], on which they are nominally based on. Instead of defining the different statistical measures as properties, there is a single measure property of "ls-qb:value", with the different measurements defined as dimensions. On the other hand, none of the partitioning dimensional properties are defined (and indeed, none of the partitioned data is available as data from http://stats.lod2.eu/), even though it is visualized there.

Another observation about stats.lod2.eu is that its access mechanisms always return either just the VoID, or just the (partial) Data Cube descriptions for a dataset. This already tells that combining the two different statistics presentation and addressing mechanisms is not without problems. Based on this, it was decided that the description used by Aether should either fully function like VoID statistics and partitions, or like Data Cube slices and measurements. From the options, VoID was chosen as it is the current commonly acknowledged base.

For the purposes of the Aether tool, is was worth noting that the statistics properties of VoID fall in two camps: one concerning entities without regard to triples (the class partition and the entities and classes statistics) and the other concerning triples and their parts (the property partition and the distinct triples, properties, subjects and objects statistics). From the specification, it is unclear if or how these interact with each other (e.g. what would an entities count mean for a property partition, or a distinct object count for a class partition).

For Aether, this proved problematic as there was a desire to support a drill-down interaction, where the user could select any partition from the visualizations, with all visualizations then updating to contain only the contents matching that partition. To solve the problem, a triple-centric approach was taken, creating new statistics and partitions that explicitly relate the triple and entity worlds to each other. For example, separate partitions were created for subject, property and object classes, each only containing classes whose instances appear in the corresponding position in a triple belonging to the current partition.

In the end, this led to the creation of the void-ext vocabulary at http://ldf.fi/void-ext, which extends the VoID vocabulary with a total of 18 statistics and 14 partitions. In this paper, in place of discussing the properties individually, they are presented later alongside the discussion of the user interface.

3 The Aether Tool

The Aether tool itself divides into two functionalities. The first of these allows the creation of an extended VoID description from any SPARQL 1.1 conformant endpoint[5]. The feasibility of this approach depends on the SPARQL endpoint and

[5] The queries used can be read from the source starting at http://github.com/jiemakel/aether/blob/1.0.0/app/scripts/void/voidService.coffee#L230.

the various dimensions of the dataset. To give some examples, a dataset of 30 000 triples residing in a TDB-backed Fuseki SPARQL endpoint was processed in 7 s. Two datasets of some 200 000 triples containing mostly uniform instance data took 3 and 7 min, respectively. An instance dataset of 750 000 triples was processed in 45 min. On the other hand, about the same time was required to process an ontology of 350 000 triples. And when that same ontology was processed from a purely memory-backed model instead of a TDB-backed one, processing time skyrocketed to a whopping 12 h, due to the memory-backed model providing less useful statistics to Fuseki's SPARQL optimizer. The largest dataset thus far processed using the SPARQL queries, comprising of the 23 million triples of the Finnish edition of DBPedia 3.9, took almost 5 h.

For processing larger datasets, an offline tool can be used. Using this tool, a description of for example the 2.2 billion triples in the complete international version of DBPedia 3.9 was created in approximately 42 h. Unfortunately, the offline tool is tied to a custom triple store implementation that is not yet publicly available, and thus also neither is the tool.

The other part of the Aether tool is the visualization interface, of which a part was already depicted in Fig. 1. In whole, the interface is divided into a configuration selector, plus six parts divulging statistics about the dataset.

At the top of the interface is the configuration selector, which allows the reading of a VoID description from a SPARQL endpoint, or also actually querying that endpoint itself live for the requested statistics. A second endpoint or description can also be specified, to which the primary statistics will be compared.

The first part of the interface containing statistics is termed General Information. Shown are for example the total amount of triples and distinct RDF nodes, as well as the amount of classes and literal datatypes and languages. Distinct triple part counts are also given, as are pie charts on how the RDF nodes divide between blank nodes, IRIs and literals, along with bar charts showing the length distribution of IRIs and literals, respectively.

The next section of the interface is an auxiliary part termed Namespace Information, which associates all namespaces encountered with prefixes so that the rest of the visualizations can show only short forms of the IRIs.

Then follow four parts relating to subdivisions by triple part: property, resource object, literal object and subject. For sections other than literal objects, bar charts are drawn on divisions by most referenced IRI, namespace and class. For literal objects on the other hand, the most referenced literals, datatypes and languages are presented. In addition, the chart for most referenced properties contains additional embedded information, relating the individual properties to their corresponding numbers of distinct subjects, resource objects and literals.

All items shown in any visualization among these four parts is also clickable, causing the whole description to update to show only information pertaining to that partition (e.g. showing statistics constrained to only those triples where the property is from the foaf namespace). Double-clicking on the other hand causes a suitable live query to be launched against the SPARQL endpoint that is the source of the data, if one is available.

4 Examples of Use

Many of the visualizations have already been found useful for divulging interesting information about a dataset. For example, when viewing statistics about the European cultural aggregator Europeana, the RDF node counts show a huge number of IRI resources, but looking at the property graph, it can be seen that all primary metadata in Europeana is actually encoded as literals! The number of IRI references comes from applying the Europeana Data Model, which requires aggregate and proxy IRIs to be minted for each work. In fact, there seem to be only about 20 million objects in Europeana, even if there are 120 million IRIs. Most literals also do not seem to have appropriate language codes.

Comparing statistics for a dataset between versions on the other hand can tell about the growth of that dataset. For example, between 2014-02-15 & 2013-11-24, the Virtual Internet Authority File VIAF has grown by 178,673 persons. In the same 3 months, 15,884 new links to DBPedia have been created and 576,387 more entity identifiers have been deprecated (merged with others). Using the tool, one can also quickly find that the person with the most distinct names in VIAF is the 13th century Persian poet and mystic Rumi, who is now known by 419 names, 6 more than in November.

For more examples, as well as to see these ones live in the interface, head to the application at http://demo.seco.tkk.fi/aether/.

References

1. Alexander, K., Cyganiak, R., Hausenblas, M., Zhao, J.: Describing linked datasets with the VoID vocabulary. W3C Interest Group Note, March 2011
2. Alexander, K., Cyganiak, R., Hausenblas, M., Zhao, J.: Describing linked datasets. [8]
3. Auer, Sören, Demter, Jan, Martin, Michael, Lehmann, Jens: LODStats – an extensible framework for high-performance dataset analytics. In: ten Teije, Annette, Völker, Johanna, Handschuh, Siegfried, Stuckenschmidt, Heiner, d'Acquin, Mathieu, Nikolov, Andriy, Aussenac-Gilles, Nathalie, Hernandez, Nathalie (eds.) EKAW 2012. LNCS, vol. 7603, pp. 353–362. Springer, Heidelberg (2012)
4. Toupikov, N., Umbrich, J., Delbru, R., Hausenblas, M., Tummarello, G.: Ding! dataset ranking using formal descriptions. [8]
5. Görlitz, O., Staab, S.: Splendid: Sparql endpoint federation exploiting void descriptions. In: Hartig, O., Harth, A., Sequeda, J. (eds.): COLD. CEUR Workshop Proceedings, vol. 782. CEUR-WS.org (2011)
6. Langegger, A., Wöß, W.: Rdfstats - an extensible rdf statistics generator and library. In: Tjoa, A.M., Wagner, R. (eds.): DEXA Workshops, pp. 79–83. IEEE Computer Society (2009)
7. Cyganiak, R., Reynolds, D., Tennison, J.: The RDF data cube vocabulary. W3C Recommendation, January 2014
8. Bizer, C., Heath, T., Berners-Lee, T., Idehen, K. (eds.): Proceedings of the WWW2009 Workshop on Linked Data on the Web, LDOW 2009, Madrid, Spain, 20 April 2009 (Bizer, C., Heath, T., Berners-Lee, T., Idehen, K. (eds.): LDOW. CEUR Workshop Proceedings, vol. 538. CEUR-WS.org (2009)

SPARQL SAHA, a Configurable Linked Data Editor and Browser as a Service

Eetu Mäkelä(✉) and Eero Hyvönen

Semantic Computing Research Group (SeCo), Aalto University, Espoo, Finland
{eetu.makela,eero.hyvonen}@aalto.fi
http://www.seco.tkk.fi/

Abstract. SPARQL SAHA is a linked data editor and browser that can be used as a service, targeting any available SPARQL endpoint. Besides being available as a web service, the primary differentiating features of the tool are its configurability to match the underlying data, and the fact that the usability of its user interface has been verified by dozens of non-experts using the tool in multiple multi-year projects.

1 Introduction

As part of the Linked Data ecosystem, both linked data browsers as well as editors are needed. The Semantic Web Wiki alone lists 45 distinct entries in its browser subcategories[1], and 35 tools in its editor category[2]. Among such a large number of tools, it would seem hard for a new tool to distinguish itself. However, after surveying the competition it was deduced that the SPARQL SAHA linked data editor and browser presented in this paper still has a particular combination of features that contributes to others' work. The tool is available online.[3]

First, SPARQL SAHA operates *as a service*[4], being able to be pointed against any SPARQL-compliant endpoint for both querying and updating. Further, the usability of the tool has been verified by dozens of non-experts using the tool in multiple multi-year projects. Finally, the tool is also fully multilingual.

Originally, SAHA was a dedicated application with its own storage [1]. The tool was created as a generic web-based RDF metadata editor that would (1) be easily adaptable to various schemas, (2) support multiple simultaneous users, and (3) be understandable and usable by laymen. It was only later as part of a general push toward more modular applications [2] that the tool was modified to work on top of a standard SPARQL endpoint, a major topic of this paper. In doing so, it was discovered that this also increased the usability and

[1] http://www.w3.org/2001/sw/wiki/Category:Special_Browser

[2] http://www.w3.org/2001/sw/wiki/Category:Editor

[3] This work is part of the Linked Data Finland project funded by the Finnish Funding Agency for Innovation (Tekes) of 20 partners.

[4] online at http://demo.seco.tkk.fi/ssaha/, with sources available at http://code.google.com/p/saha/

V. Presutti et al. (Eds.): ESWC Satellite Events 2014, LNCS 8798, pp. 434–438, 2014.
DOI: 10.1007/978-3-319-11955-7_62

adaptability of the tool, as now there was an additional, configurable layer of SPARQL queries mapping the raw data into its various presentation forms.

To evaluate the usability of SAHA, it has been used in a number of projects [3–5] by non-experts in RDF or Linked Data. The longest term and broadest of these is the BookSampo project [5], where dozens of volunteer librarians from Finnish public libraries have been indexing Finnish fiction literature using the editor since 2008. The user interface highlights presented here come mostly from the experiences gained in that project.

2 The User Interface of the SAHA Metadata Editor

Functionally, the main user interface of SAHA is divided into four distinct views. The first of these is the *index view*, which shows an overview of the class hierarchy used in the project along with corresponding instance counts. Clicking on any of the classes brings up the second *instance view*, which shows instances of the class under question. Together, these two views allow indexers and browsers to get an overview of the contents of the dataset.

In the BookSampo project, the instance view has also been used as simple work lists, with librarians dividing work for example alphabetically inside the instance list. This sort of ad-hoc collaboration is supported in the editor environment by a project-wide chat functionality, visible on all pages on the top right of the interface. Problems arising from multiple persons editing a resource at the same time are averted by a locking mechanism.

For quick navigation to resources of interest, all views in SAHA include a common keyword search functionality in the top part of the user interface. Typically, this search is configured to target all properties of all resources, so that for example indexers can quickly search for "author Waltari" to find books authored by Mika Waltari instead of the person record itself.

Selecting an instance moves the UI into the third view, the *browsing view*, where properties of the selected resource are visualized, along with a list showing any other resources referring to it. Clicking on any of the resources listed loads the view with that resource, enabling associative browsing of the dataset.

However, to better support contextualization and quick browsing, in all interface components, all resources also show their direct properties in a pop-up preview when the mouse is moved over them. Feedback from library indexers has shown this to be an extremely important functionality for them.

From the browsing view, the user can finally enter the *editing view*, which mirrors the browsing view with editable components, as show in Fig. 1. The user is here editing metadata about Mika Waltari's historical novel Sinuhe the Egyptian. The view shows both all properties that the resource has, as well as all properties associated with classes the resource is an instance of.

For object references, SAHA utilizes semantic autocompletion [6]. When the user tries to find a concept, SAHA uses at the same time web services to fetch concepts from configured external repositories, as well as the local project. Results are shown in one autocompletion result list regardless of origin, and their

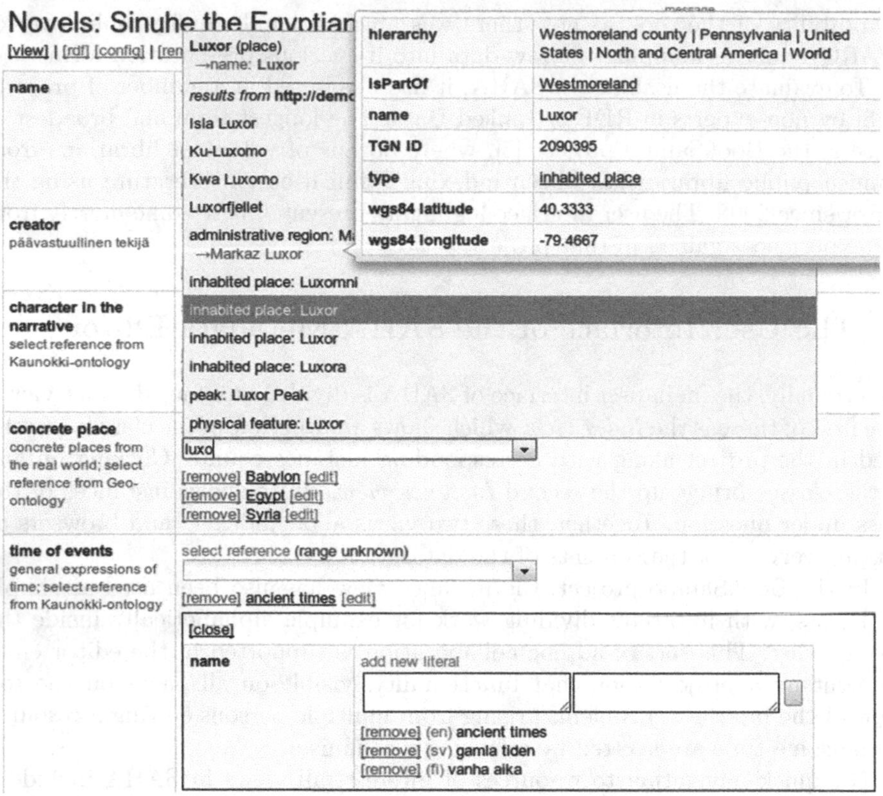

Fig. 1. The SAHA metadata editor, showing both semantic autocompletion as well as a pop-up preview presentation of one of the autocompletion results.

properties can also be inspected using the pop-up preview presentations. In the situation depicted in Fig. 1, for example, this is extremely useful when the user must choose which of the many Luxors returned from both local and external RDF sources is the correct annotation for this book. The preview of places also includes a map visualization, but this is cut off in the figure. For geodata, SAHA also supports the editing of points, polylines, and polygons on maps.

For the purposes of the BookSampo project, the SAHA editor was improved with an inline editor feature. The idea is simple: a resource referenced through an object property can be edited inline in a small version of the editor inside the existing view. Specifically, this functionality was developed to ease the use of the auxiliary resources required in the RDF data model to group information together, such as when associating an issue number with information that a book has been published in a particular literature series. However, there seemed to be no reason to restrict the functionality, so this possibility is now available for all linked object resources. In Fig. 1, this is shown for the property "time of events" whose value "ancient times" has been opened inline for editing.

3 Flexibility from Configurability and Using SPARQL

To be easily usable for a variety of projects, the SAHA editor provides a configuration interface with sensible defaults, with the configuration options also serializable as RDF and thus transferable along with the project data and schema.

For each property and class combination, the order in which the properties are displayed can be configured by simply dragging and dropping the fields. In addition, each object property can also be linked to external repositories from which to draw references from, while literal properties can be shown either with language-tagging support or without.

The move to using configurable SPARQL queries to populate all views considerably increased the flexibility of the editor. For example in the BookSampo project, certain metaclasses that caused confusion could be hidden from the class hierarchy. Also, while most projects wanted to group the list of resources referring to an object by the referring property, in BookSampo the librarians were so used to a pure alphabetical list that they wanted the functionality reverted.

The configurability of the SPARQL queries also came into use in tuning the scalability of the system when suddenly the BookSampo dataset grew to 1.5 times its former size as the project also started to cover children's literature. Here, response times on the now 6.6 million triple dataset decreased threefold by tuning the generic default queries to the exact data model semantics of the dataset. In the end, this resulted in performance faster than the original dedicated SAHA.

In the BookSampo project, operating on top of a SPARQL endpoint also allowed the creation of custom reports, basically SPARQL queries whose results are linked to the SAHA editor. For example, queries have been crafted to list multiple books having the same name and author as candidates for merging, as well as to list orphaned resources no longer referenced from any primary item.

4 SAHA as a Linked Data Browser

In addition to its use as an editor, SAHA can also be used as a simple linked data browser and publishing platform. That is, the resource view of SAHA supports content negotiation and is able to present either an RDF view or the human-oriented browser view in response. In this mode, the tool has been used to publish for example a World War I -related data collection [3]. Further, the tool was chosen as the linked data browser to be used for the national Linked Data Finland LDF.fi portal[5], after experimenting with multiple other choices such as URIBurner[6] and Pubby[7]. Here, the primary reasons for selecting the tool were: (1) the pop-up preview functionality of the tool provided a better user experience than was available from competitors, (2) by configuring the SPARQL queries, the tool could be adapted to the sometimes quirky data modeling conventions used

[5] http://www.ldf.fi/

[6] http://uriburner.com/

[7] http://wifo5-03.informatik.uni-mannheim.de/pubby/

by some of the datasets to be published and (3) the tool supported linked data browsing of material also in cases where the IRIs did not match their publication location, also an unfortunate case in some of the datasets.

5 Related Work

As stated earlier, there are both many other editors as well as browsers for linked data. Based on the survey conducted for this work, of the editors the closest to SAHA would be SKOSjs[8], which also works as a web application on top of SPARQL endpoints, and features multilanguage support. However, where SAHA is directed mostly at indexing instances, SKOSjs is geared towards managing a SKOS vocabulary hierarchy. Thus, the two tools actually complement each other.

Of browsers, the closest matches seemed to be Pubby[9] and Graphity [7], which can both operate on top of a SPARQL endpoint to publish data, and where Graphity also had ways by which to configure the presentation of that data. For both tools however the SPARQL endpoint is fixed in configuration, thus disallowing using the tool as a service.

References

1. Kurki, J., Hyvönen, E.: Collaborative metadata editor integrated with ontology services and faceted portals. In: Workshop on Ontology Repositories and Editors for the Semantic Web (ORES 2010), the Extended Semantic Web Conference ESWC 2010, CEUR Workshop Proceedings, vol. 596, June 2010
2. Mäkelä, E., Viljanen, K., Alm, O., Tuominen, J., Valkeapää, O., Kauppinen, T., Kurki, J., Sinkkilä, R., Kansala, T., Lindroos, R., Suominen, O., Ruotsalo, T., Hyvönen, E.: Enabling the semantic web with ready-to-use web widgets. In: Nixon, L.J.B., Cuel, R., Bergamini, C. (eds.): FIRST. CEUR Workshop Proceedings, vol. 293, pp. 56–69. CEUR-WS.org (2007)
3. Lindquist, T., Hyvönen, E., Trnroos, J., Mäkelä, E.: Leveraging linked data to enhance subject access - a case study of the University of Colorado Boulder's World War I collection online. [8]
4. Hyvönen, E., Alm, O., Kuittinen, H.: Using an ontology of historical events in semantic portals for cultural heritage. In: Proceedings of the Cultural Heritage on the Semantic Web Workshop at the 6th International Semantic Web Conference (ISWC 2007), 12 November 2007
5. Mäkelä, E., Hypén, K., Hyvönen, E.: Improving fiction literature access by linked open data -based collaborative knowledge storage - the BookSampo project. [8]
6. Hyvönen, E., Mäkelä, E.: Semantic autocompletion. In: Mizoguchi, R., Shi, Z.-Z., Giunchiglia, F. (eds.) ASWC 2006. LNCS, vol. 4185, pp. 739–751. Springer, Heidelberg (2006)
7. Jusevičius, M., Smirnovas, A., poraitis, J.: Graphity - a generic linked data platform. In: Proceedings of the Linked Enterprise Data Patterns Workshop 2011 (2011)
8. World Library and Information Congress: 78th IFLA General Conference and Assembly, Helsinki, Finland, 11–17 August 2012. Proceedings, World Library and Information Congress (2012)

[8] http://github.com/tkurz/skosjs

[9] http://wifo5-03.informatik.uni-mannheim.de/pubby/

LinkLion: A Link Repository for the Web of Data

Markus Nentwig[1(✉)], Tommaso Soru[2], Axel-Cyrille Ngonga Ngomo[2], and Erhard Rahm[1]

[1] Database Group, Department of Computer Science, University of Leipzig, Leipzig, Germany
{nentwig,rahm}@informatik.uni-leipzig.de

[2] AKSW, Department of Computer Science, University of Leipzig, Leipzig, Germany
{tsoru,ngonga}@informatik.uni-leipzig.de

Abstract. Links between knowledge bases build the backbone of the Web of Data. Consequently, numerous applications have been developed to compute, evaluate and infer links. Still, the results of many of these applications remain inaccessible to the tools and frameworks that rely upon it. We address this problem by presenting LinkLion, a repository for links between knowledge bases. Our repository is designed as an open-access and open-source portal for the management and distribution of link discovery results. Users are empowered to upload links and specify how these were created. Moreover, users and applications can select and download sets of links via dumps or SPARQL queries. Currently, our portal contains 12.6 million links of 10 different types distributed across 3184 mappings that link 449 datasets. In this demo, we will present the repository as well as different means to access and extend the data it contains. The repository can be found at http://www.linklion.org.

1 Introduction

In addition to being central for question answering across several datasets, links also play a key role in various other domains such as data fusion and federated SPARQL queries. It is a well-known problem that links make up less than 3 % of the RDF triples on the Web of Data [4]. This problem is being addressed by link discovery and ontology matching tools and frameworks [2,3]. However, due to the architectural choices behind the Web of Data, the results of a link discovery (LD) framework cannot be added directly to the datasets involved in the link discovery process. Further, the direct addition of links to a knowledge base fails to provide means to track the source of these links for later reference. Moreover, the availability of some endpoints still remains a major issue,[1] making the direct addition of linking results to some endpoints unattractive.

We address these drawbacks by presenting the open-source link repository LinkLion. The main goal of LinkLion is to facilitate the publication, retrieval

[1] http://labs.mondeca.com/sparqlEndpointsStatus.html

V. Presutti et al. (Eds.): ESWC Satellite Events 2014, LNCS 8798, pp. 439–443, 2014.
DOI: 10.1007/978-3-319-11955-7_63

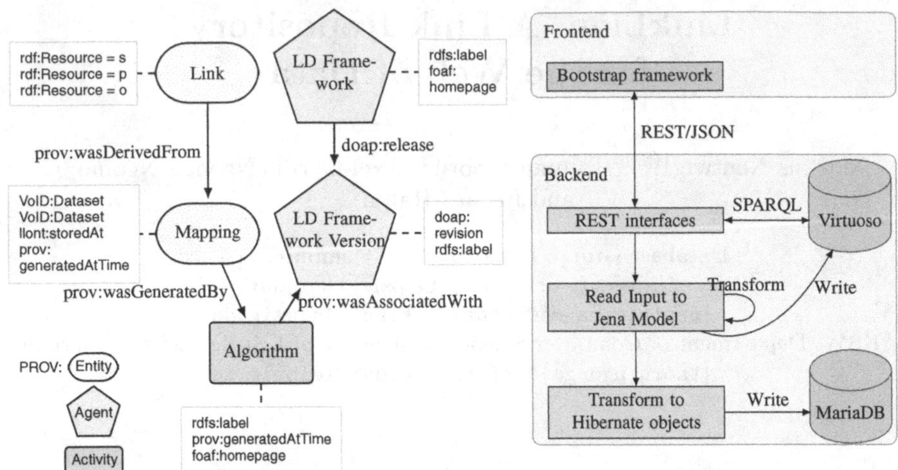

(a) Overview of the LinkLion ontology. New classes such as Link, Mapping, Algorithm and LD Framework are specified as subclasses of the PROV vocabulary.

(b) Visualization of front and back end to store the mappings in the Virtuoso and MariaDB.

Fig. 1. Overview LinkLion ontology and architecture.

and use of links between knowledge bases. Our repository thus provides dedicated functionality for the upload, storage, querying and download of large sets of links. Currently, it contains 63 million triples which describe 12.6 million links of 10 different types (e.g., `owl:sameAs`, `dbo:spokenIn`, `foaf:made`, `spatial:P`)[2] distributed on 3184 mappings that link 449 datasets. These links were retrieved from the Web as well as computed by tools such as LIMES [3] and Silk [6]. Our repository provides a SPARQL query interface as well as commodity interfaces to access the mappings. In contrast to other portals such as BioPortal[3], LinkLion focuses exclusively on links and provides dedicated functionality for manipulating them. Moreover, we do not limit ourselves to a single domain such as the life sciences. In the following, we give a brief overview of the repository and show the use cases that will be presented during the demo. The repository can be accessed at http://www.linklion.org. The code of the repository is available at http://github.com/AKSW/LinkingLodPortal. The SPARQL endpoint can be found at http://www.linklion.org:8890/sparql.

2 Implementation

An overview of LinkLion's architecture is given in Fig. 1b. The back end consists of a triple store in which we save data according to the vocabulary shown in Fig. 1a.

[2] We used the prefixes available at http://prefix.cc.

[3] http://www.bioontology.org/BioPortal

The ontology[4] was designed with usability and reuse in mind. Especially, we wanted to allow end users of the portal to select dedicated portions of certain mappings at will. This meant designing an ontology that allowed amongst others (1) retrieving all links that pertain to a particular resource or set of resources, (2) gathering all mappings between datasets of interest as well as (3) getting aggregated information on how particular links came about. We implemented this vision by storing the output of a link discovery tool under an instance of the mapping class. Individual mappings can be described by metadata including the datasets that they link, the tool (incl. a version number) used to generate the links and the creation date of the mapping. We refrained from using blank nodes for links. Instead, we gave each link a unique ID. Note that we reused existing vocabularies (especially PROV[5], VoID[6] and DOAP[7]) as much as we could. The use of a triple store pays off as end users can choose to provide more metadata such as the link specification used or parameters of the algorithm they used to discover the link without us having to alter our schema. For the sake of scalability, we yet also provide the core of the data in the triple store as SQL dump. The functionality of the back end is exposed by RESTful interfaces, which allow a programmatic access to LinkLion from code written in virtually any modern programming language.

The front end of our repository provides an easy way to use some of the functionality of LinkLion (see Fig. 2a). First, it allows users to upload new mappings. Users are asked to provide a source file in the N-Triples format[8]. well as the algorithm used within this framework have to be provided (note that we consider humans to also be linking frameworks). The data (and especially the mapping) given by the user is then checked for consistency and uploaded into the underlying triple store. The content of the triple store can be browsed directly from the web page (see Fig. 2b). Especially, the front end includes search functionality and pagination which allow end users to search for mappings that link to or from a dataset of interest. The upload and browsing functionality will be presented during the demo.

3 Use Cases

In this section, we present and motivate a selection of use cases that will be presented during the demo session.

3.1 Gather All Links and Mappings to a Given Resource

Gathering and fusing all information on a resource of interest is of central importance to applications such as Question Answering systems, Linked Data Browsers

[4] Available at http://www.linklion.org/ontology
[5] http://www.w3.org/TR/prov-o/
[6] http://www.w3.org/TR/void/
[7] https://github.com/edumbill/doap/
[8] http://www.w3.org/2001/sw/RDFCore/ntriples/

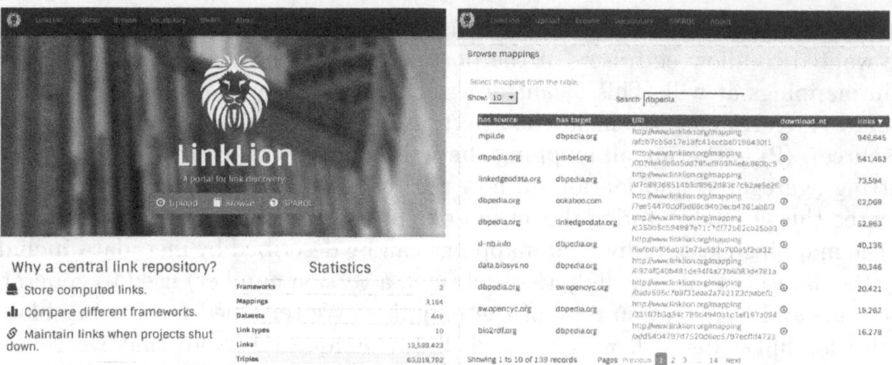

(a) LINKLION Homepage with statistics regarding the content.

(b) Mapping Browser. The search for DBpedia returns 139 mappings.

Fig. 2. Front-end views.

and Quality Assessment tools. LINKLION allows to gather all links pertaining to a particular resource (**dbpedia:Thailand** in our example) by means of the following SPARQL query. By using this information, novel repair-based algorithms for link discovery such as COLIBRI can find errors or inconsistencies in the data [5].

```
SELECT ?link WHERE { { ?link rdf:subject dbpedia:Thailand }
                UNION { ?link rdf:object dbpedia:Thailand } }
```

The portal also allows gather all mappings that contain links pertaining to a particular resource, e.g.. **dbpedia:Thailand**, as shown below.

```
SELECT DISTINCT ?mapping WHERE { ?link prov:wasDerivedFrom ?mapping .
                               { ?link rdf:subject dbpedia:Thailand }
                         UNION { ?link rdf:object dbpedia:Thailand } }
```

3.2 Get Support for a Link

Ensemble learning techniques have been shown to improve the results of manifold machine-learning applications such as Named Entity Recognition frameworks. Our repository facilitates the use of ensemble learning for combining the results of different link discovery tools. Especially, LINKLION allows us to retrieve (if any) the list of mappings that contain a given link, as well as the algorithms and the frameworks that generated it. In the following example, the support for **dbpedia: Thailand owl:sameAs** < http://sws.geonames.org/1605651/ > is queried.

```
SELECT ?mapping ?algorithm ?framework WHERE {
    ?mapping prov:wasGeneratedBy ?algorithm .
    ?algorithm prov:wasAssociatedWith ?framework .
    ?link prov:wasDerivedFrom ?mapping ;
          rdf:predicate owl:sameAs .
    { ?link rdf:subject dbpedia:Thailand;
            rdf:object <http://sws.geonames.org/1605651/> }
    UNION { ?link rdf:object dbpedia:Thailand;
                  rdf:subject <http://sws.geonames.org/1605651/> } }
```

3.3 Link Composition

With the growth of the Linked Data Web, it becomes ever more important to regard link discovery as a holistic process that goes beyond linking a pair of knowledge bases. Algorithms based on composition can exploit sequences of links to enrich their mapping composition graphs [1]. Moreover, algorithms which link several knowledge bases at the same time [5] can achieve higher accuracies. By using LinkLion, composition and concurrent linking algorithms are now enabled to gather the data they require without having to manage all the links by themselves. In the query below, all resources related to `dbpedia:Thailand` over two links are retrieved from the repository.

```
SELECT DISTINCT ?resource WHERE { {
    ?link rdf:subject dbpedia:Thailand ; rdf:object ?x .
    ?link2 rdf:subject ?x ; rdf:object ?resource }
    UNION { ?link rdf:object dbpedia:Thailand ; rdf:subject ?x .
            ?link2 rdf:object ?x ; rdf:subject ?resource } }
```

4 Summary

This paper presents LinkLion, a repository for links between knowledge bases of the Web of Data. The repository enables users to upload results of a link discovery process and furthermore allows them to add information on how the results were created. LinkLion therefore provides management and distribution capabilities through a both open-access and open-source web interface. Resulting sets of links can be reviewed in the portal and via SPARQL queries, additionally the results can be downloaded via dumps. In future work, LinkLion will be extended to support a closely collaboration with external link discovery frameworks and applications.

References

1. Hartung, M., Groß, A., Rahm, E.: Composition methods for link discovery. In: BTW (2013)
2. Kirsten, T., Gross, A., Hartung, M., Rahm, E.: GOMMA: a component-based infrastructure for managing and analyzing life science ontologies and their evolution. J. Biomed. Semant. **2**, 6 (2011)
3. Ngonga Ngomo, A.-C.: On link discovery using a hybrid approach. J. Data Semant. **1**(4), 203–217 (2012)
4. Ngonga Ngomo, A.-C., Auer, S.: LIMES: a time-efficient approach for large-scale link discovery on the web of data. In: Proceedings of the 22nd International Joint Conference on Artificial Intelligence, IJCAI'11, vol. 3, pp. 2312–2317. AAAI Press (2011)
5. Ngonga Ngomo, A.-C., Sherif, M.A., Lyko, K.: Unsupervised link discovery through knowledge base repair. In: Presutti, V., d'Amato, C., Gandon, F., d'Aquin, M., Staab, S., Tordai, A. (eds.) ESWC 2014. LNCS, vol. 8465, pp. 380–394. Springer, Heidelberg (2014)
6. Volz, J., Bizer, C., Gaedke, M., Kobilarov, G.: Silk - a link discovery framework for the web of data. In: Bizer, C., Heath, T., Berners-Lee, T., Idehen, K. (eds.) LDOW. CEUR Workshop Proceedings, vol. 538. CEUR-WS.org (2009)

Big, Linked and Open Data: Applications in the German Aerospace Center

C. Nikolaou[1], K. Kyzirakos[1], K. Bereta[1], K. Dogani[1(✉)], S. Giannakopoulou[1], P. Smeros[1], G. Garbis[1], M. Koubarakis[1], D.E. Molina[2], O.C. Dumitru[2], G. Schwarz[2], and M.Datcu[2]

[1] National and Kapodistrian University of Athens, Athens, Greece
{charnik,konstantina.bereta,kallirroi,ggarbis,koubarak}@di.uoa.gr
[2] German Aerospace Center (DLR), Cologne, Germany
mihai.datcu@dlr.de

Abstract. Earth Observation satellites acquire huge volumes of high resolution images continuously increasing the size of the archives and the variety of EO products. However, only a small part of this data is exploited. In this paper, we present how we take advantage of the TerraSAR-X images of the German Aerospace Center in order to build applications on top of EO data.

1 Introduction and Motivation

Advances in remote sensing technologies have enabled public and commercial organizations to send an ever-increasing number of satellites in orbit around Earth. As a result, Earth Observation (EO) data has been constantly increasing in volume in the last few years, and it is currently reaching petabytes (PBs) in many satellite archives. However, it is estimated that up to 95 % of the data present in existing archives has never been accessed.

EO data is the classical case of big data, and linked data is an excellent technology for moving EO data out of their silos, integrating them and building applications on top of them. In the last few years, linked geospatial data has received attention as researchers and practitioners have started tapping the wealth of geospatial information available on the Web. As a result, the linked open data (LOD) cloud has been rapidly populated with geospatial data (e.g., OpenStreetMap) some of it describing EO products (e.g., CORINE Land Cover, Urban Atlas). The abundance of this data can prove useful to the new missions (e.g., Sentinels) as a means to increase the usability of EO products produced by these missions. At last, but not least, combining linked open data with knowledge discovered from EO products offers a great chance for finding and locating interesting information in order to support emerging applications such as change detection, image time series, urban analytics, etc.

This work was funded by the FP7 projects TELEIOS (257662) and LEO (611141).

V. Presutti et al. (Eds.): ESWC Satellite Events 2014, LNCS 8798, pp. 444–449, 2014.
DOI: 10.1007/978-3-319-11955-7_64

TELEIOS[1] is a recent European project that addressed the need for scalable access to PBs of EO data and the effective discovery of knowledge hidden in them. TELEIOS was the first project internationally that introduced the linked data paradigm to the EO domain, and developed prototype applications that are based on transforming EO products into RDF, and combining them with linked geospatial data. TELEIOS advanced the state of the art in knowledge discovery from satellite images by developing a novel knowledge discovery framework and applying it to synthetic aperture radar images obtained by the satellite TerraSAR-X of the German Aerospace Center (DLR), a TELEIOS partner. In [3] we outlined the knowledge discovery framework that is currently employed by DLR and discussed how it can be used together with ontologies and linked geospatial data for the development of a Virtual Earth Observatory for TerraSAR-X data that goes beyond existing EO portals by allowing a user to express such complex queries as "Find all satellite images with patches containing water limited on the north by a port".

In this paper, we present a new framework that sets the foundations of the development of richer tools and applications that focus on increasing the exploitation of EO products. The proposed framework allows a user to express complex queries by combining metadata information of EO images (e.g., date and time of acquisition), image content expressed as low-level features (e.g., certain feature vectors) and/or semantic labels (e.g., ports, bridges), as well as other publicly available geospatial information expressed in RDF as linked open data. The contribution of this framework is not only based on the discovered knowledge, but also on presenting the results in a user friendly interface (e.g., diagrams for data analytics, thematic maps) that could be usable in a large number of related applications.

2 Knowledge Discovery from EO Products

In this section we briefly present the knowledge discovery (KD) framework for EO images that is currently being employed by DLR for SAR images obtained by the satellite TerraSAR-X. The main steps of the process for knowledge discovery are the following:

1. *Tiling the image into patches.* TerraSAR-X images are divided into patches and descriptors are extracted for each one. The size of the generated patches depends on the resolution of the image and its pixel spacing [5].
2. *Patch content analysis.* This step takes as input the image patches produced by the previous step and generates feature vectors for each patch [5].
3. *Patch annotation.* In this step, a tool implementing a support vector machine classifier with relevance feedback (SVM-RF) is used to classify feature vectors into semantic classes in a semi-automatic manner [2]. The user may provide to the classifier (SVM) positive and negative examples of patches with respect to a specific semantic class and is responsible for mapping a semantic class to a

[1] http://www.earthobservatory.eu/

semantic label. The semantic labels are organized in a two-level classification scheme. This scheme, as well as the basic concepts of the KD framework (e.g., Patch), have been encoded as an RDFS ontology (Fig. 1) developed in TELEIOS [3]. We will refer to this ontology as the "DLR ontology"[2].

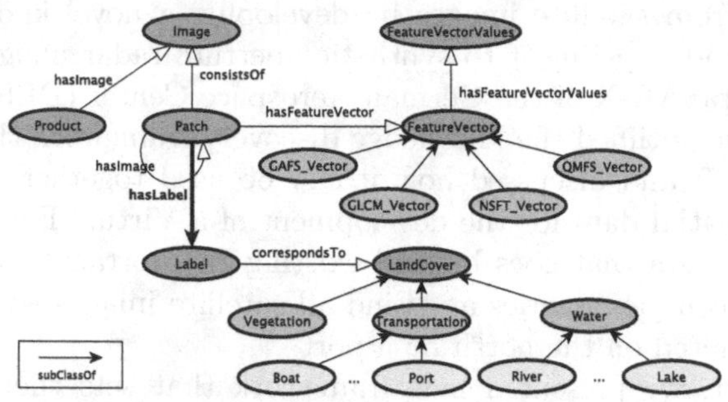

Fig. 1. The DLR ontology

After the tiling and feature extraction procedures are finished, each patch is characterized by a semantic annotation. The enrichment of EO products also involves a transformation step to the data model RDF based on the DLR ontology.

3 Applications on Top of EO Data

In this section we describe the applications we have built on top of EO products and we explain how these tools can be used to make the discovered knowledge easily accessible by a larger group of users.

3.1 Spatial Data Analytics

Enriching EO products with auxiliary data offers to users querying functionalities that go beyond the ones currently available to them. The RDF description of the EO products is stored in the RDF store Strabon [4] together with other available linked open data, like the Urban Atlals[3] (UA) dataset or CORINE Land Cover[4] (CLC).

Strabon endpoint provides a web interface where users not only can execute complex queries combining EO products and linked data, but also visualize the results in diagrams (pie charts, area charts, column charts, etc.) and produce interesting spatial data analytics. Figure 2a shows the stSPARQL [4] query used

[2] http://www.earthobservatory.eu/ontologies/dlrOntology.owl
[3] http://www.eea.europa.eu/data-and-maps/data/urban-atlas
[4] http://www.eea.europa.eu/publications/COR0-landcover

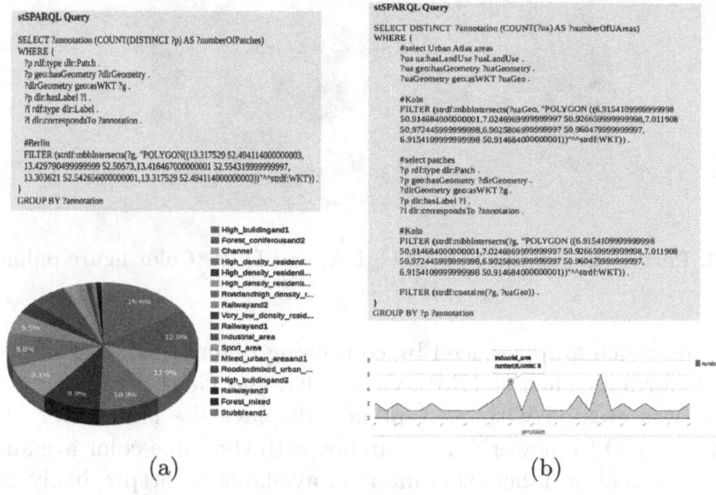

(a) (b)

Fig. 2. (a) Land use of Berlin and (b) number of Urban Atlas areas contained by a specific annotation of DLR.

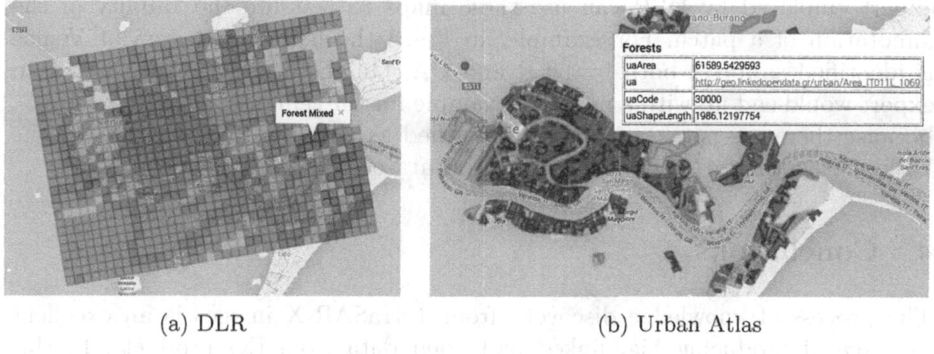

(a) DLR (b) Urban Atlas

Fig. 3. The land cover of Venice visualized in Sextant

to discover the distribution of land use of Berlin according to the KD framework and the pie chart that visualizes the result of this query. It is seen that a large part of Berlin is covered with high buildings and coniferous forests. The stSPARQL query displayed in Fig. 2b returns the number of UA areas that lie in DLR tiles with specific semantic annotation for the city of Cologne. For example, the patches characterized as "Industrial_area" by DLR contain five UA areas. An online demo providing the functionality described above is available at http://test.strabon.di.uoa.gr/DLR.

3.2 Visualizing Images of DLR in Sextant

Sextant [1,6] is a web-based tool for the visualization and exploration of linked spatiotemporal data and the creation, sharing, and collaborative editing of

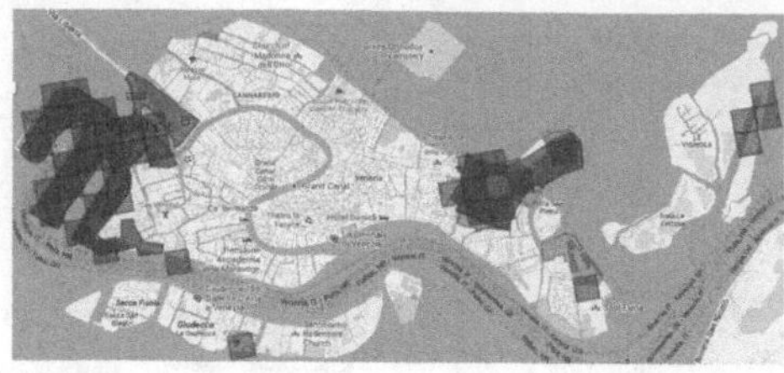

Fig. 4. Port areas identified by CLC, UA, and DLR (Color figure online)

thematic maps which are produced by combining different sources of such data and other file formats, such as KML, GeoJSON, and GeoTIFF.

Figure 3a was created with Sextant and displays the land cover of Venice according to the KD framework. The patches with the same color are annotated with the same semantic label (this map[5] is available at http://bit.ly/Sextant_Map). Figure 3b depicts the land use of Venice according to the Urban Atlas dataset.

The spatial resolution of the second map is much more accurate, so an EO expert employed by DLR can use these maps to reassure the validity of the annotation of a patch. For example, in Fig. 3 the highlighted area of Venice is identified as forest both by DLR and UA. On the other hand, in Fig. 4 an expert would end up with a negative example for the semantic class "port area", because there are patches (in grey) identified as port by DLR, but not by the Urban Atlas (in red) and CLC (in green) dataset.

4 Conclusions

The process of knowledge discovery from TerraSAR-X images is an excellent example of producing big, linked and open data from EO products. In this paper, we presented the applications we built on top of this data to make them easily accessible and usable by a larger group of users.

References

1. Bereta, K., Charalampos, N., Karpathiotakis, M., Kyzirakos, K., Koubarakis, M.: SexTant: visualizing time-evolving linked geospatial data. In: ISWC (2013)
2. Dumitru, C.O., Singh, J., Datcu, M.: Selection of relevant features and terrasar-x products for classification of high resolution sar images. In: 9th European Conference on Synthetic Aperture Radar, 2012, EUSAR, pp. 243–246. VDE (2012)
3. Koubarakis, M., et al.: Building virtual earth observatories using ontologies, linked geospatial data and knowledge discovery algorithms. In: Image Information Mining Conference (2012)

[5] To see the map click on the "Zoom To All" option in the last item of the main menu.

4. Kyzirakos, K., Karpathiotakis, M., Koubarakis, M.: Strabon: a semantic geospatial DBMS. In: Cudré-Mauroux, P., Heflin, J., Sirin, E., Tudorache, T., Euzenat, J., Hauswirth, M., Parreira, J.X., Hendler, J., Schreiber, G., Bernstein, A., Blomqvist, E. (eds.) ISWC 2012, Part I. LNCS, vol. 7649, pp. 295–311. Springer, Heidelberg (2012)
5. Molina, D.E., Cui, S., Dumitru, C.O., Datcu, M., members, C.: KDD Prototype - Phase II. Del. 3.2.2, TELEIOS project (2013)
6. Nikolaou, C., Dogani, K., Kyzirakos, K., Koubarakis, M.: Sextant: browsing and mapping the ocean of linked geospatial data. In: Cimiano, P., Fernández, M., Lopez, V., Schlobach, S., Völker, J. (eds.) ESWC 2013. LNCS, vol. 7955, pp. 209–213. Springer, Heidelberg (2013)

VideoLecturesMashup: Using Media Fragments and Semantic Annotations to Enable Topic-Centred e-Learning

Lyndon Nixon[1(✉)], Tanja Zdolsek[2], Ana Fabjan[2], and Peter Kese[3]

[1] MODUL University, Vienna, Austria
lyndon.nixon@modul.ac.at
[2] Jozef Stefan Institute, Ljubljana, Slovenia
tanja.zdolsek@ijs.si
[3] VIIDEA d.o.o., Kranj, Slovenia
peter@viidea.com

Abstract. In this demo, we present the VideoLecturesMashup, which delivers re-mixes of learning materials from the VideoLectures.NET portal based on shared topics across different lectures. Learners need more efficient access to teaching on specific topics which could be part of a larger lecture (focused on a different topic) and occur across lectures from different collections in distinct domains. Current e-learning video portals can not address this need, either to quickly dip into a shorter part focused on a specific topic of a longer lecture or to explore what is taught about a certain topic easily across collections. Through application of video analysis, semantic annotation and media fragment URIs, we have implemented a first demo of VideoLecturesMashup.

1 Introduction

Currently the VideoLectures.NET portal hosts more than 16.000 video lectures from prominent universities and conferences mainly from natural and technical sciences. Most lectures are 1–1.5 h long linked with slides and enriched with metadata and additional textual contents. Videolectures.NET is being visited by more than 15.000 unique visitors from all over the world daily, which provides a very efficient distribution and dissemination channel.

However, visitors typically have limited time to find and watch the materials they want and the topics they search for may be orthogonal to the materials themselves (be the subject of different parts of multiple learning resources rather than the subject of a specific complete learning resource). Visitors would benefit from easier and quicker access to those different parts in the form of a single, integrated presentation of learning materials, which in turn could drive more repeated access and win new users, including in new contexts, e.g. dynamic provision of such learning resource mashups would be particularly useful in mobile consumption contexts (where the user typically has more limited time and a restricted browsing interface). These mash-ups could subsequently form a new distribution channel for VideoLectures.NET contents.

V. Presutti et al. (Eds.): ESWC Satellite Events 2014, LNCS 8798, pp. 450–454, 2014.
DOI: 10.1007/978-3-319-11955-7_65

Hence we have proposed a use case in the MediaMixer project for the VideoLecturesMashup which will be a dedicated channel on the VideoLectures.NET portal capable of accepting a specific learning topic as input and producing as a result a mash up of fragments of learning materials from the site addressing that topic, ordered in a meaningful way.

2 Technology Used

Currently, the search and retrieval on VideoLectures.NET works on text matching over complete materials titles and descriptions. Not even the internal descriptions that are currently maintained (e.g. slide titles and contents) can be used in the site search. These internal descriptions (where content of the videos is tied to specific, mainly temporal, fragments) need to be more detailed, and the slide boundaries in the presentation (which can be calculated) linked to the correct temporal boundaries in the video (since a slide may be shown before the speaker starts to reference it, or they reference it before it is shown). This will require additional analysis processes being applied to the learning materials video to generate this annotation. This can usually not be included during recording, even signaling when the speaker refers to the next slide is difficult for a cameraperson probably not knowledgeable about the speakers subject. Thus in post-processing of audio, video and the associated slides, VideoLectures.NET must incorporate:

1. automatic textual transcription from speaker audio (ASR). We make use of the transLectures-UPV toolkit (TLK)[1], an open source set of ASR tools for video lectures.
2. concept extraction from slides (not just titles but textual content extracted via OCR technology). We are looking at the use of the solution from the Hasso Plattner Institute Potsdam[2] which is already used in yovisto video search (http://yovisto.com).
3. video analysis e.g. identification of spatial fragments of video with the speaker, slides and other objects. Here we use a set of tools courtesy of the research centre CERTH[3].

This richer annotation uses semantic technology, since associating a spatial or temporal fragment [1] to semantic concept (rather than, e.g. a simple text label) gives additionally the possibility to link that fragment to that concepts synonyms or related concepts in a semantic search and retrieval system. A metadata schema for the annotations has been selected, as well as a choice of vocabularies which contain the relevant concepts and provide (semantic) links to related concepts (e.g. within a taxonomy or classification scheme). An appropriate repository was provided to store the resulting (semantic) metadata and allow for efficient indexing and retrieval by a search agent. It is used alongside the current storage

---

[1] http://www.translectures.eu/tlk/

[2] http://www.yanghaojin.com/research/ACM-MM-GC-DEMO/

[3] http://multimedia.iti.gr/mediamixer/demonstrator.html

solution with the use of shared unique IDs for learning resources to provide a link between data in both stores. Automatic analysis handles timing of slide changes in the video, for example, however manual correction may likely still be important for the results of automatic concept detection. It may be that the accuracy of the processes is sufficient to rely on it in user search - however irrelevant results may be less tolerated in a mash up situation. Given the need for specialist understanding of the topic, one future option is to incentivize the learning resource creator to correct the annotation of their learning resource. Another is to rely on crowdsourcing, whether Mechanical Turk or the learning resource viewers themselves. Given the availability of richer annotation of the learning materials, a semantic search and retrieval module is provided for the fragment selection. Given the association of media fragments to semantic concepts, this module is able to match the input topic to concepts in the annotations via the use of appropriate ontologies (logical models of how different concepts relate to one another). There are three core functions performed by such a module:

1. the input topic is internally modelled as a semantic concept;
2. the annotated learning resources are internally indexed in terms of the concepts they are associated to, and
3. the module is able to calculate a match via semantic proximity between the concepts in the input topic and the concepts in a learning resource fragments annotation.

This semantic search module replaces in VideoLecturesMashup the text based search module used by VideoLectures.NET The results list no longer contains complete resources but fragments in terms of spatial or temporal divisions of the learning resources video. This required that VideoLectures.NET incorporates on both its media server and its embedded video player the necessary support for the Media Fragments specification [2].

3 VideoLecturesMashup Demonstrator

The first version of the VideoLecturesMashup demonstrator at http://mediamixer.videolectures.net shows the retrieval of media fragments based on user search.

Accessing the online demo the user sees a search bar and can conduct a search on keywords for their topic of interest. For instance, when entering as search key-word ‘Learning’ the user gets 12 video matches. For each video, users see a thumbnail and some metadata (title of the lecture, name of the lecturer, year of the lecture, number of views). Underneath, the fragments of the video which match the search term are listed, in this case we find a total of 35 fragments mentioning ‘statistics’ (Fig. 1(a)).

The user can click on one of the listed videos or directly on the listed fragments to watch the video/fragments. For example, as shown in Fig. 1(b), if a user clicks on the first video on the list, then the system will show the whole lecture title on the top, below the information of which categories the video is

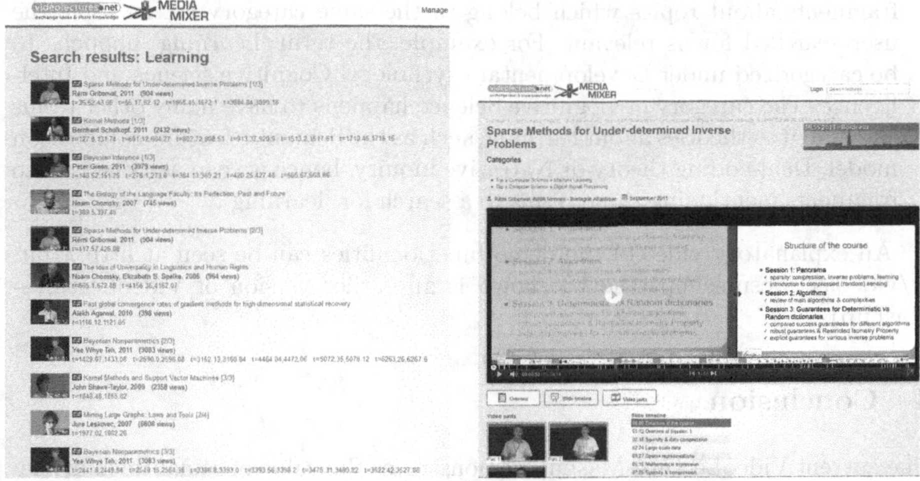

(a) User interface showing matching video fragments for 'Learning'

(b) Video fragment playback and information

Fig. 1. VideoLecturesMashup

categorized in, and information about the lecturer. On the right, it shows a picture banner, which shows at which event the watched lecture was given. After all this metadata the VideoLectures.NET player, which composed of the usual VideoLectures.NET layout (video on the left and sync slides on the right), is presented. Below the player, five features are presented: overview (short description, slide timeline), description (longer description), slide timeline (all slide timelines, a result of the video with slides synchronization), authors (description of the lecturer) and fragments (list of the matched fragments with timing).

With the integration of semantic search, the following aspects become feasible for the learner:

1. Finding video fragments via multilingual search. Since DBPedia extracts metadata from Wikipedia in all available languages, it also stores links between resources across the different language pages. Thus the term 'Learning' used in an English language lecture can still be found when the user searches for 'Lernen' (German).
2. Finding video fragments across synonyms. Since DBPedia also captures the information of Wikipedia's disambiguation and redirection pages, it can associate a resource with other terms which have been considered synonyms or clarifications of that resource. Again, a search for 'Learn' disambiguates to the term 'Learning' or for 'Acquisition' (in psychology) redirects to 'Learning', based on the already available DBPedia metadata.
3. Finding video fragments on related subjects or topics. DBPedia has a very complete categorization scheme, putting almost all resources into one or more categories, which themselves are organised in a large taxonomy. We consider

fragments about topics which belong to the same category as the topic the user searched for as relevant. For example, the term 'Learning' happens to be categorized under Developmental psychology, Cognitive science and Intelligence. The category of Cognitive Science happens to have many other terms associated to theories about learning, such as the Semantic feature-comparison model, Dual-coding theory or Narrative inquiry, hence we can associate video fragments mentioning these terms to a search for 'learning'.

An explanatory video of the demo functionalities can be seen at http://bit.ly/videolecturesmashup (the UI shown is an earlier version of VideoLectures-Mashup).

4 Conclusion

The current VideoLecturesMashup demonstrates the value of semantic multimedia and media fragment technology in enabling an e-learning video platform to offer learners a topic-centred path into parts of larger video lectures across various collections. As such, it provides a different structure to learning than current MOOCs which focus on individual courses which are curated with selected content from the outset. The learner's experience with re-mixes of materials needs further evaluation in terms of resulting satisfaction and further improvement of the visual interface will be part of this[4].

Acknowledgments. This work was supported by the MediaMixer project, funded by the EU Framework Programme 7 (http://www.mediamixer.eu). MediaMixer offers a free community portal with access to materials about semantic multimedia technologies (http://community.mediamixer.eu)

References

1. Troncy, R., Hardman, L., van Ossenbruggen, J., Hausenblas, M.: Identifying spatial and temporal media fragments on the web. In: W3C Video on the Web Workshop (2007)
2. Van Deursen, D., Troncy, R., Mannens, E., Pfeiffer, S., Lafon, Y., Van de Walle, R.: Implementing the media fragments URI specification. In: WWW 2010 Developers Track, Raleigh (USA) (2010)

[4] MediaMixer together with VideoLectures.NET ran a Grand Challenge at the ACM Multimedia 2013 conference to find new solutions for the temporal segmentation of video lectures. The winning proposal has an appealing visualisation of video fragment interlinking which we now examine as a potential UI extension for VideoLectures-Mashup. Demo at http://portal.klewel.com/graph/.

Securing Access to Sensitive RDF Data

V. Papakonstantinou(✉), G. Flouris, I. Fundulaki, and H. Kondylakis

Institute of Computer Science - Foundation for Research and Technology, Heraklion, Greece
{papv,fgeo,fundul,kondylak}@ics.forth.gr

Abstract. Given the increasing amount of sensitive RDF data available on the Web, it becomes critical to guarantee secure access to this content. The problem becomes even more challenging in the presence of RDFS inference, where inferred knowledge needs to be protected in the same way as explicit one. State of the art models for RDF access control annotate triples with concrete values that denote whether a triple can be accessed or not. In such approaches, the computation of the corresponding values for the inferred triples is hard-coded; this creates several problems in the presence of updates in the data, or, most importantly, when the access control policies change. We answer the above challenges by proposing an abstract model where the access labels are abstract tokens, and the computation of inferred labels is modelled through abstract operators. We demonstrate our model through the **HACEA** (**H**ealth **A**ccess **C**ontrol **E**nforcement **A**pplication) that provides simple access control/privacy functionalities in the context of a medical use case.

Keywords: Access control · RDF · Abstract access control models · eHealth

1 Introduction

The potential of the Web of Data is jeopardized by the fact that many of the datasets published by businesses and organizations worldwide may contain sensitive data, and, consequently, owners may be reluctant to reveal this information, unless they can be certain about the proper enforcement of the desired access rights of different accessing entities to (parts of) their data. Thus, the issue of *securing* content and *ensuring the selective exposure of information* to different classes of users is becoming all the more important. This has led to an increased interest in technologies related to *privacy* and *access control* in the context of the Web of Data. Such technologies will allow datasets with potentially sensitive content to be published, thus bringing the Web of Data to its full potential.

Most state of the art approaches for RDF access control [1–4] are based on the use of *annotation models* where each triple is associated with a *concrete value*, which is an access label designating whether the triple can be accessed or not. These models assign to the inferred triples (i.e., the ones that have been obtained

V. Presutti et al. (Eds.): ESWC Satellite Events 2014, LNCS 8798, pp. 455–460, 2014.
DOI: 10.1007/978-3-319-11955-7_66

through RDFS inference [5]) a label computed using *pre-specified* semantics. In these annotation models, a change in the assigned access label of an *explicit* triple would require a complete re-computation of the access labels of all triples obtained through inference, because there is no way of knowing which inferred triples are affected by said change. If this recomputation is not performed, then the dataset is not correctly annotated, and the system might eventually reveal data, that a requestor is not allowed to access [6].

To tackle the above problem we propose an *abstract access control model* [7,8] to provide secure access to *RDF graphs*. The model is defined by a set of *abstract tokens* and *abstract operators*, which are used to compute the access labels of *inferred* RDF triples. Essentially, our model allows us to record *how* the access label of an inferred triple is computed (rather than just the result of the computation). As a result, the proposed model (contrary to state of the art annotation models), does not commit to a specific assignment of values as access labels of triples, or to a predefined semantics for computing the access labels of the inferred triples (this is similar to *how provenance models* [9], proposed for relational data provenance). Note that, in a medical application context, it is often the case that explicit, fine-grained information need not be disclosed, whereas implicit, coarse-grained information can be accessible without jeopardizing the privacy of the data owner (patient). Therefore, we opted for treating implicit data as first-class citizens with respect to access control.

To demonstrate the use of the proposed abstract access control model, we created the **HACEA** (**H**ealth **A**ccess **C**ontrol **E**nforcement **A**pplication) based on a realistic medical scenario. **HACEA** is built on top of our access control system $A_{bs}ACEF$ and provides simple access control/privacy functionalities in the context of a medical use case.

2 Access Control Enforcement Using Abstract Models

In this section we give a brief introduction to the proposed abstract access control model; further details can be found in [7,8]. The model is comprised of *abstract tokens* and *abstract operators*. Abstract tokens encode the accessibility information of explicit RDF triples, and are assigned through *authorisations*. Authorisations are comprised of a *query* and an *abstract annotation token* and assign to all triples in the result of the SPARQL construct query the annotation token. The only abstract operator considered in our case is the *binary abstract inference accumulator* operator (denoted by $\odot$), which is used to compute the labels of inferred triples.

We represent *annotated* triples as *quadruples* of the form (s, p, o, l) where s, p, o are the RDF triple's *subject*, *property* and *object* and l is an *access label*. An access label is either an *access token* from the set of abstract tokens, or a *complex expression*; the latter is composed of the tokens and operators that describe *how* the access label of said triple is computed. These expressions are computed *once* (i.e., when triples are loaded in the repository) and are recomputed only when updates (either of the data or the authorizations) occur.

To determine whether a triple can be accessed by a requestor we compute the *actual value* of its associated abstract expression, by means of a *concrete policy.* A concrete policy is composed of a set of *mappings* that assign *concrete* values to the abstract tokens and operators; these values are used to compute the actual (concrete) value of the associated abstract expression. To determine whether a triple is accessible, an *access function* is defined by the policy and is evaluated on the computed concrete value. Note that each concrete policy is associated with a *requestor* and a *purpose*, to determine the triples that are accessible for said requestor for the defined purpose.

Access control enforcement using abstract models is done as follows: first, during the *annotation phase*, the SPARQL queries of the authorizations are evaluated against the dataset in order to annotate each triple with an abstract access token (producing a set of quadruples). Then, the RDFS inference rules, *extended for quadruples*, are applied to compute the *closure* of this RDF dataset, which includes all inferred triples, along with their access labels, which are complex expressions that use the *inference accumulator* operator.

During the *evaluation phase*, when a requestor specifies a query and a purpose for gaining access to a set of RDF triples that pertain to a specific user, the system selects the concrete policy that matches the request, and computes *on the fly* the concrete value of the triples' access labels; the access function determines whether said triples will be accessed by the requestor (or not).

3 HACEA

Figure 1 shows the architecture of the access control system $A_{bs}ACEF$, on top of which we have build the **HACEA** demo. The system is comprised of the AUTH,

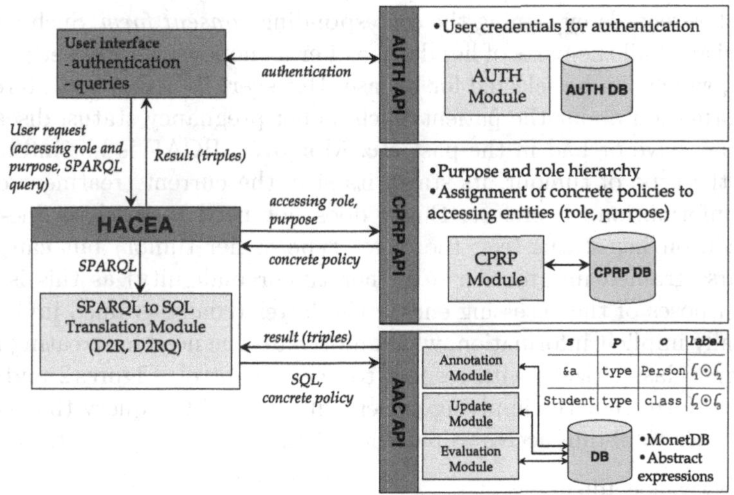

Fig. 1. System architecture

CPRP and AAC modules. The AUTH module stores the user credentials and is the module responsible for user authentication. The CPRP module is responsible for the management of *concrete policies* and is used to associate concrete policies with their corresponding user, requestor and purpose.

Last but not least, the AAC module is the backbone of our system and is comprised of different submodules described below. First, the *Annotation Module*, which is responsible for the *annotation phase* presented in [8]. The *update* module is used for updating annotated quadruples as discussed in [8]. Finally, the *evaluation* module takes as input an SQL query expressed by a requestor, and a concrete policy that matches the request (i.e., requestor, user and purpose which is returned by the CPRP module) and returns the accessible triples. MonetDB[1], a column store RDBMS, is used as the system's backend.

4 Demonstration Scenario

We will demonstrate our access control enforcement approach through **HACEA**. Due to lack of space, we will discuss one representative data access scenario and how it is supported by our demo. A short video[2] and a more detailed description[3] are also available online.

Our demo is based on accessing sensitive patients' information, which is stored in a *Personal Health Record (PHR)*; our demo will be used to allow a patient to authorize a third party (e.g., doctor, nurse, public or private entity) to access to her data through a *consent form.*

Our main example scenario assumes a *public service* (namely, Breast Cancer Action Fund - BCAF) which provides funding to cancer patients. Such a service would require access to the patient's PHR in order to verify that the patient has a malignant tumour indicating breast cancer and provide the benefit. Thus, in order to get a discount, an applying patient (say, Emily Robinson) should allow access to her records by signing the corresponding *consent form.* Such a consent form consists of all the parts of her data, as her menopausal state, her pregnancy state etc., which can be selected for release. However, BCAF is not interested in other information about the patient, such as her pregnancy status, diseases the patient may have or had in the past etc. Moreover, BCAF is not interested in knowing the type of tumour, its stage, its size, the current treatment or other detailed information. Therefore, Emily does not need to disclose fine-grained information on her status (e.g. the exact type of her tumor) but can provide more coarse-grained information (e.g., her tumor malignity) as this is enough for the purposes of the accessing entity; the latter (coarse-grained information) is essentially implicit information, which motivates the need for treating implicit data as first-class citizens with respect to access control. Figures 2 and 3 show the consent form that the applying patient fills in, and the query that BCAF is using in order to obtain access to patient's data.

[1] http://www.monetdb.org
[2] http://youtu.be/-wYbiWvTfyE
[3] http://planet-data.eu/sites/default/files/PD_WhitePaper_HealthCare.pdf

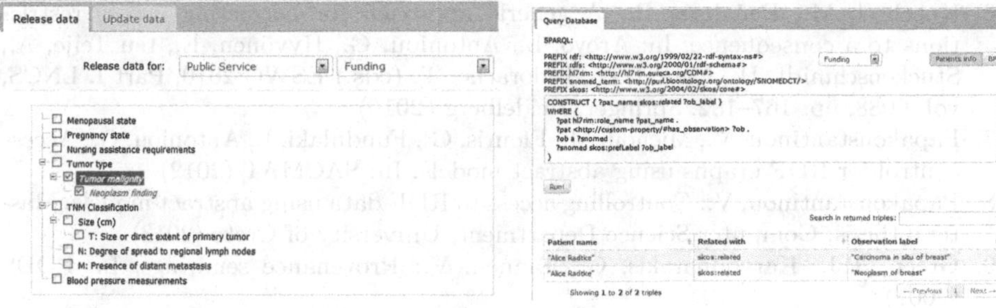

Fig. 2. Releasing data

Fig. 3. Querying data

The dataset that we used for demonstrating **HACEA** consists of a set of 10.000 patients and their corresponding health records, created by the Advanced Patient Data Generator (APDG) tool[4]. The APDG is a generator developed in the context of the EU project EURECA which uses clinical and epidemiological background knowledge to generate a set of realistic patient records. The used dataset is represented in RDF format and expressed according to the HL7-RIM[5] schema and SNOMED-CT[6] terms both of which are well-established medical ontologies. This allows the uniform expression of the data using well-defined and commonly accepted terminologies.

Acknowledgments. This work was partially supported by the EU projects Planet-Data (FP7:ICT-2009.3.4, #257641) and p-Medicine (FP7-ICT-2009.5.3, #270089).

References

1. Abel, F., De Coi, J.L., Henze, N., Koesling, A.W., Krause, D., Olmedilla, D.: Enabling advanced and context-dependent access control in RDF stores. In: Aberer, K., Choi, K.-S., Noy, N., Allemang, D., Lee, K.-I., Nixon, L.J.B., Golbeck, J., Mika, P., Maynard, D., Mizoguchi, R., Schreiber, G., Cudré-Mauroux, P. (eds.) ASWC 2007 and ISWC 2007. LNCS, vol. 4825, pp. 1–14. Springer, Heidelberg (2007)
2. Dietzold, S., Auer, S.: Access control on RDF triple store from a Semantic Wiki perspective. In: SFSW (2006)
3. Jain, A., Farkas, C.: Secure resource description framework. In: SACMAT (2006)
4. Kim, J.-H., Jung, K., Park, S.: An introduction to authorization conflict problem in RDF access control. In: Lovrek, I., Howlett, R.J., Jain, L.C. (eds.) KES 2008, Part II. LNCS (LNAI), vol. 5178, pp. 583–592. Springer, Heidelberg (2008)
5. Brickley, D., Guha, R.: RDF Vocabulary Description Language 1.0: RDF Schema (2004). www.w3.org/TR/2004/REC-rdf-schema-20040210

[4] http://wasp.cs.vu.nl/apdg

[5] www.hl7.org/implement/standards/rim.cfm

[6] www.nlm.nih.gov/research/umls/Snomed/snomed_main.html

6. Knechtel, M., Peñaloza, R.: A generic approach for correcting access restrictions to a consequence. In: Aroyo, L., Antoniou, G., Hyvönen, E., ten Teije, A., Stuckenschmidt, H., Cabral, L., Tudorache, T. (eds.) ESWC 2010, Part I. LNCS, vol. 6088, pp. 167–182. Springer, Heidelberg (2010)
7. Papakonstantinou, V., Michou, M., Flouris, G., Fundulaki, I., Antoniou, G.: Access control for RDF graphs using abstract models. In: SACMAT (2012)
8. Papakonstantinou, V.: Controlling access to RDF data using abstract models. Master's thesis, Computer Science Department, University of Crete (2013)
9. Green, T.J., Karvounarakis, G., Tannen, V.: Provenance semirings. In: PODS (2007)

SCS Connector - Quantifying and Visualising Semantic Paths Between Entity Pairs

Bernardo Pereira Nunes[1(✉)], José Herrera[1], Davide Taibi[2], Giseli Rabello Lopes[1], Marco A. Casanova[1], and Stefan Dietze[3]

[1] Department of Informatics, Pontifical Catholic University of Rio de Janeiro, Rio de Janeiro, RJ 22451-900, Brazil
{bnunes,jherrera,grlopes,casanova}@inf.puc-rio.br

[2] Institute for Educational Technology, Italian National Research Council, Palermo, Italy
davide.taibi@itd.cnr.it

[3] L3S Research Center, Leibniz University Hannover, Appelstr. 9a, 3016 Hannover, Germany
dietze@l3s.de

Abstract. A key challenge of the Semantic Web lies in the creation of semantic links between Web resources. The creation of links serves as a mean to semantically enrich Web resources, connecting disparate information sources and facilitating data reuse and sharing. As the amount of data on the Web is ever increasing, automated methods to unveil links between Web resources are required. In this paper, we introduce a tool, called *SCS Connector*, that assists users to uncover links between entity pairs within and across datasets. *SCS Connector* provides a Web-based user interface and a RESTful API that enable users to interactively visualise and analyse paths between an entity pair (e_i, e_j) through known links that can reveal meaningful relationships between (e_i, e_j) according to a semantic connectivity score (SCS).

Keywords: Semantic connectivity score · Graph visualisation · Semantic associations · Relationship discovery · Semantic UI

1 Introduction

The adoption of Linked Data for publishing and interlinking structured data has brought a range of benefits to data providers and consumers such as data interoperability, reuse and sharing. However, as the amount of data on the Web is in constant growth and change, the links between Web resources become outdated and automated methods are required to create new links within and across datasets.

A key challenge in the provision of a well-interlinked graph of Web data lies in the identification and linkage of not only existing entities, but also in the interlinking of new entities. The linkage of entities provides data consumers

V. Presutti et al. (Eds.): ESWC Satellite Events 2014, LNCS 8798, pp. 461–466, 2014.
DOI: 10.1007/978-3-319-11955-7_67

with a richer representation of the data and the possibility of exploiting and uncovering information by traversing the Web of Data graph.

Over the past years most of the entity interlinking approaches has focused on recognising strict equivalences between entities through the creation of `owl:sameAs` links across datasets. Consequently, little attention has been drawn to identify related entities intra- and inter-datasets. For instance, by creating `skos:related` or `so:related` references between entities that are related at some extent.

In this paper, we present a tool, called *SCS Connector*, that is responsible for uncovering meaningful relationships between entity pairs within and across datasets. *SCS Connector* provides a Web-based user interface and a RESTful API that enable users to interactively visualise and analyse paths between an entity pair (e_i, e_j) through known links that can reveal some meaningful relationship between (e_i, e_j) according to a semantic connectivity score. The tool was developed based on our previous works [5–7] that introduced the *semantic connectivity score* (SCS) to measure the relatedness between entity pairs in reference datasets.

The remainder of the paper is organised as follows. Section 2 reviews the literature. Section 3 describes the most relevant features of the *SCS Connector* tool. Section 4 concludes the paper.

2 Related Work

RelFinder [4] is a tool that aims at finding relationships between a set of specified entities and providing a mechanism to explore the semantic links between entities. Similarly, OntoRelFinder [12] explores the semantic links between entity pairs but outperforms RelFinder since it relies on the schema paths to find the semantic links. Scarlet [10,11] is another tool to identify semantic links that focuses on finding correspondences between entities belonging to a set of external ontologies. In a different perspective, Han et al. [3] focuses on finding related entities with respect to a given entity and semantic links.

The number of Web-based applications using semantic technologies to improve search, retrieval and recommendation of Web resources has dramatically increased. For instance, Passant [8,9] introduces a recommender system that takes advantage of the semantic links between Web resources to recommend resources laterally related to a resource of interest to a given user. Another system is presented by Souvik et al. [1] that recommends movies based on a linear regression algorithm that uses a set of features to determine whether a movie is related (or not) to a given one.

SCS Connector differs from the related works outlined since it provides to the end-user a *semantic connectivity score* (SCS) (see Sect. 3.1) that measures how related an entity pair is. Furthermore, *SCS Connector* provides a user interface that allows users to explore the semantic paths between an entity pair as well as the adjacency matrix representing the entity pair graph, enabling users to compute new semantic measures to compare them against the SCS approach.

3 SCS Connector Tool

SCS Connector aims at finding and measuring semantic relationships between entity pairs. Uncovering semantic links between disparate entities open up new opportunities to link a variety of resources on the Web. In this section, we describe the most relevant features of *SCS Connector* along with technical explanations describing the strategies used to discover semantic paths between entity pairs.

3.1 Semantic Connectivity Score (SCS)

Let $G = (E, P)$ be an RDF graph, where E and P are a finite set of entities and properties, respectively. A property $p_i \in P$ represents a link between a pair of entities (e_i, e_j), where e_i and $e_j \in E$. Thus, given an entity pair (e_1, e_n), we say that they are related iff there exists at least one path connecting them. For instance, there is one path connecting (e_1, e_n) represented by $\rho_1(e_1, e_n) = \{(e_1, e_2), (e_2, e_3), \ldots, (e_{n-1}, e_n)\}$. Note that, as properties are often found in its inverse form [2], we consider the graph G as undirected, where $\rho_1(e_1, e_n) = \rho_1(e_n, e_1)$.

Thus, to quantify the relationships and possibly uncover semantic links between entity pairs, our tool uses the *semantic connectivity score* (SCS) previously introduced in [5]. The score function SCS between a pair of entities (e_i, e_j) is computed by Eq. 1 that considers the semantic paths found $\rho_1(e_i, e_j), \rho_2(e_i, e_j), \ldots, \rho_m(e_i, e_j)$, where m is the total number of paths having a defined maximum length. Although in [5] is established a maximum path length in which the score will be computed, in our tool, it can be freely specified by the user. A semantic relationship exists iff $SCS(e_i, e_j) > 0$. Moreover, if $e_i = e_j$, then $SCS(e_i, e_j) = 1$.

$$SCS(e_i, e_j) = 1 - \frac{1}{1 + (\sum_{l=1}^{\tau} \beta^l \cdot |paths_{(e_i,e_j)}^{<l>}|)} \quad (1)$$

where $|paths_{(e_i,e_j)}^{<l>}|$ is the number of paths of length l between entities e_i and e_j, τ is the maximum length of paths $\rho_k(e_i, e_j)$ considered (default is $\tau = 4$), and $0 < \beta \leq 1$ is a positive damping factor. The damping factor β^l is responsible for exponentially penalising longer paths. The final score is normalised to range between $[0, 1)$.

3.2 Finding Paths Between Entity Pairs

To find paths between two specified entities, we adopted a similar preprocessing strategy applied by RelFinder [4]. Briefly, the preprocessing strategy computes the maximal connected subgraphs of G (see Sect. 3.1). Thus, only entities in the same connected subgraph have a (semantic) path linking them. In this case, SPARQL queries are issued to the RDF graph (in our case, DBpedia graph) to retrieve all semantic paths connecting two entities up to a maximum predefined length. Although, by default, the maximum path length is set to 4, the user can set this parameter to search for shorter/longer paths.

As a running example, suppose that a user wants to find paths between the entities `dbpedia:Barack_Obama` and `dbpedia:Michelle_Obama` and sets the maximum path length to 2. Thus, to find all paths up to a maximum length, the tool starts searching for direct links between the specified entities using the SPARQL queries below:

```
SELECT * WHERE {dbpedia:Barack_Obama ?p dbpedia:Michelle_Obama}
SELECT * WHERE {dbpedia:Michelle_Obama ?p dbpedia:Barack_Obama}
```

To find the paths with maximum length 2, *SCS Connector* issues the following queries:

```
SELECT * WHERE {dbpedia:Barack_Obama ?p1 ?e . ?e ?p2 dbpedia:Michelle_Obama}
SELECT * WHERE {dbpedia:Michelle_Obama ?p1 ?e . ?e ?p2 dbpedia:Barack_Obama}
SELECT * WHERE {dbpedia:Barack_Obama ?p1 ?e . dbpedia:Michelle_Obama ?p2 ?e}
SELECT * WHERE {?e ?p1 dbpedia:Barack_Obama . ?e ?p2 dbpedia:Michelle_Obama}
```

Note that `?e` and `?p1,?p2` are used to find semantic paths of length 2 and represents entities and properties, respectively. In this example, we omitted the clause FILTER from the SPARQL queries. However, *SCS Connector* also allows user to filter out some ontological classes from the paths linking an entity pair (e_i, e_j).

Finally, according to the existing paths between the entities (e_i, e_j), a *SCS score* is assigned representing how linked both entities are. If there is no direct links between the specified entity pair and the $SCSscore$ is above a given threshold, there is a high chance to exist a new link between the entity pairs.

3.3 Exposing the Paths Between Entity Pairs

SCS Connector is a flexible cross-browser Web application implemented in PHP and Java to interactively visualise and analyse the semantic paths between entity pairs. The semantic paths are exposed through a *graph visualisation* and a *RESTful API* service.

Graph visualisation. The paths found (see Sect. 3.2) are rendered and displayed in the form of a graph, where the vertices and edges are represented by entities and properties, respectively. The paths are also represented and displayed as a squared adjacency matrix, where the entries of the matrix determines whether there is an edge linking entities or not. The $SCSscore$ quantifies how related the entity pair is.

RESTful API. SCS Connector also provides a RESTful API to support the development of new data interlinking approaches. The API is available in two formats: JSON and XML. The API can be accessed via REST at http://lod2.inf.puc-rio.br/scs/similarities.json?entity1=db:Barack_Obama&entity2=db:Michelle_Obama.

4 Conclusions

This paper introduced SCS Connector, a Web-based application to assist users on the discovery of semantic links between entity pairs. SCS Connector enables users to interactively visualise and analyse the semantic paths and also use the results obtained to develop further services. The tool is available at http://research.ccead.puc-rio.br/scs.

Acknowledgments. This work was partly supported by CNPq, under grants 160326/2012-5, 301497/2006-0, 475717/2011-2 and 57128/2009-9, by FAPERJ, under grants E-26/170028/2008 and E-26/103.070/2011.

References

1. Debnath, S., Ganguly, N., Mitra, P.: Feature weighting in content based recommendation system using social network analysis. In: Proceedings of the 17th international conference on World Wide Web, WWW '08, pp. 1041–1042. ACM, New York, NY, USA (2008)
2. Graves, A., Adali, S., Hendler, J.: A method to rank nodes in an RDF graph. In: Proceedings of the 7th International Semantic Web Conference (Posters and Demos), Karlsruhe, Germany. CEUR Workshop, vol. 401, 28 October 2008. CEUR-WS.org
3. Han, Y.-J., Park, S.-B., Lee, S.-J., Park, S.Y., Kim, K.Y.: Ranking entities similar to an entity for a given relationship. In: Zhang, B.-T., Orgun, M.A. (eds.) PRICAI 2010. LNCS, vol. 6230, pp. 409–420. Springer, Heidelberg (2010)
4. Lehmann, J., Schüppel, J., Auer, S.: Discovering unknown connections - the DBpedia relationship finder. In: CSSW, pp. 99–110 (2007)
5. Nunes, B.P., Dietze, S., Casanova, M.A., Kawase, R., Fetahu, B., Nejdl, W.: Combining a co-occurrence-based and a semantic measure for entity linking. In: Cimiano, P., Corcho, O., Presutti, V., Hollink, L., Rudolph, S. (eds.) ESWC 2013. LNCS, vol. 7882, pp. 548–562. Springer, Heidelberg (2013)
6. Nunes, B.P., Kawase, R., Dietze, S., Taibi, D., Casanova, M.A., Nejdl, W.: Can Entities be Friends? In: Proceedings of the WOLE Workshop in Conjuction with the 11th ISWC. CEUR Workshop, vol. 906, pp. 45–57 (2012). CEUR-WS.org
7. Nunes, B.P., Kawase, R., Fetahu, B., Dietze, S., Casanova, M.A., Maynard, D.: Interlinking documents based on semantic graphs. Proc. Comput. Sci. **22**(0), 231–240 (2013). In: Proceedings of the 17th International Conference in Knowledge Based and Intelligent Information and Engineering Systems - KES2013
8. Passant, A.: Dbrec — music recommendations using DBpedia. In: Patel-Schneider, P.F., Pan, Y., Hitzler, P., Mika, P., Zhang, L., Pan, J.Z., Horrocks, I., Glimm, B. (eds.) ISWC 2010, Part II. LNCS, vol. 6497, pp. 209–224. Springer, Heidelberg (2010)
9. Passant, A.: Measuring semantic distance on linking data and using it for resources recommendations. In: AAAI Spring Symposium: Linked Data Meets AI (2010)
10. Sabou, M., d'Aquin, M., Motta, E.: Exploring the semantic web as background knowledge for ontology matching. J. Data Semant. **11**, 156–190 (2008)

11. Sabou, M., d'Aquin, M., Motta, E.: Relation discovery from the semantic web. In: Proceedings of the 7th ISWC (posters and demos). CEUR Workshop, vol. 401 (2008). CEUR-WS.org
12. Seo, D., Koo, H., Lee, S., Kim, P., Jung, H., Sung, W.-K.: Efficient finding relationship between individuals in a mass ontology database. In: FGIT-UNESST, pp. 281–286 (2011)

Distant Supervision for Relation Extraction Using Ontology Class Hierarchy-Based Features

Pedro H.R. Assis and Marco A. Casanova(✉)

Department of Informatics, PUC-Rio, Rio de Janeiro, RJ, Brazil
{passis,casanova}@inf.puc-rio.br

Abstract. Relation extraction is a key step in the problem of structuring natural language text. This paper demonstrates a multi-class classifier for relation extraction, constructed using the distant supervision approach, along with resources of the Semantic Web. In particular, the classifier uses a feature based on the class hierarchy of an ontology that, in conjunction with basic lexical features, improves accuracy and recall. The paper contains extensive experiments, using a corpus extracted from the Wikipedia and the DBpedia ontology, to demonstrate the usefulness of the new feature.

Keywords: Relation extraction · Distant supervision · Semantic web · Machine learning · Natural language processing

1 Introduction

A large amount of the data on the Web is stored in natural language format or unstructured text. While this format provides information targeting towards human consumption, several algorithms for data analysis are not applicable since they require structured data.

In order to render a structure from natural language text, a key problem is relation extraction, namely, the problem of finding relationships between entities present in the text. The most successful approaches to the relation extraction problem apply supervised machine learning to compute classifiers using features extracted from hand-labeled sentences comprising a training corpus [1,2,4]. However, supervised methods create several problems, such as the limited number of examples in the training corpus, due to expensive cost of production, and the domain dependency on corpus annotations. Such limitations prevent using supervised machine learning to construct web-scale knowledge bases.

An alternative paradigm for relation extraction was introduced in [5]. The distant supervision approach addresses the problem of creating a considerable number of examples by automatically generating training data from heuristically matching a database relation to text. Recent approaches to relation extraction use resources of the Semantic Web to improve accuracy of the classifiers and, conversely, to generate new Semantic Web resources [3].

V. Presutti et al. (Eds.): ESWC Satellite Events 2014, LNCS 8798, pp. 467–471, 2014.
DOI: 10.1007/978-3-319-11955-7_68

In this paper, we demonstrate a multi-class classifier for relation extraction, constructed using the distant supervision approach, along with resources of the Semantic Web. In particular, the classifier uses a feature based on the class hierarchy of an ontology that, in conjunction with basic lexical features, improves accuracy and recall.

We conducted two types of experiments, adopting the automatic held-out evaluation strategy and human evaluation (we recall that the term *held-out evaluation* refers to experiments where part of the data is held out for testing and the rest of the data is used to train a classifier). In the held-out evaluation experiments, the multi-class classifier identified a total of 88 relations, out of the 480 relations featured in the version of the DBPedia adopted, with an F-measure greater than 70 %, whereas in the human evaluation experiments it achieved an average accuracy greater than 70 % for 9 out of the top 10 relations, in the number of instances.

2 Heuristic Labeling, Lexical Features and Class-Based Features

Heuristic Labeling. Let O be an ontology, defined as a set of RDF triples. We define a subset $T \subseteq O$ such that $t_i = (e_1, r_i, e_2) \in T$ iff r_i is an object property of O and there are triples $(e_1, \text{rdf:type}, K_1)$ and $(e_2, \text{rdf:type}, K_2)$ in O, where K_1 and K_2 are classes of O.

Let C be a corpus of n sentences and assume that each sentence is annotated with two entities defined in O. A sentence s is *heuristically labeled* with a relation r_i iff s is annotated with entities e_1 and e_2 and $(e_1, r_i, e_2) \in T$. For example, suppose that the triple *(Led Zeppelin, genre, Heavy Metal Music)* is in T and assume that both entities are instances of classes of the ontology O. Consider the sentence "***Led Zeppelin** is a british rock band that plays **heavy metal music***", where the text in boldface are annotated with references to the entities "Led Zeppelin" and "Heavy Metal Music". Then, we label this sentence as an example of the relation *genre*.

Lexical Features. Each labeled sentence in C is described by a 12-dimension *feature vector*. Out of the 12 dimensions, 10 are *lexical* and 2 are *class-based*, defined in this and the next subsections.

Let s be a sentence and divide s into 5 components $s = (w_l, e_1, w_m, e_2, w_r)$, where w_l comprehends the subsentence to the left of the entity e_1, w_m represents the subsentence between the entities e_1 and e_2 and w_r comprehends the subsentence to the right of e_2. The *lexical features* of s contemplate the sequence of words in w_l, w_m, and w_r. Not all words in w_l and w_r are used, though. In fact, let $w_l(1)$ and $w_l(2)$ denote the first and the first and the second rightmost words in w_l, respectively, and let $w_r(1)$ and $w_r(2)$ denote the first and the first and the second leftmost words in w_r, respectively. Table 1 defines the 10 lexical features adopted and illustrates them with the sentence.

Table 1. Lexical features and examples

Dimension	Description	Example from s_A
f_1	The sequence of words of w_m	", on the Acropolis in?"
f_2	Part-of-speech tags of w_m	PREP ELSE NOUN PREP
f_3	The sequence of words of $w_l(1)$	"the"
f_4	Part-of-speech tags of $w_l(1)$	ELSE
f_5	The sequence of words of $w_l(2)$	"temple, the"
f_6	Part-of-speech tags of $w_l(2)$	NOUN ELSE
f_7	The sequence of words of $w_r(1)$	"takes"
f_8	Part-of-speech tags of $w_r(1)$	VERB
f_9	The sequence of words of $w_r(2)$	"takes its"
f_{10}	Part-of-speech tags of $w_r(2)$	VERB ELSE

s_A = *"Her most famous temple, the* ***Parthenon****, on the Acropolis in* ***Athens*** *takes its name from that title."*

Class-Based Feature. One of the main contributions of this paper is to use as a feature of an entity e the class that best represents e in the class hierarchy of an ontology. The chosen class must not be too general, in a sense that we want to avoid loosing specificities of the semantics of e that are not shared with other entities that belong to the upper classes. On the other hand, a class which is too specific is not a good choice as well. Very specific classes restrict the accuracy of classifiers since there are more entities for a more general class. Therefore, we propose to use as a feature for e the class associate with e that intuitively lies in the mid-level of the tree.

More precisely, let H be a tree representing an ontology class hierarchy and assume that h is the height of H. Let C_k be the class of entity e that the entity annotation tool returns (we assume that the tool returns only one class). Assume that the path in H from the root to C_k is $C_0, \ldots C_i, \ldots, C_k$. Then, the *class-based feature* of entity e is the class C_i, where $i = min(k, h/2)$. Note that we take the minimum of $h/2$ and k since the level of C_k may be smaller than half of the height h of H.

3 Experiments

In this work, we adopted DBpedia as our source of relation instances and the English Wikipedia as a source of unstructured text. We created the annotations of the sentences extracted from Wikipedia by matching links to others articles, occurring in the text, to entities in DBpedia, discarding any imprecision in our results due to ambiguity on entity recognition. We selected only sentences in Wikipedia that contained at least two annotations, thereby generating a corpus

Table 2. Top 10 relations for a classifier trained with lexical and class-based features.

Class	Precision	Recall	F-measure
/areaOfSearch	1.00	0.97	0.98
/ground	0.97	1.00	0.98
/mission	0.99	0.96	0.97
/sport	0.97	0.97	0.97
/targetSpaceStation	1.00	0.93	0.97
/academicDiscipline	0.93	0.99	0.96
/discoverer	0.99	0.93	0.96
/locatedInArea	0.93	0.98	0.96
/programmeFormat	0.93	0.99	0.96
/politicalPartyInLegislature	1.00	0.91	0.95

Table 3. Average accuracy for the top 10 relation in examples in our dataset for human evaluation of a sample of 100 predictions.

Relation	Accuracy
http://www.dbpedia.org/ontology/country	0.73 %
http://www.dbpedia.org/ontology/family	0.75 %
http://www.dbpedia.org/ontology/isPartOf	0.90 %
http://www.dbpedia.org/ontology/birthPlace	0.76 %
http://www.dbpedia.org/ontology/genre	0.77 %
http://www.dbpedia.org/ontology/location	0.76 %
http://www.dbpedia.org/ontology/type	0.80 %
http://www.dbpedia.org/ontology/order	0.81 %
http://www.dbpedia.org/ontology/occupation	0.87 %
http://www.dbpedia.org/ontology/hometown	0.68 %

of nearly 2.2 million sentences. From these annotated sentences, we extracted feature vectors that were used as input to a Logistic Regression classifier.

We conducted held-out evaluation experiments and human evaluation experiments. Recall that held-out evaluation refers to experiments where part of the data is held out for testing and the remaining is used for training a classifier. We ran held-out experiments with classifiers constructed using only lexical features, only class-based features and both sets of features to measure the impact of the class-based feature proposed in this work. We compared the performance of the classifiers thus obtained by counting the number of classes each classifier identified with F-measure greater than 70 %.

We considered as baseline the number of classes with F-measure greater than 70 % that the classifier trained only with lexical features identified. In our experiments, such classifier identified 9 classes. The classifier trained using only the class-based feature proposed in this work identified a total of 60 classes with F-measure greater than 70 %. The classifier trained using both lexical and class-based features identified a total of 88 classes, again with F-measure greater than 70 %. Compared to the baseline, it achieved an almost 10-fold increase in the number of classes identified with F-measure greater than 70 %. Table 2 shows the top 10 classes.

For the human evaluation, we extracted random samples of 100 sentences for each of the top 10 relations in the number of examples in our dataset. Those samples were forwarded to two evaluators. Table 3 shows the accuracy of each prediction of the samples, carried out manually.

4 Demonstration

To demonstrate the multi-class classifier for relation extraction, we created a tool that accepts a sentence, annotated with the URIs of two DBpedia instances, extracts all features described in Sect. 2, generates a feature vector that is used as an input to the classifier, and returns a relation between the two instances. A demonstration video can be watched at
https://www.youtube.com/watch?v=jwMXkHeUwhM

References

1. Curran, J., Clark, S.: Language independent NER using a maximum entropy tagger. In: Proceedings of the 7th Conference on Natural Language Learning, vol. 4, pp. 164–167 (2003)
2. Finkel, J., Grenager, T., Manning, C.: Incorporating non-local information into information extraction systems by Gibbs sampling. In: Proceedings of the 43rd Annual Meeting on Association for Computational Linguistics, pp. 363–370 (2005)
3. Gerber, D., Ngomo, A.-C.: Bootstrapping the Linked Data Web, 1st Work. Web Scale Know. Extraction ISWC (2011)
4. Nguyen, T., Kan, M.: Keyphrase Extraction, pp. 317–326. Scientific Publications, Singapore (2007)
5. Mintz, M., Bills, S., Snow, R., Jurafsky, D.: Distant supervision for relation extraction without labeled data. In: Proceedings of the Joint Conference of the 47th Annual Meeting of the ACL and the 4th International Joint Conference on Natural Language Processing of the AFNLP, vol. 2, pp. 1003–1011 (2009)

Augmenting TV Newscasts via Entity Expansion

José Luis Redondo-García[2(✉)], Michiel Hildebrand[1], Lilia Perez Romero[1], and Raphaël Troncy[2]

[1] CWI, Amsterdam, The Netherlands
{M.Hildebrand,L.Perez}@cwi.nl
[2] EURECOM, Sophia Antipolis, France
{redondo,raphael.troncy}@eurecom.fr

Abstract. We present an approach that leverages on the knowledge present on the Web for identifying and enriching relevant items inside a News video and displaying them in a timely and user friendly fashion. This second screen prototype (i) collects and offers information about persons, locations, organizations and concepts occurring in the newscast, and (ii) combines them for enriching the underlying story along five main dimensions: expert's opinions, timeline, in depth, in other sources, and geo-localized comments from other viewers. Starting from preliminary insights coming from the named entities spotted on the subtitles, we expand this initial context to a broader event representation by relying in the knowledge of other Web documents talking about the same fact. An online demo of the proposed solution is available at http://www.linkedtv.project.cwi.nl/news/.

Keywords: Video annotation · Entity expansion · News enrichment

1 Introduction

Second screen applications are a popular approach to enrich the TV viewing experience. Within the LinkedTV project we developed a second screen application for News broadcasts. The functionality and the design of this application is the result of a user-centred design process involving focus groups, interviews, iterative design and evaluation [2]. The initial design and evaluation of the prototype was done with manually curated content. This was deliberately chosen, as we did not want the quality of the content impact the evaluation of the design. However in practice, the manual curation of the content is not feasible, as it is too time consuming for a broadcaster.

This paper provides a solution to automatically generate the content for the LinkedTV News second screen application. The application supports two modes of interaction. The passive mode gives the user access to factual information about persons, locations and organisations that are related to a news item, as shown in the screenshot on the left side of Fig. 1. To generate the content for

V. Presutti et al. (Eds.): ESWC Satellite Events 2014, LNCS 8798, pp. 472–476, 2014.
DOI: 10.1007/978-3-319-11955-7_69

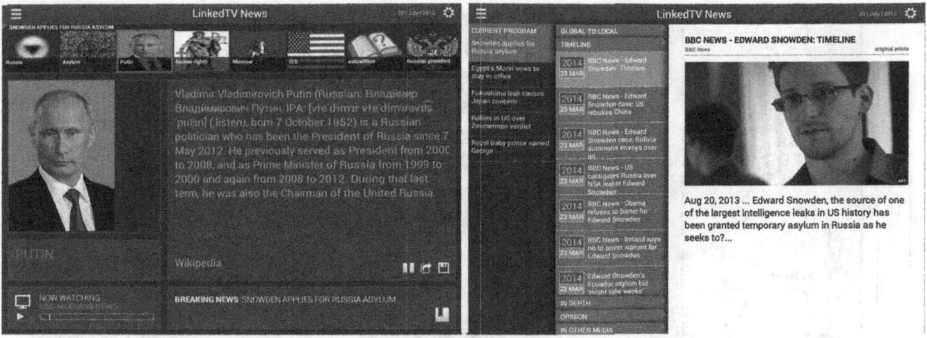

Fig. 1. Demo screen captures corresponding to the (1) passive mode and the (2) active mode. Access the demo at http://www.linkedtv.project.cwi.nl/news/ for more details.

this passive mode we therefore need a logic able to identify entities that could be highly relevant to the user. A typical approach is to use Named Entity Recognition (NER) over the textual information attached to particular video fragment. By linking the entities to real world objects using web identifiers (Named Entity Disambiguation) we get access to the factual information about these entities. A growing number of APIs provide such a service, like AlchemyAPI[1] or DBpedia Spotlight[2]. In the manual curation of the content we, however, experienced that relevant entities do not only occur in the subtitles, but can also be related to the video indirectly. Therefore, we propose an extension of the traditional entity extraction method on the subtitles that studies additional Web documents related to the main video. In particular, our solution uses a representative set of concepts found in the subtitles to retrieve extra Web documents that are annotated as well, in order to extend and better rank the initial set of entities and propose the main N candidates to be displayed in the interface.

The active mode of the LinkedTV news second screen application allows the user to explore background and related information to a news item, as shown on the right side of Fig. 2. The interface provides 5 browsing dimensions that will be populated by relying on a Google Custom Search Engine[3] and a method to generate the queries that are tailored to specific requirements of the content in the different dimensions.

2 LinkedTV News Companion Application

In the passive mode the LinkedTV news application operates as a second screen that is synced with the TV program. This mode supports the user with looking up factual information about the entities that occur in the news. The screenshot on the left side of Fig. 1 shows entities per news item and is refreshed when the

[1] http://www.alchemyapi.com/
[2] http://www.spotlight.dbpedia.org/
[3] https://www.google.com/cse/

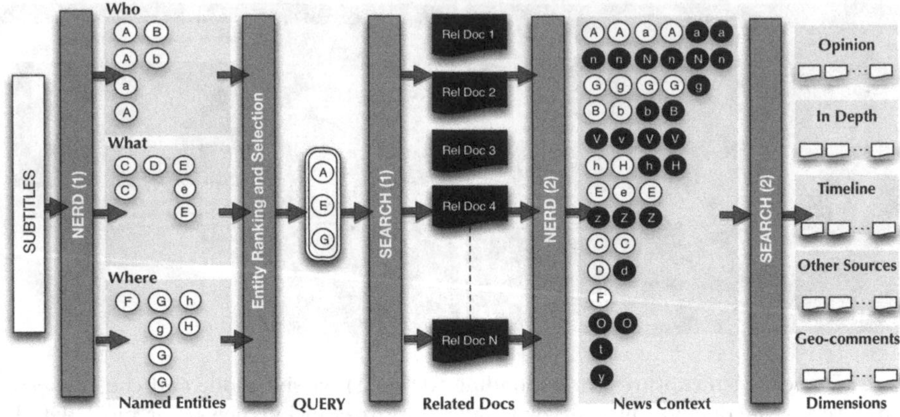

Fig. 2. Schema of named entity expansion algorithm.

next news item start. The interface contains three parts. At the top it contains a carousel of the entities related to the news item. The middle of the interface shows the entity slide with information about the active entity, taken from DBPedia. The bottom part of the interface provides information about the current news item, controls for the video and a button to bookmark the current news item.

The bookmark button in the passive mode provides a simple form of interaction that allows the user to store news item to watch later, when passing to the active mode and exploring the bookmarked news items. The screenshot on the right side of Fig. 1 shows the interface of the active mode. The left column of the interface shows a list of bookmarked items, the item on Edward Snowden is selected. The left column shows the article that is currently selected. The middle column shows the five browsing dimensions based on information needs from end users: the timeline gives an overview of past events, the opinion dimension gives access to articles in which journalists express their opinion about the topic, in other sources different perspectives on the news can be found as expressed by different news providers, in depth dimensions allows exploration of more detailed background, and the geo-localized dimension shows how people in different places in the world respond to the news item.

2.1 Entity Extraction and Expansion for the Passive Mode

For the passive mode we need to find the elements of the news, for example, basic information about the location or people involved. The logic that feeds the information displayed in this passive mode is crucial not only because it complements what the user is watching in every moment, but also because it generates the concepts that launch further enrichments in the active mode. To reconstruct the semantic context associated with one particular news video, we perform named-entity recognition over the corresponding subtitles using the NERD framework [3]. The output of this phase is a collection of entities annotated using the NERD Ontology[4]. This set includes a list of ranked entities that are explicitly mentioned during the video.

The set of entities obtained from a traditional named entity extraction operation is normally insufficient and incomplete for expressing the context of a news event. Sometimes the relevant concepts are simply not mentioned in the transcripts while being crucial for understanding the story. We perform then a process named *entity expansion*, which relies on the idea of retrieving and analyzing additional documents from the Web where the same event is also described. By increasing the size of set of documents to analyse, we increase the completeness of the context and the representativeness of the list of entities, reinforcing relevant entities and finding new ones that are potentially interesting regarding that news item. The entire logic is illustrated in Fig. 2.

Query Generation. The *Five W's* is a popular concept of information gathering in journalistic reporting. It captures the main aspects of a story: who, when, what, where, and why [1]. We try to represent the news item in terms of four of those five W's in order to generate a query that retrieves documents associated to the same event. In order to achieve this, the original entities are mapped to the NERD Core ontology. From those ten different categories, we generalize to three classes: the Who from `nerd:Person` and `nerd:Organization`, the Where from `nerd:Location`, and the What from the rest of NERD types after discarding `nerd:Time` and `nerd:Amount`. The When or so-called temporal dimension does not need to be computed since it is considered to be provided by the video publisher. The final query is the result of concatenating the labels of the most relevant entities in the sets Who, What, Where in that particular order, for a given time period t. This query will be injected into a document search engine (in our case, the Google) where additional descriptions about the news event can be found.

Entity Clustering. In this phase, the additional documents which have just been retrieved are processed and analyzed in order to extend and re-rank the original set of entities and consequently get a better insight about the event. They are again analyzed by the NERD framework in order to extract more named entities. Once finished, we performed a centroid-based clustering operation over the entities retrieved, considering as centroid the entity with the most frequent disambiguation URL's and most repeated label. The output of this phase is a list of clusters containing different instances of the same concept.

Entity Ranking. The final step of the expansion consists of ranking the different named entities obtained so far according to its relative frequency in the transcripts of the event video, relative frequency over the additional document; and average relevance according to the named entity extractors. The final output of the entity expansion operation is a list of entities together with their ranking score and the frequency in both the main video and in the collected documents retrieved from the search engine.

4 http://www.nerd.eurecom.fr/ontology/nerd-v0.5.n3

2.2 Related Content for the Active Mode

The active mode of the application acts as a hub where the viewers can access extra documents for complementing what is being told in the main news video. A similar logic to the one explained in Sect. 2.1 is applied over the main entities coming from the expansion process for building custom queries in Google CSE, but relaxing or emphasizing some particular *W's* and operating over particular lists of Web resources. For the **Timeline** we rely on a query created by including only the most relevant entity inside the pattern "The" + entity + "case", without any time constraint. For example, in news item about the recent polemic of Edward Snowden we would have the text "The Edward Snowden case". For **In other sources**, we launch a query generated from the set of expanded entities over a curated list of resources including mainly journals and broadcasters Web sites. In our example the query looked like "Asylum Snowden Russia". The **Opinion** dimension includes a list of documents obtained by executing the same query in the previous dimension, but operating over a different list of curated sources that considers only subdomains specialized in opinion documents. The **Geo-localized** data is obtained by launching the same query into the Twitter API, filtering by location and reducing the temporal dimension t to the last 7 days. And the **In depth** section gathers documents obtained by attaching to the label of the most relevant entity from the entity expansion results the keyword "in depth", and removing any temporal restriction or Web source limitation. In our example the query would be "Edward Snowden in depth".

3 Discussion

The preliminary results indicate that we are able to offer to the viewer a relevant set of entities that expands the initial concepts detected by traditional named entity recognition approaches. Many details not explicitly mentioned in the video but present in the context of the newscasts are now available to the viewer to be consumed, either while he is watching the news in passive mode or he browses additional insights in the active mode. We are currently working on formally evaluating the entity expansion method and relevance ranking algorithms.

Acknowlegdements. This work was partially supported by the European Union's 7th Framework Programme via the project LinkedTV (GA 287911).

References

1. Li, L.-J., Fei-Fei, L.: What, where and who? classifying events by scene and object recognition. In: IEEE 11th International Conference on Computer Vision (ICCV'07), pp. 1–8 (2007)
2. Romero, L.P., Ahn, R., Hardman, L.: Linkedtv news: designing a second screen companion for web-enriched news broadcasts. Technical report, Eindhoven University of Technology (2013)
3. Rizzo, G., Troncy, R.: NERD: A framework for unifying named entity recognition and disambiguation extraction tools. In: 13th European Chapter of the Association for Computational Linguistics (EACL'12), Avignon, France (2012)

Geographic Summaries from Crowdsourced Data

Giuseppe Rizzo[1,2(✉)], Giacomo Falcone[1], Rosa Meo[1], Ruggero G. Pensa[1], Raphaël Troncy[2], and Vuk Milicic[2]

[1] Università di Torino, Turin, Italy
{giuseppe.rizzo,rosa.meo,ruggero.pensa}@di.unito.it
[2] EURECOM, Sophia Antipolis, France
{raphael.troncy,vuk.milicic}@eurecom.fr

Abstract. In this paper, we present a research prototype for creating geographic summaries using the whereabouts of Foursquare users. Exploiting the density of the venue types in a particular region, the system adds a layer over any typical cartography geographic maps service, creating a first glance summary over the venues sampled from the Foursquare knowledge base. Each summary is represented by a convex hull. The shape is automatically computed according to the venue densities enclosed in the area. The summary is then labeled with the most prominent category or categories. The prominence is given by the observed venue category density. The prototype provides two outputs: a light-weight representation structured in GeoJSON, and a semantic description using the Open Annotation Ontology. We evaluate the quality of the summaries using the Sum of Squared Errors (SSE) and the Jaccard distance. The system is available at http://geosummly.eurecom.fr.

1 Introduction

Social media services are capturing large amount of data related to whereabouts of their users. This has become a social phenomenon, that is changing the normal communication means. This data encompasses people' actions, dynamics of cities, so that it instantaneously reports any changes in the city topologies [6]. Such amount of data can therefore be considered as the new oil for geo-spatial platforms if globally taken. Leveraging on this massive amount of user whereabouts data coming from social media services, we present an approach that automatically adds a layer over the typical cartography geographic maps, creating summaries on what crowd sensors tell about venues and points of interest. Our approach grounds on using unsupervised descriptive models and exposing the results using geospatial data interchange formats that enable reuse on the Web. The prototype makes use of Foursquare, but any location service that exposes venues together with their categories can fit the model.

A few research attempts have been carried out to extract spatial and non-spatial properties that are typical for venues from social platforms. Among them, Tomko *et al.* [7] propose a method to calculate the descriptive prominence of venue categories that are sampled from OpenStreetMap[1] for a particular region.

[1] http://www.openstreetmap.org

V. Presutti et al. (Eds.): ESWC Satellite Events 2014, LNCS 8798, pp. 477–482, 2014.
DOI: 10.1007/978-3-319-11955-7_70

They select the most prominent categories for the inclusion in the region characteristic description. The descriptive prominence of a venue is computed using the concept of contrast from background. Meo *et al.* [4] propose a statistical approach to estimate the spatial characterization of an area considering the surroundings without imposing a priori knowledge on the geographic area characterization. An area is then marked depending on the statistical distribution of the observed features gathered from OpenStreetMap. Other research attempts, leveraging on social platforms such as Foursquare and Twitter, focused on spotting and labeling geographic regions according to the user activities ([2,5]).

The remainder of this paper is organized as follows. The architecture overview of our approach is presented in Sect. 2. In Sect. 3, we detail our proposed demonstration, and in Sect. 4, we conclude and outline future work.

2 Architecture Overview

The prototype is composed of four main components, that we further explain in the following subsections. The source code and the API description are available at https://github.com/giusepperizzo/geosummly.

2.1 Foursquare Sampling

The first stage consists in collecting the venues metadata from Foursquare. To perform such an operation, we receive as input either the bounding box ($BBox$) coordinates or a GeoJSON structure. A grid division is then applied. To have a statistical significance of the sampled set [8], we make sure to have a number of cells in the grid greater than 100. We also ensure to comply with the limited authorized rate access Foursquare has set in terms of the number of venues that can be retrieved for a given area[2]. For each cell, we collect the surrounded venues and the related metadata (such as the venue category or the number of check-ins). We then represent each cell as a vector, where the feature values (f_i) are the category occurrences. We end up having a matrix NxM where N corresponds to the number of cells and M to the number of the categories used[3]). The matrix is then labeled with a timestamp. Hence, depending on the timestamp, we have different slices of the matrix.

2.2 Descriptive Models

The input of this stage is the matrix provided by the sampling component. We then consider the problem of computing geographic summaries as clustering geo-referenced objects in different 3-dimensional spaces: *latitude*, *longitude*, and f_i. We basically exploit the intrinsic spatial correlation of contiguous cells.

[2] https://developer.foursquare.com/overview/ratelimits

[3] Depending on the setting, the prototype can make use of the first or the second level of the Foursquare taxonomy https://developer.foursquare.com/categorytree.

For each of the obtained subspaces, we run DBSCAN [1]. As measure of distance among points, we consider the Euclidean distance, while *eps* and *minPts* are statistically computed using the sampled observations in a particular area. This process brings a set of clusters for each subspace that are then merged according to the objective function. Each cluster is a set of contiguous cells (a region of the space) characterized by having similar distribution in a subset of the venue categories. As an additional side-effect, clusters are potentially overlapping. This approach is a follow-up of the SUBCLU [3] algorithm[4].

2.3 Publishing Geographic Summaries

A two-step strategy is proposed for publishing the results of the descriptive models component: *Open Annotation Ontology*[5] and *GeoJSON*[6]. Both strategies are equivalent in terms of the output entropy but they target different audiences, depending on the how the description is re-used. Let's define fingerprint as a cluster and geometry as the shape of the cluster.

Open Annotation Ontology: the fingerprint is described with various properties including a name (the dominant category or set of categories for this geometry), a dimension, the absolute number of venues, and the popularity (number of check-ins). The geometry is a polygon described using the GeoSPARQL vocabulary[7]. The annotation is itself identified in order to attach additional provenance information, such as the date when the geographic summary has been computed, described with the PROV[8] vocabulary. The data is available in a SPARQL endpoint at http://geosummly.eurecom.fr/sparql. A simple URI design policy has been devised with the three top level objects resulting in the following RDF graph:

```
<http://data.geosummly.eurecom.fr/annotation/UUID>
      a   oa:Annotation ;
      oa:hasTarget <http://data.geosummly.eurecom.fr/geometry/UUID> ;
      oa:hasBody <http://data.geosummly.eurecom.fr/fingerprint/UUID> ;
      prov:startedAtTime "2014-03-19T11:54:13.567Z"^^xsd:dateTime ;
      prov:wasAttributedTo <http://geosummly.eurecom.fr/> .
```

GeoJSON: the fingerprint is enclosed in a feature object where the geometry is represented using the MultiPoint class and the metadata is serialized as properties of the object together with the arrays of the enclosed venues.

2.4 Visualization

The visualization allows to browse the summaries generated for a spatial area, adding a layer over the typical cartography geographic maps. A zoom interaction

[4] The algorithm technical details are omitted, the focus of this paper being a demonstration.

[5] http://www.w3.org/ns/oa#

[6] http://geojson.org/geojson-spec.html

[7] http://schemas.opengis.net/geosparql

[8] http://www.w3.org/ns/prov#

enables to explore the venues enclosed in any cluster. This component can use either the GeoJSON or the RDF representations as described above. In addition, the states of different views are persistent through URLs that can be easily shared.

3 Demonstration

This section illustrates the proposed framework in action with the geographic data sets released for the 2014 BigData Challenge[9]. Two data sets are used to demonstrate our prototype: (i) Milan Grid[10] and (ii) Trentino Grid[11]. Both areas are divided in cells of $d = 200$ m, where d is the edge of a squared cell, resulting in having 10 K cells for Milan, and 33 K cells for Trentino. The Foursquare sampling stage produced respectively 57, 136 and 21, 796 distinct venues. The probability distribution functions of the categories along the cells show major differences in the two data sets: we mainly observed a major drop in the venue distribution of the Trentino area according to the surface size, that has challenged the performance of our descriptive models algorithm. Figure 1 reports the geographic summary of the Milan extent.

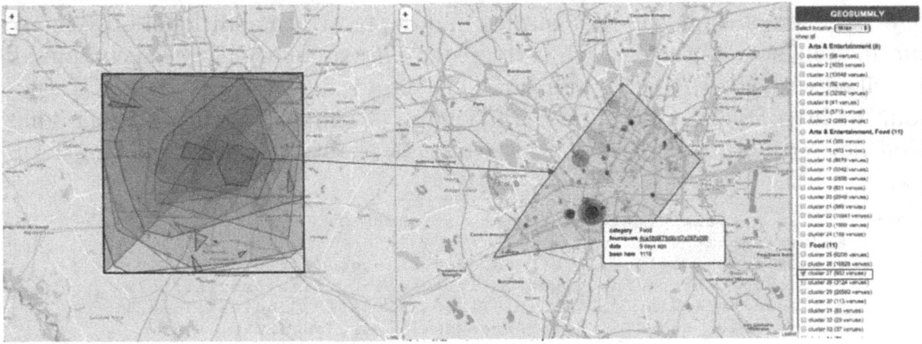

Fig. 1. First glance summary of the Milan extent at left, a zoom in a cluster on the right

We perform a two-fold evaluation strategy and we report the results for the Milan extent[12]: (i) a statistical validation where we measured the total Sum of Squared Errors (SSE_{total}) of both areas using the original data sets. We randomize them 500 times each, ensuring the same category density distributions. We measure the distance from the SSE_{total} computed from the two grids and

---

[9] http://www.telecomitalia.com/tit/en/bigdatachallenge.html

[10] coordinates: (45.5677, 9.0114, 45.3566, 9.3126).

[11] coordinates: (46.5363, 10.9143, 45.6727, 11.8312).

[12] The figures observed for Trentino are in the same order of magnitude (not included for space reason).

the SSE_{total} of the randomly created data sets. The SSE_{total} on the randomized data sets is 68.6637, while the SSE_{total} obtained from the two grids is 2.2175. Hence, we can conservatively claim that there is less than 3 % chance that the clusters occur by chance in the real data. (ii) an output-based evaluation where we perform a 10-fold cross-validation on both data sets and for each fold, we randomly pick up half of the objects (hold-out). We end up with two sets for each fold that constitute two different views of the entire data set. We then compute the clusters from the respective views and we measure the overlap using the Jaccard distance. We observe an average overlap of 81.30 % that satisfies the 70 % acceptance threshold.

4 Conclusion

This approach provides a first glance summary of a spatial area, exploiting user endeavors collected from Foursquare. To ease the reuse of the summaries on the Web, the prototype generates both a developer friendly (GeoJSON) output and a machine readable one using the Open Annotation ontology. The proposed prototype works on any geographic area from which Foursquare venues are available. As future work, we plan to integrate the categories from OpenStreetMap. We also plan to collect users' feedback for better tuning the descriptive models component. We finally plan to investigate more about the inclusion rate of two or more overlapping fingerprints, and the user zooming level that triggers different visualization scenarios.

Acknowledgments. This work was supported by the SMAT-F2 project funded by Regione Piemonte, the European Fund for the Regional Development (F.E.S.R.), and the EIT ICTLabs 3cixty project.

References

1. Ester, M., Kriegel, H.P., Sander, J., Xu, X.: A density-based algorithm for discovering clusters in large spatial databases with noise. In: 2nd International Conference on Knowledge Discovery and Data Mining (KDD'96) (1996)
2. Ferrari, L., Rosi, A., Mamei, M., Zambonelli, F.: Extracting urban patterns from location-based social networks. In: 3rd ACM SIGSPATIAL International Workshop on Location-Based Social Networks (LBSN '11) (2011)
3. Kailing, K., Kriegel, H.P., Kröger, P.: Density-connected subspace clustering for high-dimensional data. In: 4th SIAM International Conference on Data Mining (SIAM'04) (2004)
4. Meo, R., Roglia, E., Bottino, A.: The exploitation of data from remote and human sensors for environment monitoring in the SMAT project. Sensors **12**(12), 17504–17535 (2012)
5. Noulas, A., Scellato, S., Mascolo, C., Pontil, M.: Exploiting semantic annotations for clustering geographic areas and users in location-based social networks. In: ICWSM International Workshop on Social Mobile Web (SMW'11) (2011)

6. Phithakkitnukoon, S., Olivier, P.: Sensing urban social geography using online social networking data. In: 5th International AAAI Conference on Weblogs and Social Media (ICWSM'11) (2011)
7. Tomko, M., Purves, R.S.: Venice, city of canals: characterizing regions through content classification. Trans. GIS **13**(3), 295–314 (2009)
8. Walpole, R., Myers, R.: Probability and Statistics for Engineers and Scientists, 8th edn. Pearson Education International, Upper Saddle River (2007)

Dendro: Collaborative Research Data Management Built on Linked Open Data

João Rocha da Silva[1(✉)], João Aguiar Castro[1], Cristina Ribeiro[2], and João Correia Lopes[2]

[1] Faculdade de Engenharia da Universidade do Porto/INESC TEC, Porto, Portugal
{joaorosilva,joaoaguiarcastro}@gmail.com

[2] DEI—Faculdade de Engenharia da Universidade do Porto/INESC TEC, Porto, Portugal
{mcr,jlopes}@fe.up.pt

Abstract. Research datasets in the so-called "long-tail of science" are easily lost after their primary use. Support for preservation, if available, is hard to fit in the research agenda. Our previous work has provided evidence that dataset creators are motivated to spend time on data description, especially if this also facilitates data exchange within a group or a project. This activity should take place early in the data generation process, when it can be regarded as an actual part of data creation. We present the first prototype of the Dendro platform, designed to help researchers use concepts from domain-specific ontologies to collaboratively describe and share datasets within their groups. Unlike existing solutions, ontologies are used at the core of the data storage and querying layer, enabling users to establish meaningful domain-specific links between data, for any domain. The platform is currently being tested with research groups from the University of Porto.

1 Introduction

Research data is diverse and requires specific knowledge to be interpreted, driving user communities to create metadata recommendations. Metadata for datasets, as for any other kind of resource, requires a tradeoff between a comprehensive description and control of the production cost [8]. This is more drastic in the "long-tail of science" as institutions often lack financial resources for data curation [4]. As metadata schemas grow to encompass the needs of different groups, their descriptors may become unnecessary or irrelevant to others, even in similar domains, leading to an overall lack of interoperability [1,2]. This motivated some research groups to adapt and combine sets of descriptors from several metadata schemas in order to suit the needs of their applications, creating *Application Profiles* [3] to describe research datasets.

We focus on data description in the early stages of research, much like ADMIRAL [5], and propose that researchers choose their own set of metadata descriptors from existing ontologies. Dendro, our platform, innovates by integrating research datasets in the Semantic Web and allowing users to describe them

V. Presutti et al. (Eds.): ESWC Satellite Events 2014, LNCS 8798, pp. 483–487, 2014.
DOI: 10.1007/978-3-319-11955-7_71

using concepts captured in ontologies. We combine this dynamic approach with the advantages of a triple-based data model proposed in the same context [6]. To simplify the workflow, we do not attempt to represent the contents of files as sets of RDF triples (as done in VoID[1] for example) instead focusing on describing and relating the files and folders themselves.

Dendro is designed to support researchers in their daily data management activities. With a generic data model that allows on-demand metadata descriptor selection by the user, it is completely built on both generic and domain-specific ontologies. OpenLink Virtuoso and SPARQL are at the core of its data layer, enabling metadata descriptions to be exposed on the Web and queried through Virtuoso's SPARQL endpoint.

2 Enabling Collaboration and Interoperability

Dendro was designed from the start as an user-friendly interface layer for users without data management knowledge. Users build a knowledge base using ontologies *in the background*, allowing them to focus on choosing the *properties* with the right semantics for their descriptions without being concerned with design and implementation issues that arise from ontology use. Given its collaborative nature, the solution can be classified as a semantic wiki built on a triple store. It differs from other semantic wikis like Semantic Mediawiki, for example, that stores amalgamated sets of triples as "pages" in its relational database. According to the documentation[2], Semantic Mediawiki can use a triple store to provide a SPARQL endpoint, but the synchronization between the relational database and the triple store uses dedicated business logic—a trait shared by other linked open data compatible systems.

Based on our own past developments in Semantic Mediawiki [7], we concluded that its interface is not designed to allow users to combine descriptors from several ontologies when describing a page[3]. Dendro, on the other hand, makes it easier to describe any kind of resource using combinations of descriptors not specified *a priori*. The ontology-based data model enables data management personnel without coding skills to contribute by building and loading additional ontologies into *their* Dendro, which can then be shared on the web to document the descriptions and reused by others in the Dendro instances that they manage.

3 A Walkthrough of the Solution

In this section we will provide an overview of the main features provided by Dendro in its current form. We demonstrate the usage of Dendro in the daily

[1] http://www.w3.org/TR/void/

[2] http://semantic-mediawiki.org/wiki/Help:Using_SPARQL_and_RDF_stores

[3] A *description template* must be specified *a priori* for each type of description page.

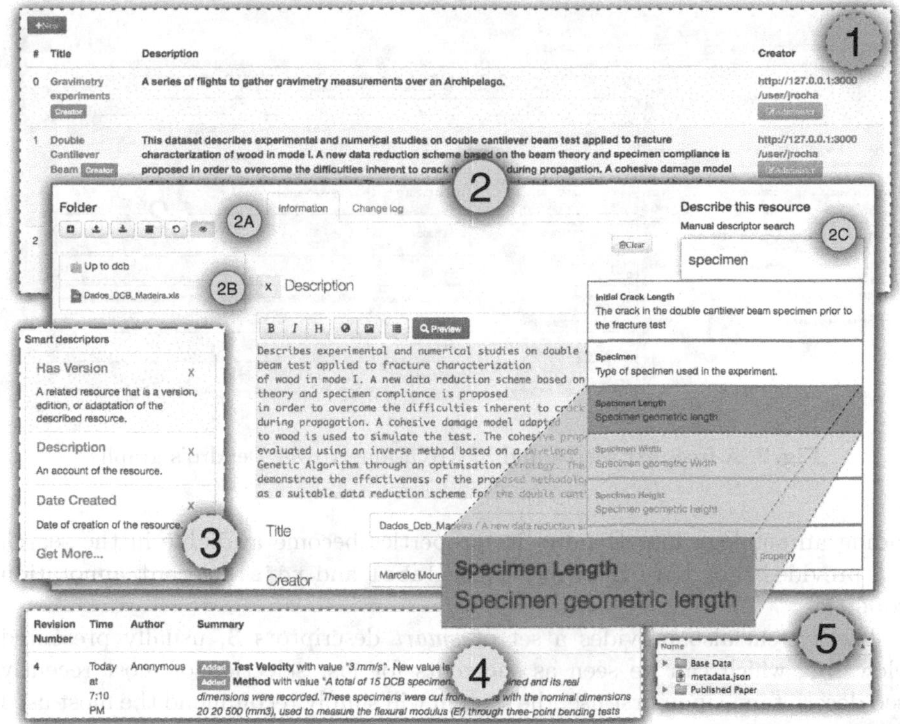

Fig. 1. Using Dendro to describe a mechanical engineering dataset

research data management activities within research groups from two very distinct domains—fracture mechanics experiments (mechanical engineering) and pollutant analysis (analytical chemistry)[4].

Figure 1 is a composite of screenshots showing how Dendro can be used to describe a dataset from the mechanical engineering domain. Area **1** shows the *project list* that allows users to see the projects that they have created in the system (i.e. there is an instance of `dcterms:creator` in the graph, with the project as its subject and the user as its object). Area **2** shows the main description interface. Note the list of options available to the user (area **2A**, from left to right: create folder, upload file(s), download folder, backup folder, restore folder, and show/hide deleted files). The file list **2B** shows the contents of the current folder and allows the user to navigate in the system. The *autocomplete* box **2C** is used to retrieve descriptors from the ontologies currently loaded in the Dendro instance, based on the values of their `rdfs:label` and `rdfs:comment` annotation properties—upon selection, the descriptor is added to the description area to be filled in. All descriptors originate from ontologies available on the web. Upon

[4] Video demonstrations for Dendro are available; short version (4 min): http://goo.gl/ug4FTh. Long version (40 min): http://goo.gl/SvdXhd

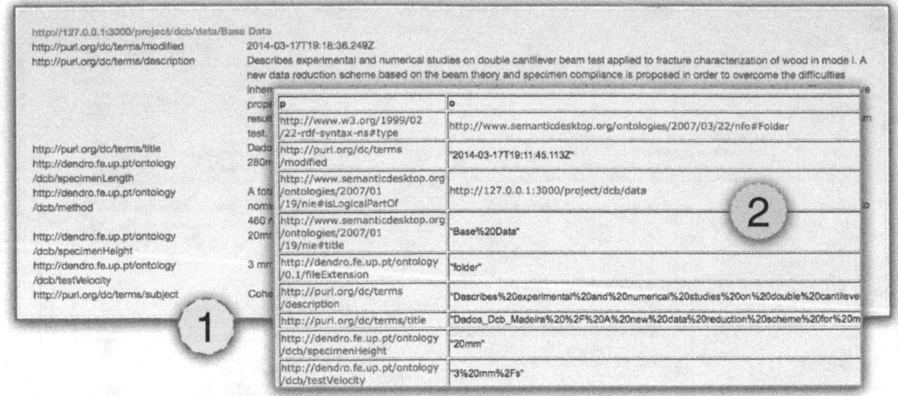

Fig. 2. A free-text search and SPARQL query over Dendro's graph

loading an ontology into Dendro, its properties become available in the search box, provided they have their own `rdfs:label` and `rdfs:comment` annotation properties.

The system also provides a set of *smart* descriptors **3**, usually presented below **2C**, which can be seen as shortcuts for fast selection of most recently used descriptors. Upon first use, the system will simply recommend the most used descriptors in the system. When the user selects a descriptor, the system will give preference to descriptors from the same ontology. When the user selects another descriptor from a different ontology, the recommendation is broadened to the descriptors from the now two *active* ontologies. All changes to descriptor values are versioned, as can be seen in area **4**. Finally, the system supports recursive backup and restore of directory structures (including metadata) through `ZIP` files. Area **5** shows the contents of a complete backup of the current project—note the `metadata.json` file at the root, which contains all the metadata for all resources in the project's directory tree.

Figure 2 shows the resource described in Fig. 1 among the results of a full-text search for the term "fracture mechanics" over the Dendro system (**1**). The search is powered by an ElasticSearch index that indexes every resource in the graph by its literals and that is continuously updated. Area **2** shows a partial view of the results of a SPARQL query used to retrieve the metadata for the same resource—SPARQL queries such as this are used internally by Dendro to retrieve and modify data in the underlying OpenLink Virtuoso graph database.

4 Conclusions and Future Work

Dendro is a research data management platform designed to provide researchers with a collaborative environment for storing and describing their datasets. Ontologies are used as sources for properties, picked by researchers to describe their research data.

Dendro differs from other research data management platforms in its "all semantic web" approach. By employing a triple-based data model and OpenLink Virtuoso, each resource can have an arbitrary set of descriptors. As they interact with the system, Dendro users are actually building a Linked Open Data graph of interconnected research-related resources, while data access is performed internally via SPARQL all accross the platform.

Dendro development is informed by the requirements of a panel of researchers from the University of Porto, and preliminary tests have shown a good match between their data management needs and the services of the platform. We regard it as an effective practical application of semantic web technologies, as well as a catalyst for the creation of domain-specific lightweight ontologies.

Acknowledgements. This work is supported by project NORTE-07-0124-FEDER-000059, financed by the North Portugal Regional Operational Programme (ON.2–O Novo Norte), under the National Strategic Reference Framework (NSRF), through the European Regional Development Fund (ERDF), and by national funds, through the Portuguese funding agency, Fundação para a Ciêancia e a Tecnologia (FCT). João Rocha da Silva is also supported by research grant SFRH/BD/77092/2011, provided by the Portuguese funding agency, Fundação para a Ciência e a Tecnologia (FCT).

References

1. Castro, J., Ribeiro, C., Rocha, J.: Designing an application profile using qualified dublin core: a case study with fracture mechanics datasets. In: Proceedings of the DC-2013 Conference, pp. 47–52 (2013)
2. Chan, L.: Metadata interoperability and standardization - a study of methodology Part I. D-Lib Mag. **12**, 1–34 (2006)
3. Heery, R., Patel, M.: Application profiles: mixing and matching metadata schemas. Ariadne Issue 25, September 2000. http://www.ariadne.ac.uk/issue25/app-profiles/
4. Heidorn, P.B.: Shedding light on the dark data in the long tail of science. Libr. Trends **57**(2), 280–299 (2008)
5. Hodson, S.: ADMIRAL: A Data Management Infrastructure for Research Activities in the Life sciences. University of Oxford, Technical report (2011)
6. Li, Y.-F., Kennedy, G., Ngoran, F., Wu, P.: An ontology-centric architecture for extensible scientific data management systems. Future Gener. Comput. Syst. **29**(2), 1–38 (2013)
7. Rocha, J., Barbosa, J., Gouveia, M., Ribeiro, C., Correia Lopes, J.: UPBox and DataNotes: a collaborative data management environment for the long tail of research data. In: iPres 2013 Conference Proceedings (2013)
8. Treloar, A., Wilkinson, R.: Rethinking metadata creation and management in a data-driven research world. In: 2008 IEEE Fourth International Conference on eScience, pp. 782–789, December 2008

Analyzing Linked Data Quality with LiQuate

Edna Ruckhaus(✉), Maria-Esther Vidal, Simón Castillo, Oscar Burguillos, and Oriana Baldizan

Universidad Simón Bolívar, Caracas, Venezuela
{eruckhaus,mvidal,scastillo,oburguillos,obaldizan}@ldc.usb.ve

Abstract. The number of datasets in the Linking Open Data (LOD) cloud as well as LOD-based applications have exploded in the last years. However, because of data source heterogeneity, published data may suffer of redundancy, inconsistencies, or may be incomplete; thus, results generated by LOD-based applications may be imprecise, ambiguous, or unreliable. We demonstrate the capabilities of LiQuate (Linked Data Quality Assessment), a tool that relies on Bayesian Networks to analyze the quality of data and links in the LOD cloud.

1 Introduction

Linking Open Data initiatives have made a diversity of collections available, and facilitate scientists the mining of linked datasets to discover patterns or suggest potential new associations. To ensure trustworthy results, linked data must meet high quality standards. However, data in the LOD cloud has not been necessarily curated, and tools are required to detect possible quality problems and ambiguities produced by redundancy, inconsistencies, and incompleteness of both data and links [2]. We developed LiQuate, a tool able to identify potential quality problems and ambiguities among data and links. LiQuate relies on statistical reasoning to analyze the quality of data based on completeness and potential redundancies or inconsistencies. A Bayesian Network models the dependencies among resources that belong to a set of linked datasets [1,3]; conditional probability tables annotate the nodes of the network and represent joint probability distributions of relationships among resources. Queries against the Bayesian Network represent the probability that different resources have redundant labels or that a link between two resources is missing; thus, the returned probabilities can suggest ambiguities or possible incompleteness in the data or links. We demonstrate the data quality validation capabilities of LiQuate and the benefits of the approach on the Biomedical datasets: *Drugbank Website*[1], *LinkedCT*[2], *D2R Diseasome*[3], *D2R Dailymed*[4], *D2R Drugbank*[5], *Bio2RDF Drugbank*[6], and

[1] http://www.drugbank.ca/
[2] http://linkedct.org/
[3] http://wifo5-04.informatik.uni-mannheim.de/diseasome
[4] http://wifo5-03.informatik.uni-mannheim.de/dailymed/
[5] http://wifo5-04.informatik.uni-mannheim.de/drugbank/
[6] http://download.bio2rdf.org/current/drugbank/drugbank.html

V. Presutti et al. (Eds.): ESWC Satellite Events 2014, LNCS 8798, pp. 488–493, 2014.
DOI: 10.1007/978-3-319-11955-7_72

DBPedia[7]. This demo illustrates how queries to a Bayesian Network that models RDF data and dependencies among properties, can be used to study quality problems related to both incompleteness of links, and ambiguities among labels and links. We show the following key issues: redundancy among drug labels in the *LinkedCT* dataset, and incompleteness and inconsistencies of links in Biomedical datasets. The demo is published at http://liquate.ldc.usb.ve.

2 The LiQuate System

As a proof of concept, LiQuate has been built on top of the Biomedical linked datasets that maintain data related to clinical trials, interventions, conditions, drugs, diseases, and the relationships among them. LiQuate exploits visualization services implemented by the D3.js JavaScript library[8]. Figure 1 illustrates the LiQuate architecture. LiQuate receives a *quality validation request* which is expressed as one or more evidence queries against the Bayesian Network. The answer of a *quality validation request* is a number in the range [0.0:1.0] that indicates the probability that a given quality problem occurs among the data. Currently, three types of quality validation requests can be expressed: (*i*) probability that labels or names of a given (type of) resource are redundant, (*ii*) probability of incomplete links among a given set of resources, and (*iii*) probability of inconsistent links. LiQuate is comprised of two components: the LiQuate Bayesian Network Builder and the Ambiguity Detector. The LiQuate Bayesian Network Builder is a semi-automatic off-line process; it relies on an expert's knowledge about the properties in the RDF linked datasets that are going to be represented in the Bayesian Network. Relevant data is retrieved from SPARQL endpoints, and stored in a relational database to compute the histograms that implement the conditional probability tables (CPTs) associated with the nodes of the network. The demo is focused on the Ambiguity Detector: a probabilistic model that supports the analysis of the three above mentioned linked data quality problems. The Ambiguity Detector is in turn comprised of three components: (*1*) the Quality Validation Request Analyzer, (*2*) the Bayesian Network Query Translator, and (*3*) the Bayesian Network Inference Engine. The Quality Validation Request Analyzer receives a user request and determines if it can be satisfied with the existing Bayesian Network. The Bayesian Network Query Translator considers the user request and generates the set of queries that must be posed against the Bayesian Network. It also gathers the answers of these queries and generates an answer to the user request. Finally, the Bayesian Network Inference Engine is responsible of performing the inference process required to answer each of the queries posed against the Bayesian Network. This engine is implemented by the *SamIam* Bayesian Inference Tool[9].

[7] http://wiki.dbpedia.org/Downloads32
[8] http://d3js.org/
[9] http://reasoning.cs.ucla.edu/samiam/help/recursiveconditioning.html

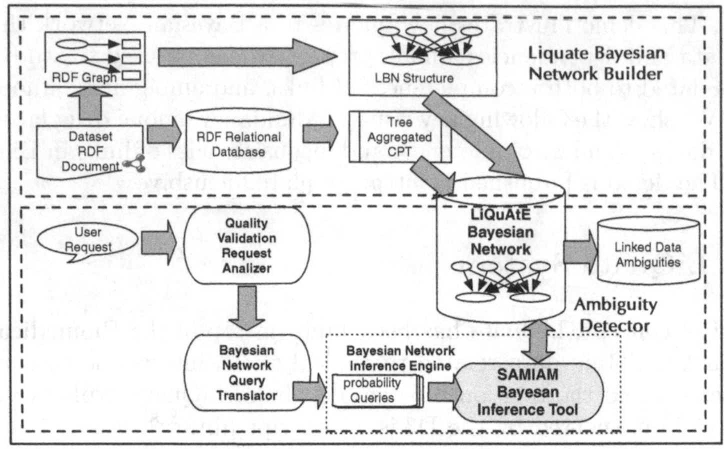

Fig. 1. The LiQuate system architecture.

3 Demonstration of Use Cases

As of September 2011, LinkedCT contains 106,308 trials, 2.7 million entities and over 25 million RDF triples. Additionally, we consider the following datasets that are linked to LinkedCT: (*i*) Drugbank (over 765,936 triples), (*ii*) Diseasome (around 91,182 triples), and (*iii*) DBPedia (links from LinkedCT 25,476). We built local RDF storage with LinkedCT triples and the triples from these three datasets that are related to LinkedCT. The Bayesian network and its corresponding CPT's were computed and stored in the *SamIam* Bayesian Inference Tool. The generated network is comprised of 17 nodes and the aggregated CPTs are of up to 167, 616 entries; for the cases to be shown, the average response time of LiQuate is 4, 715 ms. Figure 2(a) illustrates the description of Biomedical linked datasets, and Fig. 2(b) presents the Bayesian Network that represents the dependencies between these properties and links. `Concept Network Browser` plots[10] and `Force-Directed Graphs`[11] are used for visualization.

We demonstrate the following use cases:

Ambiguities between labels of Interventions or Drugs: Starting with Alemtuzumab as an exemplar, we retrieve the intersection of Monoclonal antibodies and Antineoplastic agents. This creates a dataset of 12 drugs: Alemtuzumab, Bevacizumab, Brentuximab vedotin, Cetuximab, Catumaxomab, Edrecolomab, Gemtuzumab, Ipilimumab, Ofatumumab, Panitumumab, Rituximab, and Trastuzumab. These drugs are frequently tested in clinical trials, and there are up to 723 clinical trials with a given intervention, e.g., the intervention that

[10] http://www.findtheconversation.com/concept-map
[11] http://bl.ocks.org/mbostock/4062045

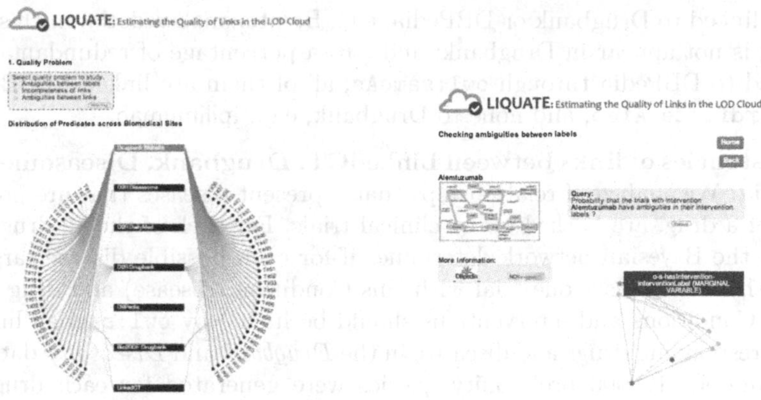

(a) LinkedCT, DrugBank (website, and two endpoints), Diseasome, and DBPedia visualized as a `Concept Network Browser` plot. Predicates published by the Drugbank Website are highlighted.

(b) Bayesian Network for LinkedCT, DrugBank, Diseasome, and DBPedia visualized by using a `Force-Directed Graph`; nodes colored in orange and in blue correspond to marginal and evidence variables, respectively

Fig. 2. Biomedical linked datasets and a LiQuate bayesian network.

corresponds to the drug Alemtuzumab is present in 112 different clinical trials, and all of these should be linked to the drug DB00087 (Alemtuzumab) in Drugbank in order for the datasets to be unambiguous. This use case illustrates the execution of a query that could indicate possible uncontrolled redundancy in the datasets. The Bayesian Network used to infer the percentage of ambiguity is visualized by using a `Force-Directed Graph`; nodes colored in orange and in blue correspond to marginal and evidence variables, respectively.

Incompleteness of links between LinkedCT, Drugbank, Diseasome, and DBPedia: We consider the family of the 12 drugs described above, and for each of the partitions induced by redundant labels we consider the `owl:sameAs` and `rdfs:seeAlso` links. A partition represents all of the clinical trials that are of interventional type and that have the same intervention (drug) label. For each intervention *id* that belongs to a partition, a query to the Bayesian Network is executed in order to determine if `owl:sameAs` links have been established for this intervention. General *results* are also presented for each of the 12 drugs. Examples of these *results* are: (*i*) a percentage of redundant labels are not linked through `owl:sameAs` to neither Drugbank or DBPedia, but 100 % of the labels are linked through `rdfs:seeAlso`, e.g., Bevacizumab; (*ii*) none of the redundant labels is linked to Drugbank or DBPedia, e.g., Brentuximab vedotin, in this case, the drug is not appear in Drugbank; and (*iii*) a percentage of redundant labels are linked to DBPedia through `owl:sameAs`, all of them are linked to DBPedia through `rdfs:seeAlso`, and none to Drugbank, e.g., Ipilimumab.

Inconsistencies of links between LinkedCT, Drugbank, Diseasome, and DBPedia: We analyze if relationships that represent diseases that are possible targets of a drug, are backed up by clinical trials. For each of the 12 drugs, the query to the Bayesian network determines if for each possible disease target of a drug, there is at least one trial with this Condition (disease) and drug intervention. Conditions and interventions should be linked by `owl:sameAs` links to their corresponding drugs and diseases, in the *Drugbank* and *Diseasome* datasets. Approximately, 10, 000 probability queries were generated for each drug and disease and all the combinations of linked (through `owl:sameAs`) conditions and interventions. The marginal node is `s-s-hascondition-hasintervention`, and the evidence is a disease, drug, condition, intervention, and the existence of `owl:sameAs` links among them. The result is that 13,5 % of the drugs and targeted diseases are supported by clinical trials that can be found through `owl:sameAs` links. Similarly, another hypothesis is that drugs that can possibly treat diseases (*possibleDrug* links) are supported by the same number of clinical trials. The result is 13, 5 % and this number suggests that both links *possibleDiseaseTarget* and *possibleDrug* are the inverse of each other. Particularly, for the dataset of 12 drugs we can observe the following: the drugs Brentuximab vedotin, Ipilimumab and Ofatumumab do not appear in Drugbank while these drugs have been studied in a large number of clinical trials. The rest of these 12 drugs do appear in Drugbank, but are associated with much less diseases through the property *possibleDiseaseTarget* in Drugbank, than to conditions through a clinical trial in LinkedCT. For example, the drug Cetuximab can possibly target eighteen diseases while this drug has been tested in completed clinical trials for 82 conditions; only four of the eighteen diseases in the property *possibleDiseaseTarget* in Drugbank, are included in the list of 82 conditions in LinkedCT. This ambiguity can be also observed in the rest of the drugs.

4 Conclusions

We present LiQuate, a data and link validation tool that relies on a Bayesian Network to identify redundancies, incompleteness and inconsistencies. We demonstrate the main quality validation capabilities of LiQuate, and illustrate different quality problems that may currently occur in the LOD cloud. Particularly, we can observe some ambiguities that suggest the experts to check for uncontrolled redundancy, incompleteness or inconsistency: (*i*) the same label or name of intervention is assigned to different resources, (*ii*) incomplete `owl:sameAs` and `rdfs:seeAlso` links between datasets, and (*iii*) associations between drugs and diseases in Drugbank may not be supported by trials in LinkedCT.

References

1. Getoor, L., Taskar, B., Koller, D.: Selectivity estimation using probabilistic models. SIGMOD Rec. **30**(2), 461–472 (2001)
2. Guéret, C., Groth, P., Stadler, C., Lehmann, J.: Assessing linked data mappings using network measures. In: Simperl, E., Cimiano, P., Polleres, A., Corcho, O., Presutti, V. (eds.) ESWC 2012. LNCS, vol. 7295, pp. 87–102. Springer, Heidelberg (2012)
3. Ruckhaus, E., Vidal, M.-E.: LiQuate-estimating the quality of links in the linking open data cloud. In: Lacroix, Z., Ruckhaus, E., Vidal, M.-E. (eds.) RED 2012. LNCS, vol. 8194, pp. 56–82. Springer, Heidelberg (2013)

Collaborative Semantic Management and Automated Analysis of Scientific Literature

Bahar Sateli and René Witte(✉)

Semantic Software Lab, Department of Computer Science and Software Engineering, Concordia University, Montréal, QC, Canada
{sateli,witte}@semanticsoftware.info

Abstract. The overabundance of literature available in online repositories is an ongoing challenge for scientists that have to efficiently manage and analyze content for their information needs. Most of the existing literature management systems merely provide support for storing bibliographical metadata, tagging, and simple annotation capabilities. In this demo paper, we go beyond these approaches by demonstrating how an innovative combination of semantic web technologies with natural language processing can mitigate the information overload by helping in curating and organizing scientific literature. We present the *Zeeva* system as a first prototype that demonstrates how we can turn existing papers into a queryable knowledge base.

1 Introduction

Every research group faces the task of managing research literature pertinent to ongoing projects. This includes storing and indexing publications that are required as background or foundation for a specific topic, finding and discussing related work, as well as sharing and linking research techniques, data, and software. Existing bibliographical tools – whether online or locally installed – mainly focus on managing bibliographic metadata, together with some limited form of social support, like tagging or free-text comments. But they all lack further support when it comes to explicitly model, store, and query a paper's *content*, such as *goals, claims, methods,* or *results.* While strategies for the semantic markup of newly created publications have been proposed before [1], no tools exist that would help researchers dealing with existing papers, in particular by integrating automated text analysis workflows.

Our overall research goal is to improve the management of scientific literature, in particular for individual researchers and research groups. Our hypothesis is that semantic technologies, including semantic wikis and text mining, can improve several tasks that users are facing on a daily basis. To investigate the feasibility and impact of semantic literature management support, we have been developing *Zeeva*, a first prototype that integrates wiki-based collaboration with semantic knowledge representation and text mining in a coherent, user-friendly interface.

V. Presutti et al. (Eds.): ESWC Satellite Events 2014, LNCS 8798, pp. 494–498, 2014.
DOI: 10.1007/978-3-319-11955-7_73

2 Zeeva System Architecture

The Zeeva system (Fig. 1) features a wiki as its front-end. Powered by the highly scalable MediaWiki[1] engine, users interact with the Zeeva wiki using their Web browser. They can view and edit the wiki content using a simple markup language, called *wiki markup*. Semantic capabilities are provided through the Semantic MediaWiki (SMW) [2] extension. SMW allows special markup to be inserted into wiki pages in order to embed metadata about the page's content. The metadata is subsequently transformed internally into RDF[2] triples. In addition, the Zeeva wiki has a special extension, called *Zeeva Facts*, which allows wiki users to seamlessly interact with natural language processing (NLP) pipelines directly within the wiki environment to automatically analyze scientific publications.

The NLP services in Zeeva are provided by the Semantic Assistants [3], an open source framework that can publish various NLP pipelines, implemented based on the General Architecture for Text Engineering (GATE) [4], as W3C standard web services. The service-oriented architecture of the Semantic Assistants framework allows us to add or remove arbitrary NLP pipelines from the Zeeva wiki to experiment different use cases without any modifications to its wiki engine.

When users invoke NLP services through the wiki interface, a RESTful request is sent to the Semantic Assistants server via the Zeeva Facts extension. The Semantic Assistants server then fetches the content of the paper from the provided URL and executes the user-selected NLP pipelines on the retrieved text. The NLP results are passed on to the Semantic Assistants Wiki-NLP connector [5], which transforms them into wiki-friendly markup and stores them in the wiki database. Each semantic wiki markup internally translates into a semantic triple, with the wiki page as the subject, the declared property as the predicate, and the given value as the object. SMW stores the generated triples in the wiki repository that can be later queried both within the wiki and from

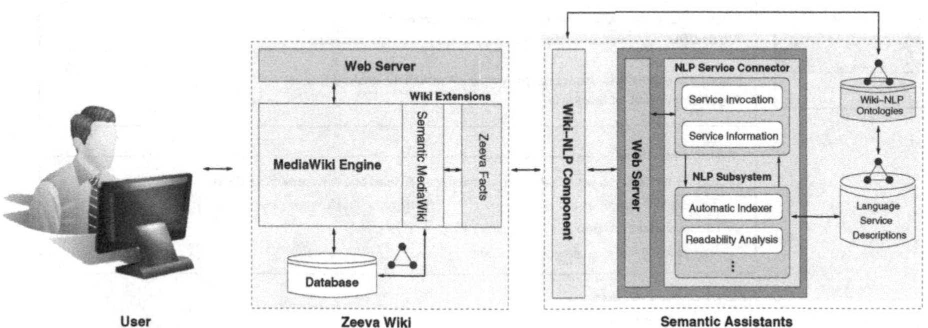

Fig. 1. A high-level overview of the Zeeva system architecture

[1] MediaWiki, http://www.mediawiki.org
[2] Resource Description Framework, http://www.w3.org/RDF/

external applications through an RDF feed. Currently, the Zeeva system does not employ any ontology specific to the literature analysis domain on its backend, rather it uses the SWIVT[3] ontology provided by the SMW extension.

3 Demonstration

In this demo,[4] we show how a number of concrete tasks, like finding contributions of an author over a set of gathered papers, are supported in Zeeva. In particular, we explain how a researcher can use the Zeeva system to interact with the NLP services (Fig. 2) in order to automatically extract structural and rhetorical entities from scientific publications. During the demonstration, visitors can see how we make use of MediaWiki's *templating* mechanism to transform NLP pipelines output to semantic triples in real-time. Zeeva's pre-defined templates, like the one illustrated in Fig. 3, define *(i)* the look and feel of the results when embedded in wiki pages, and *(ii)* the semantic metadata that should be attached to each pipeline output.

In real-world scenarios, research projects are typically collaborative work between two or more researchers. Therefore, one key requirement in the design of the Zeeva system has been the creation of a shared space, where all researchers of a team have access to the most up-to-date information and can easily keep track of content modifications. During the demo, we will show how multiple researchers can interact through the wiki, while always having an up-to-date view of the knowledge created by other users of the system using the SMW inline queries.

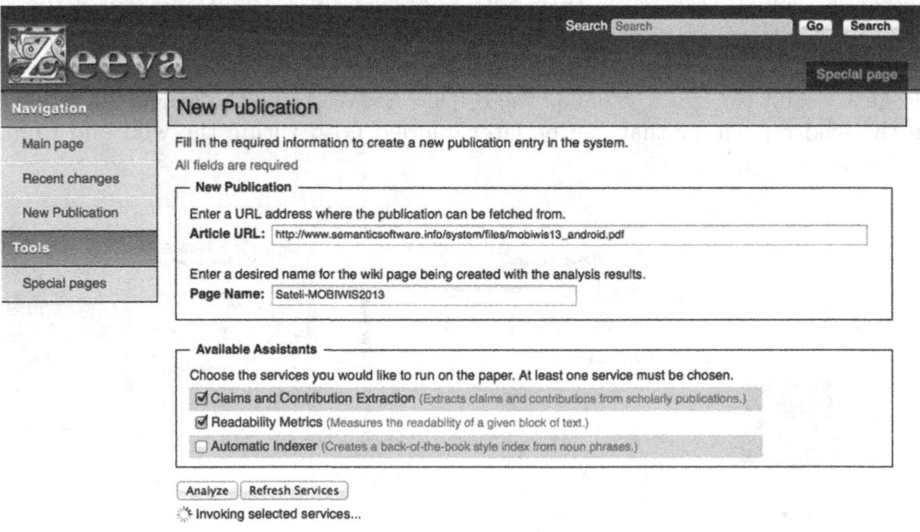

Fig. 2. Invoking integrated text mining assistants in the Zeeva wiki

[3] Semantic Wiki Vocabulary and Terminology, http://semantic-mediawiki.org/swivt/

[4] Please see http://www.semanticsoftware.info/eswc2014 for demo screencasts.

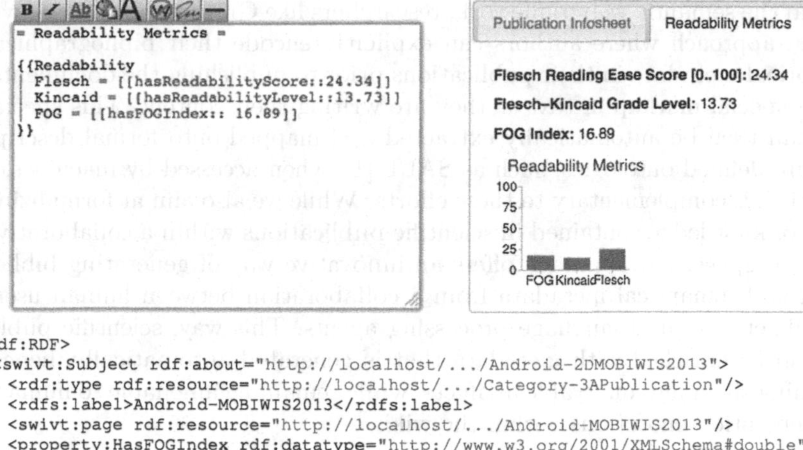

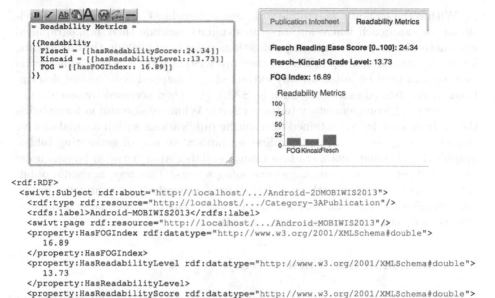

```
<rdf:RDF>
  <swivt:Subject rdf:about="http://localhost/.../Android-2DMOBIWIS2013">
    <rdf:type rdf:resource="http://localhost/.../Category-3APublication"/>
    <rdfs:label>Android-MOBIWIS2013</rdfs:label>
    <swivt:page rdf:resource="http://localhost/.../Android-MOBIWIS2013"/>
    <property:HasFOGIndex rdf:datatype="http://www.w3.org/2001/XMLSchema#double">
      16.89
    </property:HasFOGIndex>
    <property:HasReadabilityLevel rdf:datatype="http://www.w3.org/2001/XMLSchema#double">
      13.73
    </property:HasReadabilityLevel>
    <property:HasReadabilityScore rdf:datatype="http://www.w3.org/2001/XMLSchema#double">
      24.34
    </property:HasReadabilityScore>
    <!-- additional properties not shown in this excerpt -->
  </swivt:Subject>
  </property:HasTitle>
</rdf:RDF>
```

Fig. 3. Wiki template with semantic properties (left), preview in browser (right) and the RDF document (bottom) generated by Semantic MediaWiki

Finally, we will show how the Zeeva wiki can be transformed from an analysis platform to a queryable knowledge base. We will show how the results of human-AI collaboration on the Zeeva wiki can be exported to standalone RDF documents (Fig. 3) that can be directly queried with SPARQL queries.

4 Related Work

A large body of research exists that deals with improving access to the ever-increasing amount of scientific literature. Within the scope of this demo paper, we focus on collaborative solutions and semantic web ontologies.

Wiki-based systems, such as WikiPapers[5] and AcaWiki,[6] are recent efforts for collaborative literature analysis. Any user can register on these websites and submit summaries or reviews of peer-reviewed articles to the wiki. The goal of these systems is to collect a community-driven, comprehensive compilation of bibliographical and semantical metadata and make them available to the general public.

---

[5] WikiPapers, http://wikipapers.referata.com

[6] AcaWiki, http://www.acawiki.org

Within the semantic web framework, researchers like Groza et al. [1] are envisioning an approach where authors can explicitly encode their bibliographical and rhetorical metadata in their publications prior to publishing the documents, i.e., using special markup in text as they are writing their content. This special markup can then be automatically extracted and mapped onto formal descriptions in pre-defined ontologies, such as SALT [1], when accessed by machines.

Our work is complementary to these efforts. While we also aim at formalizing the body of knowledge contained in scientific publications within a collaborative (wiki-based) space, our approach offers an innovative way of generating bibliographical and semantical metadata from a collaboration between human users and 'intelligent' natural language processing agents. This way, scientific publications can be enriched with metadata that is generated automatically, hence, transforming them into queryable artifacts, while remaining amenable to human-created semantic annotations within the wiki.

5 Conclusion and Future Work

Currently existing literature management tools provide limited support for research groups when dealing with knowledge-intensive tasks, like literature surveys. We propose Zeeva, a proof-of-concept system that demonstrates how the next generation of literature management tools can go beyond simply storing bibliographical data and support research groups by transforming publications into an active knowledge base. Zeeva's embedded "Semantic Assistants" play the role of intelligent agents that collaboratively work with human users on scientific publications text analysis. Future work includes the addition of further text mining pipelines, as well as designing and integrating an ontology specific to the scientific literature analysis domain. In addition, we plan to perform user studies to measure the impact of the semantic support in real-world scenarios.

References

1. Groza, T., Handschuh, S., Möller, K., Decker, S.: SALT - semantically annotated LaTeX for scientific publications. In: Franconi, E., Kifer, M., May, W. (eds.) ESWC 2007. LNCS, vol. 4519, pp. 518–532. Springer, Heidelberg (2007)
2. Krötzsch, M., Vrandečić, D., Völkel, M.: Semantic MediaWiki. In: Cruz, I., Decker, S., Allemang, D., Preist, C., Schwabe, D., Mika, P., Uschold, M., Aroyo, L.M. (eds.) ISWC 2006. LNCS, vol. 4273, pp. 935–942. Springer, Heidelberg (2006)
3. Witte, R., Gitzinger, T.: Semantic Assistants – user-centric natural language processing services for desktop clients. In: Domingue, J., Anutariya, C. (eds.) ASWC 2008. LNCS, vol. 5367, pp. 360–374. Springer, Heidelberg (2008)
4. Cunningham, H., et al.: Text Processing with GATE (Version 6). University of Sheffield, Department of Computer Science (2011)
5. Sateli, B., Witte, R.: Natural language processing for MediaWiki: the Semantic Assistants approach. In: The 8th International Symposium on Wikis and Open Collaboration (WikiSym 2012), Linz, Austria. ACM (2012)

di.me: Ontologies for a Pervasive Information System

Simon Scerri[1(✉)], Ismael Rivera[1], Jeremy Debattista[1], Simon Thiel[2], Keith Cortis[1], Judie Attard[1], Christian Knecht[2], Andreas Schuller[2], and Fabian Hermann[2]

[1] INSIGHT Centre for Data Analytics, Galway, Ireland
{simon.scerri,ismael.rivera,jeremy.debattista, keith.cortis,judie.attard}@deri.org

[2] Fraunhofer-Gesellschaft zur Forderung der angewandten Forschung e.V., Stuttgart, Germany
{simon.thiel,christian.knecht,andreas.schuller, fabian.hermann}@iao.fraunhofer.de

Abstract. The di.me userware is a pervasive personal information management system that successfully adopted ontologies to provide various intelligent features. Supported by a suitable user interface, di.me provides ontology-driven support for the (i) integration of personal information from multiple personal sources, (ii) privacy-aware sharing of personal data, (iii) context-awareness and personal situation recognition, and (iv) creation of personalised rules that operate over live events to provide notifications, effect system changes or share data.

1 Introduction

Di.me is an example of a pervasive information system as described in [5], i.e., a dynamic environment composed of multiple personal information sources, that is capable of perceiving contextual information and supporting mobility. The di.me functionality, as included in the freely-available open-source system[1], demonstrates the value of using ontologies as representation formats for a wide variety of abstract concepts and information elements deriving from multiple devices and online accounts.

The above claim is validated particularly by the personalisable Rule Manager, which builds atop the other three ontology-driven features to enable people to construct *email filter*-style rules that extend to their entire digital sphere. If the current user interface (UI) is extended, these rules could enable users to design rules that switch a device to 'Silent' mode when entering the office/cinema, change their online presence to 'Available' when leaving, or provide notifications when someone refers to them on the social network post. Before providing examples of supported rules, and the other di.me features, we first provide a short overview of the ontologies that drive them.

[1] http://vmuscs05.deri.ie:8443/dime-communications/static/ui/dime/index.html

V. Presutti et al. (Eds.): ESWC Satellite Events 2014, LNCS 8798, pp. 499–504, 2014.
DOI: 10.1007/978-3-319-11955-7_74

2 Modelling the Personal Information Sphere

Many vocabularies in the di.me Ontology Framework were initially engineered for the Social Semantic Desktop[2]. In the digital.me[3] (di.me) project, they were extended in three directions to cover additional: (a) personal sources (beside one desktop), (b) personal information (e.g., microposts and social network interactions, placemarks, etc.) and (c) domains (e.g., privacy, trust, context and presence, histories and rules). Below is an overview[4] of the main vocabularies used to represent the personal di.me knowledge base, and an indication of how they enable the described di.me features.

Information gathered from personal sources is semantically lifted, i.e., transformed into an ontology-based representation of the Personal Information Model, as an instance of the PIMO Ontology. This process is in part supported by metadata crawlers at the integration stage of personal devices or online accounts, and in part by listeners which detect item creation/modification/deletion items in the entire personal information sphere. Thus, the semantic model maintains an integrated and up-to-date personal knowledge base, based on data stored on devices and online accounts, represented by the Device (DDO) and Account (DAO) ontologies. The extracted information items are represented by the Information Element (NIE) domain ontologies, which model files (NFO), events (NCAL), addressbooks (NCO), messages (NMO), etc., on personal devices; as well as social network data and activities (DLPO) [6]. The Contact ontology (NCO) is also the model behind the profile integration described in Sect. 3. The Sharing ontology (NSO) extends the Privacy Preference Ontology[5] to represent the concepts needed for the functionality described in Sect. 4, supported by the Annotation Ontology's (NAO) modelling of agent trust and item privacy levels.

The Context ontology (DCON) attaches context-dependant semantics to various items, e.g. a specific file is being modified, a specific person is nearby. To enable the situation recognition feature described in Sect. 5, a single DCON instance maintains a centralised representation of a person's activities, e.g., events (NCAL instances) extracted from a calendar service, files being edited and applications running (NFO instances), locations checked-in and people tagged on a social network (DLPO instances), etc. The Presence ontology (DPO) facilitates the interpretation of context information having a broad range (e.g., temperature, date/time) by mapping discrete values retrieved from sensors to pre-defined categories (e.g., 'Hot', 'Late Evening', 'Weekend'). To compare context information at different times, the user History ontology (DUHO) persists time-stamped DCON instances in separate, non-conflicting named graphs.

Finally, the context-driven rule functionality described in Sect. 6 is enabled by the Rule Management Ontology (DRMO). Through the UI, a large part

[2] http://nepomuk.semanticdesktop.org/

[3] http://dime-project.eu/

[4] For in-depth ontology descriptions please refer to: http://www.semanticdesktop.org/ontologies/. For a documentation of the ontologies' integration in di.me, please refer to: http://github.com/dime-project/meta/wiki/Ontology-Framework.

[5] http://vocab.deri.ie/ppo#

of the above mentioned Personal Information Model elements can be wrapped within DRMO instances as filters. When di.me detects that all filters apply, it triggers the desired user-defined actions. The UI allows for great flexibility, and both concepts (e.g., person) and instances (e.g., a specific known person) can be selected as rule filters. Filters can be custom-described depending on their type, e.g., when selecting a specific person (a PIMO instance) as a filter, one can specify that the person must be nearby (a DCON property). However, if the person concept is selected (signifying 'any person'), it can be further constrained, e.g., to only apply to members of a specific group (a PIMO property).

3 Multi-source Personal Information Integration

An example of ontology-driven information integration in di.me is provided by the Person/Contact merging feature, which in contrast to other methods, does not rely solely on syntactic similaries. It also takes into account the semantics attached to the various profile attributes derived from multiple sources (e.g. address book, social networks) [3]. When linking additional sources to di.me, e.g., a social network account, profiles for all contacts are semantically lifted onto the NCO ontology, and then compared to existing profiles. Matches that are identified are suggested for merging, as shown in Fig. 1-left.

4 Privacy-Aware Sharing of Personal Data

The NSO ontology enables the representation of two virtual concepts: *Databoxes* and *Profile Cards*. Databoxes are able to represent ad-hoc, user-created collections of PIM items (e.g., documents, images, archive files, etc.), organised by context (e.g., related to a topic, project, or task). Similarly, Profile Cards refer to subsets of the user's personal identification attributes (e.g., names, pictures, email addresses, etc.), manually designed for different purposes. Both Databoxes and Profile Cards can be shared through a system of whitelists and blacklists

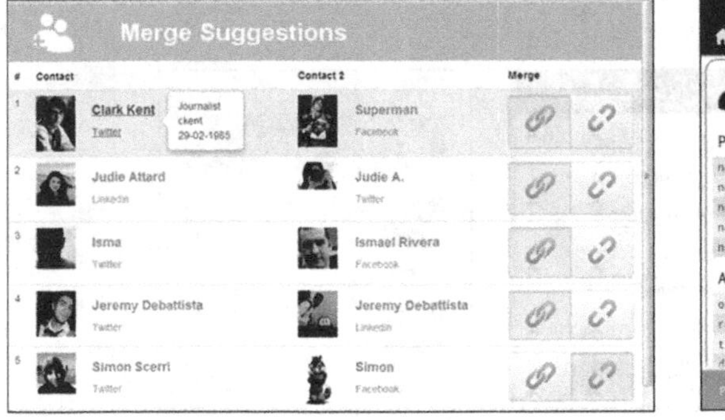

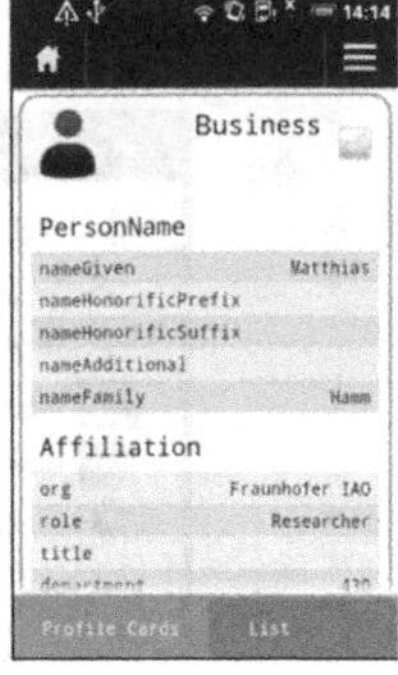

Fig. 1. Duplicate contact detection (Web UI) and a 'Business' Profile Card (mobile UI)

(e.g., share with a group of people, but exclude some members). An example of a custom profile card, or alternate personal identity, targeted towards business contacts is shown in Fig. 1-right.

To counteract risks associated with the increased cognitive complexity of sharing modularised data in this manner, di.me provides various warnings based on person trust levels and item privacy levels (NAO Ontology). Both levels can be adjusted manually through the UI, but also automatically based on perceived sharing activities and social network interactions (trust changed) and on provenance (privacy level changed).

5 Situation Training and Recognition

Personal situations can be saved on the spot and labelled accordingly (e.g. "Working@Office"). On saving, registered context elements are automatically added to the situation (DCON instance), each with an initial weight of zero. These weights are automatically adjusted whenever a suggested situation is confirmed by the user [2]. Future versions of di.me could allow the removal of elements deemed irrelevant to the situation (e.g., Sunny weather), and also manually modify their weights.

Figure 2 shows the UI components responsible for visualising a specific situation (left), and the situation suggestion bar (right). As indicated by the varied weights, the '@Conference' situation has already been trained, and the elements which have the relevance are the detected 'Working' activity (0.9) and the 'Convention Centre' placemark (0.8). The situation suggestion bar shows ranked results (by % score) of the context matching algorithm [1], which continously compares the live context information with the stored situations. Through this bar, users can manually confirm which situations are recurring. Situations are only automatically activated when matching scores are greater than 80 %.

6 Personalisable Context-Driven Rules

The di.me Rule Manager is accessible through the Settings tab. It is a 'lego-like' UI that enables owners to drag-and-drop objects and apply filters. Figure 3

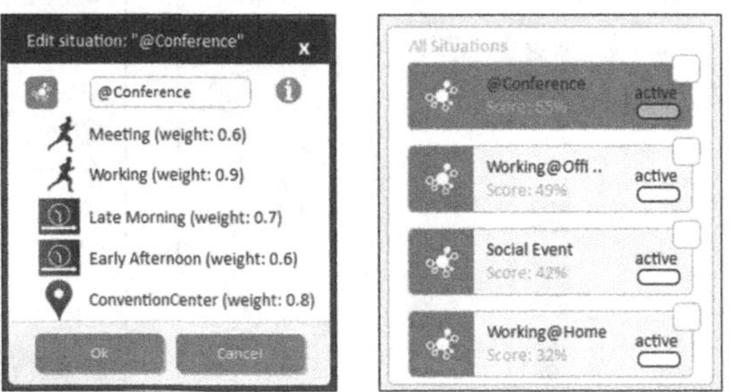

Fig. 2. Situation management and suggestions

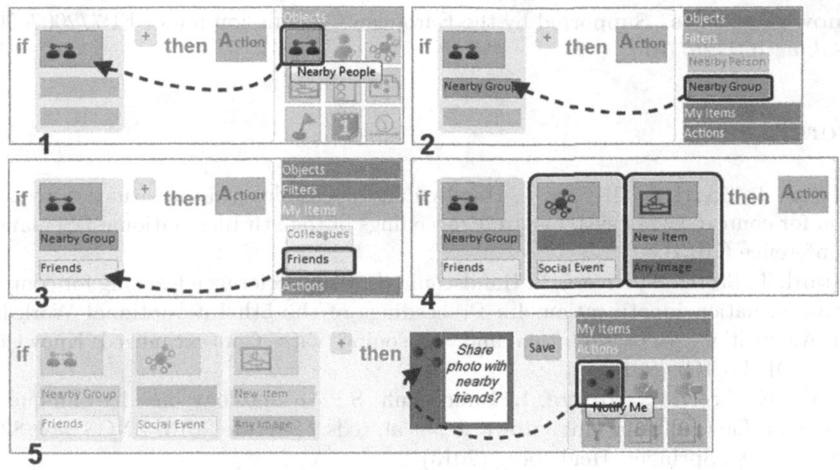

Fig. 3. The steps required to create a custom rule through the lego-like Rule Manager

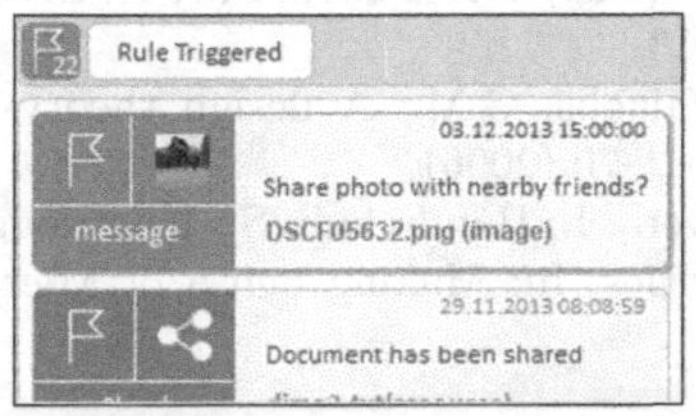

Fig. 4. Notification for a triggered rule

shows the steps required to build the following rule: *IF* (friends are nearby) *&* (I'm at a social event) *&* (I take a photo) *THEN* [Ask if I want to share it with my friends].

Step one shows objects that may be used as rule blocks. In this example, the 'Nearby People' is dragged to the corresponding coloured-box on the left-hand side. The Rule Manager then loads relevant filters. In this case (Step 2), 'Nearby Group' is selected. Available groups are then shown, and a specific one is selected (Step 3). This constitutes the first completed block. Step 4 shows how the rule looks like after two other blocks are added: (i) the situation social event is active, and (ii) a new image (photo) is created. To finalise the rule, an action is selected (Step 5). An accompanying message is required for notification purposes when the rule is triggered.

Each saved rule is stored as an instance of DRMO. At runtime, di.me builds a rule network for efficient rule matching. The system continously listens out for each context and system event, and checks these against the network. Rules are trigerred when the event processor detects that an entire path in the network has been activated [4]. Notification for the triggered rule is shown in Fig. 4.

Acknowledgments. Supported by the European Commission under FP7/2007–2013 (*digital.me* ICT-257787).

References

1. Attard, J., Scerri, S., Rivera, I., Handschuh, S.: Ontology-based situation recognition for context-aware systems. In: Proceedings of the 9th International I-Semantics Conference (2013)
2. Attard, J., Scerri, S., Rivera, I., Handschuh, S.: User preference learning for context-aware situation identification. In: Proceedings of the 5th International Workshop on Acquisition, Representation and Reasoning with Contextualized Knowledge (ARCOE-LogIC) (2013)
3. Cortis, K., Scerri, S., Rivera, I., Handschuh, S.: An ontology-based technique for online profile resolution. In: Jatowt, A., et al. (eds.) SocInfo 2013. LNCS, vol. 8238, pp. 284–298. Springer, Heidelberg (2013)
4. Debattista, J., Scerri, S., Rivera, I., Handschuh, S.: Processing ubiquitous personal event streams to provide user-controlled support. In: Lin, X., Manolopoulos, Y., Srivastava, D., Huang, G. (eds.) WISE 2013, Part II. LNCS, vol. 8181, pp. 375–384. Springer, Heidelberg (2013)
5. Kourouthanassis, P.E., Giaglis, G.M.: A design theory for pervasive information systems. In: IWUC, pp. 62–70 (2006)
6. Scerri, S., Cortis, K., Rivera, I., Handschuh, S.: Knowledge discovery in distributed social web sharing activities. In: Making Sense of Microposts (#MSM2012), pp. 26–33 (2012)

IDE Integrated RDF Exploration, Access and RDF-Based Code Typing with LITEQ

Stefan Scheglmann[1(✉)], Ralf Lämmel[2], Martin Leinberger[1], Steffen Staab[1], Matthias Thimm[1], and Evelyne Viegas[3]

[1] Institute for Web Science and Technologies, University of Koblenz-Landau, Koblenz, Germany
schegi@uni-koblenz.de

[2] The Software Languages Team, University of Koblenz-Landau, Koblenz, Germany

[3] Microsoft Research Redmond, Redmond, USA

Abstract. In order to access RDF data in Software development, one needs to deal with challenges concerning the integration of one or several RDF data sources into a host programming language. LITEQ allows for exploring an RDF data source and mapping the data schema and the data itself from this RDF data source into the programming environment for easy reuse by the developer. Core to LITEQ is a novel kind of path query language, NPQL, that allows for both extensional queries returning data and intensional queries returning class descriptions. This demo presents a prototype of LITEQ that supports such a type mapping as well as autocompletion for NPQL queries.

1 Introduction

The Resource Description Framework (RDF) is the core technology used in many machine-readable information sources on the Web. RDF has primarily been developed for consumption by applications rather than for direct use by humans. While the flexibility of RDF facilitates the design and publication of data on the Web, it complicates the integration of RDF data sources into applications. For example, it is almost impossible for a developer to know the structure of the data source beforehand. Additionally, there is an impedance mismatch between the way classes or types are used in programming languages compared to how classes are structuring RDF data, cf. [1–4].

To address these challenges, we present LITEQ, a paradigm for querying RDF data, mapping it for use in a host language, and strongly typing it for harvesting the full benefits of advanced compiler technology. It contains mechanisms to map RDF types into code types and allows for embedding query expressions into a host programming language. In addition it is developed with an autocompletion feature in mind so that the autocompletion together with static types can be used to alleviate problems with the unknown structure of RDF data.

In this demo, we present a prototype implementing the language independent LITEQ paradigm for the F# [5] programming language. It builds on top of the

V. Presutti et al. (Eds.): ESWC Satellite Events 2014, LNCS 8798, pp. 505–510, 2014.
DOI: 10.1007/978-3-319-11955-7_75

F# type provider[1] mechanism, which makes the prototype usable in arbitrary IDEs supporting the F# language. In this demo paper, we demonstrate the feasibility and usability of the LITEQ prototype and its integration into an IDE like Visual Studio.

2 Accessing RDF Data in Software Development

To illustrate both the challenges encountered by a developer when integrating and reusing RDF data in a programming environment and the contributions of LITEQ, we present some tasks which are prerequisites for working with any data source.

T1 Schema exploration: Initially the structure and the content of data sources are unknown to the developer. In order to identify RDF types that are important for main functionalities of a target application, the developer has to explore the data source and gather information about selected RDF types that he later wants to access in his application.

T2 Code type creation: Once the developer has enough information, he can design and implement his code types and their hierarchy in the host language.

T3 Data querying: Then, the developer uses the schema information in to define queries.

T4 Object creation and manipulation: Given the extensional queries, the developer can retrieve RDF objects and map them into program objects as well as access and manipulate their values.

In the conventional way, the developer could explore the Schema (T1) using a series of SPARQL queries. He can manually write down his own code types based on the RDF types (T2) and formulate SPARQL queries as plain strings in his code (T3). He can then use the results of his written queries to instantiate his previously created classes and actually work with his types (T4). There are several problems with such an approach: Exploring a schema in SPARQL is cumbersome and requires advanced knowledge of SPARQL. Also, creating the types in the code is a recurring task. Lastly, formulating SPARQL queries as plain strings is problematic as errors of all kind will only surface at runtime.

3 Node Path Query Language (NPQL)

Core to LITEQ is a novel path query language, NPQL, that combines type mapping, data querying, and autocompletion to solve the challenges formulated in the previous section. This query language does not stand for itself but is supposed to be embedded into a host language (Fig. 1).

NPQL Syntax. Every NPQL expression starts with an URI representing an RDF class. Three different kind of operators allow for the traversal of the RDF schema:

[1] http://msdn.microsoft.com/en-us/library/hh156509.aspx

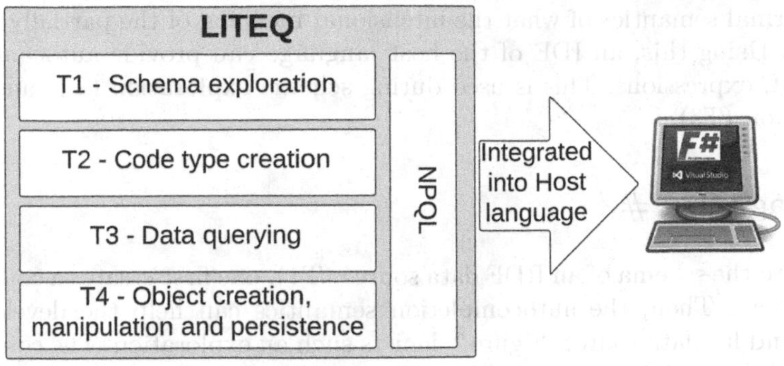

Fig. 1. Integrated into a host language, NPQL can be used to solve the 4 presented tasks.

(Op 1) The subtype navigation operator "$\triangledown$" refines the current selected RDF type to one of its direct subclasses.
(OP 2) The property navigation operator "$\triangleright$" expects a property that may be reached from the currently selected RDF type. This property is used as an edge to navigate to the next node, which is defined as the range type of that property.
(OP 3) The property restriction operator "$\triangleleft$" expects a property and uses this property to restrict the extension of the currently selected RDF node. However, it does not traverse the RDF graph further[2].

Using the FOAF vocabulary, an example could be the expression 1, which uses a subtype navigation to navigate from `foaf:Agent` to `foaf:Person` and a property navigation via the `foaf:workplaceHomepage` property to the final `foaf:Document` type.

$$\texttt{foaf:Agent} \triangledown \texttt{foaf:Person} \triangleright \texttt{workplaceHomepage} \quad (1)$$

NPQL Semantics: Depending on the context of use, NPQL expressions are evaluated using one or two of the three different semantics:
(Sem 1) The *extensional semantics* of NPQL provides us with an evaluation function, that evaluates an NPQL expression to a set of URIs (the extension). This semantics is used during data querying (T4).
(Sem 2) The *intensional semantics* provides us with an evaluation function, that maps an NPQL expression to an URI. This RDF type URI can be used in order to gather all necessary information, like hierarchy and properties, and to generate the corresponding code type. This semantics is used during code type creation (T2) but also during the retrieval and manipulation of RDF objects (T4).
(Sem 3) The *autocompletion semantics* can complete suggestions for partially written queries. This is possible, because at every step of query writing, we can

[2] It is a topic of our future research whether it may be of advantage to dynamically form a description logics like anonymous class expression $ex : Creature \sqcap \exists ex : hasOwner$ and uses this for typing in the host programming language.

give a formal semantics of what the intensional meaning of the partially written query is. Using this, an IDE of the host language can provide autocompletion for NPQL expressions. This is used during schema exploration (T1) and query formulation (T3).

4 Usage in F#

To explore the schema of an RDF data source (T1), one first creates a connection to the store. Then, the autocompletion semantics can help the developer to understand his data source. Figure 2 depicts such an exploration. The connection is created using the `RDFStore` object. The developer looks at the properties of `foaf:Person`, which is a subtype of `foaf:Agent`.

The store connection can also be used to access types from the store directly (T2). Again, this type selection is supported by autocompletion. Figure 3 shows expressions that create code types for `foaf:Person` and `foaf:Organization` using the intensional semantics of LITEQ.

Querying data (T3), like all `foaf:Persons` with a `Skype ID` can also be done using NPQL. Figure 4 shows such a query using the property restriction to restrict the set of all `foaf:Person` typed URIs to those who have a `Skype ID`. By applying an extensional evaluation of the expression, a sequence of person instances is returned. These instances are typed according to the intensional semantics.

The developer can also use the code types, such as the instances returned in the statement shown in Fig. 4, to modify the data in the store (T4). Returned types, such as shown in Fig. 3 can be used to instantiate new entities. Figure 5 depicts such an instantiation and manipulation of a new `foaf:Person`. Every change made to such an object is automatically propagated to the underlying Triplestore.

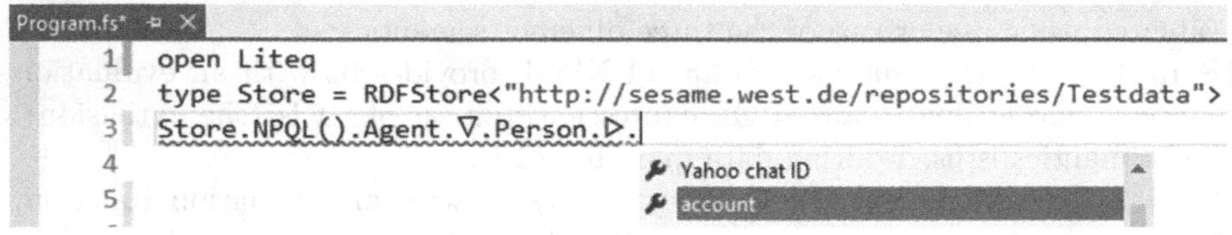

Fig. 2. Build-in autocompletion used for exploring a data source.

```
type Person = Store.Person.Intension
type Organization = Store.Organization.Intension
```

Fig. 3. Intensionally evaluated queries that yield types.

```
// Retrieve all persons that have a Skype Id
let personsWithSkypeAccounts = Store.NPQL().Person.◁.``Skype ID``.Extension
```

Fig. 4. Querying for all persons with a Skype ID.

```
let newPerson = new Person(newPersonUri)
newPerson.firstName <- [ "Jacob" ]
newPerson.familyName <- [ "Jansson" ]
newPerson.``Skype ID`` <- [ "jacob.jansson" ; "someguy42" ]
```

Fig. 5. Creation and manipulation of a new Person instance.

5 Implementation

The prototype shown in the screenshots is written in F# and builds on its type provider technology. To enable the NPQL query-object and usable types, the schema of the store is analyzed on IDE startup. Based on this analysis, the type provider can generate the classes that are necessary to integrate NPQL query expressions and intensional types. Intensional and extensional evaluation semantics as well as mappings that convert NPQL expressions to SPARQL queries are encoded in this type provider. Every part of the query is essentially a method, adding a triple pattern to a query. The extensional evaluation is then implemented as a SPARQL query that includes all those triple patterns.

Links to the current implementation, a technical report with an extended discussion of the NPQL semantics as well as a screencast of the current LITEQ implementation, showing the autocompletion can be found at http://west.uni-koblenz.de/Research/systems/liteq.

6 Conclusion and Further Work

In this demo paper we presented an implementation of LITEQ for the F# programming language. LITEQ allows for querying, code type creation, and data access of RDF data from within the host language IDE and tries to alleviate the arising challenges. It facilitates a syntax-checked query language, the node path query language (NPQL) to explore, navigate, and query unknown RDF data sources via SPARQL endpoints. The prototypical implementation of LITEQ makes use of the strong type system of F#. Thus, type safety is guaranteed and the generated types are treated as built-in types.

Acknowledgments. This work has been supported by Microsoft.

References

1. Eisenberg, V., Kanza, Y.: Ruby on semantic web. In: Abiteboul, S., Böhm, K., Koch, C., Tan, K.-L. (eds.) ICDE 2011, pp. 1324–1327. IEEE Computer Society (2011)
2. Hart, L., Emery, P.: OWL Full and UML 2.0 Compared (2004). http://uk.builder.com/whitepapers/0and39026692and60093347p-39001028qand00.htm
3. Kalyanpur, A., Pastor, D.J., Battle, S., Padget, J.A.: Automatic mapping of OWL ontologies into Java. In: SEKE 2004 (2004)
4. Rahmani, T., Oberle, D., Dahms, M.: An adjustable transformation from OWL to ecore. In: Petriu, D.C., Rouquette, N., Haugen, Ø. (eds.) MODELS 2010, Part II. LNCS, vol. 6395, pp. 243–257. Springer, Heidelberg (2010)
5. Syme, D., Battocchi, K., Takeda, K., Malayeri, D., Fisher, J., Hu, J., Liu, T., McNamaa, B., Quirk, D., Taveggia, M., Chae, W., Matsveyeu, U., Petricek, T.: F# 3.0 – Strongly Typed Language Support for Internet-Scale Information Sources. Technical report MSR-TR-2012-101, Microsoft Research (2012)

Browsing DBpedia Entities with Summaries

Andreas Thalhammer(✉) and Achim Rettinger

AIFB, Karlsruhe Institute of Technology, Karlsruhe, Germany
{thalhammer,rettinger}@kit.edu

Abstract. The term "Linked Data" describes online-retrievable formal descriptions of entities and their links to each other. Machines and humans alike can retrieve these descriptions and discover information about links to other entities. However, for human users it becomes difficult to browse descriptions of single entities because, in many cases, they are referenced in more than a thousand statements.

In this demo paper we present SUMMARUM, a system that ranks triples and enables entity summaries for improved navigation within Linked Data. In its current implementation, the system focuses on DBpedia with the summaries being based on the PageRank scores of the involved entities.

Keywords: Entity summarization · DBpedia · Linked data · Statement ranking

1 Introduction

The goal of the Linked Data movement is to enrich the Web with structured data. While the formal nature of these knowledge descriptions targets machines as immediate consumers, the final product is typically consumed by humans. Examples like Wikipedia Infoboxes show that, in many cases, next to textual descriptions users also want to browse structured data in order to get a quick overview about common or main facts of a data object. However, state-of-the-art interfaces like the one of DBpedia deliver all known facts about an entity in a single Web page. Often, the first thing users see when browsing a DBpedia entity are the values of `dbpedia-owl:abstract` in ten different languages. As a first attempt to overcome this issue, we introduce SUMMARUM, a system that ranks triples in accordance to popularity and enables entity summaries for improved navigation within Linked Data. In its current implementation, the system focuses on DBpedia with the summaries being based on the PageRank scores of the involved entities. We also adopted navigation elements from Semantic MediaWiki [3] in order to enable more flexible browsing.

The system is available at http://km.aifb.kit.edu/services/summa/.

2 Related Work

The field of browsing Linked Data entities has already been explored thoroughly. For the sake of conciseness, we focus on the most related and/or recent work in this field.

V. Presutti et al. (Eds.): ESWC Satellite Events 2014, LNCS 8798, pp. 511–515, 2014.
DOI: 10.1007/978-3-319-11955-7_76

Recent efforts for producing user-friendly interfaces for Linked Data entities include the new *DBpedia interface* (currently available via DBpedia Live)[1] and Magnus Manske's *Reasonator* tool[2] which is based on Wikidata.[3] In the new DBpedia interface, all property-value pairs are ordered in the traditional DBpedia fashion, with values sorted alphabetically in accordance to their labels. In the Reasonator tool, the listings of statements do not seem to implement a particular order.

Similar tools are *aemoo* [4] and *LODPeas* [2]. *aemoo* focuses on schema information: of which class is an entity and to which other classes does the currently browsed entity relate. Further interaction with the related classes enables to detect additional entities of the respective type which can be browsed. *LODPeas* enables to browse further entites that are related to the currently browsed entity. The system makes use of a "concurrence index" which enables to suggest entities that share common property-value pairs. Both systems are focused on presenting entities that are not necessarily directly attached to the currently browsed entity.

Semantic MediaWiki [3] offers search by property-value pairs[4], e.g. by specifying `[[Born In::Hawaii]]`. We adopt this scheme in order to enable users to discover entities which share a specific attribute with the currently browsed one. Thus, browsing `dbpedia:Barack_Obama`, it is possible to discover who else was born in `dbpedia:Hawaii`.

The three major search engines, *Google*, *Yahoo*, and *Bing* also offer summaries of entities. Bing and Google also retrieve lists of entities that are focused on a property-value pairs, e.g. "movies `directed by Quentin Tarantino`". However, this seems to work only in specific domains as querying for "people `born in Hawaii`" does not result in a list of entities.

3 DBpedia PageRank

For our popularity-based approach, we computed the PageRank [1] scores for each DBpedia entity. As a basis for this, we used DBpedia's Wikipedia Pagelinks (en)[5] dataset. This dataset contains triples of the form "Wikipedia page A links to Wikipedia page B". We only use these untyped links, i.e. do not make use of typed links (e.g., `dbpedia-owl:birthplace`) for computation and thus, the computed scores reflect the PageRank of the associated Wikipedia pages. However, we call the dataset "DBpedia PageRank" as the link extraction is performed by the DBpedia framework and the resources are identified with DBpedia URIs.

For the computation of PageRank we used the original formula as described in [1] with a damping factor of 0.85. The number of iterations was set to 40

[1] http://live.dbpedia.org/
[2] http://tools.wmflabs.org/reasonator/
[3] http://wikidata.org
[4] http://semantic-mediawiki.org/wiki/Help:Semantic_search
[5] Wikipedia Pagelinks (en) – http://wiki.dbpedia.org/Downloads39#wikipedia-pagelinks

while the score changes from 20 iterations onwards were marginal and thus, suggest convergence. We publish the computed PageRank scores for the English language DBpedia versions 3.8 and 3.9 at http://people.aifb.kit.edu/ath/#DBpedia_PageRank. The dataset is available in tab-separated values and also in Turtle format. For the Turtle representation we used the vRank vocabulary[6] [5].

4 Implementation

The SUMMARUM system is implemented as a Web Service which accepts three query parameters as input:

entity* the URI of a DBpedia entity that the user wants to browse.
k* the maximum number of statements the user wants to retrieve about the entity.
predicate the URI of a DBpedia predicate. If this parameter is present, the system focuses on statements that involve the given entity in combination with the given predicate.

The parameters marked with the star symbol (*) are mandatory. The *predicate* parameter is optional. As an example, it can be used to retrieve a ranked list of statements with `dbpedia-owl:birthPlace` as a predicate combined with the entity `dbpedia:Hawaii`.

The system currently focuses on statements that involve two DBpedia entities[7] and, as such, does not consider statements with literal values, classes, or external resources. For each entity we use its incoming and outgoing typed links. Thus, the result is a mix of statements where the summarized entity is either in the subject or object position. This also includes results of queries where the *predicate* parameter was given. For example, using `dbpedia-owl:order` in combination with `dbpedia:Apodiformes` will retrieve statements where the entity is in the subject or object position of `dbpedia-owl:order`.

The decision on whether to include a statement in the top-k summary or not depends on the rank position. The score of a statement is the sum of the PageRank scores of the subject and the object. It has to be noted that, with the focus on a specific entity, its own score is not needed for the ranking and appears superfluous as the entity's score influences each ranked statement equally. In fact, we add the score for reasons of consistency as we publish each statement's score in the Turtle output of the service. Using only the subject's (resp. object's) score for ranking the statement would produce the same ranking but two different versions of the statement's score depending on whether the subject or the object is currently in focus.

In many cases, there are more than one statement with the same subject-object pair. Often, this is due to the distinction between DBpedia "property" and "ontology" predicates. For these cases, we apply a simple heuristic to decide

[6] vRank – http://purl.org/voc/vrank
[7] All DBpedia resources with the prefix http://dbpedia.org/resource

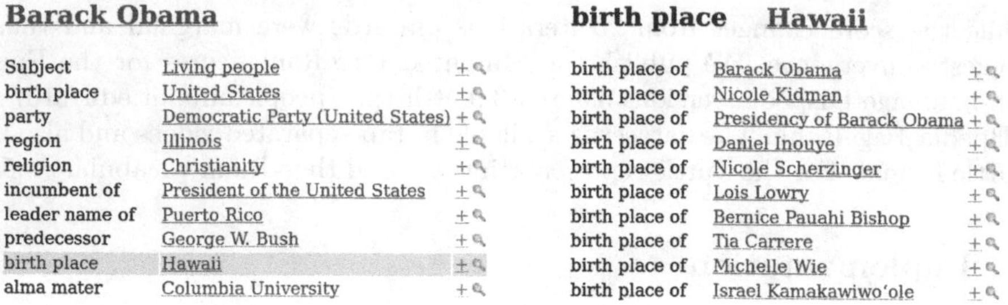

Barack Obama

Subject	Living people	±
birth place	United States	±
party	Democratic Party (United States)	±
region	Illinois	±
religion	Christianity	±
incumbent of	President of the United States	±
leader name of	Puerto Rico	±
predecessor	George W. Bush	±
birth place	Hawaii	±
alma mater	Columbia University	±

birth place Hawaii

birth place of	Barack Obama	±
birth place of	Nicole Kidman	±
birth place of	Presidency of Barack Obama	±
birth place of	Daniel Inouye	±
birth place of	Nicole Scherzinger	±
birth place of	Lois Lowry	±
birth place of	Bernice Pauahi Bishop	±
birth place of	Tia Carrere	±
birth place of	Michelle Wie	±
birth place of	Israel Kamakawiwo'ole	±

Fig. 1. HTML summary of `dbpedia:Barack_Obama` (left) and the ranked list of statements with `dbpedia-owl:birthPlace` and `dbpedia:Hawaii` (right).

which statement we present: First, we prefer statements with the entity in the subject role over those with the entity in the object role. Second, we prefer the DBpedia "ontology" over "property" predicates. In all other cases, we select the first statement with the respective subject-object pair.

The SUMMARUM system supports two types of output via content negotiation: HTML (`text/html`) and Turtle (`text/turtle`).

The HTML version is intended for human consumption and thus, includes only a list of ranked statements without scores. The option for browsing entities in combination with predicates resembles the search interface of Semantic MediaWiki. Figure 1 shows two screenshots of the HTML interface.

The Turtle version can be used by machines for further processing or different interfaces and also includes the scores of the statements. For the representation, we use reification of statements in combination with the vRank vocabulary [5]. An example for the output is given in Listing 1.[8]

Listing 1. Example result in Turtle (the namespaces are omitted).

```
[ rdf:type rdf:Statement ;
  rdf:subject <http://dbpedia.org/resource/Barack_Obama>;
  rdf:predicate <http://dbpedia.org/ontology/birthPlace>;
  rdf:object <http://dbpedia.org/resource/Hawaii>;
  vrank:hasRank [ vrank:rankValue"291.5535"^^xsd:float ]] .
```

5 Conclusion and Future Work

Our work adds popularity-based entity summaries to known Linked Data browsing interfaces in order to enhance user experience. We show a live demonstration online and also provide machine-readable output for further reuse of the rankings.

In future versions of SUMMARUM we would like to address the following points:

[8] Query: http://km.aifb.kit.edu/services/summa/summarum?entity=http://dbpedia.org/resource/Hawaii&predicate=http://dbpedia.org/ontology/birthPlace&k=1

Predicates. In our next major release we plan to focus on the predicate component of the triple.

Literal values. We plan to include literal values as descriptors of the entities. The selection of these values is planned to be based on predicate-statistics about the entity's RDF-type.

i18n and time. One of our further contributions will be the exploitation and combination of browsing context for region, language, and timeline-focused summaries.

Data sources. We are investigating on how to extend the summarization engine with further data sources such as Freebase and Wikidata.

Visualization and media. The HTML output of the system is currently very basic. We plan to put significant effort into the design of a more appealing show case.

Evaluation. We plan to extend our previous efforts [6] in designing evaluation scenarios for entity summarization.

Acknowledgements. The research leading to these results has received funding from the European Union Seventh Framework Programme (FP7/2007-2013) under grant agreement no. 611346.

References

1. Brin, S., Page, L.: The anatomy of a large-scale hypertextual web search engine. In: Proceedings of the 7th International Conference on World Wide Web 7, WWW7, pp. 107–117. Elsevier Science Publishers B. V., Amsterdam (1998)
2. Hogan, A., Munoz, E., Umbrich, J.: Lodpeas: like peas in a lod (cloud). In: Proceedings of the Billion Triple Challenge (2012)
3. Krötzsch, M., Vrandečić, D., Völkel, M.: Semantic MediaWiki. In: Cruz, I., Decker, S., Allemang, D., Preist, C., Schwabe, D., Mika, P., Uschold, M., Aroyo, L.M. (eds.) ISWC 2006. LNCS, vol. 4273, pp. 935–942. Springer, Heidelberg (2006)
4. Musetti, A., Nuzzolese, A.G., Draicchio, F., Presutti, V., Blomqvist, E., Gangemi, A., Ciancarini, P.: Aemoo: exploratory search based on knowledge patterns over the semantic web. In: Semantic Web Challenge (2012)
5. Roa-Valverde, A., Thalhammer, A., Toma, I., Sicilia, M.-A.: Towards a formal model for sharing and reusing ranking computations. In: Proceedings of the 6th International Workshop on Ranking in Databases In conjunction with VLDB 2012 (2012)
6. Thalhammer, A., Knuth, M., Sack, H.: Evaluating entity summarization using a game-based ground truth. In: Cudré-Mauroux, P., Heflin, J., Sirin, E., Tudorache, T., Euzenat, J., Hauswirth, M., Parreira, J.X., Hendler, J., Schreiber, G., Bernstein, A., Blomqvist, E. (eds.) ISWC 2012, Part II. LNCS, vol. 7650, pp. 350–361. Springer, Heidelberg (2012)

Using Semantic Technologies for Scalable Multi-channel Communication

Ioan Toma(✉), Christoph Fuchs, Corneliu Stanciu, and Dieter Fensel

Semantic Technology Institute (STI) - Innsbruck, ICT Technologiepark, Technikerstrasse 21a, 6020 Innsbruck, Austria
{ioan.toma,christoph.fuchs,corneliu.stanciu,dieter.fensel}@sti2.at

Abstract. The development of the Web in the direction of user-generated content, information sharing, online collaboration and social media, have drastically increased the number of communication channels that can be used to interact with potential customers. In this demonstration we present the latest developments of our multi-channel communication solution, which enables touristic service providers, e.g. hoteliers and touristic associations, in dealing with the challenge of improving and maintaining their communication needs. We make use of semantic technologies, i.e. semantic analysis, semantic annotations, ontologies, semantic matching and rules in order to automate several multi-channel communication tasks.

1 Introduction

The rapid advance of ICT technologies and their increasing importance in the tourism domain brings an exponential growth in on-line communication opportunities. Being able to communicate and engage via a multitude of Internet, Web, Web2.0, social and mobile channels becomes more and more important for touristic service providers. The growing number of communication channels and interaction opportunities generates new challenges in terms of scalability. Hoteliers require new skills and more efficient access means to scale and filter the exponentially increased offer. A scalable communication solution is needed in order to address the growth of the multichannel monster [1].

The Online Communication group[1] is developing a new approach for the hospitality industry that enables scalable communication, collaboration and value exchange (i.e. booking) of users (i.e. tourists) through the multitude of on-line interaction possibilities. In this demonstration we present the latest developments of our platform. We show how semantic technologies are being used to automate several multi-channel communication tasks including flexible dissemination of content on multiple channels, collection and understanding of feedback as well engagement with possible customers. Our solution integrates and includes support for several platforms e.g. Facebook, Twitter, LinkedIn, YouTube, Flickr, Google+, WordPress and Typo3. The remainder of this paper is structured as follows: Sect. 2 presents the overall architecture and how semantic technologies

[1] oc.sti2.at

V. Presutti et al. (Eds.): ESWC Satellite Events 2014, LNCS 8798, pp. 516–520, 2014.
DOI: 10.1007/978-3-319-11955-7_77

are used. Finally, Sect. 3 introduces the demonstration plan describing what the visitors will see and learn from our demo.

2 Architecture and Key Technologies

In order to build a scalable multi-channel communication solution, we specify and realize the concepts of the channel model, weaving process of content and channels and communication patterns. As depicted in Fig. 1, our platform includes two major components: (1) *dacodi*, and (2) the *weaver*.

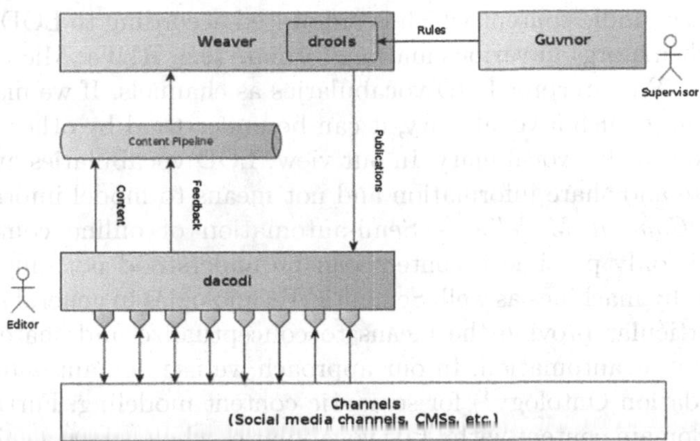

Fig. 1. The Big Picture of the architecture.

dacodi [2] is used to perform the actual distribution of content in various channels, to collect and analyze feedback from those channels and to engage in conversations. *dacodi* implements a set of wrappers to 3rd party APIs of the platforms that are supported including Facebook, Twitter, LinkedIn, YouTube, Flickr, Google+, WordPress and Typo3. Using *dacodi* one can have a federated view of social media stream, a central feedback collection, statistics and analytics on disseminated content as well as means to engage with the audience i.e. replying to comments, etc.

The *weaver* is responsible for the intelligent mapping of information items to the appropriate channels. It performs rule-based dissemination to social media channels using the underlying publishing functionality provided by *dacodi*. The *weaver* fits the right content in the right channels using the semantic annotations of the content (e.g. schema.org). It also handles fetched content and feedback from dacodi as a knowledge base.

Semantic technologies play four distinct roles in our approach enabling efficient and effective multi-channels communication. More precisely we use:

1. *Semantic Text Analysis* - Semantic Text Analysis enables our solution to "understand" the natural language statements in a communication act.

Semantic Text Analysis is commonly implemented by using Natural Language Processing (NLP) techniques. Among the various NLP techniques, opinion mining and sentiment analysis are especially important for online communication. Opinions and sentiments are identified using elements of computational linguistics, text analytics, and machine learning (e.g. latent semantic analysis, support vector machines, etc.). We make use of viralheat[2] for opinion and sentiment analysis.

2. *Semantic Channels* - The paradigm shift with respect to semantic technologies towards the Web of Data vision and its implementation Linked Open Data (LOD) provides new opportunities to integrate more data centric communication channels. Central to LOD are vocabularies and languages. Our solution can handle content which is annotated according to LOD vocabularies (e.g. schema.org) in various markup formats (e.g. RDFa, Microformats, or Microdata). We interpret LOD vocabularies as channels. If we map an information item in such a vocabulary, it can be understood by other agents that are common to this vocabulary. In our view, LOD vocabularies are means to disseminate and share information and not means to model information.
3. *Semantic Content Modeling* - Semi-automation of online communication processes is only possible if content can be understood not only by human agents, but by machines as well. Semantic Technologies in general and Ontologies in particular provide the means to conceptualize and share content, a prerequisite for automation. In our approach we use domain ontologies (e.g. Accommodation Ontology[3]) for semantic content modeling. Furthermore we also map domain content with LOD vocabularies when we see a gain in broadening our range of communication through them.
4. *Semantic Matching* - Content and channels are brought together via a weaving process. Through the use of semantics, channels and content are matched automatically. We have implemented a rule-based approach using drools[4]. Rules are fired depending on the semantic annotations of the content to be disseminated. Content is thus matched, transformed and updated to the right channels. Typical transformations include the shortening of text to fit into tweets, attachment and resizing of pictures, and the transformation and adaptation of videos or slides where needed.

Several approaches and tools for multi-channel communication exist such as Vitrue[5], CrowdFactory[6], HubSpot[7], Radian6[8] or MeltWater Buzz[9]. However, none of these tools abstract and distinguish the communication or channel model from the conceptual descriptions of the information and provide support

[2] https://www.viralheat.com/
[3] http://ontologies.sti-innsbruck.at/acco/ns.html
[4] https://www.jboss.org/drools/
[5] vitrue.com
[6] eu.marketo.com
[7] hubspot.com
[8] radian6.com
[9] buzz.meltwater.com

to automate communication tasks. In our approach we use semantic technologies to address the challenges of multi-channel communication.

3 Demonstration Plan

In this demonstration we present the latest developments of our solution, showing how various channels including Facebook, Twitter, LinkedIn, YouTube, Flickr Google+, WordPress and Typo3 can be registered with our platform, how information items can be disseminated by one click through this multitude of channels, and how feedback is collected and engagement with the users is supported. We will show how semantic technologies are used in our solution to achieve scalability. The demonstration is based on a simple use case, namely automatic announcement of events. This is a typical scenario in which a touristic service provider (e.g. touristic association) wants to disseminate information on multiple channels about the events in their touristic areas. The tourist service provider also wants to see the results of the dissemination actions, to check the received feedback and to engage in conversation with the interested parties. Several challenges are faced in such a scenario including where to disseminate the information (e.g. on the web site, Facebook, Twitter, and other social media, mailing lists, etc.) and when (repeated announcements in time, interrelation between time and channel, etc.). We show that such challenges can be addressed using semantic technologies.

The demo will present to the visitor, playing the role of a touristic service provider, a Web interface to register social channels accounts in dacodi and to manage them. The visitor can also specify the incoming channels, i.e. information sources from where the content is fetched, and then processed and published by our platform. In our demo we use yelp.com as one incoming channel. Events available in yelp.com are semantically annotated according to schema.org/Event, annotations which are used by our solution to decide on which channels and when the content is disseminated. Semantic annotations according to popular vocabularies (e.g. schema.org) and ontologies (e.g. Accommodation Ontology) are used as a basis for automation of multi-channel communication tasks.

The weaver component performs rule-based dissemination to social media channels. The weaver rules can be defined using our interface (see Fig. 2) based on Drools Guvnor[10]. Information items come either from registered incoming channels such as yelp.com, or can be defined using our user interface. Before publishing an information item, the item can be previewed and if needed modified by the user. After the information is published in multiple channels with a single click, our platform periodically checks for feedback, collects it from various platforms, aggregates and visualizes it (see Fig. 3). Using semantic text analysis, our platform can detect opinions and sentiments in the feedback. Any interested user can try our on-line demo at https://dev.dacodi.sti2.at/.

10 http://www.jboss.org/drools/drools-guvnor.html

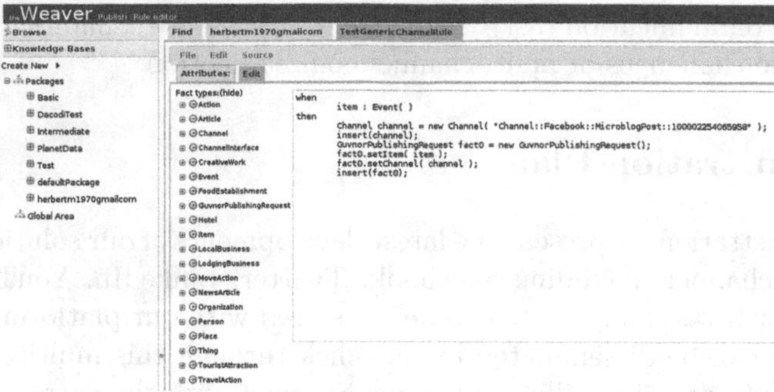

Fig. 2. Definition of rules using the Weaver GUI.

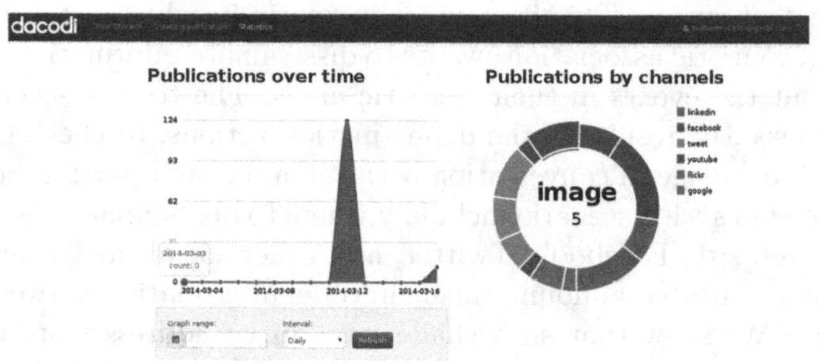

Fig. 3. Aggregate feedback.

Acknowledgment. The work presented in this paper is partly funded by FP7 projects PlanetData, MSEE, Prelida and LDBC. We would like to thank all the members of the Online Communication (http://oc.sti2.at/) working group for their valuable feedback and suggestions.

References

1. Mulpuru, S., Harteveldt, H.H., Roberge, D.: Five retail ecommerce trends to watch in 2011. Technical report, Forrester Research Report (2011)
2. Toma, I., Fensel, D., Oberhauser, A., Fuchs, C., Stanciu, C.V., Larizgoitia, I.: Sesa: a scalable multi-channel communication and booking solution for e-commerce in the tourism domain. In: ICEBE, pp. 288–293. IEEE (2013)

Author Index